SULTAN MOHAY UD DEEN,

Eldest Legitimate Son of Tippoo Sultan.

A
JOURNEY FROM MADRAS

A

JOURNEY FROM MADRAS

THROUGH THE COUNTRIES OF

MYSORE, CANARA AND MALABAR

BUCHANAN FRANCIS, M.D.

IN THREE VOLUMES.

VOL. III.

Published by

Gyan Publishing House
5, Ansari Road
Daryaganj, New Delhi-110002
Phone: 011-47034999, 9811692060
E-mail: books@gyanbooks.com

Distribution Network
gyanbooks.com
India, USA, Canada, UK, Australia, France

ISBN : 978-81-212-9694-6 (Set)
ISBN : 978-81-212-9691-5 (PB)
First Published, 1807

2nd Impression 2023

Printed at: Gyan Press, Delhi.

A JOURNEY FROM MADRAS (VOL. III)
Author: BUCHANAN FRANCIS

A

JOURNEY FROM MADRAS

THROUGH THE COUNTRIES OF

MYSORE, CANARA, AND MALABAR,

PERFORMED UNDER THE ORDERS OF

THE MOST NOBLE THE MARQUIS WELLESLEY,

GOVERNOR GENERAL OF INDIA,

FOR THE EXPRESS PURPOSE OF INVESTIGATING THE STATE OF

AGRICULTURE, ARTS, AND COMMERCE; THE RELIGION, MANNERS, AND CUSTOMS; THE HISTORY NATURAL AND CIVIL, AND ANTIQUITIES,

IN THE DOMINIONS OF

THE RAJAH OF MYSORE,

AND THE COUNTRIES ACQUIRED BY

THE HONOURABLE EAST INDIA COMPANY,

IN THE LATE AND FORMER WARS, FROM TIPPOO SULTAUN.

BY FRANCIS BUCHANAN, M. D.

FELLOW OF THE ROYAL SOCIETY, AND OF THE SOCIETY OF ANTIQUARIES OF LONDON;
FELLOW OF THE ASIATIC SOCIETY OF CALCUTTA; AND IN THE MEDICAL SERVICE
OF THE HONOURABLE COMPANY ON THE BENGAL ESTABLISHMENT.

PUBLISHED UNDER THE AUTHORITY AND PATRONAGE OF

THE HONOURABLE THE DIRECTORS OF THE EAST INDIA COMPANY.

ILLUSTRATED BY A MAP AND NUMEROUS OTHER ENGRAVINGS.

IN THREE VOLUMES.

VOL. III.

1807.

CONTENTS.

APPENDIX.

ERRATA TO VOL. III.

Page.	Line.
25,	5, for *Bahadary*, read *Bahadury*.
25,	11, 12, 16, } for *Hunas*, read *Hanas*.
26,	2, 3, } for *Hunas*, read *Hanas*.
33,	16, for *Inams*, read *Enams*.
35,	23, for $1\frac{13}{1000}$, read $1\frac{13}{100}$.
41,	second marginal note, for *grams*, read *grains*.
139,	9, for *Is*, read *I*.
284,	first marginal note, omit *Manday Gudday*.
398,	second marginal note, for *abour*, read *labour*.
463,	second marginal note, there should be no point at *Anarun*.

A

JOURNEY FROM MADRAS, &c.

CHAPTER XIV.

JOURNEY THROUGH THE SOUTHERN PARTS OF CANARA.

CHAPTER XIV.

Jan. 15.

Mr. Ravenshaw's answers to my queries.

BEFORE I proceed to give an account of my journey through the province of *Canara*, I shall prepare my reader, by detailing the answers which were sent to my queries by Mr. Ravenshaw, the collector of the southern division; a young gentleman who does credit to the school of Colonel Read, and to Mr. Hurdis, under whom he was formed to business.

Query 1st. What proportion of your district consists of land that has always been uncultivated? Of this, what part might, with proper management, be converted into rice-ground? what part into coconut or *Betel-nut* gardens? What proportion of this waste land is now cleared for grass, what is under forest, and what is enclosed for plantations of timber trees, firewood, &c.

Answer. No account of the extent of jungles (forests) has ever been taken. All the surveys that have been made only went to ascertain the cultivated lands, and those capable of culture, but not at present cultivated, and which are 111,965½ *Morays*. Of this, 24,181 *Morays* are cleared for grass, 7,043 have a capability of being converted into rice ground, and 1,789 are fit for gardens. No

CHAPTER XIV. Jan. 15.

account is kept of the quantity enclosed for timber, but all the remainder would answer for the purpose. N. B. The average *Moray* is 45 *Guntas*, each 33 feet square, or 49,005 square feet, and is therefore nearly $1\frac{13}{100}$ acre.

Q. 2d. What proportion of your district consists of rice-land? Of this, what proportion has been cultivated last year, what has been waste or unoccupied?

A. 247,218 *Morays;* of which 225,782 were cultivated, and the remainder was waste, owing to a want of tenants. Of that which was cultivated, 1,591 *Morays* were overflowed, and the crops destroyed.

Q. 3d. What proportion of your district consists of garden grounds? In these, how many coco-nut or *Betel-nut*-trees, and trees for supporting pepper vines, are planted? Is the estimate of these founded on any recent survey, or from an old valuation?

A. The number of trees contained in the gardens, according to the public accompts, are, coco-nut 695,060, *Betel-nut* 1,155,850, *Mangos* 59,772, sundries 54,362, pepper vines 368,828. This estimate is formed from an old survey made in the year $179\frac{2}{3}$. The number of trees, of each description, is at least double of what is here mentioned.

Q. 4th. How many ploughs are there in your district?

A. 71,716.

Q. 5th. How many slaves of all ages, and both sexes?

A. 7924.

Q. 6th. How many houses?

A. 71,856.

Q. 7th. Of these, how many are inhabited by Christians?

A. 2,545.

Q. 8th. How many by Mussulmans, including *Moplays?*

A. 5,223.

Q. 9th. How many by *Bráhmans,* including *Namburis?*

Jan. 15.

A. 7,187, exclusive of *Kankánies*, the *Bráhmans* of which nation are confounded with the other casts.

Q. 10th. How many by *Jain?*

A. 2,700.

Q. 11th. How many by those who wear the *Lingam?*

A. 880.

Q. 12th. How many by *Nairs?*

A. 788.

Q. 13th. How many by *Massady Buntars?*

A. 7,123.

Q. 14th. How many by *Jain Buntars?*

A. 1,060.

Q. 15th. How many by *Kankánies?*

A. 2,434.

Q. 16th. How many animals of the cow kind are there in your district?

A. Cows 62,130, males 98,860, calves 59,109.

Q. 17th. How many animals of the buffalo kind?

A. Females 12,129, males 43,596, calves 6,882.

Q. 18th. What quantity of seed rice is sown annually? As the *Hany* differs in different districts, it will be necessary to state this in *Morays* of *Mangalore*, or at least to state the proportion which the *Hany* of each district has to that measure.

A. 2,36,374 *Morays* of 60 *Mangalore Hanies.* N. B. This *Moray* contains 3,847½ cubical inches; the seed therefore is about 423,000 bushels.

Q. 19th. What goods are exported by the sea from your portion of *Canara*, and to what annual amount?

Q. 20th. What goods are imported by sea, and to what annual amount?

Q. 21st. What goods are exported from your division of *Canara* by land, and to what annual amount?

CHAPTER XIV.

Jan. 15.

Q. 22d. What goods are imported by land, and to what annual amount?

A. Annexed are statements of the exports and imports by sea, from the revenue accompts, for two years during the government of the *Sultan;* and for one year, since the country has come under the government of the Company.

General statement of commerce by sea.

The particulars of this commerce will be seen by consulting these: I shall, however, state the general result.

Account of the exports and imports into *Mangalore Taluc* (district) by sea.

	Imports.			Exports.		
	Pagodas	*Fans.*	*Anas.*	*Pagodas*	*Fans.*	*Anas.*
Fusly or revenue year 1203	39,118	5	$14\frac{3}{4}$	58,581	4	$2\frac{1}{2}$
Ditto - - - - 1205	13,641	6	2	68,903	0	8
Ditto - - - - 1210	84,461	7	19	1,72,427	2	10

From this will be evident, the immense benefit that the country has received by a change of government.

Commerce by land.

No custom-house accompt has been forwarded of the exports and imports by land; but Mr. Ravenshaw states the former to consist chiefly of salt, salt-fish, *Betel-nut,* ginger, coco-nuts, coco-nut oil, and raw-silk, to the annual amount of 20,388 *Pagodas.* The imports are chiefly cloths, cotton, thread, blankets, tobacco, and black cattle, with a small quantity of pepper, and sandal wood, to the amount of 37,455 *Pagodas.* The balance, in favour of the division of the province under Mr. Ravenshaw, is therefore 70,899 *Pagodas,* each worth at the mint price very nearly 8*s.* $0\frac{3}{4}$*d.*

Along with these answers to my queries, Mr. Ravenshaw most obligingly sent me some valuable statements relative to the quantity of seed required for rice lands, and to the quantity of produce,

[To face page 4.

ACCOUNT of SEA CUSTOMS collected in the Year *Anundasumaswara* or *Fusly* 1203 in the *Talook* of *Mangalore*.

No.	ARTICLES.	IMPORTED. Weighing Articles. Candies.	Maunds.	Seers.	Measuring Articles. Corges of 42 Moorays.	Moorays.	Hanies.	Extra Articles.	Pieces.	Parcels.	Corge, or Score by Number.		Price. Pagodas.	Fanams.	Anas.	Customs. Pagodas.	Fanams.	Anas.	EXPORTED. Weighing Articles. Candies.	Maunds.	Seers.	Measuring Articles. Corges of 42 Moorays.	Moorays.	Hanies.	Extra Articles.	Scores.	Pieces.	Parcels.	Price. Pagodas.	Fanams.	Anas.	Customs. Pagodas.	Fanams.	Anas.	Total Customs. Pagodas.	Fanams.	Anas.
1	*Chaul*, or Rice				16	20	21						771	8	8	21	9	5				1127	21						56677	7	8	11142		11	1116		3
2	*Suparee*, or Betle-Nut	12	15										133	8	12	1	2	12	74	9	10								781	8	8	301		9	303	3	1
3	*Nelipany Dogah*, or Silk Thread		6										296			15	4	7																	15		7
4	*Cheeni Sucar*, or Sugar	51											1122			105	2	2																	105		2
5	*Kuddy Sucar*, or Sugar Candy	9	12	20									435	1	9½	25	7	5																	25	7	5
6	*Huthy*, or *Kismiss*, or Plums	13	15										171	8	12	21	4	9																	21	4	9
7	*Gandagum*, or Brimstone	13	5										112	6	4	17	6	4																	17	6	4
8	*Jeera*, or Cummin Seed	9	14	20									141	6		17	8	4																	17	8	4
9	*Hing*, or Assafœtida	1	12	30									114	6	4	5	6	4																	5	6	4
10	*Badam*, or Almonds	12	3	10									206	7	10	22	7	2																	22	7	2
11	*Kunnoo Cuda*	5	10										52	5		6	6	7																	6	6	7
12	*Ganja*, or Flowers of Hemp	6	19										317	5		19	9	10																	19	9	10
13	*Cajura*, or Dates	122	11										615	2	8	106	6	6	9	4									46			3	5	1½	110		5
14	*Kurd*, or Dry Dates	11	14	20									93	8		11	6	2																	11	6	2
15	*Somu*, a Seed like Anise	7	19	20									65	7	13	8	1	2																	8		2
16	*Tumbacu*, or Tobacco	110	30										1871	6	6	143	5	8	3										51			1	5	11	115		1
17	*Gope Chundun*, a kind of Earth	21	7	20									90	8	7	16	6	9																	16		9
18	*Pungee*, or Onions	35											158	1	4	25	4	3		17									2	1	5		1	1	25		9
19	*Imly*, or Tamarinds	29	6										137		5	17	8	5																	17		5
20	*Loah*, or Iron	18											137	8		11	5	8	6	8									47	2	8	1	5	14	12		6
21	*Copra*, or Dry Cocoa-nut Kernels	96	7	20									674	6	4	83	3	12																	83		12
22	*Sis*, or Lead	1	1	30									19	5	9	2		6																	2		6
23	*Tambe*, or Brass		11	30									26	6	14	1	7	12																	1	7	12
24	*Copper Sheets*, or Tutenague		17	20									18	6	10	1	6	7																	1	6	7
25	*Aridall*		9	20									11	3	2	1		5																	1		5
26	*Cuttalla*	1											55			2	9	8																	2		8
27	*Vutsnagur*		3										15	7	8		6	3																		6	3
28	*Jeeluck Mathon*, a Wood	1	15										13	1	4	2	9			4									1	5			1	10	3		10
29	*Kuchorah*, a Root		4										4	5			4	5																		4	5
30	*Lobanah*		11	20									25	3		1	3	11																	1	4	10
31	*Safeid Dogu*, or White Thread		9										14	4			7	9																		7	9
32	*Sabuskgy*		14	20									7	3	3½		7	13																		7	13
33	*Mahlabaleb*	3	5										31			3	9	3																	3		3
34	*Ghee*, or Melted Butter		7										9	4	8		5	6																			8
35	*Puthung Lukdy*, or Red Wood		1	30									3	1	15½		2	8																			8
36	*Opium*		1										14			1	1	10																	1		10
37	*Lavangam*, or Cloves		9	30									6	2	8	3	8	12																	3	8	12
38	*Dunnah*, or Coriander Seeds	5	7	30									53	8	13	4	7	8																	4	7	8
39	*Kutha*, or Cordage	4	11										22	7	8	2	4	8																	2	4	8
40	*Tell*, or Oil	5	16										40	8		4	1	10																	4	1	10
41	*Shora Nasnah*, Salt Petre		10										5	7	8		2	8																			8
42	*Cadoy Pullah*																			10									7	8	12		3	5			5
43	*Nega Hesaru*																			2	20								1	1	4			15			14
44	*Call Merchy*, or Black Pepper																		5	10									195			11	8	7	11	8	7
45	*Alldy*, or Saffron																		19	16	10								175	3	3½	9	8	10	9	8	10
46	*Undachunee*, Cassia																		5	11	20								40	3	15	2	5	6	2	5	6
47	*Rui*, or Cotton	26		20									539	7	11	30	2	2																	30		2
48	*Gudi Jugory*																		36	16									230	6		9	5	1	9	5	1
49	*Lal Merche*, or Capsicum																		3	1									22		4	1	5	11	1	5	11
50	*Gungal*, a Rosin or Frankincense		18	30									23		5	1	2																		1	2	
51	*Adruck*, or Ginger																		1										5				3	11			13
52	*Shawls*										1½	3	145			6	6	14																	6	6	14
53	*Taffetah*, Taffetas										34½	9½	1410	6	4	128	5	11																	128	5	11
54	*Averungu Sal Suddy*, Cloth										21½	4	527	4	8	82	8																		82	8	
55	*Kimcab*, Silk Cloth										3½		457	9	8	16	9	14																	16	9	14
56	*Kistnung Cushe*, Ditto										1½	1	113	9		5	4	7																	5	4	7
57	*Mushroo*, Cloth										62½		2359	2	12	140	5	8																	140	5	8
58	*Pithambri Suddy*, or two sorts of Cloth										2½	1	95			5	6																		5		
59	*Muldery*, Cloth										32	3	904	6	8	69	2	3																	69		3
60	*Sushmung Mucky Sari*, Ditto										6½	2½	471	8	12	34	1																		34	1	
61	Ditto, *Roomaul*, or Handkerchief										13	4	369	6		27	6	2																	27		2
62	*Kaipunch*, Cloth	7	3										285	3	12	13	4	2																	13	4	2
63	*Hunnah*, or Looking Glasses										6½	1½	45	8	11	6	4	13																	6	4	13
64	*Saruttyn Chints*, Cloth										32½	4½	347	2	8	27	7	1																	27	7	1
65	*Pullung Posh*, or Sheets, ditto										16		130			12	5	7																	12	5	7
66	*Suy Hachey*, ditto										32½	3½	465	9	15	30	8	12																	30	8	12
67	*Cangu*, or Blue Cloth										574½		10049	3	12	517	9	2										4½		50	5		1	7		51[illegible]	6	9
68	*Huccuny Lerngy*, Cloth										38½	1	695	4	12	40	9	1																	40		4
69	*Kutchy* or *Pu...*, two sorts of ditto										173		4323	6	4	178		12																	178		12
70	*Jamkhanah*, or Carpet										8½		44	6	4	3	2	11																	3		11
71	*Sarri Nermuddy*, Cloth										20	4½	238		12½	16	4	9																	16	4	9
72	*Karwah*, Coarse Cotton Cloth										54	1	385	1	1	30	1	4																	30		4
73	*Dubutty*, Cloth										41	4	300			20	10																		20	10	
74	*Pugdy*, or Turbans										17	1½	1457	2	4	42	3	6																	42	3	6
75	*Kumbuzuthy*, Cloth											3	15				7	2																		7	2
76	*Amaroo*, ditto											4	9				5	1																		5	1
77	*Jurubuty Calla Kamelie*										2½	2	45		8	3	6	2																	3	6	2
78	*Salloo Suddy*, Cloth										1½	2½	72	6	14	3	8	14																	3	8	14
79	*Thennay*, ditto										1½	4	16	3	2	1		15																	1		15
80	*Kunarah Uudah*, ditto											4	1	3	8		1	4																		1	4
81	*Baray*, Chints										1	1	6	3			6	10																		6	10
82	*Sufeid Shellah*, or White Cloth										1½	3	15	4		1		7																	1		7
83	*Soosi Cuppe*, Cloth										3		25	5		1	2	6																	1	2	8
84	*Cattagy*, ditto										9½	1½	270	4	4	19	6	9																	19	6	9
85	*Nasruby*, ditto										12½	1½	691	9	5	76	9																		76		
86	*Namuck*, or Salt, (*Candies* 64½ 6)												755	3	12	31	7	8																	31	7	9
87	*Nuhalah*										9	11	200	3	10	13	3	13										9		5		10		2	14	13	8	10
88	*Narrell*, or Cocoa-nuts							186990					6			65	7																		65	7	
89	*Comple Moss*, Fish							31½					206	8	7	8	8	1																	8		1
90	*Barra*, or Mats							31000					93			5	8	2																	5	8	2
91	*Cupdah Cuttoyer*, Cloth Bundles							8					385			10	8	4																	10	3	4
92	*Talwar Tag*, or Swords							24					7	6			9	12																			12
93	*Caguth Rumee*, or Paper Reams							22					23	3	12	4	1	8																	4		8
94	*Jareeb Ramzay*, Goat					1							27				7	11																			11
95	*Chopatty*, or Tea in Boxes							8					34			1	5																		1		
96	*Mangurry Cat*, or Fish Fins																									15			45			2	8	2	2		2
97	*Adedy*, or Leather																									140			21			1	5	2	1		2
98	*Banah*, or Sarsecloth									1			8				2	8																			8
99	*Cirkah Pipy*, or Vinegar Pipes							19½					32	6	4	1	4	11																	1	4	11
100	*Coadrah*, or clean Rice Bags																									50			50			3	7	8	3	7	8
101	*Machay*, or Salt Fish, (118 Bundles)							14200					316	3		30	8	14								1578			75	9		3	3		34	1	14
102	*Chatha Sufeid Romall*, or Handkerchiefs										94½		147	5		8	8	9																	8		9
103	*Kunghi*, or Combs										26		20	3	2	1	9	3																	1		3
104	*Kragany Rech*, China Ware										3		4	7			2	13										3½								2	13
105	*Lally Kunrah Babut Hyne*, or Looking Glasses										14½		6	6	15		4	3																		4	3
106	*Hynee*, Spectacles										2		1	5	10			15																			15
107	*Mashooru Topi*										10		18	7	8	1	1	4																	1		4
108	*Pasalka Tarase*										6½		8	4	8		3	1																			1
109	*Vernusah*, or Fans										6		3	7	8		9	4																			4
110	*Sitally Wattah*							40					6	2	8		3	12																			12
111	*Sui*, or Needles							24000					15	6	4		9	6																			6
112	*Chumdale Buddy*, or Leather Pots										2		1	5	10			15																			15
113	*Chapli Jodah*, or Malabar Shoes										1		1	5	10			15																			15
114	*Push Cuttaday*							3					5	6	4		3	6																			6
115	*Phanus*, or Lanterns							3					5	7	8		2	4																			4
116	*Bdumann Sidum*							16					3	8	12		1	2																			2
117	*Taffeta Chattery*, or Silk Umbrellas							1					1	8	12		1	9																			
118	*Pugany Kuttoru* Cloth, and *Baddu*							37000					113	6	4	6	9	6																	6		6
119	Anchorage Duties for Boats (Different kinds of Vessels)							15								5	6	4																			4
120	Ditto for *Sibaky*							2																													
121	Ditto for Boats							1								3	6	4																			11
122	Ditto *Munchees*							1								3	6	4																			4
123	Ditto *Salvaddy*							9								1	1	4										1									4
124	Ditto *Ghashek*							19								6	7	8																			8
125	Ditto *Bella*							4								6	2	8																			8
126	Ditto *Manjee*							61								39	3	2																	39		2
127	Ditto *Pattamare*							13								49	9	6																	40		6
128	Ditto *Migh Herry*							22								22																			22		
129	Ditto *Dony*							35								16	3	12																	17	3	19
	Total												39115	8	11¼	2000	[illegible]	10												56581	4½		11404	3	6	1400[illegible]	5	

ACCOUNT of SEA CUSTOMS collected in the Year *Nalasamaswar* or *Fusly* 1205, in the *Tullook* of *Mangalore*.

No.	ARTICLES.	IMPORTED. Weighing Articles. Candies.	Maunds.	Seers.	Measuring Articles. Corges of 12 Moorays.	Moorays.	Dunnes.	Extra Articles.	Pieces.	Parcels.	Corge, or Score by Number.		Price. Pagodas.	Fanams.	Jeetals.	Customs. Pagodas.	Fanams.	Jeetals.	EXPORTED. Weighing Articles. Candies.	Maunds.	Seers.	Measuring Articles. Corges of 12 Moorays.	Moorays.	Dunnes.	Extra Articles.	Scores.	Pieces.	Parcels.	Price. Pagodas.	Fanams.	Jeetals.	Customs. Pagodas.	Fanams.	Jeetals.	Total Customs. Pagodas.	Fanams.	Jeetals.
1	*Bura*, or Rice																					3719	17	21					67,8[illegible]	5		10232	7	7	10,300		7
2	*Supary*, or Betle-nut	58											90			24			31	8	20								314	2	8	99	7	10	12[illegible]	1	10
3	*Brahminy Daga*, Silk Thread		1	20									31	1		3																					2
4	*Cheeny Sacar*, or Sugar	21	4	11									240		4	30	8	12																			12
5	*Chatlih*, or Tutenague		9	20									34	8	12	1																			2	8	
6	*Sesu*, or Lead		5	20									34	5	4		2	1																	1		9
7	*Arsleth*		6	20									12	3	5		3	12																			12
8	*Karpoor*, or Camphor		17										120			1	1	10																		8	10
9	*Lobaun*, or Incense		17	20									43	7	1	5		1																		1	15
10	*Shora Numuck*, or Salt Petre	3	12										41			6																			6		
11	*Nagdet*		4	20									5	1	12			8																	6		8
12	*Jeera*, or Cummin Seed	4	11										81	5		8		1		9	20																11
13	*Kala Muchy*, or Black Pepper																		6	12									218	7	8	11			9		
14	*Katha*	15	6										37	8	8	1	4	10																	11	3	10
15	*Moom*, or Wax	1	12										32			1	6	11																			14
16	*Kojme*, or Dates	13	12	20									88		17	12	7	2	4	1	20								29		11	1			1		12
17	*Kurick*	6											36	1	1	3		8																	11	6	4
18	*Puttang Lakdy*, or Red Wood		15	20									9	1	12		3	4																	3	3	4
19	*Alaly*																		27	18	30								207	1	12	1	12				7
20	*Sunup*, or Twine	1	10	20									10	5	14	1	5	4																	15		4
21	*Hespaty*, or Canvas	17	10										1137			41																			1		6
22	*Tumbauk*, or Tobacco	14	6	20									151	7		13	7																		42		
23	*Kudry Sacur*, or Sugar Candy		5															1																	13	7	15
24	*Goialoo Bainh*		5	20									3	1	1		1	1																			12
25	*Papada Kaluzy*	5											10			1		1																			13
26	*Isabgole*		3										1	1	11		1																		1	7	9
27	*Ruie*, or Cotton	42	6	10									816		8	17																					
28	*Humley*, or Tamarinds		10															1																	47	6	1
29	*Lal Mirch*, or Capsicum																																			3	14
30	*Guda*, or Jaggery																			10									55	1	4	1			1		
31	*Kathe*, or Cordage	7	19																19	11	3								79	1	8	3	9				11
32	*Pojie*, or Onions	6	6	20									4	7		1		11																	4		3
33	*Lasoon*, or Garlick												22	1			1																		3		6
34	*Sippy Chadan*	11	8																1										6				2	6			3
35	*Coppree*, or Cocoa-nut Kernels	68											69	7		6	1																		6		14
36	*Tell*, or Oil	21	9	20									398			71	1	11																	71		13
37	*Kaingollie*												170	3	8	15		15																	15		15
38	*Shevd*																			16									9	5		1	1				14
39	*Sufid Baptah*, or Cloth											3	321			12	3	11																	19	5	9
40	*Hustroo*, ditto										3½	1½	178		8	13																			14	5	7
41	*Hogah Shaddy* ditto										2¼		90			51	8	7																	35		5
42	*Brahminy Sacy*, ditto											1	7	5		3																			3		4
43	*Nerubhy*, ditto												5	5				4																			
44	*Charkana Sacy*, ditto												43			4	8																		4		1
45	*Hichy Sacy*, ditto													6	4			1																			9
46	*Soosy, Chinta*										14		199			12	1																		12	1	15
47	*Palangpos*, or Counterpanes										18	3	114	5	10	14	1	14																	14	1	6
48	*Cutlay*, Cloth												22			1		6																	1	8	10
49	*Jamkana*, or Carpet										41		446	1	15	30	8	10																	30	9	14
50	*Chitty Pugdy*, Turbans										7	3	57		12	4	7	12																	4	7	11
51	*Shaddy*, or Womens' Cloth										1	1	11		12			11																			4
52	*Langy Puncddy*, Cloth										1	3½	49	5	10	2	4	10								3			152	5			4	12	8	5	6
53	*Pursany*, ditto												22					6																		9	13
54	*Shila*, ditto										11		221	6	14	10		14																	10	7	3
55	*Mumpadd Katha*, ditto										11		159	6		8	7	6																	6	7	11
56	*Colihy Punchaddy*, ditto										9		1011		8	26		11																	36		14
57	*Pandy Moodduk*, ditto										11		247	5		10	8	11																	16		6
58	*Pang*, ditto										42	1	94			4	3	6																	4		10
59	*Dowkary Chariney*, ditto										1		26		8		3	11																	1		15
60	*Tarcuny*, ditto											1½	21	8	8		7	15																			1
61	*Kussy*												10	7	8			1							3				1	3	8		1				
62	*Kagha*, or Blue Cloth										120		2400			115																			115	3	5
63	*Seary Neruddy*, Cloth										9½	1	78	4	4	5	7	5																	5	7	9
64	*Dubbelly*, ditto										10		70	4	12	6		8																	6		8
65	*Kerzuk*, ditto										1		11	5	8		5	8																		5	8
66	*Sufid Rusall*, ditto											4	5		10		1	11																		1	11
67	*Cholay Langy*, ditto										5½	4	122	6	4	5	3	11																	5	3	11
68	*Bengally Rusall*, ditto											1	16	8	12			7																		6	7
69	*Wuthelle*				13	28	21						320	8	9	13	1	1				3	18						103	6		3	9	15	23	4	
70	*Kugath Bunny*							16					41			3																			3		
71	*Comidonse*, Fish							3					18				7	8																		7	9
72	*Narrell*, or Cocoa-nut							17100					58				1																		7	1	
73	*Shirka Potty*							7½					11	5	8		5	10																		5	10
74	*Merdy* or *Bumbly*, Fish Bundles							12606					393	2	4	39	1	14																	39	1	14
75	*Chinduck Aattoe*							Cunhs																													4
76	*Netorouck*, or Salt Bundles							4½ 9¼ ¼					669	1	8	31	1	2							50				62	5		2	1	4	31		4
77	*Muudy Jenne Bobuk*												46	6	4	2	6	14																	2	6	14
78	Anchorage Duties for *Dow Dunghie*, Boats							10								110	5	1																	110	2	4
79	Ditto, for *Kutulag* ditto							1								22	1	4																	22	1	4
80	Ditto, for *Sibudy* ditto							2								4																			4		
81	Ditto, for *Walluh* ditto							1								1	3																		1	3	
82	Ditto, for *Manchill* ditto							4								4	5																		4	5	
83	Ditto, for *Puttumars* ditto							37								47		10																	47		10
84	Ditto, for *Muque* ditto							22								16																			16		
85	Ditto, for *Hoolly* ditto							5								14		10																	14		10
86	Ditto, for *Choolnak* ditto							15								8	4	6																	8	4	6
87	Ditto, for *Koomby* ditto							1									8	10																		8	10
88	Ditto, for *Tany* ditto							96								8	2	8																	8	2	8
	Total												13641	6	2	1025	1	9											68903		3	10347	7	15	11372	9	1

ACCOUNT of SEA CUSTOMS collected in the Year *Rowdry* or *Fusly* 1210, in the *Tallook* of *Mangalore*.

No.	ARTICLES.	IMPORTED. Weighing Articles. Candies.	Maunds.	Seers.	Measuring Articles. / Pieces	Price. Pagodas.	Customs. Pagodas.	Total Customs. Pagodas.	Fanams.	Annas.
1	Chawl, or Rice	—	—	—	Corges of 42 Moorahs 68, Moorahs 20	1397	26	1420	8	9
2	Call Mirchy, or Black Pepper	15	17	—	—	1621	16	1024	[illegible]	2
3	Supary, or Beetle-nut	51	14	—	—	78	8	398	[illegible]	4
4	Kalkandu, or Sugar Candy	19	12	30	—	712	16	46	[illegible]	8
5	Cutchu	—	15	10	—	8	1	1	[illegible]	5
6	Kapoor, or Camphor	—	17	7½	—	328	16	11	[illegible]	15
7	Lobaun, or Incense	—	8	10	—	23	[illegible]	1	[illegible]	12
8	Jeerah, or Cummin Seeds	8	15	—	—	173	18	19	[illegible]	8
9	Nauntutee, or Tin	—	5	20	—	13	—	—	[illegible]	14
10	Lack, or Sealing Wax	—	5	—	—	7	—	[illegible]	6	10
11	Cutbhu	12	7	30	—	778	14	31	7	7
12	Bringe	—	3	32	—	4	—	—	[illegible]	3
13	Hing, or Assafoetida	1	6	28	—	159	8	[illegible]	[illegible]	12
14	Tombe, Pittal, & Kansund	3	18	—	—	388	18	15	[illegible]	1
15	Reshamy Dhaga, or Silk Thread	—	[illegible]	9	—	236	20	20	[illegible]	15
16	Moombutty, or Candles	8	2	27	—	384	12	12	[illegible]	15
17	Dhalchini	15	8	12	—	198	25	26	[illegible]	14
18	Jane Mashoo	6	14	—	—	56	11	[illegible]	[illegible]	7
19	Saboon, or Soap	17	9	—	—	211	21	21	[illegible]	3
20	Tobacco	104	[illegible]	10	—	1590	128	136	[illegible]	[illegible]
21	Sompoo	11	18	10	—	113	13	15	[illegible]	9
22	Gunjay, or dry Flowers of Hemp	17	11	—	—	331	21	21	[illegible]	—
23	Chikoo, or Cinnamon	—	1	—	—	—	—	[illegible]	[illegible]	1
24	Anguty	13	8	38	—	1013	50	50	[illegible]	11
25	Dhunia, or Coriander Seeds	1	11	21	—	16	1	[illegible]	[illegible]	9
26	Pomm, or Onions	107	1	—	—	488	68	68	[illegible]	—
27	Tel, or Oil	374	8	[illegible]	—	398	332	332	6	1
28	Copra, or Coco-nut Kernels	143	2	[illegible]	—	1277	112	113	[illegible]	5
29	Lusun, or Garlick	1	4	—	—	[illegible]	—	7	[illegible]	3
30	Gudd, or Jaggery	8	15	25	—	18	1	8	[illegible]	2
31	Cadu, or Cordage	160	18	5	—	951	95	202	6	10
32	Imly, or Tamarinds	19	[illegible]	—	—	91	12	12	[illegible]	4
33	Lala Mirchy, or Capsicum	3	14	30	—	20	1	[illegible]	[illegible]	2
34	Tobree Bongee Reed	1	6	10	—	8	1	1	[illegible]	7
35	Suffaid Dhaga, or White Thread	—	5	7½	—	11	—	1	[illegible]	14
36	Khajoor, or Dates	55	3	10	—	419	64	67	5	1
37	Nilly, or Blue coloured Indigo	—	—	3	—	—	—	—	[illegible]	2
38	Inglium, or Red Ink	—	8	—	—	4	—	—	8	8
39	Sujjee	—	[illegible]	—	—	6	—	—	4	7
40	Gond, or Gum Arabic	3	17	10	—	18	[illegible]	[illegible]	[illegible]	15
41	Mohgool	—	7	30	—	13	—	—	8	3
42	Cusscuss, Poppy Seed	—	—	30	—	—	—	—	[illegible]	13
43	Jadwar	1	3	30	—	22	[illegible]	5	[illegible]	13
44	Hingadik	—	2	—	—	6	—	—	[illegible]	5
45	Sandly Tel, or Sandal Oil	—	13	7½	—	172	10	37	5	4
46	Pocnado Roy, or White Cotton	—	17	30	—	18	1	1	[illegible]	—
47	Gulaby Phul, or Roses	—	—	10	—	—	—	—	6	1
48	Elachy, or Cardamoms	—	—	13	—	1	—	—	8	4
49	Aroony Gendy	—	7	30	—	5	—	—	[illegible]	2
50	Gunda Beer	—	—	10	—	4	—	—	[illegible]	12
51	Sukjee Khar	—	1	[illegible]	—	2	—	—	[illegible]	2
52	Munjit, or Madder	4	3	10	—	70	8	21	2	2
53	Badam, or Almonds	8	11	20	—	91	11	11	2	10
54	Anar, or Pomgranate	1	14	—	—	16	[illegible]	3	[illegible]	4
55	Alwa, or Sweetmeats	—	6	20	—	6	—	—	[illegible]	6
56	Kautua Cow	—	9	20	—	8	—	—	[illegible]	7
57	Gunny Surkee	—	7	28	—	6	—	—	8	7
58	Phitkari, or Alum	—	9	30	—	4	—	—	[illegible]	1
59	Gongolino, Rottie	—	4	30	—	2	—	—	[illegible]	0
60	Copper Stick	[illegible]	2	10	—	118	9	9	[illegible]	10
61	Kuttuck Rokhy	—	1	—	—	[illegible]	—	—	[illegible]	8
62	Baila Arraby	—	1	30	—	2	—	1	[illegible]	10
63	Tundy	—	3	—	—	[illegible]	—	—	[illegible]	3
64	Pimpy	—	[illegible]	30	—	8	—	—	[illegible]	10
65	Cumundy Auch	—	3	10	—	3	—	—	[illegible]	7
66	Ghee, or boiled Butter	51	1	25	—	1533	8	9	[illegible]	13
67	Pasputch Cow	3	17	25	—	33	6	6	[illegible]	5
68	Khajoor, or Dates	188	4	—	—	1078	184	190	—	2
69	Pannee, or Rose Water	1	17	—	—	21	2	2	[illegible]	14
70	Sandal Wood	—	3	35	—	4	—	6	8	14
71	Cloves	—	3	30	—	72	3	3	4	14
72	Pulley	1	1	3	—	66	2	3	[illegible]	15
73	Ajwain, a Seed like Anise	1	7	20	—	12	1	1	8	5
74	Opium	—	—	30	—	5	—	—	[illegible]	15
75	Long Capur	—	4	30	—	6	—	—	[illegible]	9
76	Sheesy Lobaun	—	5	10	—	1	—	—	[illegible]	13
77	Budda Sop	1	3	20	—	11	1	[illegible]	[illegible]	13
78	Kalla Dal	4	17	20	—	37	3	5	5	9
79	Ruhe, or Cotton	6	18	20	—	145	8	8	8	—
80	Loha, or Iron	—	—	27½	—	1	—	3	1	3
81	Omagu	—	3	32	—	—	—	—	[illegible]	2
82	Kooty Coir	1	4	20	—	3	—	—	[illegible]	3
83	Sabuda Lavanah	—	—	25	—	—	—	—	[illegible]	4
84	Harbany	6	—	20	—	13	[illegible]	2	[illegible]	9
85	China Sugar, or Sugar	300	12	—	—	3937	450	530	[illegible]	13
86	Tanjini Chitty, Taffetas	—	—	—	24	934	97	97	4	13
87	Anaringa Shaly, Cloth	—	—	—	1½	61	[illegible]	3	7	12
88	Mungu Soosy, ditto	—	—	—	16	411	12	44	[illegible]	10
89	Pullada Tan, ditto	—	—	—	3	139	13	10	8	—
90	Punnaky Soddy, ditto	—	—	—	3	84	8	5	[illegible]	3
91	Punnaky Dopatta, ditto	—	—	—	14	464	15	35	[illegible]	11
92	Reshamy Sary, ditto	—	—	—	16	295	38	39	7	10
93	Cossey, ditto	—	—	—	67	1446	163	164	[illegible]	9
94	Naunsuk, ditto	—	—	—	1½	182	21	23	[illegible]	6
95	Reshamy Rumals, ditto	—	—	—	9	261	24	23	8	4
96	Hindy Sus, ditto	—	—	—	33	409	37	27	—	9
97	Kuttey Cheetee, ditto	—	—	—	22	314	31	31	[illegible]	15
98	Putmapore, ditto	—	—	—	15	103	13	13	[illegible]	14
99	Manapaut Cossey, ditto	—	—	—	103	7406	116	146	[illegible]	12
100	Punnaky Shalah, ditto	—	—	—	40	513	89	96	[illegible]	3
101	Dobatties, ditto	—	—	—	43	316	48	49	—	11
102	Cumbly, ditto	—	—	—	638	18804	1857	1863	[illegible]	15
103	Aunkus, ditto	—	—	—	54	129	25	26	[illegible]	12
104	Mowree Lungy, ditto	—	—	—	29	1159	28	28	[illegible]	7
105	Nowree Undal, ditto	—	—	—	8	41	5	5	[illegible]	8
106	Suffaid Chilleh, ditto	—	—	—	8	181	10	16	[illegible]	12
107	Dina Puggy, or Turbans	—	—	—	8	147	5	9	[illegible]	8
108	Datta Bowghtama, Cloth	—	—	—	6	71	5	7	[illegible]	[illegible]
109	Ubar Puchady, ditto	—	—	—	4	49	4	4	[illegible]	[illegible]
110	Cadtree, ditto	—	—	—	47	464	46	15	[illegible]	[illegible]
111	Pounnay Mundurgatty, ditto	—	—	—	30	341	25	29	[illegible]	14
112	Saxoo, ditto	—	—	—	11	146	10	18	[illegible]	13
113	Sufaid Dam, ditto	—	—	—	22	163	16	18	[illegible]	6
114	Dobady, ditto	—	—	—	45	384	31	34	[illegible]	9
115	Kootiny, ditto	—	—	—	31	183	28	28	[illegible]	11
116	Tarshanty Dummal, ditto	—	—	—	4	173	9	[illegible]	[illegible]	10
117	Nasuh	—	—	—	3	367	13	18	[illegible]	11
118	Cashmerh Lungy, Cloth	—	—	—	1	3	—	[illegible]	[illegible]	7
119	Culleguy Soddy, ditto	—	—	—	23	619	60	60	4	2
120	Kasteh, or ..., ditto	—	—	—	—	22	1	[illegible]	[illegible]	10
121	Reshamy Lon, ditto	—	—	—	3	114	9	[illegible]	[illegible]	6
122	Handkerc, ditto	—	—	—	—	—	—	—	[illegible]	—
123	Reshamy Dupatt, ditto	—	—	—	—	—	—	1	[illegible]	4
124	Chint ..., ditto	—	—	—	11	—	1	[illegible]	[illegible]	1

[*This* ACCOUNT *is continued on the annexed Sheet.*]

ACCOUNT (*continued*) of SEA CUSTOMS collected in the Year *Rowdry* or *Fusly* 1210, in the *Tallook* of *Mangalore*.

No.	ARTICLES.	Imported: Weighing / Measuring Articles	Imported: Extra Articles	Imported: Pieces / Parcels	Imported: Corge, or Score by Number	Imported Price: Pagodas	Fanams	Annas	Imported Customs: Pagodas	Fanams	Annas	Exported: Weighing / Measuring Articles	Exported: Extra Articles	Exported: Pieces / Parcels	Exported: Corge, or Score by Number	Exported Price: Pagodas	Fanams	Annas	Exported Customs: Pagodas	Fanams	Annas	Total Customs: Pagodas	Fanams	Annas
125	*Ruyap dy Nagady Paldy*, Cloth				114½ 6	1873	6	1	124		6				2¼	2	6	1			13	123	1	3
126	*Bengally Buttery Cantano*, ditto				18 1½	465	4	4	23	9	6				1 3	17	3	8		5	5	23	3	13
127	*Sugoh Puthel*, ditto				6	10	1	14		6													6	
128	*Puttey Kam*, ditto				5 1½	10		1	5	4												5	4	
129	*Colshy Puchody*, ditto				90½	1015		5	58	4	1											58	4	1
130	*Morrelly Puchody*, ditto					10	1	4		8	8												8	8
131	*Shuttrunjee*, Carpets				1 9	14	7	1	1	5	11											1	8	11
132	*Teraay*, Cloth				2½ 4	37	6	10	3		14											3		14
133	*Cuchin Lerbasey*, ditto				3½	33	8	4	3		1											3		1
134	*Pala Caddry*, ditto					6	8	12		8	5												8	5
135	*Hynsh*, or Looking Glasses				8 1½	45	1	7	8	8	10											8	8	10
136	*Goolaby Seeba*, Rose Water Glasses		118			22	5		1	8	2											1	8	2
137	*Chataé Ruccréés*, or Mats		232800			486			49	2	5											49	9	5
138	*Machchy*, or Fish		27113			473	6	10	56	4	2		100			6	7	8		2	15	58	7	2
139	*Lassiah Saball*		41			5	8	8		9	3												3	3
140	Paper, Reams		196			390			41	3	5		31½			58	5		3	2	1	44	6	7
141	*Comptoneen*, Fish		23½			216	9	12	7	9	1											7	5	1
142	Coconut		806585			4296	6	8	277	2	7											277	2	7
143	*Choomp Patty*, or Box		47			367	5		4	1	2											4	1	2
144	Wine, or Leaguer of Liquors		47			1120			67	5	10											67	5	10
145	*Jogery*, Bundles		19			1	1	14			9													9
146	*Baldeck Burah*, or large Mats		113			38	7	14	1	8	7											1	8	7
147	*Pundid*		229				9	13	4		12		31			8	5	8		2	3	4	9	15
148	*Kutcha Supary*, or raw Betle Nut		247550			61	8	14	7		9		19000			4	7	8		3	5	7	8	14
149	*Acroot*, or Walnuts		23000			8	6	4		7	5												7	5
150	*Sirke Bye*, or Vinegar Boxes		81			14	8	12		7	6												7	6
151	Horse		2			9				7	12												7	12
152	*Sullet Thanum*		55½			312	7	8	40	3	5											40	3	5
153	*Round Tackah*			1		3	5			3	6												3	6
154	*Mungala Ghever Romalls*, Handkerchiefs				761	1068	1	12	138	2	11											138	5	11
155	*Jooti*, or Shoes				6½	23	2		1	6	4			25½					21		7	[illegible]	2	14
156	*Poth Cussy Muny Bar*				77½	31	1	5	2	1	2											[illegible]	1	2
157	*Pathee*, or Copper	9 30½				6	6	4	1	2	9											1	9	9
158	Fans				13½	8	9			4	6												4	6
159	*Deru*, Coconut		60161			188	5	12	13	5	10											13	5	10
160	*Oodjore*, or Mats of Coconut Leaves		2436			64	1	9	1	3	10											4	3	10
161	*Pidual Cavay*					1	8	10			15													15
162	*Lacchha Kutyph*				4½	12	8	2		8	9												8	9
163	*Caugath*, or Paper Bundles		72½			51	4	4	3	4	13											3	1	13
164	Ivory				2½	1	5	10		1	1												1	1
165	Wood				133½	55		3	3	5	15												5	15
166	*Goonas*		67			2	9	6		2	11												2	11
167	Small Boxes				16½ 1	5	3	8		3	10												3	10
168	*Kulabuth Topy*, or Caps				2½	1	5	10		1	1												1	1
169	*Byarahet Munomur*				3		8	11			9													9
170	*Sollah*						5	4			5													5
171	*Adabar Pangany*				2½	18	5	6	1	2	10				1		3	9			3	1	2	13
172	*Fisbellie Cutyph*				3½	3	4	6		2	5												2	5
173	*Loky*, or Iron Box				6		6	1			7													7
174	Cages		4			1	8	12		1	4												1	4
175	*Sorohah*				3½ 3	4	4	13		3	3												3	3
176	*Thotty Bursh*				307	98	3	12	6	5	11											6	5	11
177	*Oonnuck*, or Spectacles				14½	34	6	14	2	4	7												4	7
178	Silk Umbrellas				4	57		14	3	9	9											3	9	9
179	Empty Boxes				1½	10	5	6		6	14												6	14
180	*Nocky*				1½	10	6	4		6	8												6	8
181	*Pittleyha Tobuck*, or Iron Vessels		3			1	8	12		1	4												1	4
182	Wooden Boxes				42½	3	8	6		2	4												2	4
183	*Cockbady Punnasa*				1		7	3			5													8
184	*Jacola Much*		2				8	8			5													5
185	*Bengalli Durrah*				10	1	9	8			15													15
186	*Pongany Doby*				405 4½	76	1	12	5	3	9				3¼	1		7			10	5	3	12
187	*Cudmy Topi*, or Hat Feathers				21½ 4	43	7	8	2	9	10											2	9	10
188	Penknives				3½ 2	3	9	11		2	14												2	14
189	Needles		19000			5				3	6												3	6
190	*Sufeth Saddy*, or Tape				14	9	1	14		1	7												1	7
191	Looking Glasses covered with Paper				94½ 2	43	8	3	2	8	13				40½	7	8	2			11	3	4	8
192	*Dobne*, Coarse Needles				19½		6	4			7													7
193	*Battaline*	3				1	4	12		1												1		
194	*Sunk Thugdee*				55½ 1	32	6		2	2												2	4	
195	Iron *Good goody*				1½ 3	5	1	1		1	6												1	6
196	*Kungay*, or Wood Combs				34	2		15		2	4												2	4
197	Ditto, Ivory ditto				67½	38	2	7	2	5	15											2	5	15
198	*Pothnung Lochoddy*		25			1	8	12		1	5												1	5
199	Wooden Shoes		7				5	5			5													5
200	*Chaas Till Turah*				1 2	5	6	4		3	13												3	13
201	Iron Weights				1½ 8	4	4	11		3													3	
202	*Pisar*, or Shoes				2	2	1	14		1	8												1	8
203	*Chadrung*, or Dice		5				9	6			9													9
204	*Bongdey*, or Bracelets				1 4	1		5			11													11
205	*Lockdy Pullah*				2 3	1	3	10			14													14
206	*Kagudi Shoory*, Paper Umbrellas				49½ 1	111	8	8	7	8	12											7	8	12
207	*Goodgoodale Rully*				3		6	4			7													7
208	*Jacreh Golah*, or Fish Hooks				100		6	4			7													7
209	Brass covered Red Looking Glasses				1	3	1	4		2	9												2	2
210	*Pottachy—Cutt*		12			1	5	10		1	1												1	1
211	*Duggah Bootuah*		1000			3	5	9		2	3												2	3
212	*Chiaa Tuppy*				1	3	1	4		2	2												2	2
213	Stones for grinding Sandal		24				8	6			10													10
214	*Soorur Puns*		3			2	8	2		1	15												1	15
215	Ditto, *Muty gur Dubby*				6	3	7	2		2	8												2	8
216	Plantains		1540			1	7	12		1	4												1	4
217	*Soona Gudah*		470			1	7	12		1	4												1	4
218	*Gos Buckengahi Tuba*		7680			16	5	10	1	1	4											1	1	4
219	*Hoodiny Tokray*				9	1	8	12		1	4												1	4
220	*Goo Bengalli*		680				5	4			5													5
221	*Chilley Deruss*					8	1	4		4	14												4	11
222	*Lackhybubuh Cungay*														80	1	8	12		1	2		1	2
223	*Hurjal*, or Saffron											39 5 37				414	9	14	27	1	15	27	1	13
224	*Chidruck*											1				9	5			6			6	
225	*Hasty's Gurry*, Bundles												21			9				4	4		4	4
226	*Adaldy*												200			22			2	1		2	1	
227	*Choodreh*												3			3	2	8		1	13		1	13
228	*Gunny Bindeh*												227			20	4	6	1	9		1	8	
229	*Wukulla*	128 21 30				3436	9		184	2	6	3 19				63	5	8	4	2	12	185	8	2
230	*Chorudaky*					2295	9	8	222	9	13					9339	8	7	622	6	5	845	6	6
231	*Neemuck*, or Salt	Garce, Loge, Loge: 31 5¼ 0¼				2619	4	8	115	3	3											115	2	3
232	*Chop*, or *Markunpoa* Cloths								7	7	13											7	7	13
233	*Daw Dunghee*, Duties on Anchorage		32						232													232		
234	Long Boat, ditto		8						19	3												19	3	
235	*Puttewars*, Boats, ditto		261						222	7	12											230	7	12
236	*Munjee*, ditto		196						114	2	14											114	2	14
237	*Chambauk*, ditto		28						11	2	8											11	2	8
238	*Toney*, Canoes, ditto		172						58		4											59		4
239	Small Boats, ditto		1						7	9	8											7	9	8
240	*Sebadah*, ditto		9						9	8	5											9	8	5
241	*Coundry*, ditto		24						10	6	14											10	6	14
242	*Munchill*, ditto		14						14	5	9											14	5	9
243	*Kouly*, ditto		50						21	9	13											21	9	13
244	*Serady*, ditto		11						5	8	2											5	8	2
245	*Neraddy*, ditto		5						9	1	14											9	1	14
246	*Mahugherry*, ditto		26						8	7	13											8	7	13
247	*Mukoly Bellah*, ditto		5						9	8	14											9	8	14
	Total					84461	7		[illegible]	8	15					17212	[illegible]	[illegible]	[illegible]			3766	5	14

JOHN G. RAVENSHAW.

of which I shall hereafter avail myself. He also favoured me with a statement of the population made up about this time; and reliance may be placed on its accuracy with respect to numbers. I have taken the liberty of altering the orthography, to make it conformable to the other parts of my account. The different casts are detailed in the usual confused manner, with which they are spoken of by the native officers of revenue.

CHAPTER XIV.

Jan. 15.
Population.

Kaneh Shumareh, or statement of Casts, Men, Boys, Women, and Girls in the ten *Talucs* or districts of the Southern division of the province of *Canara.*

No.	Casts or Trades.	Houses.	Men.	Boys.	Women.	Girls.	Total.
1	*Bráhmans.* Nearly all but that of holding the plough - - - - - - - - -	6867	12677	6932	13192	4080	36881
2	*Coochastully.* The same - - - - -	320	762	450	799	275	2286
3	*Kankánies.* Bankers, shopkeepers, and traders	2434	4724	2419	4495	1436	13074
4	*Pennecar* a 2d sort. Same, but in a lower line	152	242	112	281	82	717
5	*Novaisgar.* Cultivators, and shopkeepers - -	277	544	269	542	140	1501
6	*Stanicas.* Employed in low offices at heathen temples - - - - - -	880	1466	744	1396	450	4029
7	*Gujjer.* Merchants from *Gujjerat* - -	4	38	—	8	5	51
8	*Hurry Chitties.* Merchants - - - -	161	293	129	291	83	796
9	*Lingabantar.* Merchants, usually called *Banijigar*	328	573	205	535	151	1464
10	*Rajputs.* Messengers, soldiers, and robbers -	47	91	38	79	23	231
11	*Satanies.* Adorn the idol *Vishnu* - - -	6	10	3	9	4	26
12	*Daseris.* Religious mendicants - -	114	181	67	154	74	476
13	*Vairágis.* Ditto - - - - -	6	11	4	7	5	27
14	*Jainas.* Cultivators - - - - -	2700	5108	2307	4763	1914	14092
15	*Bunts.* Ditto - - - - -	8133	19349	7775	19041	6654	52819
16	*Davadygar (Devaganica).* Musicians - -	1583	2893	1079	2968	918	7853
17	*Nairs.* Farmers - - - -	788	1718	748	1800	620	4886
18	*Moplays.* Farmers and merchants - -	3835	6383	3402	6776	2582	19143
19	*Moylar.* Similar to the *Stanica,* No. 6. - -	160	206	111	318	87	722
20	*Carwar.* Generally seamen - - -	28	33	8	36	5	82
21	Mussulmans. Exclusive of *Moplays,* and artists	1388	2276	1200	2377	832	6685
22	*Cunians.* Fortune-tellers, exorcists - -	145	234	118	233	83	668
23	*Chuplygur.* Day labourers (a Mussulman word)	43	72	24	73	20	189
24	*Pomebut.* Attendants on the idols of destructive spirits - - - - - -	224	414	147	367	124	1052
25	*Coilaury.* Cultivators, and servants - -	523	1037	410	1052	417	2916
26	*Carda Kankánies.* Ditto - - - -	719	1385	598	1336	399	3718
27	*Kankány Walleygar.* Messengers, &c. - -	275	511	205	517	125	1358
28	*Chuptagar.* Carpenters, woodcutters, &c. -	259	406	176	439	126	1147

CHAPTER XIV.

Jan. 15.

No.	Casts or Trades.	Houses.	Men.	Boys.	Women.	Girls.	Total.
29	*Baat.* Persons employed by the great to sing their praises - - - - - -	8	16	11	17	12	56
30	*Gauda Barla Wocul.* Cultivators - -	3271	6218	3587	6264	2708	18777
31	*Biluaras.* People who extract the juice of palms	11397	20222	8087	19376	6079	53764
32	*Marattahs (Súdras of that Désa).* Cultivators	1943	3298	1689	3152	1285	9424
33	*Bedor.* A savage race, who eat cats, and with great propriety are called murderers - -	16	29	13	23	14	79
34	*Kshatriyas* (pretenders to the 2d. cast). Messengers, robbers, &c. - - - -	289	657	295	640	170	1762
35	*Mogayar.* Fishermen, boatmen - -	2410	4017	1530	4166	1349	11062
36	*Parsis.* Merchants - - - -	1	8	—	—	—	8
37	*Tælics.* Oil-makers - - - - -	755	1266	553	1283	506	3608
38	*Garludda Kankánies.* Gardeners, and cultivators	114	193	65	167	40	465
39	Christians. Cultivators, merchants, &c. -	2545	3701	1968	3603	1605	10877
40	*Conegeyer.* Cultivators - - -	63	89	58	97	31	275
41	*Cabbadi.* Sellers of butter, and milk - -	23	31	12	33	16	92
42	*Currey Cudemdacr.* A low cast of cultivators -	206	437	261	393	182	1273
43	*Malayala Biluaras. (Tiars)* Toddy-sellers -	128	219	83	219	62	583
44	*Mar, Marattahs.* Cultivators - -	41	74	55	69	22	220
45	*Malay-cudis.* Cultivators living on the hills -	579	885	404	863	247	2399
46	*Hola Davaru (Halypecas?).* Cultivators -	155	330	150	334	124	938
47	*Bhyru.* Day labourers - - -	265	402	190	377	175	1144
48	*Cundlagar.* Farmers - - -	57	106	71	102	38	317
49	*Upar.* Pioneers - - - -	6	9	3	6	—	18
50	*Garwady.* Snake-catchers - - -	1	4	2	1	—	7
51	*Govaygar* (natives of *Goa*). Merchants -	46	115	77	94	44	330
52	*Autgar.* A sort of actors, who represent the ancient wars of India - - -	3	7	1	5	2	15
53	*Conchittigar.* Farmers - - -	18	21	18	21	10	70
54	*Comutty (Vaisyas).* Merchants of the 3d pure cast - - - - - -	12	18	6	27	5	56
55	*Pacanat.* Collectors, and venders of drugs -	12	17	18	17	8	60
56	*Dumbar.* Tumblers. - - -	5	20	10	25	8	63
57	*Bardsegar.* Labourers, and cultivators - -	31	46	26	50	38	160
58	*Baylall.* Farmers - - - - -	18	47	11	52	19	129
59	*Rachewar.* Messengers, soldiers, robbers -	5	8	2	8	3	21
60	*Gursor.* A set of people living in forests, on what they can procure wild there - -	6	6	—	6	2	14
61	*Rarney.* Day labourers - - -	14	18	7	14	5	44
62	*Barsagur.* Farmers - - - - -	24	54	35	56	18	163
63	*Mar Daerd (Whalliaru?).* Day labourers, Messengers, &c. - - - - -	1198	1634	833	1594	603	4664
64	*Cundacar.* Land measurers - - - -	5	12	9	10	2	83
65	*Buy.* Palanquin-bearers - - -	171	284	134	278	98	794
66	*Mally Buy.* Fishermen - - -	7	11	8	10	4	33
67	*Coomaru Marattahs.* Farmers - -	5	13	3	10	8	34
68	*Telinga Bulgewars.* Traders, and labourers. *Teliga Banijigaru* of *Karnata* - - -	32	48	30	55	22	155
69	*Cunabi.* Farmers of pure *Súdra* descent -	179	447	200	361	136	1144

CHAPTER XIV.

Jan. 15.

No.	Casts or Trades.	Houses.	Men.	Boys.	Women.	Girls	Total.
70	*Mocarey (Mogayar* No. 35.). Boatmen	135	218	124	247	98	687
71	*Gollors.* Various services	173	299	146	291	106	842
72	*Jogies.* Religious mendicants	200	332	160	319	102	913
73	*Bandarey.* Shopkeepers, servants	112	229	89	213	67	598
74	*Curubaru.* Cattle-drivers, and dealers	49	68	24	70	21	18
75	*Busive (Baswa).* Prostitutes of the sect who worship the *Linga*	33	16	14	71	16	117
76	*Jotygur.* Gardeners	75	166	83	148	38	435
77	*Neckar (Nuccal).* Jugglers, &c.	16	21	7	23	4	55
78	*Buda Budiky.* Beggars	15	21	25	30	11	87
79	*Lingawer.* Ditto	12	14	7	13	10	44
80	*Telingas.* Merchants from *Telingana*	19	34	30	35	15	114
81	*Polut.* Cultivators	48	83	37	92	25	237
82	*Savunts.* Ditto	2	4	2	3	1	10
83	*Carady.* Various services	18	33	10	34	9	36
84	*Mooshgey.* Farmers	6	8	3	7	8	26
85	*Ambigor.* Boatmen	12	22	16	22	6	66
86	*Duckey.* Beggars, worshippers of *Buddha*	11	15	5	17	5	42
87	*Seddar.* Ditto	36	66	17	66	14	163
88	*Veor.* Ditto	14	23	9	24	13	69
89	*Mistries.* Head carpenters	14	26	13	23	4	66
90	*Chowdeky.* Beggars	1	1	2	2	—	5
91	*Ruddi.* Farmers	7	14	2	13	—	29
92	*Mallewar.* Farmers, who wear the *Lingam*	689	1376	623	1257	472	3728
93	*Puroo.* Merchants' servants	16	28	13	23	9	73
94	*Cunnucungal.* Day labourers	1	4	3	4	3	14
95	*Sopucoragur (Corar).* Ditto	158	267	118	258	106	749
96	*Dererd (Whalliaru).* Slaves employed in cultivation	12278	16751	7528	16633	6446	47358
97	*Dobe.* Washermen	517	912	352	855	284	2403
98	*Hujam.* Barbers	517	912	352	855	284	2403
99	*Chummar.* Workers in leather	193	386	187	378	149	1100
100	*Sungtrash.* Stone-cutters	27	48	16	42	16	122
101	*Sunar.* Gold and silver smiths	1329	2714	1194	2640	1017	7565
102	*Cassar.* Workers in brass	127	234	95	223	73	625
103	*Lohar.* Blacksmiths	127	210	101	201	95	607
104	*Julai.* Weavers	847	1367	707	1335	543	3952
105	*Canara Kumbhara.* Pot-makers	2188	3892	1570	3646	1350	10458
106	*Buddai.* Carpenters	602	986	529	1027	382	2924
107	*Rungary.* Dyers	1	4	—	2	—	6
108	*Borudir.* Mat-makers	65	111	55	106	39	311
109	*Tambutgars.* Coppersmiths	5	13	9	12	5	39
110	*Chitrigar.* Painters	5	9	5	9	4	27
111	*Pinjar.* Cotton-cleaners	16	27	12	28	4	71
112	*Shiculdars.* Cutlers	10	26	6	23	7	62
113	*Zeendar.* Saddlers	32	62	26	62	25	175
114	*Dirzi.* Taylors	125	252	119	245	87	703
115	*Toipha.* Dancers and musicians	156	140	96	345	142	723
116	*Jetty.* Wrestlers	2	5	3	4	1	13

CHAPTER XIV.

Jan. 15.

No.	Casts or Trades.	Houses.	Men.	Boys.	Women.	Girls.	Total.
117	*Killabund.* Architects, literally constructors of forts - - - - - -	4	3	—	7	4	14
118	*Tapegar.* Jewellers - - -	1	2	2	2	1	7
119	*Jilligar.* People who search wells, and *tanks* for lost money. - - - - -	5	7	5	4	2	18
120	*Moothaley.* - - - - - - -	26	35	21	27	24	107
121	*Adagathur Mogayar.* Boatmen and fishermen -	31	51	18	61	14	144
122	*Corchey.* Day labourers - - -	3	11	4	7	11	33
	Grand total - -	79856	141681	64952	140302	49737	396672

The general result is, that in the southern division of *Canara* there are 79,856 houses, inhabited by 396,672 persons; of whom

Males, Men -	141,681	
Boys -	64,952	
		206,633
Females, Women	140,302	
Girls -	49,737	
		190,039

Polygamy not owing to an excess of females.

This excess of males above the female population, which also has been found to prevail in the *Bara-mahal*, and other parts of the peninsula where an accurate census has been taken, entirely overthrows the doctrine upon which some ingenious reasoners have attempted to account for the prevalence of polygamy in warm climates.

Jan. 16. State of the country.

16th *January*, 1801.—I went about two miles, said to be two cosses and a half, to a place called *Urigara*, or the *bank*. Immediately beyond *Carai* I was ferried over a very wide inlet of the sea, which separates the province of *Malabar* from that of *Canara;* but the country called *Malayala* by the natives extends a considerable way farther north. My road all the way led along a narrow bank of sand, between the sea and the inlet. The surf, although larger than any that I have seen on this coast, is by no means so violent

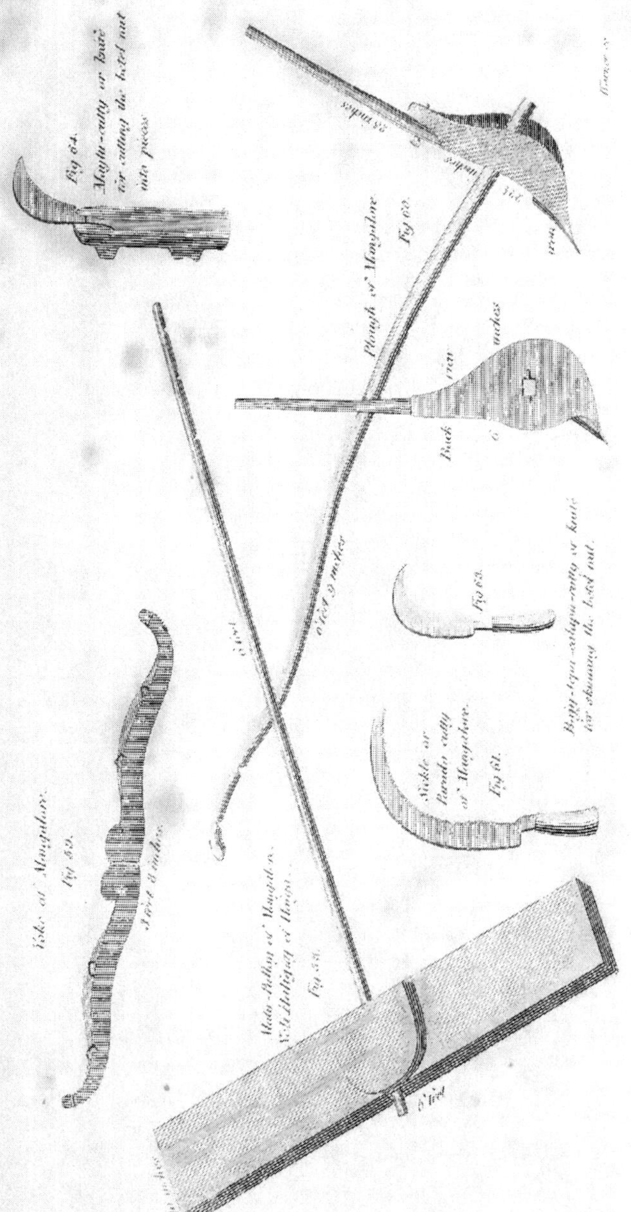
Yoke of Mangalore.
Fig 59.
3 feet 8 inches
Fig 64.
Maytu-cutty or knife for cutting the betel nut into pieces
Fig 58.
6 feet
6 feet 9 inches
Plough of Mangalore.
Fig 60.
23 inches
inches
iron
Sickle or Parudu cutty of Mangalore.
Fig 61.
Fig 63.
Back
iron
6
inches
for skinning the betel nut.
6 feet

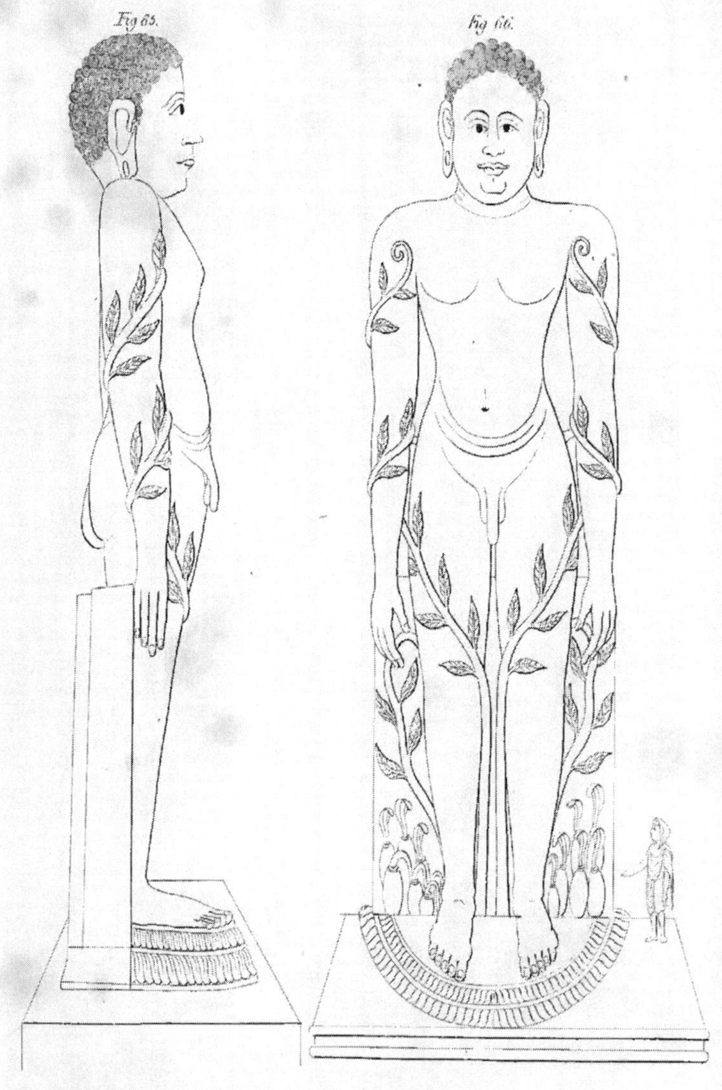

Image at Carculla in Canara.

Fig. 67.

Image of Sankara Narayana at Gaukarna.

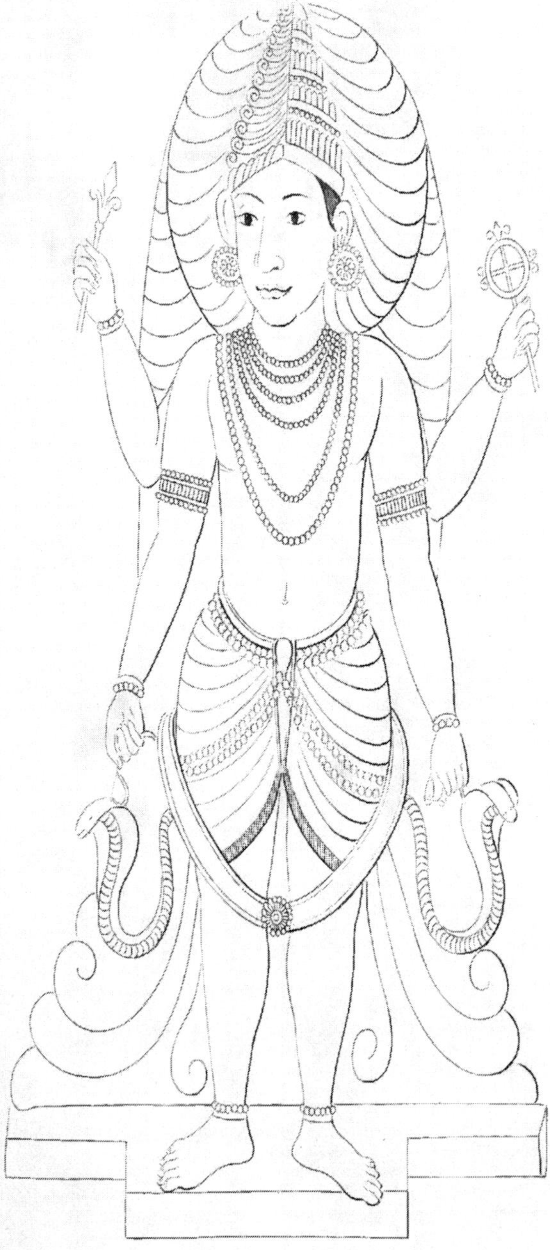

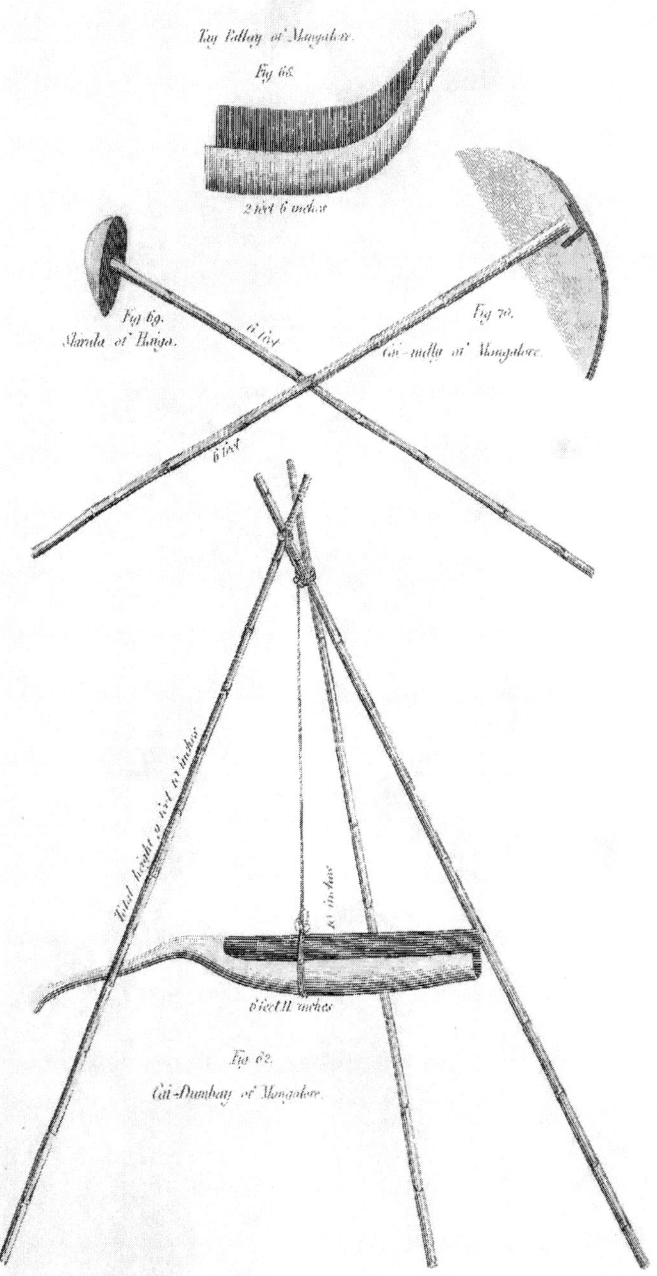
Tay Pallay of Mangalore.
Fig 68.
2 feet 6 inches
Fig 69.
Fig 70.
Cai-mally of Mangalore.
6 feet
6 feet
6 feet 11 inches
Fig 62.
Cai-Dumbay of Mangalore.

Rivner sc.

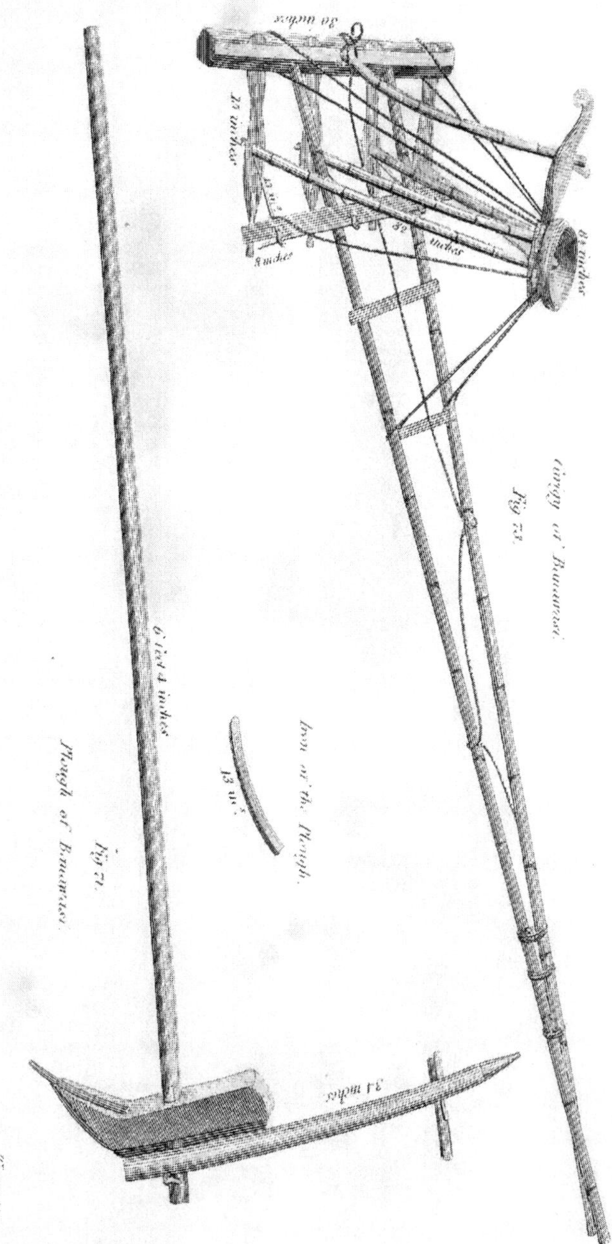
84 inches
Gorigy of Banawasi.
Fig 73.
32 inches
30 inches
13 in.s
8 inches
25 inches
Iron of the Plough.
13 in.s
34 inches
6 feet 4 inches
Fig 71.
Plough of Banawasi.
Warner sc.

Small mill for cleaning cotton at Hurri-hara.

Fig. 74.

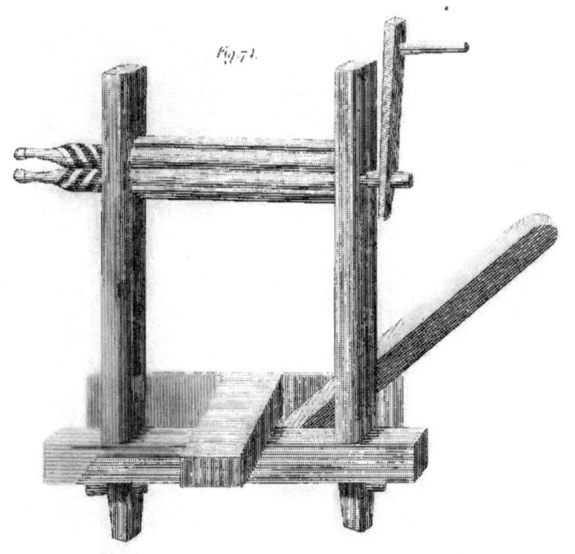

Fig. 83.

Basire sc.

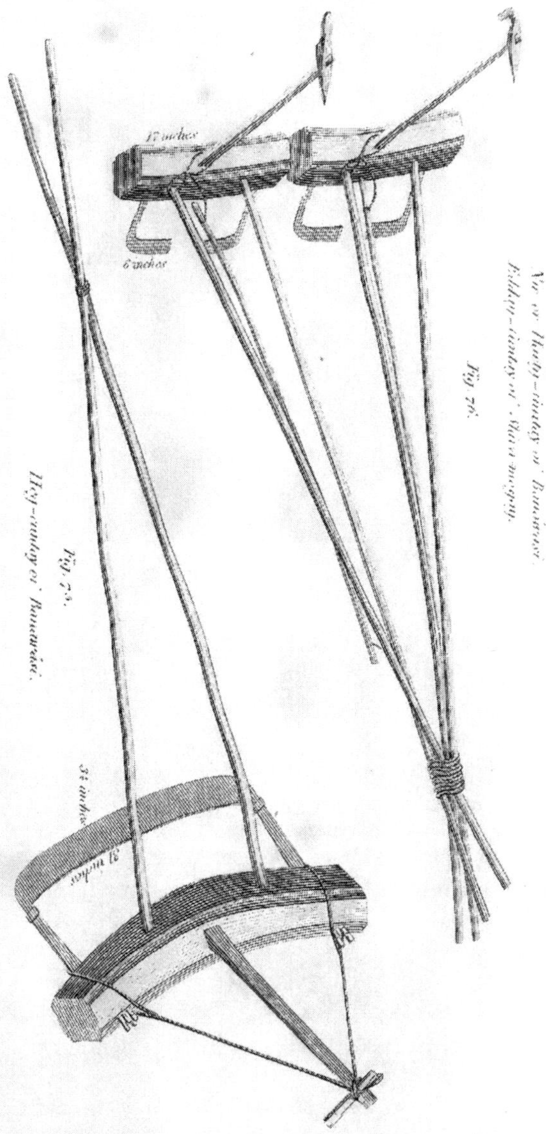

Ner or Hurty-cuntay or' Banawasi.
Edday-cuntay or' Shiva-mogay.

Fig. 76.

Fig. 75.

Hey-cuntay or' Banawasi.

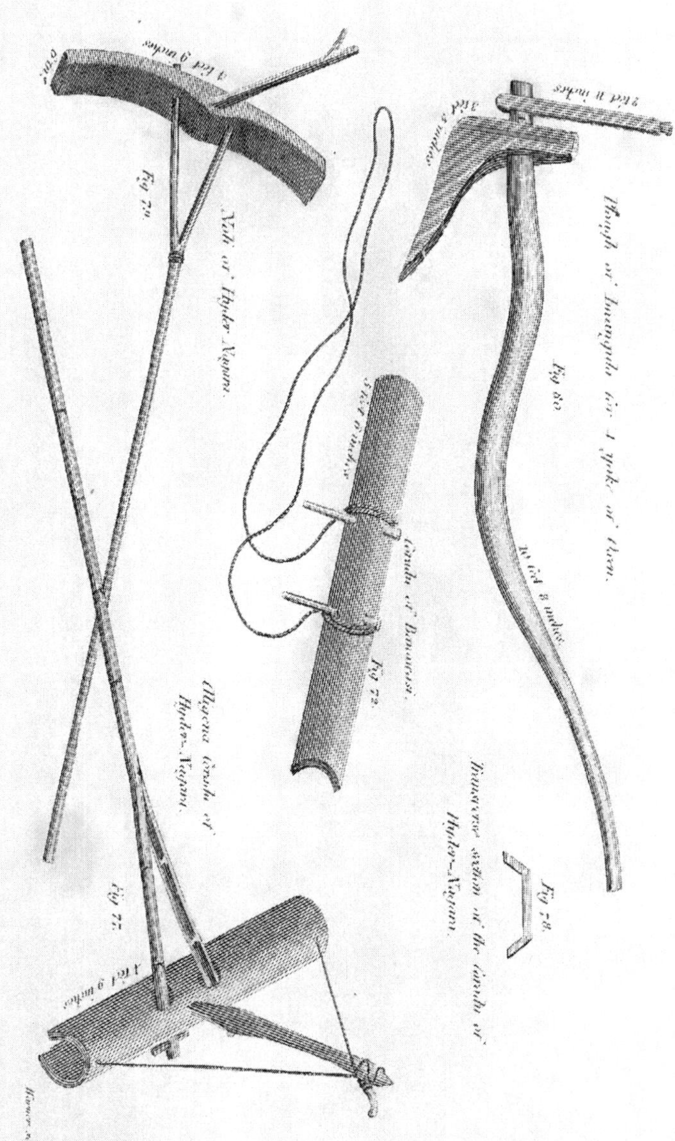
Fig 79.
Fig 80
10 feet 8 inches
Fig 72.
Fig 78.
Transverse section of the Candu of Hyder-Nagam.
Fig 77.
4 feet 9 inches

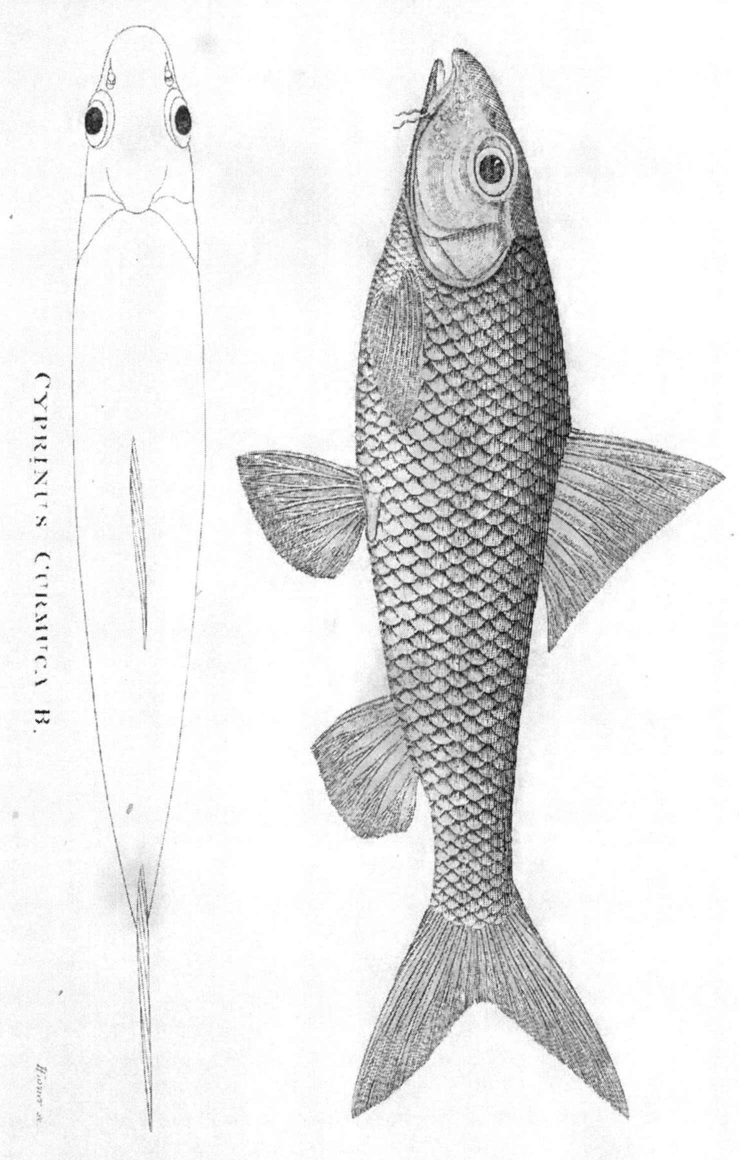

CYPRINUS CURMUCA B.

CYPRINUS ARIZA, B.

PLATE XXXII.

CYPRINUS BENDELISIS.

Warner sc.

Fig. 81.

Vertical section of a glass furnace at Mutcodu.

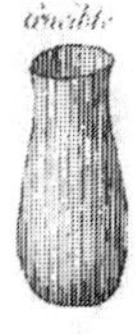

Fig. 82.

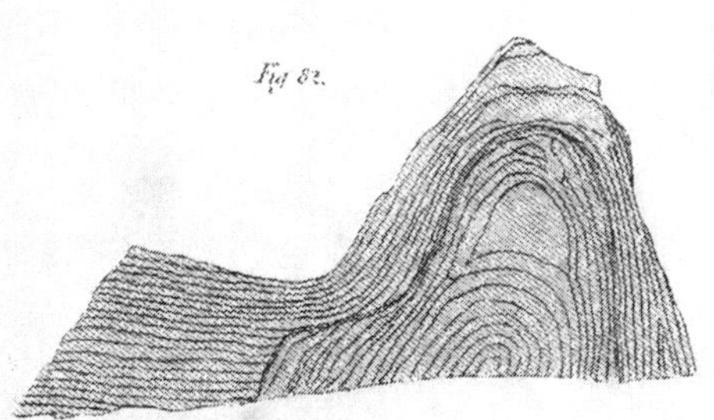

Disposition of the layers of ore within the matrix at Doda Rashy Mine.

Fig. 83.

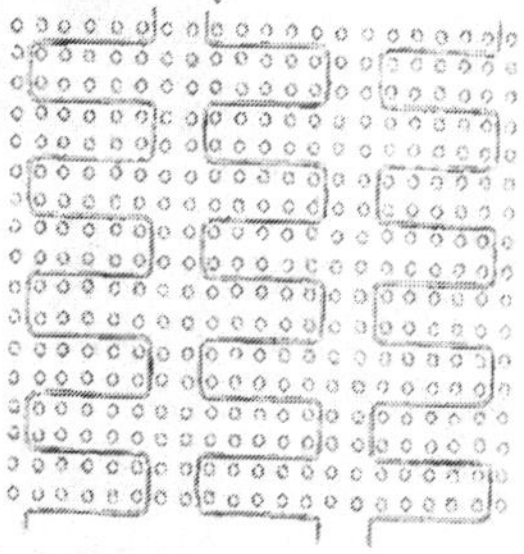

Plan of the channels in a sugar field at Kelamangulam.

Fig. 84.

Colossal image at Sravana Belgula.

MOIZ UD DEEN,

Second legitimate Son of Tippoo Sultan.

Fig 6.

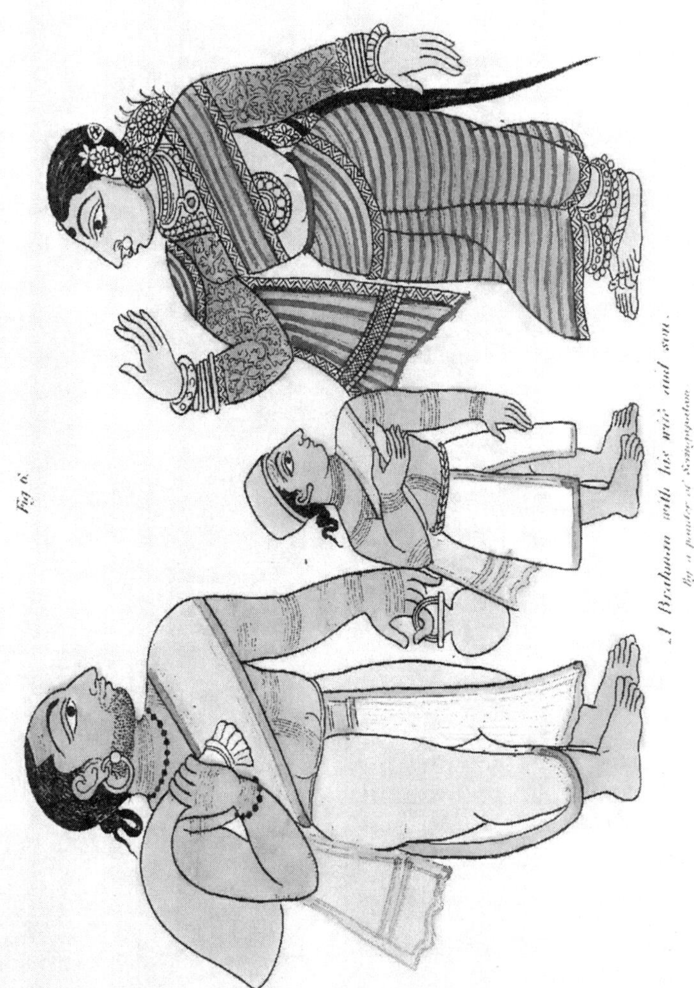

A Brahman with his wife and son.

By a painter of Seringapatam

as at Madras; and small fishing canoes go through it with ease. At *Urigara* the sand bank increases in width, and admits of some rice fields, and plantations of coco-nut trees. There is here no village; but there are a few huts inhabited by *Moplays*, who now possess the sea-coast of this part of *Malayala*, as the *Nairs* do the interior. On the side of the inlet, opposite from *Urigara*, is *Nilé-swara*, now a *Moplay* village, but formerly the residence of a *Rájá*, who derived his title from the place, which is called after one of the names of the god *Siva*. Although the *Nairs* are still more numerous than the *Moplays*, yet during *Tippoo's* authority, while not protected by government, the *Hindus* were forced to skulk in the woods, and all such as could be caught were circumcised. It must be observed, that however involuntary this conversion may be, it is perfectly effectual, and the convert immediately becomes a good Mussulman, as otherwise he would have no cast at all; and, although the doctrine of cast be no part of the faith of Muhammed, it has in India been fully adopted by the low ranks of Mussulmans. On entering *Canara*, an immediate change in the police takes place. No person is here permitted to swagger about with arms: these may be kept in the house for protection against thieves; but they must not be brought into public, for the encouragement of assassination.

CHAPTER XIV. Jan. 16.

17th *January*.—I went about ten miles to *Hosso-durga*, or *Pungal-cotay*; both of which signify the new fort, the former in the dialect of *Karnáta*, and the latter in the *Malayala* language. The country near the sea, most of the way that I came to-day, is low and sandy; but much of it is rice-land, intermixed with which is much sandy land, too poor, the natives say, to produce coco-nut palms. The whole appears to be much neglected, owing to a want of inhabitants.

Jan. 17. Appearance of the country.

Towards *Hosso-durga*, the dry-field rises into gentle swells; yet it is too hard and dry for plantations. It is now waste; but, when there were plenty of people, it was cultivated for *Ragy (Cynosurus*

CHAPTER XIV.

Jan. 17.

corocanus), *Horse-gram (Dolichos biflorus)*, *Sesamum*, and different pulses. The hill-rice is here unknown; the soil, however, is exactly the same as that which is used to the southward for this grain.

Hosso-durga.

The fort is large, and well built of the *Laterite* common all over *Malayala*. The bastions being round, it is more capable of defence than the native forts in general, in which the defences are usually square. It occupies a fine rising ground, looks well at a distance, and commands a noble prospect. The only inhabitants are a few *Puttar Bráhmans*, who serve a temple, and whose ancestors were placed there by the *Ikeri Rájá*, who built the fort.

History of the *Niléswara Rájás*.

According to the report of the *Nairs* here, all this part of the country originally belonged to *Colata-nada;* but from the river of *Cavai* to that near *Beäcul* had been long alienated, from the house of *Colastri*, to the *Niléswara Rájá*, a chief of the *Tamuri* family. In the year 905 (*A. D.* 17$\frac{29}{30}$), *Ráma Varmá Rájá* of *Niléswara* was invaded by the *Ikeri Rájá*, who in the following year built the fort. After a struggle of twelve years, the *Nair* prince was compelled to become tributary. His country was divided into three *Nadas*, or districts, for each of which he agreed to pay annually 530 *Ikeri Pagodas*, or 213*l.* 12*s.* 3*d.* On paying this sum the *Rájás* were allowed to retain the entire management of their country, and seem at least so early to have established a regular land-tax in lieu of their claims on the moveable property of all persons dying in their territory. These claims they entirely relinquished, and took one half of the landlord's *(Jenmcar's)* profit on rice-lands, and one fifth of his profit on gardens. On the destruction of the *Ikeri* family, *Hyder* took possession of this country, and increased the tribute to 1500 *Pagodas* for each district; but allowed the *Rájá*, as collector, an establishment of 650 *Pagodas* a year; so that, in fact, each district paid 1283$\frac{1}{3}$ *Pagodas*, or 517*l.* 2*s.* 4$\frac{1}{2}$*d.* Some time afterwards, some landlords *(Jenmcars)* having made complaints of violent oppression against the *Rájá*, he resisted the people sent by *Hyder* to investigate the matter, and a war ensued, which ended in the

CHAPTER XIV.

Jan. 17.

Rájá's being forced to an exile in *Travancore*. *Hyder* then took the country under his own management, and increased the rate of the land-tax; but, as usual, he made this more palatable by granting considerable allowances to the temples and *Bráhmans*. As soon as *Tippoo* obtained authority in the country, these were stopped; but, since the province was conquered by the Company, a part of the allowances have been given to the priests *(Pújáris)* who officiate in the temples. When General Mathews took *Bangalore*, the *Rájá* came back from *Travancore*, and seized on the country. After the *Sultan* had triumphantly made the peace of *Mangalore*, he was opposed with such success by this petty *Rájá*, that he was forced to consent that the *Rájá* should manage the country, and pay only the same tribute which had been exacted by *Hyder*. In the year 961 (*A. D.* $178\frac{5}{6}$), the *Rájá*, having been lulled into security, was inveigled, by repeated promises of safety and friendship, to visit *Budr' uz Zamánkhán*, governor of *Beücul*, who hanged him instantly, and, having marched all his forces into the country, before any measure could be taken to resist him, reduced the whole to the obedience of his master. The younger brother of *Ráma Varmá* made his escape to *Travancore*, and remained there until Lord Cornwallis invaded *Seringapatam*. He then came to *Tellichery*, from whence he received supplies of arms. In the year 966 (*A. D.* $179\frac{0}{1}$), he returned with these to *Niléswara*, raised an insurrection, and compelled the *Sultan* to allow him the management of the country, on condition of paying the former tribute. After the fall of *Seringapatam*, when Major Monro arrived to take charge of *Canara* as collector, the *Rájá* was sick, but sent his sister's son, or heir, to wait on that gentleman; who very prudently told the *Rájá*, that his case would be laid before the government for their decision. In the mean while, the country was put entirely under the management of *Tahsildars*, exactly on the plan introduced by Colonel Read, under whom Major Monro had been instructed in civil affairs. The *Rájá* has thus been deprived of all power; and the favourable time

CHAPTER XIV.

Jan. 17.

was chosen, when the terror inspired by the fall of *Seringapatam* rendered this easy to be done. The *Rájá* has been allowed, for his support, a remission of the land-tax on all his *Cherical* lands, or private estate. The *Nairs*, however, complain of a want of good faith in the British officers. They allege, that General Hartley, on his return from *Seringapatam*, promised the *Rájá* that he should be continued in the management of the country.

The dominions of the *Niléswara Rájá* extended from the sea to the *Ghats;* and, according to the report of the same *Nairs*, are exceedingly depopulated by war, and by a famine that ensued while they were forced to retire into the woods to avoid circumcision. The inner parts of the country are much overgrown with woods, and are very thinly inhabited. Like the other parts of *Malayala*, they consist of alternate low hills and narrow vallies. In cultivation, more slaves than free men are employed.

Jan. 18. Appearance of the country.

18th *January*.—I went an easy stage to *Beäcul*. From *Pungalcotay*, to a river bounding the country of the *Niléswara Rájá* to the north, the road leads along a ridge, sloping very gently towards the sea, and rather steeper towards a narrow valley now covered with the second crop of rice. Beyond this are low hills. The soil of the ridge is extremely sandy, and the country is very bare. The river is not wide, and has at its mouth some low land well planted with coco-nut trees.

Between the river and *Beäcul* the low hills come close down to the sea side, and are very little intermixed with rice land. In the whole way I crossed only one narrow field. The hills, however, are not steep, and seem all to be capable of being laboured by the plough; but no traces of cultivation are visible.

Beäcul.

Beäcul is a strong native fort, placed, like *Cananore*, on a high point projecting into the sea towards the south, and having within it a bay. The town stands north from the fort, and contains forty or fifty houses scattered about in great confusion. The inhabitants are chiefly *Moplays* and *Mucuas*, with a few *Tiars*, and people of

Kankána, who have been long settled in *Canara* as shop-keepers. The country extending between the river south from *Beäcul*, and that near *Chandra-giri*, was divided into two districts (*Nadas*), which continued subject to the *Cherical Rájás*, as representatives of the house of *Colastri*, until the invasion by the *Ikeri Rájá*. Beggars begin to swarm here, as is the case almost every where in India in which I have been, except *Malabar*, where I scarcely met with one.

CHAPTER XIV.

Jan. 18.

Produce of the rice-grounds.

The *Tahsildar* (collector) says, that in the part of *Malayala* which is contained in *Canara*, the rice-lands near the sea produce annually only one crop, and yield from 5 to 10 seeds, or from 12½ to 25 bushels an acre. In the vallies of the inland country the produce is greater; the land that produces one crop only gives from 12 to 15 seeds, or from 24 to 37½ bushels an acre; that which gives two crops, produces the same quantity in the first, and from 8 to 10 seeds in the second, or from 20 to 25 bushels an acre. More grain is raised in the country than the small number of inhabitants can consume. The people are accused by the *Tahsildar* of excessive indolence, and of drunkenness; vices which he attributes to the constant troubles that prevailed during the government of the *Sultan*.

Revenue.

Trimula Row, the *Tahsildar*, says, that the nominal value of this part of *Malayala* which is contained in *Canara*, according to the revenue accompts of *Tippoo's* officers, was 8000 *Bahádary Varáhas*, or 32,000 *Rupees*. Although Major Monro did not make any formal remission of this rent, he only levied 6000 *Pagodas*, or 24,000 *Rupees*, and did not keep the remainder as a balance against the cultivators, which would have depressed their spirits. He took from each man, what in his present circumstances he could afford to pay, and did not, for the sake of a nominal revenue on paper, prevent all exertion in the cultivator, by holding over his head the terror of a balance which he could never hope to clear. The rice ground now is not taxed by any share of the *Varum*, or neat rent; but each field pays so much, according to its supposed value; and this tax

CHAPTER XIV. Jan. 18.

is alleged to consume the whole rent. Very few of the landlords *(Jenmcars)* remain, and even the mortgagees *(Canumcars)* are willing to give up all the land, which they cannot cultivate with their own stock, to any one who will pay the land-tax. The gardens here pay not only a tax on the trees, as in *Malabar*, but also a tax on the extent of ground which they occupy; yet by *Trimula Row* they are reckoned by far the most profitable heritage for the cultivators. He thinks that the taxes on the cultivator are heavier here than those in *Arcot*. I must observe, that with all these complaints there is little of the rice-land waste; while there is no tax on the cultivation of dry grains, and very little of them is sown.

Niléswara Rájá.

Trimula Row says, that *Poduga* and *Cavi*, the two districts formerly belonging to *Cherical*, had been entirely subdued; but that the *Niléswara Rájás* had constantly disputed the authority of *Tippoo*. They frequently were able to retain the management, on condition of paying tribute, and then again were frequently driven into exile. The *Rájá* asked nothing more, from Major Monro, than a remission of the taxes on the *Cherical* lands, which was last year granted; but it is uncertain whether or not this favour will be continued.

Jan. 19. Appearance of the country.

19th *January*.—I went to a temple dedicated to *Iswara*, at a place called *Pulla*. The first part of my journey was over a sandy spit, separating a salt water lake from the sea. Beyond this, the country rises into open rising lands, all the way to *Chandra-giri* river, which is the northern boundary of *Malayala*. This rising land is in very few places too steep for the plough, and these places are in general rocky. The whole of this land is totally waste, and looks very ill, being covered with long withered grass. There are traces of its having been formerly cultivated; and, no doubt, with manure it would be productive of dry grains. For the cultivation of rice, tanks or reservoirs might easily be constructed; but, with the present paucity of inhabitants, it would be madness to cultivate any thing, except the richest spots. Intermixed with this rising land are a few plots of rice-ground, surrounded by palm gardens and the houses of the *Nairs;* but the proportion of this rich land does not seem to be above a hundredth part of the country. CHAPTER XIV.

Chandra-giri is a large square fort, situated high above the river on its southern bank. It was built, like the other forts before-mentioned, by *Sivuppa Náyaka,* the first prince of the house of *Ikeri* that established his authority in this part of *Canara.* Jan. 19. *Chandra-giri.*

At low water the river is shallow, but very wide. The country on its north side is by the *Hindus* called *Tulava,* and resembles that through which I passed on the south side of the river. I left to my right another fort named *Casselgoda,* which also was built by *Sivuppa,* when he subjected the petty *Rájás* of *Tulava. Pulla,* where I stopped, is on the banks of a salt water lake, communicating both with the sea and with the *Chandra-giri* river. South boundary of *Tulava.*

20th *January.*—I went about ten miles to *Kanya-pura,* and about half way crossed a river of considerable width; yet at low water it is shallow. The country through which I passed resembles much the part of *Tulava* that I saw yesterday, but the plantations of coco-nuts were rather more numerous. The rice grounds are more neatly cultivated than those in *Malayala,* and the water for the second crop is conducted to them with great care. In many places, where the ground is too high to give a second crop of rice, a crop of *Ricinus,* or of sweet potatoes *(Convolvulus),* is taken. Near the sea, sugar-cane is cultivated. Many traces of former gardens are to be seen from the road, which shows that this kind of cultivation may be greatly extended. Jan. 20. Face of the country.

Kanya-pura is seated on the south bank of a river which surrounds the fort and town of *Cumly.* This is situated on a high peninsula in a salt water lake, which is separated from the sea by a spit of sand. Two rivers fall into this kind of lake, and contain between them the peninsula on which *Cumly* stands. By far the greater part of the coast is occupied by a chain of salt water lakes; but the necks of land interposed render them of little use for an inland navigation. *Kanya-pura* contains about 200 houses, and *Kanya-pura,* and *Cumly.*

CHAPTER XIV.

Jan. 20.

Cumly about 150. The inhabitants are chiefly *Moplays*, *Mucuas*, *Mogayers*, and *Kankanies*. The interior parts are chiefly occupied by the *Bráhmans* of *Tulava*, and the *Bunts*, or *Buntar*.

Bráhmans of Tulava.

The *Tulava Bráhmans* resemble the *Namburis*, and consider themselves as the proper lords of the country.

Massadi Bunts.

The *Buntar* are the highest rank of *Súdras* in *Tulava*, and resemble the *Nairs* of *Malayala*. Having assembled some reputable persons of this cast, they gave me the following account of their customs. They are of three kinds: *Massadi Bunts*, or *Buntar* properly so called; *Jain*; and *Parivarada Buntar*. The *Massadi Bunts* are those whom I here examined. They can eat and drink with the *Nairs*; but the two casts have no sexual intercourse. They do not pretend to be by birth soldiers; their proper duty is the cultivation of the land. They can keep accompts, but are not admitted to any higher kind of learning. They have head-men, called *Mocustas*, one for every district. The office is hereditary in the males by the female line; the same mode of succession prevailing here, as in *Malayala*. At present, this office merely confers dignity; the officers of government having assumed all the jurisdiction that formerly belonged to the *Mocustas*, who settled disputes not only relative to casts, but also concerning property. In general, all the brothers and unmarried sisters of a family live together in the same house. All the property belonging to the family is considered as common, and is managed, for the good of the whole, by the oldest male. A man's own children are not his heirs. During his life-time he may give them money; but all of which he dies possessed goes to his sisters, and to their children. If a man has a mother's-brother's-daughter, he must marry her; but he may take two or three wives beside. The ceremony is performed by the girl's father, or other near kinsman. When a man marries several wives, none of them can leave him without his consent; but when discord runs high, he in general sends one of the disputants back to her brother's house; and then she is at liberty to marry again. A man at any time, if he dislikes his wife, may send her back to her brother's house; and he can do no more if she has committed adultery. In all these cases, or when a widow returns to her brother's house on her husband's death, she is accompanied by her children, and may marry again, unless she has committed adultery with a person of low cast; but if that crime has been committed with a *Bráhman*, *Kshatri*, *Vaisya*, or *Bunt*, she is well received, her children become her brother's heirs, and no man will have any objection to marry her. The *Buntar* are permitted to eat animal food, and to drink spirituous liquors. They burn the dead. They seem to be entirely ignorant of a state of future existence; only they believe, that such men as die accidental deaths become *Pysáchi*, or evil spirits, and are exceedingly troublesome, by making extraordinary noises in families, and occasioning fits, and other diseases, especially in women. To expel these, the *Buntar* apply to the *Nucaru*, who are a class similar to the *Cunian* of *Malayala*, and who pretend by means of incantations (*Mantrams*) to have a power over the spirits. For the same purpose, sacrifices are offered to various *Saktis*, which differ in almost every different village. Those worshipped here are *Dumawutty*, *Iberabuta*, or the twin devils, and *Birnala*. Besides the sacrifices offered to these idols, to free the people from the attacks of the *Pysáchi*, *Iberabuta* and *Birnala* must be appeased by an annual, and *Dumawutty* by a monthly sacrifice. If these are omitted, the enraged devils kill both man and beast. *Siva*, however, is the proper deity of the cast; yet the *Buntar* pray also to *Vishnu*. They call the *Tulava Bráhmans* their *Puróhitas*; but on no occasion do these read *Mantrams* for their followers. All that they can do is to receive *Dharma*, or charity, and to bestow consecrated ashes and holy water.

CHAPTER XIV. Jan. 20.

Cumly Rájá.

All this south part of *Tulava* formerly belonged to the *Cumly Rájá*, who pretends to be a *Kshatri* from the north of India. The manners of his family are the same with those of the *Rájás* of *Malayala*. All the males keep *Nair* girls; but their children, who are

CHAPTER XIV. Jan. 20.

called *Tambans*, have no right to the succession. The eldest daughter in the female line cohabits with a *Tulava Bráhman;* her sons become *Rájás*, and her eldest daughter continues the line of the family. Whenever she pleases, she changes her *Bráhman.* The younger daughters also cohabit with *Bráhmans*, and produce a race of people called *Bayllal*, who have no right to the succession. The dominions of this family extended from the *Chandra-giri* river to that on the north side of *Cumly*, and produced an annual revenue of 15,000 *Ikeri Pagodas*, or 6044*l.* 3*s.* 4*d.* The *Rájá* lives now in the country; but he has neither lands nor authority. Before the last war he lived at *Tellichery*, on a pension from the Company; which has been doubled since we got possession of the country of his ancestors.

Invasion by the *Coorg Rájá.*

The interior parts are said to be naturally very fertile in rice, but they suffered much in the last war. The *Coorg Rájá*, during the siege of *Seringapatam*, under pretence of assisting the English, made an incursion into the country, and swept away all the inhabitants that he could seize. He has given them possessions in his own country; but they are very desirous of returning home, although I do not hear that he uses them ill.

State of the natives in *Tuluva.*

The people of *Tulava*, although longer subjected to a foreign yoke than those of *Malabar*, never have been so entirely subdued as the greater part of the *Hindus*, and have always been able successfully to resist the pretensions of their governors to be proprietors of the soil. Their native chiefs have, indeed, been in general able to retain more or less of the management of the country; and on the fall of *Seringapatam*, I am here informed, were very much disposed to try how far they could assert their independence. Two months are said to have elapsed, after the arrival of Major Monro in the country, before that gentleman could induce the people to meet him for the purpose of settling the revenue; but the decisive measures adopted to punish all those who presumed to disturb the peace, an assumed severity of manner to prevent the hopes of success from cajolery, and a strict forbearance from making promises or concessions for the sake of a temporary submission, have saved *Canara* from anarchy, and destructive, though petty warfare.

Jan. 21. Appearance of the country.

21st *January.*—I ferried over the lake to the peninsula on which *Cumly* stands, and which was formerly joined to *Kanya-pura* by a bridge. The situation of the fort is very fine, and the town has formerly been pretty considerable. The two rivers leave a narrow isthmus of rice-fields. At present, both the rivers and the lake are salt; but in the rainy season they are quite fresh, and at that time, when no boats can venture to sea, might afford a fine supply of fish: this, however, is an article of food which, except by persons of very low cast, is seldom used. Having crossed the north branch, I went along the sea-beach, having on my right high sandy downs, which prevented me from seeing the country, until I arrived at the banks of a wide but fordable river. On the north side of this is a large straggling town called *Manjéswara*. It contains many good houses, chiefly inhabited by *Moplays*, *Buntar*, and *Biluars.* Having crossed the plain on which *Manjéswara* stands, and forded a small river, I took up my quarters at a town named *Hosso-betta*, or the *new-strength*, which is situated on a steep bank that overhangs the last mentioned river.

Byrasu Wodears, a *Jain* family.

Immediately after crossing the northern branch of the *Cumly* river, you enter a country that formerly belonged to a *Jain* family called *Byrasu Wodear*, which resided at *Carculla*. The *Jain* here say, that this family were overthrown by *Sivuppa Náyaka* of *Ikeri*, who divided the country into small districts, each producing an annual revenue of from one to three thousand *Pagodas*. Over each of these was placed a petty *Rájá* of the *Jain* religion. Ever since, the country has been constantly on the decline, having been continually in a state of insurrection or confusion.

Petty *Rájás* of *Tulava.*

Bungar Rájá.

The dominions of the first of these *Jain* chiefs that I entered were those of the *Bungar Rájá*. *Tippoo* hanged the last person who

CHAPTER XIV.

possessed this dignity; and his children cultivate some land at *Nandavara*, a village in the territory of the family.

Jan. 21. *Rájá of Vitly.*

Hosso-betta is also frequently called *Vitly Manjèswara*, from its having belonged to another *Jain* chief named *Hegady Rájá* of *Vitly*. By the intervention of other districts it is however entirely separated from the other territory which belonged to the *Vitly Rájás*, the last of whom was hanged here about three months ago. Before the war, he had lived at *Tellichery*, and received from the Company a monthly pension of 200 *Rupees*. When the army of General Harris approached *Seringapatam*, the *Rájá* came here, and, having collected a rabble, plundered the country with great success, and then returned to *Tellichery*. After *Canara* became subject to the Company, the people, who had been thus wantonly plundered, applied for redress, and *Hegady* was required to restore their property. This he refused, and, having procured 800 muskets, it is said from *Mousa*, he returned to *Vitly*, dressed up some ruffians like *Sepoys*, and assumed the authority of a sovereign prince. For almost a year he was able to skulk about the woods, and support himself by plunder; but having been then taken, he was immediately hanged, ever since which the country has been perfectly quiet.

Kankánies expelled from Goa.

The principal inhabitants of *Hosso-betta*, and indeed of many of the towns in *Tulava*, are *Kankánies*, or people descended from natives of *Kankána*. They say, that they fled hither, to avoid a persecution at *Govay (Goa)*, their native country. An order arrived from the king of Portugal to convert all the natives. The viceroy, when this order arrived, was, they say, a very lenient good man, and permitted all the natives who chose to retire to carry their effects with them, and allowed them fifteen days to arrange their affairs. Accordingly, all the rich people, *Bráhmans* and *Súdras*, retired to *Tulava*, with such of their property as they could in that time realise, and they now chiefly subsist by trade. Both *Bráhmans* and *Súdras* are called by the national appellation of *Kankánies*, and the other *Bráhmans* will have no communion with these exiles. They are, however, in flourishing circumstances; and I saw some of their marriage processions passing to-day, attended by a number of exceedingly well dressed people, and very handsome girls. The poor *Kankánies* who remained behind at *Goa* were, of course, all converted to what was called Christianity. Jan. 21.

22d *January.*—I went a short stage to *Ulala*, a large town on the south side of the lake of *Mangalore*, and formerly the residence of a petty prince. I first passed through *Harawurry Manjéswara*, which is immediately north from the *Manjéswara* that belonged to the *Vitly Rájá;* but it is situated in the district surrounding *Mangalore*, which was not divided among the petty *Rájás*, but was immediately under the government of the lieutenant of the *Ikeri Rájá* who commanded at *Mangalore*. Jan. 22. *Ulala.* *Harawurry Manjéswara.*

I afterwards crossed over the lake to the town, where I remained until the 29th. The lake is a fine body of salt water, separated from the sea by a beach of sand. In this, formerly, there was one opening; the depth of water in which was such, that ships of a considerable burthen, after their cargo had been removed, could enter the lake. Last year a new opening formed in the beach, which has proved very injurious to the harbour. The depth of the old opening has diminished, and that of the new one has never become great; so that now, even at high water, and in easy weather, vessels drawing more than ten feet cannot enter. Harbour of *Mangalore.*

For a native place of strength, the fort of *Mangalore* was well constructed; but was destroyed by *Tippoo*, after he had found how little his fortresses were calculated to resist European soldiers, and with what difficulty he could retake any of them, that were garrisoned by a few British troops. The town, called also *Codeal Bundar*, is large, and is built round the sides of the peninsula, in the elevated center of which the fort was placed. The lake, by which the peninsula is formed, is a most beautiful piece of salt water. The *Mangalore.*

CHAPTER XIV.

boats that ply on it are execrable; and the fishermen by whom they are managed are a very indolent drunken race.

Jan. 22. Customs of the *Mogayer*.

These fishermen are called *Mogayer*, and are a cast of *Tulava* origin. They resemble the *Mucuas* of *Malayala*, but the one cast will have no communion with the other. The *Mogayer* are boatmen, fishermen, porters, and palanquin bearers. All of this cast can eat and intermarry together. They pretend to be *Súdras* of a pure descent, which is rather doubtful; and assume a superiority over the *Halepecas*, one of the most common casts of cultivators in *Tulava;* but they acknowledge themselves greatly inferior to the *Bunts*. They have head-men called *Gurucaras*, whose office is hereditary in the males by the female line. With the assistance of a council, the head-man settles disputes, and punishes all transgressions against the rules of cast. The only fault that is punishable with excommunication is when a woman commits fornication with a person of a lower cast; but for adultery with either a man of the cast, or of one that is higher, a woman is seldom turned away by her husband; and even if she be, she is by no means disgraced, but returns to her brother's house, and may be married again whenever she finds a new lover. The men may take several wives, and the whole ceremony of marriage consists in giving the girl some ornaments. After accepting these, she must live in his house, nor can she leave it without her husband's consent; but, whenever he pleases, he may send her back to her brother. The children always follow the mother, and are the heirs to her brothers, and not to their father. If a man's sister be living in the house, she has the entire management of it, and his wives have no authority. The *Mogayer* are permitted to eat animal food, and to drink intoxicating liquors. Some few of them can read, and write accompts. Those of them who are rich burn, those who are poor bury their dead. The spirits of good men go to *Moesha*, which, according to the *Bráhmans*, is the heaven where *Vishnu* resides; but the *Mogayer*

CHAPTER XIV. Jan. 22.

know of no other. After death, bad men are supposed to be taken by *Emma Dharma Raja*, the judge of the infernal regions. Some of the *Mogayers* pray to *Vishnu*, and some to *Siva*; but the proper deity of the cast is a goddess named *Restali Mahastumma*, who is represented by an image in the form of a woman. The priest *(Pújari)* is a *Biluar*, whose office is hereditary in the males of the female line. The women of this family live with laymen, and the daughters of these are kept by the priest. This is the only kind of priest that these people have. The *Brahmans* indeed accept *Dharma* (duty) from them; but they do not attend at any of their ceremonies, to read *Mantrams*. The goddess has other worshippers, *Buntar*, and oil-makers. She never occasions any trouble to her votaries, if they pray and offer sacrifices; but, if these are neglected, she inflicts sickness on the impious persons. Men who have incurred her displeasure, and who in consequence have become sick, make a vow to suspend themselves by hooks passed through the skin of their backs, and thus to be swung round before her temple. This expiation is performed at the *Játram*, or great annual feast, when many bloody sacrifices are offered. Women who suppose that the goddess has inflicted on them barrenness, or other great infirmity, vow to walk barefooted on red-hot coals before the temple. If the goddess hears their prayers, she prevents the coals from burning their feet. My informants impudently assert, that the ceremony is frequently performed. A quantity of red-hot coals are spread before the temple; and the woman, after having fasted a whole day, walks three times slowly with bare feet over the fire. The *Mogayers* suppose themselves liable to various diseases from the influence of evil spirits, called *Jacny*, and *Teiteno*, which resemble those called *Paisáchi*. These are not to be expelled by sacrifices; but the *Mogayer* apply to some *Biluaras*, and Mussulmans, who possess invocations *(Mantrams)* fit for the purpose.

Christians of *Kankána* settled in *Tulava*.

The princes of the house of *Ikeri* had given great encouragement to the Christians, and had induced 80,000 of them to settle in

CHAPTER XIV. Jan. 22.

Tulava. They are all of *Kankána* descent, and retained the language, dress, and manners of the people of that country. The clergy, it is true, adopted the dress of the order to which they belonged; but they are all natives descended from *Kankána* families, and were purposely educated in a seminary at *Goa*, where they were instructed in the Portuguese and Latin languages, and in the doctrines of the Church of Rome. In *Tulava* they had 27 churches, each provided with a vicar, and the whole under the control of a vicar-general, subject to the authority of the archbishop of *Goa*. *Tippoo* threw the priests into dungeons, forcibly converted to *Islámism* the laity, and destroyed all the churches. As the Christian religion does not prevent the readmission into the church of such delinquents, these involuntary Mussulmans have in general reconciled themselves with the clergy, who now of course are at liberty, and 15,000 have already returned to *Mangalore* and its vicinity; 10,000 made their escape to *Malabar*, from whence they are returning home as quickly as their poverty will admit. The clergy are now busy with their flocks, whose poverty, however, has hitherto prevented them from rebuilding any of their churches. During the government of *Hyder*, these Christians were possessed of considerable estates in land, all of which were confiscated by *Tippoo*, and immediately bestowed on persons of other casts, from whom it would be difficult to resume them. These poor people have none of the vices usually attributed to the native Portuguese; and their superior industry is more readily acknowledged by the neighbouring *Hindus*, than avowed by themselves. The vicar-general was long confined in *Jamál-ábád*. He speaks Latin neither correctly nor with fluency, and seems very desirous of obtaining what he calls a domineering power over the sect, that his authority may be equal to that of the native *Gurus*; so as to keep his flock in good order, not only by the spiritual means of excommunication, but also by the temporal expedients of fine and corporal punishment.

The coins in common currency here are,

CHAPTER XIV.

Jan. 22. Coin.

Gold.

The *Ikeri Varaha,* or *Pagoda* struck by the princes of *Ikeri,* exchanges for - - - - - - *Rupees* 4
The *Bahadary Varaha,* or *Pagoda* struck by *Hyder* - 4
The *Sultany* ditto, *Pagoda* coined by *Tippoo* - - 4
The *Krishna Raja* ditto, *Pagoda* coined by the present *Mysore Raja* - - - - - - - - 4
The *Puli Varaha,* star *Pagoda* of *Madras* - - $3\frac{1}{2}$
The *Feringy Petta Varaha,* or *Porto-novo Pagoda* - - 3
The *Sultany, Canter'-Raya,* or *Ikeri Hunas* or *Fanams* - $\frac{1}{5}$
The *Vir'-Raya Huna,* or *Fanam* coined by the *Coorg Raja* - $\frac{1}{4}$

Silver.

Suráti Rupiya, the *Rupee* coined at *Surat,* worth silver *Fanams* $5\frac{1}{2}$
Company *Rupiya,* the *Madras Rupee* lately introduced, ditto $5\frac{1}{2}$
Bily Huna, the same silver *Fanam* that is current in *Malabar.* In the *Bázár* it exchanges for 10 *Dudus,* or *Dubs,* but in revenue is taken for 14.

Copper.

Both the *Any Dudus,* or *Tippoo's* copper *Dubs,* and the *Bombay Paisa,* coined in England, are current here; and these with their fractions, $\frac{1}{3}$, $\frac{1}{2}$, and $\frac{1}{4}$, are the only small coin in use. *Cowries,* or small shells, are not in circulation.

In payment for goods, or debts, every person must receive these coins at the above rate of exchange. The money-changers give silver for gold at the regulated price; but they take a small *Batta,* or exchange, when they give gold for silver. They give copper for silver at the regulated price; but demand $10\frac{1}{2}$ *Dubs* for the silver *Fanam.*

Accompts.

Merchants accompts are commonly kept in *Sultany Pagodas,*

CHAPTER XIV. Jan. 22.

Rupees, and *Anas*, or fractions of 16 parts; others are kept in *Pagodas*, a nominal *Huna* of 10 to the *Pagoda*, and *Anas*, or 16 parts of these *Hunas*.

I shall make my alculations by reducing all sums to *Sultany Pagodas*, and taking these at their mint value of a little more than 8*s*.

Weights.

Weights. The *Seer (Sida)* used for weighing ought to equal 24 *Bombay Rupees*, those in common currency having from 178 to 179 grains. I weighed a *Seer* in common use in the market *(Bazar)*, and found, that it contained 4297 grains, which is more than the standard of 24 *Rupees*. The *Seer* is divided into halves, quarters, eighths, and sixteenths.

The *Maund (Mana)* by which goods are sold in the market, contains 46 *Seers*, or $28\frac{14}{100}$ lb.

The *Maund* by which the merchants purchase weighs 16 *Rupees* more, or is $28\frac{55}{100}$ lb. This is the weight by which the Company buys and sells.

Jagory is both bought and sold by a *Maund* of 40 *Seers*, or $24\frac{47}{100}$ lb.

The *Candy (Baru)* contains 20 *Maunds*, and varies, accordingly, from 571 lb. to $489\frac{1}{2}$ lb. These calculations are founded on the weight of the *Rupee*. If the *Seer* that I weighed were taken as a standard, we must to the above mentioned weights add about one-third per cent.

Grain Measures.

Dry-measure. These differ not only in every village, but also as they are used for retailing grain in the market, for purchasing grain from the farmer, or for sowing the seed. These differences have, no doubt, been introduced in order to confuse the officers of revenue.

For retailing in the market here, the *Seer (Sida)* is formed by mixing equal quantities of salt and of the nine most common grains;

and then, by taking of the mixture 84 *Bombay Rupees* weight. This quantity, when heaped, fills a *Seer* measure, and is $73\frac{681}{1000}$ cubical inches. The *Moray*, or *Mudi*, contains 38 *Seers*, or about $1\frac{1}{10}$ bushel. CHAPTER XIV. Jan. 22.

The grain measure by which the farmers sell their crops is thus formed:

$64\frac{125}{1000}$ cubical inches = 1 *Hany*.
14 *Hanies* - - = 1 *Cullishigay*.
3 *Cullishigays* - = 1 *Mudi* or *Moray*, or $1\frac{2511}{10000}$ bushel.

Grain, salt, and sometimes pepper, are sold by measure. Of this last a *Pucka Seer*, or $73\frac{681}{1000}$ cubical inches, is reckoned to weigh $51\frac{1}{2}$ *Bombay Rupees*.

In *Tulava* the era of *Sáliváhanam* is in use, and at *Mangalore* this is reckoned the year 1722; but in the north it is reckoned the year 1723, and the people there are certainly the most learned. The year of *Tulava* is solar. I here give an almanack for the current year, according to the *Bráhmans* of *Carculla*, who agree with those above the *Ghats* concerning the time of the era. Calendar.

Tulava Months.		European Months.		*Tulava* Months.		European Months.	
Era of *Sál.*1723			*A. D.* 1800.	Era of *Sal.*1723			*A. D.* 1800.
Sughi - -	1	13	March.	*Sughi* - -	18	30	March.
	2	14			19	31	
	3	15			20	1	April.
	4	16			21	2	
	5	17			22	3	
	6	18			23	4	
	7	19			24	5	
	8	20			25	6	
	9	21			26	7	
	10	22			27	8	
	11	23			28	9	
	12	24			29	10	
	13	25			30	11	
	14	26			31	12	
	15	27		*Puggu* - -	1	13	
	16	28			2	14	
	17	29			3	15	

CHAPTER XIV.

Jan. 22.

Tulava Months.		European Months.		*Tulava* Months.		European Months.	
Era of *Sál.* 1723			*A. D.* 1800.	Era of *Sál.* 1723			*A. D.* 1800.
Puggu - -	4	16	April.	*Baysha* - -	21	3	June.
	5	17			22	4	
	6	18			23	5	
	7	19			24	6	
	8	20			25	7	
	9	21			26	8	
	10	22			27	9	
	11	23			28	10	
	12	24			29	11	
	13	25			30	12	
	14	26			31	13	
	15	27			32	14	
	16	28		*Catialu* - -	1	15	
	17	29			2	16	
	18	30			3	17	
	19	1	May.		4	18	
	20	2			5	19	
	21	3			6	20	
	22	4			7	21	
	23	5			8	22	
	24	6			9	23	
	25	7			10	24	
	26	8			11	25	
	27	9			12	26	
	28	10			13	27	
	29	11			14	28	
	30	12			15	29	
	31	13			16	30	
Baysha - -	1	14			17	1	July.
	2	15			18	2	
	3	16			19	3	
	4	17			20	4	
	5	18			21	5	
	6	19			22	6	
	7	20			23	7	
	8	21			24	8	
	9	22			25	9	
	10	23			26	10	
	11	24			27	11	
	12	25			28	12	
	13	26			29	13	
	14	27			30	14	
	15	28			31	15	
	16	29			32	16	
	17	30		*Ati* - - -	1	17	
	18	31			2	18	
	19	1	June.		3	19	
	20	2			4	20	

CHAPTER XIV.

Jan. 22.

Tulava Months.		European Months.		*Tulava* Months.		European Months.	
Era of *Sál.*1723			*A. D.* 1800.	Era of *Sál.*1723			*A. D.* 1800.
Ati - - -	5	21	July.	*Sonay* - -	22	7	September.
	6	22			23	8	
	7	23			24	9	
	8	24			25	10	
	9	25			26	11	
	10	26			27	12	
	11	27			28	13	
	12	28			29	14	
	13	29			30	15	
	14	30		*Cannay* - -	1	16	
	15	31			2	17	
	16	1	August.		3	18	
	17	2			4	19	
	18	3			5	20	
	19	4			6	21	
	20	5			7	22	
	21	6			8	23	
	22	7			9	24	
	23	8			10	25	
	24	9			11	26	
	25	10			12	27	
	26	11			13	28	
	27	12			14	29	
	28	13			15	30	
	29	14			16	1	October.
	30	15			17	2	
	31	16			18	3	
Sonay - -	1	17			19	4	
	2	18			20	5	
	3	19			21	6	
	4	20			22	7	
	5	21			23	8	
	6	22			24	9	
	7	23			25	10	
	8	24			26	11	
	9	25			27	12	
	10	26			28	13	
	11	27			29	14	
	12	28			30	15	
	13	29		*Buntäelu* -	1	16	
	14	30			2	17	
	15	31			3	18	
	16	1	September.		4	19	
	17	2			5	20	
	18	3			6	21	
	19	4			7	22	
	20	5			8	23	
	21	6			9	24	

CHAPTER XIV.

Jan. 22.

Tulava Months.		European Months.	
Era of *Sál*. 1723			*A. D.* 1800.
Buntäela -	10	25	October.
	11	26	
	12	27	
	13	28	
	14	29	
	15	30	
	16	31	
	17	1	November.
	18	2	
	19	3	
	20	4	
	21	5	
	22	6	
	23	7	
	24	8	
	25	9	
	26	10	
	27	11	
	28	12	
	29	13	
Jarday - -	1	14	
	2	15	
	3	16	
	4	17	
	5	18	
	6	19	
	7	20	
	8	21	
	9	22	
	10	23	
	11	24	
	12	25	
	13	26	
	14	27	
	15	28	
	16	29	
	17	30	
	18	1	December.
	19	2	
	20	3	
	21	4	
	22	5	
	23	6	
	24	7	
	25	8	
	26	9	
	27	10	
	28	11	

Tulava Months.		European Months.	
Era of *Sál*. 1723			*A. D.* 1800.
Jarday - -	29	12	December.
	30	13	
Perarday -	1	14	
	2	15	
	3	16	
	4	17	
	5	18	
	6	19	
	7	20	
	8	21	
	9	22	
	10	23	
	11	24	
	12	25	
	13	26	
	14	27	
	15	28	
	16	29	
	17	30	
	18	31	
	19	1	January 1801.
	20	2	
	21	3	
	22	4	
	23	5	
	24	6	
	25	7	
	26	8	
	27	9	
	28	10	
	29	11	
Pointalu -	1	12	
	2	13	
	3	14	
	4	15	
	5	16	
	6	17	
	7	18	
	8	19	
	9	20	
	10	21	
	11	22	
	12	23	
	13	24	
	14	25	
	15	26	
	16	27	
	17	28	

CHAPTER XIV.

Jan. 22.

Tulava Months.		European Months.		*Tulava* Months.		European Months.	
Era of *Sál.* 1723			*A. D.* 1801.	Era of *Sál.* 1723			*A. D.* 1801.
Pointalu -	18	29	January.	*Mahi* - -	10	20	February.
	19	30			11	21	
	20	31			12	22	
	21	1	February.		13	23	
	22	2			14	24	
	23	3			15	25	
	24	4			16	26	
	25	5			17	27	
	26	6			18	28	
	27	7			19	1	March.
	28	8			20	2	
	29	9			21	3	
	30	10			22	4	
Mahi - -	1	11			23	5	
	2	12			24	6	
	3	13			25	7	
	4	14			26	8	
	5	15			27	9	
	6	16			28	10	
	7	17			29	11	
	8	18			30	12	
	9	19					

Pretensions of the *Tulava Bráhmans.*

The *Bráhmans* of *Tulava*, like the *Namburis*, pretend, that the country was created expressly for their use by *Parasu-ráma*, and that they are the only persons entitled to be called *Baliky*, or proprietors of the soil. It would not appear, however, that in *Tulava* this story was ever so successful as it has been in *Malayala*. The *Bráhmans* indeed say, that they did not like the country, and were always running away to a city named *Ahichaytra*, which seems to be in *Telingána*. At length a prince, named *Myuru Varmá*, made all those here adopt some new customs; after which the *Panch-Drávida Bráhmans* of *Ahichaytra*, and they, could no longer live in communion. They allege, that *Myuru Varmá* reinstated them again in the whole property of *Tulava*.

Actual tenures.

At present, however, the greater part of the country belongs to *Bunts*, and other *Súdras*, who style themselves proprietors *(Balikies)*, although the *Bráhmans* are willing only to give them the title of

CHAPTER XIV. Jan. 22.

Mulacaras, or tenants. The property, if ever it belonged to the *Brahmans*, has been entirely alienated; nor is there even a pretence set up, of the *Brahmans* having a power of redemption.

Mulacaras, Balikies, or proprietors.

The *Balikies, Mulacaras*, or proprietors, are answerable for the land-tax, called here *Shista*, and by the Mussulmans *Shist*. The estate is always called by the *Baliki* or proprietor's name, although it is often mortgaged to its full value.

Aduvacaras, or mortgagees.

The mortgagee is here called *Aduvacara*, from *Aduva*, a mortgage. The mortgagee pays the amount of the land-tax to the landlord *(Baliky)*, who gives it to government. The remainder of the profit is retained by the mortgagee for the interest of the money that he has advanced, which is in general at the rate of $12\frac{1}{2}$ *per cent. per annum:* in some places, however, it is only 10 *per cent.* Land is never mortgaged without a regular writing, wherein is mentioned the sum for which the estate is mortgaged. It may be resumed, by paying up this sum, whenever the landlord pleases; but, if the mortgagee has planted any trees, he must be paid for them at a certain fixed rate, which is known to be equal to the expense that he must have incurred. Many of the landlords retain their own estates, and cultivate much of them with their own stock; but about an eighth of the country has been mortgaged. Some landlords have mortgaged the whole of their estates, and, having had no hopes of being able to redeem them, have entirely left the country. The estates still, however, go by their names, and the tax is paid in their names by the mortgagees.

Gaynicaras, or tenants.

Both proprietors and mortgagees let part of their lands to tenants, or *Gaynicaras*. In this district, the tenant gives a writing, obliging himself to pay a certain rent, but receives no lease in return; and, whenever the land-holder pleases, may be ejected from his farm. In other districts, however, especially that of *Barcuru*, the tenant has a lease in perpetuity, of which he can only be deprived by his, or his heirs, failing to pay the stipulated rent. Some of this rent is paid in rice, and some in money.

CHAPTER XIV.

Jan. 22.

Encouragement given to improvement.

When a tenant undertakes to plant a garden, he obtains a writing from the landlord, by which he is ensured of the payment of the expenses incurred, should the garden be resumed; and he pays no rent *(Gayni)* for a number of years sufficient to allow the garden to become productive. The amount of the expenses to be paid is settled by arbitration. When rice-land has been waste, the tenant for two or three years pays nothing, except the tax. This is the account given by the landlords.

The tenants ought, on rice-lands, to have one-half of the produce; so, at least, the proprietors say. The proprietors let very few of their gardens, this being a profitable kind of farming.

In this district *(Taluc)* there are no waste lands; but some fields, actually cultivated, were by Major Monro allowed to be considered as waste, on account of the clamours made by the natives of their poverty.

Hindu worship, how supported.

Although all the *Inams*, or charity lands, were ordered by *Tippoo* to be resumed, yet some belonging to temples have been concealed, as is acknowleged both by the *Tahsildar* and by the *Hindu* landlords. This has not been disturbed by Major Monro, nor his successor Mr. Ravenshaw; and an allowance is made by the government to both heathen temples and mosques. The principal *Hindu* temple here receives annually 120 *Pagodas*, and its lands produce 360, in all 480 *Pagodas*, or 193*l.* 8*s.* 3*d.* The people are very anxious for its being restored to its former splendour. Major Monro seems to have thought that very moderate expenses should be incurred in supporting the religious ceremonies of the natives, the allowances that he has made for the temples being in general very small. I do not find that this economy has had any bad effect; and it is impossible for a European to be more respected by *Hindus*, than Major Monro is by those who were lately under his authority.

All the lands of *Tulava* are private property, and pay a land-tax.

In *Tulava* the state has no lands; the whole is private property. All the land-tax is now paid in money; but before the conquest

CHAPTER XIV. Jan. 22.

part of it was demanded in rice, and other articles of consumption for the troops, at a low rate, which was fixed by the officers of government. The accompts contain solely the tax which each proprietor ought to pay. When a man alienates part of his lands, he agrees with the purchaser to take a part of the tax, and then the revenue of the new proprietor is entered in the public accompts under his name. The sum which he is to pay is always mentioned in the title deeds; and the government has a right to prevent any division, that is not in proportion to the value of the lands alienated; otherwise the revenue might suffer greatly. The proprietors allege, that the tax amounts to more than the rent, and that they are obliged to borrow money, or to give part of the profit from the lands cultivated with their own stock, to enable them to satisfy the claims of government. Those whom I had assembled to give me information, and most of whom were as fat as pigs, gravely told me, that they were reduced to live upon *Kanji*, or rice-soup. From what they say, therefore, no estimate can be formed of the share of the rent which they pay to government. Every one thinks himself bound to conceal the truth, and none more so than the native officers of revenue. Every step, indeed, seems to have been taken, by a chaos of weights and measures, and by plausible but false accompts, to keep the state of the country a profound mystery.

Circumstances of the cultivator.

To judge from appearances, the occupiers of land in *Tulava* are richer than even those of *Malabar*, who are, no doubt, in easier circumstances than those in *Coimbetore*, or those above the *Ghats*. The universal cry of poverty, however, that prevails in every part of India, and the care, owing to long oppression, with which every thing is concealed, render it very difficult to know the real circumstances of the cultivator. We may safely however conclude, from the violent contest for landed property of every kind in *Canara*, that each occupant has still a considerable interest in the soil, besides the reward due to him for cultivating whatever his stock enables him to do. It is indeed sincerely to be wished, that this property may long continue unmolested; as no country can thrive where the absolute property of the soil is vested in the state.

Jan. 22. Farms and stock.

Cultivators who are rich keep from twenty to twenty-five ploughs, but at least one half of the actual farmers have only one. Those who keep two, three, and four ploughs, are common. Near the sea there are many plantations, and some cultivators take care of these only; but, in general, each cultivator has some rice-ground, and some gardens. In the interior parts of the country very few have gardens. A farmer with four ploughs requires constantly six men, four women, and eight oxen. To transplant his rice, he must also hire women; ten are required to plant in two days a *Moray* land. The wages of these ten for two days is said to amount to 40 *Hanies*, or almost the value of the seed; which seems to be exaggerated. A farm, thus stocked, ought to contain 8 *Morays* sowing. Some people cultivate 10 *Morays*, but they do it imperfectly. The land, either for rice or pulse, it must be observed, is cultivated twice a year. I made many measurements to endeavour to satisfy myself with respect to the extent of what is called a *Moray*, or *Mudi* sowing; but, owing to some artifices of the natives, the results differed so essentially, that I can place no reliance on my own measurements, and am inclined to think the extent very indefinite. The average *Moray*, according to Mr. Ravenshaw's answer to my queries, is $1\frac{11}{1000}$ acre. At this rate, the eight *Morays* cultivated by four ploughs would amount to little more than 9 acres, which is absurd. The least that can be allowed for a plough is, I am persuaded, six or seven acres.

Price of labour. *Culialu*, or hired servants.

The cultivation is chiefly carried on by *Culialu*, or hired servants; but there are also some *Muladalu*, bought men, or slaves. A hired man gets daily 2 *Hanies* of clean rice, or annually $21\frac{3}{4}$ bushels, together with $1\frac{1}{2}$ *Rupee's* worth of cloth, a *Pagoda* in cash, and a house. A hired woman gets $1\frac{1}{2}$ *Rupee* for cloth, and $\frac{3}{4}$ of the man's allowance of grain. In planting season, the women hired by the day get two *Hanies* of rice, or $128\frac{1}{4}$ cubical inches. These wages are very

CHAPTER XIV. Jan. 22.

high, and may enable the hired servants to keep a family in the greatest abundance. It is evident from hence, that the stock required to cultivate eight *Morays* of land was excessively exaggerated by the proprietors. The wages, in grain alone, would amount to 156½ *Morays* of rice for 8 *Morays* sowing; so that, to pay even them, would require at least 40 seeds. We may safely allow six *Morays* for each plough fully wrought; but the number of ploughs in the whole district amount to rather less than one to 3 *Morays* of rice ground in actual cultivation, according to the revenue accompts; owing, probably, to a want of cattle and other stock. At the end of the year, the hired servant may change his service, if he be free from debt; but that is seldom the case. When he gets deeply involved, his master may sell his sisters' children to discharge the amount, and his services may be transferred to any other man who chooses to take him and pay his debts to his master. In fact, he differs little from a slave, only his allowance is larger, but then the master is not obliged to provide for him in sickness nor in old age.

Slaves.

A male slave is allowed daily 1½ *Hany* of rice, or three-fourths of the allowance for a hired servant; a woman receives one *Hany*. The man gets 1½ *Rupee's* worth of cloth, and 2 *Rupees* in cash; the woman is allowed only the cloth. They receive also a trifling allowance of oil, salt, and other seasonings. A small allowance is given to children and old people. When a slave wishes to marry, he receives 5 *Pagodas* (2 guineas) to defray the expense. The wife works with the husband's master. On the husband's death, if the wife was a slave, all the children belong to her mother's master; but, if she was formerly free, she and all her children belong to her husband's master. A good slave sells for 10 *Pagodas*, or about 4 guineas. If he has a wife who was formerly free, and two or three children, the value is doubled. The slave may be hired out; and the renter both exacts his labour, and finds him in subsistence. Slaves are also mortgaged; but the mortgager is not obliged to supply the place of a slave that dies; and in case of accidents, the debt becomes extinguished; which is an excellent regulation. Free men of low cast, if they are in debt or trouble, sometimes sell their sister's children, who are their heirs. They have no authority over their own children, who belong to their maternal uncles.

CHAPTER XIV. Jan. 22.

In this country the hill ground is never cultivated, except for gardens; the whole may therefore be divided into rice-land and garden ground.

Rice-land of three kinds.

The rice land is of three kinds; *Bylu*, *Majelu*, and *Betta*. *Bylu* ground is that in the lower part of vallies which are watered by small streams, from whence canals are dug to convey the water to the fields, which by this irrigation are able to give annually two crops. The *Majelu* land is higher than the *Bylu*, and is provided with small reservoirs, which ensure one crop, even when the rains last only two or three months. From some of these reservoirs, the water is let out by a sluice. It is raised from others by means of the *Yatam*, or by a basket suspended between ropes. The *Betta* land is the highest part of the rice ground, and is provided with neither streams nor reservoir; so that the crop depends entirely on the rain. In some places there is another kind of rice ground called *Potla*. During the rainy season, it is so inundated, that it cannot then be cultivated; and, as the water dries, the rice is transplanted.

Bylu rice-land produces three crops annually.

On the *Bylu* land there are three crops in the year, 1st. *Yenalu*, 2d. *Sughi*, and 3d *Colaky*. This last is only produced by a few spots particularly favoured with water. The accompanying table will explain several particulars relative to the cultivation of rice.

CHAPTER XIV.

Jan. 22.

Table explaining the Cultivation of Rice at *Mangalore*.

Kind.	Quality.	Soil.	Crop for which it is used.	Months required for this crop.	Manner of cultivation.	Increase in a good crop. Folds.	Produce of an Acre, supposing it to sow $1\frac{1}{4}$ Bushel.
Bily Ayki - -	White and small -	*Bylu*	*Yenalu*	5	transplanted	20	25
Ditto - - -	Ditto - - -	ditto	*Colaky*	3	sprouted seed	5	$6\frac{1}{4}$
Ditto - - -	Ditto - - -	*Majelu*	*Yenalu*	5	ditto	12	15
Jirigay Saly - -	Very small - -	*Bylu*	ditto	5	transplanted	15	$18\frac{3}{4}$
Amutty - - -	Large and black -	ditto	ditto	5	sprouted seed	20	25
Cagi Ayki - -	Ditto - - -	ditto	ditto	5	ditto	15	$18\frac{3}{4}$
Ditto - - -	Ditto - - -	ditto	*Colaky*	3	ditto	5	$6\frac{1}{4}$
Atticaráya - -	Red and low priced	ditto	*Sughi*	$3\frac{1}{2}$	ditto	10	$12\frac{1}{2}$
Kiny Vettu - -	- - - -	*Majelu*	*Yenalu*	3	ditto	10	$12\frac{1}{2}$
Ditto - - -	- - - -	*Bettu*	ditto	3	ditto	8	10
Sampa Saly - -	- - - -	*Majelu*	ditto	$3\frac{1}{2}$	ditto	10	$12\frac{1}{2}$
Soma Saly - -	- - - -	ditto	ditto	$3\frac{1}{6}$	ditto	10	$12\frac{1}{2}$
Ditto - - -	- - - -	*Bettu*	ditto	$3\frac{1}{2}$	ditto	8	10
Tungalu - - -	- - - -	ditto	ditto	3	ditto	8	10
Attigary - - -	- - - -	*Potla*	- -	5	transplanted	10	$12\frac{1}{2}$

Yenalu crop transplanted.

The kinds of rice that are transplanted for the *Yenalu* crop on *Bylu* land are cultivated as follows. Between the 14th of May and the 14th of June, water the ground intended for raising the seedlings for two days, and then plough it twice; all the water, except two inches in depth, being let off at each ploughing. The two ploughings must be repeated every other day, until the eighth time. The field, before the last ploughing, is manured with ashes, and with dung, in which, while in the cow-house, the leaves of every kind of bush and tree have been mixed. The mud is then smoothed with the *Mutu Pallay*, or plank drawn by oxen (Plate XXII. Fig. 58.). The seed, prepared by causing it to sprout, is then sown very thick, the water being three inches deep. Next day the water is let off. On the fifth day, when the shoots come up, they get as much water as covers the half next the ground; and every day, as the plants grow, the quantity of water is increased. On the ninth day the water is let entirely off, and is not given again until the eleventh day. If worms affect the plants, about the end of the third week the water is again let off for three days, and some ashes are sprinkled over the field to kill these destructive animals. The seedlings must be transplanted between the 30th and 35th days.

On the day that the seed is sown, the ground for receiving the seedlings when transplanted begins to be ploughed, and in the course of the month gets four double ploughings. The plough in use here (Plate XXII. Fig. 60.) is neater than usual in India, but is an implement equally wretched. In the intervals between the ploughings, the field is kept inundated. At the time of ploughing, two or three inches only of water are allowed to remain. After every ploughing, the soil is smoothed with the plank drawn by oxen. Between the 4th and 15th of July all the water except one inch is let off, and the seedlings are transplanted. On the third day the field is drained; and for two days it is allowed to dry. On the sixth it receives 2 inches of water, and then is continued inundated until the crop ripens. Between the 5th and 16th of August the weeds are removed by the hand. In October, or at the beginning of November, the straw is cut with the grain, and, till it be dry, is allowed to lie on the ground. In Figure 61, the sickle is delineated. The rice is thrashed by beating handfulls of the straw against a grating of *Bamboos*, which is placed sloping from a stone to the ground: the grain falls through the grating. This operation is performed in the square surrounded by the farm-houses; for here, as well as in most parts of India, there are no barns. The rough rice is dried in the sun, and much attention is paid to this operation with what is intended for seed. The straw is spread out to the sun as much as possible; but, owing to the rain, is seldom got in well. The seed is kept in *Morays*, or straw bags, which are hung up in the smoke of the kitchen. The rice intended for consumption is put up in heaps, placed on straw, and covered with thatch.

CHAPTER XIV. Jan. 22.

The husks are beaten off in the course of two or three months, and immediately sold. The rough rice is put into large pots, overnight, with so much water as will cover it. In the morning it is boiled until the husks begin to open. It is then dried in the sun, and beaten in a small hole in the ground, or in a stone with a long pestle, the end of which is covered with iron. For the use of *Bráhmans*, a little is beaten without having been boiled; but it does not preserve long.

Yenalu crop sown *Mola.*

The rices that are cultivated as sprouted seed for the *Yenalu* crop on *Bylu* land are thus managed. The ploughings and manure are conducted exactly in the same manner as in the field on which the seedlings are raised; but, in order to gain time, they are made fifteen days later. The seed is prepared by putting the *Moray*, or straw bag, in which it has been kept, into water from the evening until next day at noon. The bag is then removed into the house, and in the morning of the fourth day is opened, the seed is sprinkled with dung and water, and immediately sown. After having been sown, it is managed like the seedlings; but the weeds are removed about the 26th of July. The quantity of seed required on the same ground for the sprouted seed cultivation, is to that required for transplantation, as two to three.

Sughi crop.

In the *Sughi* crop on *Bylu* land the rice is mostly cultivated as sprouted seed. It is inferior in quality to the rice of the *Yenalu* crop, and is chiefly reserved for home consumption. Being reaped in the hot and dry season, the straw, though short, is well dried, and is a valuable supply of fodder. The sprouted seed for this crop is thus cultivated. Between the 16th of October and the 14th of November, immediately after the *Yenalu* crop has been reaped, the ploughings commence; and are carried on exactly as before described; only in place of one man's standing on the plank drawn by oxen, the ground being now harder, three or four men must stand on this instrument; a most barbarous and expensive manner of adding weight; but in India it is seldom that an attempt is made

CHAPTER XIV.

Jan. 22.

to accomplish any thing by machinery, that can be performed by human labour. The quantity of manure required for this crop is larger than that which is given to the first. If this crop be transplanted, it only produces six seeds.

Colaky crop of rice.

The seed of the rices that are cultivated for the *Colaky* crop is sown sprouted. Between the 12th of January and the 10th of February, immediately after having cut the *Sughi* crop, the ploughing for the *Colaky* commences, and the field is managed exactly as in the *Sughi* crop. In most places the water must be raised by the *Yatam*, called here the *Panay*, or by the instrument called *Cai-dumbay* (Plate XXV. Fig. 62), which makes the cultivation very expensive. The *Cai-dumbay* cannot raise water more than three feet, and is a means of irrigation very inferior to the basket suspended by ropes and wrought by two men. This crop requires a great deal of manure, otherwise it injures the following crop called *Yenalu*.

Colaky crop of other *grams*.

In place of this third crop of rice, where the quantity of water is too small, a crop of *Urudu (Phaseolus minimoo* Roxb: MSS.), *Padingi (Phaseolus Mungo)*, or *Cudu (Dolichos biflorus)*, is taken from the *Bylu* land. In some villages, but not in this immediate neighbourhood, a crop of *Enama (Sesamum)* is taken. For the three leguminous plants the ground in five days gets five double ploughings, and after each is smoothed with the plank drawn by oxen. It is then manured with dung and ashes, and the seed is sown broadcast, and covered by the plough; after which the soil is again smoothed with the plank drawn by oxen. Then, if the field be not sufficiently moist, it must be divided into small plots surrounded by little banks, and once in fifteen days it must receive water. The quantity of the seed required for these pulses, is one-fourth of that required for rice in the sprouted seed cultivation, or about five-sixteenths of a bushel an acre. The produce is about 8 seeds, or $2\frac{1}{2}$ bushels an acre.

CHAPTER XIV. Jan. 22.

In order to prevent the torrents of water, which in the rainy season run down from the hills, from injuring the *Bylu* land, a strong mound is formed round the bottom of the hills; and a channel above this mound conveys all the superfluous water into the sea, or into rivers. Coco-nut trees are frequently planted under the bank, or mound, in order to give it strength.

Majelu land. All the rices cultivated on the second sort of rice land, called *Majelu*, are sown sprouted; only, any seedlings, that may happen to remain after planting the *Bylu* fields are put into the *Majelu*. The cultivation on this is exactly the same, and at the same season, as the *Yenalu*, or first crop on *Bylu* land. The water, in case of a deficiency of rain, is supplied from small tanks, which reserve a supply for fourteen or fifteen days after the rains are over. The seed required for this kind of land is said to be one third more, than that required for the same extent of *Bylu;* but, on actual measurement, I found that a *Moray* of seed required considerably more *Majelu* than it did of *Bylu*. On a small portion of *Majelu* land, a second crop of *Cudu (Dolichos biflorus)* is taken. It is sown between the 16th of October and the 13th of November, and its produce is nearly the same as when cultivated on *Bylu* land.

Betta land rice. The third sort of rice land, called *Betta*, is the same with the lower *Parum*, or hill-land of *Malayala*, which is there chiefly used for gardens. The rice cultivated on this is always sown sprouted, exactly in the same manner as the *Yenalu*, or first crop; only it requires two more ploughings, and a greater quantity of manure. The seed ought to be 1¼ of that which is required for the same extent of *Bylu;* but this also, I found, was not confirmed by actual measurement. This rice is kept for home consumption; for that of the *Yenalu*, or first crop from *Bylu*, or the lowest land, is the kind commonly exported.

Sugar-cane. It is upon this kind of ground that sugar-cane is cultivated; but very small quantities only are raised, and that entirely by the native

Christians. Their method is as follows. Between the 14th of December and the 11th of January the ground, for four successive days, has a double ploughing, and, after each, is smoothed with the plank drawn by oxen. Then, with a hoe, called *Haray* (Plate XXI. Fig. 56), parallel channels are formed, at the distance of every 8 or 10 cubits. At right angles to these, and contiguous to each other, are formed trenches three quarters of a cubit deep, half a cubit wide at the bottom, and one cubit and a half at the top. The field is then manured with dung and straw; which, after they have been spread on the field, are burned; so that, in fact, the manure is ashes. The canes for seed are then cut into pieces, from half to three quarters of a cubit long; and these are soaked in water a whole day and a night. On the day after the manure has been burned on the field, the soil in the bottom of the trenches is loosened with the hoe, and mixed with the ashes; and with these united the joints of the cane are slightly covered. They are placed horizontally, two and two, in lines parallel to the trenches; and the ends of one pair touch the ends of the two adjacent pairs. The field is then watered, the channels being filled from a tank, or well, by means of the machine called *Yatam*. Except when there is rain, it must be watered every fourth day, speaking as a medical man; that is to say, if it be watered on the 1st day of a month, it will be watered again on the 4th, 7th, 10th, and so forth. A compost having been formed of rich mould, dung, and dry grass, it is burned; and on the 15th day from planting the ashes are spread over the field. At the end of the month, the weeds are removed by the hand, and with a small instrument named *Sulingy*. At the same time, the young canes are again manured with the burnt compost. At the end of the second month, if the cane has a sickly colour, it is again manured. The rains commence about that time, and then the earth from the intermediate ridges is gathered up round the young canes; which thus, in place of being in trenches, stand on the top of ridges. The field must then be well fenced.

CHAPTER XIV.

Jan. 22.

The dried leaves must be removed by the hand, which is all the farther trouble required, no watering being necessary after the rainy season is over. Jackalls eat the cane, and must be carefully watched. The cane is fit for cutting in 11 or 12 months. There are two kinds; the *Bily*, and *Cari Cabbu;* or white, and black canes. The former is the *Restali*, and the latter the *Putta Putty* of the country above the *Ghats*. The same ground will not produce sugar-cane every year; between every two crops of cane there must be two crops of rice. A piece of land that sows one *Moray* of rice, will produce 4000 canes, which are about six feet long, and sell to the *Jagory* boilers at from half to one *Rupee* a hundred. The *Moray* sowing of *Betta* land is here about 30,000 square feet; so that, according to the price of sugar cane, the acre produces from about 58 to 29 *Rupees*, or from about 5*l.* 17*s.* to 2*l.* 18*s.* 6*d.* The land-tax is the same as when the field is cultivated for rice. The want of firewood is the greatest obstacle to this cultivation; the *trash*, or expressed stems, is not sufficient to boil the juice into *Jagory*, while that operation is performed in earthen pots placed over an open fire. If all the land in *Codeal Taluc* (district) that is fit for the purpose, were employed to raise sugar-cane, it would yearly produce 1000 *Pagodas* worth of cane; that is to say, there are about 1125 *Mudis* sowing of land, that once in three years might be cultivated. The quantity in the neighbouring district on the south side of the river is much greater. The *Jagory* made here is hard, but black, and of a bad quality. It sells at 3 *Maunds* for the *Pagoda*, or at 12*s.* 3½*d.* a hundred-weight.

Kitchen-stuffs.

Between the rows of sugar-cane are raised some cucurbitaceous plants, and some kitchen stuffs, that soon come to maturity.

On *Betta*, or the highest of rice-land, where the water may be had by digging to a little depth, some people, chiefly Christians, cultivate capsicum, and *Banguns (Solanum Melongena)*, as a second crop after rice. In good soils, these require to be watered once in three days; in bad soils, they must be allowed water every other day.

Jan. 22. *Potla* land.

The kind of land called *Potla*, or *Mojaru*, is situated in deep places near the banks of rivers; and is so much overflowed in the rainy season, that, until the violence of this is over, it cannot be cultivated. Even in the dry season, it would in general be overflowed by the tide at high water; so that it is necessary to make banks to exclude the sea. The rice which it produces is always transplanted. Between the 17th of August and the 15th of September the seed is sown, and is managed in the same manner as the transplanted rice on *Bylu* land; only the season is different. The same quantity of seed is required for the same extent of *Bylu* ground; that is, one-half more than would be required for sowing broad-cast. This is a very precarious crop, being subject to be totally ruined by either too little or too much rain.

Poor land of every denomination requires more seed than richer land of the same kind.

Manure.

The leaves of every kind of tree and bush, except such as are prickly, are used for manure. The cattle are kept in the house all night, and their dung is collected for the same use. It is kept in pits, and every day's collection is covered with leaves; the whole dunghill thus forming alternate strata of dung and leaves, which soon rot. The ashes and sweepings of the family are kept in a separate pit. The soil of towns is never used as manure.

Palm gardens, soil fit for them.

In *Tulava* the coco-nut and *Betel-nut* are the only productions of the gardens that are taxed. The gardens are formed on hilly ground which has a red soil; but, as the trees require to be watered, such places only are considered fit for the purpose, as afford water by digging wells to no great depth, or as can be watered by forming reservoirs. The water of the wells is raised by the machine called *Yatam*; but the gardens thus supplied, although requiring a great deal of trouble, are equally valuable with those watered from tanks; for as these sometimes fail in the hot season, the crop for that year is lost, although the trees do not perish.

Cultivation of the *Areca* palm.

Here the *Areca* or *Betel-nut* palm forms separate plantations,

CHAPTER XIV. Jan. 22.

which are surrounded by some rows of the coco-nut tree, and is not scattered about the gardens, as in *Malabar*. The following is the manner of making one of these plantations, as described by the proprietors. Between the 17th of December, and the 13th of February, the seed must be collected from trees that are at least fifty years old. Having been kept four days in the house, it is tied up in a *Moray*, or straw-bag, and is immersed for 25 days in the water of a well. In the mean time a small plot of rice ground is repeatedly ploughed until it be reduced to a fine mud, and is well manured with dung and ashes. In this mud the nuts are placed close to one another, with their eyes uppermost, and one half of them above the earth. Then the plot is covered with straw, and is watered once a day for a month. A piece of dry ground is then dug up with the hoe, and manured with dung and ashes. Into this the nuts, which have now sprouted, are transplanted at half a cubit's distance from each other. The nuts only are covered, and the sprouts are left projecting. For two months, if the soil be moist, it must be watered once in four days; if it be dry, once in three days is sufficient. Another piece of ground is in the mean time prepared; and at the end of the two months the young seedlings are removed thither, and placed at the distance of one cubit from each other. In this nursery they remain eight months; and once in four days, when there is no rain, they are watered. In the mean while the garden is prepared by inclosing it with a dry hedge of prickly bushes. Within the hedge a row of coco-nut palms is planted, each being 24 cubits from the other. Within these, at 10 cubits distance from each other, are formed pits, two cubits in diameter, and two cubits deep. In the bottom of each of these is put a young *Areca*; all its roots are covered with fine mould, and it is manured with a little dung. This is between the 19th of October and the 16th of November, at the close of the rainy season. Every fourth day the pits must be watered, while the sun is excluded by branches and leaves. At the end of six months some dung must be given, and the weeds removed by the hand. Whenever there is no rain the waterings are to be continued; and twice a year the trees must be manured, and the weeds ought to be removed from near their roots. In two years the pits are filled up with the manure. At the end of five years another set of pits is made, one between every two of the old ones; and in these is placed another set of young plants, and managed as the first set. At this second planting some plantain trees *(Musas)* are set in the garden, but not above forty for the hundred *Arecas*. Near the hedge, in a line with the coco-nut palms, are also put some *Jack (Artocarpus integrifolia)* and *Mango (Mangifera indica)* trees. When ten years old, the *Areca* begins to produce fruit; but until the fifteenth year does not arrive at perfection. For thirty-five years it continues in full bearing. From its 50th year until its death, which happens in from its 70th to its 100th year, the quantity of fruit gradually diminishes, but its quality rather improves. The trees in full fruit produce annually three bunches, which ripen in succession between the 19th of October and the 16th of December. Each bunch contains from 30 to 100 nuts; so that, according to the natives, 200 nuts may be taken as the average produce of an *Areca* when it is in vigour. When the *Mango* and *Jack* trees have grown up, the pepper vines are usually put round them. Some people plant them also against the *Areca*, but they diminish its produce. *Yams (Dioscoreas)* are planted near the hedge.

Jan. 22.

Manner of collecting and preserving the Betel-nut.

The *Betel-nut* is collected by a set of people called *Devadigas*, who are sometimes kept as servants, and sometimes hired for the crop season, at 1¼ silver *Fanam* a day (5½*d.*), part of which is paid in rice. A *Devadiga* in the forenoon cuts 25 bunches, and in the afternoon assists the family to prepare the nuts. If the season promise to be favourable, that is to say, not too rainy, when the nuts are three quarters ripe, they are cut for *Wan'-Adiky*, or *dry-betel*. Immediately after they are cut, the husk is separated, and the nuts are then put into a pot, with as much water as will cover them, and boiled until the eyes *(Corculla)* fall out. They are then cut

CHAPTER XIV. Jan. 22.

into eight pieces, and dried in the sun four days, being removed into the house at night, or on the appearance of rain. It is of great advantage to the *Betel* to be dried on a gray granite rock *(Bily Cullu)*; but where that cannot be procured, it is dried on a piece of ground that is purposely made hard and smooth. For this operation, the *Devadiga* requires the assistance of four people, generally the women of the house; and they prepare daily 12 *Seers* measure of *Wan'-Adiky* ($1\frac{455}{1000}$ peck). When the weather threatens to be rainy, the nuts are allowed to ripen on the tree for *Nir'-Adiky*, or *wet-betel*, which is thus prepared. The nuts, with the husk on, just as they are taken from the bunch, are put into large jars full of water, and the mouths of these are closely shut. In this state they cannot be preserved longer than four or five months, and are therefore taken for immediate consumption. A quantity adequate to supply the demand is daily taken out of the jar, and skinned as wanted. The knives used in preparing *Betel-nut* are delineated in Plate XXII. Fig. 63, 64.

Expense of cultivation.

A garden of 300 *Arecas*, which is one of a middling size, if it be watered by a well, requires the labour of six people, but of three only if it be watered by a tank. In the rainy season, however, while the cultivation of rice is chiefly carried on, the three men who are employed to raise the water have nothing to do in the garden, and are employed on the rice ground; even the three other men may be a few hours daily employed at any other kind of work. In fact, I suspect that the men, who spoke of six servants and four ploughs being requisite to cultivate 8 *Morays* of rice-land, ought to have added to the account an *Areca* garden of 300 trees. These men get $1\frac{1}{2}$ *Pagoda* a year in money, 2 *Rupees* worth of cloth, and eat three times a day in their master's house.

Black pepper.

The pepper is managed as follows. Between the 24th of May and the 22d of June, the ground near the tree upon which it is to be trained is dug with a hoe. Then two, three, or four cuttings of the pepper vine, each a cubit long, are put in the ground, one end them being allowed to project. They are then covered with grass. This is done when the rainy season commences. A month afterwards they get a little dung. As the vines shoot, they are tied to the tree. When the dry season commences, they must be watered every second day, until a year old, after which they require water once in four days. Twice a year also they must get manure of dung and leaves; and long grass, or bushes, must be prevented from growing near their roots; but there is no occasion to dig or plough the whole ground. They begin to bear in the fifth year; but are not in full crop until the eighth. If the worms attack the vine, they die in twelve or fifteen years; but otherwise they live twenty-five, and all the while produce good crops. When any vine dies, a new one is planted in its stead. Here they are trained upon the *Pongary* or *Hongary (Erythrina)*, the *Nuriga (Moringa)*, *Jack (Artocarpus)*, *Mango (Mangifera)*, *Areca*, coco-nut, and tamarind. The first is, however, most commonly employed, and in this country lives fifty years. It is not customary here to prune the trees upon which the pepper is trained. Each tree, according to the number of vines that it can support, produces from two to four *Pucka Seers* measure, or from $\frac{5413}{10000}$ parts to $1,\frac{0966}{10000}$ of a Winchester gallon, which will weigh from $2,\frac{625}{1000}$ lb. to $5,\frac{25}{100}$ lb. When one or two berries begin to appear red, the whole are collected by pinching off the *amenta*. A man, in one day, can take the fruit from three trees, that is to say, can cure about 12 pounds of pepper. It is kept all night in the house. Next day the berries are rubbed off with the hands, and picked clean. They are then dried three days on mats, or on a piece of smooth hard ground, and every night are taken into the house. The pepper is then fit for sale, and the common price is one *Vir'-Ráya Fanam* for the *Seer*, which is at the rate of 106½ *Rupees* a *Candy* of 560 lb. the weight here in use; or at the rate of 120 *Rupees* nearly for the *Candy* of 640 lb. which the cultivators in *Malabar* employ. The export price is on an average 136 *Rupees*

CHAPTER XIV.

for the small *Candy;* but in this the merchants profit and the customs are included.

Jan. 22. Sale of black pepper.

The crop season is between the 15th of January and the 13th of February. Some people take advances; but the practice does not seem to be so prevalent as in *Malabar*, and the terms are somewhat more reasonable, although abundantly severe on the imprudent cultivator. If the advance be made six months before the time of delivery, the borrower gets three fourths of the value of the pepper; so that the lender has a profit of one *Rupee* for every three advanced, or 33⅓ *per cent.* If, however, there is a delivery short of the stipulated quantity, the merchant gets back only a proportional part of the advance, with interest at the rate of three fourths of a *Rupee* for the *Pagoda per annum*, that is to say, 18¾ *per cent.*

Coco-nut plantations.

Although I examined both the cultivators and extractors of palm wine concerning the plantations of coco-nut trees, the account that I can give of them is not at all satisfactory; what they said being in some places evidently false, and in others contradictory.

Account of them by the proprietors who cultivate their own gardens.

The cultivators say, that the seed must be allowed one whole year on the tree to ripen, and must be the produce of a palm above fifty years old. After being plucked, it is kept four months in a place which is sheltered from the sun and rain. Then it is put in a well, and kept a month under water. A small plot of dry ground is then dug, and manured with dung and ashes. In this the coco-nuts are placed, at one cubit's distance from each other, and buried so as just to be covered above the eyes, which are placed uppermost. The plot must be near a tank or rivulet, from which with a wooden scoop, *Tay-pallay* (Plate XXV. Fig. 68.), the water is thrown into it every other day when there is no rain. If there be rain, pains must be taken to prevent too much from lodging on the plot. These operations may be performed at any season; so that the young plants, after remaining in the plot from 12 to 15 months, may be fit for transplanting between the 22d of July and the 20th of August. In this month square pits two cubits in width, two cubits deep, and at 24 cubits distance, are dug; and in the bottom of each is placed a coco-nut with its young shoot, which then is about three feet high. Round it are placed a *Seer* of salt, some ashes, and as much fine mould as will rise four inches above the nut and roots. The young plant must be watered every other day, until the second leaves expand, which will be in about six weeks. In dry weather they must, for at least five years, be watered once in four days. In low grounds near the sea or inlets, the trees after this age require no watering: but on high ground, during the dry season, they must be watered as long as they live. In both situations the trees must be manured twice a year with ashes, dung, and leaves; and, if at a distance from the sea-water, they must at the same time get a little salt. When the first set are from five to ten years old, another set is planted in the spaces between them. They arrive at full perfection in twelve years, and continue in vigour until sixty. Those in plantations near the sea die at this age. These require no trouble; but after five years of age to be manured once in six months; and here no plantation is hoed or ploughed. Every second year, in the rainy season, between the 24th of May and the 16th of November, those trees which grow in low places near the sea are let for six months to the people who extract the juice. During this time, owing to the quantity of rain, the nuts in such situations do not ripen. In the year in which juice is extracted, the tree gives four bunches of nuts; in the intermediate year it gives six bunches. According to the farmers, a garden on high ground, that contains 500 trees, if watered by a tank, requires twenty men to work it; if watered by a well, it requires thirty men in the rainy, and forty in the dry season. This, however, must be an excessive exaggeration. In the dry season these trees may once in three years be let for extracting juice; but the practice is not common. Each tree, while in vigour, ought annually to produce fifty nuts. Those on the low ground produce more, but on the high-land they live much longer,

CHAPTER XIV. They there continue in full vigour until sixty years old, and for about ninety more gradually decay.

Jan. 22. Account given by the *Biluaras*, who extract the juice. The men who extract the juice in general hire the trees when these are fit for their purpose. The rate that they give seems very low, being only one fourth of a *Rupee* for three trees near the salt-water, and one fourth of a *Rupee* for four or five trees growing on hill-land; and there must be some mistake, as both to the north and south the rate for each tree is half a *Rupee*. It is true, that here the trees are never exhausted, and, even in the year in which juice is taken, produce a crop of nuts. According to the *Biluaras* the trees near the sea can at all times yield juice, those growing on hills produce it only in the rainy season; which is directly contrary to the assertion of the cultivators. The juice is partly sold, for drink, while fermenting; partly distilled into a liquor called *Gungasir;* and partly boiled into *Jagory*.

Customs of this cast. The people who follow the business of extracting juice from palm trees, in their native language of *Tulava*, are called *Biluaras;* but in that of *Karnáta*, which the people of rank here commonly use, they are called *Halépeca Devaru*. Their proper business is to extract juice from palm trees, to boil it down to *Jagory*, or to distil it into spirituous liquor; but many of them also cultivate the ground, a few as masters, but many more as *Culialu*, or hired servants. Some of this cast have now settled above the *Ghats*. These will marry the daughters of the people remaining in *Tulava;* but those here will not marry a girl from *Karnáta*, because the property there goes to a man's children, but here it goes to the children of his sisters; and, if he married a girl from *Karnáta*, her brothers would not receive the children. The *Biluaras* pretend to be *Súdras*, but acknowledge their inferiority to the *Bunts*. The business of the cast is settled by a person called *Guricara*, who is appointed for the purpose by the government, and who, with the assistance of a council of elders, has the power of excommunication, and of inflicting corporal punishment. None of this cast can read. They are permitted to eat animal food, but ought not to drink intoxicating liquor. The men are allowed a plurality of women, who live in their houses; but on the husband's death the widows, with their children, return to their brother's houses, and the eldest son of the eldest sister of the deceased person becomes master of his house and property. If a man fall into poverty, his children go to their uncle's house, before their father's death. Girls continue to be marriageable after the age of puberty; and a widow, or divorced woman, may marry again. A man may turn away his wife when he pleases; but a woman cannot leave her husband without his consent. This however, by committing adultery with any person of the cast, she can in general procure; for few husbands retain their wives when unfaithful; and she is not disgraced, but may get another husband, or at any rate she can live with her brother. Those who are in easy circumstances burn their dead; those who die poor are buried. The spirits of good men are supposed to go to a heaven called *Sorgum*, those of bad men are sent to a place of punishment called *Nuraka.* They seem to have no idea of transmigration. A few of them worship *Vishnu;* the greater part, however, never pray to any of the great gods, but content themselves with an annual sacrifice to *Marima*, and the other *Saktis*, by which they hope to avert the evils that are occasioned by these agents of *Siva.* Their women are liable to disorders that are attributed to the influence of *Paisáchi*, or evil spirits. These are not appeased by sacrifices; but the *Biluaras* apply to the *Cunian*, whose *Mantrams*, they fancy, are capable of casting out these devils. None of the *Biluaras* have *Puróhitas* to read *Mantrams* or *Sástrams* on occasion of any ceremony, such as marriage, or the commemoration of their deceased parents; nor have those who confine their worship to the *Saktis* any *Guru;* but those who pray to *Vishnu* are subject to the *Sri Vaishnavam Bráhmans*, who accept of their *Dhurma*, or duty, and bestow on them *Upadésa*, *Chakrántikam*, holy-water, and the like.

CHAPTER XIV.

Jan. 22.

Account of the coco-nut plantations by the tenants.

But to return to the gardens. The tenants *(Gaynigaras)* not only differ from the *Biluaras*, but also give a different account from the proprietors *(Mulucaras)*. They say, that when they are disposed to plant a garden, they agree with a proprietor for a piece of ground suited to the purpose. They agree to give him a fixed annual rent in money; and so long as they pay this, the garden cannot on any pretence be resumed. In case of a deficiency of rent, the proprietor may resume the garden; but he must pay the tenant for all improvements made by planting. The value of each kind of tree is fixed, and is not left to arbitration, as was alleged by the proprietors. For coco-nut palms the value differs, according to their age, from one to three *Rupees*. A *Betel-nut* palm is valued at one fourth of a *Rupee;* ten or twelve fruit trees at one *Rupee;* a tree covered with pepper vines one *Rupee.* The expense of rearing all these must be as great here as in *Malabar;* and we may safely conclude, that these values at least equal the expense incurred. A tenant cannot sell his garden; but he may at any time go to the proprietor and compel him to take it off his hands, and to pay the value of the trees. The tenants sometimes hire gardens that have been brought to maturity. In this case, they pay a certain sum for each palm, but nothing for any of the other articles that are reared in the garden. The proprietor continues to cultivate the garden, and to keep up the number of the trees. This seems to be a reason for the low state at which the cultivation of pepper is in *Tulava;* as the proprietor is not at all interested in increasing the number of vines.

Betel-leaf.

Betel-leaf (Piper Betle) is here cultivated in separate gardens, as is the case in most parts of India, except in *Malabar.* For this purpose, a red stony soil on the side of a rising ground is preferred. Some of the gardens are watered from tanks; others, by means of the *Yatam*, from wells, in which the water stands from 12 to 24 feet under the surface. Between the 23d of April and the 23d of May the ground is first dug, and is then formed into beds six cubits wide, which are separated by trenches three fourths of a cubit broad, and half a cubit deep. In the centre of each trench, at four finger-breadths from each other, are planted, in a row, cuttings of the *Betel-vine*, each a cubit in length. If there is no rain, they must be slightly watered five times a day, and then covered with branches to keep off the sun. At the end of the first and second months, a little fresh red soil, mixed with small stones, are put in the bottoms of the trenches. At the end of the third month a row of branches, at six or eight cubits from each other, is planted on each side of every trench. The branches are intended to grow up to trees as supports to the vines. Those chosen are the *Pongary* *(Erythrina)*, the *Nuriga (Moringa)*, and the *Agashay (Æschynomene grandiflora)*. At the same time, a little more earth and some dung are put into the trenches. In the sixth month more earth and dung is given; and, *Bamboos* having been tied horizontally along the rows of branches, the young *Betel-vines* are tied up to these. At the same time, in the middle of every second bed, a channel is formed, which every other day is filled with water; and from thence, by means of the *Tay-pallay* (Plate XXV. Fig. 68), the water must be thrown on the plants. Every month, a little dung and red earth is put to the roots of the vines, and these are tied up to the *Bamboos* and trees. When a year old, the garden begins to produce leaves for sale; after which, once in two months, it requires to be manured, and in dry weather to be watered once in two days. In the centre of each of the beds that have no channels, is then put a row of plantain trees. The garden is generally surrounded by a quickset hedge, at other times by a dead hedge of prickly bushes, and in the interval between the fence and vines are planted *Capsicums*, and other kitchen stuffs. Every four years the *Betel-vines* die; but in their stead others are immediately planted, a new trench being dug in the situation of each old one. In eighteen or twenty years, the soil having been exhausted, all that is near the trees is removed, and in its place fresh red earth is brought into the garden.

CHAPTER XIV. Jan. 22.

The trees last for fifty or sixty years; but when, by accident, one dies sooner, a fresh branch is planted to supply its loss. These substitutes, however, do not thrive. When, from old age, the whole trees begin to decay, the garden is abandoned, and a new one is formed in another place. If the garden receive its supply of water from a reservoir, the cultivator, each time that he plants, pays to the proprietor 10 gold *Fanams*, or $2\frac{1}{2}$ *Rupees* for every 1000 vines. In the three intermediate years he pays nothing. If the water be supplied from a well, the rent is only half of the above mentioned sum.

Cattle and fodder.

The cattle employed in labour here are chiefly bred in the inland districts about *Subhra-mani*, and are no larger than those of *Malabar*. From the month of January, until the commencement of the rainy season, they are supported on fodder. Between the 17th of November and the 16th of December a bad hay is made of the long grass which grows naturally on some hills that are purposely kept clear of bushes. This hay is chopped, and is boiled with rice husks for three hours; of this the oxen are allowed a quantity morning and evening; half a *Maund* (14 lb.), the people say, would be a good allowance. At night they get rice straw to the amount of about three fourths of a *Maund* (21 lb.), as the people whom I consulted conjecture; but, from the appearance of the cattle, the quantity allowed cannot be near so much. The people indeed merely spoke by guess, no *Hindu*, so far as ever I heard, having thought of weighing fodder. At the end of the dry season the cattle, as usual in India, become very poor; but in the rainy season those here are fat, and the cows are entirely supported by pasturing on the hills: at night the working cattle are allowed rice straw. An ox is wrought from sun rise until noon only, and is allowed the afternoon to pasture. Epidemic diseases are sometimes very destructive, and are attributed to a contagion which is supposed always to originate above the *Ghats*. An old man says, that he remembers twenty times the prevalence of this epidemic; but that seems to be speaking in round numbers: for the five last years there has been no disease of the kind. A good cow gives twice a day half a *Seer* of milk. For this purpose few female buffaloes are kept, but a great many males are employed in the plough. Swine are kept by some of the low casts; but the pork of tame swine is an abomination with the *Bunts*, as with all the higher ranks of *Hindus*, although many of them are fond of the meat of the wild hog. No horses, sheep, goats, nor asses are bred in *Tulava;* nor have its inhabitants any carts.

CHAPTER XIV. Jan. 22.

Salt.

Salt is made on this coast by a process similar to that used in *Malabar;* but the quantity manufactured is very inadequate to the demand of the country. A low piece of ground covered by the flood, but dry at low water, is chosen, and surrounded by a bank that is capable of excluding the tide. By means of a tunnel passing through the bank, and formed of a hollow coco-nut tree, the salt water can at pleasure be admitted. A sufficient quantity having been received, the tunnel is shut; and, when the water has evaporated, the soil is very strongly impregnated with salt. Brine is formed, as usual in India, by filtering salt water through this saline earth. The brine is exposed to the sun in small plots, levelled, and rendered impenetrable to water by a coating of clay and sand well beaten together, and rubbed smooth with a stone. To form the salt requires 28 hours evaporation; and it can be made only between the 26th of March and the 23d of May. The man who makes it gets from the government an advance of five *Pagodas* in cash, and of rice to the same amount. He repays the money, but not the rice, and pays on an average a tax of 43 *Pagodas;* so that, in fact, government gets from him 38 *Pagodas* (15*l.* 16*s.* 3*d.*) for an ordinary salt-field. Larger or smaller ones pay in proportion. The manufacturer sells his salt as he pleases. It is mixed with a considerable quantity of earthy impurities, but not with more than the common salt of *Bengal* contains. The grains are large and cubical, and often adhere together in large porous masses. It seems to be

CHAPTER XIV. Jan. 22. very deliquescent. The common price is 1120 *Seers* for the *Pagoda.* The *Seer* measures $76\frac{1}{2}$ cubical inches; the bushel therefore, including the duties, costs less than $2\frac{1}{2}d.$

No mines. No iron is made in the province of *Canara.*

Commerce. Having assembled the principal traders of this place, they say, not only that the trade of the place has decayed greatly since the time of *Hyder*, which may possibly be true; but they also assert, contrary to the evidence of the custom-house accompts, that since the fall of *Tippoo* the imports have diminished greatly. They acknowledge, however, that under this prince the merchants suffered terrible oppressions, and that under his government the greater part of them were ruined. *Hyder* had collected them together with great pains, and he always allowed a *Lac* of *Rupees* (10,073*l.* 12*s.* $2\frac{1}{2}d.$) to be in advance to honest and industrious, but poor men; by which means such valuable persons were induced to come from great distances, and to settle at this place. The principal merchants in *Hyder's* time were *Moplays* and *Kankánies*; a few came from *Guzzerat.* Since the Company has acquired the government of the country, many men of substance have come from *Surat*, *Cutch*, *Bombay*, and other places to the north. These men are chiefly of the *Vaisya* cast, but a good many *Parsis* are among them. The shopkeepers are still mostly *Moplays* and *Kankánies.* The *Bunts* are now beginning to pursue commerce. The vessels employed in trade chiefly belong to other ports.

Exports. Rice is the grand article of export. It is sent to *Muscat*, *Bombay*, *Goa*, and *Malabar.* The duties on its exportation were lowered by Major Monro; but that has made no material difference in the price, and the cultivators are not sensible of any benefit from this measure. The average price, including duties and shipping charges, varies, according to its quantity, from 24 to $18\frac{1}{2}$ *Pagodas* a *Corge* of 42 *Morays.* This makes the price from almost 3*s.* $6\frac{1}{2}d.$ to 2*s.* $8\frac{3}{4}d.$ a bushel. The cultivators, of course, sell it lower; about 2 *Morays* for a *Pagoda* may be the average price that they get for good rice, which is 3*s.* 1*d.* a bushel. The coarser kinds are lower in proportion.

Jan. 22.

Next to rice, *Supári* or *Betel-nut* is the chief export. It is sent to *Surat*, *Bombay*, and *Cutch*. The export price of the raw nut is 14 *Pagodas* a *Candy*, or 1*l.* 2*s.* 4½*d.* a hundred-weight. That of the boiled nut is 15 *Pagodas*, or 1*l.* 3*s.* 11¾*d.* a hundred-weight.

Black-pepper the merchants reckon the next greatest article of export; but, to judge from the custom-house accompts, it would seem to be more considerable. Its average price is 34 *Pagodas* a *Candy*, or 3*l.* 1*s.* 1*d.* a hundred-weight. The customs on pepper are lower here than in *Malabar*, and no rent nor tax is exacted from the cultivator; yet the price at *Mangalore* is higher than at *Tellichery*, and the cultivation is more neglected.

Sandal wood is sent to *Bombay;* but it is all the produce of the country above the *Ghats.*

Cassia, called here *Dhál'-China*, or cinnamon, is sent to *Muscat*, *Cutch*, *Surat*, and *Bombay;* and is exported at 9 *Pagodas* the *Candy*, or 14*s.* 4½*d.* the hundred-weight. The buds of this tree are called *Cabob China*, which seems to be the origin of the European word *Cubeb.* They are exported to the same places.

Turmeric grows in the country, and is exported to *Muscat*, *Cutch*, *Surat*, and *Bombay*, at the rate of 8 *Pagodas* a *Candy*, or 12*s.* 9½*d.* a hundred-weight.

Imports.

The chief imports, according to these merchants, are blue cotton cloths from *Surat*, *Cutch*, and *Madras.* The *Surat* cloth is the most common. It is 36 cubits long, two broad, and of a very dark colour, and sells for from 18 to 50 *Pagodas* a *Corge*, or from 3⅘ to 10 *Rupees* a piece.

Coarse white cotton cloth from *Cutch*, *Bavanagur*, and other places north from *Bombay.*

Salt from *Bombay* and *Goa.* The former sells at 70 *Pagodas* a *Cumbu*, and the latter at 50 *Pagodas:* the former is a little more than 3¼*d.* and the latter than 2½*d.* a bushel.

CHAPTER XIV.

Jan. 22.

Raw-silk, for the use of the manufacturers above the *Ghats*, is imported from *China* and *Bengal*; and from *Muscat* a kind of red dye, called *Munjisht*, which I believe is a species of madder.

Sugar is imported from *Bengal* and *China*, and oil and *Ghee* (boiled butter) from *Surat*.

Much of the cloth used in the country is brought from above the *Ghats*; partly by the merchants of this place, and partly by those of *Bangalore* and *Cuddapa*.

CHAPTER XV.

JOURNEY FROM MANGALORE TO BEIDURU.

CHAPTER XV.

Jan. 29. *Feringy-petta.*

JANUARY 29th.—I went about ten miles to *Arcola*, which is also called *Feringy-petta*, having formerly been chiefly inhabited by the Christians of *Kankána*, invited to reside here by the princes of the house of *Ikeri*. Its situation, on the northern bank of the southern *Mangalore* river, is very fine, and it was formerly a large town. After *Tippoo* had taken General Mathews, he destroyed the town, and carried away its inhabitants. One end only of the church remains, which however shows that it has been a neat building. Its situation is remarkably fine.

Mangalore river. Appearance of the country.

Even now the river contains a great deal of water, and in the rainy season it is very large. Its banks, like those of the *Panyani* river, are very beautiful and rich. Indeed the whole country entirely resembles *Malabar*, only the sides of the hills have been formed into terraces with less industry. As no hill-rice is cultivated in this vicinity, the terraces are formed at the roots of the hills only, where the gardens in *Malabar* are situated. According to the report of the natives, not one fourth part of the ground fit for gardens is now planted. They say, that *Tippoo*, in order to remove every inducement for Europeans to frequent the country, destroyed all the pepper vines, and all the trees on which these were supported. Much of the rice land is so well watered by springs and rivulets, that it produces a constant succession of crops of that grain; one crop being sown as soon as the preceding one has been cut. Although here the steep sides of the hills are not formed into terraces,

CHAPTER XV. Jan. 29. as in *Malabar*, yet the gently sloping lands are formed into rice-fields that are cultivated once a year. In *Malabar* they would be either planted, or reserved for the cultivation of hill-rice, *Sesamum*, or the like; and would yield a crop once only in three years.

Jan. 30. Stupid guides. 30th *January.*—Yesterday a considerable part of my baggage lost its way; and although accompanied by two guides, and travelling on the most public road in *Canara*, I did not discover my tents until two o'clock this morning. The guides and attendants, in excuse for their stupidity, alleged, that they were misled by the reports of the natives, who had informed them of my having passed places which I never had been near. The cattle were so much fatigued that I would not proceed; so I employed the day in collecting plants.

Jan. 31. Appearance of the country. 31st *January.*—In the morning I went three *Sultany* cosses to *Nagara Agrarum*. The road in general is bad even for oxen. The country is similar to that between *Mangalore* and *Arcola*. Most of the hills are clear; but many palms of the *Borassus* kind are scattered throughout the country, and the little vallies are finely watered with clear perennial rivulets. These are confined by dams; so that it is said, that about one fourth part of all the low rice land in *Buntwala* district *(Taluc)* produces annually three crops of rice.

Buntwala. About a coss from *Nagara* I passed through an open town named *Buntwala*, which at present contains about 200 houses. In the last war the *Coorg Rájá* destroyed about 200 houses, and carried away one half of the inhabitants. Many new houses are building; and, as I passed through, I observed, that the people were deeply engaged in the bustle of commerce, and from their appearance were in good circumstances. They carry on a great trade between *Mangalore* on the one hand, and *Hásina, Bailuru, Wostara, Singa-pura-petta, Narasingha-pura,* and *Attigupa* on the other. From the neighbouring country they also collect much rice for exportation.

Nétravati river. The town is situated on the north bank of the river passing

Arcola, and which is named the *Nétrawati*. Since I left *Animalaya*, this is the first river that I have found possessing a name. The tide flows no higher than *Arcola;* but canoes carrying 100 *Morays*, or about 130 bushels of rice, can at all seasons ascend five or six cosses above *Nagara*. The channel is very wide, and full of rocks, which in the dry season form many islands, among which the river winds with a gentle current. In the rainy season, canoes can ascend six cosses farther than they can do at present. There are two branches of the river, which join five cosses above *Nagara*. The northern branch is the largest, and comes from the same place that gives rise to the *Tunga* and *Bhadra* rivers.

Jan. 31.

All the way I observed many iron guns lying near the road; and was told that *Tippoo*, when he destroyed *Mangalore* fort, ordered all the guns to be transported to *Seringapatam;* but the people entrusted with performing this duty were bought off by the labourers, and found out various pretexts for leaving most of the guns on the road. By the natives they are considered as totally useless.

Nagara Agrarum.

Nagara Agrarum, as its name implies, is a village, inhabited by *Bráhmans*, of whose houses it at present contains thirty. They were brought here 70 or 80 years ago, and land was assigned for their support by *Colala Vencatashya*, a *Bráhman* in the service of *Sómasékara Náyaka*, the son of *Sivuppa Náyaka*, the first prince of the house of *Ikeri*. The *Tahsildár* of *Buntwala* resides here; for, being a *Bráhman*, he naturally prefers the society of *Nagara* to that of the traders of *Buntwala*. His district *(Taluc)* contains four *Rájáships; Choutar, Bungar, Ajelar*, and *Mular*. These *Rájás* were all *Jain*. The families are still extant, but have neither authority nor public revenue. They support themselves by their private estates.

Soil of Tulava.

The soil of *Tulava* gradually grows worse for grain, as it is distant from the sea. The best in quality extends from *Mangalore* to *Buntwala;* the next from thence to *Punjalcutta;* and the worst from thence again to the hills. There the rains are so excessive, that they injure the crops of rice, as indeed happens in *Malabar;* but it

CHAPTER XV.

is allowed, that this inland portion of the country is very favourable for plantations.

Feb. 1. Appearance of the country.

1st *February.*—I went three cosses to *Cavila-cutty.* The hills are much higher than those to the westward, and some of them are covered with tall thick forests, in which are found *Teak (Theka)* and wild *Mango (Mangifera)* trees, and the palm which Linnæus called *Caryota.* These hills abound with tigers, which have of late killed several passengers. The road all the way is tolerably well formed, but the engineer has paid no attention to avoid hills: some parts of it are excessively steep. I passed many oxen, loaded with salt, going to the *Mysore* dominions, and met many coming from thence loaded with iron.

Irrigation.

The road, part of the way, led along the south side of a small river called *Bambilu.* A dam has been formed on it, which confines a great body of water, so that it serves also as a reservoir.

Cavila-Cutty.

My halting-place was at a small temple dedicated to *Culimanatia*, one of the *Saktis.* Near it is a small temple belonging to the *Jain*, and a tree, which is surrounded by a terrace for the repose of passengers. Such a tree, in the languages of *Karnáta* and *Tulava*, is called a *Cutty;* and the names of many places in both countries have this word for their termination. The tree here is named *Cavila-Cutty* from its standing in *Cavila,* a district that belonged formerly to the *Mular Rájá.* The representative of the family lives at *Bylangudy*, on the road between *Jamál-ábád* and *Subhramani.*

Depredations of the *Coorg Rájá.*

In the last war this vicinity was plundered by the *Coorg Rájá;* and, among others, the house of the *Jain* priest was destroyed. The *Rájá* wished to replenish his dominions with inhabitants; many of his subjects having perished in his wars with *Tippoo.* From most villages he contented himself with levying a contribution of fourteen or fifteen persons; but he carried off a much larger proportion of the *Bráhmans* from the *Agrarums*, or villages granted to them in charity. This did not proceed from any partiality that the *Rájá* has for the sacred order, as he is supposed rather to be averse to the whole cast, and at any rate does not reverence them as his *Gurus*, for he is a *Sivabhaktar*. His severity, which the *Bráhmans* consider as worse than ordinary impiety, arose from their obstinacy. Relying on the sacred nature of their cast, the *Bráhmans* would come to no composition, and the *Coorg* officers carried away every one of them whom they could seize. In *Tulava* their loss will not be severely felt; for there the *Agrarum Bráhmans* possess none of the industry that distinguishes those of *Pali-ghat*, and in *Coorg* necessity will probably induce them to follow some useful employment.

Singular customs of the *Moylar*.

In the temples of *Tulava* there prevails a very singular custom, which has given origin to a cast named *Moylar*. Any woman of the four pure casts, *Bráhman*, *Kshatri*, *Vaisya*, or *Súdra*, who is tired of her husband, or who (being a widow, and consequently incapable of marriage,) is tired of a life of celibacy, goes to a temple, and eats some of the rice that is offered to the idol. She is then taken before the officers of government, who assemble some people of her cast to inquire into the cause of her resolution; and, if she be of the *Bráhman* cast, to give her an option, of living either in the temple or out of its precincts. If she choose the former, she gets a daily allowance of rice, and annually a piece of cloth. She must sweep the temple, fan the idol with a *Tibet* cow's tail *(Bos gruiens)*, and confine her amours to the *Bráhmans*. In fact, she generally becomes a concubine to some officer of revenue, who gives her a trifle in addition to her public allowance, and who will flog her severely if she grant favours to any other person. The male children of these women are called *Moylar*, but are fond of assuming the title of *Stánika*, and wear the *Bráhmanical* thread. As many of them as can procure employment live about the temples, sweep the areas, sprinkle them with an infusion of cow-dung, carry flambeaus before the gods, and perform other similar low offices. The others are reduced to betake themselves to agriculture, or some honest employment. The daughters are partly brought up to live like

CHAPTER XV. their mothers, and the remainder are given in marriage to the *Stánikas.*

Feb. 1. The *Bráhmany* women who do not choose to live in the temple, and the women of the three lower casts, cohabit with any man of pure descent that they please; but they must pay annually to the temple from one sixteenth to half a *Pagoda.* Their children also are called *Moylar;* those descended from *Bráhmany* women can marry the daughters of the *Moylar* who live in the temples; but neither of them ever intermarry with persons descended from a woman of inferior cast. It is remarkable in this cast, where, from the corrupt example of their mothers, the chastity of the women might be considered as doubtful, that a man's children are his heirs; while in most other casts the custom of *Tulava* requires a man's sister's children, by way of securing the succession in the family. The *Moylar* differ much in their customs, each endeavouring to follow those of the cast from which his mother derived her origin. Thus the descendants of a *Bráhmany* prostitute wear the thread, eat no animal food, drink no spirituous liquors, and make marks on their faces and bodies similar to those which are used by the sacred cast. They are not, however, permitted to read the *Védas,* nor the eighteen *Puránas.* Indeed but very of them learn to keep accompts, or to read songs written in the vulgar language. Contrary to the custom of the *Bráhmans,* a widow is permitted to marry. They burn the dead, and believe in the transmigration of souls, but seem to have very crude notions on this subject. They are, indeed, very ignorant of the doctrine of the *Bráhmans,* who utterly despise them, and will not act as their *Gurus* to give them *Upadésa.* They will attend, however, at the ceremonies of the *Moylar,* and read the services proper on the occasion, and will accept from them both *Dhana* and *Dharma.*

Strata of Tulava. The *strata* of *Tulava,* near the sea-coast, resemble entirely those of *Malayala,* and consist of *Laterite* or *brickstone,* with a very few rocks of granite interspersed. This granite is covered with a dark black crust, and is totally free from veins of quartz, or of felspar. In many places large masses of the granite immersed in the *Laterite* are in a state of decay; the black mica has entirely disappeared, and the white felspar has crumbled into powder, leaving the quartz in angular masses. These sometimes form so large a share of the whole rock, that, after the decay of the other component parts of the granite, they firmly adhere.

CHAPTER XV. Feb. 1.

On arriving in the *Cavila* district, the granite shows itself more abundantly; and among that which, as usual, has no *strata*, I observed some disposed in *strata* running east and west, and which were truncated at the end, like much of that which is found above the *Ghats*. Even this was free from veins of quartz.

Feb. 2. Appearance of the country.

2d *February*.—I went three *Sultany* cosses to *Bellata Angady*, or the white market; a place very improperly named, as it contains only one shop, and in that nothing but *Betel* is sold. The country is not so steep as that through which I came yesterday; but it contains much less rice-land, which is the only part of this country that is considered as of any value. I am persuaded, however, that for cotton or dry crops much of it might be cultivated by the plough; but the population at present is too small to admit of all the rice-land being cultivated; and, while that continues to be the case, it would be madness to attempt any other. On the hills many trees have now grown up; but it would appear, that formerly they had been all cleared; and to keep the bushes down, and to destroy vermin, the grass is still annually burned. To-day many buffaloes and sheep have passed, coming for sale from the dominions of *Mysore;* and many oxen have passed from the same quarter, laden with iron, cloth, and grain.

Bungar Rájás.

At no great distance from the shop near which I encamped, is a *Matam* belonging to the *Sivabhaktar;* and from thence a town formerly extended, almost two miles west, to a temple of the *Jain*. Midway is a ruinous fort, formerly the residence of the *Bungar Rájás*, to whom much of the neighbouring country belonged. The

CHAPTER XV. Feb. 2.

fort and city were destroyed by *Sivuppa Náyaka*, the first prince of the house of *Ikeri* who established his power in *Tulava*. From this it is clear, that the petty *Jain Rájás* existed before the time of that conqueror; and so indeed do the people of this place say, in contradiction to the story which those of *Hosso-betta* told. The tradition here is, that the petty *Jain Rájás* existed long before the time of *Sivuppa Náyaka*, and were entirely independent of each other. Under the *Ikeri Rájás* they paid no tax of any kind for their *Umblica* lands, or private estates. For at least a portion of these *Hyder* continued to allow an exemption from taxes; but the *Sultan* taxed their whole lands at the same rate as the rest of the province, and this tax they continue to pay. During the siege of *Seringapatam*, the commandant of *Jamál-ábád* hanged the *Bungar Rájá*, as he was suspected of an inclination to favour the English. His children live at *Nandavanram*, south from *Buntwala*, and cultivate their lands in that neighbourhood.

Irrigation.

On the river at *Bellata Angady* is a dam, which is rebuilt every year, at the commencement of the dry season, and is formed of piles, stones, and earth. It sends off a large stream of water, the whole of which is wasted on one small *Betel-nut* garden.

Feb. 3. Appearance of the country.

3d *February*.—I went a short journey to *Jamál-ábád*, which originally was called *Narasingha Angady*. The country through which I passed to-day is almost entirely covered with wood; but much of it has a good soil, and might be watered by means of the small river which we twice crossed. The road is very good.

History of *Jamál-ábád*, or *Narasingha Angady*.

The tradition here is, that a *Bráhman* named *Narasingha Ráyá*, the founder of a dynasty who governed the whole of *Tulava* immediately after that of *Myura Varmá* became extinct, built a town on the banks of the river here, and called it *Narasingha Angady* after his own name. Toward the foot of the rock, at present occupied by the fortress, he erected a citadel; and this was the residence of the family, of which I have found no traces in any other place. From the extinction of this family, which must have happened many ages ago, the place continued totally unoccupied, until *Tippoo* was returning in triumph, after the peace which he granted to the English at *Mangalore*. As he encamped where the town now stands, he observed the immense rock placed to the westward; and having sent two officers *(Hirkaras)* to survey it, he determined to build a fortress on its summit. Money was transmitted from the capital immediately on his arrival there, and the work having been completed, a number of people were collected and sent to inhabit the town, which was called *Jamál-ábád*. The *Sultan* afterwards destroyed the fort at *Mangalore*, as being too accessible for Europeans, and made his new town the residence of an *Asoph*, who governed the province of *Canara*. In the fort was placed a *Khiladar*, or commandant, with a garrison of 400 men. In the town there were then about 1000 houses, and it enjoyed a considerable trade. On the late invasion of *Mysore*, the *Coorg Rájá* destroyed the town, and carried away one half of its inhabitants. The remainder made their escape into the woods, and only about 20 houses have been rebuilt; for the former inhabitants, having been mostly collected by force from different places, when dispersed by the *Coorg Rájá*, returned to their native villages. The immense rock on which the fort stands is wholly inaccessible, except by one narrow way, and may be deemed impregnable. The nature of the access to it, however, renders the descent, in face of an enemy, nearly as difficult as the ascent; so that a very small body of men, with artillery, are adequate to blockade a strong garrison; which renders the place of little use, except as a safeguard for treasure or records. After the fall of *Seringapatam*, a party of British troops summoned the place to surrender; and informed the commandant, that if he submitted immediately, the whole arrears of the garrison should be paid; but that no quarter would be given, should the garrison, by a useless resistance, occasion a wanton effusion of blood. The garrison, however, continued obstinate for about a month and a half, until some mortars were brought up. After three days bombardment, the

CHAPTER XV. Feb. 3.

soldiers ran off, the commandant poisoned himself, and the principal officers who submitted to be taken were hanged. Sometime afterwards, a person named *Timma Náyaka*, who had been a petty military officer at *Beäcul*, and who, by promising to procure recruits for the *Bombay* army, had been admitted into the Company's service, persuaded about 200 of the recruits to desert, and with them went to join an insurgent of the name of *Suba Row*. This was a *Bráhman*, who had been a clerk *(Surishtadár)* at *Coimbetore;* and who, with a view of raising a disturbance, had set up a pretended *Futty Hyder*. The man that pretended to be *Futty Hyder*, who is a natural son of the late *Sultan*, remained at a temple near *Bylangudy*, a town on the *Ghats* towards *Subhramani;* while the *Bráhman* occupied a cave at no great distance, and detached *Timma Náyaka* with his recruits to surprise *Jamál-ábád*. In this they succeeded. A young officer had relieved the garrison, and was sleeping that night in a house at the foot of the rock, with all his men, except a native corporal's *(Náyaka's)* party, intending probably next day to march into the fort; but *Timma Náyaka* came upon them unawares, and put the whole party to death; after which he persuaded the corporal to give up the gate, and took possession without loss. While the neighbourhood was awed by their success, *Suba Row*, with his pretended *Futty Hyder*, descended from their hills, and plundered several villages. They then advanced to *Buntwala*, where they defeated the *Tahsildár*, who, to oppose their ravages, had collected some armed messengers *(Peons)*. Elated with this advantage, they attacked a person called *Rájá Hegada* of *Dharmastulla*, whom they wounded at a place called *Potur;* but two of the neighbouring *Tahsildárs*, having procured thirty regular *Sepoys*, soon came up, and immediately dispersed the rabble. The two leaders, however, made their escape to the mountains, where they are still skulking. A military force was sent from *Mangalore*, that a proper example might be made of *Timma Náyaka* and his party, and two attempts were in vain made by Europeans to take the fort

CHAPTER XV. Feb. 3.

by assault. The place was then blockaded for three months; when, all the provisions having been exhausted, the people in the fort contrived to let themselves down the back of the rock by means of chains, ropes, blankets, and the like. They immediately dispersed; but many of them were secured by the country people, and hanged. For some time *Timma Náyaka* concealed himself in disguise; but at length he was recognised by an old friend, a *Nair*, at *Beäcul.* This man, under pretence of cutting a *Bamboo*, borrowed *Timma's* sword, without seeming to know him, but addressing him as a stranger. No sooner had he disarmed his old acquaintance, than he rushed on him, and threatened him with instant death, unless he followed quietly. The culprit was thus delivered over to justice, and the *Nair* as a reward received 500 *Rupees.* The fellow has the impudence to complain of its insufficiency, and has persuaded some gentlemen to support his demands for more, by pretending that, in attacking so desperate a man, he has performed extraordinary deeds of valour. The fort, in order to prevent it from falling into the hands of ruffians, is now garrisoned; for, as I have said before, in a military point of view it is of little use.

Malayar, and their manner of cultivating the hills.

In this neighbourhood, the hills that are cultivated after the *Cotucadu* or *Cumri* manner are all private property. The *Mulucaras*, or proprietors, have alienated the whole right of cultivating them to a rude tribe, called *Malayar*, or *Malay-cudies.* The *Malayar*, who dwells on any hill of this kind has the exclusive hereditary right of cultivating it; but, while not occupied by this labour, he and his family must work for the proprietor *(Mulacara)*, at the allowance of provisions usually given to slaves. The *Malayar* may give up his possession when he pleases, which secures him from being ill used by the proprietor; for such people on an estate add greatly to its value. They work for their master ten months in the year; but, having six or seven miles to come and go from their hills to their master's fields, they labour only six hours in the day. In this neighbourhood no tax is imposed on this kind of land; but in some

CHAPTER XV. Feb. 3.

districts the *Malayar* pay annually a small sum to government for each hill.

The following is the manner in which this sort of cultivation, called *Cumri*, is performed. In the beginning of the dry season, the *Malayar* cuts down all the trees and bushes from a certain space of ground, and before the rains set in he burns them. The ground is then dug with a sharp *Bamboo*, and sown with *Shamay (Panicum miliare)*, *Ragy (Cynosurus Corocanus)*, rice, and various cucurbitaceous plants. The grains are sown separately; but seeds of the cucurbitaceous fruits are mixed with all the farinaceous crops. With the *Ragy* are also mixed the seed of *Hibary (Cytisus Cajan)*, and of *Abary (Dolichos Lablab)*. Next year another piece of ground must be cleared, the former not being fit for cultivation in less than twelve years. In *Tulava*, this is the only kind of cultivation of dry grains, although much of the ground seems fit for the purpose; but the natives have a notion, that no high ground can produce any thing unless a great deal of timber has been burned on it.

Hills of *Tulava* considered as useless. Hay.

They therefore consider the greater part of the country as totally useless, except for pasture or hay, and very little of it produces the proper grass. One kind of grass only that is produced in *Tulava* is eatable; and when I proposed to the natives to destroy the bad kinds, and sow the seed of the good, they were filled with astonishment at what they considered as the extravagance of the project. Where the hills are not too steep for the plough, I am persuaded that this might be done to great advantage; and the quantity of live stock and manure might be thus quadrupled. The hay at present is very bad, and sapless; for the grass, in its natural state, withers from maturity, before the rainy season is over; and before that period the hay could not be preserved. This, however, might be easily remedied, by cutting the grass while young, and allowing a second crop to come up, so as to be in juice at the commencement of the fair weather. The first crop would make good manure. This project the natives consider as equally extravagant with the former;

nor indeed can it be expected, that in their circumstances they should attempt any innovation of the kind, until convinced, by an experiment made before their eyes, that it would succeed.

Feb. 4.

Appearance of the country.

4th *February*.—I returned by the same road to the *Jain* temple at *Bellata Angady*, and then turned towards the north, and came to *Padanguddy* in a district named *Majura*, which formerly belonged to the *Bungar Rájás*. The country through which I came from *Bellata Angady* is clear, and the road good; the hills being low, and of gentle declivity. The quantity of rice ground is inconsiderable, and by the way I saw hardly any gardens. Near the temple is a very fine reservoir, made, exactly like those above the *Ghats*, by building a mound of stone across the head of a narrow valley, which it supplies with water. The value of the rice ground, from its small extent, seems not to have been a sufficient inducement with them to construct such a work; which, was made, probably from ostentation, by a *Linga Banijigar*, named *Luddi Guruvaia*.

Feb. 5.

5th *February*.—I went three cosses to *Sopina Angady*. From *Padanguddy*, to the banks of the northern branch of the *Mangalore* river at *Einuru*, the country is much like what I saw yesterday, but more woody. Between the river and *Sopina Angady*, the hills are steeper, and consequently the road is very bad.

Jain.

Einuru is a small town, containing eight temples belonging to the *Jain*, and one to the *Siva Bráhmans*. The former have an annual allowance of 14 *Pagodas*, and the latter one of 10 *Pagodas*. As in this country the worshippers of *Jain* are more numerous than those of *Siva*, the temples of the former ought to have the best endowments; but while the native officers of government are mostly *Bráhmans*, pretences will never be wanting for depressing these heretical temples.

At *Einuru* is an immense colossal image of one of the gods worshipped by the *Jain*. It is formed of one solid piece of granite and stands in the open air.

CHAPTER XV.

Feb. 5. Tigers.

Sopina Angady has only three shops; but the houses of the proprietors are very large, and the occupants seem to be in easy circumstances. Here is a *Jain* temple, with an excellent house for the priest *(Pújári)*. The place was formerly much infested with tigers; but a year ago the inhabitants collected, and cleared away so much of the wood, that they now have no trouble from these animals. They clear the country by cutting down the brush-wood, and burning it when it has dried. If this be repeated two or three years successively, the large trees also decay. The country is afterwards preserved clear by annually burning the grass. A few bushes always spring up, but not more than is sufficient to supply the farmers with leaves for manure.

Feb. 6. Appearance of the country.

6th *February*.—I went two cosses to *Mudu*, or East *Biddery*, and by the way crossed a branch of the northern *Mangalore* river, which descends from the *Ghats*. On the way, two tigers were seen by some of my people. Although the country is well cleared, it contains very little rice ground; and, as the hills are considered as totally useless, this is in fact one of the poorest countries that I have ever seen.

Choutar Rájás.

Mudu Biddery was formerly subject to the *Choutar Rájás*, and their descendants have still a house in the place. The tradition, as given me here by a *Bráhman* native officer, and apparently a well informed man, is, that the *Jain Rájás* of *Tulava* were independent of each other, and of all other powers, and were descended from the kings of *Vijaya-nagara* by *Jain* women. They derived their territories from their parents, as appanages free from all claims of tribute. I think it probable, that the *Bráhman* confounds the *Baylala Ráyas*, who were sovereigns of *Karnáta*, and who were *Jain*, with the family who afterwards founded *Vijaya-nagar*, who governed the same dominions, and who were worshippers of *Vishnu*.

About 150 years ago, when under the *Choutar Rájás*, the place contained 18 *Busties* or temples of the *Jain*, and a throne occupied by one of the chief *Gurus* of this sect of *Bráhmans.* It also contained 6 *Gudies*, or temples belonging to the *Bráhmans* who follow the *Puránas*, and 700 houses, mostly occupied by *Bráhmans* of the two sects. At that time, a dissension happening between the *Rájás* of *Carculla* and *Choutar*, the *Siva-Bhaktar* were called in, and subjected the country in the name of the kings of *Vijaya-nagara;* but in fact it continued subject to the princes of *Ikeri*, until these were overthrown by *Hyder*. Ever since the overthrow of the *Choutar*, the place has been on the decline, and the allowances formerly granted to the *Guru* have been stopped. The temples still, however, continued to enjoy their land; and in the government of *Hyder*, those of the *Jain* had possessions to the amount of 360 *Pagodas* a year. These were entirely resumed by *Tippoo*, who gave, in place of them, an annual pension of 90 *Pagodas;* but he destroyed most of the *Bráhmans* houses, and now the whole place contains only a hundred families. Major Monro increased the pension of the *Jain* temples to 207 *Pagodas;* but Mr. Ravenshaw has reduced it to what *Tippoo* allowed, and it is to be collected in the same manner, that is to say, by a small tax levied on the farmers. As this is to be done by officers who abhor the *Jain* as detestable heretics, very little of the pension will reach their hands. The free lands formerly occupied by the *Jain* have been totally resumed, and they have not been allowed to cultivate it on payment of the land-tax, as all the other persons holding land of this kind have been permitted to do. This is owing to the ill will of those *Bráhmans* who act as revenue officers.

Account of the *Jain*, or *Arhita* sect.

Having invited *Pandita Achárya Swámi*, the *Guru* of the *Jain*, to visit me, he came, attended by his most intelligent disciples, and gave me the following account of his sect.

The proper name of the sect is *Arhita (worthy);* and they acknowledge, that they are one of the twenty-one sects who were considered by *Sankara Achárya* as heretical. Like other *Hindus*, they are divided into *Bráhman*, *Kshatri*, *Vaisya*, and *Súdra*. These

CHAPTER XV. Feb. 6.

casts cannot intermarry; but, provided she be of pure descent, a man of a high cast is not disgraced by having connection with a woman of inferior birth. A similar indulgence is not granted to the women of the higher casts. The men are allowed a plurality of wives, which they must marry before the age of puberty. The man and woman must not be of the same family in the male line. Widows ought not to burn themselves with the bodies of their husbands; but it is those of the *Súdras* only that are permitted to take a second husband. The *Bráhmans* and *Vaisyas* in *Tulava*, and every cast above the *Ghats*, consider their own children as their heirs; but the *Rájás* and *Súdras* of *Tulava*, being possessors of land, follow the custom of the country, and their sisters' children are their heirs. Even the *Súdras* are not permitted to eat animal food, nor to drink spirituous liquors; nor, except for the *Kshatriyas* when engaged in war, is it lawful for any one to kill an animal. They all burn the dead.

Opinions of the *Jain*, or *Arhita* tribes.

The *Védas*, and the eighteen *Puránas* of the other *Bráhmans*, the *Arhita* reject as heretical. They say, that these books were composed by a saint *(Rishi)* named *Vyása*, whom the other *Bráhmans* consider as an incarnation of the deity. The chief book of which the doctrine is followed by the *Arhita* is named *Yoga*. It is written in the *Sanskrit* language, and character of *Karnáta*, and is explained by 24 *Puránas*, all written by its author, who was named *Vrishava Sayana*, a saint *(Rishi)*, who by long continued prayer had obtained a knowledge of divine things. They admit, that all *Bráhmans* are by birth of equal rank, and are willing to show their books to the *Bráhmans* who heretically follow the doctrine of the *Védas;* but they will not allow any of the lower classes to inspect their sacred writings.

The gods of the *Arhita* are the spirits of perfect men, who, owing to their great virtue, have become exempt from all change and misfortune, and are all of equal rank and power. They are collectively called by various titles; such as *Jinéswara*, (the lord *Jina)*,

Arhita (the worthy), and *Siddha* (the holy); but each is called by a particular name, or names, for many of them have above 1000 appellations. These *Siddha* reside in a heaven called *Moesha;* and it is by their worship only, that future happiness can be obtained. The first person who by his virtue arrived at this elevated station was *Adi Paraméswara* (the first supreme being); and by worshipping him, the favour of all the *Siddha* may be procured He has 1008 names, the most common of which among his adorers is *Jinéswara,* the god *Jina.*

CHAPTER XV.

Feb. 6.

The servants of the *Siddha* are *Dévatas,* or the spirits of good and great men, who, although not so perfect as to obtain an exemption from all future change, yet live in an inferior heaven called *Swargam;* where for a certain length of time they enjoy great power and happiness, according to the merit of the good works which they performed when living as men. *Swargam* is situated higher in the regions of the air than the summit of *Mount Méru* (the north pole); and men ought to worship its inhabitants, as they possess the power of bestowing temporal blessings. Concerning the great gods of the eighteen *Puránas* and *Védas,* the *Arhita* say, that *Vishnu* was a *Rájá,* who, having performed certain good works, was again born a *Rájá* named *Ráma.* At first, he was a great hero and conqueror; but afterwards he retired from the pleasures of the world, became a *Sannyási,* and lived a life of such purity that he obtained *Siddha* under the name of *Jina,* which he had assumed when he gave up his earthly kingdom. *Mahéswara,* or *Siva,* and *Brahmá* are at present *Dévatas;* but are inferior in rank and power to *Indra,* who is the chief of all the happy beings that reside in *Swargam.* In this heaven are sixteen stages, containing so many different kinds of *Dévatas,* who live in a degree of bliss in proportion to their elevation. An inferior kind of *Dévatas,* called *Ventaru,* live on mount *Méru;* but their power and happiness are greatly inferior to those of the *Dévatas* of *Swargam.* *Marimá, Putalimá,* and the other

CHAPTER XV. *Saktis*, are *Ventarus* living on *Mahá Méru;* but they are of a malevolent disposition.

Feb. 6. Below *Mahá Méru* and the earth, is situated *Bhuvana*, or hell, the residence of the spirits of wicked men. These are called *Rákshas* and *Asuras;* and, although endowed with great power, they are miserable. *Bhuvana* is divided into ten places of punishment, which are severe in proportion to the crimes of their respective inhabitants.

The heaven and earth in general, including *Mahá Méru*, and *Bhuvana*, are supposed never to have been created, and to be eternal; but this portion *(Khanda)* of the earth called *Arya*, or *Bhárata*, is liable to destruction and re-production. It is destroyed by a poisonous wind that kills every thing; after which a shower of fire consumes the whole *Khanda*. It is again restored by a shower of butter *(Ghee)*, followed by one of milk, and that by one of the juice of sugar-cane. Men and animals then come from the other five portions *(Khandas)* of the earth, and inhabit the new *Arya* or *Bharata-khanda*. The books of the *Arhita* mention many *Dwipas*, islands or continents, surrounding *Mahá Méru*, of which the one that we inhabit is called *Jambu-dwipa*. People, from this, can go as far as *Manushotra*, a mountain in *Pushkarara-dwipa*, between which and *Jambu-dwipa* are two seas, and an island named *Daticy shunda*. *Jambu-dwipa* is divided into six *Khandas*, and not into nine, as is done by the *Bráhmans* who follow the *Védas*. The inhabitants of five of these portions are called *Mléchas*, or barbarians. *Arya* or *Bharata* is divided into 56 *Désas*, or nations, as is done by the other *Bráhmans*. As *Arabia* and *China* are two of these nations, *Arya* would seem to include all the world that was tolerably known to the *Arhita* who composed the books of this sect.

Every animal, from *Indra* down to the meanest insect, or the most wicked *Ráksha*, has existed from all eternity; and, according to the nature of its actions, will continue to undergo changes from a higher to a lower rank, or from a lower to a higher dignity, until at length it becomes perfect, and obtains a place among the *Siddha*. Before a *Súdra* can hope for this exemption from evil, he must be born as one of the three higher casts; but, in order to become a *Bráhman*, it is not necessary that he should be purified by being born of a cow, as many of the followers of *Vyása* pretend. The *Arhita* however allow, that to kill an animal of the cow kind is equally sinful as the murder of the human species. The death of any other animal, although a crime, is not of so atrocious a nature. The *Arhita*, of course, never offer sacrifices, but worship the gods and *Dévatas* by prayer, and offerings of flowers, fruits, and incense.

Feb. 6.

The *Saugata* and *Jaina* not the same sect.

By the *Bráhmans* who follow the doctrine of *Vyása*, the *Arhita* are frequently confounded with the *Saugata*, or worshippers of *Buddha*; but this arises from ignorance. So far are the *Arhita* from acknowledging *Buddha* as their teacher, that they do not think that he is now even a *Dévata*; but allege, that, as a punishment for his errors, he is undergoing various low metamorphoses. Their doctrine however, it must be observed, has in many points a strong resemblance to that which is taught in *Ava* by the followers of *Buddha*.

The *Jain Bráhmans* abstain from lay affairs, and dress like those who follow the doctrine of *Vyása*. They have *Gurus*, who are all *Sannyásis*; that is to say, have relinquished the world, and all carnal pleasures, These *Gurus* in general acknowledge as their superior, the one who lives at *Sravana Belgula*, near *Seringapatam*; but *Pandita Achárya Swámí* pretends to be at least his equal. In each *Matam*, or convent, there is only one *Sannyási*, who, when death approaches, gives the proper *Upadésa* to one of his followers, who must relinquish the world and all its enjoyments, except perhaps an indulgence in the pride of devotion. The office is not confined to the *Bráhmans*; none but the *Súdras* are excluded from this highest of dignities; for all the *Sannyásis*, after death, are supposed to become *Siddha*, and of course do not worship the *Dévatas*, who are greatly their

CHAPTER XV.

Feb. 6.

inferiors. The *Sannyásis* never shave, but pull out all their hair by the roots. They never wear a turban, and are allowed to eat and drink but once a day. In fact, they are very abstemious; and the old *Swámí*, who, from his infirmities, expected daily to become a god, mortified the flesh exceedingly. The *Gurus* have the power of fining all their followers who cheat or lie, or who commit murder and adultery. The fines are given to the gods, that is, to his priest *(Pújári)*. These *Gurus* excommunicate all those who eat animal food, or fornicate with persons that are not *Jain;* which, of course, are looked upon as greater crimes than those which are only punished by fine. The married *Bráhmans* act as *Pújáris* for the gods, and as *Puróhitas* for the inferior casts. The follower may choose for his *Puróhita* any *Bráhman* that he pleases. The *Bráhman* receives *Dhana*, and on this occasion reads prayers *(Mantrams);* as he does also at the marriages, funerals, and commemorations of the deceased ancestors of his followers.

The *Jain* extend throughout *India;* but at present, except in *Tulava*, they are not any where numerous. They allege, that formerly they extended over the whole of *Arya* or *Bharata-khanda;* and that all those who ever had any just pretensions to be of *Kshatri* descent, were of their sect. It, no doubt, appears clear, that, until the time of *Ráma Anuja Achárya* many powerful princes in the south of *India* were their followers. They say, that formerly they were very numerous in *Arabia;* but that about 2500 years ago a terrible persecution took place at *Mecca*, by order of a king named *Parsua Battáraka*, which forced great numbers to come to this country. Their ideas of history and chronology, however, as usual with *Bráhmans*, are so very confused, that they suppose *Parsua Battáraka* to have been the founder of the Mussulman faith. None of them have the smallest trace of the *Arabian* features, but are in every respect complete *Hindus*.

Feb. 7.

Appearance of the country.

7th *February*.—I went three cosses to *Carculla*. The first part of the road led through a tolerably level country; but, as usual, nothing more

CHAPTER XV. Feb. 7.

was cultivated than low places, which wind through among the swelling lands, and are very narrow. The higher part, which is bare, seems to be capable of cultivation for cotton or dry grains. Nearer *Carculla* the hills are steep and rocky, and some of them are overgrown with trees. The road is wide, and has a fine row of trees on each side. In this part of the country are many traces of inclosures; and it is said, that formerly there were here several villages, which have been deserted ever since *Hyder* raised the taxes.

Byrasu Wodears, and the Jain Rájás.

Carculla is an open town, containing about 200 houses, which mostly belong to shopkeepers. Near it are the ruins of the palace of the *Byrasu Wodears*, the most powerful of the *Jain Rájás* of *Tulava*. The *Jain*, who are the chief inhabitants of the place, do not pretend that their prince had any authority over the *Rájás* of the south; the whole tradition, therefore, at *Hosso-betta* seems to be erroneous. That place, however, may have belonged to the *Byrasu Wodears;* as the territories of the *Rájás* of *Tulava* were probably as much intermixed as those of the chiefs of *Malayála*. The revenues of this family, it is said, amounted to 17,000 *Pagodas*, or 6850*l.* 4*s.* 7½*d.*

Doctrines of the *Jain*, and their history.

The *Jain* altogether deny the creation of *Tulava* by *Parasu Ráma*, or any gift of it made by that personage to the *Bráhmans*. From a book called *Amonoro Charitra*, which gives an account of *Jenadutta Ráya*, the ancestor of the *Byrasu Wodears*, they say that he was born at *Uttara Madura* (the *Matra* of Major Rennell), near the *Jamuna* river. He was of the family of the sun; and, having incurred the displeasure of the *Rájá* his father, in order to avoid being put to death, was obliged to fly. Having come to a village near *Nagara*, he founded a city named *Hombucha*, and soon after conquered a place called *Culisha*. He afterwards descended to *Sisila*, near *Subhramani*, and finally established himself at *Carculla*. His son was the first *Byrasu Wodear*, and all his descendants assumed that title. The book gives no account of the time when these events happened, nor of the princes who were previously in the country. In

CHAPTER XV. Feb. 7. one of the temples here there is an inscription on stone, in the language and old character of *Karnáta*, of which a copy in the modern character has been delivered to the government of Bengal (MSS. Inscriptions No. 1.). From this it would appear, that *the protected by Padmawati* (a title by which, it is well known, *Jenadutta* is meant) reigned at *Carculla* in the year of *Saliváhanam* 1256 (*A. D.* 133¼). From this it would seem probable, that in the beginning of the fourteenth century a *Rájá* of the *Jain* religion governed *Matra*, now one of the chief seats of the followers of the *Védas*. The latest inscription here belonging to this family is on a colossal image. A copy (No. 2.), in the old character, has been also delivered to the Bengal government. It is dated in the year of *Saliváhanam* 1353 (*A. D.* 1431). The family were overthrown by *Sivuppa Nayaka* of *Ikeri*, and have since become extinct. The tradition is, that before the arrival of *Jenadutta* there were many *Rájás* of the *Kshatri* cast, and who, of course, according to the *Jain*, were of their religion. These, they say, were all tributaries, or *Polygars*, under the kings of *Vijaya-nagara*. These *Jain* say, that the *Tulava Bráhmans* who follow the *Védas* were first introduced by *Myuru Varmmá*, who was a *Jain* prince that lived about a thousand years ago at *Barcuru*, and governed all *Tulava* without any superior; but of this prince the *Jain* have no written account.

Among the *Jain* there are two kinds of temples; one covered with a roof, and called *Busty;* the other an open area, surrounded by a wall, and called *Betta*, which signifies a hill. The temples of *Siva* and *Vishnu*, the great gods of the followers of the *Védas*, are here called *Gudies*. In the *Busties* are worshipped the images of 24 persons, who have obtained *Siddharu*, or become gods. These images are all naked, and exactly of the same form; but they are called by different names, according to the *Siddharu* which they are designed to represent. These idols are in the form of a man sitting. In the temples called *Betta* the only image of a *Siddha* is that of a person called *Gomuta Ráya*, who while on earth was a powerful king.

The images of *Gomuta Ráya* are naked, and always of a colossal size. That here, of which two views are given (Plate XXIII. Fig. 65, 66.), is made of one piece of granite, the extreme dimensions of which, above ground, are 38 feet in height, 10½ feet in breadth, and 10 feet in thickness. How much is below ground I cannot say; but it is probably sunk at least three feet, as it has no lateral support. According to an inscription on the stone itself, it was made by *Vira Pandia*, son of *Bhairava-Indra*, 369 years ago. A copy of this inscription has been delivered to the government of Bengal. Feb. 7.

The *Jain* deny the creation of man, as well as of the world. They allow, that *Brahmá* was the son of a king, and that he is a *Dévata*, and the favourite servant of *Gomuta Ráya;* but they altogether deny his creative power. *Brahmá* and the other *Dévatas* are worshipped, as I have said, by the *Jain*, who have not become *Sannyásis;* but all the images of these supposed beings that are to be found in the great temples of the *Jain (Busties,* or *Bettas)*, are represented in a posture of adoration, as worshipping the *Siddha* to whom the temple is dedicated. These images, however, of the *Dévatas* are not objects of worship, but merely ornamental; and the deity has not been induced to reside in the stone by the powerful invocations of a *Bráhman*. When a *Jain* wishes to adore one of these inferior spirits, he goes to the temple that is dedicated to its peculiar worship. *Jain* or *Ráma* is never represented by an idol in a temple of the kind called *Busty*, although he is acknowledged to be a *Siddha;* and although *Ganésa* and *Hanumanta* are acknowledged to be *Dévatas*, these favourites of the followers of *Vyása* have no images in the temples of the *Arhita*.

The *Jain* have no tradition concerning a great deluge that destroyed a large proportion of the inhabitants of the earth; but they believe, that occasionally most of the people of *Arya* are destroyed by a shower of fire. Some have always escaped to the other portions of the earth, and have returned to repeople their native country, after it has been renovated by showers of butter, milk,

CHAPTER XV. Feb. 7.

and of the juice of the sugar-cane. The accounts of the world, and of the various changes which the *Jain* suppose it to have undergone, are contained in a book called *Lóka Swarupa.* An account of *Gomuta Ráya* is given in a book called *Gomuta Ráya Charitra.* The *Camunda Ráya Purána* contains a history of the 24 *Siddháru* which are worshipped in the temples called *Busties.* These books may be read by any person; and the *Jain* of *Carculla* entered into an agreement with me to copy them for my use. I paid them the price, but I have not yet received the books.

Feb. 8.

8th *February.*—I remained at *Carculla* in order to investigate some matters relative to agriculture.

Divisions of rice ground.

Here the distinctions of rice ground differ somewhat from those in the south. *Bylu* is that which receives from rivulets a supply of water sufficient to ensure two crops. *Majelu* has one crop ensured by the same means. Small reservoirs, in case of a scarcity of rain, secure one crop from *Betta* land. *Bana Betta* is that which depends on the rains alone; so that, if these give over early, the crop is entirely lost. *Potla* is land overflowed by rivers. The sprouted seed is here by far the most common cultivation in both crops, and in all soils, except in some called *Nunjinay Gudday,* in which worms abound. In this the seed is sown broad-cast without preparation. Scarcely any rice is here transplanted, and sprouted seed is sown even on *Potla* land. The quantity of seed required for the same extent of ground, of whatever kind, is nearly the same; only *Bylu* land requires a little more, as part of the seed is choaked by sinking too deep in the mud. This is directly contrary to the assertion of the people at *Mangalore;* but the farmers here say, that the information given at that place was correct; and that near the sea the *Bylu* land requires the least seed, while in inland places it requires more than the *Majelu* or *Betta.*

If the rains continue late, a crop of pulse or *Sesamum* may be procured from both kinds of *Betta* land; but, if the dry weather commences early, they can only be obtained from *Majelu,* the others being too dry. On the *Majelu* land here a very small quantity of sugar-cane is raised; but the whole of this is of very small extent. At the head of a *Bylu* field here, there is a large reservoir; but very little use is made of its water, at least for the purpose of agriculture. The people say, that they do not make reservoirs, because the rains are so heavy that they would break the mounds, and that the soil soaks up the water so fast, that, very soon after the rainy season is over, they would become dry. The farmers of *Carculla* seem to be an obstinate and ignorant set of men.

CHAPTER XV.

Feb. 8.

Betel gardens.

The *Betel-leaf* is raised on the *Areca*, and this is planted in separate gardens. It does not injure the produce of the tree. These gardens are made both on the low grounds, and on hills where there is a command of water. They are allowed much manure; but, if on hilly ground, require no red earth. They are always watered, as at *Mangalore;* their cultivation must be therefore much more expensive than in *Malabar*, where they are only watered when young. All the gardens belong to the landlords, who occasionally mortgage them, but very rarely let them out for rent. The revenue, although nominally raised by so much a tree, has nothing to do with the actual number. It is levied by an old valuation; in making of which three trees were called one; and, if double the original number has been planted, no additional tax is paid. A thousand nominal trees on good land were rated at so much, and those on worse soils are rated lower in proportion.

Turmeric and ginger.

In the *Hitelu*, or back-yard of the house, are cultivated turmeric, ginger, *Capsicum*, greens, roots, and other things called *Tarkári*. The quantity of turmeric and ginger raised in the neighbourhood is considerable. The soil proper for these plants is *Betta* land which is free from stones. Between the 24th of May and the 22d of June the ground is ploughed four times, and smoothed with a hoe. The whole is then divided by trenches, one cubit wide, half a cubit deep, and one cubit distant; and the earth which is taken from the trenches is thrown on the ridges. Then bits of the roots,

CHAPTER XV.

Feb. 8.

each containing an eye, are planted in the ridges at half a cubit's distance from each other. These are then covered with *Casara Sopu*, or the small branches and leaves of the *Strychnos Nux vomica*, which is the most common tree on the hills of *Tulava*. At the end of a month, the leaves having rotted, the small sticks are removed. Dung is then put over the plants, and a little more earth is thrown up from the trenches. In the month preceding the winter solstice, the roots are fit for taking up. The large roots, containing eyes, are kept for seed; and, being tied up in a straw bag, are hung upon a tree until the next season for planting. The smaller roots are fit for sale. The turmeric and ginger are cultivated exactly in the same manner. The roots of the turmeric intended for sale are boiled for twelve hours, and afterwards dried fifteen days in the sun.

Betel-nut reared in large quantities by *Bráhmans.*

About 250 years ago a *Márattah Bráhman* came here, and observed that many hills were quite waste, which might be cultivated for *Betel-nut* by making reservoirs at the head of a valley; so that the water might be preserved, and distributed upon the sides of the hills. He applied to *Byrasu Wodear*, then sovereign of the country, for some of these hills; and having obtained a grant of them, he began his plantations with great success. By degrees this man's descendants increased to fifty families; and these were joined by many of the same sect and country, who all betook themselves to this kind of cultivation; so that between *Subhramani* and *Gaukarna* they amounted to seven hundred families. In their plantations *Betel-nut* was the great article; but they also contained many coconut palms, and some black pepper, and *Mango* and *Jack* trees. Each of the last produces from two to three hundred fruit; and these are so little in demand, that they are given to the cattle. They are not palatable to the ox; but at the season in which they ripen, any thing will be devoured, as the cattle are then starving. The prohibition against exporting *Betel-nut* by sea, which the late *Sultan* issued, reduced the price so much, that many of the plantations were allowed to go to ruin; and the number of *Bráhmans* was reduced to four hundred families. The markets being now open, and a brisk trade carried on between the coast and *Madras*, and *Goa*, which are the principal markets for the nut, the *Bráhmans* are with great spirit returning to this object of industry. The influence of *Mousa* and his *Moplays* does not extend this length. The principal merchant is *Murtur Sangaia*, a *Banijigar*, who lives at *Hara-punya-hully*, but has factories in every part of the peninsula.

CHAPTER XV.

Feb. 8.

Weather in *Tulava.*

The most judicious old men that I could find here gave me the following account of the weather. Between the 13th of March and the 13th of May they have slight showers, lasting three or four hours a day. These come three or four days successively, with equal intervals of dry weather, and accompany easterly winds. In the first month the winds night and day are easterly; in the latter part of this time the winds are from the southward, and in the west there is much thunder. Between the 14th of May and the 16th of August there come from the west strong winds, and heavy rains. The land winds are not at all perceptible. Between the 17th of August and the 15th of October there are gentle showers from the eastward. Except when it rains, the winds are westerly. From the 16th of October to the 13th of November there are slight showers from the eastward. The rain is sometimes, however, so heavy as to injure the crops. Except when it rains, the winds are variable. In the four following months there is no rain, and the air is reckoned cold by the natives. At present, the days are hot and the nights cool. The winds in the day come from the sea, and in the night from the land.

Feb. 9.

Appearance of the country.

9th *February.*—I went three cosses to *Beiluru*, a place where there were a few houses of cultivators, but no shops nor market. There is a small temple of *Siva* there, with an annual allowance to the *Pújári* of six *Pagodas*. The country is rather woody, and little rice ground can be seen from the road. The granite rocks make a conspicuous figure on the high lands.

CHAPTER XV.

Feb. 9. Obstinacy of the guides.

Although the guides were natives of the place, and the road was well marked, yet they contrived to make a part of my baggage wander about from four in the morning, until two in the afternoon. Occasionally I meet with such accidents; from what other principle but obstinacy in the guides, I cannot say. This place is in the district of *Barcuru*, which formerly gave a title to one of the *Jain Rájás* of *Tulava*.

Feb. 10. Hills capable of cultivation.

10th *February*.—I went three cosses to *Haryadika*. The country is similar to that through which I came yesterday. The farmers here say, that all the hills, wherever the soil is free from rock, might be converted into *Betta-land*. The quantity of such grounds, they say, is very considerable; at least three times as much as is cultivated; but, they add, the expense is great, and the returns are small. About a fourth part of what was formerly cultivated is now waste, for want of people and stock. Until that be fully occupied, no experiments on new land would be proper. The people say, that they would be willing to bring this new land into cultivation on the following conditions. The whole expense attending the various operations being collected into a sum, they should pay no revenue to government until that was reimbursed by the usual amount of the land-tax, which is from one to three *Sultany Fanams* for a *Moray* sowing, or from rather more than $6\frac{1}{2}d.$ to almost $1s.\ 11d.$ an acre.

Tenures, produce, and rent, of rice-land.

The proprietors here say, that they let their rice lands to tenants *(Gaynicaras)*, and are obliged to advance stock to a new man. In the course of four years the value of the stock is repaid by instalments. The rent is paid in rice, so much for each *Moray* sowing. The best *Bylu-land* pays 4 *Morays* of rice for both crops; the next in quality pays 3 *Morays;* and the worst 2. The best *Majelu* pays $2\frac{1}{2}$ *Morays;* the second quality $1\frac{1}{2}$; and the third 1 *Moray*. The best *Betta* land pays 2 *Morays;* the second $1\frac{1}{2}$; the third 1; and the fourth $\frac{1}{2}$ a *Moray*. The *Moray* of rice, if of the coarsest quality, is at present worth $2s.\ 8\frac{1}{4}d.$; and each

Feb. 10.

Moray of rent, for a *Moray's* sowing, is at the rate of about 2*s.* 4½*d.* an acre. The tenant, according to these people's account, has about one half of the produce; which therefore, in the worst *Betta* land, must be three seeds, or $3\frac{696}{1000}$ bushels an acre. These people say, that when the rice is cheap the whole rent is not equal to the land-tax. At present, they acknowledge that they have a little profit. Taking the statement which they give as fair, their present profit will be evident, even allowing their whole rice to be of the coarsest kind. The worst *Betta* land pays 6½*d.* tax an acre, and the rent is 1*s.* 2¼*d.*; so that the tax does not amount to half the rent; and I am inclined to think, that the average price of all the kinds of rice is never lower than the present value of the coarsest.

Haryadiká.

At *Haryadiká* there is only one shop; and on the approach of my people the owner ran away. There is a large temple of one of the *Saktis;* this is attended by one of the *Tulava Bráhmans* as *Pújári,* on which account no bloody sacrifices are performed. There was formerly a *Jain* temple here of the kind called *Busty,* but it has gone to ruin, and the number of the *Jain* is daily diminishing. The image in the temple was of copper. With many other similar idols from different parts of the country, it was carried to *Jamál-ábád.* By orders from the late *Sultan,* some of them were converted into money, and others cast into guns.

Feb. 11. Appearance of the country.

11th *February.*—In the morning I went three cosses to *Udipu.* The country, to the vicinity of this place, is similar to that which I passed through on the two preceding days. The *strata* of granite, however, are mostly covered by the *Laterite.* The roads are execrable; but, like many of those in *Canara,* are shaded by fine rows of trees, especially of the *Vateria indica;* which, being now in full blossom, makes the most beautiful avenues that I have ever seen.

On getting within sight of the sea near *Udipu,* the country becomes more level; and round the town it is finely cultivated, and the rice fields are beautifully intermixed with palm gardens. Such a delightful situation has been chosen as the chief seat of the *Tulava Bráhmans* of the *Madual* sect.

Feb. 11. *Madual Bráhmans* of *Tulava*. *Panch Drávida*, or five *Drávidas*.

Having assembled the men who, among the followers of *Madua Achárya* in *Tulava*, were reckoned the most eminent for their knowledge, they gave me the following information. The *Tulava Bráhmans* belong to the *Panch Drávida* division of the sacred tribe, and are a mixture composed of emigrants from each of the nations or tongues that compose this division. These are, *Andray*, or the nations speaking the *Telinga*, or *Andray* language, which occupy the north-eastern parts of the peninsula; *Karnátaca*, those who speak the language which we call *Canarese*, and who inhabit the country south from the *Krishna* river, and above the *Ghat* mountains; *Maháraslitra*, who speak the *Maráttah* language, and occupy the north-western parts of the peninsula; *Gurjara*, or *Carjura*, or the *Bráhmans* of *Guzerat*, who also have a peculiar dialect, very different from the language of the *Maráttuhs;* and *Drávida*, or those who speak the *Tamul* language, and occupy the southern parts of the peninsula below the *Ghats*. *Drávida* proper, or the *Désam* so called, is confined to the country between *Madras* and the mountains; but the name is extended, first to all the country occupied by people who speak the *Tamul* language, and then to the whole of the *Bráhmans* of this division. Although the whole of the *Tulava Bráhmans* form a kind of separate nation, yet each subdivision confines its marriages to its own original nation; and, contrary to the custom of the *Namburis*, a *Karnátaca Tulava Bráhman* has no objection to marry the daughter of a *Bráhman* of *Karnáta* who never has left his own country.

Origin of the *Tulava Bráhmans*.

They allege, that originally they were assembled here from all their native countries by *Parasu Ráma*, who created *Tulava* for their use, in the same manner as he created *Malayála* for the *Namburis*. The language of *Tulava* has a strong resemblance to that of *Malayála*, and the written characters are the same; but in the language of *Tulava* there is a very great admixture of words from all the countries containing the five southern nations of India.

Feb. 11. *Batta Achárya.*

Originally, the *Tulava Bráhmans* were followers of *Batta Achárya,* who flourished at *Ahichaytra,* on the banks of the *Godávery.* An account of his life, which they of course consider as prophetical, is to be found in the *Skandha Purána,* one of the eighteen books written by *Vyása. Batta Achárya* had great success against 18 of the 21 heretical sects, some of which admitted, and others denied, the authority of the *Védas.*

Sankara Achárya.

Afterwards *Sankara Achárya* disputed with the followers of *Batta,* and, having convicted them of numerous errors, gained many proselytes; and many of the *Tulava Bráhmans* continue to follow his doctrines, and receive the *Sringa-giri Swamalu* as their *Guru,* and as the successor of *Sankara Achárya.* In this *Yugam,* or age, there have been three appearances of *Sankara Achárya.* First, he was born at *Sivuli,* in *Tulava,* about 1500 years ago, and established the *Matam* or college at *Sringa-giri.* His next appearance was some hundreds of years afterwards; when he was born in *Malayála,* and lived at *Sri Rangam,* near *Tritchenopoly.* Lastly, he was born about 600 years ago at *Paducachaytra,* in *Tulava.* In the *Skandha Purána,* composed, as my informants imagine, many myriads of millions of years ago, an account of all his transactions in these three incarnations is to be found, and also an account of the great success which he had against the heretical sects.

Madua.

Madua Achárya was last born at *Paducachaytra,* in the year of this *Kali-yugam* 4300, or 601 years ago. In the time of the five sons of *Pandú,* he had appeared as one of these brothers, named *Bhíma;* in the time of *Ráma* he had been *Hanumanta;* and in the *Kali-yugam* preceding this (for the *Bráhmans* suppose a constant succession of the four *Yugams)* he had appeared as the *Madua Achárya* of that degenerate age. When he appeared last, he not only confuted the heretical sects, but obtained a great victory in dispute over *Sankara Achárya,* who had forced all the *Madual Bráhmans* outwardly to adopt

CHAPTER XV. Feb. 11.

his opinions; and he thus restored his sect to its proper splendour. The *Hindus* will seldom allow their own sect to have had any origin; but insist rather, that it has existed from all eternity, or at the very least from the first origin of things. The *Maduals* say, that all the different sects were created in the beginning by *Náráyana*, and have continued ever since, sometimes one prevailing and sometimes another; and the prevailing sect has always forced the others, at least in appearance, to comply with their doctrine.

Doctrine of the *Madual.*

The *Madual* allege, that there is one supreme God, *Náráyana* or *Vishnu*. His son is *Brahmá*, who is the father of *Siva*. Both of these ought to be worshipped, but *Brahmá* only mentally; as temples and regular forms of prayer to that deity are not lawful. They look with abhorrence upon the doctrine of the spirits of good men being absorbed into the deity, in which they differ from both *Smartal* and *Sri Vaishnavam*. *Moesha* they consider as the highest heaven; and men who, by their piety, obtain a place there, are ever afterwards exempted from change; but still they are greatly inferior to *Náráyana*, or the other great gods; and, according to their merit, enjoy different ranks. The *Madual* pray to the *Dévatas* who reside in *Swargham*, which they say is the same with *Mahá Méru;* and when they are sick they pray to the destructive spirits, such as *Marimá*, *Putalimá*, and *Kalimá*. These are not considered to be different names for the wife of *Siva*, as the *Smartal* allege, but beings that live in the stars, clouds, and lower regions of the heavens. The *Madual Bráhmans* of *Tulava* act as *Pújáris* in the temples of these spirits, and offer sacrifices of paste made in the form of animals, but will not consent to the shedding of blood. In this country there are eight *Sannyásis*, each of whom has a *Matam* at *Udipu*, and each has a disciple who from his infancy is brought up to celibacy and other mortifications, and is destined to be his successor. These eight *Sannyásis* are the *Gurus* of the whole sect in *Tulava;* and each maintains a number of disciples, who are permitted to marry, but who are men of great Indian learning, and who read, and perform all manner of services for their master. These *Sannyásis* are not conceived to be any portion of the deity; nor is it even believed, that in general they obtain after death a seat in *Moesha*. To attain this, a *Bráhman* must completely adhere to every rule of his order, which is attended with so much difficulty, that human nature is seldom adequate to the task. No other cast has any kind of chance to procure a place so near the gods; and my informants seem to doubt, whether it be even possible for any person of low rank ever to be born a *Bráhman*. Temporal blessings they consider as those which the three lower casts ought chiefly to expect; and, by means of charity given to their superiors, they may have an abundance of these low pleasures.

CHAPTER XV. Feb. 11.

Government.

The eight *Gurus*, each in his turn for two years, act as priests (*Pújáris*) in the temple of *Krishna* at *Udipu*. During this time the officiating *Sannyási* must not only defray the expenses of worship, but must feed all his disciples, and every *Bráhman* that comes to the place. To do this handsomely, will require above 20,000 *Pagodas* (8054*l.* 14*s.* 8$\frac{1}{4}$*d.*); and the very least, for which it can be done, is 13,000 *Pagodas* (5238*l.* 4*s.* 8$\frac{1}{2}$*d.*). In order to raise such great sums, each *Sannyási*, with his disciples, during the fourteen years that he is out of office, wanders about the country, and, wherever he goes, levies contributions under the name of *Bhiksha*, or begging. Out of these alms he not only supports a considerable equipage, and feeds all his disciples, but can save a sum sufficient to defray the expense which he must incur during the two years that he performs the office of *Pújári*. Except in *Tulava*, these *Sannyásis* have no authority as *Gurus*; for above the *Ghats* there are three *Matams*, whose *Sannyásis* possess the sole authority of bestowing *Chakrántikam* and *Upadésa*, and of punishing transgressions against the rule of cast. Each *Sannyási* of *Tulava* has certain families, who are hereditarily annexed to his *Matam*, as to that of their *Guru*. As, however, the officiating *Pújári* never goes out of the

CHAPTER XV. Feb. 11. temple, and as the others are generally absent, begging, the eight have mutually appointed two persons to act as judges. These have the power of excommunication, which implies the whole wealth of the sect being at their mercy. They also levy fines, and cleanse sinners by prayers *(Mantrams)*, cow's urine, and other things esteemed pure. The *Gurus* reserve to themselves the exclusive right of bestowing *Chakrántikam* and *Upadésa.* They never, at any ceremony, read *Mantrams*, that office being reserved for the married *Bráhmans;* and each man by hereditary right belongs to some *Bráhman*, who is his *Puróhita.* The *Sannyásis* do not require a *Puróhita;* for they are considered as sufficiently holy to be exempted from all the ceremonies and customs usually observed by *Bráhmans.* They do not wear the thread; all meats become to them indifferent; and they do not celebrate the ceremonies in honour of their deceased parents. A *Puróhita* may sell or mortgage the families that belong to him, and may give them to a *Bráhman* of any sect; for the prayers *(Mantrams)* and portions of scripture *(Sastrams)* read by any person of the sacred order, whatever his theological opinions may be, are considered as equally efficacious. This does not proceed from any gentleness or facility of temper among the *Bráhmans*, who abound in the *Odium theologicum.* It is, however, between the *Madual* and *Sri Vaishnavam*, although both are worshippers of *Vishnu*, that the most violent antipathy prevails. The *Smartal*, although followers of *Siva*, agree much better with the *Madual;* and, in *Tulava* and *Malayála* especially, these two live on tolerable terms. In *Tulava*, indeed, it is not unusual for one temple to be common to both gods; and in most places there the temples of *Vishnu* and of *Siva* are built near each other, and the same *Rath*, or chariot, serves for the *Jútram*, or procession, of both idols.

To the east of the *Ghats*, the *Madual Bráhmans* scorn to serve as *Pújáris*, even in the temples of *Vishnu*, and are the proudest of the whole sacred order. This scorn, however, is perhaps affected; as when *Madua Achárya* appeared, the *Sri Vaishnavam* were in possession of the temples, and have always been favourites with the persons in authority.

Customs.

The *Bráhmans* of *Tulava* are allowed a plurality of wives, which must be of the same nation with themselves, but of a different *Gótram*, or family, and which must be married before the signs of puberty appear. Their widows cannot marry, but may become *Moylar*, as already described. It is looked upon as disreputable for a *Bráhman* to keep a woman of this kind, and he would lose cast by having a connection with a dancing girl, or with a *Moylar*, that did not belong to a temple; but all such women as are consecrated to the gods cohabit with some *Bráhman* or other. The *Bráhmans* of *Tulava* burn the dead, and their widows ought to be burned along with them; but this practice has gone entirely into disuse. They can neither eat animal food, nor drink spirituous liquors. A man's own children, even in landed property, are his heirs.

History of *Tulava*.

I next questioned these *Bráhmans* concerning the history of the country; and they produced a book called *Gráma Paditti*, which they say is historical. It is written in *Sanskrit*, and is presumed to have been composed by *Vishnu*, who assumed a human form, under the name of *Védi Vyása*, and promulgated the *Védas*, the eighteen *Puránas*, the *Gráma Paditti*, and other sacred writings. From this work the *Bráhmans* say, that *Tulava* was created, and given entirely to them, 1 *Arbuda*, 95 *Crowds*, 58 *Lacs*, and 80 thousand of years, before the extinction of the *Pándu* family. The last of these ended his reign in the year of the *Kali-yugam* 1036,

or	- - - - - -	3,865 years ago.
Add 80 thousand	- -	80,000
58 *Lacs*	- -	5,800,000
95 *Crowds*	-	950,000,000
1 *Arbuta*	-	1,000,000,000
		1,955,883,865 years since the creation of

CHAPTER XV. Feb. 11.

Tulava, according to the *Gráma Paditti.* The candid reader will not expect, that in a work comprehending the accounts of such a long duration of time a few thousand years, earlier or later, in the chronology of these degenerate times can be considered as of any consequence. This having been premised, and the accounts of the *Hindu* gods and *heroes* having been left in becoming obscurity, we find from the *Gráma Paditti*, that 1115 years after the family of the *Pándus* became extinct, *Ananda Ráya* governed *Tulava.* He and his eight brothers (or rather kinsmen in the male line) reigned 200 years, or until the year of the *Kali-yugam* 2351. *Vakia Rájá* and his ten sons (descendants) reigned 112 years, till *Kali-yugam* 2463. *Maursushy* and his ten sons governed 137 years, till *Kali-yugam* 2600. *Cadumba Ráya* 45 years, till *Kali-yugam* 2645. *Myuru Varmá* 10 years, till *Kali-yugam* 2655. *Hubushica*, chief of the savages called *Coragoru*, or *Corar*, governed 12 years, till *Kali-yugam* 2657. *Lócáditya Ráya*, son of *Myuru Varmá*, expelled the *Coragoru*, and governed *Tulava*, *Malayála*, and *Haiga* 21 years, till *Kali-yugam* 2678. After his death, eighty-one of his cousins, among whom the chief was *Cadumba Ráya* of *Wudia-nagara*, governed 24 years, till *Kali-yugam* 2702. *Balhica Ráya*, and twenty-nine other petty princes, governed 46 years, till the *Kali-yugam* 2748. *Abhiri*, and ten *Rájás* governed 99 years, till *Kali-yugam* 2847. The descendants of *Mona Rájá* then reigned 200 years, till *Kali-yugam* 3047, or till 53 years before the birth of Christ. At this time *Mahummud Surtala*, a *Mlécha*, who was a spy, visited the whole country as far as *Rámészwara.* It must be observed, that, according to these *Bráhmans*, *Mlécha* properly means an *Arab*, *Turc* a *Tartar*, and *Yavana* an European; but all the three terms are frequently applied to the nations living toward the north and west of *Hindustan*, without distinction of country or religion. Nine *Belalla Ráyas* governed 6 years, till *Kali-yugam* 3053, or 47 years before the birth of Christ. The *Turc* then returned, took *Anagundi*, and governed 540 years, till the *Kali-yugam* 3593, or *A. D.* 493. The followers of *Vyása*

CHAPTER XV. Feb. 11.

here, it must be observed, cut short the government of the *Belalla* family, who are more detestable than *Mléchas*, as having been followers of the *Arhita* or *Jain Bráhmans*. *Campi Ráya* of *Penu-conda* drove out the *Mléchas*, and governed 13 years over the whole country south of the *Krishna*, till the year *Kali-yugam* 3606, or *A. D.* 506. This prince sent an officer named *Sankara Déva Ráya* to visit *Tulava*. In his train was a messenger *(Peon)* named *Hucabuca*, a *Curuba* by cast. This fellow, having received assistance from the *Yavanas*, took *Anagundi*, and having built a city near it, which he called *Vijaya-nagara*, or the city of victory, he assumed the title of *Hari-hara Ráya*. This account of the origin of the family of *Vijaya-nagara* may be attributed to the following circumstance. The *Bráhmans* of *Tulava* had hitherto been exempted from taxes; but *Hari-hara*, on the conquest of the country, imposed an annual tax upon them, to the amount of 12,000 *Morays* of rice. *Déva Swámi*, a tributary prince, was ordered to collect this tax; but, his conscience having revolted at the thoughts of exacting tribute from the *Bráhmans*, he was dismissed, and their tax was increased to 2578 *Pagodas* in money. The history of the *Gráma Paditti* ends with this grievous event; but the *Bráhmans* say, that thirteen princes of the family of *Hari-hara* governed for about 150 years, or from *A. D.* 493 to 643. Unfortunately for the exactness of this chronology, many inscriptions on stone, made in the reigns of these princes, are scattered throughout their dominions. Copies of five of these have been delivered to the Bengal government. The date of the first is in the era of *Salivahanam* 1297, or *A. D.* 1375, and of the latest *E. S.* 1400, or *A. D.* 1478. With this correction of about eight centuries and a half, *Muhammad Surutala* may have been a Mussulman, and probably some of the followers of *Muhammad Ghizni*. The *Yavana* dynasty of *Anagundi* is, however, a matter of great curiosity, and not yet well understood.

Krishna Ráyalu.

These *Bráhmans* say, that the celebrated *Krishna Ráyalu*, of *Vijaya-nagara*, was not of the family of *Hari-hara*, but governed the

CHAPTER XV. Feb. 11.

same dominions after the overthrow of the former dynasty. He was descended from the nurse of one of the five princes called *Pándus*, who lived at the commencement of the present *Kali-yugam*. *Dharma Ráya*, the last of these five brothers, died in the year 36 of that era, or 4865 years ago.

Jain Rájás, or Polygars.

The country of *Tulava* was first subject to the kings of *Anagundi*, and then to the princes of *Ikeri*; by whom, these *Bráhmans* suppose, the *Jain Polygars* were appointed; but they pretend an almost total ignorance of these chiefs, and a sovereign contempt for their sect.

Possessions of the *Bráhmans.*

They allege, although there were *Jain Rájás* in many parts of *Tulava*, that there never was one at *Barcuru*; but that it, and all the *Grámas* in *Tulava*, were governed by *Bráhmans* immediately dependent on the sovereign, and over whom these infidel chiefs had no control. The thoughts of being subject to a *Jain* are indeed horrible to a follower of *Vyása*; nor will it ever be acknowledged, where there is a possibility of denial. When pushed to account for the introduction of so many *Jain* into a country made expressly for the *Bráhmans* who follow the true doctrine of *Vyása*, they say, that *Hubashica* drove all the *Bráhmans* out of the country; and that, when *Lókáditya* regained his paternal dominions, he only brought a few *Bráhmans* from *Ahichaytra*, where he resided during his exile, and gave them the 32 *Grámas*, which they enjoyed without molestation till *Hari-hara* imposed the illegal tax. I think it probable, that *Lókáditya*, in order to procure assistance to regain his throne, changed the religion which he inherited from his father *Myuru Varmá* who, according to the *Jain* of *Mudu Bidery*, was of their sect; and having become a follower of *Batta Achárya*, then teaching the doctrine of *Vyása* with great success on the banks of the *Gódávéry*, he brought with him the first colony of *Tulava Bráhmans*, and gave them a gift *(Enam)* of thirty-two villages. In imitation of the *Namburis*, they afterwards set up the story of *Parasu Ráma*; but it does not seem to have succeeded so well with them as with their southern neighbours.

CHAPTER XV.

Feb. 11. *Udipu*, and its history.

Udipu is a town which contains about 200 houses, and stands about a coss from the sea near a small river called the *Pápa-násaní*, which comes from a *Tank* at *Carculla*, passes about two miles to the south of the town, and falls into the sea at a fort named *Duriá Bahádar*. Near *Udipu* is a small fort, which formerly was the residence of *Chittupadi Baylala*, the chief *Bráhman* of the town *(Gráma)*. Each of the 32 *Grámas* belonging to the *Tulava Bráhmans* was governed and defended by an hereditary chief of their own sect, who was in every respect, but the name, a *Polygar*, or petty chief; some of them assumed the title of *Baylala*; others that of *Hegada*, which signifies mighty.

At *Udipu* are three *Gudies*, or temples, which are placed in a common square, and surrounded by 14 *Matams*, or convents, belonging to an equal number of *Sannyásis*, who are *Gurus* to different sects of *Bráhmans*. Eight of these *Matams* belong to the eight *Madual Sannyásis*, who in their turn officiate as priests in the temple of *Krishna*, which is one of the three that stand in the square. Two other *Matams* belong to *Sannyásis* of the same sect; each of the predecessors of whom, as well as the eight others, received an image from *Madua Achárya;* but they have few followers, and are not entitled to officiate at the temple. Three other *Matams* belong to the three *Sannyásis*, who are the *Gurus* of all the *Madual Bráhmans* to the eastward of the mountains. The fourteenth *Matam* belongs to the *Sringa-giri Swámi*. These *Matams* are large buildings; and, considered as houses belonging to *Hindus*, improved by neither Mussulman nor European arts, they are stately edifices. Some pains have even been taken to admit air, as they have many windows. Apertures indeed "for the purpose of intromitting air and light," although scarcely deserving the appellation of windows, are more common in the houses of *Tulava*, than I have any where else seen among the mere natives of *Hindustán*. The *Matams* are designed chiefly as storehouses, in which the *Sannyasis* may deposit the produce of their begging till they want it for consumption. Being

CHAPTER XV.

Feb. 11.

too expensive guests, they very seldom reside in one place more than a few days. The temples, as usual, are but poor buildings, and, like almost all those of *Malayala* and *Tulava*, have pent roofs. Those here are roofed, with copper, which must have cost much money; but, being very rudely wrought, it makes no show.

Customs of the *Corar*.

Having assembled some of the *Corar*, or *Corawar*, who under their chief *Hubashica* are said to have once been masters of *Tulava*, I found, that they are now all slaves, and have lost every tradition of their former power. Their language differs considerably from that of any other tribe in the peninsula. When their masters choose to employ them, they get one meal of victuals, and the men have daily one *Hany* of rice, and the women three quarters of a *Hany*. This is a very good allowance; but, when the master has no use for their labour, they must support themselves as well as they can. This they endeavour to do by making *Coir*, or rope from coco-nut husks, various kinds of baskets from *Ratans* and climbing plants, and mud walls. They pick up the scraps and offals of other people's meals, and skin dead oxen, and dress the hides. They build their huts near towns or villages. Their dress is very simple, and consists in general of a girdle, in which they stick a bunch of grass before, and another behind. Some of the men have a fragment of cloth round their waist; but very few of the women ever procure this covering. They are not, however, without many ornaments of beads, and the like; and, even when possessed of some wealth, do not alter their rude dress. Some few of them are permitted to rent lands as *Gaynigaras*. In spite of this wretched life, they are a good looking people, and therefore probably are abundantly fed. They have no hereditary chiefs, and disputes among them are settled by assemblies of the people. If they can get them, they take several wives; and the women are marriageable both before and after puberty, and during widowhood. They will not marry a woman of any other cast; and they are considered of so base an origin, that a man of any other cast, who cohabits with one of their women, is inevitably excommunicated, and afterwards not even a *Corar* will admit his society. The marriages are indissoluble, and a woman who commits adultery is only flogged. Her paramour, if he be a *Corar*, is fined. The master pays the expense of the marriage feast. When a man dies, his wives, with all their children, return to the huts of their respective mothers and brothers, and belong to their masters. They will eat the offals of any other cast, and can eat beef, carrion, tigers, crows, and other impure things; they reject however dogs and snakes. They can lawfully drink intoxicating liquors. They burn the dead, and seem to know nothing of a state of future existence, nor do they believe in *Paisachi*, or evil spirits. Their deity is called *Buta*, and is represented by a stone, which is kept in a square surrounded by a wall. To this stone, in all cases of sickness, they sacrifice fowls, or make offerings of fruit or grain, and every man offers his own worship *(Pújá)*; so that they have no officiating priest, and they acknowledge the authority of no *Guru*. They follow all the oxen and buffaloes of the village, as so much of the live stock, when these are driven in procession at a great festival which the farmers annually celebrate.

CHAPTER XV. Feb. 11.

Feb. 12. Appearance of the country.

12th *February*.—I went three cosses to *Brahmá-wara*. The rice grounds extend from *Udipu* to the sea; their extent towards the north and south is not considerable. I soon came to gently rising hills, free of woods; but the road was finely sheltered by avenues of the beautiful *Vateria indica*, called here *Dupada Maram*, or the resin tree. I passed first through *Kalyána-pura*, which was formerly a large place; but during *Tippoo's* government it has been almost intirely ruined. I then crossed a very wide, but shallow river, named the *Suvarna*. Its source is from a lake or tank near *Carculla;* but it owes its magnitude entirely to the water of the sea. Near the *Suvarna* are many fine plantations of coco-nut palms, and also some rice grounds. *Barcuru* is near *Brahmá-wara ;* but for a long time, even previous to the irruption of *Sivuppa Nayaka*, it has been ruined. The fortress was erected by *Hari-hara*, first king of

CHAPTER XV. Feb. 12.

Vijaya-nagara. It still gives its name to the district *(Taluc)*, the *Tahsildar* of which resides at *Brahmá-wara.* This is a small place containing only about 60 houses, but in its neighbourhood there is much rice ground.

Cultivation and produce of rice lands.

I have received much information relative to the produce of the rice grounds in this neighbourhood; partly from Mr. Ravenshaw, and partly from the people employed to measure and value the district. In the annexed Tables I give some of this information, with the measures reduced to the English standards. It must be observed, that the *Gunta*, or chain used by the surveyors, ought to have been 33 English feet in length; but, owing to the rudeness of the workmanship, it had stretched to 33 feet $10\frac{1}{2}$ inches: by the standard, the acre would be equal to 40 *Guntas;* but, by the actual chain, it would be equal to only $37\frac{24}{100}$ *Guntas.* I calculate, however, by the standard measure. The *Mudi*, or *Moray* in use here, is that of the market of *Mangalore;* but is divided, when speaking of seed, into 60 *Hanies;* and, when speaking of produce, into 40 *Hanies;* but the produce is in general estimated in rice, after deducting the expense of beating and cleaning. It would appear from all circumstances, that the quantity of seed which is sown on the same extent of ground, even of the same kind, differs much. Whether this proceed from the natives having found by experience, that such or such a field gives most profits when sown with a certain quantity of seed; or whether it arises from a want of precision and economy that attends all rude states of agriculture, I cannot take upon myself to affirm; but the latter cause seems the most probable. The seed is here sown much thinner than in *Malabar;* which, although a kind of saving that is common in every part of India, seems to be very injudicious: the crops in general appear to me to be proportionably scanty. Of the gross produce of estates, one half is here, as in most parts of India, considered as a proper reward for the labour of the cultivator, and the use of his stock; and is perhaps sufficient, considering that his cattle pay nothing,

A Statement, showing the quantity of Seed required, and the Produce, both in respect to quantity and value, of two Rice Estates in *Serour* Village of *Tonbretta Magany*; the grain having been cut down, beaten, and measured, in presence of the Valuators. The materials furnished by Mr. Ravenshaw.

Estates.	Measurement.		Seed. Quantity according to the report of the Cultivators. Reduced to the Mudy of 40 Baws.	Reduced to English measure.	Proportion. One Mudy sows,	One Acre requires,	Gross Produce. Of rough Rice.		Clean Rice, deducting the expense of beating and cleaning. Quantity		Value at 2½ Pagodas for 40 Mudies.		Average increase of rough rice.	Average produce of one Acre. Quantity. Rough rice.	Clean rice, deducting expense of cleaning.	Value of the preceding Column.
	Cawns, Ann.	Acres dec.	Mud. Har.	Bush. dec.	Cawns Ann.	Bush. dec.	Mud. Har.	Bush. dec.	Mud. Har.	Bush. dec.	Pag. Rup. Fan.	£. s. d.	Folds.	Bush. dec.	Bush. dec.	£. s. d.
Ram Pandary Landlord.																
1 sort *Byle* land - -	182 14	4,578	4 20	5,9345	41 0	1,2936	109 0	141,845	46 0	59,976	16 1 2	5 15 11½	22 [illegible]	31,06	13,102	1 13 0
2 ditto *Magele* land - -	52 25½	1,354	2 10	2,98725	23 4	2,233	96 4	99,89	11 25½	15,154	3 2 2½	1 7 7½	11 [illegible]	25,665	11,446	1 8 10
3 ditto *Batta* or *Mockey* land	209 6	5,234	6 0	7,8234	37 10	1,4928	23 28	30,096	9 19	12,339	2 3 3½	1 3 10½	3 [illegible]	5,896	4,337	0 5 11
Total -	445 8½	11,180	12 30	16,64515	35 0	1,6731	158 32	206,021	67 4½	87,421	20 3 8½	10 7 5½	19 [illegible]	18,51	7,854	1 0 3
Ante Tolar Landlord.																
1 sort *Byle* land - -	197 6	4,931	4 5	3,873685	47 12	1,089	264 0	343,585	108 26	141,813	34 0 6½	12 14 3	64	69,733	22,843	2 17 6½
2 ditto *Mockey* land - -	400 10	10,015	7 25	10,2531	50 12	1,023	128 32½	167,346	51 41	67,1	16 0 1½	6 9 3	16 [illegible]	16,748	6,699	0 16 10½
Total -	597 16	14,946	12 0	14,126725	49 12	1,0465	392 32½	511,531	160 17	208,913	50 0 2	20 4 0	32 [illegible]	34,225	13,89	1 14 11½
General Total	1043 1½	26,076	24 30	32,311875	42 0	1,24	551 24½	717,552	227 21½	296,332	71 0 1½	30 11 5½	22 [illegible]	27,5	11,36	1 8 7½

A Statement, showing the Seed required for Rice-ground, and its Produce, in seven Estates of five different Villages in *Tonbretty Maugany* of *Barcura Talac*. The materials furnished by Mr. Ravenshaw.

Villages.	Landlords.	Measurement.		Seed rough rice. Total.		For One Acre.	Produce in Rice, deducting the expense of beating. Gross.		Average. Of One Mudy sown.	Of One Acre. Quantity.	Value.
		Cawns. Ann.	Acres, dec.	Mud. Har.	Bush. dec.	Bush. dec.	Mud. Har.	Bush. dec.	Mud. Har.	Bush. dec.	£. s. d.
Heggoda -	*Maddoo Rao* -	3249 19	131,0927	136 27½	178,	1,3582	967 25	1239,912	7 5	9,612	0 18 7
Ober - -	*Seebura Narayana*	19828 10	198,2335	357 22½	465,83	0,9315	3230 20	4958,129	10 20	10,011	0 19 6
Brichy -	*Manju Shetty* -	1362 4	26,3564	26 17½	34,6276	1,2984	199 30	260,173	7 22	9,735	0 18 11
Hammana -	*Podegar* - - -	1507 14	37,6727	33 15	43,462	1,153	299 —	376,35	9 —	9,983	0 19 4
Betardy -	*Ama Shetty* - -	2480 14	61,0843	62 17½	81,303	1,332	456 20	594,8	7 5	9,747	0 18 10
	Shambery - -	479 18	11,9955	16 22½	24,1728	2,015	109 —	141,813	5 33	11,833	1 2 10½
	Timmy Hebba -	272 13	6,8204	5 29½	7,5691	1,11	56 20	73,576	9 29	16,757	1 0 13½
	Total - -	30938 —	773,4	640 25	834,4	1,078	5303 —	7634,835	9 8	9,955	0 19 2

Measurement and Valuation of two Villages in *Barcuru Talac*, furnished by *Vencatraut Row*, the Appraiser employed by Government.

Village.	Landlord.	Byle lands. Measurement.		Seed rough rice. Gross.	Per Acre.	Produce in clean Rice after deducting the expense of cleaning. Gross.	Per Acre. Quantity.	Value.	Magele lands. Measurement.		Seed rough rice. Gross.	Per Acre.	Produce in clean Rice after deducting the expense of cleaning. Gross.	Per Acre. Quantity.	Value.
		Cawns. Ann.	Acres, dec.	Mud. Har.	Bush. dec.	Mud. Har.	Bush. dec.	£. s. d.	Cawns. Ann.	Acres, dec.	Mud. Har.	Bush. dec.	Mud. Har.	Bush. dec.	£. s. d.
Coligy -	Ram Chandra Nyghe	343 13	12,846	7 0	0,2(964)	195 20	13,823	1 4 9	411 2	10,47	4 5	0,596	69 20	8,835	0 17 9
	Luga Baykda - -	663 11	16,679	8 0	0,625	196 20	12,587	1 4 6	387 9	9,68	8 20	1,142	67 0	9,001	0 17 5
	Siteram Chey - -	338 13	8,471	4 25	0,704	76 22	11,709	0 18 1	232 2	5,80	2 10	0,505	41 0	9,138	0 17 9
	Uspei Chitty - -	773 18	13,349	11 5	0,749	186 23	12,159	1 4 3	244 6	6,09	3 5	0,539	44 10	9,472	0 18 2
	Krishna Ebala - -	86 1	2,151	1 20	0,979	21 22	13,012	1 5 2	34 6	0,85	0 20	0,757	6 0	9,085	0 17 7
	Dagaya Bygante -	15 12	0,393	0 10	0,837	4 0	13,099	1 5 7	. . .	. . .	. . .	. . .	. . .	. . .	. . .
	Total - -	2297 5	59,59	39 20	0,811	577 22	12,548	1 4 3	1309 9	32,66	18 29	0,687	227 30	9,036	0 17 6
Dewara -	Rangow - - - -	1027 7	25,687	21 10	1,037	256 0	10,073	1 5 1	342 5	8,56	7 0	1,065	38 0	8,833	0 17 0
	Rama Sastri - -	. . .	. . .	. . .	. . .	. . .	. . .	. . .	. . .	. . .	. . .	. . .	. . .	. . .	. . .
	Ariendaya - - -	123 1	3,077	2 20	1,058	30 20	10,402	1 4 3	. . .	. . .	. . .	. . .	. . .	. . .	. . .
	Madoo Row - -	121 3	3,022	2 5	0,812	30 0	12,881	1 4 11	. . .	. . .	. . .	. . .	. . .	. . .	. . .
	Total - -	1271 13	31,79	25 35	1,06	316 20	12,052	1 5 0	342 5	8,56	7 0	1,063	38 0	8,825	0 17 0
	General total	3569 —	91,728	53 15	0,859	894 0	12,592	1 4 8	1651 14	41,22	25 20	0,804	265 30	9,009	0 17 5

Village.	Landlord.	Batta, Vana-Batta, and Mockey lands. Measurement.		Seed rough rice. Gross.	Per Acre.	Produce in Clean Rice after deducting the expense of cleaning. Gross.	Per Acre. Quantity.	Value.	Total of Rice lands. Measurement.		Seed rough rice. Gross.	Per Acre.	Produce in clean Rice after deducting the expense of cleaning. Gross.	Per Acre. Quantity.	Value.
		Cawns. Ann.	Acres, dec.	Mud. Har.	Bush. dec.	Mud. Har.	Bush. dec.	£. s. d.	Cawns. Ann.	Acres, dec.	Mud. Har.	Bush. dec.	Mud. Har.	Bush. dec.	£. s. d.
Coligy -	Ram Chandra Nyghe	228 10	5,71	4 37	1,01	15 10	3,462	0 6 8	1133 11	28,78	15 22	0,704	211 10	9,557	0 19 3
	Luga Baykda - -	256 1	6,40	5 10	0,852	18 20	3,783	0 7 3	1312 3	32,740	19 15	0,769	236 0	9,866	0 19 11
	Siteram Chey - -	124 4	3,1	1 30	0,738	18 10	3,539	0 6 10	695 9	17,380	8 25	0,616	125 20	9,52	0 18 2
	Uspei Chitty - -	233 0	5,85	4 5	0,695	25 10	3,737	0 7 2	1356 7	33,905	18 15	0,706	255 0	9,797	0 19 11
	Krishna Ebala - -	62 9	1,56	1 0	0,852	5 0	4,162	0 8 0	183 1	4,573	3 0	0,854	32 20	9,03	0 17 10
	Dagaya Bygante -	. . .	. . .	. . .	. . .	. . .	. . .	. . .	15 12	0,393	0 10	0,836	4 0	13,099	1 5 7
	Total - -	1009 10	25,2	14 29	0,753	71 10	3,634	0 7 1	4716 8	117,91	65 22	0,721	876 20	9,63	0 18 8
Dewara -	Rangow - - - -	643 14	16,1	10 30	0,699	49 20	3,62	0 7 0	2013 10	50,349	39 0	1,037	358 20	9,33	0 17 11
	Rama Sastri - -	381 4	9,599	5 0	0,667	28 0	3,735	0 7 4	384 4	9,599	5 0	0,667	28 0	3,735	0 7 4
	Ariendaya - - -	8 13	0,22	0 15	2,213	0 20	3,935	0 5 8	131 14	3,299	2 35	1,138	31 0	10,372	1 6 8
	Madoo Row - -	21 13	0,53	0 15	0,935	2 0	4,776	0 9 2	143 2	3,578	2 20	0,910	32 0	11,647	1 2 6
	Total - -	1058 12	26,47	16 20	0,611	75 10	2,869	0 7 2	2612 14	66,82	49 15	0,662	449 20	8,265	0 16 10
	General total	2068 6	51,7	31 2	0,782	146 20	3,285	0 7 1	7329 6	154,74	114 37	0,81	1326 10	3,48	0 18 1

CHAPTER XV.

Feb. 12.

that his other stock is of little or no value, and that the quantity of seed is very small. Owing to the present great want of people and stock, the cultivators, however, do not in general pay so much; and, according to the valuation of five villages in this neighbourhood, I find, that out of 2048 *Pagodas*, the gross value of their produce, the cultivators retain 1295 *Pagodas*. The share of the government amounts in general to one quarter of the gross produce; and in these villages is 671 *Pagodas*, of which 37 are alienated in *Enam*, or charity lands, as they are called. What remains to the landlord is 82 *Pagodas;* but part of their lands are waste, and the *Enams* are nominally higher than what is here stated; so that, apparently, some of the landlords, who are supposed to pay these charities, are losers by their estates. At present, they are all cultivators; and, when the country is repeopled, there can be little doubt, that, should they not encumber themselves with mortgages, they will enjoy one fourth of the gross produce of their estates; for a part of the present great share of the cultivators arises from the interest of money which they have advanced on their farms; and this also should be considered as a part of the profits of the landlord.

Feb. 13. Language and inhabitants.

13th *February.*—I went three cosses to *Hirtitty*, one of the fourteen small villages that are called by the common name of *Cotta.* The whole of this almost is occupied by *Bráhmans*, who pretend to be of *Parasu Ráma's* colony, although almost the only language spoken by them is that of *Karnáta.* Very few of them understand the peculiar dialect of *Tulava.* It must be observed, however, that, this country having been long subject to princes residing above the *Ghats*, all persons of rank speak the language of *Karnáta;* and from having been subject to these princes, and from its having been the place where all intercourse between them and Europeans was conducted, the province has got the name of the coast of *Canara*, a corruption of *Karnáta.* In the towns on the sea-coast the Mussulman language is more commonly understood, than in any other part of the peninsula that I have visited.

CHAPTER XV.

Feb. 13. Appearance of the country.

The road from *Brahmá-wara* to *Hirtitty* for the most part passes along a low sandy ridge, on either side of which are extensive rice-grounds; for the *Bráhmans*, as usual, have appropriated to themselves the finest parts of *Tulava*. The country looks well; for even the greater part of the sandy height is inclosed, and planted for timber and fewel. Except where the cattle were forced to swim over a very wide river, called *Mabucullu*, the road was comparatively excellent. This river descends from the *Ghats*, and in the rainy season brings down a great body of fresh water; but, where the road crosses, it is at this season quite salt. The tide goes up from the sea about three cosses; and canoes, in the rainy season, can ascend six cosses from the mouth. The banks are well planted with coco-nut trees, which in *Tulava* seem confined chiefly to such places.

Feb. 14. Mr. Read's district.

14th *February*.—I went three cosses to *Kunda-pura*, where I entered the northern division of *Canara*, which is under the management of Mr. Read, a young gentleman brought up in the same school with Mr. Ravenshaw. I had not the good fortune to meet with him; but he was so obliging as to send me very satisfactory answers to the queries that I proposed in writing, of which I shall avail myself in the following account.

Face of the country.

The country between *Hirtitty* and *Kunda-pura* resembles that between *Brahmá-wara* and *Hirtitty*; only there is by the way neither river nor coco-nut plantations; and, in proportion, the extent of rice-ground is smaller. The whole road is excellent, and fit for any kind of carriage, except in one place, where, in the descents to a low narrow valley, stairs have been formed. By the natives these are considered as an excellent improvement on a road, although they are very inconvenient even for cattle that are carrying back-loads.

Feb. 15. *Kunda-pura.*

15th *February*.—I was detained at *Kunda-pura*, as being the only place where I could get a supply of necessaries, till I reached *Nagara*; and also in expectation of meeting a *Bráhman* named *Rámuppa Varmica*, who is said to be the most intelligent person in the country concerning its former state.

CHAPTER XV. Feb. 15.

Kunda-pura is situated on the south side of a river, which in different places, according to the villages which it passes, is called by different names. This river is in general the boundary between the northern and southern divisions of *Canara;* but *Kunda-pura* is under the collector of the northern division. The villages or towns on the banks of this river are the places where all the goods coming from, or going to *Nagara* are shipped, and landed. The custom-house is at *Kunda-pura;* but the principal shipping place is farther up the river at *Bassururu.* On the north side of the river the *Sultan* had a dock; but the water on the bar, even at spring tides, does not exceed 9 cubits, or 13½ feet. The river, or rather lake, at *Kunda-pura* has only one opening into the sea. It is very extensive, and the only ferry-boats on it are wretched canoes. Five fresh water rivers come from the hills, and, meeting the tide in this lake, intersect the whole level ground, and form a number of islands. I have not seen a more beautiful country than this; and an old fort, situated a little higher up than the town, commands one of the finest prospects that I ever beheld. The people here seem to have no knowledge of any thing that happened before the conquest by *Sivuppa Nayaka;* since which it is, that the place has risen into any kind of consequence. The origin of its rise was probably a small fort built by the Portuguese. Round this General Mathews drew lines, as a defence for his stores, when he went up to *Nagara.* These were afterwards somewhat strengthened by *Tippoo*, but were always poor defences. The town contains about 250 houses, and is never remembered to have been larger. It is the head quarters of a battalion of *Bombay Sepoys*, by the officers of which I was most kindly received.

Hu-minu, or flower-fish.

Colonel Williamson informed me, that at no great distance there was a tank of fresh water, in which was a kind of fish that the *Sultan* reserved for his own use, and which by the natives was named *Hu-minu*, or the flower-fish. It is a large fish, full of blood, and very fat, but is only fit for use when salted. For this purpose it is excellent, a circumstance very rare with fresh-water fish; so that

CHAPTER XV. Feb. 15.

the propagating of this species in different parts of the country would seem to be an object worthy of attention. My time would not admit of seeing any of them taken, as the fishery cannot be carried on without some days preparation.

Customs of the *Bacadaru* and *Batadaru*.

In the northern parts of *Tulava* are two casts, called *Bacadaru* and *Batadaru*, both of whom are slaves; both speak no other language than that of *Karnáta*, and both follow exactly the same customs. Each disputes for a pre-eminence of rank, and they will not eat nor intermarry with one another, except in certain cases of adultery, when, a ceremony of purification having been undergone, a slave of the one cast may marry a female of the other.

Although they do not use leaves to cover their nudities, they seem to be poorer and worse looking than the *Corar*, whom I lately described. Their masters give annually to each slave, male or female, one piece of cloth worth a *Rupee*, together with a knife. Each family has a house, and 10 *Hanies* sowing of rice-land, or about a quarter of an acre. At marriages they get one *Mudy* of rice ($\frac{1}{10}$ bushel), worth about 2*s.*, and half a *Pagoda*, or 4*s.* in money. When their master has no occasion for their work, they get no wages, but hire themselves out as labourers in the best manner they can; for they have not the resource of basket-making, nor of the other little arts which the *Corar* practise. The master is bound, however, to prevent the aged or infirm from perishing of want. When they work for their master, a man gets daily $1\frac{1}{2}$ *Hany* of rice to carry home, with $\frac{1}{2}$ a *Hany* ready dressed, in all 2 *Hanies*, or rather more than one-sixteenth of a bushel; a woman gets $1\frac{1}{4}$ *Hany* of rice to carry home, and $\frac{1}{2}$ *Hany* ready dressed; and a boy gets 1 *Hany* of rice.

These casts have no hereditary chiefs; but quarrels are amicably settled by eight or ten prudent men, who assemble the parties, and, with the assistance of a little drink, discuss the business. They never expel any one from the cast; even women who commit fornication with strange men are not subjected to this disgrace. If

CHAPTER XV.

Feb. 15.

the seducer has been a *Súdra*, or man of pure birth, the husband is not at all offended at the preference which his wife has given to a superior. If he be a slave, the husband turns her away; but then she is taken to wife by her paramour, even though he be of a different cast. In order to purify her for this purpose, the paramour builds a small hut of straw, and, having put the woman into it, sets it on fire. She makes her escape, as fast as she can, to another village, where the same ceremony is again repeated, till she has been burned out eight times; she is then considered as an honest woman. The men may lawfully keep several wives, but either party may at pleasure give up the connection. Girls after the age of puberty, widows, and divorced women, are all allowed to marry. These casts can eat goats, sheep, fowls, and fish; but no other kind of animal food. They may lawfully intoxicate themselves. None of them can read, nor have they any kind of *Guru*, or priest. In every house is a stone representing the *Penates* called *Buta*, which, according to the *Bráhmans*, means a devil, or evil spirit. Two or three times a year the family perform worship *(Pújá)* to this stone, by oiling it, and covering it with flowers. Fowls are also sacrificed to *Buta*, whose worship generally costs the family from two to three *Pagodas* a year; but the sacrifices are the most expensive part, and these the votary eats. It must be observed, that the *Hindus* of pure descent seldom eat animal food, except such as has been sacrificed to the gods; a custom that seems to have also prevailed among the Grecians, in whose language the same word ἱερεῖον signifies a sacrifice, and an animal whose flesh is fit for eating. When the annual worship of *Buta* is neglected, he is supposed to occasion sickness and trouble. The spirits of the dead, both of those who have been good or bad, and of those who died naturally or by accident, are supposed to become *Pysachi*, and are troublesome, unless a sacrifice is made to *Buta*, who takes the spirit to himself, and then it gives the living no more trouble.

CHAPTER XV.

Feb. 16. Appearance of the country.

16th *February.*—I was obliged to set out without seeing *Ramuppa Varmikâ;* and, after having crossed the lake, I went three cosses to *Kira-manéswara*, a temple dedicated to *Siva.* I passed first between the sea and a branch of the *Kunda-pura* lake, and afterwards my road led along a rising ground near the sea. I saw many plantations of coco-nut trees; but, owing to the want of inhabitants, they are very poor. About fifty years ago an epidemic fever raged in the country, and carried off a great number of the people. A few months ago the same complaint again destroyed many. The natives say, that before the third day it resembled a common fever; then the patient became delirious, and on the fifth day died. About ten years ago a predatory band of *Marattahs*, under the command of *Balu Row*, came this way, destroyed entirely the *Agrarum* at *Kira-manéswara;* and the inhabitants, who remained after the epidemic, were swept away from all the neighbouring country.

Face of the country.

The quantity of rice ground is small, and a great part of the country is covered with low woods, in which are to be seen the enclosures of former gardens. The road is good, but is not ornamented with rows of trees, as usual to the southward. The sea-coast, like that between *Mangalore* and *Kunda-pura*, is chiefly occupied by villages of *Bráhmans;* the interior parts of the country belong to *Buntar.* This is a part of *Tulava*, but the language of *Karnata* is that in most common use. The water in wells is no where at any great depth from the surface. The temple here is a sorry building. It had formerly lands to the yearly value of 100 *Pagodas*, or of about 40 guineas. Last year it received in money an allowance of 5 *Pagodas.*

Feb. 17. Appearance of the country.

17th *February.*—Early in the morning I was joined by the learned *Bráhman Ramuppa Varmika*, who accompanied me to *Beiduru*, three cosses distant. By the way we crossed three rivers; the first, called the *Edamavany*, is the most considerable; the second also is not fordable, and is called *Angaru;* the third is small, and joins the

Feb. 17.

second at some distance to the westward. Its channel is in many places shut up, and converted into places for making salt; for the tide in all the three rivers, reaches a considerable way into the country. On this day's route there is much rice ground, and the crops look well.

Beiduru.

Beiduru is an open village, containing about 120 houses. It had once a fort, and was then a large place, which belonged to a *Jain* princess, named *Byra Dévi.* This family was destroyed by the *Siva-bhaktars*, and the place has ever since been on the decline. The cultivators now are *Bráhmans*, and *Nadavar*, who are a kind of *Bunts*, but they do not speak the language of *Tulava.* The *Jainar* are quite extinct. One temple of the kind called *Busty* continued until the time of *Hyder;* when the *Pújári*, being no longer able to procure a subsistence, left the place.

Inscriptions at a temple of *Siva.*

The temple at present here is one dedicated to *Siva.* There are about it several inscriptions on stone, that contain the grants of lands with which the temple was endowed. One, which was a good deal defaced, so as not to be wholly legible, is dated in the year of *Salivahanam* 1445 (*A. D.* $152\frac{2}{3}$), in the time of *Devarasu Wodear*, *Rájá* of *Sanghita-pura;* and son of *Sanga-raya Wodear*, who held his *Ráyada* of *Krishna Ráya*, the chief of *Rájás* in wealth, a *Rájá* equal to *Paraméswara*, a hero greater than the *Trivira*, &c. &c. *Sanghita-pura*, in the vulgar language called *Hadwully*, is four cosses east from *Batuculla*, and was formerly the residence of a governor appointed by the kings of *Vijaya-nagara. Devarasu Wodear* must either have been one of these, or an ancestor of *Byra Dévi. Krishna Ráya* is, no doubt, the celebrated *Ráyalu* of that name.

In another inscription, of which a copy has been presented to the Bengal government, it is stated, that in the year of *Salivahanam* 1429 (*A. D.* $150\frac{6}{7}$), and in the reign of *Jebila Narasingha Ráya*, the great king of *Vijaya-nagara*, *Kedaly Baswappa Arsa Wodear* having been appointed to the *Ráyada* of *Barcuru*, with orders to restore the lands of the god, and of the *Bráhmans*, certain merchants

CHAPTER XV.

Feb. 17.

of *Bideruru (Nagara)* founded an inn for the accommodation of six travelling *Bráhmans*, and for this purpose purchased certain lands, which are specified in the inscription.

Ramuppa Varmika, a learned Bráhman.

Ramuppa Varmika says, that his family have been hereditary *Shanabogas*, or accomptants of *Barcuru* district, ever since the time of the *Belalla Ráyas;* which dynasty, according to him, commenced their reign here in the year 637 of *Salivahanam* or *A. D.* 71$\frac{4}{5}$. *Ramuppa*, however, possesses no revenue accompts previous to the conquest of the country by *Hari-hara Ráyalu*, in the year of *Sal.* 1258 (*A. D.* 133$\frac{5}{6}$).

His account of the *Rájás* who have governed *Tulava.*

Ramuppa has a book in *Sanskrit*, called *Vidiarayana Sicca*; and from thence, and his family papers, he has made out a *Ráya Paditti*, or succession of the *Rájás* who have governed *Tulava.* Of this I here give a translation, with observations, partly made by himself, and partly from what I could collect from inscriptions. From these it will appear, that not much dependence can be placed on some of his dates. Great difficulty occurs in comparing the native accounts with those of the Mussulman writers, who corrupt the *Hindu* names most extravagantly, and hold all knowledge of the infidels in so much contempt, that very little can be gathered from what they say.

"*Srí.*"

"Succession of *Rájás.*"

"The reign of the *Yudishtira* family commenced on Friday, the 6th day of the moon, in the month *Chaitra*, in *Privndi*, the 1st of the *Kali-yugam.*"

"After this, *Parikshitta Ráya* was king here."

Then follows a *Slokam* on his *Putapesheca*, which is a ceremony somewhat similar to our coronation and anointing.

"From *Parikshitta Ráya* to *Nanda Ráya's* coronation, there had elapsed of the *Kali-yugam* 1115 years," B. C. 198$\frac{4}{5}$.

"After this, under *Nanda Ráya* and his family, in all nine princes, there passed 200 years."

"After that, under ten princes of the *Vahanicula* family, passed 112 years."

"After that, under ten princes of the *Moviuan Navaiada* family, passed 137 years."

"After that, one *Cadumba Ráya* had 45 years possession, till the year of the *Kali-yugam* 1609," B. C. 149½.

"After that, in the year *Vicruti*, of the *Kali-yugam* 1631 (B. C. 147½) *Myuru Varmá* brought the *Bráhmans* from *Ahichaytra*, or *Eichetra*, and gave them 18 *Grámas* or villages. In this 22 years were employed, till the year of the *Kali-yugam* 1631."

"After that, *Myuru Varmá* possessed the kingdom for 10 years."

"After that, *Trinétra Kadumba Ráya*, son of *Myuru Varmá*, sat on the throne of the kingdom for 12 years."

"After that, from the year *Virodicrutu Myuru Varmá* governed with his son for 10 years, till 1663 years of the *Kali-yugam* had elapsed," (B. C. 143$\frac{9}{10}$).

"After that, *Myuru Varmá* gave *Cadumba Ráya's* sister in marriage to *Lókáditya* at *Gaukarna*, and destroyed the *Hubashica* family. This occupied 15 years."

"After this, the countries of *Parasu Ráma* being without *Bráhmans*, *Cadumba Ráya* and *Lókáditya* brought good *Bráhmans*, and kept them in the country in the year *Sarcajitu*, being of the *Kali-yugam* 1689," (B. C. 1413).

"After this, under twenty-one *Jeantri Cadumba Ráyas*, there passed 242 years."

From an inscription from *Bellagami*, which has been presented to the government of Bengal, it would appear, that a *Trinétra Cadumba* was sovereign prince in the year of *Sal.* 90 (*A. D.* 16½), or 1579 years after the time assigned for *Trinétra Cadumba* in this *Ráya Paditti*. These princes, however, were probably the same; and in order to make the time of the possessions of the *Bráhmans* in *Tulava* much more ancient than it really is, the succession of dynasties has either been altered; or a number of families, that

CHAPTER XV.

Feb. 17.

never existed, have been introduced to fill up the space between the *Cadumba Ráyas* and the *Belalla* family, of whom many traces remain. In the northern parts of *Karnáta* the *Cadumba* family seem long to have retained considerable power, as I procured two inscriptions, belonging to them, after the time of *Trinétra Cadumba.* The one is a grant of land to the *Kudali Swámalu* in the reign of *Purandara Ráya* of the *Cadumba* family, who governed at *Banawási* in the year of *Sal.* 1043, or *A. D.* 112$\frac{2}{1}$. The other is from a temple near *Savanuru* in the reign of a *Cadumba Ráya*, and in the year of *Sal.* 1130, or *A. D.* 120$\frac{4}{5}$. Copies of these inscriptions have been delivered to the Bengal government.

"After the *Cadumba Ráyas* there elapsed, under thirty-two *Banhica Ráyas*, 456 years."

"After that, under *Rájás* of the *Abhira* family, there passed 1199 years."

"After that, the *Monayer* family possessed the kingdom 200 years."

"3786 years of the *Kali-yugam* had now elapsed; of which the particulars are,

3044 years of the *Yudishtira* era.
135 years of the *Vikrama* era.
607 years of the era of *Salivahanam.*

3786 total of *Kali-yugam*," *A. D.* 68$\frac{4}{5}$.

Belalla family.

"From the year 607 of *Salivahanam*, *Belalla Ráyaru*, and persons of the same family, being in all nine princes, governed 209 years. Above and below the *Ghats* they governed 98 years, and below the *Ghats* they continued to govern 111 years more."

"Above the *Ghats* were the following princes:"

"The *Yavanas* at *Anagundi* possessed the kingdom for 54 years."

Who were these *Yavanas?* This word properly signifies an European; but as the *Hindus* speak with great confusion concerning the northern and western nations, it is often confounded with the

Melenchas and *Turcs*, or *Arabs* and *Tartars;* and all the three terms are frequently applied to the Mussulmans. But the *Yavanas* of *Anagundi* could not be Mussulmans, as their government by this account lasted from *A. D.* 782 till 836; and there is strong reason to believe, that *Ramuppa* is not essentially mistaken in the time at which the *Belalla Rāyas* lived. Although he says that they only governed 98 years above the *Ghats*, this must not be understood literally. *Anagundi*, where *Vijaya-nagara* was afterwards built, was probably their first seat of government; and after their being expelled by the *Yavanas*, according to the accounts given verbally by *Ramuppa*, they retired to *Hully-bedu*, or *Goni-bedu*, a town situated above the *Ghats*. They governed *Tulava* by officers called *Rāyaru*, who resided at *Barcuru*, and were also masters of all the southern parts of *Karnāta*. They were of *Andray* or *Telinga* descent, and originally of the *Jain* religion. One of them having been killed by the Mussulmans, who then were making predatory excursions into the *Deccan*, his son removed the seat of government to *Tonuru*, near *Seringapatam;* and soon after this period *Tulava* seems to have withdrawn its allegiance, instigated perhaps to rebellion by his having thrown aside the religion of his fathers, and adopted that taught by *Rāma Anuja*, as I have related in the seventh Chapter. After this conversion he resided at *Bailuru;* and from an inscription there, it would appear, that he rebuilt the temple of *Cayshava Permal* there, in the year of *Sal.* 1039, or *A. D.* 111$\frac{6}{7}$; while, from the inscription No. 13, it would appear, that his son, *Hoisela Narasingha Rāya*, continued to govern in the year of *Sal.* 1095, or *A. D.* 117$\frac{3}{4}$. The government of the *Yavanas* of *Anagundi*, and of the *Hindu* princes who followed them, must have been confined to the northern and eastern parts of the peninsula: for we have already seen, that the *Cadamba Rāyas* continued to have possessions in the north-west of *Karnāta*.

CHAPTER XV. Feb. 17.

"After the *Yavanas*, the *Campina Rāma Rāyas* had the kingdom 30 years."

CHAPTER XV.

Feb. 17.

"Then *Daria Soructa* cut off the head of *Campina Comora Rámanátha* in the year of the *Kali-yugam* 3951." (*A. D.* $8\frac{49}{50}$).

"After that, *Boji Ráya* possessed the kingdom 63 years; and under nine princes of his family were passed 145 years. Total of the reigns of the ten princes of this family 213 years." (*A. D.* $106\frac{2}{7}$).

"After that, under eighteen princes of *Andray* descent, the ancestors of *Pratápa Rudra*, there passed 211 years."

"After this, *Pratápa Rudra* possessed the kingdom 54 years, till the year of the *Kali-yugam* 4429," (*A. D.* $132\frac{1}{2}$) "then the kingdoms of *Andray* were in the possession of the *Mlécha*, who, increasing in power, seized on the dominions of *Pratápa Rudra.* They took his towns, and gained his kingdom, wealth, and umbrella.

Kings of *Vijaya-nagara*, who rose on the ruins of the *Andray*.

Then *Hucca* and *Buca*, both the *Bundara Cavilas*" (guards of the treasury) "of *Pratápa Rudra*, came to *Sri Mahá Vidyáranya Mahá Swami*" (who according to *Ramuppa* was *Guru* to the late king, and the eleventh successor of *Sankara Achárya* on the throne of *Sringa-giri*), "and solicited his favour. The *Mahá Swámi* visited God, and acted according to his orders. He built *Vijaya-nagara* city" (*Pattana*). "In seven years the whole city was fully built. In the year *Datu*, being 1258 of the era of *Salivahanam*" (*A. D.* $133\frac{1}{6}$), "in the 7th day of the moon in *Vaisákha*, being Wednesday, under the constellation *Mocca*, in *Abijun Muhurta*" (*Muhurta* is a division of the day containing $3\frac{3}{4}$ *Hindu* hours), "and in *Singha Laghana*" (*Laghana* is a space of time equal to $\frac{1}{2}$ a *Pahar*, or $\frac{1}{4}$ of a natural day), "he took both *Hucca* and *Buca*, the guards of the treasury of *Pratápa Rudra*. To the man *Hucca* he gave *Puttavuncutty*" (a ceremony like our coronation), "and gave him the name of *Hari-hara Ráyaru*. The whole kingdom was given to him in the year of the *Kali-yugam* 4437," or *A. D.* $133\frac{1}{6}$.

There is reason to believe, that in the reigns of *Pratápa Rudra* and his ancestors the seat of government was *Woragulla* (*Warancul* of the Mussulmans), the chief place in *Andray* or *Telingana*. In many accounts, the last of the family is called *Woragulla Pratápa*

Ráya. He probably governed *Telingana*, or the country of warriors, and the northern parts of *Karnáta* which were not subject to the *Belalla* family. We learn from Scot's translation of *Ferishta's* history of the *Deccan*, that in the year 1309 *Ala ad Dien*, Mussulman king of *Dhely*, sent *Mallek Naib* to invade *Telingana*, and obliged *Ludder Deo, Rájá* of *Warancul*, to become tributary. In 1310 *Mallek Naib* advanced into *Carnatic*, and took *Rájá Bellaul Deo* prisoner; and in 1312 he again over-run these countries, and obliged *Telingana* and *Carnatic* to become tributary to the throne of *Dhely*. This chronology agrees very well with that of the *Ráya Paditti*, which makes the final overthrow of the kingdoms of *Andray* by the *Mlé-chas* to have happened in 1327, or 13 years after this last expedition of *Mallek Naib*, who had then rendered them tributary. It must be observed, that the *Belalla* family still continued to be in 1312 the principal rulers in *Karnáta;* but the *Ráya Paditti* considers them also as of *Andray*, as they originally came from that country. It is true, that *Pratápa Rudra* is not mentioned by *Ferishta*, by whom the *Rájá* of *Warancul* is called *Ludder Deo;* but for this we may account, either from the sovereign contempt in which these infidel princes were held by the Mussulmans, who rarely gave themselves the trouble to inquire about their true names or customs; or *Ludder Deo* may be a corruption of some of the numerous titles, which, like all *Hindus* of his rank, this prince assumed.

CHAPTER XV. Feb. 17.

Soon after this, we learn from *Ferishta*, that the government of *Dhely* declined into the usual debility of an *Indian* dynasty that has been established for any length of time; and many chiefs declared themselves independent of the king's authority. Among these, the most remarkable was the founder of a dynasty, who governed the Mussulman conquests in the *Deccan*, and who were called the *Bhaminee Sultáns.* This enterprising man, in the year 1347, was able to throw off all appearance of submission, and assumed at *Beder* all the insignia of sovereign authority. He was of-

CHAPTER XV. Feb. 17. course obliged to manage with discretion the neighbouring *Hindus;* and *Hucca* and *Buca*, two of the principal officers of *Pratápa Rudra*, took this opportunity of establishing a kingdom in the southern parts of the countries which formerly belonged to princes of *Andray* descent; and to the southern provinces of *Pratápa Rudra*, they added those of the latter *Belalla Ráyas*. *Rumuppa* says, that after the overthrow of their master, these two men undertook a pilgrimage to *Ráméswara;* and, while on their way, met the *Guru* of the late king at *Humpay*, a village on the opposite side of the river from *Anagundi*, where afterwards *Vijaya-nagara* was built. Having conferred with this mighty *Bráhman*, he retired into a celebrated temple of *Siva*, who is worshipped at *Humpay* under the name of *Vira-pacsha*. Here the god was consulted; and the *Bráhman* declared, that he was ordered by the deity to crown *Hucca*, and to build the city *Vijaya-nagara*, or the city of victory. This name the Mussulmans corrupt into *Beejanuggur;* and *Ferishta* gravely tells us, that it derives its name from *Beeja*, a *Hindu* prince; and that it had been founded by the family who governed it in 1365, about 700 years previous to that time. Of his judgment in antiquities an opinion may be drawn from his also gravely relating, that *Deccan* (that is the south country) derives its name from *Deccan*, the son of *Hind*, the son of *Ham*, the son of *Noah*. In this author we need not wonder at any corruptions of names; for he changes the name of the river on which *Vijaya-nagara* stands, from *Tunga-bhadra*, or contractedly *Tung'bhadra*, into *Tummedru;* and he corrupts the celebrated *Vikramáditya* into *Bickermajeet*.

The *Ráya Puditti*, having detailed the princes who governed the country above the *Ghats*, returns to mention those who governed the sea-coast, while it was separated from *Karnáta*.

"Here below the *Ghats Belalla Ráya* entered upon the government in the year of *Salivahanam* 637" (*A. D.* 71$\frac{4}{5}$). "He and his descendants, nine princes, and eleven persons of the same family, from *Pratápa Rudra* to *Viruppa Wodearu*, in all twenty princes, occupied the country for 461 years, till the year of *Salivahanam* 1068." (*A. D.* 1145). CHAPTER XV.

N. B. This *Pratápa Rudra* is evidently a very different personage from the prince destroyed by the *Mlêchas* in 132½. Feb. 17.

"Then in the intermediate time between the year of *Salivahanam* 1068, and the year *Paradavi* 1175 (*A. D.* 125$\frac{2}{3}$), for a space of 107 years, there was no person in the possession of the kingdom. Some of the servants of the *Bellala Ráyas* strengthened themselves, and this *inter-regnum* was passed in one person's plundering another."

"In the year of *Salivahanam* 1175, being *Paridavi*, the devils (*Butagallu*) brought *Panda Ráya* to the government of *Baracuru* kingdom, and gave him *Puttuvuncutty*, calling him by the name of *Buta Panda Ráya*. He alone possessed the kingdom 42 years. Of the same family *Víra Pratápa Ráya* governed 19 years, and *Déva Ráya* 21 years. Total three princes 82 years."

"There had then passed of the era of *Salivahanam* 1257 years." *A. D.* 133$\frac{4}{5}$.

I have already mentioned the probable cause of the overthrow of the *Belalla* family's authority in *Tulava*. These servants of the king, who strengthened themselves, were according to *Ramuppa* the ancestors of the *Jain Rájás*, such as the *Choutar*, *Bungar*, *Byrasu Wodears*, &c. &c. who have in this journal been often mentioned; and of the truth of this, I think, there can be little doubt. When the king changed his religion, and assumed the name of *Vishnu Vardhana Ráya*, as I have already related, these petty *Jain Rájás* refused to submit to his authority, or to pay any tribute. Many idle stories are told concerning the manner in which the *Butagallu*, or devils, introduced *Panda Ráya*, and rendered all the *Jain* princes subject to his authority. It would appear, that he came from *Pandava*, the district contiguous to Cape *Comorin*; and he is said to have introduced from thence the singular mode of succession that prevails in *Tulava*, as well as in *Malayála*. The *Ráya Paditti* then proceeds thus.

CHAPTER XV.

Feb. 17.

" In this manner in the year of *Salivahanam* 1257, being the year *Yuva*, *Déva Ráya Mahá Ráya*, of the family of *Buta Panda Ráya*, commanded *Baracuru* kingdom. In the year *Dat'hu*, by the favour of *Srí Vidyáranya Mahá Swámi*, the founder of *Vijaya-nagara* city, and the crowner of *Hari-hara Ráya*, *Déva Ráyaru* delivered *Baracuru* kingdom to *Hari-hara Ráya*. There had then elapsed of the era of *Salivahanam* 1258 years.

" From the year of *Salivahanam* 1258, being the year *Dhatu*, on Wednesday the 7th of the moon, in *Vaisákha*, after *Hari-hara Ráya*, were the following *Ráyaru*."

Family of *Hari-hara*.

In the original here follows a *Slókam*, containing the first letter of every *Rájá's* name, as the commencement of a word. It must be observed, that each of these princes is spoken of by the title of *Ráyaru*, the *Karnátaka* plural of *Ráya*. This is the same word with the *Rylu*, or *Rayalu* of the *Telingas*, contracted by Mussulmans into *Ryl*, and commonly applied exclusively to the kings of *Vijaya-nagara*. In the south, however, every person of very high rank is spoken of in the plural number; and the princes of all the great dynasties that have governed *Karnáta* are commonly called *Ráyaru* by its native inhabitants.

" In this manner 13 *Ráyaru* princes possessed the kingdom for 150 years."

" Particulars.		Until the æra of *Sal.*	Until the year of Christ.
15 years	*Hari-hara Ráya* - - - -	1273	$135\frac{2}{1}$
22	*Buca Ráya* - - - -	1295	$137\frac{3}{7}$
31	*Hari-hara Ráya* - - - -	1326	$140\frac{1}{4}$
4	*Virapaksha Ráya* - - - -	1330	$140\frac{1}{8}$
1	*Buca Ráya* - - - -	1331	$140\frac{8}{9}$
7	*Déva Ráya* and *Ráma Ráya* -	1338	$141\frac{5}{6}$
11	*Virapaksha Ráya* - - -	1349	$142\frac{6}{7}$
28	*Déva Ráya* and *Virapaksha Ráya*	1377	$145\frac{4}{5}$
4	*Maruppa Ráya* - - -	1381	$145\frac{8}{9}$
27	*Ráma Ráya* and *Virapaksha Ráya*	1408	$148\frac{5}{6}$

"Total thirteen princes governed till the year *Crodi* for 150 years. It was then of the era of *Salivahanam* 1407." *A. D.* 148$\frac{4}{5}$.

Feb. 17.

Although this is detailed with great minuteness, little reliance can be placed on its exactitude. From an inscription, a copy of which I presented to the Bengal government, we learn, that *Buca Ráya* was king in *Salivahanam* 1297, *A. D.* 137$\frac{4}{5}$, two years after the end of his reign according to the *Ráya Paditti.* Another inscription, also presented to government, is in the reign of *Déva Ráya,* and is dated in the year of *Sal.* 1332, *A. D.* 14$\frac{09}{10}$, which agrees with the chronology of the *Ráya Paditti.* In this last *Ráma Ráya* is stated to have reigned conjointly with *Déva;* but it is evident from the inscription, that he had not been admitted to partake in the royal dignity for some time after the other's accession. Another inscription, also procured by me, is dated in the year *Sal.* 1352, *A. D.* 14$\frac{29}{30}$ in the reign of *Pratápa Déva Ráya,* son of *Vijaya Ráya.* This also agrees with the chronology of the *Ráya Paditti.* This prince's father was never sovereign. Another inscription is dated in the year of *Sal.* 1400, *A. D.* 147$\frac{7}{8}$, in the reign of *Virapaksha Mahá Ráyaru.* This also agrees with the chronology of the *Ráya Paditti;* but that mentions a *Ráma Ráya,* as governing along with *Virapaksha,* which is not countenanced by the inscription. It must, however, be observed, that these inscriptions seem to be among the *Hindus,* what the legends on the coins are among the Mussulmans; and so long as a nominal king is retained, all inscriptions and legends are made in his name; but the historian or chronologer must also mention the person actually possessed of the power of government; and *Ráma Ráya* was perhaps a minister, like the *Peshwa* at the *Poonah,* who confines his sovereign, the descendant of *Sevajee,* and governs the *Marattah* states with absolute authority. The general agreement between these inscriptions, collected in parts of the country very remote from the residence of *Ramuppa,* confirms beyond a doubt his account of the dynasty of *Vijaya-nagara;* and the accounts given of the great antiquity of that city by *Ferishta*

CHAPTER XV. Feb. 17.

must be looked upon as entirely fabulous. Of the actions which the princes of this dynasty performed, we have in that author's history of the *Deccan* several accounts, apparently strongly tinctured by zeal for the Mussulman doctrines. Owing to his corruptions of names, and probably owing to his frequently mistaking the general or minister for the sovereign (for *Ráya* is a title applied to all *Hindus* of distinction, as well as to kings) we very seldom can reconcile his names with those of the *Ráya Paditti*, or of inscriptions. He says, that in the year 1365 *Roy Kishen Roy* was king of *Beejanuggur*, and his ancestors had possessed the kingdom for 700 years. This was in the reign of *Buca Ráya*, son of the founder of the dynasty and of the city. From the year 1398 to the year 1420 *Dewal Roy* of *Beejanuggur* is frequently mentioned. This may have been *Déva Ráya* the First, who may have been employed as a general long before his accession in 1408. *Deo Roy* of *Beejanuggur* is mentioned in 1437 and 1443, and is no doubt *Déva Ráya* the Second, who during these times was sovereign.

Usurpers who governed at *Vijaya-nagara.*

As the two dynasties of the *Bhaminee Sultáns*, and the *Ráyarus* of *Vijaya-nagara* commenced nearly about the same time, their fall also happened at the same period. From *Ferishta* we have the following account of the manner in which the servants of the *Hindu* princes usurped their authority. *Hemraje*, or as he in one place is called *Ram Ráje*, was minister of *Beejanuggur*. He was a man of abilities, and gained some advantages over the declining power of the *Bhaminee Sultáns*. In order to protract his authority, he poïsoned the young prince, son of *Sheo Roy*, and placed on the throne a younger brother. In making an excursion into the Mussulman territories, in the year 1492, he was met by *Adil Shah*, founder of the dynasty of *Beejapoor (Vijaya-pura)*, and defeated. In this engagement the young *Rájá* was killed, and *Hemraje* assumed sovereign power. It must be observed, that *Sheo Roy* is a manner of writing *Siva Ráya*; and *Virapaksha* is one of the names of the god *Siva*. *Virapaksha Ráya*, the last of the thirteen *Ráyaru*, may therefore be meant by *Sheo Roy;* and *Hemraje*, or *Rám Raye*, the usurping minister, may be the *Ráma Ráya* mentioned in the *Ráya Paditti* as conjoined in authority with *Virupacsha.* The dates agree very well. Feb. 17. On his usurping sovereign authority, it is likely, that, as usual in India, he assumed some new name, and was called *Prouwuda Ráya,* the name by which the first usurper is known among the *Hindus.* Of these the *Ráya Paditti* gives the following account.

"From the year *Visua Vasu* of *Saliváhanam* 1408 (*A. D.* 1485), the servants (*Cadaëvaru*) of the *Ráyaru*, being seven men, possessed the kingdom 103 years.

Particulars.	Till year of *Sal.*	Till year of Christ.
12 years *Prouwuda Ráya* - - -	1420	149$\frac{7}{8}$
10 ditto *Vira Narasingha Ráya* -	1420	150$\frac{7}{8}$
12 ditto *Solva Narasingha Ráya* -	1442	15$\frac{19}{20}$
43 ditto *Achuta Ráya*, and *Krishna Ráya*	1485	156$\frac{2}{3}$
26 ditto *Sadásiva Ráya*, and *Ráma Ráya*	1511	158$\frac{8}{9}$

"Total 7 men and 103 years."

Here, in the original, follows a *Slókam*, or *Anagram* on these seven princes. Among a set of usurpers struggling for authority, we cannot expect much regularity; and it is hardly possible, that two of them could unite exactly at the same time, reign together for 43 years, and then die together; but to a *Hindu* chronologist such difficulties do not present themselves as extraordinary. Several of these princes were men of abilities, and *Krishna Ráyaru* was by far the greatest *Hindu* monarch that has appeared in modern times. Of this we need not require a stronger proof, than his living in the immediate frontier of the countries whose history *Ferishta* is writing, and yet his never being mentioned by that author. In his reign no victories over the idolaters were to be celebrated; and it would have been unbecoming a Mussulman to disclose the disasters of the faithful.

CHAPTER XV.

Feb. 17. Government of the kings of *Vijaya-nagara* in *Tulava.*

The account given orally by *Ramuppa* of the manner in which this country was governed by the kings of *Vijaya-nagara* is as follows. *Hucca* and *Buca* were of the *Curuba* cast, the customs of which low tribe I have already described. They were of *Telinga* extraction; all the officers of their court were of the same nation; and the remaining *Rájás* of *Anagundi* still retain that language. When *Hucca* had assumed the name of *Hari-hara*, and became very powerful, the *Rájá* of *Tulava* made a submission, in appearance voluntary, and did not attempt any resistance. It is not known what has become of his descendants; but they seem to have been entirely deprived of power; and *Hari-hara* appointed three deputies to command the military force, and to collect the revenue from the *Jain Rájás*, and other tributaries. The deputy, who resided at the former capital, *Barcuru*, or *Baracuru*, had the title of *Ráyaru;* the one who governed *Mangaluru* was styled *Wodear;* and an inferior person governed the small district belonging to *Bagwady*. These offices were not hereditary. The *Jain Rájás* were confirmed in the hereditary possession of their territories, and were allowed for their support certain estates, called *Umbli* lands, free from revenue. They collected the revenues of the other parts of their territories, and paid them in to the deputy under whom they lived; and over all persons living within their respective territories they possessed most ample authority. Each supported a certain number of troops, with which in time of war he was bound to assist his liege lord. Their common title was *Manatana Dévaru*. The *Manatana*, however, were not allowed to exercise any authority over the 32 *Grámas* which *Cadumba Ráya* had bestowed on the *Bráhmans.* The revenues of *Cotta* and *Shivuli*, two of these, were collected by the officers of the deputies. The remaining thirty were under the government of an equal number of *Bráhmans*, who held their offices by hereditary right. These were called *Hegadas*, or *Baylalas*, and also enjoyed *Umbli* lands; but their jurisdiction was much less extensive than that of the *Jain Rájás*. They could not inflict capital punishment, nor confiscate a man's property, nor erase his house. CHAPTER XV. Feb. 17.

It would appear, that before the time of *Hari-hara* no land-tax existed in *Tulava;* and this country, after its rebellion from the *Belalla Rayas,* was probably in a state of anarchy and confusion similar to that of *Malayála* after its division among the captains of *Cheruman Permal.* The settlement and valuation made by *Hari-hara* is said to be still extant, and *Ramuppa* gives the following account of the plan adopted by that prince. The whole produce having been estimated, out of every thirty measures the government took 5, the *Bráhmans* got 1½, the gods 1, the proprietors 7½; and 15, or one-half, was allowed to the cultivator. The whole lands of the *Bráhmans* were valued in the same manner as the others; but the revenue was remitted on such part of them as was dedicated to the support of the temples, or of public worship. This system of revenue continues to the present day; only the shares of the god and the *Bráhmans* are supposed to have been taken by the government, who grant annual sums for the support of public worship; and the *Umbli* lands are now taxed, in the same manner as the others.

Concerning the usurpers of the throne of *Vijaya-nagara* I collected from inscriptions, copies of which I presented to the government of Bengal, the following information. From that which I procured at *Beidura,* it would appear that *Jebila Narasingha Ráya* was king in the year of *Sal.* 1429. This is probably the *Vira Narasingha* of the *Ráya Paditti,* whose reign ended in the following year. In another inscription, *Achuta Ráya Narasingha Ráya,* and *Krishna Ráya* are mentioned as sovereigns conjunctly. The copyist has made the date 1337, but he evidently ought to have made it 1437. From this it would appear, that *Achuta* and *Krishna* had been conjoined with their predecessor, *Solva Narasingha,* so early as the seventh year of his reign, although the *Ráya Paditti* does not make their government commence until his terminated. In an inscription

CHAPTER XV.

Feb. 17.

at this place, of which I have no copy, *Krishna Ráya* is mentioned as sovereign in the year of *Sal.* 1445, or *A. D.* $152\frac{3}{4}$. In another inscription, *Vira Pratápa Achuta Ráya* is sovereign in the year of *Sal.* 1452, or *A. D.* $15\frac{30}{31}$; and in another *Achuta Ráya* and *Krishna Ráya* are joint sovereigns in the year of *Sal.* 1454, or *A. D.* $153\frac{2}{3}$. In another still, *Achuta Ráya* is mentioned alone in the intermediate year 1453. With the long and glorious reign of these two princes the fortune of *Vijaya-nagara* departed. In another inscription at *Banawási*, is mentioned a *Vencatadri Deva* as sovereign in the year of *Sal.* 1474, or *A. D.* 1551. This name is not to be found in the *Ráya Paditti;* and *Vencatadri* was either some person struggling for the supreme authority, or some tributary who had entirely thrown off his allegiance. In another inscription *Vira Pratápa Sadásiva Déva Mahá Ráya* is mentioned as king in the year of *Sal.* 1477, or *A. D.* $155\frac{5}{6}$; and he is again mentioned in another inscription as king, and as son of *Achuta Ráya.* The date to this inscription is *Sal.* 1412; but that is an evident error in the copyist, and it must be in the original 1512. This, it is true, according to the *Ráya Paditti,* is one year after the death of his colleague *Ráma Ráya,* and the destruction of *Vijaya-nagara;* but the representatives of this family still exist, and for a long time their rebellious *Polygars* continued to show an external deference for their dignity, although they refused all submission to their authority. Upon the whole, from these two inscriptions it would appear, that although *Achuta* and *Krishna* are mentioned as joint sovereigns, whose reign did not terminate till *Sal.* 1485; yet *Achuta* died earlier, and was succeeded by his son *Sadásiva,* so early at least as *Sal.* 1477; but his name was obscured, by the lustre of his first colleague's reputation, till the death of this celebrated prince.

Probably owing to the reason which I have before mentioned, the account of these princes in *Ferishta* is extremely imperfect. He makes the first usurper to be succeeded by his son *Rám Ráye,* against whom three of the Mussulman princes united in 1564, and killed him in the first engagement. After which the capital city was destroyed, and each of the *Zemeendars (Polygars)* assumed in his own district an independant power. This account makes the destruction of *Vijaya-nagara* 24 years earlier than the end of the reign of *Ráma Ráya* according to the *Ráya Paditti.* Which is in the right, I cannot say; but the matter may probably be decided by means of some of the numerous inscriptions that are to be found in the country. It does not appear clear, whether or not the line of *Hari-hara* has become extinct, nor whether the present *Rájá* of *Anagundi* be descended from him, or from one of the usurpers who seized on *Vijaya-nagara*, but who still continued to govern in the name of the royal family, as their servants.

Feb. 17.

Rájás of Kilidi, or Ikeri.

Ramuppa now takes leave of the family of the *Ráyaru*, and proceeds to give an account of one of the chief *Polygars*, who on the decline of *Vijaya-nagara* assumed independence.

"Until the year *Dhatu* of *Salivahanam* 1510 (*A. D.* 158$\frac{7}{8}$) *Sadásiva Ráya*, and *Ráma Ráya* possessed the kingdom, as servants of the *Ráyaru*. In the mean while *Sadásiva Ráya* gave to *Sadásiva Gauda*, son of *Baswuppa*, the *Gauda* of *Kilidi*, a government *(Subayena)* in *Karnátaka Désa*, namely, *Guty*, *Baracuru*, and *Mangaluru*. These three towns were given into the possession of *Sadásiva Gauda*, and his name was changed into *Sadásiva Ráya Náyaka*, after the name of the *Ráyaru* who gave him the power *Suluntra* (of governing by a deputy), and put it into his possession. From the year *Durmuti* 1482 (*A. D.* 15$\frac{59}{60}$), to the year *Chitrabanu* 1685 (*A. D.* 176$\frac{2}{3}$), sixteen persons, styling themselves *Rájás* of *Kilidi* or *Ikeri*, possessed the government 203 years. Particulars."

"Seven persons governed 77 years, styling themselves servants *(Cadaëvaru)* of *Vijaya-nagara*. Particulars."

"16 years *Sadásiva Náyaka*;" began to reign 1482. *A. D.* 1559.

"9 years his younger brother *Bhadruppa Náyaka*:" began to govern 1498. *A. D.* 157$\frac{5}{6}$.

CHAPTER XV.

Feb. 17.

" 11 years *Doda* (great) *Sunkana Náyaka*, the son of *Sadásiva Náyaka's* first wife." He began to govern 1507. *A. D.* 158$\frac{4}{5}$.

" 7 years *Chica* (little) *Sunkana Náyaka*, the son of *Sadásiva's* second wife." He began to reign in 1518, *A. D.* 159$\frac{5}{6}$.

" 1 year *Siduppa Náyaka*, son of *Chica Sunkana Náyaka*." He began to reign in 1525. *A. D.* 159$\frac{2}{3}$.

" 22 years *Vencatuppa Náyaka*, son of *Doda Sunkana Náyaka*." He began to govern in 1526, *A. D.* 159$\frac{3}{4}$.

"This *Vencatuppa's* son, *Bhadruppa Náyaka*, and his son *Bhadruppa Náyaka*, governed for 23 years nominally as servants of the *Ráyaru*, and 12 years as sovereign princes. They began to reign in 1548, *A. D.* 162$\frac{5}{6}$.

" In all, as servants of the *Ráyaru*, 7 princes governed 77 years."

"After this, from the year *Dhatu* 1559 (*A. D.* 163$\frac{6}{7}$), till the year *Chitrabanu* 1685 (*A. D.* 176$\frac{2}{3}$), nine *Rájás* governed in their own name 126 years. Particulars."

"The above mentioned *Bhadruppa Náyakas* 23 years; but, deducting 11 years before they governed independently, they reigned in their own name

" 12 years." This began in 1559, *A. D.* 163$\frac{6}{7}$.

" 22 years *Sivuppa Náyaka*, son of *Chica Sunkana Náyaka*." He began to reign 1571. *A. D.* 164$\frac{8}{9}$.

" 10 years his eldest son *Bhadruppa Náyaka*." He began to reign 1593. *A. D.* 167$\frac{0}{1}$.

" 5 years *Hutso* (*Mad*) *Sómasikhara Náyaka*, younger son of *Sivuppa Náyaka*." He began to reign in 1603. *A. D.* 168$\frac{0}{1}$.

" 12 *Doda Chinna Magi*, wife of *Sómasikhara Náyaka*." She began to govern in 1608. *A. D.* 168$\frac{5}{6}$.

" 16 years *Basvruppa Náyaka*, her adopted son." He began to reign 1620. *A. D.* 169$\frac{7}{8}$.

" 26 years *Sómasikhara Náyaka*, his eldest son." He began to reign 1636. *A. D.* 171$\frac{3}{4}$.

"31 years *Budi* (wise) *Baswuppa Náyaka*, son of *Virabhadra*, younger brother of *Sómasikhara*." He began to govern 1662, *A. D.* 17¼.

"2 years *Chinna* (little) *Baswuppa Náyaka*, adopted son of *Viru Magi*, widow of *Budi Baswuppa*." He began to govern in 1675. *A. D.* 175⅔.

"8 years *Sómasikhara Náyaka*, another adopted son of *Viru Magi*." He began to govern in 1677. *A. D.* 175$\frac{4}{7}$.

"In all, ten independent princes of *Kilidi* governed 126 years."

Ramuppa says, that *Doda Sunkana Náyaka* resigned his government to his younger brother, and undertook a pilgrimage to *Kási*, or *Benares*. From thence he went to *Dhely*, where he encountered and killed *Ancusha Khán*, a celebrated prize-fighter. On account of his gallantry he received many honours and lands from the king. The whole of these lands he gave in charity to the *Bráhmans*, and returned home, where he lived in retirement, without making any attempt to resume his authority. His younger brother, in return, left the government to his nephew. This nephew *Vencatuppa*, and his son and grandson, the two *Bhadruppa Náyakas*, being weak men, and mere cyphers, the whole business of the country was managed by their cousin *Sivuppa*, who acted as *Dalawai*, or minister. On their death without children, he succeeded to the sovereignty as lawful heir, and seems to have been the greatest prince of the house. It was he who finally reduced the *Jain Rájás* of *Tulava*, and added to the family dominions the whole province of *Canara*; for, on the overthrow of *Vijaya-nagara*, the *Jain Polygars* had assumed independence. His successor, *Sómasikhara*, was mad, and during the paroxysms of his disease committed great enormities. He ripped up pregnant women with his own hands, and for the gratification of his lust seized every beautiful girl that he met. At length he was assassinated by a *Bráhman* named *Saumya*, who was one of his servants. The rank of the assassin did not save him, and he was put to death by the *Sivabhactars*, who were much attached to this

CHAPTER XV. Feb. 17. family of princes, as being of their own sect, and which by this murder seems to have become extinct. *Doda Chinna Magi*, the widow of *Sómasikhara*, assumed the government; but having no children, she adopted *Baswuppa*, the son of *Marcupa Chitty*, a *Banijiga* merchant of *Bideruru (Bednore)*, where the seat of government then was. The male descendants of this adopted son also ended in *Budi Baswuppa*, who left two widows, *Chinna Magi*, and *Vira Magi*. The latter, although inferior in rank, being a bold woman, put her superior in confinement; and, having adopted a young man named *Chinna Baswuppa*, she governed in his name, and was called *Ránî*. The publicity of her amorous intrigues was so scandalous, that the young *Rájá* ventured to remonstrate with her concerning this part of her conduct. He was immediately removed by a violent death, and a boy was adopted in his stead, and called *Sómasikhara*. *Hyder*, taking advantage of the disgust occasioned by her immoral conduct, subjected to his own authority the dominions of the *Sivabhactars* of *Ikeri*, and shut up the *Ránî* and her adopted son in the fort of *Madhu-giri*. From thence they were taken by the *Marattahs*, but died before the purpose for which the *Marattahs* intended them could be carried into execution. The *Ráya Paditti* proceeds thus.

Mussulman conquest.

"In the year *Chitrabanu*, of *Salivahanam* 1685 (*A. D.* 176$\frac{2}{3}$), on the 3d of the moon in *Maga*, on Friday at the 18th hour, the *Nabob Hyder Aly Khán's* troops took possession of *Bideruru* city; from which time this name was lost, and the place was called *Hyder Nagara*. This *Nabob Hyder Ali Khán* governed (that is to say the dominions of *Ikeri*) from *Chitrubanu*, of *Salivahanam* 1685, till the 3d of the moon in *Paushya* of the year *Shobacrutu*, *Salivahanam* 1706 (*A. D.* 178$\frac{3}{4}$), 20 years and 11 months."

"From the same year *Shobacrutu*, till Saturday the last of the moon in *Chaitra*, of the year *Sidarti*, of *Sal.* 1722 (*A. D.* 1$\frac{799}{800}$), governed *Tip pooSultán* 16 years 3 months, and 28 days.

British government.

"On Monday the *Amávásya* in *Chaitra*, in the same year *Sidarty*, 1722, the Company's forces took possession of *Sri Ranga-Pattana*."

CHAPTER XV.

Feb. 17.

It must be observed, that Saturday is the real date; but, that being an unlucky day, the *Bráhman* changes the day of taking possession into Monday. In order, however, to show that it was on the same day with the fall of *Tippoo*, he tells us, that the one event happened on the last day of the month, and the other on the *Amávásya*, which is the same thing. Such discordances therefore in *Hindu* chronology must not be considered by the antiquary as any proof of either error or ignorance.

CHAPTER XVI.

JOURNEY THROUGH THE NORTHERN PARTS OF CANARA.

CHAPTER XVI. Feb. 18.

FEBRUARY 18th.—I went four cosses to *Batuculla*, which means the *round town*. A very steep barren ridge separates *Beiduru* from a fine level, which is watered by the *Combara*, a small slow-running stream, that in several places is dammed up for the irrigation of the fields. Here was formerly a market *(Bazar)* named *Hosso-petta*, which General Mathews destroyed. After passing this level, I came to a very barren country, but not remarkably hilly. It is covered with stunted trees, and intersected by a small rapid stream, the *Sancada-gonda*, and farther on by a narrow cultivated valley. *Batuculla* stands on the north bank of a small river, the *Sancada-holay*, which waters a very beautiful valley surrounded on every side by hills, and in an excellent state of cultivation. At the public expense eight dams are yearly made in order to water the rice grounds. They are constructed of earth, and are only intended to collect the stream in the dry season. In the rains they would be of no use, and the violence of the stream would then sweep away the strongest works. The dams are repaired between the 17th of November and the 16th of December, and are carried away in the two months which precede the summer solstice. There are here many coco-nut gardens, and these in the best condition of any that I have seen in *Canara*. They are well inclosed with stone walls. Their produce is partly shipped for *Mangalore*, or *Rája-pura*, and partly sent to the country above the *Ghats*.

Batuculla. *Batuculla* is a large open town containing 500 houses. It has two mosques; one of which receives from the Company an allowance of

100 *Pagodas*, and the other half as much. These places of worship are situated in a quarter of the town inhabited by Mussulmans alone. Many of these are wealthy, and go on commercial speculations to different parts of the coast; but this is their home, and here they leave their families. In this part of the country there are no *Buntar*, nor does the language of *Tulava* extend so far to the north. In fact, *Batuculla* is properly in a country called *Haiga*; and the most common farmers are a kind of *Bráhmans*, named *Haiga* after the country, and a low cast of *Hindus* called *Halepecas*. There are here 76 *Gudies*, or temples belonging to the followers of the *Vyása*. Last year the officers of revenue, being all *Bráhmans*, began by their own authority to levy money, under pretence of applying it to the support of these places of worship; but some of them having been flogged, and dismissed from the service, a stop was put to this dangerous practice, and the priests (*Pújáris*) must content themselves with voluntary contributions. Major Monro does not seem to have thought it necessary to be so liberal to the temples, as Major Macleod and Mr. Hurdis have been. I do not perceive that his economy has been attended with any bad effect; and his conduct, on the whole, seems to have gained the good opinion of every honest industrious man that lived under his authority.

Country called *Haiga*.

Money levied for the support of public worship.

Thinking to obtain some information from the *Bráhmans* in a place where they were so numerous, I sent for some of them. They denied having ever been subject to the *Jain*, and said, that this and four other districts were each governed by an independent officer, sent immediately from *Nagara*, meaning the capital above the *Ghats*; for the present *Nagara* is a name of very recent origin. These four territories were *Shiraly*, *Chindawera*, *Garsopa*, and *Mirzee*, and each occupied the whole country from the sea to the *Ghats*. They afterwards confessed, however, that this was only during the government of the *Sivabhactars*; and that *Batuculla* formerly belonged to *Byra Devi*, a *Jain* princess, whose dominions extended

Account of the country by the *Bráhmans*.

CHAPTER XVI. Feb. 18. almost to *Barcuru*, which belonged to a *Jain Rájá* of the name of *Budarsu*. These *Bráhmans* having told me that at all their temples I should find inscriptions, I set out in search of them, and was a good deal disappointed to find none at the two chief *Gudies;* and I inquired at several others, but was informed that they had no such thing. In the course of my walk I met with two *Jain* temples of the kind called *Bustics*, the only remains of sixty-eight that were formerly in the place. The one had an inscription dated in the year of *Sal.* 1468, *A. D.* 154$\frac{5}{6}$, in the reign of *Runga-ráya*. He is not mentioned in the *Ráya Paditti*, but in the inscription is said to have been brother's son of *Krishna Ráya*, by whom he was probably employed as a deputy. The date is toward the end of the time assigned by *Ramuppa* for the reign of *Krishna Ráya*. At the other *Busty* is an inscription, dated *Sal.* 1479, *A. D.* 155$\frac{6}{7}$, in the reign of *Sri Vira Sadásiva Ráya*. A copy of this has been delivered to the Bengal government. From the *Pújári* of the *Busty*, one of the few *Jain* now remaining in the place, I obtained the following account.

Account by the *Jain*.

All the country between *Carcul* and *Cumty* belonged to a family of *Jain Rájás*, called by the common name of *Byrasu Wodears;* but each had a particular name, several of which the *Pújári* mentioned. The founder of this family, as we have already seen, was *Jenaditta*, a fugitive prince from the north of India. The last of these *Wodears* having no son, the greater part of his dominions was divided among his seven daughters, all of whom were called *Byra Devi;* and it is concerning them, that *Ferishta* has related an absurd fable. From these ladies *Barcuru* was taken by a *Jain* prince, whom the *Bráhmans* called *Budarsu*. The *Byra Devi* of this place built a fort, the ruins of which may still be traced. In her time the town was very large. During the war conducted by Lord Cornwallis it suffered much from a plundering band of *Marattahs*, but is again recovering fast. The *Pújári* showed me the ruins of a *Busty* built by one of the *Wodears*. The workmanship of the pillars and carving

Feb. 18. A fine stone.

is superior to any thing that I have seen in India, probably owing to the nature of the stone, which cuts better than the granite in common use, and preserves its angles better than the common pot-stone, of which many temples are constructed. The quarry is four cosses to the eastward. The stone is what Mr. Kirwan calls *Sienite* in a slaty form, and consists of hornblende slate, with layers of white quartz, and a little felspar interposed. In some pieces these are occasionally wanting, and the plates of hornblende are connected only by fibres of the same nature crossing the interstices between plate and plate. In some places again, the plates are waved, somewhat like the layers of timber at a knot, and there the quantity of quartz and felspar generally exceeds that of the hornblende.

Errors in the accounts of the *Bráhmans* and *Jain*.

As the *Bráhmans* err in denying their former dependance on the *Jain*, and endeavour as much as possible to conceal the former existence of such odious infidels; on the other side the *Jain* go into the contrary extreme, and deny altogether the dependance of their *Rájás* on the kings of *Vijaya-nagara*, which from many inscriptions, and other circumstances, is quite indubitable. The *Belalla* family, who, till the time of *Vishnu Verdana Ráya's* conversion, were undoubtedly *Jain*, probably governed their dominions, like other *Hindu* princes, by chiefs paying tribute, and holding their lands by military tenure. We have seen that, when their sovereign changed his religion, these chiefs threw off their allegiance, and continued in an independent anarchy, till subjected by *Buta Panda*, and soon after by *Hari-hara*. The princes of the throne of *Vijaya-nagara*, although favourers of the *Bráhmans* who follow *Vyása*, did not venture to dispossess the *Jain Rájás*, but employed them as their vassals, both in the civil and military government of the country. When the government at *Vijaya-nagara* became weak under *Sadásiva*, and fell into utter contempt by the death of *Ráma Ráya*, the *Jain Rájás* again asserted their independence; and in the inscription here, dated in the year $155\frac{6}{7}$, the *Byra Devi* no longer

CHAPTER XVI. Feb. 18.

acknowledges any superior. It was at this time that *Sadásiva Náyaka* of *Killidi* obtained a grant of *Tulava* from the king; and, taking advantage of the weakness of a female reign, he attacked the *Jain* without mercy. It must be observed, that the *Jain* are extremely obnoxious to the *Sivabhactars*, as they altogether deny the divinity of *Iswara;* but the *Bráhmans* who serve as priests *(Pújáris)* in his temples are favourites, although among the *Sivabhactars* they are not the order dedicated to the care of religin. In this part of the country the princes of *Ikeri* seem to have almost extirpated the *Jain;* but toward the south they met with a more obstinate resistance, and made no considerable conquests there, until the government of *Sivuppa*, who reigned from 1642 till 1670, and had the management of public affairs from about the year 1625. Even he was obliged to permit the *Jain Rájás* of the south to retain their authority as his vassals; and until the more vigorous government of *Hyder* they continued in power.

Feb. 19. Face of the country.

19th *February.—Honawera* being too far distant for two days journey with my cattle, I went a short stage of one coss and a half to *Shiraly.* The country, after ascending the little hill above *Batuculla*, is not steep; but much of the soil is very poor, in many places the *Laterite* being almost entirely naked. In some other places the soil is very good; and, although not level, a part of it has been formed into *Betta* land for the cultivation of rice; which confirms the account given by the people of *Haryadiká*, concerning the possibility of rendering all the hills of *Canara* arable. In general, however, they are considered as not fit for this purpose. At *Shiraly* is a river called *Shiraly-tari*, which comes from a temple on the *Ghats* that is named *Bhimeswara.* The tide comes up to *Shiraly*, a mile from the sea, and forces the traveller to swim his cattle. The banks at the ferry are rather stony; but round the village, there is much rice land, and good plantations of coco-nut trees. A great quantity of salt is made in the neighbourhood. *Shiraly* is a poor village, with three or four shops.

CHAPTER XVI.

Feb. 20.

20th *February*.—I went three cosses to *Beiluru*, which signifies the *cleared place*, and is a common name in countries where the dialect of *Karnata* prevails. My tents were, however, pitched in a very stately grove of the *Calophyllum inophyllum*, which in this part of the country is much planted near the villages. It grows to a large size, especially in sandy places near the sea. The common lamp oil of the country is expressed from its seed, by means of a mill turned by oxen. It is here called *Hoingay*, the name by which above the *Ghats* the *Robinia mitis* is known. In *Tulava* and *Malayala* it is called *Puna*, by us commonly written *Poon*. I suspect that the *Poon* of the eastern islands is different.

Poon, or *Puna*, the *Inophyllum* of Linnæus.

Appearance of the country.

From *Shiraly* to *Beiluru* the plain, between the sea and the low hills, varies in breadth from half a mile to a mile and a half. Its soil is in general good, and almost the whole of it is cultivated for rice; but few parts yield two crops annually. The sea-shore is skirted with groves of coco-nut palms, and the view is very beautiful. This plain is only watered by two small streams, the one of which is a branch of the *Shiraly*. Among the low hills are said to be, as usual, many narrow rice vallies. About three-quarters of a coss from *Beiluru* is *Murodéswara*, a temple standing on a lofty promontory that has been fortified, and at high water is insulated by a narrow channel. To the south of the promontory is a small bay sheltered by some rocks, which appear above the water, and afford protection to boats. Near this is a small village containing shops (*Bazars*). South-west from the promontory is a peaked island, which I suppose is what our seamen call Hog Island: the natives call it *Jaliconda*. In the offing from *Murodéswara* is a very large rock; and still farther west an island, which I suppose is what the seamen call Pigeon Island. It seems to be five or six leagues from the continent, and is pretty high, with a flat top. By the natives it is called *Naytrany Guda*, which last word signifies a hill. They say, that it has trees, with a small stream of fresh water, and good landing on its western side. Its caves are frequented by many wild

CHAPTER XVI. Feb. 20.

pigeons, whence the European name is probably derived. It is frequented also by boats for coral, with which its shores abound; and they likewise supply all the neighbouring continent with quick lime.

Worship of *Jetiga*.

To this island many people also go to pray, offer coco-nuts, and sacrifice to a stone pillar called *Jetiga*, which represents a *Buta*, or male devil. As this spirit is supposed to destroy the boats of those who neglect him, he is chiefly worshipped by traders and fishermen. On the continent there is another pillar called *Jetiga*; but as this devil is less troublesome than the one on the island, he receives fewer marks of attention.

Face of the country.

At *Beiluru* the inhabitants, living in scattered houses unprotected by forts, suffered much in the *Marattah* invasion; and there is not remaining above one half of the people that would be requisite to cultivate the ground. Owing to this cause, a great part of the coco-nut palms have died. A good tree is reckoned to produce annually 50 nuts. The rice lands near the sea, contrary to the common rule in *Malayala*, are reckoned more productive than those inland; but the soil here near the sea is not so sandy as that to the south, and the beach is quite firm; whereas to the south it is very heavy. The roads here are in general good; but that is entirely owing to the nature of the country, no pains having been bestowed on them by the natives. Every now and then the traveller comes to a river, hill, or rock totally impracticable for a carriage of any kind, and very difficult even for cattle that are carrying back loads.

Feb. 21.

21st *February*.—I went four cosses to the south side of the *Honawera* lake, and encamped in a coco-nut grove close by the ferry, which is above a mile wide, and without previous notice it is impossible to procure a conveyance capable of transporting cattle. The country from *Beiluru* to *Cassergoda*, about two miles from the ferry, is one of the most barren that I ever saw. It consists of low hills of *Laterite*, which extend down to the sea, and are almost destitute of soil. In some places a few stunted trees may be seen; but in general the rock is thinly scattered with tufts of grass, or of thorny plants. On the whole route there are only two narrow vallies. In these there are a few inhabitants, and a little good rice-land. On descending to *Cassergoda* the traveller enters a plain, which, after having been in the desert, looks well; but its soil is very poor, and it wants cultivators, especially to plant coco-nut palms, for which it is best fitted.

CHAPTER XVI.

Feb. 21.

Lake of Honawera.

The lake is of great extent, and, like that at *Kunda-pura*, contains many islands, some of which are cultivated. It reaches almost to the *Ghats*, and in the dry season is quite salt; but it receives many small streams, which during the rainy monsoon become torrents, and render the whole fresh. By the natives it is commonly called a river, but lake is a more proper term. The lake abounds with fish; but many more are taken in the sea, and, when salted, form a considerable article of commerce with the inland country. Each fishing-boat pays annually to government from four to six *Rupees*.

Garsopa.

Garsopa is a district including all the lands on the south side of the lake, and part of those on the north. The chief town, of the same name, stood at the extremity of the lake on its south side. This is now in ruins, and ought to be distinguished from a fort of the same name above the *Ghats*, which is laid down by Major Rennell.

Honawera, or Onore.

Honawera, or *Onore*, as we call it, was totally demolished by *Tippoo* after he had recovered it by the treaty of *Mangalore*. It was formerly a place of great commerce, and *Hyder* had established at it a dock for building ships of war. In the lake remain the wrecks of some which were sunk by our troops, after the fort was taken by assault. There is now a custom-house at the place, and some poor people have made offers of rebuilding the town if government would assist them. Five shops only have been rebuilt, and these are not in the situation of the former town. Boats now come from *Goa* and

CHAPTER XVI. Feb. 21. *Raja-pura;* and from merchants who live scattered near the bank of the lake, they purchase rice, pepper, coco-nuts, *Betel-nuts*, salt-fish, &c.

Pirates. The piratical boats from the *Marattah* coast are a great impediment to commerce; they hover especially round Pigeon Island, and have even the impudence to enter the rivers and inlets of the coast. Eight days ago they cut out from this place two boats; fifteen days ago one boat from *Manky;* and five days previous to that a fourth from *Batuculla.*

Fortified Island. A little way north from the entrance into *Honawera* lake is *Baswa Rasa Durga*, called by us Fortified Island. Its works were erected by *Sivuppa Náyaka* of *Ikeri*, and it contains coco-nut palms and plantain trees, with abundance of fresh water. Boats can occasionally go to it in the south-west monsoon; I imagine that vessels might even then find shelter in the channel between it and the continent. It produces the best quality of *Cavi*, or reddle, which is used by the natives for painting their houses.

The country called *Haiga*, or *Haira*, formerly belonging to *Rávana.* All the country, as far as *Gaukarna* inclusive, is called *Haiga*, and seems formerly to have been under the influence of *Rávana*, king of *Lanca*, or *Ceylon*. *Tritchenopoly* is said to have been the station of his most northern garrison on the eastern side of the peninsula. It is probable, that on the west side his dominions extended much farther. Although a king governing the *Racshasa*, or devils, he seems to have been a pious *Hindu;* and four temples, dedicated to *Siva* in *Haiga*, are said to have been erected by him. Their names are *Mahaboléswara* at *Gaukarna; Murodéswara*, which I passed yesterday; *Shumbéswara*, on the south side of the lake; and *Daréswara*, half a coss from *Hulledy-pura*. He also built *Sujéswara*, which is in *Kankána.*

Feb. 22. Appearance of the country. 22d *February.*—I crossed the inlet or lake, and went two cosses to *Hulledy-pura*, where the *Tahsildar* of *Honawera* resides. The road leads over a plain of rice-ground. The soil is poor, and much intersected and spoiled by creeks containing salt-water; this, however, might be easily excluded by dams. *Hulledy-pura* is an open town containing 352 houses, and is situated east from a considerable creek that runs through the plain. Its present name, signifying turmeric-town, was given to it by *Hyder;* for its original appellation, *Handy-pura,* signifying hog-town, was an abomination to the Mussulman. CHAPTER XVI. Feb. 22.

23d *February.*—I remained at *Hulledy-pura,* with a view of taking an account of the agriculture of the country, as an example of that which prevails in *Haiga.* Is found most of the cultivators to be *Bráhmans,* cunning as foxes, and much alarmed concerning my intentions in questioning them on such subjects. Great reliance, therefore, cannot be placed on what they said, especially as their answers were very contradictory. Feb. 23.

Tenures. Most of the cultivated lands in *Haiga* are private property; but the hills and forests belong to the government. Every man pays a certain *Shistu, Caicagada,* or land-tax, for the whole of his property *in cumulo,* and cultivates it in whatever manner he pleases. This prevents a traveller from being able to ascertain how far the tax is reasonable or oppressive. The proprietors are called *Mulugaras,* and are chiefly *Bráhmans.* Most of them cultivate their lands on their own account; but some let a part out to *Gaynigaras,* or renters; for *Gayni* signifies rent. Very few are encumbered with mortgages; the *Bráhmans* of *Haiga,* like most *Hindus,* being in many respects good economists.

Size of farms, and quantity of stock. Those who keep twenty ploughs are reckoned very wealthy; men in moderate circumstances have from four to six; but a very great number possess only one plough. The *Bráhmans* perform no labour with their own hands. One of them says, that he has four ploughs, with eight oxen, and keeps four male and four female servants. The *extra* expenses of harvest and weeding amount to 20 *Morays* of rough rice. He sows 20 *Morays* on low land, and 2 *Colagas* on hill land, and has a coco-nut garden containing 200 trees.

CHAPTER XVI.

Feb. 23.

Allowance for slaves.

In the farms of the *Bráhmans* most of the labour is performed by slaves. These people get daily $1\frac{1}{2}$ *Hany* of rice: a woman receives 1 *Hany*. Each gets yearly $2\frac{1}{2}$ *Rupees* worth of cloth, and they are allowed time to build a hut for themselves in the coco-nut garden. They have no other allowance, and out of this pittance must support their infants and aged people. The woman's share is nearly 15 bushels a year, worth rather less than $14\frac{1}{4}$ *Rupees;* to this if we add her allowance for clothes, she gets $16\frac{3}{4}$ *Rupees* a year, equal to 1*l.* 16*s.* $8\frac{1}{2}$*d.* The man's allowance is $22\frac{1}{2}$ bushels, or $23\frac{3}{4}$ *Rupees*, or 2*l.* 3*s.* $0\frac{1}{2}$*d.*

Wages of free servants.

A male free servant, hired by the day, gets 2 *Hanies* of rice. Both work from seven in the morning until five in the evening; but at noon they are allowed half an hour to eat some victuals that are dressed in the family as part of their allowance; and every cast can eat the food which a *Bráhman* has prepared.

Leases, rent, and land-tax.

The leases granted to tenants *(Gaynigaras)* are in general for from four to ten years. For each crop of rice they pay, for every *Moray* sown, 2 *Morays* of rice for land of the first quality; $1\frac{1}{2}$ for middling land; and 1 *Moray* of rice for the worst land: out of this the proprietor pays the taxes. The proprietor ought to find security for the payment of the land-tax. If he does not, a revenue officer is sent to superintend the harvest, to sell the produce, and to deduct the revenue from the proceeds. This is a miserable system, and one of a true *Hindustany* invention; as the person sent to collect the harvest received an allowance from the farmer; and thus one of the idle tatterdemalions that formed part of the clamorous suite of some great man had for a while the cravings of his appetite satisfied. If a man has given security, and fails in payment, on the third day after the term the security is called upon, and confined until the revenue is paid. The estate is never sold on account of arrears; and where the crop has failed from bad seasons, or other unavoidable causes, a deduction from the rent is generally allowed.

Feb. 23. Value of estates.

Estates that pay 20 *Pagodas* as land-tax, sell for about 100 *Pagodas*. The same quantity of land may be mortgaged for 50 *Pagodas*. The lender gets the whole profits of the estate for interest; but, whenever the borrower pleases to repay the debt, he may resume his land.

Both these circumstances, of estates being saleable, and capable of being let on mortgage, show, that they are of more value to the proprietors than what might be esteemed as an adequate reward for the labour and expense of cultivation. This is also evinced by the number of disputes that happen concerning succession. These, in the first instance, are determined by the *Tahsildar*, with the assistance of a *Panchaity*, or assembly of respectable neighbours. The decision is sent to the collector, who, as he sees reason, either confirms it finally, or investigates farther into the matter. Here a man's sons generally divide the estate equally among them; but the eldest manages the whole, and they live all together. When it comes to be divided among a number of cousins, owing to more than one brother of a family having children, the estate is commonly let, and the rent divided.

Quantity of seed required for an acre.

I measured three fields. The first containing 76,280 square feet, was rated in the public accompts at $3\frac{1}{2}$ *Morays* sowing, which would make the seed at the rate of $2,\frac{441}{1000}$ bushels an acre. The next plot measured 10,135 square feet, and was said to sow 8 *Hanies*, which is at the rate of $1,\frac{4}{10}$ bushel an acre. The third plot measured 21,356 square feet, and was said to require 20 *Hanies* of seed, which is at the rate of $1,\frac{668}{1000}$ bushel an acre. These agree so ill, that much dependance cannot be placed on the estimate; but, having no better grounds to proceed upon, I must take the average, or $2\frac{194}{1000}$ bushel as the seed required for one acre. This is nearly the same quantity with that used in the southern parts of *Malabar;* but much greater than would appear to be the case in Mr. Ravenshaw's district.

Divisions of rice-grounds.

In this neighbourhood there are three kinds of rice-ground; *Mackey*, *Bylu*, and *Caru*. The first is the higher ground, which

CHAPTER XVI.

Feb. 23.

gives only one crop in the year. The *Bylu* ground gives either two crops of rice, or one of rice and one of pulse. The *Caru* in the rainy season is so deeply inundated, that it cannot then be cultivated; and in the dry season gives one crop. The crop of rice produced in the rains is called *Catica;* that which grows in the dry season is called *Sughi.*

Quality and price of different rices.

In the accompanying Table, several particulars, relative to the cultivation of rice are detailed. The rice raised on *Mackey* ground is of a very inferior quality to that raised on the lower fields, and is that which is given to slaves and day labourers. Its average price is 12 *Pagodas* a *Corge*, or $21\frac{1}{4}$ pence a bushel; while that of the other is 20 *Pagodas* a *Corge*, or $35\frac{1}{2}$ pence a bushel.

Table explaining the cultivation of Rice at *Hulledy-pura.*

Kinds.	Soils for which each is fitted.	Crop in which each is sown.	Months each requires to grow.	Produce after deducting Seed.					
				Of one *Moray* sown.			Of one Acre.		
				Good crop.	Middling crop.	Poor crop.	Good crop.	Middling crop.	Poor crop.
				Morays	*Morays*	*Morays*	Bushels	Bushels	Bushels
Hany Samy	*Mackey* - -	*Catica*	$2\frac{1}{2}$	6	4	2	$19\frac{3}{4}$	$13\frac{1}{8}$	$6\frac{1}{2}$
Cochiga -	*Mackey* - -	*Catica*	$2\frac{1}{2}$	6	4	2	$19\frac{3}{4}$	$13\frac{1}{8}$	$6\frac{1}{2}$
Aria - -	*Bylu* - - -	*Catica*	4	10	8	8	33	$26\frac{1}{4}$	$13\frac{1}{8}$
Hulluga -	*Bylu* - - -	*Catica*	5	10	8	8	33	$26\frac{1}{4}$	$13\frac{1}{8}$
Cansu Surity	*Bylu* and *Caru*	*Sughi*	4	12	9	9	$39\frac{1}{2}$	$29\frac{1}{2}$	$16\frac{1}{2}$
Chituca -	*Bylu* and *Caru*	*Sughi*	4	9	6	6	$29\frac{1}{2}$	$19\frac{3}{4}$	$13\frac{1}{8}$

On *Mackie* land.

The only mode of cultivation used here for *Mackey* land is that called *Mola*, or sprouted-seed. In the month preceding, and that following the summer solstice, when the rains commence, the field is ploughed five times in the course of fifteen days, and all the while the water is confined. Before the last ploughing it is manured with dung from the cow-house. After the ploughings the field is smoothed with the *Noli-haligay*, or plank drawn by oxen (Plate XXII. Fig. 58.). It is then harrowed with the *Haligay*, which is the same with the *Halivay* of *Seringapatam* (Plate IV. Fig. 9.); and at the same time roots and weeds are pulled out by the hand. The water is then allowed to run off, and the prepared seed is sown broad-cast. If in three days any rain fall, the seed is lost, and the field must be sown again. For a month the water is allowed to run off as fast as it falls, after which it is confined on the rice until the crop is ripe. At the end of one moon and a half the weeds are removed by the hand.

Management of the grain.

The straw is cut with the grain. That intended for seed is immediately thrashed, and dried seven days in the sun. That intended for eating is put in heaps for eight days, and defended from the rain by thatch. The grain is then either beaten off with a stick, or trodden by oxen; and for three days is dried in the sun. The whole is preserved in *Morays* or straw bags, and kept in the house, till it can be boiled, and cleaned from the husks; for the farmer here never sells rough rice *(Paddy)*. All the grain that is cut in the rainy season is boiled, in order to facilitate the separation of the husks.

Catica crop of rice on *Bylu* land.

The *Catica* crop on *Bylu* land is mostly sown sprouted-seed: a very little only is transplanted. The manner of preparing the seed here is, to steep the straw bag containing it in water for an hour twice a day. In the intervals it is placed on a flat stone which stands in the house, and it is pressed down by another. The large-grained seeds require three days of this treatment, and are sown on the fourth day. The small-grained seeds are steeped two days, and sown on the third. For the *Catica* crop on *Bylu* land the five ploughings are given at the same season as for that on *Mackey* land. After the fifth ploughing the field in the course of five days is manured, and ploughed again twice, having all the while had the water confined on it. The mud is then smoothed with the rake drawn by oxen; the water is let off, and the prepared seed is sown broad-cast. It is managed afterwards exactly like the crop on *Mackie* land; and, as it ripens toward the end of the rainy season, the straw

CHAPTER XVI.

is in general well preserved. The rice however, to enable the husks to be easily removed, must be always boiled.

Feb. 23.

Sughi crop of rice on *Bylu* land.

The *Sughi* crop on *Bylu* land is entirely sown sprouted-seed. In the two months following the autumnal equinox, the field is ploughed eight times, then manured with cow-house dung, and ploughed a ninth time. It is then smoothed with the rake drawn by oxen, having been all the while inundated. The water is then drawn off by an instrument named *Cainully* (Plate XXV. Fig. 70.), which is wrought by a man like a rake. Small furrows are then made in the mud, to allow the water to drain off thoroughly, which is done by a small wooden instrument named *Shirula* (Plate XXV. Fig. 69.). In the month preceding the winter solstice the seed is sown. On the ninth day a little water is given; and, as the rice grows, the quantity is gradually increased. Till the end of the first month, the rain water in general is not expended; afterwards, by means of the machine called *Yatam*, the fields are supplied from small reservoirs and wells, or still more commonly from rivulets or springs, the water of which is raised by dams, and spread over the fields. These dams are very simple, consisting of earth and the branches of trees, with a few stones intermixed. The government in general is at the expense of making the reservoirs and dams.

Cultivation of rice on *Caru* land.

In the rainy season the *Caru* land is covered with water to the depth of from three to six feet; and on that account cannot be then cultivated. Afterwards it is cultivated exactly in the same manner as the *Bylu* land for the *Sughi* crop; and, although it yields only one crop in the year, the produce is not greater.

Cultivation of dry grains on *Bylu* land.

Upon some of the *Bylu* land, where there is not a supply of water for two crops of rice, a crop of some of the dry grains is taken in the *Sughi* season. The quantity of seed for all the kinds is the same, 2 *Colagas* for a *Moray* land, or $0,\frac{292}{1000}$ bushel an acre.

CHAPTER XVI.

Feb. 23.

Of the grains cultivated,

Ellu, or *Sesamum* produces 10 *Colagas*, or $1,\frac{463}{1000}$ bushel an acre.
Udu, *Phaseolus minimoo* R: produces 12 *Colagas*, or $1,\frac{755}{1000}$ bushel an acre.
Hessaru Bily (white) *Phaseolus mungo*, produces 14 *Colagas*, or $2,\frac{047}{1000}$ bushels an acre.
Pachy (green) produces 10 *Colagas*, or $1,\frac{463}{1000}$ bushel an acre.

For all these, the ground is ploughed five times in the month which precedes the shortest day; but the *Hessaru* is sown fifteen days later than the *Ellu*, and the *Udu* fifteen days later than the *Hessaru*. Before the last ploughing, the field is manured with ashes. The seed is sown broad-cast, and covered with the rake drawn by oxen. A month after seed time, the weeds are removed by the hand. Cattle will eat the straw of all the three pulses, but it is reckoned a worse fodder than the straw of rice.

Sugar-cane.

Sugar-cane is raised on *Mackey* land; but four years must intervene between every two crops; and for the first two years after cane, the rice does not thrive. The kind of cane used here is called *Bily-cabo*, which above the *Ghats* is called *Mara-cabo*. Inland they cultivate the *Cari-cabo*, which above the *Ghats* is called *Puttaputty*. In the month preceding the vernal equinox, the field is dug to the depth of ten inches with the hoe called *Cutari*. It is then ploughed five times, and smoothed with the rake drawn by oxen. Channels for conveying the water are then made, parallel to each other, and at the distance of three cubits. They are about nine inches wide, as much deep, and raised a little above the surface, the field being level. The intermediate beds are formed into ridges perpendicular to the channels, and resembling those of a potatoe field when it has been horse-hoed. The field is then covered with bushes, grass, dry cow-dung, and especially with dried parasitical plants, such as *Epidendra*, *Limodora*, &c. and the whole of these are burned to ashes as a manure. On the third day after this the canes intended for planting are cut into pieces, each containing three joints, and these are soaked in water for two days. Then in each furrow between two ridges are placed longitudinally two rows of these cuttings. Each

CHAPTER XVI. Feb. 23. piece leaves an interval of four inches between it and the next piece of the same row. The rows are placed near the bottom of the furrows, and are slightly covered with earth; and the furrows are then filled with water. All this must be performed before the new year commences at the equinox. Next day the furrows are again watered, and this is repeated on the eighth day, and afterwards once every four days. Two months after planting the field is weeded, and the ridges are repaired with a small hoe called *Halucatay*. The field is then manured with ashes, and with mud taken out of places where water lies deep. After this the watering is repeated once in four days till the commencement of the rainy season, when the ridges are thrown down, and new ones formed at the roots of each row of canes. In nine months these ripen without farther trouble. The water is in general raised, by the machine called *Yatam*, from wells in which it is found at the depth of from three to twelve feet from the surface. Three men are required to water and cultivate one *Moray* land, of which 1,$\frac{79}{100}$ are equal to an acre; but at the time they are so employed the farm requires little other work. The canes are very small, being from 2 to $2\frac{1}{2}$ cubits long, and about the thickness of a man's thumb. The juice is expressed by a mill, which consists of three cylinders moved by a perpetual screw. The force is applied to the centre cylinder by two capstan bars, wrought by six or eight men; and the whole machine is extremely rude. A *Moray* land produces 10 *Maunds* of *Jagory*, worth in all 5 *Pagodas*. This is at the rate of 4,$\frac{33}{100}$ hundred-weight an acre, worth about 3*l.* 10*s.* My informants seem to have greatly under-rated the quantity of *Jagory*.

In the very satisfactory answers which Mr. Read, the collector, has been so good as to send to my queries, he observes as follows: "As the land on which the sugar-cane is reared is all rice-ground, its cultivation might be increased to a very considerable extent; but not without lessening the quantity of rice, because, the market for sugar being neither so extensive nor so profitable, by any means,

Feb. 23.

as that for rice, few farmers would be at the expense of levelling and preparing ground for sugar-cane only They, probably, even now plant as much of their grounds with the sugar-cane as they think they can readily sell; but I do not think this cultivation will be ever much increased, because the late reduction in the export duties on rice, together with the increased demand for that article, make its cultivation of still more importance to the farmer than it was heretofore."

In this *Grámam* of *Hulledy-pura* there are 144 *Mulagaras*, or proprietors, whose estates in the revenue accompts are said to amount to 1443$\frac{2}{3}$ *Morays* sowing, or 805$\frac{3}{4}$ acres. They have besides, by actual enumeration, 7499 coco-nut palms, and 226 *Arecas*, young and old. The *Shistu*, or land-tax, is 1084$\frac{5\frac{1}{2}}{10}$ *Bahadury Pagodas*, or 436*l*. 16*s*. 11*d*.

Betta, or hill-land.

The land called here *Betta*, or *Hackelu*, like the *Parum* of *Malabar*, is formed into terraces; but on these rice is not cultivated. The only crops that it produces are *Sesamum* and *Udu* (*Phaseolus minimoo* Roxb:). On this kind of ground, after the soil has been ploughed three times, and manured with ashes, these grains are sown broad-cast in the second month after the summer solstice. The seed is covered with a hoe called *Ella-kudali*. The produce is much the same as on *Bylu* land; but there are no means by which the extent of *Betta* ground can be estimated.

Cumri cultivation.

In the hilly parts of the country, many people of a *Marattah* extraction use the *Cumri*, or *Cotu-cadu* cultivation. In the first season, after burning the woods, they sow *Ragy (Cynosurus)*, *Tovary (Cytisus cajan)*, and *Harulu (Ricinus)*. Next year they have from the same ground a crop of *Shamay* (*Panicum miliare* Lamarck.). These hills are not private property, and pay no land-tax; but those who sow them pay, for the right of cultivation, a poll-tax of half a *Pagoda*, or nearly 4*s*. On account of poverty, many of them at present are exempted from this tax.

CHAPTER XVI. Feb. 23.

I could here procure no satisfactory account of the garden cultivation, and shall not state what was said on the subject; but shall defer describing the gardens of *Haiga* until another opportunity.

Implements and cattle.

The only cattle in *Haiga* are buffaloes and oxen, about an equal number of each of which are used in the plough. This implement is here of the same form as that in the neighbourhood of *Seringapatam*. In *Haiga* they have no carts. Many of the cattle are imported from the countries adjacent to the *Ghats* near *Nagara*, and even these are of the poorest kind, nor are they larger than those of *Malayala* or *Tulava*. In the dry season, although fed with hay and straw, they are scarcely able to crawl. In the rainy season they grow fat, and strong, on the natural grass of the hills. Working oxen get the powder which separates from rice while it is beaten; buffaloes get the cake which is left after squeezing the oil from coco-nut kernels. The natives are ignorant that the cake which is formed in the same manner from *Sesamum* seed could be given to their cattle. Milk, and butter, or *Ghee*, are very dear, owing to the small number of cows, and their wretched condition.

Manure.

At night the cattle in every part of *Haiga* are kept in the house, where they are daily well littered with fresh materials. The litter and dung are carefully reserved, as a manure for rice-land; and the manure that is made from each kind of litter is kept in a separate dunghill. In the two months preceding, and in that following the winter solstice, the litter is dry grass, and the manure formed with it is called *Caradada Gobra*. Dry leaves of every kind of tree, except those that are prickly, and those of the *Govay (Goa)* or *Anacardium occidentale* Lin: are used as litter in the three following months, and form a manure which is called *Daryghena Gobra*. During the six remaining months, mostly of wet weather, the fresh leaves of trees are used for litter, and make a dung called *Hudi Gobra*, which is esteemed the best. The ashes of the family are kept in a separate pit, and are applied to different purposes. The cakes made of cow-dung are little used as fewel in this part of the country; but, to increase the quantity of manure, the women and boys follow the cattle while at pasture, and pick up the dung.

CHAPTER XVI. Feb. 23.

Weights.

The *Seer* weight at *Hulledy-pura* is the same with that of *Mangalore.* It ought to weigh 24 *Bombay Rupees;* but, these being a scarce article with the shopkeepers, in their stead *Dubs*, or *Dudus*, are commonly used, and are somewhat heavier.

The *Maund* for the common articles in the market *(Bazar)*	=40 *Seers*,	or $24\frac{55}{100}$ lb.
The *Maund* of pepper - -	=42 do.	or $26\frac{99}{100}$ lb.
of *Betel-nut* - -	=$45\frac{1}{2}$ do.	or $27\frac{92}{100}$ lb.
of dry coco-nut kernels	=48 do.	or $29\frac{46}{100}$ lb.
of *Jagory* - -	=44 do.	or $26\frac{82}{100}$ lb.

Dry-measure.

There are in use here two kinds of grain measure; one for the farmers, and one for the merchants. The basis of the farmer's measure is the *Hany*, containing $87\frac{3}{4}$ cubical inches.

2 *Hanies*	=1 *Colaga* - - -	=Bushel 0,08163
20 *Colagas*	=1 *Moray* or *Mudy* for common use	=Bushel 1,632
$22\frac{1}{2}$ *Colagas*	=1 *Moray* for sale - -	=Bushel 1,8136
15 *Colagas*	=1 *Moray* for seed - -	=Bushel 1,224

The basis of the measure by which merchants deal is the *Sida* of $32\frac{1}{2}$ cubical inches.

6 *Sidas*	=1 *Colaga* -	=Bushel $0,\frac{0907}{10000}$
20 *Colagas*	=1 *Moray*, or *Mudi*	=Bushel $1,\frac{814}{1000}$
30 *Morays*	=1 *Corge* -	=Bushel $54,\frac{419}{1000}$

The market *(Bazar) Mudy*, or *Moray*, and that of the farmers for sale, ought to be the same; but they differ $\frac{22}{1000}$ parts of a bushel. Any exact coincidence, however, cannot be expected from the rude implements which the *Hindus* employ in forming their measures. The different quantities that are called by the same denomination, when used for different purposes, seem to have been contrived

CHAPTER XVI. with a view of increasing the difficulty of the government in acquiring a knowledge of the real state of the country.

Feb. 23. Money. The common currency here consists of *Ikeri*, *Sultany*, and *Bahadury Varahas*, *Hoons*, or *Pagodas*; *Surat* and *Madras Rupees*, which are considered as of equal value, and pass for one quarter of a *Pagoda*; Silver *Fanams*, of the same kind as are current in *Malabar*, but here five and a half are only equal to one *Rupee*; and the *Any Dudu*, or elephant *Dubs*, coined by *Tippoo*, ten of which pass for one *Fanam*. The revenue is collected in a much greater variety of coins, according to a rate fixed by the collector, which private people also have adopted in their dealings; in forming it, therefore, due regard to justice has been observed.

Commerce. Having assembled the principal traders from the neighbourhood, they said, that in the government of *Hyder* the trade of *Honawera* was very considerable.

Pepper. The Company had established a factory, where they annually procured from above the *Ghats* about 750 *Candies* (520 lb.) of pepper, and 150 *Candies* the produce of the low country. The greater part of the pepper from above the *Ghats* was sold directly by *Hyder*. The chief of the factory contracted with individuals for the produce of *Billighy*, and of the low country, and advanced sometimes one-half, and at others the whole of the price, which varied from 110 to 120 *Rupees* a *Candy* of 520 lb. The merchants again began to make advances to the cultivators in the month after the autumnal equinox, which is about four months before crop season. These advances were always less in amount than what the merchant received from the Company; and the use of the balance, and two *Rupees* on each *Candy*, are alleged to have been all the profit which he received. The advances were not made to individuals; but the merchant gave a certain sum into the hands of some respectable *Gauda*, or chief of a village, who contracted to deliver a certain quantity of pepper at *Honawera*, at two *Rupees* a *Candy* less than the

Feb. 23.

Company's price. What profits these *Gaudas* had, the merchants do not know. There were no export duties; and nobody, except the Company, exported pepper.

Sandal-wood.

Hyder sold to the Company the whole of the sandal wood. None of it is produced below the *Ghats;* and the quantity then brought annually to *Honawera* was from two to three hundred *Candies* of 600 lb.

Cardamoms.

No cardamoms ever came this way.

Betel-nut, or *Areca.*

All the *Betel-nut* exported from *Honawera* was the produce of the low country between *Batuculla* and *Mirzee*, and amounted annually to 1000 *Candies* of 560 lb. worth 10,000 *Pagodas* (4034*l.* 19*s.* 7*d.*): of this the Company took a considerable quantity, both raw and boiled; and, for whatever they wanted, they had always a preference.

Coco-nuts.

The trade in coco-nuts, both whole, and in the state called *Copra*, or dried kernels, was in the hands of individuals. The value annually exported was about 12,000 *Rupees* (1206*l.* 1*s.* 1½*d.*). Owing to the great number of inhabitants, rice was then imported; at present it is the chief article of export. There never were in this country any manufactures. The oppressions of the late *Sultan* soon destroyed the whole trade; and the merchants are now just beginning to appear from their lurking-places, or to return from the countries to which they had fled. The exports at present, besides rice, are a little pepper, *Betel-nut*, and coco-nut; which are purchased by boats from *Goa*, *Bombay*, and *Raja-pura*. The *Marattah* pirates are a great obstacle to the inhabitants building boats for the exportation of goods.

The present price of staple articles here is:

	Pagodas
Rice for slaves per *Corge*	13
coarse	15
fine	22½
Betel-nut boiled, per *Candy*	15

CHAPTER XVI.

Feb. 23.

Betel-nut raw per *Candy*, *Pagodas*	-	11
Coco-nut *Copra* - -	-	10
whole per 1000 -	-	6
Black-pepper, per *Candy* -	-	30
Jagory of sugar-cane, *Maunds* 2½	-	1

Feb. 24. Appearance of the country.

24th *February*.—I went a long journey, called four cosses, and encamped on the south side of a river opposite to *Mirzee*. About two cosses from *Hulledy-pura*, I came to a town named *Cumty*. It seems to have been formerly a place of some note. Its lanes are straight, and fenced with stone walls, and it has many coco-nut gardens. Twice it had the misfortune of having *Tippoo's* army encamped in its vicinity; and on both occasions it was burned down by some of the irregulars. On its south side is a plain, intersected by a salt-water creek, which allows much salt to be made. The soil of the plain, which extends all the way from *Hulledy-pura*, is very sandy. For a coss north from *Cumty*, the ground is high, with very little cultivation; but a great part of it seems to be fit for being formed into *Mackey*, or at least into *Betta* land. Between this and the river is a very fine plain, called *Hegada*, from a small town near which I encamped. The low lands here are subject to being inundated by the swelling of the river, which frequently spoils the *Catica* crop of rice when the farmers attempt to cultivate it. The appearance of the farm-houses at *Hegada* denotes that the inhabitants are in a much more comfortable situation than is usual in India. The river is called *Tari-holay*, and abounds with fine oysters. At this place, which is three cosses from the sea, it is at this season about 600 yards wide. The tide and salt-water go up about three cosses farther. Its northern bank is high, and was formerly occupied by a fort and town called *Midijay*, corrupted by the Mussulmans into *Mirzee*, *Merzee*, and *Merjawn*. This place suffered much in a siege which it stood against *Hyder*; and in the oppressive government of his son it was entirely deserted. The river formed the northern boundary of the dominions of a *Jain* family, who resided at *Cumty*, and possessed the country as far south as *Honawera*. CHAPTER XVI.

Feb. 24. Plantations.

There being in this neighbourhood many palm gardens, I assembled the cultivators, and obtained from them the following account:

Coco-nut.

In this part of the country the sandy downs near the sea are not much esteemed for the cultivation of the coco-nut. Here the farmers prefer the banks of salt-water inlets; and near these the rising grounds are generally planted, and the houses are built in the gardens. About towns, many gardens are enclosed with stone walls; in villages, the proprietors are contented with fences of earth, like those in *Malabar*. Once in two years the whole garden is dug, and fresh earth at the same time is spread throughout, by the industrious, to the depth of two inches; but lazy people allow only a little to the roots of each tree. The garden gets no other manure, except some salt to the young seedlings when these are transplanted. For six months in the year they must be watered once in four days. A young tree, fit for transplanting, costs two *Dubs* (about a penny), and is set in place of an old one which has died; so that the garden is never suffered to decay. In a good soil, the trees when ten years old begin to produce fruit, but in bad soils they are much later. Common reckoning says, that a coco-nut palm lives 100 years; but some die at 20, and many at all intermediate ages. At all times plantains and *Yams (Dioscorea)* are raised in the coco-nut gardens. Rich people never draw juice from their coco-nut trees, except in one year when they are young. For some years before the young palms can bring the fruit to maturity, they produce flowers; but, by extracting juice for one year, their coming to perfection is hastened. If any disease happen to the tree, rich men, to give relief to the sickly plant, do not extract juice, as is usual in some places, but with a sharp iron they bore a hole into the pith above the diseased part. Poor people, not being able to raise money to pay the wages of their workmen, give them

CHAPTER XVI. Feb. 24.

annually a certain number of trees for extracting juice, with which they can procure a daily subsistence. This compels the poor man, once in four or five years, to take juice from his trees. Besides, although this practice soon kills the tree, it gives much more immediate profit, especially in poor soils. In good soils, the nuts are of equal value with the juice; as a good tree in such a situation gives on an average, 80 full grown nuts, worth 25 *Rupees* a thousand; and 100 trees in such a soil, good and bad, young and old, produce 3000 nuts, which is at the rate of three quarters of a *Rupee* for each. In an indifferent soil the same number of trees produce only 1000 nuts, which is only at the rate of a quarter of a *Rupee* for each; but the coco-nut trees, good and bad, produce each a *Rupee* worth of juice, one-half of which goes to the extractor, and one-half is clear profit to the proprietor. One man can collect the juice of forty trees, and his share of the produce, being 20 *Rupees* (2*l.* 0*s.* 3¼*d.*), is reckoned a sufficient maintenance for a man, his wife and children; for the people who extract the juice of palms are of a very low cast.

Betel-nut, or *Areca*.

The *Betel-nut* gardens are cultivated, at a distance from the banks of rivers, in the upper ends of narrow vallies, which contain *Bylu* land. The best soil is red, and contains shining particles, which I take to be mica. This soil is called *Cagadala*. Next in value to this is *Gujiny*, which is a black loose earth. The worst soil is called *Betta*, and is a hard earth composed of decayed or broken *Laterite*. The *Cagadala* is found in the bottoms of the vallies at their upper end, and is watered from a small reservoir, whence the water sometimes runs off by sluices, and sometimes is raised into the channels by the machine called *Yatam*. The *Gujiny* is found very low and level, where the hills forming the valley begin to recede a little from each other. In such land the water at all seasons of the year stands in the ditches, but is of a quality pernicious to the *Areca*, which must be watered from springs or rivulets. The *Betta* land forms the upper parts of the declivities of the hills, and must be irrigated, by the hand, with water drawn from wells that are dug in the valley below. The garden must be fenced with a wall of stone or mud, on the upper side of which a deep drain must be formed to carry off the water, which during the rainy season descends from the hills in torrents. In this respect the *Cagadala* requires most trouble, and its watering is more expensive than that of the *Gujiny;* yet, owing to its being more productive, it is more profitable. The produce of the *Betta* land is still smaller than that of the *Gujiny*, and its cultivation is attended with much more trouble; yet it is worth while to plant the whole that is near a man's house; for to a certain extent the family can perform the watering without great inconvenience.

Immediately before the winter solstice, the nuts for seed are cut, and are exposed three days to the sun, and three nights to the dew. In the mean time, a plot of *Cagadala* soil is dug for a seed-bed. In this the seeds are placed at four inches distance, and are half immersed in the ground. They are then covered with dung; and, that having been covered with straw, they are watered every other day until the second month after the vernal equinox. The rainy season then commences; and a drain must be dug to prevent the water from lying upon the bed. In the first or second month after the autumnal equinox, another piece of ground is hoed, and in this are placed the nuts which are then said to be *Mola*, as they have shoots sprouting from them a cubit long. The nuts in this bed are placed at about the distance of a foot from each other, and are buried an inch under ground. Every other day, during the dry season, they are well manured and watered. In this bed they remain fifteen months; and in the month preceding the winter solstice, they are manured with dung made from dry grass-litter; while in the month following the vernal equinox, the manure, which they receive, is that formed of dry leaves. During the month before and the month after the autumnal equinox, the young palms are *(Sussi)* fit for planting.

CHAPTER XVI. Feb. 24.

The garden having been properly inclosed, and secured from the torrents of the rainy season; and tanks, wells, or canals for supplying it with water, having been formed; the *Cagadala* soil is levelled into terraces like rice-ground, and formed into beds seven cubits wide. Between every two beds is a deep channel, to carry off the rain water; and in the middle of each is a small channel to convey the water that is to refresh the palms; and which, as it runs along, a man throws out on their roots with a *spatha*, that has fallen from the trees. On each side of the bed is planted a row of the *Arecas*, distant from each other five cubits, and between every two *Arecas* is set a young plantain tree. The garden is then manured with dung made from fresh leaves, and ever afterwards during the dry season it must be watered once in two days. For the first four years, it must be dug over in the month preceding the autumnal equinox, and at three different seasons must be manured with the three different kinds of manure. Afterwards, it is manured once a year only, in the second month after the autumnal equinox; and it is once in two years only that it requires to be dug. The *Betel-nut* is improved by the plantain trees, which keep the earth cool and moist; and therefore these are always continued, except where it is intended to train up the *Betel-leaf* vine upon the *Areca*, which is the manner wherein that plant is here cultivated. In this case, in the tenth year, the plantain trees are removed; and in the second month after midsummer, five cuttings of the *Betel-vine*, each containing three joints, are placed round every *Betel-palm*, while one of their ends is buried in the ground. They are then manured with the leaves of the *Nelli (Phyllanthus emblica)*. Immediately after the autumnal equinox, the ground round the young vines must be hoed, and manured with dung made from fresh leaves. Ever afterwards, it must be manured three times a year. As the vines grow, they must be tied up to the palms. In eighteen months they begin to produce leaves fit for sale; in the third year they are full sized; two years they continue to give a full crop; in the

Betel-leaf, or Piper Betle.

following year the crop is bad, and then the vines are lifted, and new ones are planted in their stead. The *Betel-palm*, or *Areca*, in *Cagadala* soil begins to ripen fruit in ten years, is in full crop at fifteen, and continues in perfection for thirty years. They then die; and as the old ones decay, new ones are planted. Each tree yields two bunches, which ripen at different times between the autumnal equinox and winter solstice. The produce of a hundred trees, young and old, is reckoned five *Maunds* of boiled nut, or thirty-five *Bazar Colagas* by measure of nuts in the husk, as they come from the tree. The five *Maunds* are one fourth of a *Candy*, or 140 lb. The present price of boiled *Betel-nut* is fifteen *Pagodas*; each tree therefore, young and old, produces to the value of $3\frac{636}{1000}$ pence, or a hundred trees produce fifteen *Rupees*. The cultivators boil the *Betel-nut*.

In *Gujiny* ground, in order to remove the water off the soil, the drains between the beds must be one cubit and a half deep. It is irrigated once in seven days only, from the same sources that supply the *Bylu* rice-ground. In this soil, plantains and *Betel-leaf* grow in the same manner as in *Cagadala* gardens. A hundred trees, young and old, on *Gujiny* ground, are reckoned to produce four *Maunds* of boiled *Betel-nut*, worth twelve *Rupees*.

On the *Betta* land no drains nor channels are required; but round the root of every palm a small bank is formed to confine the water, which is given once in two days. In such gardens, plantains, but not *Betel-leaf*, are reared. The trees in this soil do not come into full fruit till they are twenty years of age, and a hundred produce only two *Maunds* and a half of boiled nut, worth seven *Rupees* and a half. A man and his wife can manage a garden of 500 trees; some of which will grow on *Betta*, and a proportion on either *Cagadala*, or *Gujiny*, or on both. They require no assistance at crop season; but, unless the keeper be an active man, he will require some help when the garden is hoed. The expense of first planting a garden is commonly reckoned 100 *Rupees* for every 500 trees; but in

CHAPTER XVI.

Feb. 24.

level situations it will be much less, and in steep places much more. Some people go to 50 *Pagodas* for 100 trees, or 2 *Rupees* for each. No value is put upon the future expense, which is merely that of the keeper and his wife, who get $2\frac{1}{4}$ *Hanies* of coarse rice daily, and 4 *Rupees* a year for clothing; that is to say, $37\frac{1}{4}$ bushels of rice, worth $32\frac{812}{1000}$ *Rupees*, and 4 *Rupees* in money; or in all 36 *Rupees* 13 *Anas* (3*l.* 14*s.* 3*d.*). It must be observed, however, that after the first year the plantains are adequate to the defraying of this expense, which is therefore not charged in the accompt. The farmer has therefore, on an average, 50 *Rupees* a year, for an original advance of from one to two hundred; but out of this must be deducted the revenue. His profit is much larger where he has a sale for *Betel-leaf*. It appears to me, that the gardens here are formed with more care, and at a greater expense, than in *Malabar*, where a colony of *Haiga Bráhmans* would be highly beneficial.

Feb. 25. Face of the country.

25th *February*.—In the morning, having crossed the river, I took a circle of about six miles into the country east from *Mirzee*, in order to see some forests that spontaneously produce black pepper. The whole of the country through which I passed was hilly; but I met with several narrow vallies well watered, though not fully cultivated, owing to a want of inhabitants. Many of the hills were so barren, steep, and rocky, that I was soon forced to dismount from my horse, and proceed on foot. These hills consist entirely of naked *Laterite*. Other hills, which were those I sought after, were covered with stately forests.

Pepper growing spontaneously.

The pepper-plant (*Piper nigrum*) seems to grow spontaneously on the sides of all the narrow vallies in the interior of *Haiga*, where the soil is so rich and moist as to produce lofty trees close to each other, by which a constant coolness is retained. In such places the pepper-vine runs along the ground and the roots of bushes, and propagates itself entirely by striking its roots into the soil, and then again sending out new shoots. The natives say, that without assistance it cannot ascend a tree; and that, unless it is exposed in such a situation to sun and air, it never produces flowers. In order to procure fruit from a hill which spontaneously produces the pepper-vine, the proprietor cuts all the underwood and bushes, and leaves only the large trees, and a number of the young ones sufficient to exclude the violence of sun, but to allow of a free circulation of air. Four cubits from tree to tree is reckoned a proper distance. The ends of the vines, which were lying on the ground, are then tied up to the nearest trees. Any kind of tree answers the purpose; but those of about eight inches or a foot in diameter are preferred, as it is easy to climb such for the purpose of gathering the pepper. A quantity of leaves are then placed round the root of the vine, to rot, and to serve as a manure. In the course of the year the vine, so far as it has been tied, strikes its roots into the bark of the tree; but the shoots above that, hang down. Twice a year afterwards these are tied up, and strike root, till they spread over all the large branches of the tree. In places where no vines have naturally sprung, the owner, after having dug a small spot round the tree to loosen the earth, propagates them by planting slips near the roots of the trees on which he wishes them to climb. The early part of the rainy season is the time proper for this operation. In five years, after having been managed in this manner, a hill begins to produce fruit, and in eight years is in full bearing. The vines live about thirty years; when others, that are found creeping on the ground in their natural state, are tied up in their stead; or, where these happen to be wanting, shoots or cuttings are planted near the trees. There is no difference in the quality between the pepper springing spontaneously from the seed, and that growing from cuttings; nor is the pepper growing in gardens either better or worse than that growing on a hill, managed as I am now describing. These hills producing pepper require no trouble, but the tying up of the plants, keeping the forest clear of underwood, and collecting the pepper. They are

CHAPTER XVI. Feb. 25.

manured in the following manner. In the month succeeding the vernal equinox, a hole three or four inches above the ground is made into the trunk of any very large tree that is situated near the top of the hill. Into this are put some burning coals, and, for an hour, a fire is kept up with fresh fewel. After this, the tree will burn inwardly for two days, and is then killed. A large insect immediately takes possession of the trunk, and works its nest into the wood. In the next rainy season, the whole falls down into a rotten dust, which the rain washes away, so as to disperse it over the face of the hill below. The crop season commences about the winter solstice, and it continues rather more than two months. A man can in one day gather three *Colagas*, farmer's measure, or almost one peck of the *amenta*. These are dried three days in the sun, and then are rubbed with the feet on a piece of smooth ground, to separate the grains; which, having been cleared from the husks and foot-stalks, are again dried two days in the sun, and tied up for sale in straw bags or *Morays*. Seventy-five *Colagas* of *amenta* are required to make one *Bazar Moray* (bushel $1\frac{1}{10}$) of dry pepper, which weighs 3 *Maunds* (about 84 lb.); so that a man daily collects about $3\frac{14}{25}$ lb. of dry pepper. These hills were formerly valued; and, according to their extent, each paid as a land-tax so many *Maunds* of pepper, the *Maund* containing 60 *Seers*. The same valuation is now continued; but the *Maund* is reduced to 40 *Seers*, and converted into money, at the rate of a *Pagoda*, which is in favour of the proprietor. Still one half of these hills is waste, owing to a want of hands to cultivate them; and on that account three-fourths of the revenue are remitted to the proprietors, who are also favoured by having all the rice-ground lying among these hills free from tax. This has been given them, on a supposition that its produce was only adequate to feed the people who are employed in cultivating the pepper.

Produce of the forests. *Teak.*

So far as I went, no *Teak* grows in these forests; but I am told, that

Feb. 25.

it is procurable farther inland. The landlords (*Malugaras*) pretend, that all the timber trees are their property, but that none of them are saleable.

Nutmeg.

The wild nutmeg and *Cassia* are very common. As the nutmegs ripen, the monkies always eat up the outer rind, and mace; so that I could not procure one in a perfect state. They are collected from the ground, after having been peeled by the monkies, and are sold by some poor people to the shopkeepers; but they have little flavour; and the demand for them is very small. Although they are, doubtless, of a distinct species from the nutmeg of *Amboyna*, it is probable, that by proper cultivation and manure their quality might be greatly improved; and that, in the situations where they now grow spontaneously, they might be reared as the supporters of the pepper vine; which would produce copiously, and of an excellent quality, were the same pains bestowed on it here as is done in the gardens above the *Ghats*, where by far the best pepper grows.

Laurus Cassia.

The *Cassia* belongs to government, and is in general given in lease; but at present no renter can be procured. Its quality also might, no doubt, be greatly improved; and by cutting the shoots, when of a proper size, and cleaning and rolling up the bark neatly, it might be made equal to the *Cassia* of *China*.

Strata.

On my return from the pepper hills to *Mirzee*, I passed a very fine plantation of *Betel-nut* palms, belonging to four *Bráhmans*, and containing many thousand trees. It was placed on the two steep sides of a very narrow valley, well supplied with water from springs. Here I observed the first regular *strata* since leaving *Pali-ghat*. They consisted of very soft pot-stone, probably impregnated with hornblende slate, as they seem to be a continuation of the quarries of slaty sienite, from which the temples at *Batuculla* have been supplied with stone. I have already noticed the affinity that prevails between the hornblende and pot-stone rocks in the dominions of *Mysore*. The *strata* at this garden are vertical, and run nearly north and south.

CHAPTER XVI.

Feb. 25. Appearance of the country.

Having returned to *Mirzee*, I went two cosses and a half to *Hirigutty*. Part of the country through which I passed was very barren, consisting of low hills covered with stunted trees. The soil of other parts was good; but, owing to a want of inhabitants, was much neglected. Near *Hirigutty*, there is on the northern side of the river a remarkably fine plain. It does not seem to be well cultivated, and has suffered lately from the breaking down of a dam, which has permitted a great part of it to be inundated with salt-water.

History of *Haiga*, according to its *Bráhmans*.

At *Hirigutty*, I collected several *Haiga Bráhmans*, who were said to be the best informed men concerning the history of the country. The *Shanaboga*, or accomptant of the temple of *Daréswara*, produced a book called *Bahudunda*, which, they said, was written by a certain *Subahitta*, or *Bráhmany* chief, who will hereafterwards be mentioned. On the authority of this book the *Shanaboga* said, that *Parasu Ráma* created *Haiga* at the same time that he formed *Tulava* and *Malayála*, and he then also appointed certain *Bráhmans* to inhabit these lands. *Tulava* he gave to the *Mittu Bráhmans*, and *Haiga* to those called *Nagar* and *Mutchy*. These people were not true *Bráhmans;* but they kept possession of the country till after the commencement of the *Kali-yugam*. The country was then seized upon by two casts of impure origin, the *Mogayer* and the *Whalliaru*. The former are the fishermen of *Haiga;* the latter I have had frequent occasion to mention; and to this tribe the *Rájá* belonged. At length a *Sannyási*, who had visited the country, induced *Myuru Verma* to invade it. He was king of *Banawási* and *Gutti* in *Karnata*, and by cast a *Baydar*, which is a tribe of *Telingana*. His attack was successful, and he conquered *Haiga*, *Tulava*, and *Kankána*. He then brought a colony of five thousand true *Bráhmans* from *Ahichaytra*, a city in *Telingana*, and settled them in *Haiga*. He brought others of the same origin to *Kankána* and *Tulava*. A thousand of these *Haiga Bráhmans* lost cast immediately, having omitted the performance of certain prayers *(Mantrams)* which were necessary to purify the country before they took possession. The remaining four thousand obtained the whole lands of *Haiga*, and continued to enjoy them until *Myuru Verma* was obliged to fly by *Nunda*, the son of *Utunga*, one of the *Whalliaru*, who recovered the dominions of his ancestors. This low fellow seized on the lands that had been granted to the four thousand *Bráhmans*, and forced them to retire to *Ahichaytra*. He was succeeded by his son *Chanda Sayana*, whose mother, being a dancing girl from the temples of *Karnata*, had educated him so as to have a due respect for the sacred order. Soon after his accession to power, he invited back the *Bráhmans;* and, having given up the whole of his authority to their *Subahitta*, or chief, the author of the book, he made all his *Whalliaru* the slaves of the sacred order. So long as *Chanda Sayana* lived, he was called *Rájá*, and the *Subahitta* continued to govern in his name. On his death without children, the *Subahitta* was at a loss what to do; as according to the laws of his cast he could not assume the regal title, and as there was no *Rájá* under whose authority he could act. He therefore invited *Solva Krishna Devarasu Wodearu* of *Anagundi* to take possession of *Haiga*, which had never before been subject to *Vijaya-nagara*. This prince accordingly came; but, far from allowing the *Subahitta* to enjoy any authority, he imposed a land-tax on the *Bráhmans*, and gave all the country to a *Jain Polygar*, *Itchuppa Wodear Rájá* of *Garsopa*. No date is assigned in the book for these extraordinary events, which nobody but a *Haiga Bráhman* can possibly believe. In order to conceal the long subjection to the infidel *Jain*, in which the *Bráhmans* of *Haiga* had been compelled to live, they bring down the time of *Myuru Verma* to that of the latter princes, or usurpers of the throne of *Vijaya-nagara*. Many inscriptions render it indubitable, that *Haiga* belonged to the kings of *Karnata* long before the time of *Krishna Ráyalu*. Copies of all these, which I now quote, were in the possession of the very *Bráhmans* who gave me the foregoing account. The temple at *Daréswara* has two grants engraved

CHAPTER XVI. Feb. 25.

on copper-plates. The one is dated *Sidarti* of *Sal.* 1422, on the 14th of the moon in *Bhádrapada*, in the reign of *Déva Ráya Wodearu Trilochia*, &c. &c. This title of king of the three people *(Trilochia)* is said to be peculiar to the kings of *Vijaya-nagara*, as is also the title of king of the three seas. The title of *Trilochia* seems well enough applied, as these princes governed the tribes who speak the *Telinga*, *Tamul*, and *Karnataca* languages. This date apparently does not agree well with the *Ráya Paditti;* for the last *Déva Ráya* which it mentions ended his reign in the year of *Sal.* 1377. But, as we shall afterwards see, this *Déva Ráya* may have been one of the names of the usurper who reigned in 1422. The other grant on copper is by *Solva Krishna Devarasu Wodearu Trilochia*, &c. &c. and is dated *Sal.* 1481, on the 15th of *Ashádha*, in the year *Calayucti.* This agrees very well with the chronology of *Ramuppa.* A third grant to the same temple is by *Krishna Devarasu Wodearu Trilochia*, &c. &c. in the year *Vicari* of *Sal.* 1462, on the 1st of *Kartika.* This also agrees with the chronology of *Ramuppa.* Another, in the time of *Trinetra Solva Narasingha Nayaka*, king of the three seas, and of *Anagundi*, &c. &c. is dated in *Durmati Sal.* 1424, 14th *Bhádrapada.* Among other strange titles assumed by this prince, he is said to be able to pull all other potentates by the whiskers. In it he commands *Devarasu Wodear*, probably the lieutenant of *Haiga*, to grant such and such lands to the *Bráhmans.* It is clear therefore, that before the time of *Krishna Ráyaru* the kings of *Anagundi* were sovereigns of *Haiga*, and that all the lands did not belong to the *Bráhmans.* Another grant, for erecting an inn for travellers, is dated on the same day and year, and by order of *Solva Déva Ráya Wodearu*, *Rájá* of *Nagara* (not the present *Nagara* but *Vijaya-nagara)*, *Haiga*, *Tulava*, *Kankana*, &c. &c. We here find, that the second *Narasingha* of the usurping princes is sometimes called also *Déva;* and the same probably was the case with the first *Narasingha*, which will reconcile the chronology of the first grant with that of *Ramuppa.* The inscription on stone at the temple of *Gunavunti*, in

Garsopa district, of which a copy has been presented to the Bengal government, mentions, that *Itchuppa Wodearu Pritani (Jain Rájá* of *Garsopa)* granted certain lands to that temple by order of *Pritápa Déva Ráya Trilochia*, &c. &c. of the family of *Hari-hara*, &c. &c. in *Virodi Sal.* 1332, on the 10th of *Márgasírsha*. This is *Déva Ráya* the First, and agrees very well with the chronology of *Ramuppa*.

Feb. 25.

Account from a book of the *Jain*.

A very intelligent *Bráhman* from *Batuculla* says, that he had consulted a book in the possession of a *Jain Sannyási*, which stated, that the *Byrasu Wodear* family of *Carculla* was descended from the *Belalla Ráyas*, the supreme kings of *Karnata*. The last male of this branch of the family had seven daughters, all called *Byra-Dévi*. When the *Rájá* died, his country was divided among his daughters in seven portions; and *Krishna Ráyaru* was so gallant, as to remit the whole tribute to them, as being ladies. The eldest sister, *Doda Byra Dévi*, lived at *Batuculla*. The second sister married the son and heir of *Itchuppa Wodear* of *Garsopa*, who seems to have been the tributary *Rájá* of *Haiga*. This marriage produced only one daughter; and none of her aunts having had children, she united again in her person the sovereignty of all the dominions of *Carculla*. To these she added *Haiga*; and, during the weakness of the princes of *Anagundi*, in the reign of the last usurper, she seems to have refused all marks of submission to their authority. She lived sometimes at *Garsopa*, and sometimes at *Batuculla*, until she was destroyed by the *Sivabhactars* of *Ikeri*, who were assisted by an insurrection of the *Halypecas*; and who, in conjunction with that low, barbarous tribe, almost exterminated the *Jain* of *Haiga*, and the northern districts of *Tulava*. There is still a man living at *Dharmastilla*, six cosses distant from *Jamal-ábád*, who is named *Comara Hegada*, and who is looked upon as a descendant in the male line of the *Carculla* family, and legal representative of the *Belalla Ráyas*, who began to govern *Karnata* in the year of our Lord 684. This man may very probably be of the family of the *Carculla Rájás*; but, in fact, these were descended from *Jenaditta*, a fugitive from the north of *India*;

CHAPTER XVI.

Feb. 25.

and a desire of flattering the princes of the *Jain* sect, who were the most powerful in these latter days, probably occasioned the legend, in the book of the *Sannyási*, to trace up their origin to the *Belalla* family.

Hirigutty, which has no market (*Bazar*), stands on a fine plain, about two miles from the river; and at some distance, toward the east and north, has rugged barren hills.

Feb. 26. Appearance of the country.

26th *February*.—I went three cosses to *Gaukarna*. There was a thick fog, which prevented me from seeing the country; but near the road it was a plain, consisting mostly of rice fields; many of which, by the breaking down of the bank, had been inundated with salt-water. At the western extremity of this plain is a ridge of low barren hills, which bend round to the sea, and separate the plain on the banks of the river from that on which *Gaukarna* stands, about a coss north from the mouth of the river. The plain of *Gaukarna* is well cultivated, and consists of rice fields intermixed with coco-nut gardens.

Gaukarna.

Gaukarna, or the cow's horn, is a place of great note among the *Bráhmans*, owing to a celebrated image of *Siva* called *Mahaboléswara.* The image is said to have been brought from the mountain *Coila* by *Ravana*, king of *Lanca*. He wished to carry it to his capital; but having put it down here, the idol became fixed in the place, where it stands to this day. The building, by which the idol is at present covered, is very mean. *Gaukarna* is a scattered place, buried among coco-nut palms; but enjoys some commerce, and contains 500 houses, of which *Bráhmans* occupy one half.

Account of *Haiga* by the *Bráhmans* of *Gaukarna.*

I assembled the most distinguished of these *Bráhmans*, who informed me, that the book produced yesterday by the *Shanaboga* of *Daréswara* is not considered by them as of good authority. That every *Shanaboga* has a *Bahudunda*, containing the papers and deeds belonging to his office, and which are generally preceded by such an account of past times, as the first person of the family who enjoyed the office could obtain. These *Bahudundas* the *Vaidika*

Bráhmans hold in great contempt; but, as the office of *Shanaboga* has in numerous instances continued for many generations in the same family, I am inclined to think that from this source much historical information might be procured. The *Bráhmans* here are all *Smartal*, of true *Panch Dravada* extraction, and despise the *Haiga Bráhmans*, as being greatly their inferiors. When I interrogated them concerning the history of the country, they said that it was contained in a book in their possession, called *Seinghadri Utracunda*, or the second volume of *Seinghadri*, a work composed by God in the form of *Vyása*, who wrote the eighteen *Puranas*. They suppose, that this was done long before the creation of this part of the world, and therefore look upon all the historical part as entirely prophetical. I found that none of them had ever been at pains to read the book, and they therefore spoke of its contents merely from report, or tradition. They say that it brings the history of *Kérala*, *Tulava*, *Haiva* (the *Sanskrit* name for *Haiga*), and *Kankana*, no lower down than the time of *Myuru Verma's* grandson. It is written in the character of *Tulava*, which is the same with that of *Malayála*, and in the *Sanskrit* language. It contains no dates, and seems to be, as usual, an idle rhapsody, in which are foretold the great deeds of five princes of one family, who were to be great favourers of a certain sect of *Bráhmans*. These five princes are *Trenetra Cadumba*, *Hæmanga*, *Myuru Verma*, *Locadita*, and *Chanda-Sayana*; which last the *Haiga Bráhmans* suppose to have been a *Whalliaru*. The dominion of these princes extended all over the country created by *Parasu Ráma*, from Cape *Comorin* to *Surat*. In all this country, at the accession of *Myuru Verma*, there was no true *Bráhman*; but for each division of it that prince brought a colony from *Ahichaytra*. The *Namburis* formed one of these colonies, all of which have in some measure lost cast, or at least have been degraded, by a disobedience of the orders of *Sankara Achárya*. At that time, the *Rájá* of *Ahichaytra* was a *Jain*; but he favoured the *Bráhmans* who followed *Vyása*, his wife's mother having been

CHAPTER XVI. Feb. 26. very intimate with one of these persons, and having educated her daughter in a due regard for the sect. Shortly before that time, this sect had risen into considerable reputation in *Andray*, by the efforts of *Buta Achárya*, and was afterwards spread throughout the peninsula by the teaching of the three great doctors *Sankara*, *Rama Anuja*, and *Madua*. These *Smartal Bráhmans* possessed a grant of lands engraved on a plate of copper. It is dated *Serrajittu* of *Sal*: 1450, in the 20th of *Maga*, and in the reign of *Krishna Ráya*, which agrees with the chronology of *Ramuppa*. Having been informed that there were here many inscriptions on stone, I went out in search of them.

The large tank is a very fine work, and the only structure in the place that is worth notice. Near this, in the yard of a small religious building called *Kaméswara Matam*, I found the most ancient inscription. The stone on which this is cut is at the top adorned with emblems, which indicate that its erectors have been worshippers of *Siva*. Much of it is buried under ground; only thirteen lines are at all legible, and parts of these are decayed. First come the titles of the sovereign *Cadumba Chicraverti*. These are quite different from those assumed by the kings of *Vijaya-nagara*, which are known by almost every *Bráhman*, and facilitate greatly the reading of all the inscriptions that were made during their government. The titles given to *Cadumba Chicraverti* seem to be little understood. After the titles, and a defacement of half a line, mention is made of two sons, learned and heroic men, and *Rájás* by the favour of *Rajaya* (the goddess of the earth). Then follow some unintelligible words. Then the date of the *Kali-yugam* 120, being *Vikrama*, 15th *Maga*, there being then an eclipse of the moon. These two sons gave *Dharma* (charity), by building *Kaméswara Matam*, on the west side of the temple of *Sankara Narayana*, in the name of *Sri Mahaboléswura*; and for the performance of *Bunaneia* (worship and charity) in this *Matam*, they granted certain grounds, then overset, without proprietors, and become *Harawéri* (reverted to the state) with the water-courses, house-steads, gardens, *Betta*-fields, *Chitta*-fields high and low, and the rank formerly thereunto appertaining. Here the writing is totally defaced. It probably contained the extent, name, and boundaries of the lands. From their disposing of lands belonging to the government, it is probable that the two sons, mentioned in the inscription, were sons of the king. The first cypher of the date is defaced; but from some fragments of it the *Bráhmans* think that it must be either a 1 or a 3; and from their traditions they are inclined to think that it is the former. *Cadumba Chicraverti* is the ancestor of *Myuru Verma*. This date would make him to have reigned 534 years earlier than the time assigned for the commencement of his reign by *Ramuppa;* which, I have already said, is probably much more early than the reality. The 3120, supposing that to be the true reading, would make *Cadumbà Chicraverti* to have been governing 149 years before the time in which (from an inscription that I afterwards procured) I found that his descendant *Trenetra Cadumba* actually reigned. I am persuaded, therefore, that this is the proper era of *Myuru Verma*, and the introduction of the *Bráhmans* from *Ahichaytra*; and that the *Banchica*, *Abhira*, and *Monayer* families of *Ramuppa*, are either names altogether fabricated, in order to increase the antiquity of *Myuru Verma;* or that, more probably, the order in the succession of the dynasties has been altered. This inscription, copied in imitation of the old character, has been delivered to the Bengal government. The image of *Sankara Narayana*, mentioned in this inscription, still remains in a small temple, on the east side of the *Matam;* and is a strong proof of the early prevalence of the doctrine which the *Smartal* now teach, namely, that *Siva* and *Vishnu* are different names for the same god, according to his different attributes, as destroyer and preserver of the world. A likeness of it is given in Plate XXIV.; from which it will appear, that, in order to show their identity, the same image has the emblems of both

CHAPTER XVI.

gods. The names do the same; for *Sankara* is one of the titles of *Siva*, and *Narayana* one of the names of *Vishnu*.

Feb. 26.

The next most ancient inscription that I found here was, like the others, in a private house, and exceedingly neglected. It is dated *Anunda* 1297, Friday 1st *Palguna*, in the reign of *Sri Vira Buca Ráya*, by the favour of the feet of *Virupacsha Devaru* (the *Siva* at *Humpay* opposite to *Vijaya-nagara*) king of the east, west, and south seas. This must be *Buca Ráya* the First, who would therefore appear to have reigned at least two years later than the time assigned for him by *Ramuppa*.

Another is dated in *Sal.* 1308, and contains a grant of revenue for supporting an inn, by the son of *Hari-hara Ráya*; but his name is effaced. A copy of this has been delivered to the Bengal government.

The last that I visited is dated *Suabanu Sal.* 1472, on the 23d of *Srávana*. In this, *Solva Krishna Devarasu Wodearu*, son of *Sedásiva Ráya*, and king of *Nagara* (*Vijaya-nagara*), *Haiva*, *Tulava*, *Kankana*, &c. grants lands situated in the *Ashtá-grám* of *Sashisty* district (*Desa*), in *Govay Ráyada* (principality of *Goa*). Hence it will be evident, that, while this powerful *Hindu* prince lived, the *Adil Shah Sultans* of *Vijaya-pura* were very much confined in their territories toward the south-west.

Feb. 27. Account of a *Bahudunda*, or register, kept by the hereditary accomptant.

27th *February*.—It having been mentioned to me, that the books of the hereditary *Shanaboga* here contained much curious information, I determined to stay a day, and examine them. I found that he had a *Bahudunda* of two volumes. The first commenced with some verses on medicine. Then followed some rules for the performance of the ceremonies of religion. Then came an old list of the names of all the principal traders in *Mirzee*. They were 54 in number; but the ants had eaten up the date. This was followed by an old enumeration of the inhabitants of *Mirzee* district (*Taluc*), then divided into three divisions (*Maganas*) *Gaukarna*, *Nagara*,

Feb. 27.

and *Seiganahully*. Then came an account, without date, of a contribution which a vagrant *Bráhman* had raised for the repairs of a temple. Then came the copy of a grant, originally engraven on stone, dated in 1442, the year of *Sal.* 1441 having past. By this, *Rutnuppa Wodearu*, and his son *Vijayuppa Wodearu*, having been appointed *Rájás* of *Barcuru* by *Sri Vira Krishna Ráya* on the throne of *Vijaya-nagara*, they granted to a certain *Bráhman* the *Shistu*, or land-tax, arising from certain grounds, and amounting to the annual value of 25 *Pagodas*. This year, according to *Ramuppa*, was the first of the reign of *Krishna*. Next follows a paper respecting the relief granted to a village by a Mussulman governor, under the *Sultan* of *Vijaya-pura*. Then comes a memorandum, which states that *Mahaboléswara*, the great *Pagoda* here, possessed lands to the value of 12000 *Pagodas* a year (4835 *l.* 7 *s.* $2\frac{1}{2}$ *d.*), from the time of *Madua Ráya* (probably the great doctor of the *Bráhmanical* laws) in the year of *Sal.* $138\frac{8}{9}$, until the time of *Byra Devi*. The memorandum then details all the lands, and appropriates the manner in which the revenue is to be expended. No date accompanies this memorandum; but it is looked upon by the *Bráhmans* as affording the temple a sufficient right to the specified lands, and as a clear proof that the rules for expenditure were prescribed by *Madua Ráya*. Next follows a grant of lands to the ancestors of the *Shanaboga*, from *Mahanundeléswara Krishna Devarasu Wodearu*, king of *Nagara*, *Haiva*, *Tulava*, *Kankana*, &c. in the year of *Sal.* 1452, which also is agreeable to *Ramuppa's* chronology. Then comes a copy of a *Shist*, or valuation, usually called that of *Krishna Ráyaru*; but there is nothing in the writing that shows when or by whom it was framed. It extends to the three divisions (*Maganas*) of *Mirzee* already mentioned, and includes a fourth named *Hirtitty*. From this it would appear, that those people who cultivated *Cumri* land paid $2\frac{1}{8}$ *Fanams* a head. At present they pay $2\frac{1}{2}$ *Fanams*. Gardens then were also taxed, and the government took one half of their supposed produce. Thus 1000 coco-nuts paid 3 *Pagodas*. It would

Valuation supposed to have been made by *Krishna Ráya*.

CHAPTER XVI. Feb. 27. appear, that since that time the price of this article has not increased, 6 *Pagodas* being the present value of 1000 coco-nuts. This seems to me a clear proof of the flourishing state of the country when the valuation was formed; as there can be no doubt, that the value of gold has in general decreased greatly since the time of *Krishna*, owing to the great quantities procured from America. The difference, therefore, must be made up by the more flourishing state of the country, which introduced wealth, and enhanced the price of every thing valuable: the present decayed state of the country, notwithstanding the low value of money, keeps down the price. By this valuation the pulse sown as a second crop was taxed. It had been a custom for every proprietor of a garden, at a certain festival, to wait on the officers of government, and present them with 1½ *Pagoda*. The valuation directs, that they should be exempted from this trouble, and that the money should be paid at the same time with their land-tax. The rice land paid 3 *Pagodas* for every *Cumbum* of produce. The *Cumbum* is two-thirds of a *Corge*, and at present is worth on an average about 12 *Pagodas*. Since that time an additional tax of 3¾ *Fanams* has been laid on each *Cumbum*. In this manner each estate having been valued, the land-tax was fixed on it *in cumulo;* and the same continues still to be taken, with the addition above mentioned on the rice-lands; but a great deduction is made on account of lands not occupied. When the valuation was formed, there was no tax on houses, but shops paid a duty to the *Suncha*, or custom-house.

Chronicle. The second volume of the *Shanaboga's* register commences with a kind of chronicle. *Killidi Vencatuppa Náyaka* having destroyed *Byra Devi*, information of the event was sent to *Ibrahim Adil Shah Padishah*, by *Sherif ún Mulk*, the *Vazir* residing at *Ponday*, a place near *Goa*. This officer seems to have commanded in *Kankana*, after the Mussulmans had seized on it, during the decline of the *Hindus* of *Vijaya-nagara*. The *Padishah* then ordered all the *Havildars* (military officers) commanding in *Kankana*, to join *Sherif ún Mulk*, and to fight with *Vencatuppa Náyaka.* On the 5th of *Margasirsha* *Sal.* 1529, being the year *Parabava,* they advanced as far as *Chindawera,* where they were entirely defeated. They retreated beyond the *Mirzee* river, and, having there built a strong fort, the river continued to be the boundary between the *Sivabhactars* and Mussulmans. Next year *Sherif ún Mulk* returned to *Ponday,* leaving an officer *(Havildar)* in command at *Mirzee* to collect the revenues, and remit them to *Ponday.* In the course of thirty-five years, there were twelve governors *(Havildars).* These were succeeded by officers called *Mahal Mocasi,* of whom there were ten at *Mirzee* in the course of thirty years. A *Tannadar* then governed it for eighteen months. After which *Mammud Khan* held the government for a year and a quarter. *Abdul Hassein Havildar* then governed twenty-one months, another *Havildar* nine months, and *Murtiza Khan* a similar length of time. He was displaced by two Mussulmans, who rose up, and put him in confinement. These possessed the country for eighteen months. After this *Mirzee* became subject to the *Sivabhactars,* and continued to be governed by *Karnataca Parputties* till the year *Durmutti,* fourteen years after *Hyder* had reduced *Bidderuru,* now called *Nagara.*

CHAPTER XVI.

Feb. 27.

Valuation by *Adil Shah.*

Next follows a valuation *(Shistu)* which was made by the officers of *Adil Shah,* in the *Fusly* year, or year of the *Hejira* 1044, and includes the five districts, or *Mahals,* that were subject to *Vijaya-pura,* and were named *Mirzee, Ancola, Ponday, Cadawada (Carwar),* and *Sivéswara;* and which were probably the part of the dominions of *Byra Devi,* that fell to the share of the Mussulmans. This is the valuation now in use. *Hyder* imposed no new taxes, but resumed one half of the charity lands *(Enams); Tippoo* seized upon the remainder.

I have detailed the contents of these volumes, that a judgment may be formed, of what may be usually expected in such registers, which are very numerous throughout the Peninsula.

Inscription.

In my evening walk I examined an inscription on stone. It is

CHAPTER XVI.

Feb. 27.

dated *Sal.* 1311, 1st *Phálguna*, and in the reign of *Buca Ráya Trilochia*, &c. son of *Hari-hara Ráya*, king of *Haiva*, *Tulava*, *Kankana*, &c. This must be *Buca Ráya* the First, and his reign must have continued much longer than is mentioned in the *Ráya Paditti*. He must also be the same prince mentioned in the inscription, page 170 (of this Volume), which shows that *Hari-hara* was not succeeded by his former companion *Buca*, but that he named his son and heir after that friend.

On my return, I met with an itinerant image of *Hanumanta*. He was in a palanquin, attended by a *Pújári*, and many *Vairagis*, and had tents, flags, *Thibet-tails*, and all other insignia of honour. He was on an expedition to collect the money that individuals in distress had vowed to his master *Vencata Ramanya*, the idol at *Tripathi*; and from his style of travelling seemed to have been successful. Many such collectors are constantly travelling about the Peninsula. Out of the contributions the *Pújári* (priest) defrays all the expenses of the party, and pays the balance into the treasury at *Tripathi*, which is one of the richest that the *Hindus* now possess.

Dancing women.

At the temples here dancing girls are kept, which is not done any where on the coast toward the south; for in *Tulava* and *Malayala* many of the finest women are at all times devoted to the service of the *Bráhmans*.

Feb. 28. *Gangawali* river.

28th *February*.—I went three cosses to *Ancola*. Midway is the *Gangawali*, an inlet of salt water that separates *Haiga*, or *Haiva*, from *Kankana*. Its mouth toward the sea is narrow; but inwards it forms a lake, which is from one mile to half that extent in width, except at the ferry, where it contracts to four or five hundred yards. Boats of a considerable size *(Patemars)* can come over the bar, and ascend the river for three cosses. Canoes can go three cosses farther, to the foot of the *Ghats*. The boats of *Haiga* are the rudest of any that I have ever seen, and no where worse than on this river, which possesses no trade; and the country on its banks, although very beautiful, seems rather barren.

Feb. 28.

Appearance of the country.

Between *Gaukarna* and the river, the country consists of low hills, separated by rice grounds of very small extent. Where they are of any considerable size, the soil is very sandy. Soon after leaving the *Gangawali* I crossed a smaller salt water inlet, which by overflowing it at high water injures a good deal of land.

Salt.

The salt made in this part of the country, where there are the same natural advantages as at *Goa*, is very bad, and scarcely saleable at any market; whereas at *Goa* vast quantities are made, and sent not only inland, but all over the coast. This seems to be an object that merits attention, so soon as the population shall have increased beyond what is adequate to cultivate the lands.

Appearance of *Kankana*.

The part of *Kankana* through which I have passed resembles *Haiga*. The quantity of rice-land is pretty considerable. Most of it is what in *Malabar* would be called *Parum*, yet it produces annually a crop of rice, and much of it a second crop of pulse. Although this part of *Kankana*, which is subject to the British government, and forms the district *(Taluc)* of *Ancola*, is larger than either of the districts into which *Haiga* is divided, it produces only an annual revenue of 29,000 *Pagodas;* while *Honawera* produces 51,000, and *Kunda-pura* yields 50,000. This is not attended with any advantage to the inhabitants; for the houses of the proprietors and cultivators are greatly inferior in appearance to those in *Haiga*, *Tulava*, and *Malayala*. The low revenue is not therefore owing to the people being less burthened, nor is it owing to an inferiority in natural riches, but to a long unsettled state, which has occasioned a wonderful devastation. The officers of revenue say, that one-third of even the good lands are now waste. This devastation has been owing to the constant depredations of *Marattah* chiefs, and robbers of two casts which are called *Comarapeca* and *Halepeca*. A *Comarapeca* chief, named *Ghida Ganoji*, or the short *Ganésa*, having continued in his usual practices after the conquest by the English, Major Monro sent a party of *Sepoys*, who shot him; ever since which the country has been quiet.

CHAPTER XVI.

Feb. 28. *Ancola.*

Ancola is a ruinous fort, with a small market *(Bazar)* near it. Robbers have frequently burned the market; but it is now recovering, and contains forty shops. It is not the custom here for the people to live in towns. A few shops are collected in one place; and all the other inhabitants of what is called a village are scattered upon their farms. Most of the people here are of *Karnata* extraction; and few of *Kankana* descent remain, except a particular kind of *Bráhmans,* who are all merchants, as those of *Haiga* are all cultivators. Being originally descended from *Pansh Gauda,* or *Bráhmans* of the north of *India,* those of *Kankana* are held in great contempt by the *Dravada Bráhmans,* or division of the south; one of the strongest reasons assigned for which is, that they eat fish.

March 1.

1st *March.*—I went five cosses to *Chandya.* At two computed cosses from *Ancola,* I crossed a considerable salt-water inlet called *Belicary.* The country between is level, but very sandy, and little cultivated. The banks of the *Belicary* are well planted with coconut gardens; and being broken into many islands and points are very beautiful. At the mouth, although it admits boats of some size *(Patemars),* it is not above two hundred yards wide. Small boats can ascend two cosses, to where the inlet receives from the *Ghats* a stream of fresh water. A little north from its mouth is a high island, called by the natives *Sonaka Guda,* which with a high promontory, projecting far to the west, forms a large bay, in which at this season there is scarcely any surf. Here the road for some way leads along the beach. At the head of the bay there is a fine plain between the hills toward the *Ghats,* and those forming the promontory which projects into the sea. The soil of this plain is good, but in many places is spoiled by the irruption of salt water creeks. Money has this year been advanced to make a bank, which which will be a great improvement. Toward the north the plain becomes narrower, and is overgrown with trees. Part of this has been formerly cultivated; and, if there were inhabitants, the whole might be rendered productive. Farther north the valley opens

CHAPTER XVI. March 1.

again into a fine plain, which faces the sea on the north side of the promontory. From the sea on the south of this to that on the north, is computed three cosses, or about ten miles. On our maps this part of the coast appears to be very ill laid down. *Chandya* is in the plain at some distance from the sea. At this place there is no market *(Bazar)*, but there are many scattered houses sheltered by groves of coco-nut palms.

Catechu.

In this part of *Kankana*, a little *Cut*, *Catechu*, or *Terra Japonica*, is made by some poor people, who gave me the following account of the process. The tree, or *Mimosa Catechu*, is called here *Keiri*, and grows spontaneously on all the hills of *Kankana*, but no where else in the peninsula that I observed. It is felled at any season; and, the white wood being removed, the heart is cut into small bits, and put, with one half the quantity of water by measure, into a round-bellied earthen pot. It is then boiled for about three hours; and when the decoction has become ropy, it is decanted. The same quantity of water is again added, and boiled, until it becomes ropy; when it is decanted, and a third water also is given. This extracts all the substance from the wood. The three decoctions are then mixed, and next morning boiled in small pots, until the extract becomes thick, like tar. It is afterwards allowed to remain in the pots for two days, and then has become so hard, that it will not run. Some husks of rice are then spread on the ground, and the inspissated juice is formed into balls, about the size of oranges, which are placed on the husks, or on leaves, and dried seven days in the sun. For two months afterwards they are spread out in the shade to dry, or in the rainy season for twice that length of time, and are then fit for sale. Merchants who live above the *Ghats* advance the whole price four months before the time of delivery, and give 2 *Rupees* for a *Maund* of 40 *Cutcha Seers* of 24 *Rupees* weight; that is, for a hundred-weight $9\frac{89}{100}$ *Rupees*, or nearly 1*l.* sterling. The merchants who purchase reside chiefly at *Darwara*, *Shanore*, and other parts in that neighbourhood, and are those who

CHAPTER XVI. March 1. supply the greater part of the peninsula with this article, which among the natives is in universal use. Their greatest supply comes from that part of *Kankana* which is subject to the *Marattahs*. The encouragement of this manufacture in British *Kankana* seems to merit attention. The tree is exactly the same with what I found used for the like purpose in the dominions of *Ava*, and does not agree very well with the descriptions in the *Supplementum Plantarum* of the younger Linnæus, nor in Dr. Roxburgh's manuscripts.

March 2. Appearance of the country. 2d *March.*—I went three cosses to *Sedásiva-ghur*. The road passes over two steep ridges of hills, running out into two promontories, between which is a bay sheltered by the island of *Angediva*, belonging to, and inhabited by the Portuguese. South from the island are two small hummocks, and off the southern promontory are some high rocks. The appearance of the whole from land renders it probable, that shelter might be found here for ships, even during the south-west monsoon. In the plain round this bay the soil is tolerably good. On the plain north from the two ridges it is very sandy, and much spoiled by salt water, which soaks through any such banks as can be formed of the loose materials that are procurable. The coco-nut is perhaps the production which would thrive best; but a great part of the plain is waste, and covered with bushes of the *Cassuvium*, called *Govay* by the natives, from its having been introduced from America by the Portuguese of *Goa*. The river of *Sedásiva-ghur* is a very wide and deep inlet of the sea. The passage into it is intricate, but at the height of the tide contains 25 feet water. It is sheltered in a deep bay by three islands, one of which, called by the natives *Karmaguda*, is fortified. The entrance is commanded by the fort, which is situated on a lofty hill. Much land in this vicinity has fallen into the hands of government, and, owing to the depredations of the *Comarapeca* robbers, has become waste. One of their chiefs, named *Venja Náyaka*, was the terror of the whole country, and forced even *Bráhmans* to adopt his cast. Two of his sons were hanged by *Tippoo;* but, until terrified by the firmness of Major Monro's government, he continued obstinate in his evil practices. Soon after that gentleman's arrival, he made his submission, and continues to behave like a good subject. I found him very ready to give me assistance in procuring supplies, and means to transport my baggage; and from the mildness of his manners, until informed by the officers of revenue, I had no idea of his disposition, which was barbarous in the extreme. March 2.

3d *March.*—I remained at *Sedásiva-ghur* taking some account of the state of British *Kankana*, and making preparations for my journey up the *Ghats.* The *Petta*, or town, here contains about twenty very wretched shops: all the other inhabitants live scattered on their farms. *Cadawada*, or as we usually pronounce it *Carwar*, stood about three miles above *Sedásiva-ghur*, on the opposite bank of the river. It was formerly a noted seat of European commerce, but during the *Sultán's* reign has gone to total ruin. There are here at present some merchants from the *Marattah* dominions above the *Ghats*, who say that they came chiefly with a view of purchasing salt. They also procure here a considerable quantity of *Cut*, none of which grows above the *Ghats.* They purchase it for ready money from the merchants of the country, who make the advances to the manufacturers. It is of a very good quality; and they cannot afford to give more than 10 *Sultany Pagodas* for the *Candaca*, or *Candy* of 40 *Maunds* of 48 *Seers* each; that is, 40 *Rupees* for the *Candy* of 582½ lb., or 15*s.* 5*d.* a hundred-weight. March 3. Commerce.

It would appear, that at one time all the lands of this district *(Taluc)* belonged to *Jain* landlords *(Mulagars)*; but all these have either been killed, or so oppressed that they have disappeared. After their expulsion, part of the lands were annexed to the government, and part given to landlords *(Mulagars)* called *Hubbu Bráhmans.* These are of the *Pansh Dravada* division; but are considered as having been degraded by *Sankara Achárya*, and are now reduced to a miserable state of ignorance. None of them here can give any Tenures.

CHAPTER XVI. March 3.

account of the time when they came into the country, who brought them, or whence they came. They are the common *Panchangas*, or almanac-keepers of the country, and in some temples are priests *(Pújáris)*; but *Sujéswara*, the most celebrated temple in the country, and one of those built by *Ravana* king of *Lanca*, is in possession of a colony of *Marattah Bráhmans*, who were introduced by *Mahomed Adil Shah* of *Vijaya-pura*. Of the history of the country these know nothing, except the legends concerning the foundation of their temple that are to be found in the eighteen *Puránas*. The lands formerly granted to the *Hubbu Bráhmans*, and which form by far the greater part of the country, are called *Mula* lands, and may be transferred by sale whenever the proprietor pleases. The *Hubbus* have indeed alienated a great part of it to *Marattahs*, *Kankana Bráhmans*, and *Comarapeca*. It may be also transferred on mortgage, resumable at pleasure by paying the debt. This tenure is here called *Adava*. The *Shist*, or assessment, now in use, was made by *Sherif un Mulk*, the *Vazir* of *Ponday* already mentioned; and was formed by laying so much on the land, according to its soil, and the quantity of rice seed that it was supposed capable of sowing. The proprietor may cultivate it with whatever he pleases, and may plant it with palms without any additional tax. Since the time of *Sherif un Mulk*, a small tax has been imposed on every coco-nut tree; and at different times, by imposing a per centage *(Pagadiputti)* on the amount of each person's land-tax, an increase of revenue has been made. Major Monro, according to the account of the revenue officers, considerably reduced the rate of the land-tax; but owing to his care, and strictness in the collections, the revenue which he raised was much greater than was ever before realised. The proprietors allege, that they paid more to him than they did to *Tippoo*. The two accounts are very reconcileable; as under the inspection of Mr. Monro there was little room for the corrupt practices which in the *Sultán's* government were very prevalent. Disputes about landed property are very common. An estate paying four *Pagodas* of revenue can be mortgaged for a hundred *Pagodas*, and the mortgagee pays the taxes. The same estate will sell for one hundred and fifty *Pagodas*. The government lands are let at rack rent, which is of course higher than the tax *(Shist)* paid by the proprietors *(Mulagars)*. The tenants on these lands, or *Circar Cutties*, cannot be turned out of their farms so long as they pay the rent, the leases being in perpetuity. They can neither sell nor mortgage their lease; but they may let it to an undertenant. By far the greater part of the cultivation is carried on by the proprietors *(Mulagars)* and tenants of the public *(Circar Cutties)*, and very little by lease-holders. The sizes of the farms vary from one to five ploughs. Two oxen are required to each plough, which cultivates from five to seven *Candies* of land. In general, the family of the proprietor labours the farm, but a few rich men employ hired servants. There are here no slaves. Men servants get yearly from two to six *Pagodas*, or from 16*s.* $1\frac{1}{2}$*d.* to 48*s.* $4\frac{1}{2}$*d.*; but those, who get only the first sum in money, have daily one meal of rice. March 3.

The cultivation of watered-fields, and of gardens, both on the same kind of land, is the only one known in British *Kankana*, except the *Cumri*, or *Cotu Cadu*, called here *Culumbi*. There is no ground from which two crops of rice in one year are taken; but, while most of the rice grows in the rainy season, some land called *Vaingunna* is so low, that in the rainy season it cannot be cultivated, and, after the water has evaporated, this yields a crop. All the other land is called *Surd*, and is mostly what in *Malabar* would be called *Majelu*, and what the people of *Tulava* would call *Betta*. In the accompanying Table may be seen several particulars relative to the cultivation of rice, which were taken from the accounts of the cultivators. I had no opportunity of ascertaining the quantity of land required to sow one *Candaca* of seed, nor, consequently, of judging how far the statement of the produce is credible. Rice.

CHAPTER XVI.

March 3.

Table explaining the cultivation of Rice in British *Kankana.*

Name.	Ground.	Produce of One *Candaca* sown.			Time required to ripen.	Quality.
		Suca-dan.		Rice.		
		1st Soil.	2d Soil.			
		Candacas.	*Candacas.*	*Candacas.*	Months.	
Asgha -	*Surd* - -	6	5	4	3½	Large.
Pandia -	- - -	6	5	4	3½	Ditto.
Patni -	- - -	6	5	4	3	Ditto.
Halga -	- - -	none	- -	4	3	Middle sized.
Sanmulghi	- - -	6	5	4	4	Ditto.
Wala - -	- - -	8	6	5	4	Small.
Cago - -	- - -	none	- -	10	3½	Large and coarse.
Sorutta -	*Vaingunna*	none	- -	4	4	

The *Suca-dan* is, where the seed is sown broad-cast without preparation; and in this case one-fifth more seed is required for the same ground, than when, previous to its being sown, the seed is prepared, or made to sprout, which is here called *Rau.* The *Cago* is cultivated on the lands impregnated with salt by inundations, and is the only kind that will thrive in such places. The *Wala* requires a clayey soil, and its produce is great; but the quantity of this soil is very small. All the *Surd* land requires manure. The seed season for dry-seed is the month preceding midsummer; and that for sprouted-seed is the month following. In *Vaingunna*, or inundated land, according as the water evaporates, the seed season continues during the two months previous to and one month after the winter solstice. The fields are watered from small *Tanks,* which in such low situations do not suddenly dry up, and contain the water at from one to two feet below the surface. It is raised by means of a trough, which moves upon a pivot near the centre; so that one of its ends may be immersed into the water, while its lighter end hangs over the field.

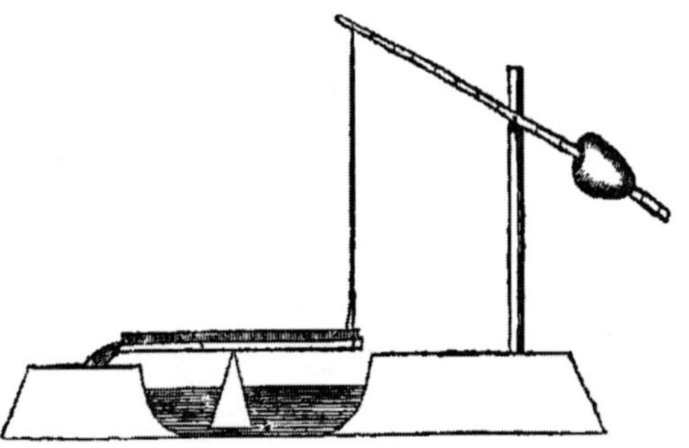

To the heavy end is annexed a *Yatam* wrought by two men, who allow this extremity of the trough to sink into the water, and to be thus filled. They then raise it by the *Yatam*, and the water runs out upon the field by the light end. Two men with a basket and ropes would throw out four times as much water, but it would be hard work.

Upon good *Surd* land may be procured a second crop of the following leguminous plants: Pulse.

Udied, Phaseolus minimoo Roxb: MSS.

Mung, Phaseolus mungo.

Cultie, Dolichos biflorus.

These are cultivated in the same manner as the pulses in *Haiga.*

In the rainy season the cattle are kept in the house, and, to increase the quantity of manure, are littered with fresh leaves. In the dry season they are shut up at night in pens, which are placed on the *Surd* lands, and are shifted once in four days. Every morning some dry soil is mixed with the foregoing night's dung, and the whole is made smooth, that the cattle may lie clean. The manure collected in the rainy season is given to the soil of the first and second quality, which are always sown with rice after the dry-seed cultivation. The ashes of the family are kept separate, but are used for the same kind of land. Manure.

The cattle here are of the same small kinds that are to be found on the coast to the southward. A great many of them are brought Cattle.

CHAPTER XVI.

March 3.

from above the *Ghats.* At this season they are in a most wretched condition, and are supported entirely on straw; for in *Kankana* no hay is made. In this part of the country few buffaloes are employed.

Customs of the *Comarapeca.*

The *Comarapeca* are a tribe of *Kankana* descent, and seem to be the *Súdras* of pure birth, who properly belong to the country; in the same manner as the *Nairs* are the pure *Súdras* of *Malayala.* By birth they are all cultivators and soldiers; and, as usual with this class of men among the *Hindus,* are all strongly inclined to be robbers. From the anarchy which has long prevailed in this neighbourhood, they had acquired an extraordinary degree of cruelty, and had even compelled many *Bráhmans* to assume their customs, and adopt their cast. They have hereditary chiefs called *Náyakas,* who, as usual, with the assistance of a council, can expel from the cast, and settle disputes among their inferiors. A man's own children are his heirs. They can read poetical legends, and are permitted to eat meat and drink spirituous liquors. Their women are not marriageable after the age of puberty. Widows ought to burn themselves with the bodies of their husbands, but this barbarity is no longer in use. Widows, and women who have been divorced for adultery with a *Bráhman* or *Comarapeca,* may be taken into a kind of left-hand marriage; but their children are despised, and no person of a pure descent will marry them. A woman cannot be divorced for any other cause than adultery; if the crime has been committed with any man but a *Bráhman,* or *Comarapeca,* she loses cast. The men may take as many wives as they please. The *Sringagiri Swamalu* is their *Guru.* He receives their *Dharma,* and bestows on them *Upadesa,* holy-water, consecrated ashes, and the like. The *Panchanga,* or astrologer of the village, is their *Puróhita,* and reads prayers *(Mantrams)* at marriages, *Namacurna* (the giving a child its name), *Tithi, Amávásya,* &c. &c. They worship the great gods, *Siva* and *Vishnu,* in temples where *Kankana Bráhmans* are *Pújáris.* They offer bloody sacrifices; and at the temples of the *Saktis,* or destructive spirits, such as *Dava Dévaru*, and *Marca Devi*, whose priests *(Pújáris)* are called *Gurus*, they swing suspended by iron hooks which are passed through the skin of their backs. The spirits of children, whose mothers die during pregnancy, are supposed to become *Butas*, or devils, and to occasion much trouble to those unfortunate persons into whom they enter. The sufferers attempt to be relieved of them by prayer and sacrifice, and some village people are imagined to be possessed of invocations *(Mantrams)* capable of expelling these evil spirits. The *Comarapecas* suppose that the spirits of good men go to *Moesha*, a pretence that is looked upon by the *Bráhmans* as very impudent; for they think that such a place is far beyond the reach of a *Súdra*. For the spirits of bad men the *Comarapeca* do not know any place of punishment, nor do they know what becomes of such after death.

March 3.

Bráhmans of Kankana.

The *Bráhmans* properly belonging to *Kankana*, and who alledge that they are the descendants of the colony to whom the country was given by *Parasu Ráma*, are of the *Pansh Gauda* division. *Goa*, called by them *Govay*, seems to have been their principal seat. After being expelled thence by the Portuguese, they dispersed, and have now mostly become traders. A few are still priests *(Pújáris)*, and a very small number call themselves *Vaidikas*. All those who are here are very ignorant, and do not pretend to say when the *Jain* and *Panch Dravada Bráhmans* came in upon them.

March 4. Appearance of the country.

4th *March*.—I went three cosses to *Gopi-chitty*. For the first part of the journey the road led through a level country, with a few small hills scattered at some distance, and a pretty good soil. It afterwards passed among low hills covered with wood. In many places here, the soil seems good, and the trees are tall; so that pepper might probably be cultivated to advantage. In many other places the hills are barren, producing nothing but bushes, or stunted trees: among them I saw no *Teak*. *Gopi-chitty* is a village containing eight houses. Owing to the disturbed state of the country, it had for twenty years been entirely deserted; but the

Gopi-chitty.

CHAPTER XVI.

March 4.

confidence of enjoying security under Major Monro's authority, has induced the present inhabitants to settle in the place, and they have already cleared a considerable extent of the rice ground, which consequently belongs entirely to the government. The lower part of the valley, toward the great river, has been destroyed by the breaking down of the dykes that kept out the tide. To repair these, would cost 25 *Pagodas*, which is more than the tenants can afford or choose to advance.

History of the part of *Kankana* subject to the British.

This part of *Kankana*, on the fall of the *Sultans* of *Vijaya-pura*, became subject to the *Rájás* of *Sudha*, which we call *Soonda*. One of these, named *Sedásiva Row*, built the fort at the mouth of the river, and called it after his own name. The dialect of *Kankana* is used by the natives of this place in their own houses; but, from having been long subject to *Vijaya-pura*, almost all of them can speak the *Marattah* language, which has a very strong affinity with the *Hinduy* that is spoken on the banks of the *Ganges*.

March 5. Appearance of the country.

5th *March*.—I went four cosses to *Caderi*, and did not see a house the whole way; but the heads of some cultivated vallies approach near the road, and extend from thence toward the river. I passed through many places that formerly have been cultivated, but are now waste, and through some places where the soil seems fit for cultivation, but which probably have never been cleared. The trees in some places are of a good size, but none of them are very valuable. The people whom I took with me for the purpose gave me the following account of such as I observed by the way.

Forests.

The most common is the prickly *Bamboo*, called *Colaki*.

Cussum, or the *Shaguda* of my MSS.

Is very hard, and strong, and is used for the cylinders of sugar-mills.

Rindela, *Chuncoa Huliva*, Buch: MSS.

Is used only for the beams of the houses of the natives.

Biba, *Holigarna*, Buch: MSS.

This is the varnish tree of *Chittigong*, and I suppose of *Ava*. The natives here are only acquainted with the caustic nature of its juice, and apply it to no use.

Cadumba, the *Nauclea purpurea* Rox:

A large tree used for planks.

Maratu, a *Chuncoa* called by Dr. Roxburgh *Terminalia alata glabra*,

Grows to a very large size, and is used for building boats and canoes.

Beiladu, *Vitex foliis ternatis*,

Of hardly any use.

Cajeru, *Strychnos Nux vomica.*

Hedu, *Nauclea Daduga* Roxb: MSS.

A large tree fit for planks.

Cumbia. The *Pelou* of the *Hort: Mal:*

Ticay, *Laurus Cassia.*

People from above the *Ghats* come to collect both the bark and the buds, which the natives call *Cabob-China.*

Paynra. Gardenia uliginosa Willd:

Of no use.

Hodogus. Arbor foliis suboppositis, estipulaceis, ovalibus, integerrimis. The timber is said to be very strong and durable, and to resist the white ants, even when buried in the ground.

Sissa. Pterocarpus Sissoo Roxb: MSS.

Is found in great plenty near the river toward the *Ghats.*

Dillenia pentagyna Roxb:

The natives have no name for it.

Jambay. Mimosa xylocarpon Roxb:

It grows to an immense size.

Bassia longifolia.

Robinia mitis.

Myrtus cumini.

The forests are the property of the gods of the villages in which they are situated, and the trees ought not to be cut without having

CHAPTER XVI. March 5.

obtained leave from the *Gauda*, or head man of the village, whose office is hereditary, and who here also is priest *(Pújári)* to the temple of the village god. The idol receives nothing for granting this permission; but the neglect of the ceremony of asking his leave brings his vengeance on the guilty person. This seems, therefore, merely a contrivance to prevent the government from claiming the property. Each village has a different god, some male, some female, but by the *Bráhmans* they are all called *Saktis* (powers), as requiring bloody sacrifices to appease their wrath.

No persons here collect honey or wax.

Caderi. Unhealthy nature of the country.

Caderi at present contains only two houses, with one man and a lad, besides women. It was formerly a place of note; but for several years a great sickness has prevailed, and has swept off nearly all the inhabitants. This is attributed to the vengeance of some enraged *Buta*, or devil; but may be accounted for from the neighbouring country having been laid waste, and being over-run with forests. On the banks of the river at *Caderi* there was a fort, which was destroyed by *Hyder*, and the garrison sent to occupy the fortified island at the mouth of the river. General Mathews, the natives say, took possession of the ruins, erected some works, and left a garrison, which held out until the peace of *Mangalore*. Most of the cultivators lived on the opposite side of the river. Those who resided near the fort were chiefly traders; and there is still a weekly fair at the place, to which many people resort. This seems to be the reason why the few remaining inhabitants continue in such a situation. They are *Bráhmans;* and from those who frequent the fair they receive considerable contributions. *Patemars*,

River of *Sedásiva-ghur.*

or large craft, can ascend almost to the fort, and canoes can go two miles above it. The water is quite fresh. The encouraging of a market *(Bazar)* here seems to be an object of importance, and a mean likely to bring back a great trade to this river, which by nature has many advantages.

CHAPTER XVI.

March 6.

Robbers suppressed.

6th *March.*—I went four cosses to *Avila-gotna,* without having seen the smallest trace of cultivation, or of inhabitants. The country is not, however, entirely a desert. Small villages are scattered through the forests, and hidden in its recesses. Formerly the inhabitants of these lived in a constant defiance of the rest of mankind, robbing whoever unfortunately came within their power, and continually on the alarm to defend themselves from their neighbours. This manner of living has however been entirely stopped. Major Monro, by taking advantage of the terror inspired by the fall of *Seringapatam,* and by an instant punishment of the first transgressor, has made every thing quiet; and there is reason to think that a defenceless man may now traverse these forests without danger from his fellow-creatures. Tigers are said to be very numerous; and, to lessen the danger to be apprehended from them, the traders who frequent the road have cleared many places where they may encamp, and these are prevented from being overgrown by annually burning the long grass. On one of these clear places I halted, having at no great distance a village of thieves.

Appearance of the country.

The country through which I passed to-day was in general level, with hills near the road toward the left, and a ridge to the right at about four or five miles distance. This ridge is that which runs out into the sea to form the southern boundary of the bay of *Sedásiva-ghur.* The trees are in general high, with many *Bamboos* intermixed. The soil is apparently good, and a large proportion of it is sufficiently level for the plough. Near *Avila-gotna* I crossed the river, which here assumes a very singular appearance. Its channel is about half a mile wide, and consists of a confused mass of rocks, gravel, and sand, intersected by small limpid streams, and overgrown with various trees and shrubs which delight in such situations. In the rainy season, it swells into tremendous torrents, but never fills the channel from bank to bank. It is then, however, quite impassable. At present its clear streams, with the fresh

CHAPTER XVI.

March 6.

verdure of the plants growing near them, are very pleasant, after having come through the forest, whose leaves at this season drop; for all the juices of the trees are dried up by the arid heat of this climate, in the same manner as they are by the cold of an European winter. The nights, however, are at present cool, but the days are burning hot. Near the sea a more equable temperature prevails.

March 7.

7th *March.*—Although before leaving *Sedásiva-ghur*, I had collected the persons who were said to be best informed concerning the road, and had procured from them a list of stages said to be distant from each other three or four cosses, that is, about ten or thirteen miles; yet to-day I came to my stage at *Déva-kara*, after less than an hour's journey.

Face of the country.

The road passes along the south side of the river; and toward the east the valley becomes narrower, and more uneven; but still much of it is fit for the plough. From the stunted appearance of the trees, I conclude that the soil is worse than that on yesterday's route. At *Déva-kara* there is a good deal of ground cleared, and formed into rice fields; but the people of eight houses, which form the village, are not able to cultivate the whole. The ground that is cleared is by no means equal either in soil or levelness, to much of what I saw waste on the two last days' journey; but it is finely watered by a stream that even now affords a great supply. The river at *Déva-kara* is a rapid stream full of small islands; but not so much broken as at *Avila-gotna*, and of course narrower. In the rainy season it is quite impassable; and then, although very rapid, swells at least ten feet above its present level.

Unhealthy nature of the country.

At the commencement of the last rainy season, this village contained twelve houses; but, twenty persons having died, four of the houses are now deserted. It is looked upon as certain death, for any stranger to attempt to settle in this place.

Robbers.

Here was the residence of a very notorious robber, who died in consequence of the wounds that he received from the party which

Major Monro sent to apprehend him. His family are now quiet cultivators, and ever since his death safety and tranquillity have been established in the country.

March 7.

Produce of rice-ground.

The people here say, that their *Surd* lands produce from 12 to 20 seeds, which is a more probable account than that given at *Sedá-siva-ghur*, unless the seed there be sown as thick as in *Malabar*.

Mr. Read's account of the districts below the *Ghats*.

As I am now about to enter *Karnata Désam*, where a new face of things will present itself, I shall here conclude the chapter, by extracting from Mr. Read's answers to my queries such as relate to that part of his district which is situated below the *Ghats*, and which comprehends the districts *(Talucs)* of *Kunda-pura* and *Honawera* in *Haiga*, and that of *Ancola* in *Kankana*.

Soil.

In these districts the proportion of land capable of being cultivated with the plough, or of being converted into gardens, Mr. Read estimates as follows:

	Now cultivated.	Capable of being so.	Sterile.
Kunda-pura	0,32	0,08	0,60
Honawera	0,26	0,12	0,62
Ancola	0,21	0,20	0,59

Revenue.

The revenue, notwithstanding so much waste land, is said to have been greater during the first year of Major Monro's management, than it was ever before known to have been. Mr. Read attributes this to an increase of rent on the lands actually in cultivation; but of this I have much doubt. In general, the natives acknowledged a remission, which naturally they would not have done had their taxes been increased; and it must be remembered, that *Tippoo* had resumed all the charity lands *(Enams)*, which during the former governments probably amounted to more than what is now waste, while the collections remitted to the treasury, and consequently brought to accompt, during the *Sultán's* government, are no rule by which an estimate can be formed of the taxes; the whole revenue department under him having been subject to the most gross peculation.

CHAPTER XVI.

March 7. Produce of waste-land.

The produce of the waste lands brought to market, Mr. Read states as follows.

The *Maund* weighs $24\frac{84}{100}$ lb. and is divided into 40 *Seers.*

	Sandal wood trees. Total.	*Teak* trees cut annually.	*Sissa* trees cut annually.	Annual produce of honey.	Annual produce of bees wax.	Annual produce wild cinnamon.	Annual produce of *Cabob China.*	Annual produce nutmegs	Annual produce of wild pepper.
				Maunds.	*Maunds.*	*Maunds.*	*Maunds.*	*Maunds.*	*Maunds.*
Kunda-pura	8758	—	1582	—	—	8 30	25 30	—	51 0
Honawera -	1017	2059	344	—	—	99 35	42 32½	12 5	533 0
Ancola - -	315	1124	572	8 0	2 7½	15 10	50 14	28 17½	474 38¾
Total -	10143	3183	2498	8 0	2 7½	123 35	118 36½	40 22½	1058 38¾

The *Cut,* and perhaps some other articles of less importance, have eluded Mr. Read's inquiries, probably from their never having been objects of revenue.

Sandal wood.

"All sandal trees," says Mr. Read, "growing upon private lands are considered as the property of the government; but it would be ridiculous to suppose, that they will always be considered as such by the occupiers of estates, who undoubtedly commit frequent depredations upon them. It would therefore be for the benefit of the Company to have the whole cut down immediately that are of a fit age, which I am told is not till they are 30 years old. The whole might be easily collected at *Onore (Honawera),* and taken up by one of the Indiamen passing from *Bombay* to *China.*" Mr. Read was probably not aware, that last year all the ripe sandal in *Mysore* had been cut, and a great danger has consequently been incurred of glutting the market; while some years hence it will probably be greatly enhanced in value. I have already mentioned, that some measure should be adopted for regulating the cutting of the sandal wood; so that a certain supply should annually be brought to market, and no more permitted to grow than can be disposed of to advantage; for it must be considered as a mere superfluous luxury, the only proper use of which is to become a source of as much revenue as possible. As the Company and the *Mysore Rájá* are in the sole possession of the countries which produce it, the arrangement might be readily made on somewhat like the following plan. An estimate of the quantity annually saleable, and of the whole produce that grows in both territories, having been formed, an agreement might be made, that each party should furnish the annual supply for a number of years, in proportion to the whole quantity that grows in his country. For instance, the *Mysore Rájá* might furnish the supply for nineteen years, and the Company for one, which I imagine is somewhat about the relative proportion of what the two territories produce. The parties, of course, would be tied down to sell no more than a certain weight each year. They might improve its quality, as much as they could; and public sales, such as the Company use in *Bengal* for opium and salt, I am persuaded would be found by far the most advantageous manner of disposing of this article. Mr. Read mentions no difference in the quality of the sandal which grows below the *Ghats*, from that which grows in *Karnata;* but all the natives that I have ever spoken with on the subject, from *Pali-ghat* to this place, look upon the produce of the low country as of little or no value, as having no smell. CHAPTER XVI. March 7.

The wild cinnamon and *Cabob China* are rented together for about 22 *Rupees* a year. The former sells in the market *(Bazar)* at 28 *Rupees* a *Candy*, and the latter at 32 *Rupees*. The *Candy* is equal to 20 *Maunds*. *Laurus cassia.*

Mr. Read values the wild pepper at one *Pagoda* a *Maund;* and says, that it is of a quality very inferior to that raised in gardens, which sells for about $1\frac{1}{2}$ *Pagoda*. All the natives with whom I conversed looked upon them as of equal value. Wild pepper.

The number of people at present employed in the *Cumri*, or *Cotu-cadu* cultivation, amounts to 2418, who pay yearly $954\frac{1}{2}$ *Pagodas*, or 3*s*. $2\frac{1}{4}$*d*. a head. It is supposed by the revenue officers, that in this manner 1900 more people might find employment. *Cumri* cultivation.

CHAPTER XVI.

March 7.

Sugar-cane.

I have already mentioned Mr. Read's opinion concerning the quantity of land in his districts below the *Ghats* that is fit for the cultivation of rice or gardens. The quantity of sugar-cane annually raised is estimated at 98,19,250 canes, and Mr. Read does not think that this cultivation ought to be farther encouraged, as it would interfere with that of rice, which is more valuable.

Stock.

The stock required for the arable lands, according to Mr. Read, is as follows.

	Ploughs belonging to			Cattle.	
	Landlords.	Tenants.	Total.	Buffaloes old and young.	Cow kind old and young.
Kunda-pura -	3180	4343	7523	5894	23462
Honawera - -	4883	1221	6104	8472	22148
Ancola - - -	2331	673	3004	2858	11055
Total -	10396	6237	16633	17224	55665

Plantations.

Mr. Read states it as Major Monro's opinion, that, had the land-tax on coco-nut plantations been more moderate, double the present quantity would have been raised. No means at present exist to ascertain the number, either actually growing, or that of plantations which have gone to decay.

Mr. Read gives the following account of the population of these districts.

CHAPTER XVI.
March 7.

	Houses, of which the following are occupied by						Persons of the following conditions.		
	Total Numbers	Christians.	Mussulmans.	*Brâhmans.*	*Sivabhacters.*	*Jain.*	Salt-makers.	Fishermen.	Slaves of both sexes.
Kunda-pura -	9049	36	485	1799	115	46	—	2628	410
Honawera - -	10554	256	704	2231	21	39	180	4842	470
Ancola - - -	6130	93	311	804	11	1	—	1832	270
Total -	25733	385	1500	4834	147	87	180	9302	1099

In the annexed Statement will be seen the exports and imports, by sea, from these districts: the first amounting to 331,532 *Rupees*, and the latter to 44,585 *Rupees*.

CHAPTER XVI.

March 7.

Statement shewing the Average annual Quantity of Goods imported and exported by Sea in the northern Division of Canara, 1800-1.

No.	Names of the Articles.	Average annual Quantity Imported.								Total Value in Rupees.	Average annual Quantity Exported.								Total Value in Rupees.
		Corges of 1470 *Pucka Seers.*	*Morays* of 51½ *Pucka Seers.*	*Candies* of 20 *Maunds.*	*Maunds* of 44 *Seers Cutcha.*	*Seers Cutcha* of 24 *Rupees.*	*Kodie*, or Scores.	*Tak* 40 Cubits.	*Adud*, or Pieces.		*Corges* of 1470 *Pucka Seers.*	*Morays* of 51½ *Pucka Seers.*	*Candies* of 20 *Maunds.*	*Maunds* of 44 *Seers Cutcha.*	*Seers Cutcha* of 24 *Rupees.*	*Kodie*, or Scores.	*Tak* 40 Cubits.	*Adud*, or Pieces.	
1	Rice, cleaned	2	5¼	—	—	—	—	—	—	118	2363¾	5¾	—	—	—	—	—	—	141837
2	*Paddy*, or rough rice	64¾	5	—	—	—	—	—	—	1687	650¾	½	—	—	—	—	—	—	19523
3	*Ragy (Cynosurus)*	—	—	—	—	—	—	—	—	—	23¼	1	—	—	—	—	—	—	716
4	*Toor Dhall* (a pulse)	—	9	—	—	—	—	—	—	27	6¼	¾	—	—	—	—	—	—	628
5	Green *Cuddalay* (ditto)	1¼	1½	—	—	—	—	—	—	218	1	—	—	—	—	—	—	—	130
6	Wheat	1½	8½	—	—	—	—	—	—	244	—	3½	—	—	—	—	—	—	14
7	*Shamay* (millet)	—	¾	—	—	—	—	—	—	2	—	1	—	—	—	—	—	—	4
8	Mustard	—		½	4	—	—	—	—	18	½	—	½	1½	—	—	—	—	59
9	*Wooduth* (a pulse)	—	—	—	—	—	—	—	—	—	14¼	—	—	—	—	—	—	—	862
10	Green *Gram* (ditto)	—	—	—	—	—	—	—	—	—	4½	¾	—	—	—	—	—	—	281
11	*Hurvaday*, or *Allahsundy* (ditto)	—	—	—	—	—	—	—	—	—	6½	2¼	—	—	—	—	—	—	364
12	*Gram* for horses (ditto)	—	—	—	—	—	—	—	—	—	14¾	—	—	—	—	—	—	—	740
13	Lamp-oil seeds *(Ricinus)*	—	2	—	—	—	—	—	—	5	—	—	—	—	—	—	—	—	—
14	*Chunam* (lime)	—	25¾	—	—	—	—	—	—	13	—	—	—	—	—	—	—	—	—
15	Salt	—	7643¼	—	—	—	—	—	—	2419	—	3105	—	—	—	—	—	—	621
16	Sweet-oil seeds *(Sesamum)*	—	6	—	—	—	—	—	—	15	—	10	—	—	—	—	—	—	25
17	*Toor* (a pulse)	—	7½	—	—	—	—	—	—	15	¼	—	—	—	—	—	—	—	19
18	*Lobay*, or white *Gram* (ditto)	—	—	—	—	—	—	—	—	—	—	¾	—	—	—	—	—	—	1
19	Oil	—	—	3	1	10	—	—	—	165	—	—	12¼	3	6½	—	—	—	731
20	*Ghee* (boiled butter)	—	—	1	2	9	—	—	—	149	—	—	—	3¼	¼	—	—	—	24
21	*Betel-nut* 1st sort	—	—	1½	¾	—	—	—	—	72	—	—	195¼	¼	10¼	—	—	—	11740
22	Ditto - 2d ditto	—	—	—	—	—	—	—	—	—	—	—	896	2½	6	—	—	—	36577
23	Ditto - 3d ditto	—	—	—	—	—	—	—	—	—	—	—	128¼	3¼	8½	—	—	—	4688
24	Ditto - 4th ditto	—	—	—	—	—	—	—	98500	78	—	—	—	—	—	—	—	1538605	620
25	Pepper	—	—	¼	4	—	—	—	—	50	—	—	278¼	3½	9	—	—	—	28030
26	Cardamoms	—	—	—	4½	5	—	—	—	138	—	—	—	—	—	—	—	—	—

27	*Jagory* of sugar-cane	—	—	12	3¾	—	—	—	—	366	—	—	54	1	—	—	—	—	1100
28	*Palmira Jagory* (bundles)	—	—	—	—	—	—	—	—	—	—	—	—	—	—	—	—	537	136
29	Turmerick	—	—	—	4½	—	—	—	—	5	—	—	17½	4¼	—	—	—	—	476
30	*Jeeryah* (a pulse)	—	—	¼	3	—	—	—	—	34	—	—	—	4	5	—	—	—	20
31	*Mathee* (ditto)	—	—	¼	2¼	—	—	—	—	8	—	—	¼	—	—	—	—	—	12
32	Coriander seed	—	16¼	3¼	½	—	—	—	—	108	—	—	6¼	4¾	—	—	—	—	201
33	*Woomum*, or *Ajewan* (a kind of anise)	—	—	¼	—	—	—	—	—	6	—	—	¼	2	—	—	—	—	4
34	Onions	—	—	10½	3	—	—	—	—	102	—	—	8½	1½	—	—	—	—	103
35	Garlick	—	—	2¼	¾	—	—	—	—	45	—	—	1¾	2¾	—	—	—	—	50
36	*Chillees*, or *Capsicum*	—	—	5½	3¼	—	—	—	—	162	—	—	66¾	1	8	—	—	—	2184
37	Cinnamon (*Cassia*)	—	—	—	—	—	—	—	—	—	—	—	4	4	—	—	—	—	81
38	Ditto flower	—	—	—	—	—	—	—	—	—	—	—	10¼	4	—	—	—	—	252
39	Dry coco-nuts	—	—	42¼	2½	—	—	—	—	1349	—	—	2½	2½	—	—	—	—	95
40	Tamarind	—	—	3¾	1½	—	—	—	—	44	—	—	11¼	2¼	—	—	—	—	114
41	*Hamsool* ditto	—	5	—	—	—	—	—	—	7	—	21¼	—	—	—	—	—	—	38
42	Ginger	—	—	1½	1¼	—	—	—	—	94	—	—	—	—	—	—	—	—	—
43	Green ginger	—	—	¾	—	—	—	—	—	4	—	—	—	—	—	—	—	—	—
44	*Cut*, or *Terra Japonica*	—	—	—	—	—	—	—	—	—	—	—	¼	—	—	—	—	—	10
45	*Coirs* (coco-nut-rope)	—	—	—	—	—	—	—	—	—	—	—	214¼	2	5	—	—	—	4170
46	*China* sugar	—	—	11¾	2½	—	—	—	—	960	—	—	2¼	2	—	—	—	—	235
47	Sugar candy	—	—	1½	3¼	5	—	—	—	270	—	—	—	—	—	—	—	—	—
48	Dry dates	—	—	61½	5	—	—	—	—	1364	—	—	—	—	—	—	—	—	—
49	Dates	—	—	312½	4¼	—	—	—	—	4522	—	—	—	—	—	—	—	—	—
50	Plumbs (raisins)	—	—	¾	2¾	5	—	—	—	72	—	—	—	—	—	—	—	—	—
51	Mace	—	—	—	¼	—	—	—	—	50	—	—	—	—	—	—	—	—	—
52	Almonds	—	—	—	2¾	—	—	—	—	6	—	—	—	—	—	—	—	—	—
53	Camphire	—	—	—	4¼	—	—	—	—	176	—	—	—	—	—	—	—	—	—
54	Benjamin	—	—	¼	3	—	—	—	—	80	—	—	—	—	—	—	—	—	—
55	*Googool Dammer* (Resin)	—	—	1	—	—	—	—	—	21	—	—	4¼	—	—	—	—	—	90
56	*Malaca* (ditto)	—	—	—	½	—	—	—	—		—	—	—	—	—	—	—	—	—
57	Brimstone	—	—	—	1½	—	—	—	—	4	—	—	¼	¼	5	—	—	—	18
58	Saltpetre	—	—	—	2	—	—	—	—	8	—	—	¼	—	—	—	—	—	25
59	*Kankana kar*	—	—	—	3¾	—	—	—	—	35	—	—	—	1	—	—	—	—	10
60	Tin	—	—	6½	1¼	—	—	—	—	1290	—	—	—	—	—	—	—	—	—
61	Soap	—	—	2	½	—	—	—	—	162	—	—	—	—	—	—	—	—	—
62	*Chendoorum*	—	—	—	3½	—	—	—	—	21	—	—	—	—	—	—	—	—	—
63	*Puppa la kar*	—	—	3	2	—	—	—	—	50	—	—	—	—	—	—	—	—	—
64	*Cupper Sooth*	—	—	—	2½	—	—	—	—	10	—	—	—	—	—	—	—	—	—
65	Wax	—	—	¼	¼	3	—	—	—	43	—	—	1	2½	1	—	—	—	180

CHAPTER XVI.
March 7.

	Names of the Articles.	Average annual Quantity Imported.									Average annual Quantity Exported.								
		Corges of 1470 *Pucka Seers.*	*Morays* of 51¼ *Pucka Seers.*	*Candies* of 20 *Maunds.*	*Maunds* of 44 *Seers Cutcha.*	*Seers Cutcha* of 24 *Rupees.*	*Kodis*, or Scores.	*Tak* 40 Cubits.	*Adud*, or Pieces.	Total Value in *Rupees.*	*Corges* of 1470 *Pucka Seers.*	*Morays* of 51¼ *Pucka Seers.*	*Candies* of 20 *Maunds.*	*Maunds* of 44 *Seers Cutcha.*	*Seers Cutcha* of 24 *Rupees.*	*Kodis*, or Scores.	*Tak* 40 Cubits.	*Adud*, or Pieces.	Total Value in *Rupees.*
6	*Moy Pull*, or *Coy*	—	—	—	4½	—	—	—	—	40	—	—	—	—	—	—	—	—	—
7	*Hing*, or *Asafœtida*	—	—	—	3	1½	—	—	—	90	—	—	—	—	—	—	—	—	—
8	*Tippeelee Moolum*	—	—	—	2½	—	—	—	—	20	—	—	—	—	—	—	—	—	—
9	Red paint	—	—	—	—	5	—	—	—	10	—	—	—	—	—	—	—	—	—
0	Green ditto	—	—	—	—	1¼	—	—	—	3	—	—	—	—	—	—	—	—	—
1	Spanish root	—	—	¼	2	—	—	—	—	56	—	—	—	—	—	—	—	—	—
2	*Issup Koole*	—	—	—	2	—	—	—	—	20	—	—	—	—	—	—	—	—	—
3	*Goornakputhay*	—	—	—	—	5	—	—	—	10	—	—	—	—	—	—	—	—	—
4	*Subjah*	—	—	—	1	—	—	—	—	1	—	—	—	—	—	—	—	—	—
5	Gum	—	—	—	3	—	—	—	—	10	—	—	—	—	—	—	—	—	—
6	*Jahpull Beez* (nutmegs)	—	—	—	3	—	—	—	—	15	—	—	—	—	—	—	—	—	—
7	*Gurd pull*	—	—	—	—	—	—	—	—	—	—	—	—	4	—	—	—	—	8
8	*Coochalay Beez*	—	—	—	—	—	—	—	—	—	—	—	—	4	—	—	—	—	4
9	*Muckah*	—	—	—	—	1	—	—	—	2	—	—	—	—	—	—	—	—	—
0	*Rogun*	—	—	—	—	1	—	—	—	4	—	—	—	—	—	—	—	—	—
1	*Cauvee*, or paint (Reddle)	—	—	5¼	2½	—	—	—	—	120	—	—	—	—	—	—	—	—	—
2	*Paring Chucka*	—	—	2	—	—	—	—	—	80	—	—	—	—	—	—	—	—	—
3	Fish *geeree*	—	—	—	—	—	—	—	—	—	—	—	1	4¼	—	—	—	—	288
4	*Cutecoorogcony*	—	—	—	½	—	—	—	—	20	—	—	—	—	—	—	—	—	—
5	Iron	—	—	—	—	—	—	—	400	80	—	—	—	—	—	—	—	140	28
6	*Gopee Chundenum*	—	—	10	3½	—	—	—	—	129	—	—	¼	3	—	—	—	—	3
7	Copper	—	—	¼	4½	4½	—	—	—	300	—	—	—	—	—	—	—	—	—
8	Brass	—	—	½	4½	—	—	—	—	145	—	—	—	—	—	—	—	—	—
9	Cotton	—	—	1	2	—	—	—	—	88	—	—	—	—	—	—	—	—	—
0	White thread	—	—	—	—	—	—	—	—	—	—	—	½	—	—	—	—	—	180
1	Twine	—	—	6¼	2½	—	—	—	—	133	—	—	—	—	—	—	—	—	—
2	*Cossumba* flower (*Carthamus*)	—	—	—	4¼	—	—	—	—	15	—	—	—	—	—	—	—	—	—
3	Silk thread	—	—	—	¼	—	—	—	—	30	—	—	—	—	—	—	—	—	—
4	Tobacco *Malabar*	—	—	105⅕	¾	3¼	—	—	—	8508	—	—	6	4¼	—	—	—	—	745
5	Steel	—	—	—	—	—	—	—	—	—	—	—	—	—	—	—	—	16	2

CHAPTER XVI.

March 7.

96	Sealing-wax	—	—	½	¼	3	—	—	—	103	—	—	—	—	—	—	—	—	—
97	*Soonda* salt	—	—	—	1½	—	—	—	—	1	—	—	—	—	—	—	—	—	—
98	*Hingdah*	—	—	—	3	—	—	—	—	30	—	—	—	—	—	—	—	—	—
99	*Budda Soop*	—	—	—	4¾	—	—	—	—	20	—	—	—	—	—	—	—	—	—
100	Sundry cloths	—	—	—	—	—	126	196½	140	—	—	—	—	—	—	33¼	49½	—	—
101	Blue cloths	—	—	—	—	—	55¾	5	—	3720	—	—	—	—	—	—	—	—	—
102	Silk cloths	—	—	—	—	—	1½	45	—	680	—	—	—	—	—	—	—	—	—
103	*Case* shawls (*Banares*)	—	—	—	—	—	—	40	—	560	—	—	—	—	—	—	—	—	—
104	Silk upper cloths	—	—	—	—	—	—	2	—	60	—	—	—	—	—	—	—	—	—
105	*Cutkah Tharree* cloths	—	—	—	—	—	1¼	—	—	65	—	—	—	—	—	—	—	—	—
106	*Nankeen*	—	—	—	—	—	6½	4½	—	400	—	—	—	—	—	—	—	—	—
107	*Nar Muddee*	—	—	—	—	—	8¼	37	—	202	—	—	—	—	—	—	—	—	—
108	Chints	—	—	—	—	—	3	5¼	—	130	—	—	—	—	—	—	—	—	—
109	White *Comblie* (blankets)	—	—	—	—	—	12¼	1	1	257	—	—	—	—	—	—	—	1	2
110	Black *Comblie* (ditto)	—	—	—	—	—	6½	—	5	80	—	—	—	—	—	—	—	—	—
111	*Musrooms*	—	—	—	—	—	1¼	57	—	698	—	—	—	—	—	—	—	—	—
112	*China Peelown*	—	—	—	—	—	1¼	3	—	290	—	—	—	—	—	—	—	—	—
113	*Soorlee Thaun*	—	—	—	—	—	¼	—	—	125	—	—	—	—	—	—	—	—	—
114	*Dummas*	—	—	—	—	—	¼	5	—	310	—	—	—	—	—	—	—	—	—
115	*Moocmall*	—	—	—	—	—	—	2	—	120	—	—	—	—	—	—	—	—	—
116	*Mooctay* cloth	—	—	—	—	—	½	40½	—	202	—	—	—	—	—	—	—	—	—
117	*China* handkerchiefs	—	—	—	—	—	3¾	36¾	—	1163	—	—	—	—	—	—	—	—	—
118	*Loongee*	—	—	—	—	—	¼	2	—	4	—	—	—	—	—	—	—	—	—
119	Silk *Kittasauls* (umbrellas)	—	—	—	—	—	½	—	4	56	—	—	—	—	—	—	—	—	—
120	*China* ditto	—	—	—	—	—	7½	—	—	70	—	—	—	—	—	—	—	—	—
121	Canvas	—	—	—	—	—	6	—	—	180	—	—	—	—	—	—	—	—	—
122	Red *Dungree*	—	—	—	—	—	2½	4	—	88	—	—	—	—	—	—	—	—	—
123	*Kinkop* (silk cloth)	—	—	—	—	—	—	2	—	100	—	—	—	—	—	—	—	—	—
124	*Umroo*	—	—	—	—	—	—	2	—	40	—	—	—	—	—	—	—	—	—
125	Silk *Womans* cloth	—	—	—	—	—	—	91½	—	940	—	—	—	—	—	—	—	—	—
126	*Kelkee* ditto ditto	—	—	—	—	—	—	21	—	147	—	—	—	—	—	—	—	—	—
127	*Howrunga Jubbee Thaun*	—	—	—	—	—	—	9	—	90	—	—	—	—	—	—	—	—	—
128	*Thod putree*	—	—	—	—	—	—	4	—	40	—	—	—	—	—	—	—	—	—
129	Turbans	—	—	—	—	—	1¼	66	—	1274	—	—	—	—	—	—	—	—	—
130	*Gunnee*, or sackcloth	—	—	—	—	—	—	—	44½	45	—	—	—	—	—	—	—	—	—
131	Glass	—	—	—	—	1	—	—	—	2	—	—	—	—	—	—	—	—	—
132	Pearl shells	—	—	—	—	—	—	—	511	22	—	—	—	—	—	—	—	—	—
133	*Rojahver Tubbucks*	—	—	—	—	—	—	—	28	42	—	—	—	—	—	—	—	—	—
134	Rose water bottles	—	—	—	—	—	1¾	—	2	37	—	—	—	—	—	—	—	—	—
135	*China* ware	—	—	—	—	—	16	—	111	431	—	—	—	—	—	—	—	—	—

CHAPTER XVI.
March 7.

No.	Names of the Articles.	Average annual Quantity Imported.								Total Value in Rupees.	Average annual Quantity Exported.								Total Value in Rupees.
		Corges of 1470 *Pucka Seers.*	*Morays* of 51½ *Pucka Seers.*	*Candies* of 20 *Maunds.*	*Maunds* of 44 *Seers Cutcha.*	*Seers Cutcha* of 24 *Rupees.*	*Kodie*, or Scores.	*Tak* 40 Cubits.	*Adud*, or Pieces.		*Corges* of 1470 *Pucka Seers.*	*Morays* of 51½ *Pucka Seers.*	*Candies* of 20 *Maunds.*	*Maunds* of 44 *Seers Cutcha.*	*Seers Cutcha* of 24 *Rupees.*	*Kodie*, or Scores.	*Tak* 40 Cubits.	*Adud*, or Pieces.	
136	Salt-fish bundles	—	—	—	—	—	—	—	2	4	—	—	—	—	—	—	—	—	—
137	Ditto by *Donies*	—	—	—	—	—	—	—	6	150	—	—	—	—	—	—	—	—	—
138	*Coomloo Mass* (a fish)	—	—	—	1¼	—	—	—	1500	50	—	—	—	—	—	—	—	—	—
139	Sheep and goats	—	—	—	—	—	—	—	2	4	—	—	—	—	—	—	—	—	—
140	Liquor pipes	—	—	—	—	—	—	—	—	—	—	—	—	—	—	—	—	109¾	—
141	Coco-nuts	—	—	—	—	—	—	—	172399	4000	—	—	—	—	—	—	—	48795	975
142	Country paper reams	—	—	—	—	—	—	—	60¾	607	—	—	—	—	—	—	—	—	—
143	*Betel-leaf* bundles	—	—	—	—	—	—	—	17½	26	—	—	—	—	—	—	—	6000	6000
144	Sugar-cane	—	—	—	—	—	—	—	5300	43	—	—	—	—	—	—	—	150	2
145	*Cadjans* (coarse mats) bundles	—	—	—	—	—	—	—	—	—	—	—	—	—	—	—	—	4½	60
146	Green plantains	—	—	—	—	—	—	—	18	5	—	—	—	—	—	—	—	—	—
147	*Bahder buttoo*	—	—	—	—	—	—	—	—	—	—	—	32¾	—	—	—	—	—	200
148	*Mummeeties*	—	—	—	—	—	—	—	—	—	—	—	—	—	—	—	—	140	140
149	Firewood boat loads	—	—	—	—	—	—	—	—	—	—	—	—	—	—	—	—	13	52
150	Basket bundles	—	—	—	—	—	—	—	10	1	—	—	—	—	—	—	—	25	12
151	Matts	—	—	—	—	—	—	—	—	—	—	—	—	—	—	—	—	318	318
152	*Buttoovah*	—	—	—	—	—	—	—	9	2	—	—	—	—	—	—	—	—	—
153	Sundry Curry-stuff bundles	—	—	—	—	—	—	—	19	39	—	—	—	—	—	—	—	5	12
154	Sandal-wood	—	—	—	—	—	—	—	—	—	—	—	803	6¼	5	—	—	—	64660
	Total value in *Rupees*									44585									331532

CHAPTER XVII.

JOURNEY FROM THE ENTRANCE INTO KARNATA TO HYDER-NAGARA, THROUGH THE PRINCIPALITIES OF SOONDA AND IKERI.

CHAPTER XVII. March 8. *Karnata Désam.*

MARCH 8th, 1801.—On leaving *Déva-kára*, the valley watered by the *Bidháti* becomes very narrow, and you enter *Karnata Désam*, which extends below the *Ghats*, and occupies all the defiles leading up to the mountains. *Karnata* has been corrupted into *Canara;* and the coasts of *Tulava* and *Haiga*, with the adjacent parts of *Malayála* and *Kankana*, as belonging to princes residing in *Karnata*, have been called the coast of *Canara.* The language and people of this *Désam* being called *Karnataca*, the Mussulmans, on conquering the peninsula, applied this name, changed into *Carnatic*, to the whole country subject to its princes, and talked of a *Carnatic* above the *Ghats*, and one below these mountains; although no part of this last division belonged to the *Karnata* of the *Hindus.* Europeans for a long time considered the country below the eastern *Ghats* as the proper *Carnatic;* and, when going to leave *Dravada* and enter the real *Karnata*, they talked of going up from the *Carnatic* to *Mysore.*

Appearance of the country.

After going two cosses near the river side, with stony hills to my right, I came to the first cultivated spot in *Karnata.* Here a small rivulet descends from the hills, and waters a narrow valley, which in the bottom is cultivated with rice, and on the sides is planted with *Betel* and coco-nut palms. For half a coss the road then passes through a forest of the kind which spontaneously produces black pepper. Beyond this I came to another narrow valley, that is

CHAPTER XVII. March 8. watered by a perennial stream, and cultivated like the former. Afterwards I went about half a coss through a forest, where the ground is very level, and capable of being converted into rice fields. At the end of this I encamped in a third valley, which is called *Barabuli*, and like the two former is finely watered, planted, and cultivated. Near it is another hill that spontaneously produces pepper; and there are many such in this part of *Karnata*, especially in the *Yella-pura* and *Chinna-pura* districts. These pepper-hills are miserably neglected. The vines are not tied up to one third part of the trees, and the whole ground is overgrown with brush-wood. From their moisture a delightful freshness prevails in these places; and were they carefully cultivated, and the trees manured, I have no doubt, but that the pepper would be of a quality as good as any other. No tree should be allowed to grow in them, but such as are of some use; and of these the country spontaneously produces many; namely, two species of *Artocarpus*, *Teak*, blackwood, *Cassia*, wild nutmegs, *Caryota urens*, and the *Bassia*, with perhaps some others that escaped my notice. At present, however, these valuable kinds are not numerous, for they are overwhelmed by such as are totally useless. By the natives these pepper forests are called *May-nasu Canu*. The people here have no idea that any thing farther should be done to them, than once in three years to cut the bushes, and once annually to tie the vines to the young trees; and even these operations are much neglected. But, to make the most of such places, they ought to be carefully cultivated, no trees ought to be permitted to grow in them but such as are of use, and the vines ought to be manured as much as possible.

Mutti. In all this day's journey, even where the soil was full of stones, the forests through which I passed were very stately. The *Mutti* (*Chuncoa Muttia* Buch: MSS.) in particular grows to a prodigious size. The natives use the ashes of its bark to eat with *Betel*, in the same manner as in other parts quick-lime is employed. Fewer of the trees lose their leaves here than nearer the sea; for a freshness and moisture are kept up by the vicinity of the mountains, which every morning are involved in clouds. March 8.

The stream of the river is here slow, and its channel is filled with rocks and small islands. Owing to the quantity of rotten leaves that it contains, the water is dirty. From the straw and leaves which adhere to the trees high above the banks, it is easy to perceive, that in the rainy season it must be an immense stream, and must then rise between eight and ten feet above its present level, which in such a country will give it a most formidable velocity. *Bidháti* river.

The climate here, although very pleasant, is reckoned extremely unhealthy. Climate.

9th *March*.—I went what was called two *Sultany* cosses, to *Cutaki*; but this estimate is formed more from the difficulty of the road than the actual distance, which cannot be above five or six miles. At first I ascended close to the river, with a high hill immediately on my right. Soon after I came to the foot of the *Ghat*, where a fine stream enters from the south through some ground fit for cultivation; but of this no traces can be observed. I then ascended a very long and steep hill, sloping up by the sides of deep glens; and having gone a little way on a level ridge, I descended a considerable way into a valley, where there is a fine perennial stream. On the banks of this are some rice ground, and a wood which spontaneously produces pepper, and which is totally neglected. I then ascended a mountain, still longer and steeper than the first; and after a very short descent came to a small lake, and a building for the accommodation of travellers. Another short ascent brought me to a plain country above the *Ghats*, and immediately afterwards I came to *Cutaki*. March 9. Road up the *Ghats*.

The road, although not so steep as that at *Pedda Náyakana Durga*, is by no means judiciously conducted, and no pains have been taken in its formation. Loaded cattle, however, can pass; and, by the

CHAPTER XVII.

natives of the peninsula, that seems to be considered as the utmost perfection that a road demands.

March 9. Soil and trees of the western *Ghats.*

Here the western *Ghats* assume an appearance very different from that at *Pedda Náyakana Durga*, or *Kaveri-pura.* The hills, although steep and stony, are by no means rugged, or broken with rocks: on the contrary, the stones are buried in a rich mould, and in many places are not to be seen without digging. Instead, therefore, of the naked, sun-burnt, rocky peaks, so common in the eastern *Ghats*, we here have fine mountains clothed with the most stately forests. I have no where seen finer trees, nor any *Bamboos* that could be compared with those which I this day observed. The *Bamboos* compose a large part of the forest, grow in detached clumps, with open spaces between, and equal in height the *Caryota urens*, one of the most stately palms, of which also there is great plenty. There is no underwood nor creepers to interrupt the traveller who might choose to wander in any direction through these woods; but the numerous tigers, and the unhealthiness of the climate, would render any long stay very uncomfortable. About midway up the *Ghats* the *Teak* becomes common; but it is very inferior in size to the following trees, which unfortunately are of less value.

Tari, Myrobalanus Taria Buch: MSS.

Jamba, Mimosa xylocarpon Roxb:

Nandy, foliis oppositis, non stipulaceis, integerrimis, subtus tomentosis.

This is reckoned to make good planks and beams.

Unda Muraga, foliis oppositis, integerrimis stipulis inter folia ut in Rubiaceis positis.

Also reckoned good for planks and beams.

Mutti, Chuncoa Muttia Buch: MSS.

Good timber.

Sampigy, Michelia Champaca.

The wood used for drums.

March 9.

Shaguddy. Shaguda Buch: MSS.

A strong timber.

Wontay. Artocarpus Bengalensis Roxb: MSS.

The fruit is about the size of an orange, and is preserved with salt. Here it is used by the natives in place of tamarinds, which are much employed by the *Hindu* cooks.

Honnay. Pterocarpus santalinus Willd:

The *Teak* in some parts of this district of *Yella-pura* is abundant, and in the rainy season may be floated down the river.

Strata of Kankana.

Below the *Ghats* the country consists of the *Laterite*, or brick-stone, so often mentioned; but it is much intermixed with granites, and talcose argilite, which seems to be nothing more than the pot-stone impregnated with more argill than usual, and assuming a slaty form.

Strata on the *Ghats.*

The *strata* on the *Ghats* are much covered with the soil; so that it is in a few places only that they are to be seen. Having no compass, I could not ascertain their course; but, so far as I could judge from the sun in a country so hilly, they appeared to run north and south, with a dip to the east of about 30 degrees. Wherever it appears on the surface, the rock, although extremely hard or tough, is in a state of decay; and owing to this decay, its stratified nature is very evident. The plates, indeed, of which the *strata* consist, are in general under a foot in thickness, and are subdivided into rhomboidal fragments by fissures which have a smooth surface. It is properly an aggregate stone, composed of quartz impregnated with hornblende. From this last it acquires its great toughness. In decay, the hornblende in some plates seems to waste faster than in others, and thus leaves the stone divided into zones, which are alternately porous and white. I am inclined to think, that all mountains of a hornblende nature are less rugged than those of granite, owing to their being more easily decomposed by the action of the air. This rock contains many small crystallized particles, apparently of iron.

CHAPTER XVII.

March 9.

Appearance of the country.

From the summit of the *Ghats* to *Cutaki*, the whole country is level enough for the plough, and the soil is apparently good; yet, except in some low narrow spaces used for rice ground and *Betel-nut* gardens, there is no cultivation. *Cutaki* is a poor little village, with seven houses.

Height of the mountains.

I perceive no difference in the temperature of air, on coming from the country below the *Ghats;* and, in fact, do not think that I have to-day ascended more than a thousand feet perpendicular height. This is perhaps the very lowest part of the mountains; but the country is said to rise rapidly all the way to the *Marattah* frontier.

Robbers.

Almost all the inhabitants of this neighbourhood are *Haiga Bráhmans,* who are a very industrious class of men, that perform all agricultural labours with their own hands. During *Tippoo's* government, thieves were in this vicinity very numerous; and many bands of a set of scoundrels, called *Sady Jambuty,* were then in the habit of coming from the *Marattah* country to plunder. The former have been entirely banished; but the *Sady Jambutty* still come in bands of twenty or thirty men, although not so commonly as in former times. On Mr. Monro's arrival, a thief of this country, finding that this was not likely to be a convenient place for his residence, withdrew to the *Marattah* territory, and formed an alliance with *Lol Sing,* a noted robber. With their united forces these two ruffians have made three incursions into this country. In their last expedition, about twelve days ago, both were taken prisoners, and are now in confinement at *Hully-halla.* When these robbers make their attack, or are known to be in the neighbourhood, the *Bráhmans,* and other peaceable inhabitants, retire from their houses with their effects, and even during the rainy season conceal themselves in the forests; for pestilence, or beasts of prey, are gentle in comparison with *Hindu* robbers, who, in order to discover concealed property, put to the torture all those who fall into their hands.

10th *March.*—I went four cosses to *Yella-pura.* The first part of the road led through a forest spontaneously producing pepper. The trees and soil are very fine; but owing to a want of cultivators, according to the report of the inhabitants, not above one fourth of the pepper is procured from it that ought to be. This forest is intersected by narrow vallies of rice-ground, with a few gardens well supplied with water from springs and rivulets. I afterwards passed through a very hilly country; but the hills are of no considerable height, and in general the soil is apparently good. The trees, however, are not so large as where the pepper grows; and it is universally agreed, that the plant will not thrive in any forest but where it is found spontaneously growing. Many places among these hills are so level that the plough might be employed; and I suppose they might be cultivated for *Car' Ragy,* as is done in similar situations at *Priya-pattana;* but the people say, that unless the ground has been formed into terraces, the rains here are so heavy as to sweep away the seed. The rains in general are fully adequate to produce one crop of rice from any land properly levelled; and therefore it might be thought that by far the greater part of the country here might be cultivated for rice; but the people have an idea that no part of the country is fit for that purpose, but what has been already cultivated. Even of this, owing to a want of cultivators, three fourths are at present waste. The gardens being more profitable, and being also private property, are better occupied; and not above one quarter of them have gone to ruin.

CHAPTER XVII. March 10. Appearance of the country.

Yella-pura is the residence of a *Tahsildar,* and contains a hundred houses with a market *(Bazar),* which is tolerably well supplied; but every kind of grain is dearer here than at *Seringapatam.*

Yella-pura and its district.

The *Tahsildar* gives me the following account of his district. Near the *Ghats* cultivation is confined to pepper and *Betel* gardens, and to rice fields, in which, as a second crop, a little *Hessaru (Phaseolus Mungo)* is raised, and occasionally a little sugar-cane. In

CHAPTER XVII. March 10. the eastern parts toward *Hully-halla*, *Sambrany*, *Madanuru*, *Mundagodu*, and *Induru*, the woods consist mostly of *Teak*, and there are no gardens. The cultivated articles on low lands are rice, *Carlay* (*Cicer Arietinum*), and *Horse-gram* (*Dolichos biflorus*), and on the dry-field *Ragy* (*Cynosurus Corocanus*), and *Ellu* (*Sesamum*). The soil every where is tolerably free from stones. Although the rains are not so heavy as below the *Ghats*, they are sufficient on level land to bring to maturity one crop of rice. Little attention is paid here to the tanks; and they are rather dams to collect the water of small streams, or of springs, and to distribute it to the fields and gardens, than reservoirs to collect the rain water.

Maynasu Canu, or forests containing spontaneous pepper.

The *Haiga Bráhmans* say, that all the forests spontaneously producing pepper, with the gardens and rice fields intermixed, are their private property. By an old valuation, a separate land-tax is affixed on each kind of ground; but on most of the properties, on account of the depopulated state of the country, from one half to three fourths of what was exacted by the *Ráyaru* have been relinquished. To manage a *Maynasu Canu* properly, requires the following labour. Once a year the branches of the pepper vines must be tied up to the trees, and these must be freed from all climbing plants, especially the *Pothos scandens* Lin. and the *Acrostichum scandens* Buch: MSS. both of which climb to the tops of the highest trees. Every third year all the bushes ought to be cut down; and every fifth year the side branches of the trees should be lopped, to render them proper supports for the vine, which thrives best on slender straight trees. Where the trees are too distant, a branch or cutting ought to be planted; and if no young shoot of the pepper is near, a cutting or two of the vine should be put into the earth near the young tree. The pepper vine thus managed lives about ten years; when it dies, another young shoot must be trained up in its stead. In doing this, care must be taken to select shoots of a good kind; for, as the birds drop all the seeds promiscuously, shoots of the three different kinds of pepper are to be found in these woods. These three kinds are

Cariguta, *Bily Maynasu*, and *Vocalu*. The first kind is the best; not that there is any difference in the quality of the pepper, but the *amenta* of the two last kinds contain very few grains. I have had no opportunity of determining, whether the difference consists in sex, species, or variety; but the natives, by examining their leaves, can distinguish the different kinds. Every kind of tree is reckoned equally fit for supporting the pepper vine; but, where the woods are too thin, the tree commonly planted is the *Bondu Bala*, because it easily takes root. As the produce could not be secured from the monkies, no fruit trees are planted. When the trees are about three cubits distant from each other, and are of a middling size, the vines thrive best. Very large trees do not answer for the pepper, but are said to be of advantage by giving shade. In fact they are very common; but I imagine more owing to the trouble of cutting them, than to any advantage that they are of to the pepper. In order to prevent the havoc which would be occasioned by the natural decay and fall of one of these immense trees, when they observe one beginning to wither, the natives cut off its branches, and a circle of bark from the bottom of the stem; by this means it decays gradually, and rots without falling down in a mass, owing to the weight of its branches. Except this rotten wood, no manure is used. Most of these steps, which I have now enumerated, are in general very much neglected. The pepper of a *Maynasu Canu* is reckoned somewhat inferior to that raised in gardens, which I consider as arising merely from a want of proper cultivation and manure. In a *Maynasu Canu*, a tree, although much larger than one in a garden, produces only one *Cutcha Seer;* while the one in the garden usually produces double that quantity. A man collects in the day the produce of twenty trees, or rather more than 12 lb., and at the same time he ties up the branches, which is all the annual labour required. He ascends the tree by means of a ladder of *Bamboos*, some of which are forty cubits long.

CHAPTER XVII.

March 11. Face of the country.

11th *March.*—I went four cosses to *Caray Hosso-hully;* that is, the new village at the tank. The whole country, so far as I saw, was totally uninhabited, and very few traces of former cultivation were observable. A few narrow vallies seem once to have been under rice. The higher grounds, I suspect, have been always a forest; although, from the stateliness of the trees, the soil would appear to be good, and in its present state much of it is not too steep for the plough, while no part seems incapable of being formed into terraces, as is done below the *Ghats.* In a small portion near *Yella-pura,* the trees of the forest were stunted, and from a want of moisture had lost their leaves; but in the greater part they were very luxuriant, and many of the kinds were, to me at least, quite unknown. In my botanical investigations, however, I had very little success; for the cutting down one of these trees is a day's work for four or five natives; and at *Yella-pura* I could procure nobody that would climb to bring me specimens. The vast number of ants, indeed, that live on the trees in India, render this a very disagreeable employment.

Caray Hosso-hully.

Caray Hosso-hully is a miserable village of six houses, collected by Major Monro as a stage between *Yella-pura* and *Soonda;* for, on his taking possession of the country, the whole way was through a continued waste. The nearest inhabited place to *Hosso-hully* is two cosses distant. The new settlers are *Marattahs,* by which appellation in the south of India the *Súdras* of *Maharastra Désam* are known. Since the conquest, many of these people have come into this province; and many more would come, were small advances made to enable them to commence cultivation; for the desolation here has introduced a wildness equal to that of an American forest. The huts here are wretched, but the people have already cleared some ground. Throughout the forests of *Soonda,* tigers and wild buffaloes are very numerous, but there are no elephants.

Irrigation.

The reservoir here has been a very fine one, and never becomes dry; but it is now so filled with bushes and long grass, that to put

CHAPTER XVII. March 11.

it in proper repair would require a thousand *Pagodas*. Its water never was employed for the cultivation of rice, but was used only to bring forward the young shoots of sugar-cane, which, till the setting in of the rainy season, require irrigation.

Bidháti river.

About two-thirds of the way from *Yella-pura* to *Hosso-hully*, I crossed the *Bidháti-holay*, which goes north, and joins a river coming from *Supa* to form the *Sedásiva-ghur* river. Its channel is wide, and in the rainy season is probably full, but at present it contains very little water.

Strata.

The *strata*, laid bare by the river, are of the same nature with those on the *Ghats*; but their dip toward the east is greater.

March 12. Appearance of the country.

12th *March*.—I went three cosses to *Sancada-gonda*. Immediately after setting out, I crossed a small branch of the *Bidháti*, which is called *Baswa-holay*; and still farther on I crossed another, named *Gudialada-holay*. The whole country is waste, and covered with forest. The soil almost every where appears to be excellent, with more low vallies, and more vestiges of former cultivation, than on the route of yesterday. This valley land is here called *Taggu*, and the rice growing on it requires five months to come to maturity. The higher lands are called *Mackey*, and the highest arable land is called *Bisu*. The rice cultivated there requires only three months to come to maturity. *Sancada-gonda* contains three houses, with some pretty rice lands in a good state. Not far from it are two other villages, each containing four houses, with some rice-land and gardens. These villages subsisted during all the trouble of *Tippoo's* government, and belong to the *Guru* of all the *Haiga Bráhmans*, who resides at *Honawully Matam*, in *Soonda*, pays the land-tax, and lets his lands to some of his disciples.

March 13.

13th *March*.—I went three cosses to the place which Europeans and Mussulmans call *Soonda*. In the vulgar language of *Karnata* it is called *Sudha*, which is a corruption from *Sudha-pura*, the *Sanskrit* appellation. The road was very circuitous; as I went first about south-west, and afterwards almost east. The hills are much

CHAPTER XVII. March 13.

steeper than those on the last two days route, and of course are less fit for the cultivation of rice; but there are many deep and narrow vallies fit for *Betel-nut* gardens; and several of these, within or near the old walls, are now occupied, and filled with *Haiga Bráhmans*, who in this country are the sole cultivators of gardens. In many places I observed the pepper growing spontaneously; but it is entirely neglected; and many of the trees that would bear it are stript of their leaves and branches, which are used as manure for the gardens. All the rivulets that I crossed to-day are said to be branches of the *Sálamala*, which comes from *Sersi;* and on going below the *Ghats* assumes the name of *Gangáwali*, and forms the boundary between *Haiga* and *Kankana*.

Guru of the *Haiga Bráhmans.*

I sent a message to the *Guru* of the *Haiga Bráhmans*, offering to visit him; but this he declined, and sent me word, that he would come to my tents at three o'clock, at which time he would have finished his devotions which then occupied his time. He did not however arrive until late in the evening, when I was eating; so that he could not enter. I found, that in place of prayer he had been employed in giving an entertainment to another *Sannyási;* and I am uncertain whether he thought that it would be consistent with his dignity to keep a European four or five hours in waiting; or whether these persons, who had relinquished the vanity of worldly pleasure, were detained so long at table by pious conversation.

Haiga Bráhmans.

The *Haiga Bráhmans* seem to have changed countries with the *Karnataca Bráhmans* of *Sudha*, who in *Haiga* are in greatest estimation, while the *Bráhmans* of that country have all the valuable property in *Sudha*, and their *Guru* has taken up his abode in its capital, at *Honawully Matam*, or the golden convent. Whatever truth may be in the story of *Myuru Verma*, the *Haiga Bráhmans* were certainly the first of the *Panch Dravada* division who penetrated among the *Jáin* of these parts. It seems to have been with the view of depriving them of their property, that the pretence of their having lost a part of their cast, or rank, was set up by the subsequent intruders, who followed the conquests of the *Vijaya-nagara* monarchs. The character which the *Haiga Bráhmans* use in writing books on science, is the *Grantha* of *Kérala*, which they say includes all the countries created by *Parasu Ráma.* The *Haiga Bráhmans*, however, consider the *Karnataca* language as their native tongue; and all accompts and inscriptions on stone, whether in the vulgar language or in *Sanskrit*, are written in the *Karnata* character, which is nearly the same with the *Andray*, or old writing of *Telingana.*

Account of the *Rájás* of *Sudha-pura* by their *Guru.*

While I was waiting for the *Sannyásis*, I assembled the most learned men of the place, among whom was the hereditary *Guru* of the *Rájás*, who has a written account of the family of *Sudha*, with a copy of each prince's seal. These men said, that in the time of the father of *Krishna Ráyaru* this country belonged to *Jain Polygars*, the descendants of the *Cadumba* family; which strongly confirms the assertion of the *Jain* of *Haiga*, when these said that *Myuru Verma* was of their sect. These *Polygars* managed the country as usual, and paid tribute to *Vencatuppati Ráya*, the father of *Achuta* and *Krishna Ráyalu*, and who was their predecessor on the throne of *Vijaya-nagara.* This, however, is probably a mistake; as from an inscription at *Gaukarna*, already mentioned, it would appear, that the name of *Krishna Ráya's* father was *Sedásiva. Vencatuppati*, having for many years obtained no children, promised the whole of his kingdom to his sister's son *Arasuppa Náyaka;* but, having afterwards had two sons born to him, he gave to the young prince, his nephew, the full sovereignty of *Sudha.* This warrior governed from the year of *Sal.* 1478 *(A. D.* 155$\frac{1}{6}$) till 1521 *(A. D.* 159$\frac{1}{9}$). He built *Sudha-pura;* and having destroyed all the *Jain Polygars*, and the priests of these heretics, he brought up the *Haiga Bráhmans* to occupy the waste lands. He was succeeded by his son, *Ram Chandra Nayaka*, who governed till 1541 *(A. D.* 161$\frac{8}{9}$). He was succeeded by his son, *Ragunata Nayaka*, who governed till 1561 *(A. D.* 163$\frac{8}{9}$). His son, *Mādŭ Linga Nayaka*, became a follower of

CHAPTER XVII. March 13.

the *Sivabhactars*, and governed till 1597 (*A. D.* 167$\frac{4}{5}$). He was succeeded by his son, *Sedásiva Ráya*, who governed till 1620 (*A. D.* 169$\frac{7}{8}$); he by his son, *Baswa Linga Rájá*, who governed till 1668 (*A. D.* 174$\frac{5}{6}$); and he by his son, *Imody Sedásiva Rájá*, who was expelled by *Hyder* in 1685 (176$\frac{2}{3}$), and took refuge in *Goa*, where his son is now living on a pension from the viceroy.

During the government of these *Rájás* the country is said to have been cultivated, and the town to have been very large. The space within the walls is said to extend each way a coss, or at least three miles, and was fully occupied by houses. The country, having been repeatedly the seat of war between *Hyder* and the *Marattahs*, has been desolated, and the houses in the town are now reduced to about fifty. In the reign of *Imody Sedásiva*, the town suffered much from an attack of the *Marattahs;* but, when *Hyder* took possession of it, there still remained 10,000 houses. The original territories of the family seem to have been the four districts (*Talucs*) above the *Ghats*, now under the management of Mr. Read; and, according to the *Guru*, they acknowledged no superior. From the *Vijaya-pura Sultans*, *Sedásiva*, grand-father of the last *Rájá*, conquered five districts (*Pansh-malu*) in *Kankana*. *Imody Sedásiva*, as has been already stated, was attacked by the *Marattahs*, and forced to pay tribute (*Chouti*). Till he was able to collect the sum demanded, the *Pansh-malu* were given in pledge to a *Marattah* chief named *Gópál Row*, who restored them when the money was paid. On *Hyder's* attack, the *Rájá* resigned the *Pansh-malu* to the viceroy of *Goa*, who settled on him an annual pension of 12000 *Putlis*, or *Venetians*, equal to 48,000 *Rupees*. This his son now enjoys; and he has besides some houses, and gardens, befitting his rank. These five districts are said to be worth annually 80,000 *Rupees*, and seem to have been the remnant of the five larger districts, at one time governed by the *Vazir* of *Ponday*, after what now composes the *Ancola* district (*Taluc*) had been wrested from the Mussulmans, and *Rájás* of *Sudha*, by the *Sivabhactars* of *Ikeri*.

CHAPTER XVII.

March 13.

Inaccuracies in this account, shown from inscriptions.

Although in many points this account seems to be true, it is by no means accurate, as I learned from inscriptions found at this place. Those of which I was able to take any account to-day are as follow:

The most ancient inscription here is at a *Jain* temple *(Busty)* dedicated to *Adéswara*, the first of the gods *(Sidaru)*. It is dated in the year of *Sal.* 722 *(A. D.* $\frac{799}{800}$), and in the reign of *Imody Sedásiva Ráya*. This being the name of the last *Rájá* of *Sudha*, it might at first sight be supposed, that he was the prince mentioned in the inscription, the thousand years of the era having been omitted in the date, as is sometimes done among the *Hindus;* but this, it must be observed, would bring down the date to the year of our Lord $1\frac{799}{800}$, and the donation is made to a *Jain* temple that has been long in ruins, and to a sect abhorred by the last dynasty. Besides, it is said that the titles used in the inscription are totally different from those used by the late *Rájás* of *Sudha*, and are of a much higher nature.

The next inscription in antiquity is at a *Jain Matam*. A copy of this, as of the preceding, has been delivered to the Bengal government. It is dated in the year of *Sal.* 727, or *A. D.* $80\frac{4}{5}$, and in the reign of *Chamunda Ráya*, who has very high titles, like those of his predecessor, and is styled the chief of all the kings of the south. He mentions the advantages that had been gained over the followers of *Buddha* by two of his ancestors, *Sedásiva* and *Belalla*. These two inscriptions, therefore, belong to the dynasty of the *Belalla Ráyas*, monarchs of *Karnata*. *Ramuppa Varmica* makes the overthrow of that dynasty, as supreme monarchs, to have happened in the year of Christ $78\frac{2}{3}$; but here we find them governing in the northern parts of *Karnata* 22 years afterwards. Although this is an inaccuracy, yet the difference is so small, that the era of the government of the *Belalla* dynasty may be considered as ascertained to have been in the eighth century of the Christian era. The *Jain* religion was then the predominant one in the peninsula, and had

CHAPTER XVII.

March 13.

been preceded by that of *Buddha*, whose followers were then persecuted by the *Jain*, as these again were afterwards by the followers of *Vyása*.

The third inscription, of which a copy has also been delivered to the Bengal government, is placed in a *Jain Matam*, and is dated in *Sal.* 1121, or *A. D.* 119$\frac{8}{9}$, in the reign of *Sedásiva Rájá* of *Sudhapura;* which shows, that this town was not founded by *Arasuppa Nayaka*, but had many centuries before his time been the residence of a *Jain Rájá*. *Sedásiva* does not acknowledge any superior, but he does not arrogate to himself such high titles as those used in the two last mentioned inscriptions. He is very lavish in praise of his *Guru*, *Sri Madabinava Butta Calanco*, who (that is to say, his predecessors in the same *Matam*) had bestowed prosperity on *Belalla Ráya*. Whether this *Sedásiva* was a descendant of the *Belalla* family, as this would incline one to think, or whether he was descended from the *Cadumba* family, as the *Guru* here supposes, is uncertain.

There are here two inscriptions by *Imody Arasuppa*, founder of the last dynasty of *Sudha Rájás*. The one is on a stone at *Honawully Matam*. The whole almost is in couplets, few of which are to be found in the inscriptions of an early date. The time of this inscription is involved in one of these *conceits*, of which I have not procured the explanation. The other inscription is at a *Matam* belonging to one of the *Udipu Sannyásis*. It is dated in the year of *Sal.* 1515, or *A. D.* 159$\frac{2}{3}$, which confirms the chronology of the family *Guru*. The donation contained in the inscription is made by *Arasuppa Nayaka*, *Rájá* of *Sudha;* by the appointment of *Sri Vira Prubu Vencatuppati*, his superior, who gets all the titles usually bestowed on the sovereigns of *Vijaya-nagara*. This, in the first place, shows, that the *Rájás* of *Sudha* were not independent, but for a time governed, at least nominally, as vassals of the kings of *Vijaya-nagara*. Indeed, the first four persons of the family assumed only the title of *Nayaka*, which is that usually given to *Polygars*.

In the year 1674, *Sedásiva* assumed the title of *Ráya*, 38 years after the *Ikeri* family had thrown off all form of respect for their ancient lords. This inscription also shows, that *Vencatuppati* could not have been the father of the celebrated *Krishna Ráyaru*; as he lived after the reign of that monarch. In fact, the date of this inscription is after the period assigned for the destruction of *Vijaya-nagara* by *Ramuppa*; and *Vencatuppati* was probably some person adopted to support the falling dynasty after the death of *Ráma Rájá*, and conjoined in the government with *Sedásiva*, usually reckoned the last king of *Vijaya-nagara*.

CHAPTER XVII. March 13.

14th *March*.—I went four *Sultany* cosses to *Sersi*. The outermost wall of *Sudha* was at least six miles from where I had encamped, and is said by the natives to be sixteen cosses, or at least forty-eight miles, in circumference. There are three lines of fortification round the town. The extent of the first, as I have already observed, was estimated by the natives at three miles square, and the whole space that it contained was closely occupied by houses. In the two spaces surrounded by the outer lines, the houses were formerly scattered in small clumps, with gardens between them.

March 14. Former extent of *Sudha*.

From the outer gate of *Sudha*, till I reached *Sersi*, I saw neither houses nor cultivation; but it was said, that there were villages in the vicinity of the road. The country is more level than that through which I came yesterday. In two places the trees of the forest were covered with pepper-vines; but these were entirely neglected. *Sersi* is a small village, but it is the residence of the *Tahsildar* under whom *Sudha* is placed. It is not centrical for the district, but is chosen on account of its being a great thoroughfare, and as having a very considerable custom-house. It has a small mud fort, in which nobody resides, although robbers are still troublesome; but to live in forts is not the custom of *Sudha*. Near it are the ruins of a fortress, which was built by *Rám Chandra Nayaka*, the second prince of the last dynasty. It is called *Chinna-pattana*, the same name with that of the city which we call *Madras*.

Appearance of the country.

CHAPTER XVII.

March 14. Former population.

The hereditary accomptant (*Shanaboga*) of the place says, that his brother is now with *Baswa Linga Rájá*, the son of *Imody Sedásiva*, at *Goa*, and confirms the account given by the *Guru*. He says also, that an enumeration of all the houses of the country was taken, in order to levy a tax for discharging the tribute which the *Marattahs* exacted. *Sersi* then contained 700 houses, and *Sudha* 100,000; but with the amount of the whole population of the country the accomptant is not acquainted. The population of the capital consisted of the court and army, with their followers; for it would appear, that the country never possessed any manufactures. The country must have been then very well cultivated, and rich, to be able to support such a capital, whose inhabitants, if this account be true, were then at least three times as numerous as the present people of the whole territory: but the account is probably exceedingly exaggerated.

Sources of two rivers.

From a garden on the west side of *Sersi*, the *Sálamala*, or *Gangawali* river takes its rise; and on its east side, from a *Tank* called *Aganasini*, issues a river of the same name, which in the lower part of its course is called the *Tari-holay*.

March 15. Cultivation in the western parts of *Soonda*.

15th *March*.—I continued at *Sersi*, taking an account of the state of the country, as an example of the western parts of *Soonda*, in which the cultivation of gardens is the chief object of the farmer.

Gardens. Situation.

In these gardens are raised promiscuously, *Betel-nut*, and *Betel-leaf*, black-pepper, cardamoms, and plantains. A great part of the ground formerly planted has now become waste, and there is some fit for the purpose that would appear never to have been cultivated; but it is only a small proportion of the whole country that can be employed in this way, and that is chiefly in the vicinity of the *Ghats*. Toward the eastern side of the province there are very few gardens. The situation required is a low narrow valley, with its head to the west, and opening toward the east; so that the hills by which it is bounded may defend it from the west and south sun.

To add to the shelter, the hills in these directions must be covered with high trees. The hills on the north side of the valley must also belong to the garden, and must be covered with trees, which are annually pruned to procure branches that serve as manure. At all seasons the garden must command a supply of water. This commonly is obtained from springs, which are numerous in this country at the head of almost every little valley. The water of these springs is collected in a small pond or reservoir, from whence it can at pleasure be let out by a channel which is conducted along the upper side of the garden. Water is also procured by forming channels from the small rivulets with which the country abounds. Some rich men fill up the whole bed of one of these rivulets, and form their plantation in the place where it was. They have thus at its upper end a reservoir formed of the remaining part of the old channel, and by one side of the garden they draw a canal to carry off the superfluous water. This incurs a very considerable expense, not only in filling up the channel, but in giving the reservoir and canal a strength sufficient to resist the torrents of the rainy season. The best soil for these gardens is the *Cagadali*, a red mould containing very small stones. I observe, however, that all kinds of soil are used. The prevalent one throughout the country is a light-coloured loam of great depth.

Formation of a new garden.

The first step in the process of making a new garden is, to surround it by a ditch, to keep off the torrents which descend from the hills. The garden is then levelled with the hoe, and the whole is formed into beds, about twenty feet wide, by drains, which are parallel to each other, and run in the direction of the length of the valley, or nearly east and west. These drains are intended to carry off superfluous moisture, and in some gardens to carry away water that at all seasons springs up from the soil wherever it is opened. The soil where this abounds is reckoned by far the best; but the water itself is very pernicious, and nothing would grow unless it were carefully removed by the drains. These are about a foot broad,

CHAPTER XVII. March 15.

and, according to the natural moisture of the soil, are from a foot to eighteen inches deep. At the same time must be formed the reservoir or canal for giving the supply of water, with the channels in which it is to run. The principal channel runs at the head of the garden, and crosses the direction of the drains. From this a small channel leads between every two drains, in the centre of each bed. Such is the disposition of some of the gardens that I examined; but, according to the various declivities in different gardens, it must be varied considerably. The season for performing this labour is during the two months which precede the autumnal equinox.

Plantain trees.

In the month following the autumnal equinox, young plantain trees are set in rows, within two feet of each side of the drains, and at the distance of twelve feet from each other. If possible, the whole garden should then be covered with branches of the *Nelli (Phyllanthus Emblica);* at any rate, some must be put near each young plantain tree; and at the same time the centre channel of each bed must be raised a cubit high, with earth brought from the neighbouring hills. When the rainy season is over, the earth is spread upon the bed, the channel is formed anew, and every fifteen days water is given once. In the operation of watering, the channel is first filled; and then, with a pot or scoop, some water is thrown on the roots of the trees.

Betel-nut palm, or *Areca.*

In the same season of the second year, a pit, of a cubit square and of the same depth, is made between every two plantain trees. In each pit is placed a young *Areca*, which is taken up from the seed-bed with much earth adhering to its root. The pit is filled with fresh earth, which is trampled down by the foot; so that one half of the pit becomes empty, and is afterwards filled with the leaves of the *Emblica.* At the same period of every even year, that is, the second, fourth, sixth, and so forth, the channels of every bed must be filled with fresh earth. In the month preceding the winter solstice, the beds must be levelled; and, new channels having been formed, the trees must be watered once every fifteen days. In the second month afterwards, the beds must be hoed, and each tree manured with rotten dung taken from the cow-house, where the litter used has been either fresh leaves or dry grass. Above this are spread the small branches and leaves of any kind of trees, and towards the root of every *Areca* a quantity of these is heaped up. In the month preceding the summer solstice, to prevent the rains from washing away the manure, the beds are covered with plantain leaves. In the uneven, or intermediate years, nothing is done in the garden, but to clear the drains and channels, and in the dry season to give the trees water. Each garden therefore is divided into two parts; in the first year one half is formed, and in the year following the other is planted.

The *Betel-nut* palm, or *Areca,* in thirteen years after it has been planted, begins to produce fruit, and in five years more arrives at perfection: it lives from fifty to a hundred years; and, when one dies, another from the nursery is put in its place. There is only one kind.

The nursery is managed as follows. In the month preceding the vernal equinox the seed is ripe. After having been cut, it is kept eight days in the house. In the mean time a bed of ground in a shady place is dug, and in this the nuts are placed nine inches from each other, and with their eyes uppermost. They must be covered with a finger breadth of earth. The bed is then covered with dry plantain leaves, and once in eight days is sprinkled with water. In the month preceding the summer solstice, the plantain leaves are removed, and young shoots are found to have come from the nuts. In the second month afterwards, leaves of the *Emblica* are spread between the young plants. In the month preceding the vernal equinox, they get a little dung. In the dry season they are watered once in from four to eight days, according to the nature of the soil. They are not removed till they are going to be finally

CHAPTER XVII. March 15. planted in the garden, which is done in their fifth year. They are then estimated worth one silver *Fanam* a hundred, $5\frac{1}{2}$ *Fanams* going to the *Rupee;* but they are seldom sold, any man lending to his neighbour when he may be in want of a few.

The crop season of an *Areca* garden continues from two months before, till one after, the winter solstice. The bunches are cut as they approach to ripeness, for the ripe nut is of no use except for seed. The husk is removed with a knife. A decoction is then made with a few nuts, a little *Chunam* (ashes of the bark of the *Chuncoa Muttia* Buch: MSS.), and some bark of the *Honay*, or *Pterocarpus santolinus.* These are bruised together, and are boiled six hours in water. A quantity of the nut cleared from the husk is then put in a pot, and into this the decoction is poured, until it rises above the nuts, which are then boiled till the eyes separate. They are now put upon a strainer of mats supported on posts, and are dried six days in the sun. At night they are covered with a mat. In this country the *Betel-nut* is never cut, but is sold entire, and is called red *Betel.* Any nuts of a bunch, that have become too ripe before it was cut, are picked out and kept separate. Their husks are removed, and they are dried in the sun without boiling. These are called raw *Betel,* and sell much lower than the other kind.

From the month preceding the winter solstice, to that following the vernal equinox, the leaves of the *Areca* fall off. Each is accompanied by its broad, leathery, membraneous petiole; which, when they are young, form collectively a green smooth body at the top of the stem. These membranes are cut off, and carefully preserved. They are about three feet long, and a cubit broad; and, in the rainy season, are used to make covers for the young bunches, or *spadices.* In the month following the summer solstice, a man mounts the *Areca,* and above every branch fixes a cover, so as entirely to keep off the rain. Some of the trees are so tall and slender, that they cannot bear the weight of the operator, and thus are deprived of covers. On these the bunches produce only from five to a hundred nuts, while two hundred nuts are reckoned the average produce of a covered bunch, and some bring five hundred to maturity. Each tree commonly yields two good bunches, or three small ones. The average produce is said to be 1 *Maund*, or 72 *Seers* of boiled nut from fifty trees, or from each $\frac{9148}{10000}$ parts of a pound. A particular set of men are employed to cover the bunches, and cut down the fruit. At each time they get two *Rupees* for every thousand bunches, and are very dexterous. Round their ancles, and under their soles, they fix a rope made of plantain stems, and thus unite their feet, which are then placed against the stem, and drawn up together, while the climber holds on with his hands. Having placed the rope and his feet firm against the stem, he first moves up one hand, and then the other, and afterwards draws up his feet again. In this manner he reaches the top of one tree, where he secures himself by taking a round turn with a rope, which he carries up in his hand. One end of this rope is tied to the middle of a short stick, upon which the man seats himself, and performs his labour, drawing up whatever he wants, from an attendant below, by means of a line that he has fixed to his girdle. When he has done with one tree, he unties his seat, secures it round his neck, and swings the tree backwards and forwards, till he can reach another, upon which he then throws himself, and again makes fast his seat. He thus passes over the whole garden, without ever coming to the ground. The trees that, from being too tall and slender, are unable to support a man's weight, have their fruit gathered by being pulled towards a neighbouring tree by means of a hook. The cultivators seem to under-rate the produce very much.

Black pepper.

When the *Betel-nut* palm is thirteen years old, the garden is planted with either black pepper, or *Betel-leaf* vines, which climb upon the *Areca*. The pepper, as I have already mentioned, is of

CHAPTER XVII. March 15. three kinds. The *Cari Maynasu* is the most productive, but requires a *Cagadali* soil. In this, the produce of a good tree covered with *Cari Maynasu*, is reckoned five *Seers* of cured pepper, or a small fraction more than three pounds. The *Sambara* and *Arsina gutti* thrive very well on *Arsina Munnu*, or a light-coloured soil; but the first produces only one *Seer*, and the latter two. The quality of all the kinds is the same. In the month following the vernal equinox, four cuttings of the pepper vine, each a cubit and a half in length, are taken for every *Areca*. One of their ends is buried five or six inches in the ground, the other is tied to the stem of its supporter. The vine requires no farther trouble, but tying its branches up once a year in the month preceding the summer solstice. It bears in six or seven years, and lives about twenty-five; so that one *Areca* requires three or four sets of vines. The crop season is during the two months which precede the vernal equinox. The fruit is collected by means of ladders; and a man does not collect, and cure, in a day more than five *Seers*, or three pounds. The pepper, as usual, is gathered when the grains are full grown, but not ripe. Here the *amenta* are gathered into a heap, which stands in the house, and there they are kept three days. They are then rubbed with the foot; and the grains, having been separated from all other matter, are then fit for sale.

White pepper. A little white pepper is made by allowing the berries to ripen. The bunches, having been kept three days in the house, are washed and bruised in a basket with the hand, till all the *amenta* and pulp are removed. The seed is then dried five days, and is fit for sale. It is twice as dear as black pepper, but the demand for it is very small, for it is used only as a medicine.

Betel-leaf. The *Betel-leaf* is cultivated exactly like the pepper, and lives the same length of time. In this country, the *Nagwally*, or female plant, for it is *dioecious*, is that chiefly used; but the *Umbadi*, or male, may also be found. Here both frequently produce fructification, which I have not seen any where else. A thousand leaves of the *Nagwally* sell for 8 *Dubs*, while the same number of leaves of the *Umbadi* bring only one fourth part of that sum.

Whenever the *Betel* and pepper vines have fairly taken root, the greater part of the plantain trees are removed.

Cardamoms.

The cardamoms *(Amomum repens)* are propagated entirely by cuttings of the root, and spread in clumps exactly like the plantain tree, or *Musa*. In the month following the autumnal equinox, a cluster of from three to five stems, with the roots adhering, are separated from a bunch, and planted in the same row, one between every two *Betel-nut* palms, in the spot from whence a plantain tree has been removed. The ground around the cardamom is manured with *Nelli (Emblica)* leaves. In the third year, about the autumnal equinox, it produces fruit. The capsules are gathered as they ripen, and are dried four days on a mat, which during the day is supported by four sticks, and exposed to the sun, but at night is taken into the house. They are then fit for sale. Whenever the whole fruit has been removed, the plants are raised, and, all the superfluous stems and roots having been separated, they are set again; but care is taken never to set a plant in the spot from whence it was raised, a change in this respect being considered as necessary. Next year these plants give no fruit, but in the year following yield capsules again, as at first. After transplantation the old stems die, and new ones spring from the roots. Each cluster produces from one quarter to one *Seer* weight of cardamoms, or from $\frac{14}{100}$ to $\frac{6}{10}$ of a pound.

Tenures.

All these gardens are private property, and all belong to *Haiga Bráhmans*. When a man wishes to make a new one, he fixes upon a spot, which must not only contain room for the trees, but must have hills for shelter, and for supplying manure, and a place for the house and kitchen garden. When a proper situation has been found, the planter purchases the whole from the government. The usual price has been ten *Pagodas*, or forty *Rupees*, for every thousand

CHAPTER XVII. March 15. trees planted. For twelve years they pay no land-tax; on the thirteenth year, every thousand trees paid, on a good soil, three *Pagodas;* and every year, until the eighteenth, an additional tax of three *Pagodas* was imposed. Afterwards the thousand trees, on a good soil, paid yearly twenty *Pagodas;* on a bad soil, the tax was only ten *Pagodas* a thousand. Nothing was exacted for the plantains, pepper, *Betel-leaf,* or cardamoms. If the proprietor become poor, and be not able to cultivate his garden, so that it runs to waste, he informs the officers of revenue, who sell the ground, and give him the price. He may sell the garden when he pleases. This property is never mortgaged. *Tippoo* raised the land-tax; owing to which burthen, and other troubles, many of the gardens are now waste. Major Monro reduced the rent to the old standard; but as yet no new gardens have been formed, and the people are expecting some farther indulgence before they begin to plant.

Labour. In this country a few slaves are kept; but most of the labour, even in the grounds of the *Bráhmans,* is performed by the proprietors, or by hired servants. The *Haiga Bráhmans* toil on their own ground at every kind of labour, but they never work for hire. The hired servants seldom receive any money in advance, and consequently at the end of the year are free to go away. No warning is necessary, either on the part of the master or of the servants. These eat three times a day in their master's house, and get annually one blanket, one handkerchief, and in money 6 *Pagodas,* or 48 *Rupees,* or 2*l.* 8*s.* 4$\frac{1}{4}$*d.* Their wives are hired by the day, and get 1$\frac{1}{2}$ *Seer* of rough rice, and 3 *Dudus,* of which 49$\frac{1}{2}$ are equal to 1 *Rupee.* In so poor a country, these wages are very high. A male slave gets daily 2 *Pucka Seers* of rough rice, with annually one blanket, one handkerchief, a piece of cotton cloth, and some oil, tamarinds, and capsicum. He gets no money, except at marriages; but these cost 16 *Pagodas,* or 6*l.* 8*s.* 11$\frac{1}{2}$*d.*, for the woman must be purchased. She, and all her children, of course become the property of her husband's master. The woman slave gets daily

$1\frac{3}{4}$ *Seer* of rough rice, a blanket, and annually a piece of cotton cloth, and a jacket. Children and old people get some ready dressed victuals at the house of the master, and are also allowed some clothing. The men work from sun-rise till sun-set, and at noon are allowed one *Hindu* hour, or about twenty-four minutes, for dinner. The women are allowed till about eight o'clock in the morning to prepare the dinner, which they then carry to the fields, and continue to work there with the men until sun-set.

Sandal-wood.

In the forests here, any person may cut whatever trees he pleases, except sandal-wood, and such as grow in forests producing pepper. The sandal trees are numbered, and put in charge of the head-man of the village. The custom of this district *(Taluc)* is, once in twelve years to cut the sandal. Three years ago a man purchased all that was fit for cutting, and procured about 100 *Maunds* of 40 *Seers* each, or about $21\frac{1}{2}$ hundred-weight.

Commerce. Exports.

Few or no merchants reside in *Soonda.* Those from below the *Ghats* come, and purchase a little pepper; but by far the greatest part of this article, and all the *Betel-nut* and cardamoms, are brought up by the *Banijigas,* who come from *Hubuli, Darwara, Hameri,* or *Haveli,* and *Umanabady* in the *Marattah* dominions. They come here in the hot and dry season, between March and June, and, going round the houses of the cultivators, give cash for the produce of the gardens. The common price of pepper is 18 *Ikeri Pagodas,* or 72 *Rupees,* for the *Nija* of 12 *Maunds,* each weighing 72 *Seers* of 24 *Dudus.* This is at the rate of $3\frac{321}{1000}$ pence a pound, or at about $82\frac{1}{2}$ *Rupees* for the *Candy* of 600 lb., which is used by the Company in *Malabar.* The cultivation of gardens being evidently more expensive here than in *Malabar,* we may, from the price given at this place, judge of the practicability of the Company's taking at a low rate all the pepper of that country, and, provided they removed the land-tax, of giving a sufficient encouragement for its cultivation. The common price of red *Betel-nut* here is one *Pagoda* for the *Maund,* or $2\frac{214}{1000}$ pence a pound. The

CHAPTER XVII. cardamoms sell for 7 *Pagodas* the *Maund* of 40 *Seers;* so that a pound costs almost 2*s.* 4*d.*

March 15. Imports. The *Marattah* merchants bring almost the whole cloth, and a great part of the grain, that is used in the country. Some they exchange with the cultivators; but the greater part is sold for ready money to shopkeepers, who again retail these articles to the people of the country. The iron used in the neighbourhood comes from *Chandra-gupty,* and other places in the dominions of *Mysore.* Their salt comes from *Canara,* and a vast quantity passes this way to the *Marattah* territory.

Betel-nut. The *Marattah* merchants, who are just now here, say, that the *Betel-nut* of this place is greatly inferior to that of *Sira,* and the neighbouring countries; which is in direct opposition to the information of the people of *Bangalore.* The taste of the people in the two countries may be different; as, for instance, the female *Betel-leaf* is here preferred, while in some other countries the male is in greater request. There is no reason to doubt the accuracy of the price current given me at *Bangalore.* The *Marattah* merchants say, that they purchase all that they can get at *Sira;* but, that being totally inadequate to supply the demand, they must take whatever they can get. They say, that none grows in the *Marattah* territories, and from hence it is carried to the most remote parts of their dominion.

Cardamoms. The cardamoms that grow here are of an inferior quality to what they get at *Sringa-giri,* that is, to the produce of *Coorg.*

Pepper. The garden pepper of *Soonda* and of *Nagara* is of equal value, and is better than that which grows spontaneously, by three *Pagodas* a *Candy,* that is, in the proportion of ten to nine. They say also, that merchants and commerce meet with every protection and encouragement in the *Marattah* dominions. Indeed, among the *Hindus,* even in the most rapacious governments, this class of people is seldom molested.

Strata of *Jaydi Munnu.* In low moist vallies here, a kind of white clay, mixed with small bits of quartz, is very commonly found under the soil of rice-grounds. Its *strata* are often several cubits in thickness, and, where it comes to the surface, render the ground very sterile. It is called *Jaydi Munnu*, and is used to white-wash the houses of the natives. It is diffused in water to separate the sand and stones, and is then mixed with a little *Chunam*, that is to say, the ashes of *Muddi* bark (*Chuncoa Muddia* Buch: MSS.); for in this vicinity there is no lime. March 15.

The *Panchanga*, or astrologer of this place, gives me the following account of the weather. In the month preceding, and the four months following, the summer solstice, the winds are westerly, and very strong, with excessive rains; so that during these five months it is rarely ever fair for an hour. In the five following months, that is, two months before and three months after the winter solstice, the winds are easterly, and of moderate force. The weather is in general fair; but during the first month there are some showers, and during the two next there are every morning heavy dews, and thick fogs. In the two months following the vernal equinox, the winds are variable, but come mostly from the south. At first they are moderate, but they increase in strength toward the end of this period, and bring on the commencement of the rainy season. At present, toward the end of the second period, the nights are rather cool, with very heavy fogs in the morning. The days are clear, and very hot. Weather.

The two most unhealthy seasons are, the two first months of the rainy season, and the four months of cool weather. At all times, however, the country is extremely unhealthy for people not inured from birth to its dangerous air; and my servants are now suffering considerably from its baneful influence. Unhealthy air.

16th *March*.—Having been employed all the 15th in taking the foregoing account, I to-day went five cosses to *Banawási*. A great deal of the country through which I passed has been formerly cleared; and the greater part, although now waste, has not yet March 16. Appearance of the country.

CHAPTER XVII. March 16.

been overgrown with trees. The woods, being young, do not in general contain tall trees; but I passed through a stately forest, in which the pepper-vine grows spontaneously. In this there was some *Teak*. The greater part of the country is not too steep for the plough; but in many places the *Laterite* rises to the surface. Where that is not the case, the soil is apparently good. *Banawási*, in *Hyder's* government, contained 500 houses, which are now reduced more than one half. Its walls are ruinous, and, although it has been a place of great celebrity, do not appear to have been ever of great extent. It is now the residence of a *Tahsildar*. The *Varadá* river, after having come from *Ikeri*, passes on the east side of the town, and falls into the *Tunga-bhadra*. At present it is very small, and muddy, with little current; but in the rainy season it is no where fordable, and might be applied to the purposes of commerce. It is only navigated, however, by the baskets covered with leather, which serve for ferry-boats.

Madu Linga, a *Hindu* antiquary.

I remained at *Banawási* two days, having met with a *Bráhman* very curious in antiquities, who was named *Madu Linga Butta*, and who was priest *(Pújári)* in the temple called *Madugéswara*, to the sanctity of which the celebrity of *Banawási* is attributed by *Madu Linga*. It is dedicated to *Maducanata*, one of the names of *Iswara*, or *Maha Déva*, of whom my antiquary is a most devout worshipper. This temple had formerly very large endowments; and, although a very mean building, is still in good repair, and much frequented. Its priest was to me the most interesting object about the place. Although a person of the most austere and mortified life, and who employs much time in the ceremonies of devotion, yet he had considerable curiosity, and had been at great pains in studying and copying the ancient inscriptions, both here, and at some places of celebrity in the neighbourhood.

Banawási.

Banawási, he says, in the first *Yugam* was called *Coumodi*; in the *Traytaia-yugam* it was called *Jainti*, or success; in the *Duapar-yugam* its name was changed to *Beindivi*; and in this age it is called

Vanavási in the *Sanskrit*, and *Banawási* in the vulgar language, as being situated in a forest. At the very commencement of this age, it was for some time the residence of *Dharma*, the youngest of the five sons of *Pandu*; and here several princes descended from *Trenetra Cadumba* held their court.

CHAPTER XVII. March 16.

Madu Linga gave me copies of the following inscriptions, which have been delivered to the Bengal government.

Inscriptions.

The most ancient by far, and, unless there be some mistake in the matter, which indeed is almost certain, the most ancient inscription any where existing, is at the temple *Madugéswara*, and contains a grant of lands to the god *Maducanata*, by *Simhunna Bupa* of *Yudishtara's* family, dated in the year of the era of *Yudishtara* 168. As the Christian era, according to the usual reckoning of the *Bráhmans*, commences in the 3102 year of *Yudishtara*, this inscription was made 4735 years ago.

Another very ancient inscription, but following the other at a great interval, is also at the temple of *Maducanata*. It is dated in the year *Jeya* of the era of *Vicrama* 96, in the reign of *Vicrama Dittya*. This answers to the 39th year of our Lord.

The next most ancient inscription, of which he gave me a copy, is at *Balagami*, a place south-east from hence in the *Mysore* territory. *Yudishtara*, or *Dharma Ráya*, dwelt at it one year; and afterwards, during the reign of *Vira Belalla*, it was for some time the capital of *Karnata*. The ruins are said to contain an immense number of inscriptions. Two of these are dated in the reign of *Yudishtara*; and the others are all in the reigns of *Jain* princes, who, early in this *Yugam*, according to *Madu Linga*, expelled the followers of the *Vedas*, and till the time of *Sankara*, and *Rám' Anuja*, continued to be the governing power. The inscription of which I am now treating contains a grant of lands to the goddess *Renuca*, mother of *Parasu Ráma*. Her temple is, however, situated at *Chandra-gupty*. The date is in the year of *Sal.* 90, or *A. D.* 16$\frac{7}{8}$, in the reign of *Trenetra Cadumba*. I have many doubts concerning the

CHAPTER XVII. March 16.

antiquity of this inscription. It is said to mention, that, before the time of this *Trenetra Cadumba*, there had been fourteen *Cadumba Ráyas*, and twenty-one of the family of the *Barbaraha;* and that after him there would be seven *Cadumba Rájás*, and *Vira Bojah Vassundara*, a *Rájá* who, according to the *Bráhmans*, has not yet appeared, but who is soon to come, and who, after having expelled all *Melenchas* and other infidels, is to restore the true worship in all parts of *Bharata-khanda*. When I stated, that the inscription must have been written after the last of the twenty-one *Jeantri Cadumba Rájás* mentioned by *Ramuppa*, as their exact number is specified in the writing, my doubts by no means discomposed the *Hindu* antiquary; he said, that this matter could have easily been ascertained by prophecy; and, in order to remove my doubts, showed me a list of monarchs extracted from the eighteen *Púranas*, in which the Mussulman kings of *Delhi* were mentioned. Any reply to this could only have given offence; but the circumstance shows, that either these books usually attributed to *Vyása* are of recent fabrication, or have suffered gross interpolations.

Madu Linga was, however, so far from looking upon the power of foretelling future events as a proof of supernatural authority derived from divine favour, that he gave me a copy of an inscription on stone, which also came from *Balagami*, and which he says is prophetical, and yet acknowledges that it was composed by a *Jain Guru*, who by intense study had acquired the art of prophecy. A copy of what is said to be the prophetical part of this inscription I delivered with the others; the remainder *Madu Linga* did not think worth copying. The prophecy he applies to the success of the British arms in India; and says, that before the year of *Sal.* 1900, the English are to possess the whole country from the snowy mountains, to *Raméswaram*. The author of the inscription in question is said to have been *Muru Jamadeya*, *Guru* to *Maha Sholia*, or *Sholun Rájá*, a *Jain* prince, who was sovereign king of the five great divisions of the world. He lived since the time of *Salivahanam;*

and my antiquary relates many extraordinary things of this infidel prince, and of his unbelieving *Guru*. I am at a great loss to account for this circumstance, as *Madu Linga* is apparently a zealous worshipper of *Siva*. I can only account for it by supposing, that he is inwardly a *Jain*, which does not prevent him from worshipping the *Linga* as a representation of a *Devata*. However that may be, he gravely relates, that *Sholia Rájá* permitted none of his subjects to die till they were a hundred years old; and also, that his *Guru* one day, about 3 o'clock in the afternoon, told the sun to stop, and the luminary immediately obeyed. After three hours the *Guru* allowed it to set, which it accordingly did at the usual time by a sudden movement to the west. The inscription in question was composed by *Muru Jamadeya*, that, when the prophecies in it came to be fulfilled, all future ages might have evident proof of his learning.

Another inscription is engraven on a stone at the temple of *Talaléswara* in *Hanagul*, a place in the *Savanuru* district *(Taluc)*, which is probably the *Shanoor* of Major Rennell. The date is involved in the conceit of a couplet, but was interpreted to be *Sal.* 1130, being the year *Jeya*. The reigning prince is *Cadumba Ráya*, and must have been a descendant of the *Jeantri Cadumba* monarchs, who even then retained a portion of their dominions.

The next inscription is at a place called *Cupatura*, which lies east from *Banawási*. It is dated *Anunda Sal.* 1297 (*A. D.* 137$\frac{4}{5}$), in the reign of *Vira Buca Ráya* of *Hasinawali*, which is the *Sanskrit* name of *Anagundi*, a city on the bank of the *Tunga-bhadra*, opposite to *Vijaya-nagara*.

The next inscription is engraven on a stone at a *Jain* temple *(Busty)* in the same place, *Cupatura*. It is dated in *Sal.* 1337, which, as I before mentioned, is probably an error of the copyist for 1437; as it is in the reign of *Achuta Ráya*, *Narasingha Ráya*, and *Krishna Ráya*.

It would appear, that until about this period the *Jain* in these parts continued numerous. Among other proofs, I may mention

CHAPTER XVII. March 16.

that a valuation of all the country between *Nagara* and *Vereda*, both included, and said to have been made by the orders of *Krishna Ráyaru*, appears to have been conducted by a *Jain* officer, *Gopa Ganda*. This valuation is engraved on stone at *Balagami*, or *Balagavi*; and a copy of it, which I procured from *Madu Linga*, accompanies the other inscriptions.

The next inscription is in a temple at *Banawási*, and is dated *Paradavi*, *Sal.* 1474, in the reign of *Vencatadri Deva Maha Ráya*.

The last inscription also is engraven on a stone at *Banawási*, and dated *Vilumbi* of *Sal.* 1501, in the reign of *Imudy Arasuppa Nayaka* of *Sudha*, which confirms the chronology of the *Guru* of that family in the account which he gave me while I was at their capital.

State of agriculture in the open part of *Soonda*.

Having assembled the cultivators in presence of the officers of government, they gave me the following account of the state of agriculture; which may be considered as applicable to the eastern and more open parts of *Soonda*.

Every village has a different measure for grain: that in use here is as follows:

Grain measures.

One *Candaca* contains 20 *Bullas*; 1 *Bulla* 4 *Seers*. The *Seer*, when heaped as usual, contains $76\frac{1}{2}$ cubical inches. The *Candaca*, therefore, is equal to $2\frac{846}{1000}$ bushels. By this *Candaca*, the farmers estimate the seed and produce; but they sell rough rice by another, the *Bulla* of which is equal to 80 *Seers*, or which contains $56\frac{9}{10}$ bushels. The value of this at present is 6 *Pagodas*, which is at the rate of $10\frac{19}{100}$ pence a bushel. Rice again, when freed from the husk, is sold by a *Candaca* whose *Bulla* contains 32 *Seers*, or which is equal to $22\frac{1}{4}$ bushels. This at present sells for $6\frac{1}{4}$ *Pagodas*, or 25 *Rupees*; which is at the rate of 2*s.* $2\frac{1}{2}$*d.* the bushel, and is said to be higher than the price at *Seringapatam*. The difference of price shows the enormous expense which attends the operation of removing the husks, owing to the ignorance of mechanism among the natives; for only one half of rough rice consists of husk.

Here, and all toward the east side of *Soonda Ráyada*, the great object of cultivation is rice; as toward the west the farmers are chiefly occupied with plantations. I measured two fields, in order, if possible, to ascertain the rate of seed and produce, but without getting any thing satisfactory. By measuring a great extent an average may be struck, as has been done by Mr. Ravenshaw; but it will be found, that some fields are alleged by the cultivators to require one half less seed than others of equal extent. Great allowances must be made, in a point even of such importance, to the ignorance of the farmers; but still I do not suppose them to be so grossly inattentive, as to make such a difference in the seed actually sown. I rather suppose, that what they call a *Candaca's* sowing has nothing to do with the real quantity of seed, which is concealed with a view of lowering their burthens. One of the fields which I measured contained 72,698 square feet for the nominal *Candaca*, which is at the rate of $1\frac{705}{1000}$ bushel an acre. The other field was at the rate of 48,749 square feet a *Candaca*, or at $2\frac{1}{2}$ bushels an acre. These fields were contiguous, and the difference appeared to me to have arisen from two plots of *Ragy* ground having been stolen into the first, which in the revenue accompts was still kept at its original rate of sowing, but actually required more seed. As a foundation for calculation, I therefore prefer the last measured field.

The rains are not so heavy as to the westward; but, in ordinary seasons and a moist soil, are sufficient to bring to maturity a crop of rice that requires six months to ripen. Where the soil is very absorbent, small tanks are formed, to keep a supply for a few days that may occasionally happen to be without rain. A few of the highest fields are cultivated with a kind of rice that ripens in three months; but the natives here consider as totally useless much land that might be easily formed into terraces, like the *Mackey* land of *Kankana*, and of which the soil is apparently good. The rice ground never gives two crops of rice in one year, although, by means of tanks, a constant succession of crops might be obtained from the lower parts of the vallies. This kind of land is divided

CHAPTER XVII. March 16. into two sorts; the *Soru*, or low fields; and the *Bisu*, or higher ones. Both are cultivated in the same way, and the only difference is in the quantity of produce.

The six months rices are cultivated on the low fields *(Soru)*; and on the best of the higher land *(Bisu)*; and are the following:

Doda Honasu.

Sana Honasu.

Mulary.

Cari Chinna Calli.

Sali Butta.

Mota Hulliga.

Sidu Sali.

Asidi Butta.

Chinta Punny. All these are large grained.

Sana Butta, a small grain, and rather more valuable than the others; but it is found to answer on very few soils. Experience shows, that certain fields agree best with certain kinds of rice, and each is of course sown with the kind only that gives most return. The natives have no rule to ascertain this *a priori;* and when a new field is brought into cultivation, they must find it out by experience. The manner of cultivating these kinds of rice is as follows. Immediately after harvest, the field is ploughed lengthwise and across. (The plough of this place is delineated in Plate XXVI. Fig. 71). The clods are then broken by drawing over the field an instrument named *Coradu*, which is yoked to a pair of oxen, and is represented in Plate XXIX. Fig. 72. The field is then allowed to rest exposed to the air until the month preceding the summer solstice, or until the rains commence, when its soil is loosened by the hoe drawn by oxen and called *Heg Cuntay* (Plate XXVIII. Fig. 75); and the seed is sown without preparation by means of a *Curigy*, or drill (Plate XXVI. Fig. 73). The four bills of this implement are secured by bolts of iron passing through a beam, to which the yoke-rope is fastened. The perforations, for the seed to pass through from the cup, are an inch in diameter; so that the seed must fall very thick. After having been sown, the field is manured with cow-dung, and smoothed with the *Coradu*. The water is allowed to run off as it falls. Eight days after having been sown, the field is hoed with the *Cuntay*, which kills the weeds without injuring the seed that is then just beginning to sprout. Eight days afterwards the young rice is four inches high, and the field is hoed between the drills with a hoe drawn by oxen, and called *Harty*, or *Nir Cuntay*, which is delineated in Plate XXVIII. Fig. 76. This kills the grass, and throws the earth toward the drills. After this, a bunch of prickly *Bamboos* is yoked to a pair of oxen, and the driver stands on a plank above the thorns, to give them weight. This is drawn over the field, and removes the grass without injuring the corn. When this is six inches high, if there be rain, the water is confined, and the field is kept inundated; but, if the weather should be dry, the field must again be hoed with the *Harty Cuntay*, and harrowed with the bunch of *Bamboos*. Whenever the field begins to be inundated, it must be again hoed with the same implement, and smoothed with the *Coradu*, which acts in some measure like a rolling-stone. At the end of the third month, the field is drained, and the weeds are removed. The water is again confined; but in fifteen days, if more weeds spring up, the field must be again drained and cleaned: this, however, is not always necessary. In the fifth month, a grass, much resembling rice, comes up, and must be carefully removed with a knife. In the seventh month the crop is reaped, and the straw is cut close by the ground. For three days it is allowed to remain on the field in handfulls. It is then thrown into loose heaps, and afterwards tied up in small sheaves, which are stacked on some airy place; and in the course of three months it is trodden out by the feet of oxen. All this time there is seldom any rain; and even when any comes, it seldom injures the reaped corn. The grain is always preserved in the husk, and beaten out as wanted for use. Any omission in these steps of cultivation produces a great

CHAPTER XVII. March 16. diminution of the produce. Ten seeds, the farmers say, is a good crop on low land, and 7 seeds on the higher fields called *Bisu.* At this rate, an acre of the former produces $25\frac{1}{2}$ bushels, worth 1*l.* 1*s.* $7\frac{1}{4}$*d.*; and of the latter, $17\frac{9}{10}$ bushels, worth nearly 15*s.* $1\frac{1}{2}$*d.* The officers of revenue say, that the produce is about a fifth part more. Much reliance cannot, however, be placed upon what either party say; as all the officers have either lands of their own, or have relations who are deeply interested.

The kind of rice that is sown on the more elevated parts of the *(Bisu)* high land, and which ripens in three months, is called *Varangully.* The grain is of the same value with the others. Its cultivation is similar, only it is sown eight days later, and all the steps of the operation must succeed each other more rapidly. The produce is from five to seven seeds.

Sugar-cane. Sugar-cane is raised on the rice-ground, but in very small quantities, and the whole is made into *Jagory.* The ground fit for it must have a *Tank* containing water enough to irrigate the field twice after it has been planted, and once before the crop is reaped. The kind used is called the *Hulocabo,* or straw cane; and it is the same with the *Maracabo* of *Bangalore.* It is planted in the second month after the winter solstice, and is cut within the year. 1400 canes give a *Maund* of *Jagory,* and a *Candaca* of land will produce 21,000 canes, or 15 *Maunds* of 44 *Seers,* each weighing 24 elephant *Dubs.* The produce of an acre, by this account, is only about 357 lb. of *Jagory.* Some people allow the cane to grow up again from the roots, and thus get what in *Jamaica* is called a crop of *Ratoons.* This produces only half of the above mentioned quantity of *Jagory.* Between every two crops of sugar must intervene two of rice, which are as productive as usual.

At *Banawási,* no second crop of any kind is taken from the rice ground.

Sterility of the higher lands. In the eastern parts of *Soonda,* a very small quantity of the grains called dry is cultivated, but none toward the west. This cultivation was formerly much more extensive; but the rice ground being most profitable, and the whole even of that not being cultivated, owing to a want of people and stock, the dry-field is of course much neglected. The fields used for dry grains are not levelled. I have already said, that all over the *Ráyada*, even in its western parts, there is a great extent of land apparently fit for the purpose; but the natives allege, that they find by experience, that the grain will thrive only in particular spots. Experience is their sole guide; they have no rule by which they can at sight discriminate the barren from the fertile land. I am inclined to think, that this is one of the absurd notions prevalent among all unskilful farmers; and that in a well watered country, such as this is, wherever the soil is not rocky, or the land too steep, it will be found productive.

CHAPTER XVII. March 16.

Cultivation of dry field fit for *Ragy*.

A certain field having been found by experience fit for the cultivation of *Ragy*, the following succession of crops in three years is taken from it; *Huts' Ellu*, *Ragy*, fallow.

Huts' Ellu, or the *Verbesina sativa* Roxb.

A month before or after midsummer, according as there is rain, the ground is ploughed three times, and smoothed twice with the *Coradu* before mentioned. The month following the autumnal equinox, the seed of the *Huts' Ellu* is sown broad-cast, ploughed in, and the field is then smoothed with the same implement. The seed is sown twice as thick as that of *Ragy*. It ripens in two months, and produces five seeds.

Ragy, or the *Cynosurus corocanus.*

Next year, in the month preceding the summer solstice, the field is ploughed with the first rain. Eight days afterwards it gets a second ploughing. On or about the 16th day it is smoothed with the same implement, and two or three days afterwards it is ploughed a third time. After another interval of two or three days, furrows, at a span's distance, are drawn throughout the field. The seed of the *Ragy* is then mixed with some cow-dung; and at a span's distance from each other, small lumps of the mass, containing from eight to twenty seeds, are dropt into the furrows. The field is then smoothed with the *Coradu* before mentioned. In about fifteen days

CHAPTER XVII. March 16.

afterwards, when the plants are four or five inches high, the field is hoed with the *Cuntay*, and afterwards harrowed with the bunch of prickly *Bamboos*. About fifteen days afterwards, the intervals between the drills are ploughed, and the field is again smoothed with the *Coradu*. In five months the *Ragy* comes to maturity, and produces 20 fold. In this, the greatest imperfection, besides the usual want of proper implements, is the neglect of manure. I measured a field, said to sow one *Colaga* and a half of *Ragy*, and found it to contain 33,516 square feet. An acre at this rate sows about $\frac{27}{100}$ parts of a bushel, and produces about $5\frac{1}{2}$ bushels of *Ragy*. Its produce of *Huts' Ellu* is half that of *Ragy*, and the seed is double.

Cultivation of dry field fit for *Horse-gram*.

By experience, other fields are found fit for the cultivation of *Huruli*, or *Horse-gram;* and *Harulu*, or the *Ricinus*. These are cultivated in a similar rotation of *Huruli*, *Harulu*, and fallow. Sometimes both crops consist of the *Harulu*.

Harulu, or *Ricinus palma christi*.

For *Harulu*, the field is ploughed four times in the month preceding and the two months following the summer solstice. At the same time it is twice smoothed with the *Coradu* above mentioned. In the last of these months furrows are drawn throughout the field at one cubit's distance, and crossing each other at right angles. In each intersection are placed two seeds, and the whole is again smoothed with the same implement. On the tenth day the plants come up; on the fifteenth the intervals between the rows must be hoed with the *Cuntay*. The plant does not rise above two cubits high, and produces four seeds. The crop season continues during the two months preceding the winter solstice. The oil is extracted entirely by boiling, and four *Seers* of seed give one of oil, but with the seed the measure is heaped. The oil is used for medicine and for the lamp. After the *Harulu* comes a fallow.

Huruli, *Horse-gram*, or *Dolichos biflorus*.

Then in the month preceding the summer solstice the field is ploughed twice, and smoothed with the *Coradu*. In the month preceding the autumnal equinox, the field is again ploughed, sown broad-cast, and smoothed with the same implement. In three months the grain ripens, and three seeds are reckoned a good crop.

Small value of this ground.

A field said to sow 3 *Seers* of *Huruli*, and $3\frac{1}{2}$ of *Harulu*, measured 24,780 square feet. The seed required for an acre will be of *Huruli* $\frac{23}{100}$ parts of a bushel, and the produce $\frac{69}{100}$ parts of a bushel, or deducting seed $\frac{46}{100}$. *Horse-gram* sells here at 15 *Seers* for the *Rupee*, or for 3*s.* $9\frac{3}{4}$*d.* a bushel. The value of the produce of an acre, deducting the seed, is therefore about 1*s.* $9\frac{1}{2}$*d.* The seed of *Harulu* required for an acre will be $\frac{269}{1000}$ parts of a bushel, producing $\frac{807}{1000}$ parts of a bushel.

Cattle.

The cattle of *Soonda* are of a rather larger breed than those of *Kankana* or *Haiga*; but they are greatly inferior to those of the country to the eastward, whence many are brought for the plough. Buffaloes are here more used than oxen. There are in *Soonda* no sheep, goats, swine, nor asses, and very few horses. In the dry season, that is, from the month preceding the shortest day, until the summer solstice, the cattle are fed on straw, and that of *Ragy* is preferred to that of rice. In the two months following the summer solstice, while there is much labour going forward, the cattle are allowed hay made of the soft grass which grows on the little banks separating the rice-fields: that of the hills is considered as totally useless. For the milch cattle the hay is boiled, and mixed with the bran of rice. During the three remaining months the cattle are allowed to pasture.

Manure.

In the dry weather, the cattle are folded on the fields; in the rainy season they are taken within doors, and as a manure for the fields their dung is collected, and mixed with ashes, and the soil of the farmer's house. Those who have no gardens allow no litter: but the *Haiga Bráhmans*, for the use of their gardens, litter the cattle at one season with fresh leaves, and at another with dry grass. The two manures thus formed are kept separate, and applied to

CHAPTER XVII. different purposes. A want of attention to manure is a striking feature in the grain farmers of *Soonda*.

March 16. Tenures. All the arable land in *Soonda* is considered as the property of the government; but the value of every estate is fixed; and so long as a tenant pays his rent, it is not customary to turn either him or his heirs out of their possessions. It is true, that he cannot transfer his right to occupy the farm by sale, but he may transfer it by *(Votay)* mortgage to any person *(Aduvacara)* who will advance money. There are two kinds of mortgage. In the one the *Aduvacara* advances nearly the value of the property, cultivates it, and pays the taxes. This loan is made for a stipulated time; and, when that expires, the money must be repaid. If the mortgagee has neglected the weeding, arbitrators will fix a certain reduction to be made from the debt, on account of the injury which his neglect has done to the property. He can claim nothing on the score of improvement; indeed, a field, once regularly brought into cultivation with rice, is supposed to be incapable of farther amelioration. The other mortgage is, where the tenant borrows money on his land, and gives a bond, stating that he has borrowed so much money on such and such lands at such an interest, generally from $1\frac{1}{2}$ to 2 *per cent. per mensem*, and that he will pay the interest monthly, and at such a period will repay the capital. The mortgager in this case continues to cultivate the lands and to pay the taxes. If he cannot discharge the debt when it becomes due, the mortgagee takes the land, pays the revenue, and keeps the profits for the interest; but it is always redeemable by the origiual tenant, should his circumstances ever enable him to repay the debt.

Land-tax. The revenue is paid entirely in money, at from one to four *Rupees* for the *Candaca*, according to the old valuation; but in some places the quantity sown is double of what is rated in the revenue accompts. The reason assigned for this is, that such lands are poor. The dry-field pays no revenue whatever; but a certain quantity is annexed to each estate of rice-land, as an encouragement for the farmer. Of the two fields that I measured, one paid at the rate of 2 *Rupees*, and the other at the rate of $2\frac{84}{100}$ *Rupees* an acre; the first equal to 4*s*. $0\frac{1}{4}$*d*., and the last to 5*s*. $8\frac{1}{2}$*d*. The gross produce I have already stated, on the report of the farmers, to be worth from 15*s*. to 1*l*. 1*s*. an acre. This calculation, and the custom of lending money on mortgage, are a clear proof that the tax is moderate, and that enough of the property remains with the actual cultivator, not only as a reward for his trouble, but to render his land a valuable property.

Size of farms.

A farmer who has five ploughs is esteemed a rich man. With these he must keep six men and six women, and ten labouring cattle; and at seed-time and harvest he must hire additional labourers. Farmers, who are not *Bráhmans*, unless their farms be large, work the whole with their own families; but rich men must hire servants, or keep slaves; and, to hold their plough, *Bráhmans* must always have people of the low casts. This is a kind of work that even a *Haiga Bráhman* will not perform.

Condition of the slaves.

	£	s.	d.
A man slave gets daily 2 *Seers* of rough rice, or yearly about 26 bushels worth - -	1	2	$0\frac{1}{2}$
A handkerchief, a blanket, and piece of cloth worth 2 *Rupees* - - - - -	0	4	$0\frac{1}{4}$
A *Pagoda* in money - - - - -	0	8	$0\frac{3}{4}$
Six *Candacas* of rough rice at harvest -	0	14	6
	2	8	$7\frac{1}{2}$
The women get one piece of cloth annually, and a meal of ready dressed victuals on the days that they work, which may amount annually to - -	0	8	1

Wages of free men.

Hired men get four *Seers* of rough rice a day, worth less than three half-pence.

Quantity of land cultivated by one plough.

The farmers say, that, with a stock of six ploughs, a man can cultivate thirteen *Candacas* of land. The officers of government

CHAPTER XVII. March 16.

say, that three *Candacas* for a plough is the common reckoning; but even this cannot be received, unless we suppose the ground more productive than the farmers confess. For, supposing all the eighteen *Candacas* to be of a good quality, and to produce ten seeds, the whole value of the crop would be 21*l.* 15*s.* 2*d.*; and the support of six men and women slaves, not to mention seed, rent, cattle, &c. &c. would come to 16*l.* 19*s.* 9*d.* The people here are far from taking any extraordinary trouble with their lands; and, I should suppose, cultivate with a similar stock as much as is done in *Bengal*, where about seven acres may be considered as the usual rate of work for one plough. We may, therefore, allow between thirty and forty *Candacas* at least for six ploughs, or double that which the officers of revenue stated.

Mr. Read's account of this part of his district.

Being now about to enter the territories of the *Mysore Rájá*, I shall conclude what I have to say concerning *Soonda*, with extracts from Mr. Read's answers to my queries, which have been collected with great precision and ability from the reports of the native officers.

Soil.

Mr. Read states the proportion of sterile and productive lands, in the four districts *(Talucs)* of *Soonda*, in the following proportions, supposing each to be divided into a hundred parts.

Talucs.	Land capable of cultivation.	Sterile lands.
Supa	12	88
Soonda, or *Sudha*	16	84
Banawási	20	80
Billighy	20	80

Produce of waste lands.

The produce of the waste lands Mr. Read states as follows. The *Maund* weighs $24\frac{14}{100}$ lb. and is divided into 40 *Seers*.

CHAPTER XVII.

March 16.

Taluc.	Sandal wood trees.	Teak trees.	Sissa trees.	Annual produce of honey.	Annual produce of wax.	Annual produce of wild cinnamon.	Annual produce of *Cabob China.*	Annual produce of wild pepper.
				Maunds.	*Maunds.*	*Maunds.*	*Maunds.*	*Maunds.*
Supa - - - -	2097	394495	59770	33 23	49 6	15 30	5 10	—
Soonda, or *Sudha*	1718	1639	1715	8 7	29 28½	2 0	1 0	—
Banawási - - -	3812	29	3069	11 24	3 13	—	—	—
Billighy - - -	5266	—	34	—	—	—	43 0	34 8
Total -	12893	396113	64588	53 14	72 7½	17 30	49 10	34 8

Wild pepper.

I know that wild pepper is collected in the *Soonda Taluc*, but it has not been reported to Mr. Read. The report of the *Marattah* merchants, I look upon as decisive, that it is not of so little value as interested persons have endeavoured to represent to the collector.

Arable lands.

The *Tahsildars* have reported, that nearly the whole of the arable lands are now cultivated; which is in direct opposition to both what I heard and what I saw.

The number of sugar-canes cut annually amount to 6,260,400, which should produce about 4471 *Maunds*, of about 30 lb. each.

Dry grains are chiefly cultivated in *Supa;* and about one twentieth part of the arable land there is employed for that purpose.

The cultivation of gardens has decreased about a third since the year 1754, when it is supposed that they were in the greatest possible prosperity.

CHAPTER XVII. March 16. Stock.

The stock employed in the country at present, according to Mr. Read, is.

Taluc.	Ploughs belonging to			Cattle.	
	Landlords.	Tenants.	Total.	Buffaloes old and young.	Cow kind old and young.
Supa - - - -	2348	2043	4391	8992	19882
Soonda - - -	1709	389	2098	3115	12234
Banawási - -	804	454	1258	3658	7818
Billighy - - -	1407	360	1767	1760	7515
Total -	6268	3246	9514	17525	47449

Population.

Mr. Read gives the following account of the population of these districts.

Taluc.	Houses, of which the following are occupied by						Slaves.
	Total	Christians.	Mussulmans.	*Bráhmans.*	*Sivabhactars.*	*Jain.*	
Supa - - - -	6929	87	515	1116	780	87	348
Soonda - - -	3396	4	178	2015	417	21	61
Banawási - -	2729	—	57	845	295	40	—
Billighy - - -	2593	—	50	692	433	14	36
Total -	15647	91	800	4568	1925	162	445

Commerce.

The exports and imports by land are very considerable, as may be seen by the accompanying Statement. The former amount to *Rupees* 9,63,833; and the latter to 1,08,045. The *Rupee* is worth nearly 2*s.*

Statement shewing the Average annual Quantity of Goods imported and exported in the northern Division of *Canara* and *Soonda* by Land, 1800-1.

No.	Names of the Articles.	Average annual Quantity Imported.									Total Value in *Rupees*.	Average annual Quantity Exported.										Total Value in *Rupees*.
		Nidge of 12 *Maunds*.	Bullock loads of 6 *Maunds*.	*Maunds* of 44 *Seers Cutcha*.	*Seers Cutcha* of 24 *Rupsweight*.	*Per man's load* (large)	*Per man's load* (small)	Potts.	*Kodi*, or Scores.	*Adud*, or Pieces.		*Nidge* of 12 *Maunds*	Bullock-load of 6 *Maunds*.	*Maunds* of 44 *Seers*.	*Seers* of 24 *Rupees* weight.	*Per man's load* (large)	*Per man's load* (small)	*Guddah*, or Potts.	*Kodi*, or Scores.	Baskets.	Pieces.	
1	Salt	—	6039	—	—	11½	18½	—		—	18128	—	18544	—	—	—	1	—	—	—	—	74176
2	Lamp-oil seed (*Castor*)	—	55½	—	—	—	—	—	—	—	140	—	—	—	—	—	—	—	—	—	—	—
3	Sweet-oil seed (*Sesamum*)	—	—	—	—	—	—	—	—	—	—	—	3	—	—	—	—	—	—	—	—	24
4	Jungle-oil seed	—	5½	—	—	—	—	—	—	—	50	—	—	—	—	—	—	—	—	—	—	—
5	Sweet-oil (*Sesamum*)	—	242½	39¼	5	—	—	1	—	—	5985	—	—	—	—	—	—	—	—	—	—	—
6	Coco-nut oil	—	15	1081½	7½	—	—	1140½	—	—	13810	—	—	—	—	—	—	1274¾	—	—	—	12740
7	Sandal oil	—	—	5¾	—	—	—	—	—	—	1265	—	—	—	—	—	—	—	—	—	—	—
8	*Chillies* (*Capsicum*)	—	506½	9¼	—	2	5	—	—	—	4070	—	—	—	—	—	—	—	—	—	—	—
9	Tamarinds	—	43	—	—	—	—	—	—	—	130	—	16	—	—	—	—	—	—	—	—	96
10	Garlick	—	1	—	—	—	—	—	—	—	6	—	—	—	—	—	—	—	—	—	—	—
11	Onion	—	29½	—	—	—	—	—	—	—	90	—	—	—	—	—	—	—	—	—	—	—
12	Mustard	—	1½	—	—	—	—	—	—	—	18	—	—	—	—	—	—	—	—	—	—	—
13	Corinnder seed	—	17½	—	—	—	—	—	—	—	158	—	—	—	—	—	—	—	—	—	—	—
14	Turmerick	—	—	—	—	—	—	—	—	—	—	—	14½	—	—	—	3	—	—	—	—	156
15	*Soonda* salt	—	2	—	—	—	—	—	—	—	12	—	—	—	—	—	—	—	—	—	—	—
16	*Cut* (*Terra Japonica*)	—	40	22	5	4	4½	—	—	—	685	—	27	22	—	—	4	—	—	—	—	555
17	Dry coco-nuts	—	7¾	2¼	—	—	—	—	—	—	147	—	158½	4	—	—	—	—	—	—	—	3820
18	Dates	—	112¼	40	—	19	8	—	—	—	1472	—	123½	76¾	—	—	—	—	—	—	—	2453
19	Dry dates	—	—	—	—	—	—	—	—	—	—	—	1	147	—	—	—	—	—	—	—	612
20	*China* sugar	—	23½	¾	—	—	1	—	—	—	1460	—	—	—	—	—	—	—	—	—	—	—
21	*Ghee* (boiled butter)	—	4	—	—	—	—	—	—	—	168	—	—	¼	6	—	—	—	—	—	—	3
22	Plumbs	—	—	—	—	—	—	—	—	—	—	—	—	1	—	—	—	—	—	—	—	18
23	Honey	—	—	—	—	—	—	—	—	—	—	—	6	—	—	—	—	1	—	—	—	114
24	Wax	—	—	—	—	—	—	—	—	—	—	—	2	169½	2½	—	2	—	—	—	—	2017
25	Cotton	—	12½	6¾	—	—	—	—	—	—	163	—	—	—	—	—	—	—	—	—	—	—
26	Cashew nuts	—	—	2¾	—	1½	—	—	—	—	8	—	1	66½	—	—	—	—	—	—	—	72

CHAPTER XVII.

March 16.

CHAPTER XVII. March 16.

No.	Names of the Articles.	Average annual Quantity Imported.									Total Value in Rupees.	Average annual Quantity Exported.										Total Value in Rupees.
		Nidge of 12 Maunds.	Bullock-load of 6 Maunds.	Maunds of 44 Seers Cutcha.	Seers Cutcha of 24 Rupsweight.	Per man's load (large)	Per man's load (small)	Potts.	Kadi, or Scores.	Adud, or Pieces.		Nidge of 12 Maunds.	Bullock-load of 6 Maunds.	Maunds of 44 Seers.	Seers of 24 Rupees weight.	Per man's load (large)	Per man's load (small)	Guddah, or Potts.	Kadi, or Scores.	Baskets.	Pieces.	
27	Cinnamon	—	—	—	—	—	—	—	—	—	—	—	4	—	—	—	—	—	—	—	—	72
28	Bastard ditto (*Cassia*)	—	—	—	—	—	—	—	—	—	—	—	10	—	—	—	—	—	—	—	—	180
29	Brimstone	—	48	—	—	—	—	—	—	—	864	—	—	—	—	—	—	—	—	—	—	—
30	Saltpetre	—	3	—	—	—	—	—	—	—	54	—	—	—	—	—	—	—	—	—	—	—
31	*Cuddakah* (a seed)	—	—	—	—	—	—	—	—	—	—	—	41	—	—	—	3½	—	—	—	—	23
32	Sundry Curry-stuffs	—	361	7¼	—	5¼	65¼	—	—	—	—	—	1241¼	—	—	—	25	—	—	—	—	—
33	Coco-nut	—	2824	—	—	906½	1103½	—	—	57	19247	—	1536	—	—	229	202	—	—	—	76774	12508
34	Toddy (palm wine)	—	—	—	—	—	—	2	—	—	4	—	—	—	—	—	—	287½	—	—	—	575
35	Iron bars	—	65½	—	—	—	—	—	—	320	1422	—	—	—	—	—	—	—	—	—	—	—
36	Iron pots	—	—	—	—	—	—	—	—	1	40	—	—	—	—	—	—	—	—	—	4	170
37	Ploughshares	—	—	—	—	—	—	—	—	57	14	—	—	—	—	—	—	—	—	—	—	—
38	Bill hooks	—	—	—	—	—	—	—	—	71	71	—	—	—	—	—	—	—	—	—	—	—
39	*Coir* (cordage made of coco-nut)	—	36½	1¼	—	15½	8½	—	—	—	474	—	4½	37	—	7	—	—	—	—	56½	143
40	White thread	—	—	—	—	—	1	—	—	—	3	—	—	—	—	—	—	—	—	—	—	—
41	Silk ditto	—	2	—	—	—	—	—	—	—	3568	—	—	—	—	—	—	—	—	—	—	—
42	Silk	—	—	—	—	—	—	—	—	14	140	—	—	—	—	—	1	—	—	—	—	200
43	Broadcloth	—	—	—	—	—	—	—	—	11	—	—	—	—	—	—	2	—	—	—	—	240
44	Sundry cloths	—	594½	—	—	56	113	—	1	89	—	—	—	—	—	—	—	—	—	—	—	—
45	Black *Cumlies* (blankets)	—	99½	—	—	1	6	—	1½	453	10615	—	—	—	—	—	—	—	—	—	—	—
46	Salt-fish	—	4½	—	—	61	66½	—	—	—	56	—	—	—	—	—	—	—	—	—	—	—
47	Red paint	—	1	—	—	—	—	—	—	—	9	—	17½	—	—	—	67	—	—	—	—	100
48	Tobacco	—	309	88½	5	—	2	—	—	—	5830	—	8½	2	—	—	—	—	—	—	—	88
49	*Jagory* (inspissated juice of sugar-cane)	—	249	316¾	—	—	—	—	—	—	1810	—	21	951	—	—	—	—	—	—	—	2154
50	*Chunam* (lime)	—	—	—	—	—	—	—	—	—	—	—	—	—	—	—	—	—	—	—	206	52
51	Sealing-wax	—	¾	—	—	—	—	—	—	—	72	—	—	—	—	—	—	—	—	—	—	—
52	*Dammer* (Rosin)	—	—	—	—	—	—	—	—	—	—	—	—	¾	—	—	—	—	—	—	—	1
53	Arrack	—	—	—	—	—	—	16	—	—	64	—	—	—	—	—	—	—	—	—	—	—
54	Sheep	—	—	—	—	—	—	—	—	983	1475	—	—	—	—	—	—	—	—	—	—	—

CHAPTER XVII.

March 16.

No.	Article																					
55	*Utchada* cloth	—	—	—	—	—	—	—	—	1139	2272	—	—	—	—	—	—	—	—	—	—	—
56	*Gunny* sackcloth	—	—	—	—	—	—	—	—	12	18	—	—	—	—	—	—	—	—	—	—	—
57	*Dungaree* (cloth)	—	—	—	—	—	—	—	—	6	3	—	—	—	—	—	—	—	—	—	—	—
58	*Cudjans* (mats)	—	—	—	—	2	1	—	—	5	4	—	—	—	—	—	—	—	—	—	—	—
59	Country *Kittisalls* (umbrellas)	—	—	—	—	4	8	—	—	—	24	—	—	—	—	—	—	—	—	—	73	10
60	*Ratton* boxes	—	—	—	—	—	—	—	—	—	—	—	—	—	—	—	—	—	—	—	—	—
61	Country paper (bundles)	—	—	—	—	—	1	—	—	—	8	—	—	—	—	—	—	—	—	—	137	5
62	Sugar-cane	—	—	—	—	—	—	—	—	—	—	—	—	—	—	—	—	—	—	—	—	—
63	Stone plates	—	8	—	—	—	—	—	—	—	32	—	—	—	—	28	—	—	—	—	—	14
64	Skins	—	—	—	—	1	—	—	—	—	8	—	—	—	—	—	—	—	—	—	2	1
65	*Jack Stones* of the *Artocarpus*	—	—	—	—	—	—	—	—	—	—	—	—	—	—	15	—	—	—	—	29	158
66	*Betel-leaf*	—	47	—	—	54	49	—	—	—	319	—	—	—	—	305½	5	—	—	—	—	31
67	*Dooleys* (litters)	—	—	—	—	—	—	—	—	—	—	—	—	—	—	—	3	—	—	—	—	1734
68	*Grec* plantains	—	—	—	—	—	—	—	—	—	—	—	—	—	—	—	—	—	—	—	14	78
69	Horses	—	—	—	—	—	—	—	—	2	—	—	—	—	—	3	2	—	—	62	—	4110
70	*Hookah* snakes	—	—	—	—	—	—	—	—	—	—	—	—	—	—	—	—	—	—	—	—	—
71	Cattle	—	—	—	—	—	—	—	—	574	11560	—	—	6	—	—	—	—	—	—	—	5
72	*Mangoes*	—	—	—	—	—	—	—	—	—	—	—	14	—	—	—	—	—	—	—	73	1470
73	*Jack* fruit	—	—	—	—	—	—	—	—	—	—	—	3	—	—	—	—	—	—	—	—	28
74	*Guavas* fruit	—	—	—	—	—	—	—	—	—	—	—	4	—	—	—	—	—	—	—	—	3
75	*Betel-nut* 1st sort	—	—	—	—	—	—	—	—	—	—	10251⅓	—	2½	9½	—	—	—	—	—	—	618081
76	Ditto - 2d ditto	—	—	—	—	—	—	—	—	—	—	1245¾	—	10	5½	—	—	—	—	—	—	59836
77	Ditto - 3d ditto	—	—	—	—	—	—	—	—	—	—	168½	—	½	¾	—	—	—	—	—	—	5356
78	Pepper	—	—	—	—	—	—	—	—	—	—	1350	—	¼	7¼	—	—	—	—	—	—	109863
79	Cardamoms	—	—	—	—	—	—	—	—	—	—	121½	—	1¾	8½	—	—	—	—	—	—	48664
80	Sandal-wood	—	—	—	—	—	—	—	—	—	—	1024	44	—	—	—	—	—	—	—	—	1024
	Total value imports *Rupees*										108045										Total value exports *Rupees*	963833

(Signed) Alexander Read, Collector.

CHAPTER XVII.

March 18. Appearance of the country. Chandra-guti.

18th *March*.—I entered the territory of the *Mysore Rájá*, and went to *Chandra-gupti*. The country through which I passed is level, and would appear to have been at one time almost entirely cultivated. A great part of it is now overgrown with trees, which have not yet had time to arrive at a great height. *Chandra-gupti*, or *Chandra-guti*, is also called simply *Guti;* care must therefore be taken to distinguish it from *Gutti*, a place of some note situated at a distance toward the north. It formed one of the first acquisitions of the house of *Ikeri*, and has a fort, which stands on a high peaked hill. The fable of the natives says, that this hill was formerly of an immense height, and prevented the moon from going round in her due course; whence the name of the place is derived. When the *Racsha Jellasunda* had defeated *Krishna*, that incarnation of the deity hid himself among the rocks of this hill. The enraged demon, not being able to discover the god, consumed the hill to its present size, very much to the satisfaction of the moon. It may perhaps be thought, that this fable may have arisen from a tradition of the hill having been formerly a volcano. For my own part, I think that these stories are so monstrous, that nothing can be drawn from them, but a commiseration for the credulity of mankind. In times far posterior to those of *Krishna* this was a place of great celebrity; the town at the foot of the hill having been the residence of *Trenetra Cadumba Ráya*, on the site of whose palace I am encamped. A well, and some faint traces of walls and buildings, still mark the spot. On the fall of this dynasty the place lost its consequence. About a hundred and fifty years ago, it suffered much from an invasion by a Mussulman named *Seyd Assaripha*. In the time of *Hyder*, *Somashecara Nayaka*, *Polygar* of *Billighy*, destroyed it. Soon afterwards the commandant *(Killadar)* betrayed the fort to *Purseram (Parasu-Ráma) Bhow;* but seven months afterwards he was compelled to restore it. From that time the inhabitants had no molestation, until the troubles occasioned by *Dundia*, who held it almost a month. It at present contains about 100 houses.

March 18. Soil of the neighbourhood.

To the eastward of the hill *Chandra-gupti*, although much of the country is waste, it is in a better condition than *Soonda*. Much of it is under *Ragy*, which pays no revenue; and between every two crops the ground is allowed three years fallow. The natives allege that the soil is very poor. I have never seen stronger stubble, and to all outward appearance the soil is rich. I suspect that the principal defect is in the cultivators; but without actual experiment, it would be rash to speak decidedly on the subject.

Iron ore.

About a coss north from *Chandra-gupti* is a hill producing iron ore, which is wrought to some extent. It is found in veins intermixed with *Laterite*, like the ore of *Angada-puram* in *Malabar*. The ore is of the same nature with what is usually smelted in the peninsula; that is to say, it is a black sand ore, which here is conglutinated by clay into a mass, and contains less extraneous matter than common. It is broken into small pieces, and the little masses of iron are picked out of the clay. Every man employed in the work pays to government two *Rupees*, or about 4*s.*; and they all have an equal share of the produce. There being no tax on the forges, is perhaps the reason why none are mentioned in the public accompts of this *Ráyada*, in which much iron is smelted. The workmen say, that in *Billighy* and *Sudha*, there is abundance of ore; but in these districts there are no people who understand the process.

Strata.

The rock on which the fort is built is a white granite without observable *strata*, exactly like that of *Jamal-ábád*, and which is common throughout *Haiga*. The nature of the minerals there and here is indeed quite similar.

Sandal wood.

In this district *(Taluc)* there is some sandal-wood of a very good quality. It grows on dry hard ground, where of course the forest trees do not arrive at any great size. It is never planted, but grows from the seed which the birds disperse. In *Hyder's* government, in order to regulate the market properly, it was cut by the officers of revenue *(Amildars)*; and, after having been divided into proper billets, was sold on the account of government. *Purseram Bhow*

CHAPTER XVII. cut all that he could, and the remainder was much injured by renting it out to merchants. All that was good for any thing was cut

March 18. last year; but three years hence there will be some more fit for the market. The quantity procured last cutting was about 40 *Candies*, of 20 *Cutcha Maunds*, each weighing about 26 lb. Its price is commonly about 30 *Pagodas*, or 120 *Rupees*, a *Candy*. The following is considered to be the proper management. The trees, after having been cut, are allowed to remain in the woods for one month. They are then taken into a house; the white wood is removed, and the sandal, or heart, is cut into billets, and stored. The roots are dug up, and oil can be extracted from them, as well as from the chips, and the cuttings of the stem. All the persons who extract the oil are Mussulmans.

March 19. 19th *March*.—I went three cosses to *Sunticopa*, or dry-ginger-village. The country through which I passed is by nature very fine; and the trees, by which much of it is overgrown, are low, a proof of its not having been long waste. The fields have never been enclosed, and the cultivation of dry grains is not at all understood, the ground being cultivated once only in four years. The rice grounds are tolerably well occupied. It probably would answer good purposes to bring here, from *Priya-pattana*, a colony to cultivate *Car' Ragy*, and to send thither a colony of *Haiga Bráhmans*, to form *Betel-nut* plantations. No tanks are required for the rice grounds; but in this district of *Chandra-guti*, there are many small ones, for the use of gardens. The rice lands suffer much from the inundations of the *Varadá*, which frequently sweep away the crops. Of course, those near the river let very low, 5 *Candacas*, or 300 *Seers* sowing, being only taxed at four *Rupees*. Where the inundations do not reach, the lands let at from two to four *Rupees* a *Candaca*. The natives acknowledge twelve seeds as the produce of land which is properly laboured and manured.

Malavaru, or *Malawars*, and their government.

The most numerous class of inhabitants are *Halepecas*, whose customs I described while in *Canara*. There are also many of rather a low class of *Sivabhactars*, called *Malavaru*, or *Malawars*. Most of the *Gaudas* are of this class; and the father of *Sedásiva Nayaka* was a *Malawar*, the *Gauda* of *Kilidi*. The people do not complain of the change of government from his descendants to *Hyder;* but they say, that not above a tenth part of the inhabitants remain. This devastation was occasioned, first by a cruel invasion of the *Marattahs* headed by the *Peshwa*, and afterwards by a sickness inflicted by the goddess *Havali*. This appears to have been a remittent fever, a disease that is still very prevalent; but of late its virulence has considerably abated.

CHAPTER XVII. March 19.

Worship of *Nandi*, or the *Baswa*, and of the *Saktis*.

In this neighbourhood the village god is *Nandi*, or the bull on which *Siva* rides. He is also called the *Baswa*, and receives no sacrifices, which are held in abhorrence by the *Sivabhactar* chiefs *(Gaudas)*. The *Halepecas* and *Whalliaru* offer bloody sacrifices to *Marima*, and the other *Saktis*, but have no temples. The votaries go to the side of some river, put up a stone which represents the deity, and offer it the blood. From this worship the *Sivabhactars* entirely abstain; and under their government the temples of the *Saktis* were called *Butagallu Champadi*, or devil's huts, a name which the Mussulmans did not change.

March 20. Appearance of the country.

20th *March*.—I went three cosses to *Kilidi*. The greater part of the country is pretty level; but the higher grounds seem to be entirely neglected, although the soil is in general apparently good. Most of the trees are small, owing to their being young; but in places where they are aged, they have grown to a large size, and support pepper vines. *Tippoo* prohibited the produce of these from being gathered, and of course the woods supporting them were neglected; but some pains having last year been bestowed, there is now a tolerable crop. In the neighbourhood of *Kilidi* are many gardens of *Areca* palms, in which pepper is raised; but among the *Arecas* neither *Betel-leaf* nor cardamoms are cultivated. The *Arecas* are planted wherever there is a supply of water, without regard to the exposure; but they are sheltered from the west and south by several rows of trees.

CHAPTER XVII.

March 20.

History of the *Kilidi* family.

I here found a *Bráhman*, named *Bayluru Dwuppa*, whose ancestors have been the hereditary writers of the chronicles of the *Kilidi* family. He engaged to give me the family book, called *Kilidi Ráya Paditti.* It is in the old dialect and character of *Karnata*, and contains 400 *Slókams*, or distichs; for, like all the other works of any note among the *Hindus*, it is poetical. He afterwards forwarded a copy of the work to *Purnea*, who was so good as to add a translation into the modern language and character, and both of them have been delivered to the Bengal government. The family of the historiographer enjoyed an *Enam*, or free land, to the amount of sixty *Pagodas* a year.

From some particulars explained to me out of this historical poem it would appear, that its chronology differs considerably from that of *Ramuppa*. The *Kilidi* family were originally hereditary chiefs *(Gaudás)* of five or six villages in this neighbourhood, and were *Sivabhactars* of the *Malavara* cast. *Bhadráconda*, the son of *Basw'-uppa Gauda*, entered into the service of *Krishna Ráyaru*, who gave him the name of *Sedásiva Nayaka*, and conferred on him the hereditary government of some districts in the year *Sal.* 1422, being *Sidarty*. *Kilidi* continued the seat of government, until *Sal.* 1436 only. From *Ikeri* it was removed to *Bidderuru*, in *Sal.* 1568 *(A. D.* 164$\frac{1}{6}$). *Viru Magi*, the last princess of the house of *Kilidi*, or *Ikeri*, says *Dwuppa*, allowed her adopted sons no power. She put the first to death when he was twenty-four years old, because he presumed to interfere with her intrigues. Soon afterwards *Medicarey Náyaka*, *Rájá* of *Chatrakal*, took a young man, a weaver by cast, and brought him up as *Basw'-uppa Náyaka*, the murdered prince. Finding, however, that he was not able to make any advantage of the young man's claims, he lent him to *Hyder*, who espoused the cause of the weaver with much seeming earnestness, and carried him about with great pomp. He accompanied the pretender through the whole country, merely as an ally; and, *Viru Magi* being detested on account of her criminal life, many of the commandants of fortresses

March 20.

were induced to deliver up their charge to the pretended *Basw'-uppa*. These were immediately garrisoned with the troops of his friend *Hyder*. The princess, conscious of the detestation in which she was held, retired with her adopted son *Somashecara* to a strong hold named *Belalla Ráya Durga*, and left her capital in charge of the *Delawai*, or prime minister, named *Virapadruppa*. On the approach of *Hyder* and the pretender, the people of *Bidderuru* deserted, and the Mussulman took possession without trouble. He laid siege to *Belalla Ráya Durga*, and after some time took the princess *(Rany)* and her adopted son prisoners. Thence he returned to the capital, on which he bestowed his own name of *Hyder Nagara;* and, disguise being no longer necessary, he began to treat the pretender with the utmost contempt, and at length induced the young man to quarrel with him, by taking his favourite dancing girls, who by intercourse with a Mussulman were defiled. Immediately after the rupture, the pretender, the princess, and her adopted son, were sent to *Madhu-giri*. Soon afterwards they were relieved by the *Marattahs*, who altogether neglected the pretender, and, knowing the weakness of his claims, dismissed him. The princess died on the road to *Poonah* of a pain in her bowels; but the *Marattahs*, with a view of taking advantage of his claims, carried the son to their capital. The people here do not know what has been his fate, and seem very little interested about the matter. The pretender, being in absolute want, applied to *Hyder*, who gave him free lands to the amount of 120 *Pagodas* a year, or 40 *Rupees* a month. He left two sons, who on the fall of *Seringapatam* collected a rabble, and began to plunder in the neighbourhood of *Hossodary* (*Wostara* of our maps, I suppose). They were soon taken by a party of British troops, and were immediately hanged as lawless robbers.

Kilidi, and the rise of *Sedásiva*.

Sedásiva built a fort at *Kilidi*, which continued to be garrisoned till the time of *Hyder*. The town never was large, and the only remarkable building is a temple of *Iswara*, which *Sedásiva* erected

CHAPTER XVII.

March 20.

by orders of the god, who appeared to him in a dream. As a curiosity, I was shown the pit whence *Sedásiva* dug out a treasure, and a sword, the commencement of his great fortune. To this he was conducted by a *Naga*, or hooded serpent, sent for the purpose by some propitious deity. While *Sedásiva* was asleep in a field, the *Naga* came, and shaded his head from the sun by raising up as an umbrella its large flat neck. The young man was awaked by a shriek from his mother, who, in looking after her son, found him under the power of the monster. He immediately started up to escape, but was opposed by the serpent, until he consented to follow it quietly, and was conducted to the place where the treasure was hid. Here the snake began to bite the ground, and make signs. At length *Sedásiva*, having dug into the earth, found a cave filled with treasure, and containing a sword. Such are the fables by which the *Hindu* chiefs endeavour to gain the admiration and respect of their countrymen, whose credulity indeed renders the means very adequate to the end proposed.

March 21. *Ságar*, and its commerce.

21st *March*.—I went three cosses to *Ikeri*, through a country entirely like that which I saw yesterday. Near *Ikeri* is a well-built town, named *Ságar*, which at present is the residence of the chief of the district *(Amildar)*. It stands on the southern bank of the *Varadá*, which is here a very small stream, as being near its source. *Ságar* has some merchants of property, who export to a considerable distance the produce of the country. The exports are pepper, *Betel-nut*, and sandal wood; about equal quantities of which go to the dominions of the *Nabob* of *Arcot*, and to the country south of the *Krishna*, lately ceded by the *Nizam* to the Company. The prices are highest in the last mentioned territory; but the expenses and duties are in proportion. The returns from both countries are chiefly made in cloths, there being no manufactures in this neighbourhood. To *Haiga* the merchants of *Ságar* send pepper, cloth, iron, and grain; they receive from thence salt, coco-nuts, and *Cut*, or *Terra Japonica*. About one half of all the returns made to this country for its produce are in cash. The merchants say, that the sandal wood of the *Ikeri Ráyada* is superior to that of either the south or east. They acknowledge the inferiority of their *Betel-nut*. According to the report of the custom-house, the quantity of *Betel-nut* exported annually from *Ságar* is about 8000 loads. That of pepper is about 500 loads. The load is about 8 *Maunds*, or $196\frac{1}{2}$ lb. CHAPTER XVII. March 21.

During the time *Ikeri* was the residence of the princes descended from *Sedásiva*, it was a very large place, and by the natives is said, in round numbers, and with the usual exaggeration, to have contained 100,000 houses. Like *Sudha*, its walls are of very great extent, and form three concentric enclosures, rather than fortifications. It had also a citadel, but of no great strength, which until eight or ten years ago continued to be garrisoned. Within it was the palace of the *Rájá*, constructed of mud and timber, like those of *Tippoo*, and by no means a large building. The wooden work has been neatly carved, and covered with false gilding. The temple of *Siva*, where the town stood, is a large edifice, and is formed of stone brought from a great distance; but, as usual, it is destitute of either elegance or grandeur. It is now repairing, and workmen have been brought from *Goa* for the purpose; even the Portuguese of India being more skilful artists than any that can be procured in this country. At *Ikeri* there remains no town, but the devastation has not been occasioned by any calamity. When the court removed to *Bidderuru*, the inhabitants willingly followed. *Ikeri* continued, however, to be the nominal capital; the *Rájás* were called by its name, and the coins were supposed to be struck there, although in fact the mint was removed. *Ikeri.*

So long as the government of the *Sivabhactar* family lasted, the coins continued to be called *Ikeri Pagodas* and *Fanams*. On the conquest, the name was changed, first by *Hyder* into *Bahadury*, and then by *Tippoo* into *Sultany*. The princes of *Mysore* never coined *Pagodas*; but *Canterua Narasingha Ráya*, the first of them who *Coins.*

CHAPTER XVII. March 21.

acquired considerable power, coined gold *Fanams*, called after his name *Canter'-ráya Fanams*, which we usually write *Cantery*. Ten of these formed a nominal *Pagoda*, which accomptants commonly use. On the fall of *Tippoo*, the *Mysore* government, having found it convenient to coin *Pagodas* of the same value with those before current, struck them at *Mysore* and *Nagara*, but restored the old name of *Ikeri*.

Forests of the *Ghâts*.

The *Ságar* district *(Taluc)* extends to the bottom of the mountains, on the declivity of which are many woods that spontaneously produce pepper. These forests are said to be very unhealthy.

Soil.

The *Amildar*, who is a man of plain manners and good sense, says, that in this neighbourhood dry grains have been often tried, but have always failed; and that the goodness of the soil is merely apparent; for in general it is very shallow, and placed on a *substratum* of *Laterite*, which renders the soil above it very unproductive of grain. Even rice thrives ill, although the deepest and richest soils are reserved for its cultivation. It must be observed, that in all the countries where it is found the opinion of the unfitness of the soil for dry grains is prevalent. The *Amildar* makes a curious observation. He says, that in the country to the eastward the surface is covered with stones; but under these there is a fine cool earth; while here, the surface is earth, but under that there is a dry rock which burns up every thing. It must, however, be observed, that the forests here are greatly superior to those farther east; owing probably to the roots of trees being able to penetrate into the crevices of the rock, and to get at water, which is here generally found at no great depth from the surface: but to the eastward, before water can be procured, the wells must be dug to a considerable depth.

Account of the *Marattahs* by the *Amildar*.

The *Amildar* says, that he was employed by the *Sultán* in a diplomatic capacity at *Poonah* when *Seringapatam* was taken. He would have been successful in procuring assistance for his then master, had the dissensions among the *Marattah* chiefs permitted them to act. *Scindia* was decidedly in favour of the *Sultán;* but was quite destitute of money; and the army which he had at *Poonah,* after having expended all the means that they possessed, had for some time been subsisted on plunder. The *Amildar* says, that *Tippoo's* government, when compared with that of the *Marattahs,* was excellent; and, notwithstanding all the evils the people suffered from the extortions of the *Asophs,* and the attacks of invading armies, they enjoyed a comparatively great security. The government never subsisted by open plunder; whereas among the *Marattah* chiefs there are very few who do not support their troops by avowed robbery. March 21.

22d *March.*—I went three cosses to *Ghenasu-guli.* The country all the way is hilly, and is considered by the natives as totally useless, although in many places the nature of thesoil would admit of the use of the plough. It does not even answer for pasture, and the coarse, rank grass that grows upon it in the rainy season cannot be made into hay. Once a year, in order to keep the country clear, it is burned. This is probably the reason of the stunted appearance of the trees. On the whole, no desert in Africa can be less productive of use to man. At *Ghenasu-guli* there is no market *(Bazar);* but there is a small village of *Haiga Bráhmans,* who, to judge from the appearance of the houses, are in easy circumstances. They cultivate some fine gardens. I here met with *Ram' Row,* chief officer *(Subadar)* of the *Nagara* principality *(Ráyada),* a very gentleman-like person, which is rather uncommon in people of his cast. He agrees entirely with the other natives, in thinking the higher lands of this *Ráyada* totally useless. March 22. Appearance of the country. *Ghenasu-guli.*

23d *March.*—I went three cosses to *Duma,* or *Dumam.* The country resembles that which I came through yesterday, and on the whole way I did not see the smallest trace of cultivation. I passed through a very long wood where pepper grows spontaneously. The trees are very fine, and the soil is apparently good; but it is quite neglected by the natives, who say that the pepper is of no value March 23. Wild pepper, and appearance of the country.

CHAPTER XVII. March 23. It is watered by the *Pada-gópí*, a rivulet that, after passing through the *Garsopa* district, falls into the inlet of the sea at *Houawera*. At *Duma* there is only one house belonging to a *Malawar Gauda*; but it is a very large one.

March 24. 24th *March*.—Although I had desired the guides to divide the road into tolerably equal stages, I found this day's journey to *Fatah-petta* very short. It was called two *Sultany* cosses. The country is rather opener than what we passed through on the two preceding days; but a large proportion of the small quantity of rice-ground is waste.

Fatah-petta. *Fatah-petta*, or the town of victory, is usually pronounced *Putty-pet*. It was built by *Hyder* in commemoration of an advantage which he gained at this place over the troops of the princess of *Ikeri*. At first he built five hundred houses; but finding that the place injured the trade of *Naggar*, and gave a facility to smuggling, he reduced the shops to fifty, and they have now decreased to twenty-five. Near the town runs a small stream, commonly called *Ram Chandra-pura* from the place where it has its source; but its proper name is the *Sarawati*. North from *Fatah-petta*, it receives a small branch, and forms the *Pada-gópí*.

Farm belonging to the *Rájás*. At this place the *Rájás* had a farm, which an overseer now cultivates on account of the government. It produces coco-nuts, *Arecas*, and rice; and is finely supplied with water by a canal, which is supplied from a perennial stream as clear as crystal. No experiment is made at this farm, nor any attempt at improving the usual cultivation of the country; which is the only rational inducement that could lead a prince to farm. On the contrary, it is in a more slovenly condition than any plantation that I have seen in the country. At this farm the *Rájás* had a *Mahal*, or palace, consisting of three squares, which are surrounded by low, mean buildings covered with tiles. These, however, contained baths, and all such conveniences as a *Hindu* chief requires. Near the palace are stables for the cattle of the farm.

CHAPTER XVII.

March 25. *Hyder Nagara, or Bidderuru.*

25th *March.*—I went two cosses to the centre of *Hyder Nagara,* through a fog so thick that I could see little of the country. It is extremely hilly, and overgrown with woods, in which there are many fortified defiles and passes, that are guarded by armed men in the service of the *Mysore Rájá.*

I remained three days at *Nagara,* where I met with a kind reception from Captain Lloyd of the *Bombay* army, who commanded the garrison in the fort.

Nagara was originally called *Bidder-hully,* or *Bamboo-village,* and consisted of a temple dedicated to *Nilcunta (Blue-neck,* one of the titles of *Siva),* and surrounded by a few houses, under the direction of a *Bráhman* chief. *Sivuppa,* son of *Chica Suncana,* removed the seat of government from *Ikeri* to this place, and changed its name into *Bidderuru,* or *Bamboo-place.* The whole revenue of the country being then expended here, it immediately became a town of great magnitude and commerce. The situation is also favourable for trade, as the *Hosso Angady* pass, leading from *Mangalore* this way, is one of the best roads in the western mountains. The town is said to have contained 20,000 houses, besides a very great number of huts; but, on account of the inequality of the ground, could never have been closely built. It was defended by a circle of woods, hills, and fortified defiles, extending a great way in circumference, and containing many *Bamboos,* from which the name of the place was derived. The space within these defences is much larger than was ever occupied by the city, and contained many hills, woods, gardens, and rice fields. Toward the centre stood the *Rájá's* palace, situated on a high hill, and surrounded by a citadel. To this *Hyder* added some new works; but, being commanded by some neighbouring hills, it never was capable of much defence. After *Hyder* took the town, its trade increased greatly; for he made it his principal arsenal, and employed many people in making arms and ammunition. He also continued the mint, and much money was coined there during his reign. He gave great encouragement

CHAPTER XVII. March 25.

to merchants, and endeavoured to introduce the cultivation of mulberries and silk, but in this he had little or no success. On the outside of the fort, he built a palace, and resided in it three years. On the invasion by General Mathews, the commandant of the fort, by way of showing an inclination to make an obstinate defence, burnt the palace; and the whole town shared the same fate during an engagement which took place on *Tippoo's* coming up with his army. It is commonly reported by our officers, that General Mathews was surprised; and, indeed, from his infatuated conduct, that would appear to have been the case; yet the people here say, that he had given them eight days previous notice of the probability of a siege, and of consequence they lost little more than their houses, as they had time to remove all their valuable effects. The palace was rebuilt by *Tippoo*, elated with the victory of which he made so cruel a use; but in the short time that has since intervened, it is now almost a ruin; for it is built entirely of mud and timber; and on these materials the excessive rains of this climate have so strong an effect, that without a very complete repair once in three or four years, no building of this kind will stand for any length of time. *Tippoo* also re-established the mint and arsenal, and recalled the people; but a great many of them did not return, being under suspense for the event of the siege of *Mangalore*.

After the peace of 1783, *Tippoo* returned to *Bidderuru*, and immediately afterwards his officers began to be troublesome to the merchants, and put a stop to all commerce with those who did not belong to the *Sultán's* dominions. At his death the town contained between fourteen and fifteen hundred houses, besides huts; one hundred and fifty new houses have been since built, and merchants are resorting to it from all quarters. It cannot be expected, however, to arrive at its former greatness, as it is neither the seat of a court, nor of any public works. It possesses no manufactures; so that its chief support will be its trade, as being a convenient thoroughfare. The mint is maintained, and every liberty granted to merchants; which seems to be all the encouragement that could with propriety be given.

March 25. Christians.

During the princesses *(Ranys)* government a hundred families of *Kankany* Christians had settled at *Bidderuru*, and subsisted chiefly by distilling and selling spirituous liquors. Their condition may be estimated by knowing, that the building of their church cost 12 *Pagodas*, or less than 5*l*. They were, however, able to support a priest, and to maintain some form of worship. In the reign of *Tippoo* they were all carried to *Seringapatam;* but, since the fall of that place, ten families have returned, and are living in great poverty. The church was pulled down by the *Cazi*, who was a furious bigot, and delighted in overthrowing what he called the temples of idolaters. There were at this place many inscriptions on stone; but they were all broken to pieces by the zealot. With the ruins of temples he built a handsome mosque, and settled in it three priests *(Moullahs)*, with whom he passed his leisure time in prayer, and exercises of religion. When he saw the Christian flag displayed on the fort, he could not endure the abomination, and immediately withdrew towards *Mecca*. The three priests remain in the mosque, where, in place of being pampered by the charity of the *Asophs*, and other officers of distinction, they drag out an existence upon an annual pension of 2 *Pagodas*, or 16*s*. Their being allowed any thing is however a great proof of *Purnea's* moderation; as they are still living in the spoils of *Hindu* temples, torn from the gods at their instigation.

Mussulman bigot.

Hujiny Swami.

During my stay here I had frequent intercourse with the *Hujiny Swami*, one of the four great chiefs of the *Sivabhactar* religion. His predecessors were the *Gurus* of the *Ikeri* family, and had obtained from them free-gift lands to the yearly amount of 3000 *Pagodas* (1208*l*. 16*s*. 8*d*.). By *Hyder* and *Tippoo* the whole was gradually taken away, and no allowance has been made to him since the country has been granted to the *Rájá* of *Mysore*. He has, it is true, a village considered as his property; but he pays rent for it like

CHAPTER XVII. March 25.

any other farmer. Whether it be owing to his poverty or to his good sense I know not, but he is quite free from pride or affectation; a kind of virtue that I do not expect among those who, like him, are considered by their followers as incarnations of the deity.

Remains of the *Ikeri* family.

The *Swami* says, that a brother of *Chinna Basw'-uppa* is still alive in the *Marattah* territories, and lives near *Savanuru*. *Somashecara*, the last adopted son of the princess, died in the *Marattah* country unmarried, but has left behind him relations who are living with the brother of *Chinna Basw'-uppa*. By the *Swami* this person is considered as the lawful heir of the family. In case of his line failing, the relations of *Somashecara* would be entitled to the succession.

Account of the *Sivabhactars* by the *Swami*.

The original *Matam* or college of the *Hujiny Swami* was at *Hara-punya-hully*; but the seat was removed to this neighbourhood in the time of *Choudeia Budreia*, who founded *Ikeri*. According to the *Swami*, *Sivabhactar* is the proper name of the cast, which arose in the following manner. *Iswara*, having been displeased that his worship was neglected on this earth, commanded *Baswa*, or the bull on which he rides, to assume a human form, and to recall mankind to the true worship. *Baswa* was very reluctant to go among such a wicked race of beings; but at last consented, and took upon himself the form of a child, and was born in the family of a *Bráhman*. Having, while a boy, performed sundry miracles, and persuaded his supposed parents of his divine nature, he was called by the name of *Baswana*. In the year *Vicrama* of the *Káli-yugam* 3875 (*A. D.* 775), he took with him his sister, and went to *Kalyán-pura*, a city in the country now belonging to the *Nizam*, but at that time the residence of a prince named *Bejala*, who was a *Jain*. While this *Rájá* was sitting in his court surrounded by all his officers, there fell from the heaven called *Coilasa* a letter, which no one present could read. The stranger, who had already obtained some reputation, was called, and read the letter, which informed the *Rájá*, that is a certain place he would find a treasure amounting to some millions of *Rupees.* The treasure having been found, *Baswana* was made prime minister, and married the daughter of a certain *Moduersa.* *Baswana's* sister now became pregnant, without having been married. She alleged, that she had been impregnated by *Iswara;* and, as a proof of her veracity, the child came from her back, in place of being born in the usual manner. The child was called *Chinna Baswana.* The *Baswa* then began publicly to teach, that the only true worship was that of *Iswara,* or *Siva;* and, having gained many proselytes, he made 196,000 *Jangamas,* some of whom were allowed to marry, and others were ordained to be *Sannyásis.* In the year *Racshasa,* of the *Kali-yugam* 3911 *(A. D.* 811) the time for the *Baswa's* remaining on earth having been expired, he went to *Capily,* a place at the junction of the *Malapahari (Malpurga)* with the *Krishna.* At that place was a celebrated image of *Iswara,* which, on the appearance of *Baswana,* opened, and desired him to enter. *Baswana* replied, that nobody would believe that he had entered into a stone, and requested that the god would assume the form of a *Jangama;* which he accordingly did, and, having clasped *Baswana* in his arms, they became as one person, and ascended to *Coilasu* on Wednesday the 1st of *Margasirsha,* at 21 hours *(Gurries)* of the night.

Chinna Baswana succeeded his uncle as minister, and three months afterwards *Bejala Rájá* was killed by three servants of that personage, named *Jagádeva, Maleya,* and *Bumuna.* He was succeeded by *Vira Vassuunta,* who is allowed by the *Swami* to have been also a *Jain.*

The *Sivabhactars* are divided into two sects; the one is called *Vira Siva,* and comprehends all the *Jangamas,* and by far the greater part of the *Banijigaru,* who are of a much higher rank than the artists and cultivators who wear the *Linga* or emblem of their deity, and who compose the second division called *Samana Sivá.* All the descendants of *Jangamas* continue to be of that class, whose proper profession, like that of the *Bráhmans,* is to subsist upon alms. The

CHAPTER XVII. March 25.

Upadésa of a *Jangama* may be given to any *Sivabhactar*, who is thus adopted into the sacred order; but this practice is condemned by those who are strict. The descendants, however, of these adopted *Jangamas* enjoy all the privileges of the sacred order. This class of men has so multiplied, that in order to procure a subsistence many of them are compelled to pursue the low occupations of the world.

The *Swami* says, that *Iswara* created the *Védas*, and also created many sects, some of which ought to follow one part of the sacred books, and some are bound to obey other portions of those writings. The *Vira Siva* ought to reject the greater part of the doctrine of the *Védas* concerning *Curma*, or ceremonials; that is to say, the offerings of *Yagam*, or sacrifice, washing of the head, *Puja*, and the like. They are, however, permitted to follow part of the *Curma*, and to give *Dhana* and *Dharma*, two kinds of alms bestowed on religious men. These ought only to be given to the *Jangamas*; but many of the laity, who are of the division called *Samana*, have been persuaded heretically to give to the *Bráhmans* both kinds of alms. The *Vira Siva* reject altogether the *Bráhmans*, and never employ them at any ceremony to read prayers (*Mantrams*). The doctrine of the *Védas*, which the *Sivabhactars* are bound to follow, is called *Gniana*, and consists in an acknowledgment of the gods, and in prayer. The *Vira Siva* follow in part only this doctrine, and confine their worship entirely to *Iswara*, his family and dependants: but the *Samana Siva* consider *Vishnu* and *Bráhma* as the same with *Iswara*, and worship them accordingly. These *Samana Siva* act as *Pújáris* in some temples, especially those of *Baswa*; but the *Swami* considers this as an abominable heresy.

The *Swami* says, that the eighteen *Puranas* were written by a very pious *Bráhman* named *Vyása*; and that ten of them contain doctrines which he considers as sound. Next in authority to the *Védas*, however, he considers twenty-eight *Agamas*, which contain an account of the doctrines taught by all sects, with warnings to avoid such as are heretical. Next in point of authority to these, is the *Baswa Purana*, written originally in the *Andray* language, by *Andray Cavi Somaderu*, at the command of *Baswana*, who did not deliver any thing in writing. The work has been translated into the *Karnataca* language by *Bhíma Cavi;* and of this translation a copy, which the *Swami* gave me, has been delivered to the Bengal government. Many commentaries have been written by different learned *Jangamas*.

At each *Matam*, or college, is a chief *Sannyási*, who gives the *Upadésa* of this rank to several children that become his disciples and servants. These *Sannyásis* are of various ranks, and some of them are even permitted to marry. They must be all children of *Jangamas*. From among these *Sannyásis*, the chief *Guru* or *Swami* of the *Matam* chooses the most pious person; and, when he is apprehensive of the approach of death, gives him the *Upadésa* peculiar to his elevated rank, and delivers over to him his book and authority. The successor, so soon as master of the *Upadésa*, is considered as being the same with *Iswara*.

The *Guru* reprimands his followers for small faults, and possesses the power of excommunication for great crimes, such as eating animal food, or drinking spirituous liquors. He also possesses the power of reconciling a man to his wife, when she has committed adultery with a man of the cast. In such cases, he reprimands the woman, but will seldom permit the husband to turn her away. If the crime has been committed with a man of another cast, the *Guru* does not interfere to prevent divorce; but the husband is not under any necessity of parting with his wife; for on paying a fine for her purification, he may retain her.

The *Swami* says, that at certain periods the fourteen *Locums* of the world are destroyed by water. The *Baswa* stands in the middle of the deluge, which reaches only half way up his thighs, and all living creatures are saved by laying hold of his hair. The world is afterwards restored by *Iswara*, who lives in *Coilasu*. It is thither

CHAPTER XVII. March 25.

that after death the spirits of good men go, and are united to the substance of God, where they are exempted from all future change. There is no other heaven, such as *Moesha*, or *Sorghum;* but there are various purgatories, and hells, in which are punished the spirits of wicked men, either for a time, or for eternity, according to the nature of their transgressions. The spirits of men who have been neither bad nor good in the extreme are born again, some as men, others as animals; on which account, except in battle, the *Siva-bhactars* kill no animal. The crime of the premeditated death of an insect is quite the same with that of a man, nor is a cow more sacred than any other animal.

Commerce.

Having assembled the principal merchants, they say, that since the time of the *Rájás* and of *Hyder*, owing to a removal of the court, and of extensive public works, the trade of the place has greatly diminished. It never was the seat of private manufactures; but still has a considerable trade, and is the residence of several wealthy merchants, who export the produce of the country. This consists of pepper, *Betel-nut*, sandal wood, and cardamoms. The merchants cannot state the quantity of any of these articles exported, either now, or at any former period. They say, that advances to the cultivators are seldom made; but, when the owner of a plantation takes advances six months before crop-time, he gets one half of the value of the estimated produce. The price of the commodity is not fixed, but it is taken at the common market-price at the time of delivery, deducting ten *per cent.* for the money advanced. The greater part of the produce is, however, bought up for ready money, immediately after crop season, and more than one half of it is purchased by merchants of the *Marattah* territory, or other distant countries; some of whom come hither in person, and others employ agents. Every merchant, whether native or foreign, has certain families with whom he commonly deals; and at the proper seasons he goes round to their houses, and collects the produce of their farms. Fairs or markets are not in use.

The *Marattah* merchants purchase pepper, cardamoms, and sandal: the *Betel* of this place, being cut, is not fit for their purpose. They bring for sale a great variety of cloths, thread, and cotton-wool, most of which are again exported from hence. They also bring wheat, *Callay (Cicer arietinum)*, and *Danya*, a carminative seed like anise. March 25. With the *Marattah* states.

The merchants of *Mangalore*, and other places below the western *Ghats*, take from hence pepper, wheat, *Callay*, *Danya*, tamarinds, capsicum, cotton-wool, cotton-thread, *Goni* (cloth made of the *Crotolaria juncea)*, cotton-cloth, blankets, iron, iron-work, and steel. They bring up salt, rice, *Horse-gram (Dolichos biflorus)*, coco-nuts, oil, turmeric, and sandal-wood. With *Tulava*.

From the ceded provinces south of the *Krishna*, the merchants import cotton-cloths, and take back *Betel-nut*, pepper, and cardamoms. With the ceded provinces.

From the *Chatrakal* principality are imported buffaloes, sheep, blankets, *Ghee* (boiled butter), and tobacco. With *Chatrakal*.

From *Gubi*, *Sira*, *Bangalore*, &c. are brought cotton cloths, tobacco, blankets, *Goni*, sheep, steel, and iron. The exports to all these places are pepper, *Betel-nut*, and cardamoms. With *Bangalore*.

Merchants from the dominions of *Arcot*, and those of the Company below the eastern *Ghats*, bring cotton cloth, with European and Chinese goods; and take back *Betel-nut* and pepper. The merchants say, that three quarters of the whole produce are purchased with ready money; and the imports brought are equal only to the amount of the remainder. With *Arcot*.

The pepper of *Nagara* is here reckoned better than that of the sea-coast; and a *Parsi* merchant says, that it sells higher at *Bombay* than the pepper of *Malabar*. The average price here is 23 *Ikeri Pagodas* for every *Niza (Nidge*, of vulgar English) of 21 *Maunds*, each weighing 40 of the *Cucha Seers* of *Mangalore*, that is used for *Jagory;* so that the *Niza* should weigh $515\frac{1}{2}$ lb., and sells for 92 *Rupees*. The carriage to *Mangalore* is one *Rupee* a *Maund*, making Pepper.

CHAPTER XVII. March 25.

the *Niza* there worth 113 *Rupees*. The Company's *Candy* of 600 lb. would therefore cost 131½ *Rupees*, beside the charges of merchandize.

Carriage.

The roads being bad, most of the goods are carried between this and *Mangalore* by porters. A man's hire between the two places is 3 *Rupees*, or 6*s*.; and he carries 3 *Maunds*, or 73½ lb. To the country toward the east and north, all goods are sent on oxen, as back loads, each carrying 8 *Maunds*, or 196½ lb. For each load the hire is 4 *Rupees* for 10 *Gavadas*, or days journies; the *Gavada* being computed at four *Sultany* cosses, or *Hardaries*, or at about 14½ British miles; so that the carriage of one hundred-weight costs almost 1 *d.* a mile.

Betel-nut.

The most important article of export from *Nágara* is *Betel-nut*, which is fit for the consumption of all the country to the eastward as far as *Madras*. The merchants cannot state the quantity. In *Tippoo's* reign the merchants were afraid to purchase, knowing that obstacles would be put in their way. The whole, therefore, fell into the hands of the dependants of the *Asophs*, at a low price, and was exported on their account to *Seringapatam*, *Bangalore*, and other cities in the *Sultán's* dominions; for the trade with foreign countries was prohibited. Owing to this, the cultivation was diminished; but the merchants think that this foolish plan had not continued so long as to occasion the loss of many of the trees; but that their produce was only diminished from a want of due cultivation. This year, all due encouragement having been given, it is expected that the produce will equal what it did at any former period. The price just now is higher than it was in *Hyder's* government, and amounts to 20 *Pagodas* a *Niza*, or *Candy*.

Cardamoms.

It is evident from the considerable exportation of cardamoms from hence, all of which are the produce of *Coorg*, that what was stated at *Tellichery* as the amount of cardamoms reared in that country, is applicable only to the quantity sent down to *Malabar*. I have reason to believe, that a much greater quantity comes through the *Mysore Rájá's* territories, although I received no proper account of the specific quantity.

March 25. Grain measure.

The grain measure in every village is different; and even in *Nagara*, that which the cultivators use is different from that by which grain is sold in the market. The *Sida*, or *Cucha Seer* of $20\frac{7}{10}$ cubical inches, is however the foundation of both.

The *Colaga* of the farmers contains $183\frac{3}{10}$ cubical inches. The *Candaca* of 20 *Colagas* is, therefore, equal to nearly $1\frac{7}{10}$ bushel. The market measure is a third larger.

Climate and weather.

The climate here is nearly the same with that of *Sudha*. In the day-time the winds, at present, are pretty strong from the westward. The same plants that one month ago were in flower, when I was at *Kunda-pura* in the same latitude, are now coming into flower here; the difference of elevation making this climate a month later than that of the sea-coast. It is remarkable, that in many parts of India, during March and April, there are on shore strong winds blowing directly from the sea; while in the offing it is a perfect calm. Thus in *Bengal* there are, at that season, very strong southerly winds; while in the bay calms prevail until May or June. On the coast of *Malabar*, the south-west monsoon does not commence blowing with strength until the beginning of the rainy season; but on shore there are strong westerly winds from about the vernal equinox.

Low lands.

The ground levelled for the cultivation of wet crops is here called *Gudday*, and is not subdivided into different kinds. The bottoms of vallies only are levelled, and are chiefly watered by the rain; but there are also some small reservoirs, from which a few days supply can be obtained in the rainy season, when there happens to be no fall for eight or ten days. For the same purpose, the water of some rivulets is turned into channels by dams; but irrigation is much neglected; and although in many places the rivulets are perennial, the farmers do not endeavour to take two crops in one year. The only crops taken from watered ground are rice and sugar-cane.

CHAPTER XVII. March 25. Different kinds of rice.

In order to give time to the cultivators, part of the rice is sow dry seed, and part is transplanted; the seasons for these two modes of cultivation being different. Every kind of rice that is sown here takes six months to grow; and they are of less variety than usual, namely, *Billy Battu*, or *Heggai*, and *Jolaghena*, which may be cultivated both ways; and *Honasena*, or *Kempa*, which can be sown only as dry-seed.

Dry-seed, or *Bara-butta* cultivation.

The *Bara-butta* cultivation is conducted as follows. In the course of the five months following the winter solstice, the field gets four single ploughings. In the second month after the vernal equinox, it is manured with leaf-dung, and ploughed once. After the next rain, the seed is mixed with dry cow-dung, sown broad-cast, and covered by the implement called *Coradu*, which differs from that of *Banawási* in having its section composed of three sides of a square, as in Plate XXIX. Fig. 78, in place of being a segment of a circle. A month after sowing, when the young rice is about four inches high, the field is turned over with a small plough, to kill the grass, and to destroy part of the young corn, which is always sown too thick. After this, the field is again smoothed with the same implement, and barrowed with a bunch of thorns, as described at *Banawási*. In the second month after the summer solstice, all the banks are repaired, to retain the water on the fields, which are then ploughed again, and smoothed with the implement called *Aligena Coradu* (Plate XXIX. Fig. 77.). A large rake, called *Halacu*, is then drawn by the hand over the field, to remove the weeds. In the month preceding the autumnal equinox, the weeds are removed by the hand. In the two months preceding the shortest day, the crop is ripe. It is cut close by the ground, and for four days is allowed to lie loose on the field. It is then stacked in heaps, with the ears inward, but without having been bound up in sheaves. In the course of three months, it is trampled out by oxen. The grain with the husk is preserved in store-houses, or straw bags, and is only made into rice as it may be wanted for immediate use.

The process for transplanted rice, called here *Nitty*, is as follows. In order to raise the seedlings, in the course of fifteen or twenty days during the month following the vernal equinox, a plot is inundated, and ploughed four times. It is then manured with any kind of fresh leaves, and with the dung made by cattle that have been littered with dried leaves. These are ploughed down, and the mud is smoothed, first with the *Noli* (Plate XXIX. Fig. 79.), and afterwards by the *Mara*, which is a square log of timber yoked in the same manner. The field is then drained so that three inches of water only remain. In any of the three months between the vernal equinox and the summer solstice, the seed is sown broad-cast. As this is the dry season, the seedling plot must be very low, so as to receive a supply of water from some rivulet. On the fifth day after the seed has been sown, the whole water is allowed to drain from the plot; and for three days this is kept dry, after which it is constantly inundated, till the seedlings are fit for transplantation. The field, into which they are to be removed, is inundated during the two months following the summer solstice, and in the course of three days during that period is ploughed four times. It is then manured, in the same manner as the plot was; and afterwards, in the course of two or three days, it is ploughed again three times. The mud is then smoothed with the *Noli*, above mentioned; and the water having been let off to the depth of three inches, the seedlings are transplanted into the field, which must be always kept under water; and a month after it has been planted, the weeds must be removed by the hand. The harvest is in the month preceding the winter solstice.

CHAPTER XVII. March 25. *Nitty*, or transplanted cultivation.

All the fields are capable of both modes of cultivation. The transplanting is reckoned most troublesome, and least productive, and requires most seed. A *Candaca* of land is an extent, that in the transplanting cultivation requires one *Candaca* of seed; in dry-seed cultivation, it requires only fifteen *Colagas*. The produce of all the three kinds of rice is nearly the same, only the *Heggai* gives rather

Produce.

CHAPTER XVII. March 25.

most. Of this grain a *Candaca* of land of the first quality, cultivated by transplanting, produces eleven or twelve *Candacas;* land of the second quality produces eight *Candacas;* and land of the third quality produces six *Candacas.* The same ground, cultivated with dry-seed, would produce from one half a *Candaca* to one *Candaca* more.

Seed and produce for an acre.

Having taken the *Shanaboga*, or accomptant, and the farmers who gave me the foregoing account, to a man's fields, who was rated in the public books as possessed of fourteen *Candacas* of land, I found that they contained 308,024 square feet, or that the *Candaca* was equal nearly to 22,000 square feet; so that the seed required for one acre, in the transplanted cultivation, would at this rate be $3\frac{376}{1000}$ bushels, which in Indian farming appears to be an excessive quantity. The owner would give no account of the quantity actually sown, nor of the usual produce; and I observed some contiguous plots, which he called *Ragy* land, and which of course paid no land-tax: but they appeared to have been cultivated with rice, and there was no observable difference between their soil or situation, and those of the neighbouring plots of *Gudday* land. The accomptant pretended ignorance; but from circumstances I am inclined to believe, that there was a collusion between him and the farmer to impose upon the government. At present, from the confused manner in which all native accompts are kept, this is too much in the accomptant's power.

I afterwards sent to discover some farmer who would be more communicative, and at length found a respectable looking *Gauda*, who declared his willingness to tell me the real quantity of seed required to sow his fields, and the quantity that he usually reaped from them. I first measured two plots, each said to require one *Colaga* in the transplanted cultivation, and two thirds of a *Colaga* when sown with dry-seed; the produce in both cases was stated to be one *Candaca* and a half; that is, 30 seeds in the former, and 45 in the latter. The first plot measured 3836 square feet; the

March 25.

second 4131; average 3983. At this rate, the *Candaca* sowing on a good soil is 79,660 square feet; and the acre in the transplanted cultivation requires $\frac{5325}{10000}$ parts of a bushel of seed; and in the dry-seed $\frac{6215}{10000}$ of a bushel. The produce in both cases is 29 bushels. I then measured $1\frac{2}{7}$ *Colaga* of poor land, which proportionably requires more seed than that of a good quality. I found, that it contained 2880 square feet; so that the *Candaca* of poor land contains nearly 47,127 square feet. This plot produces one *Candaca*, and consequently about $16\frac{36}{100}$ seeds; and an acre at this rate would require $1\frac{576}{1000}$ bushel of seed, and would produce $25\frac{72}{100}$ bushels. From this it would appear, that a *Candaca* of land is not a measure of definite extent. I think that this man spoke the truth.

Sugar-cane.

The same people who gave me the account of the cultivation of rice say, that the sugar-cane cultivated here is the *Maracabo*, or stick-cane. The ground fit for it is that which has a supply of water in the dry season. Any soil will do, but a red earth is reckoned the best. In the month preceding the vernal equinox, they plough four times; and then throughout the field, at the distance of one cubit and a half, they form with a hoe trenches one cubit wide, and one span deep. They then cover the field with straw, dry grass, and leaves, and burn them to serve as a manure. The soil in the bottom of the trenches is afterwards loosened with a hoe; and a man, with his hand, opens up the loose earth, puts in a little dung, and upon this places horizontally, and parallel to the sides of the trench, cuttings of the cane, each containing four or five joints. These he covers with a little dung and earth. The cuttings are placed in one row, in each bed, the end of the one being close to that of another. Once a day, for a month, the canes must be watered with a pot; the young plants are then about a cubit high; and, the earth round them having been previously loosened with a sharp pointed stick, a little dung should be given to their roots. After this, the ridges are thrown down, and the earth is collected toward the rows of young cane, which by this means are placed on

CHAPTER XVII. March 25.

ridges, with a trench intervening between every two rows. Until the rains commence, these trenches must every other day be filled with water. In the month preceding the autumnal equinox, in order to prevent them from being eaten by the jackalls and rats *(Bandicotes)*, the canes are tied up in bundles of from five to ten, and each of these is surrounded by a service of straw rope. In ten months they are fit for cutting, and require no farther trouble. The crop season lasts one month. Five *Colagas* of land, or about $\frac{457}{1000}$ parts of an acre, form what is considered as a large field of sugar-cane, and will produce one *Maund* and a half of *Jagory*, each *Maund* containing 40 *Seers* of 24 *Dudus* weight. At this rate, an acre of cane would produce only about $80\frac{1}{2}$ lb.; but these people do not state the produce of their rice land at more than a third of the truth; and respecting the sugar, they fall into at least an equal fault. Their mill consists of three cylinders moving by a perpetual screw, and turned by a man with a capstan bar, which is fixed to the cylinder in the centre. No addition is made to the juice when it is boiled into *Jagory*, which is done in flat iron boilers. The whole apparatus is extremely rude. On the second year a crop of *Ratoons* is taken, on the third year the roots are dug up, and the field is again planted with cane; so that it is never reinvigorated by a succession of crops. If a sugar-cane garden be to be converted into a rice field it is allowed a year's fallow before the rice is sown.

Dry grains.

On the lower part of the hills bordering on the rice grounds, are some small plots of land called *Hakelu*, or *Mackey*, which are cultivated for dry-grains. The whole is of a small extent, and of a bad quality: the *Ricinus*, for instance, does not grow more than two feet high. The grains cultivated on these fields are *Udu* (or *Phaseolus minimoo* Roxb:), *Huts' Ellu (Verbesina sativa* Roxb:), *Huruli (Ricinus palma christi)*, *Harulu (Dolichos biflorus)*, *Ragy (Cynosurus corocanus)*.

Plantations.

The garden cultivation is here of great importance, and produces about one third of the whole revenue. Much of it is conducted by

Haiga Bráhmans; but they have not, as in *Sudha*, the exclusive possession. The most favourable situation is the head of a valley, where the two hills approach each other. By raising a bank from hill to hill, a tank is formed at the upper extremity; and along the declivity of each hill a canal is made from whence all the intermediate ground on the slopes, and in the valley below, can be supplied with water, and is planted for a garden. At the junction of the hills, or lowest part of the valley, the water from both sides is again collected, and carried down to where the valley is wide, and is cultivated with rice. A western exposure is reckoned very prejudicial; but I see some very thriving gardens which face the setting sun. They are sheltered from its withering influence by tall groves of forest trees. In some cool places, where the water is near the surface, the trees grow without irrigation; but then they require a great quantity of dung, and do not produce much fruit. Gardens are also made on plains, where a tank or canal affords a supply of water. These thrive very well. The *Cagadali* soil is here likewise preferred to all others.

The seed of the *Areca* is managed in the same manner as at *Sersi.* In the month preceding the autumnal equinox of the second year, the young plants are removed into another nursery, where they are planted a cubit distant, and manured with *Nelli (Phyllanthus emblica)* leaves and dung. This nursery must be kept clear of weeds, manured twice a year, and in the dry season should receive water once in eight days. The seedlings remain in it two years, when they are fit for transplantation. The gardens are formed as at *Sersi;* but when the *Arecas* are three years old, they are removed into the garden, planted close to the drains for letting off the water, and remain there two years, when they are finally placed in the spots where they are to grow. Once in twenty or thirty years only the watering channels are filled up with fresh earth, and then are not allowed water. During that year, the garden is kept moist by occasionally filling the drains. The water in these is, however, reckoned

CHAPTER XVII. March 25.

very prejudicial, and is never thrown upon the beds. Once in two years the garden is dug near the trees, and manured. The manure is dung, above which are placed the leafy twigs of all kinds of trees. When an *Areca* dies, a new one is planted in its stead; so that in an old garden there are trees of all ages. On this account, although a *Candaca* of land will plant 300 trees, in the books of revenue these are only rated as 100 taxable *Arecas.* When the trees are sixteen years old they are employed to support pepper vines. Here few or no cardamoms arc raised. In some gardens there are a few plants, but they are not productive. After having been boiled, the *Betel-nuts* are cut into pieces. According to the report of the cultivators, a garden of a thousand rated trees in a good soil produces twenty-five *Maunds* of prepared *Betel-nut,* each *Maund* containing 60 *Seers,* of 24 *Dudus* weight. The pepper of such a garden will be four *Maunds* of the same weight. The extent of this garden is about 796,600 square feet, or about 18$\frac{1}{4}$ acres. Its produce of *Betel-nut* weighs 920$\frac{1}{2}$ lb. worth 14*l.* 9*s.* 6*d.*; and of pepper 117 lb. worth 19*s.* 4$\frac{1}{4}$*d.* A garden rated at two thousand trees is reckoned a good one; any thing less is small. Five thousand *Arecas* constitute a very great garden. Many proprietors of gardens have no rice ground. For dung, they must keep cows, and female buffaloes; but this is far from being a charge against the garden, which in the dry season supplies the cattle abundantly with grass, and in the rainy season they pasture on the hills without cost to the owner, who sells the males which he rears. Four men can work a garden of two thousand rated trees, and collect the fruit and pepper. In an ordinary situation, to bring such a garden to perfection will cost about 1000 *Pagodas,* or 403*l.* 8*s.* 11$\frac{1}{2}$*d.*, besides 100 *Pagodas* for the tank; but of this the government advances one half. The only return, until the garden becomes productive, is from the plantains. The cultivators say, that they never take advances for the produce of their gardens, but sell for ready money when it is fit for market.

March 25. Tenures of corn land.

The fields here are called the property of the government; but the government cannot legally dispossess any farmer of his lands so long as he pays the rent, which is also considered as fixed. The *Gudday*, or rice ground, only is taxed; and each farmer has annexed to this a portion of *Mackey*, or dry-field. The whole of this is of little value, and pays no tax; but it gives room for evil practices; what is really *Gudday*, being sometimes, by the connivance of the accomptants, called *Mackey*. The pasture land is common. The farmer can neither sell his land, nor let it on mortgage. If he be not able to pay his rent, he goes away; but, if either he or his descendants recover stock enough, they may return, and claim their heritage, and any new occupant would be obliged to relinquish the property. The rent is paid in money, according to a valuation made by *Sivuppa*, of the *Kilidi* family; and for each *Candaca* of ground, according to its quality, amounts to from 3 to 10 *Ikeri Fanams*. Allowing that the land of the *Gauda* of veracity was of the best quality, this rent will amount to less than one sixth of the produce, 10 *Fanams* being worth almost 6*s.* 3*d.*, and 29 *Candacas* of rough rice, at one sixth of an *Ikeri Pagoda*, the usual price, being worth nearly 1*l.* 18*s.* 11½*d.* Upon this valuation, the princess *Viru Magi* laid a *per centage*, or *Puggaday Putti*, of one fourth, making the rent of the *Candaca* of the best land 7*s.* 9¾*d.*, or nearly one fifth of the produce. To this no addition has since been made; but some new taxes were imposed both by *Hyder* and *Tippoo*. The former, however, put a stop to certain exactions that had formerly been levied by the revenue officers; so that the people, on the whole, were not higher taxed than by their native princes. The taxes imposed by *Tippoo* have been repealed, and the revenue put on the same footing as in *Hyder's* time, whose example *Purnea* seems most judiciously to follow.

Tenures of plantations.

The plantations of *Areca* can be sold or mortgaged; on which account they are looked upon as more the property of the cultivators, than the rice fields are; but this is a fallacy; for a rice field

CHAPTER XVII. March 25.

is in fact the cultivator's unalienably. If a cultivator get into debt, he must sell his garden to satisfy his creditors; but he may relinquish his rice-land for a time, and, whenever his creditors cease from molesting him, he may again obtain possession. The mortgage here is exactly similar to the wadset of Scotland; the lender of the money taking the use of the estate for the interest of his money. The tax on plantations varies, according to the nature of the soil, from 8 to 24 *Canter'-Ráya Pagodas* for every thousand rateable trees. This is from 2*l.* 9*s.* 11*d.* to 7*l.* 9*s.* 9½*d.* for about 18¼ acres planted; but conjoined with this is always much ground for the house, tank, hills, &c. &c. According to the report of the cultivators, the produce, in a good soil, of 1000 rateable trees is worth 15*l.* 8*s.* 10½*d.*; so that the cultivator would at this rate pay about one half of the produce. A garden usually mortgages for from two to three times the amount of the tax, and sells out-right for twice the amount of the mortgage. The cultivators probably detracted as much from the real produce of the gardens, as they did from that of the rice land.

Price of labour, and condition of slaves.

Most of the cultivation is carried on by the families of the cultivators: there are very few hired servants; but a good many slaves, by whom on the farms of the *Bráhmans* all the ploughing is performed. A slave gets annually 1½ *Rupee* for a blanket; 3 *Rupees* worth of cotton cloth; ¼ *Rupee* for a handkerchief; 6 *Candacas* of rough rice, worth 4 *Rupees*, to procure salt, tamarinds, &c.; and daily 1½ *Colaga* of rough rice, or annually 27½ *Candacas* (or almost 49 bushels), worth 1*l.* 16*s.* 11¾*d.*; add the annual allowances 17*s.* 7¼*d.* the total expense of maintaining a male slave one year is 2*l.* 14*s.* 7¼*d.* A woman slave gets as follows: 365 *Colagas* of rough rice, one daily, and 3 *Candacas* at harvest; in all, 21¼ *Candacas*, or 36¼ bushels, worth 14$\frac{1}{16}$ *Rupees*; 2 *Rupees* worth of cloth, and ¼ *Rupee* for a jacket; in all, nearly 16½ *Rupees*, or 1*l.* 13*s.* 2*d.* The marriage of a slave costs 10 *Pagodas*, or about four guineas. The wife belongs to the husband's master. A master cannot hinder his slave girl from marrying the slave of another man, nor does he get any price for her. The widow and children, after a slave's death, continue with his master. If a slave has no children by his first wife, he is allowed to take another. March 25.

Stock and size of farms.

The same people who gave me an account of the cultivation of rice say, that a man who has ten ploughs is reckoned a very great farmer; and a man who has three ploughs is thought to have a good stock. These three ploughs require four men, and six oxen. They seldom have occasion to hire additional labourers at seed time or harvest, one man helping another on such occasions. The annual expense of the servants amounts to 17*l.* 11*s.* 1*d.* With three ploughs they can only cultivate 15 *Candacas* of land. The produce of these, supposing them of the best quality, would be only worth 30*l.*, and the rent is 5*l.* 16*s.* $10\frac{1}{4}$*d.*; so that the farmer, for his trouble and stock, would have only 6*l.* 12*s.* $0\frac{3}{4}$*d.*, which is evidently too little. From the number of people employed to manage the three ploughs, it is indeed probable, that, besides the fifteen *Candacas* of rice-land, the same stock cultivates also a plantation of *Arecas*.

Cattle.

The cattle here, like those of the country below the *Ghats*, are remarkably small. No large ones are ever bought, as they do not live long. About an equal number of oxen and buffaloes are employed for the plough. The country breeds more than are required for its cultivation, and a considerable surplus is annually exported to the sea-coast. In this country there are neither sheep nor asses. All the chief officers of revenue keep brood mares, considerably better than the common Indian ponies, or *Tatoos.* The horses, in the present state of the breed, would not answer for our cavalry; but it might, no doubt, be improved, by sending into the province a few good stallions.

Treatment of the cattle and manure.

The cattle are kept all the year in the house. In the rainy season, they are littered with green leaves. Fresh litter is every day added, but the stable is cleaned only once a week. This dung is

CHAPTER XVII. March 25. collected in a pit, and called *Sopina Gobra*, or leaf manure. During the two months preceding and the two following the winter solstice, the cattle are littered with hill grass, and cleaned once in four days. This dung also is collected in a separate pit, and is called *Hulu*, or *Soday Gobra*. In the hot and dry season the cattle are littered with dry leaves, and cleaned once in four days; the dung is generally spread upon the hollow roads leading into the villages, where it is trodden upon by man and beast, and is thereby much improved; but it renders the villages quite loathsome. This is called *Daraghina Gobra*. The grass *(Hulu)* dung is never used for rice land; but all the three are indiscriminately used for gardens.

CHAPTER XVIII.

JOURNEY FROM HYDER-NAGARA TO HERIURU, THROUGH THE PRINCIPALITIES OF IKERI AND CHATRAKAL.

CHAPTER XVIII.

March 29. Face of the country.

MARCH 29th.—I went to *Cowldurga*, which is said to be four cosses from *Nagara*; but the stage proved very long, as the gate was at least four miles from where my tents had been pitched. The road the whole way is exceedingly rough and hilly. The hills are all covered with woods, most of which produce the wild pepper vine: but these are quite neglected; and as they are not cultivated, although the village people collect a little pepper, they pay no revenue. The want of the stimulus of rent seems to produce the neglect. I passed through a good many narrow vallies fit for the cultivation of rice, several of which were entirely waste. All the streams of these vallies fall into the river of *Honawera*.

Cowldurga, or *Bhavana-giri*.

The original name of *Cowldurga* was *Bhavana-giri*, and it is a place of great antiquity. A small fort is said to have been erected on the hill by *Dharma Rájá*, or *Yudistara*, one of the five sons of *Pandu*, who governed India at the commencement of this *Yugam*, almost 5000 years ago. The works of this old fortress are said to be still distinguishable by their solidity, and the excellence of their structure. The fortifications were much enlarged, and improved into their present form by *Sedásiva Náyaka*, the founder of the *Kilidi* family. *Hyder* repaired it, and added a cavalier, which by the Mussulmans here is called a *battery*; and he then changed the name of the place into *Cowldurga*, a name which the natives have retained out of respect to *Hyder's* memory, although they laugh at the

CHAPTER XVIII.

March 29. *Monday Gudday.*

barbarity of its derivation; for *Cowl* is a Mussulman word, originally I believe Arabic, and signifies protection or encouragement, such as is given by a good government to the subject; and *Durga* is a *Karnataca* word, signifying a fort that is situated on a rock. *Tippoo,* with the usual zeal of a Mussulman, changed the Pagan names of almost every town in his dominions; but the names which he bestowed have already fallen into disuse, and in a few years will sink into oblivion. The hill on which *Cowldurga* stands is not very high; but, the walls being numerous and lofty, it looks better than most of the hill forts of *Karnata,* of which the buildings are hardly observable at a distance, being hidden among the immense rocks on which they are placed. It is now undergoing a complete repair, and is garrisoned by the troops of the *Mysore Rájá.* The *Petta* stands at some distance, and contains about a hundred houses, which for an Indian town are well built. In the government of the *Kilidi* family, it contained six or seven hundred houses; for it is a considerable thoroughfare, and well situated for trade. The road from *Hosso-Angady-ghat* divides into two branches at *Hyder-ghur:* the one goes by *Nagara;* and that way the trade of *Bangalore, Chatrakal,* and other places toward the north-east, passes; the other branch of the road passes through *Cowldurga,* and is that by which the trade of *Seringapatam* goes to *Canara. Hyder-ghur* is a pass fortified by a wall and gate. Near it there is no cultivation; and indeed near *Cowldurga* there is very little. As, however, the pass commands one of the principal entrances into *Karnata Désam,* it seems to deserve some attention.

March 30. State of the country.

30th *March.*—I went four cosses to *Hodalla.* Near *Cowldurg,* the country is covered with thick forests. Farther on, the hills are tolerably well cleared, and the intermediate little vallies are as usual rice grounds. In fact, all this part of the country resembles entirely that below the western *Ghats.* The hills here, although apparently well fitted for this purpose, are never formed

March 30.

into terraces, as in *Malabar*. The gardens are not so numerous as near *Nagara*, and infinitely fewer than in *Malayala*. About half way, I passed through a village named *Arga*, which formerly was a large place. Its inhabitants were removed by *Hyder* to *Cowldurga*, and suffered much from the change of air; for *Arga* is in a clear open country, and *Cowldurga* is surrounded by hills and forests. East from *Arga* are two small rivulets, the *Gopinátha*, and *Kusawati*; which join, and then fall into the *Tunga*. The natives say, that at *Galagunjy-mani*, a hill near *Sringa-giri*, there is an image of *Nara-singha*, the incarnation of *Vishnu*, whose head resembles that of a lion. This image is not larger than a man. From one eye comes a small stream, called the source of the *Nétrawatí*, which falls into the sea at *Mangalore*; another stream comes from his left tusk, and is the source of the *Tunga*; and a third stream, called the source of the *Bhadra*, comes from the right tusk of this image. These streams are about the thickness of a quill, and, having united for a little way, run down a rock, when they again separate; and each, being joined by various springs and rivulets, forms a river. I have heard a similar story at several places, both above and below the *Ghats*; and the account here given I took with care from a sensible person who has been on the spot; yet there is probably some gross mistake in it, most of the people here being willing to believe any thing extraordinary, even in perfect opposition to the evidence of their senses.

Hereditary flute-player to the king.

Hodalla contains seven or eight families, who are very inadequate to cultivate all the arable lands. It was formerly the residence of a family of *Polygars*, named *Coramar*, and of *Telinga* extraction. They were hereditary flute-players to the kings of *Vijaya-nagara*. By the first chiefs of the family of *Kilidi* they were deprived of their authority, but were allowed certain lands free from taxes. The family is now extinct.

Plantations.

A man here is just now forming a garden that will plant 12000 *Betel-nut* trees, which will be rated in the public accompts as 4000.

CHAPTER XVIII.

March 30.

The cost, before it comes to produce, according to estimate, will be 4000 *Ikeri Pagodas*, or 1611*l.* 15*s.* 11¼*d.* When the garden begins to produce, the *Amildars* (chief officers) of three districts (*Talucs*), three *Sheristadars* (accomptants of districts), and two principal cultivators from each of three neighbouring districts, will form a kind of jury, and fix the revenue according to the soil and local advantages; the *maximum* being 18 *Ikeri Pagodas*, and the *minimum* being 5 *Pagodas*, for every thousand rateable trees. In every part of the country this is the practice.

March 31. State of the country.

31st *March*.—I went to *Tuduru*. The stage seemed to be short, but it is called four cosses. The road passes near a village called *Maluru*, but on the whole way I did not see a house. By far the greater part of the country is covered with stunted woods; and as the roads generally follow the low hills, these hide from the view of the traveller the greater part of what is cultivated.

Mahisi, a temple built by *Hanumanta*.

On the banks of the *Tunga*, near *Maluru*, is a celebrated temple named *Mahisi*, which signifies *the female buffalo*. It is supposed to have been built by *Hanumanta*, who, unwilling to accompany *Ráma* in his expedition against *Lanca*, assumed for concealment the form of this animal. At that time he built this temple, and dedicated it of course to *Vishnu*, his master. It is said to possess inscriptions on stone of great antiquity, of which the *Amildar* promised to send me copies. All that has come to hand, however, is one without a date, of which a copy has been given to the Bengal government.

Weather.

At *Tuduru* there is no village, and only a few scattered houses. I pitched my tents at a ruinous *Jangama's Mata*, which stands on the left bank of the *Tunga*. The stream of this river never dries, but is not applied to irrigate the fields. In the morning there were two very heavy showers of rain from the eastward, with much thunder, and little wind. At this season usually, once in eight or ten days, similar rains are said to happen. The prevailing winds come from the west, and are strong and dry.

April 1.

1st *April*.—I went four cosses to *Baikshaváni Mata*. The road is near the left bank of the *Tunga*. After leaving the cultivated country near *Tuduru*, which is pretty extensive, I entered a forest of trees and *Bamboos*, almost equalling in stature those of the western *Ghats*. Here were many fine *Teak* trees, more indeed than I have ever seen in any one place. They might be of value, could they be floated down the *Tunga* to the *Krishna*, and so to the sea; which I think might probably be done by supporting the floats with *Bamboos*. The *Tunga* at all times contains water; but in the dry season the channel, being full of rocks, will not admit floats. In the rainy season the river swells prodigiously, and is said to be in most places eight or ten feet higher than the top of the rocks. Its stream is then exceedingly rapid and muddy, and filled with large trees swept away by the flood; while in some places rocks come very near the surface. These circumstances would, no doubt, render the navigation in boats very dangerous, but they do not seem to me likely to impede well-constructed floats of timber, strengthened and buoyed up by *Bamboos*. If this should be found practicable, I know of no place that would answer better, for rearing a *Teak* forest, than the banks of the *Tunga* near *Tuduru*, where close to the river there is much excellent soil, which is considered as useless. As there are already on the spot many fine *Teak* trees, all that would be required would be, to eradicate the trees of less value, which I look upon as a necessary step to procure any considerable quantity of *Teak* in a well regulated government. In the wilds of *America*, or the dominions of *Ava*, where a few inhabitants are buried in the recesses of an immense forest, a considerable supply of timber may without trouble be procured; but in a well cultivated country, without much pains bestowed on rearing the proper trees, it is in vain to think of supplying the extensive demands of the ship-builder.

CHAPTER XVIII.

April 1.

Teak forests, and *Tunga* river.

In this forest the road is in several places defended by fortifications; for, although not hilly, it is a pass called *Uluvadi*. These fortifications were erected by *Hyder*, with a view probably of

Face of the country.

CHAPTER XVIII.

April 1. *Manday Gudday.*

stopping marauders. After leaving this pass, I came to an extensive plain of rice ground, in which stands *Manday Gudday*, a scattered town surrounding a ruinous mud fort. It formerly was considerably larger, but suffered much from *Purseram Bhow's* army, into the course of whose destructive route I have again come.

Tundu flowers, a dye.

Near the town I observed many fine trees of the *Tundu*, or *Cedrella Tuna* Roxb: MSS. Its flowers, as I have mentioned at *Bangalore*, are used for dyeing. It is said, that they are collected by Mussulmans, who gather them every morning as they fall from the tree, and afterwards dry them on mats exposed to the sun. The price at present is said to be so low, that none are collected.

Sandal.

East from the plain of *Manday Gudday*, I passed through a forest which contains much sandal-wood, but no *Teak*. Indeed, I have never seen the two trees in the same place.

Face of the country.

On passing this forest, I came to an open country, in which is situated *Baikshavâni Mata*, where there is no village; all the houses are scattered on the different farms, which is the usual custom throughout the principalities (*Ráyadas*) of *Sudha* and *Nagara*, as well as in the country below the western *Ghats*.

Sivabhactars.

The *Mata* belongs to the *Sivabhactar Jangamas*, one of whom still resides in it. The village is considered as his property, but he pays the usual taxes to government. He is dependent on the *Umblay Guru*, who lives near *Shiva-mogay*. None of these *Matas* seem to be older than the government of the *Kilidi Rájás*. Long before their accession, it is true, the greater part of the cultivators were *Sivabhactars*, and no doubt had among them many *Jangamas;* but they were probably in too great poverty to be able to erect religious buildings of any consequence.

Want of people.

The people here say, that if there were a sufficient number of cultivators the greater part of the woods might be cut, and the land, which these now occupy, might be converted into dry field; but at present about one third of the rice land is unoccupied. It would not however appear, that the country was ever sufficiently populous to cultivate more than the rice lands, with a very little of the adjacent high ground, and a few small plantations. At this distance from the *Ghats*, both *Betel-nut* and sandal-wood become scarce. Great quantities of the latter grow in the low woods between *Hodalla* and *Tuduru*.

CHAPTER XVIII.

April 1.

Weather.

Here the quantity of rain also diminishes; and rice cannot be cultivated without small reservoirs, sufficient to contain a supply of water for two months after the cessation of the rains; for the rains last four months only; and all the kinds of rice that are cultivated here require six months to grow.

April 2.

State of the country.

2d *April*.—I went a long stage, called five cosses, to *Shiva-mogay*. The first two cosses of this road are in a forest of very fine trees, many of which are *Teak*. On leaving this, I entered an open country extending very far to the eastward. The greater part of it seems to be fit for cultivation; but at present a want of inhabitants renders the greatest part of it a waste. One coss from the forest is *Gajunuru*, a fort and village on the left bank of the *Tunga*.

Battle of *Simoga*.

On the plain between this and *Shiva-mogay* was fought a battle between *Purseram Bhow*, and *Mahomet Reza*, usually called the *Binky Nabob*, or burning Lord; as, from his activity, he was usually employed by the *Sultán* to lay waste any country that might be of use to his enemies. *Purseram* had advanced as far as *Fatah Petta*, hoping that the garrison of *Nagara* would run away, and leave him the spoil of the city; but as they preserved a countenance which he did not like, he marched toward his left, in order to join Lord Cornwallis before *Seringapatám*. At this place he was met by *Mahomet Reza*, who had 5000 horse, and 10,000 foot, with eight guns. An engagement took place, in which the Mussulman was defeated, and compelled to retire to *Nagara* with the loss of four or five hundred men. This is the account of the natives of *Shiva-mogay*, little inclined to favour either party. From the field of battle, *Purseram* advanced to *Shiva-mogay*, and after a siege of two days

CHAPTER XVIII.

April 2.

took the fort. His march, as usual, was marked by devastation, famine, and murder. The town at that time contained 6000 houses, the whole of which were destroyed; the women were ravished, and the handsomest carried entirely away. Such of the men as fell into the hands of the *Marattahs* were killed, and of those who escaped the sword a large proportion perished of hunger; every eatable thing having been swept away by those whom people in Europe are pleased to call the gentle *Hindus*. These ruffians did not even spare the *Kudali Swami*, who is the *Guru* of all the *Marattah Bráhmans* of the *Smartál* sect, and who is by them considered as an actual incarnation of the deity. His *Matam*, or college, was plundered and burnt; but this cost the *Peshwa* dear. The enraged *Swami* held out threats of instant excommunication, and was only pacified by a present of 400,000 *Rupees*. *Tippoo* had the satisfaction of taking one half of this sum, which was the assessment levied from the *Swami* on account of the *Nuzzur* that Lord Cornwallis exacted.

Charity of a great *Bráhman*.

The *Swami* is said to have been of great use in the famine, and to have employed the utmost of his influence in collecting money to support the starving wretches. He daily fed 3000 *Bráhmans*, and other religious mendicants; for, according to the *Hindu* doctrine, it is the charity which is bestowed on religious men that chiefly procures favour in the eyes of the gods. In his distributions the *Swami* is said to have expended six *Lacs* of *Rupees*, or 60,441 *l.* 13*s.* 4*d.*, most of which was collected in the *Marattah* states.

Shiva-mogay, or *Simogay*.

On the fall of *Seringapatam*, the unfortunate *Shiva-mogay* became a prey to *Dundia*, who remained in it fifteen days, and plundered the inhabitants very completely. Many of the neighbouring villages he burnt. On going away, he put a garrison in the fort, which was stormed by Colonel Stephenson, who hanged the commandant. The *Amildar* who gave me the foregoing account is said to have distinguished his courage on this occasion. The town now contains about 500 houses, and is increasing fast. Its proper name is disputed. In the public accompts it is called *Shiva-mogay;* but some *Bráhmans* of the place say, that its name is properly *Shimuggay* (*Simoga* of the English). This signifies sweet-pot. Such an absurd name is said to be owing to its having been the residence of one of the saints called *Rishis*, who lived entirely on the roots of grass, which he pounded in a pot, and called the mixture his *Shimuggay*. The whole time that the *Rishi* did not employ in preparing this simple diet was of course passed in prayer and other acts of devotion.

Navigation of the *Tunga*.

From *Mangalore Hyder* brought to *Shiva-mogay* many carpenters, and built a number of lighters of about eight tons burthen. They are strong, and flat-bottomed; but, as the greater part of them have been allowed to remain on the bank where they were built, I doubt not that they were found very useless. From the account of the river, which I have given, this will readily be believed; the attempt is however no impeachment on the sagacity of *Hyder*, who, having been educated in a place remote from every kind of navigation, could have no idea of what boats could perform, nor of what obstacles would prevent their utility. The only object that could strike him was the immense advantage of carrying down the river the timber, and bulky produce of this country; from whence even the *Betel-nut* and the pepper require many cattle to go loaded, that must again return empty. To attempt dragging any thing up such a torrent as the *Tunga*, would be vain; but, after having seen the boats, and known that some of them have been actually navigated down the river, I have no doubt of its being practicable to carry down floats; and on these perhaps many bulky articles of commerce might be transported.

Manufactures.

In this neighbourhood the manufacture of cotton cloth begins; for none is made to the westward. In all the villages of this district (*Taluc*), very coarse cloths, for country use, are made by the *Whalliaru*, and by a class of the *Sivabhactars*, who are called *Bily Muggas*.

Grain measure.

Every village has different grain measures. Those of the *Kasba*, or chief town of the district (*Taluc*), are as follow:

CHAPTER XVIII.

April 2.

First, Those used by the farmers.

$90\frac{1}{7}$ cubical inches are equal to 1 *Mana*, or *Seer*.

16 *Manas* make 1 *Colaga*.

20 *Colagas* make 1 *Candaca*, which contains $13\frac{414}{1000}$ bushels.

Second, Those used in the *Bazar*, or market for retail:

18 *Sultany Seers* make 1 *Colaga*.

20 *Colagas* make 1 *Canduca*; which therefore, if the *Sultany Seer* were at the true standard, ought to contain $12\frac{425}{1000}$ bushels; but in fact the two *Candacas* are the same, and this measure is divided by the farmers into 320 *Manas*, and by the shopkeepers into 360 *Seers*.

In the open country round *Shiva-mogay*, according to the account of its intelligent and obliging *Amildar*, the hills and barren ground do not occupy more than a third of the surface. Near the river the greater part of the arable lands are rice grounds; far from it the dry-field prevails. On the whole, the quantity of ground fit for the cultivation of rice is about equal to that fit for dry grains. Not above one third of the whole arable land is now under cultivation, and the rice ground is more neglected than the dry field. This is not owing to rice being less profitable to the cultivator, but to the contrary cause; for the devastation of the *Marattahs* fell heaviest on the best parts of the country; while the inhabitants of the villages situated among the dry field were near the forests to make their escape.

Watered-lands.

The wet lands are in general of a light soil. Although the rains are less copious than at *Nagara*, so that artificial irrigation would be of great utility, little care has been taken with that branch of agriculture. The people here allege, that the plains are so small as to render the construction of reservoirs too expensive. This seems to be one of the usual excuses held out by indolence; as no where in *Karnata* have I seen so much level country. No dams have been made on the *Tunga*; and in fact its channel is so wide, and so deep under the level of the country, that they could be made only at a great expense; but then, I am persuaded, it would be found that they would irrigate a proportionably large extent of ground. The greater part of the rice is raised by the rain water alone, and of course there is only one crop; so that during six months the people are almost wholly idle. A few farmers have small reservoirs, which give a supply of water to the crop when the rains are less regular than usual; and where the reservoirs are somewhat larger, their water supplies in the hot season a few plantations of *Areca* and sugar-cane. The extent, however, of both these is so inconsiderable, as scarcely to deserve notice. The plantations of palm trees contain only coco-nuts and *Arecas*, without pepper; and their produce is of so bad a quality, that it will answer only for country consumption.

Rice.

The kinds of rice cultivated here are,

Sampigy Dala,	produce in a good crop	10 seeds.
Betta Candala,	- -	12 seeds.
Caimbutty,	- - -	9 seeds.
Sanabutty,	- -	9 seeds.

All these require six months to grow. They are all large grained, except the *Sanabutty*, which sells five *per cent.* higher than the others. The lowest ground is used for the *Sanabutty;* the highest is used for the *Caimbutty*. The *Candaca* of land is the quantity supposed to require a *Candaca* of seed, and is quite indefinite in size; more and more seed being sown in proportion to the goodness of the soil. This seems agreeable to reason; the contrary was, however, at first asserted by the cultivators, and throughout the country is indeed a usual cry with that class of people; but I was cautioned by the *Amildar* not to credit such assertions. The produce of a good and that of a bad field, each of one *Candaca*, is nearly the same; but the good one, being much smaller, and requiring less expense of cultivation, can afford a higher rent. Accompanied by the *Amildar*, I measured a field of the poorest soil, said to require eight *Colagas* of seed, and found it to contain 152,084 square feet;

CHAPTER XVIII. April 2.

so that the *Candaca* in such a soil would be 380,210 feet. The acre would therefore sow $1\frac{536}{1000}$ bushel. The produce of this field last year, which was a favourable season, was 5 *Candacas*, or $12\frac{1}{2}$ seeds, or $19\frac{1}{5}$ bushels an acre. In the preceding year the crop was bad, and produced only 3 *Candacas*, or $7\frac{1}{2}$ seeds, or $11\frac{52}{100}$ bushels an acre. This account I think is true, the *Amildar* being well informed, and apparently inclined to give me assistance. What the extent of a *Candaca* land of the two superior qualities is I did not attempt to ascertain: the people said it was much less.

The cultivation of all soils and all kinds of rice is the same, and the unprepared seed is sown by a drill. Immediately after harvest, the ground is once ploughed. When the rains commence, during the two months following the vernal equinox it is ploughed again twice, smoothed with the implement called *Coradu*, which is similar to that of *Banawási* (Plate XXIX. Fig. 72.), and then hoed twice with the *Heg Cuntay* (Plate XXVIII. Fig. 75.), which is drawn by two oxen. This removes the grass; after which the clods are broken by drawing the *Coradu* twice over the field, which in some measure serves as a rolling-stone. The dung is then spread; and after the first good rain the seed is sown with the drill or *Curigy*, and covered with the *Coradu*. At this season the rain comes in showers, between which are considerable intervals. On the third day after having been sown, the field is hoed with the *Heg Cuntay*, which here is called also *Cambutigay*. On the twentieth day, when the seedlings are nine inches high, the *Coradu* is used again; then the *Edday Cuntay* (Plate XXVIII. Fig. 76.); then the *Coradu*, and finally the harrow which is made of a bunch of thorny *Bamboos*. On the thirtieth day, more grass having sprung, the *Edday Cuntay* is again used, the rows of young corn passing between the hoes; and this must be repeated as often as the grass springs. In the third month the water is confined, and then for the last time the *Edday Cuntay* must be used. The mud raised by this is smoothed by the *Coradu*; but in this operation, the same implement is called *Aravasi*.

All these weedings are not sufficient, and the remaining grass must be removed by the hand and weeding-iron. The rice is cut with the straw, and for two days is allowed to lie loose on the field. It is then put in ricks, without having been bound in sheaves, and remains there until trodden, which may be done any time in the course of three months. It is always preserved in the husk, and when wanted for consumption is cleaned by a hand mill of the usual form, but made entirely of timber, which removes the outer husk; but the inner one, or bran, must be separated by beating in a mortar. Eight measures of clean rice, as usual in India, are equal in value to twenty of that which retains the husk.

CHAPTER XVIII.

April 2.

Second crop of pulse.

In a few places, where there is a moist black soil, the rice-ground produces a second crop of *Callay (Cicer arietinum)*, and of *Hessaru (Phaseolus mungo)*. The seed for both is one fifth of the quantity of rice that is required to sow the field; and, as the soil is rich, will probably be about half a bushel the acre. The *Callay* produces five seeds, and the *Hessaru* four. For the former, the field is ploughed once in the month preceding the winter solstice. The seed is dropt into the furrow after the plough, and in three months ripens without farther trouble; and this is no additional labour, as the field must at any rate have been ploughed. For the *Hessaru*, the field after the rice harvest must be ploughed twice. In the month following the shortest day, it must be watered from a reservoir, and smoothed with the implement called *Coradu*. As a mark for the sower, furrows are then drawn through the whole field, at the distance of four cubits; and the seed having been sown broadcast is covered by the plough. The field is then smoothed with the *Coradu*, and in four months the crop ripens.

Dry-field.

Near *Shiva-mogay* the cultivation of dry grains begins to be of importance. The following kinds are cultivated.

Ragy, or the *Cynosurus Corocanus*, with its concomitants *Avaray (Dolichos Lablab)*, *Tovary (Cytisus Cajan)*, *Punday (Hibiscus Cannabinus)*, Lin. and *Udu (Phaseolus Minimoo* Roxb: MSS.)

CHAPTER XVIII.

April 2.

Huruli, or *Dolichos biflorus.*

Shamay, or *Panicum miliare* Lamarck.

Navonay, or *Panicum italicum.*

Harica, *Paspalum frumentaceum* Roxb: MSS.

Barugu, *Panicum miliaceum.*

Harulu, *Ricinus palma christi.*

Huts' Ellu, or *Verbesina sativa* Roxb: MSS.

Wull' Ellu, or *Sesamum.*

Udu, or *Phaseolus minimoo* Roxb: by itself.

Jola, or *Holcus sorghum.*

The only ones, that are raised in a quantity deserving much attention, are the *Ragy* with its concomitants, and the *Huruli.* About three fourths of the fields are sown with the first crop, and one fourth with the last mentioned. In giving an account of the present state of the country, the others may be altogether neglected. They might, however, deserve much attention from any person who wished to try experiments for the improvement of agriculture. The best soil is reserved for *Ragy.* The *Huruli* is sown on poor soils, or on the *Ragy* fields when, owing to a want of rain, the crop of that grain has failed. Here the crop of *Huruli* is not thought to injure the following one of *Ragy,* which is contrary to the opinion that is commonly received in most parts of the country. In the present system of *Hindu* agriculture, however, very many opinions must be commonly held, without any fair trial having been made to ascertain how far they are well founded. Both *Ragy* and *Huruli* fields are sown every year without rest. The *Huruli* is a very uncertain crop; for, by either too much or too little rain it is spoiled; so that, although very high priced, it gives little profit.

Ragy.

At *Shiva-mogay* there is only one kind of *Ragy*, and one mode of cultivation. In the month following the summer solstice, the field is ploughed twice, and smoothed with the *Coradu.* It is then ploughed and smoothed again, and hoed with the *Heg Cuntay.* After this, it is harrowed with the rake drawn by oxen. Eight days afterwards,

April 2.

it is again hoed with the *Heg Cuntay*, and is allowed to rest fifteen days. Then throughout the field furrows are drawn at the distance of about seven inches, and into these the *Ragy-seed*, mixed with dung, is placed very thin with the hand; a small quantity being dropped at about every ten inches. In every seventh furrow are put the seeds of *Avaray*, *Tovary*, and *Punday* intermixed, or of *Udu* by itself. The field is then smoothed with the *Coradu*, and with the bunch of prickly *Bamboos*. In eight days, when the young plants have come up, the spaces between the rows are hoed with the *Edday Cuntay* (Plate XXVIII. Fig. 76.), and again smoothed with the *Coradu* and bunch of twigs. These operations must be repeated twice, with an interval of eight days between each time. After the third the field is harrowed with the rake drawn by oxen, and after another interval of eight days this is again repeated. In the fourth month, the weeds are removed by the hand: in five months the crop is ripe. It is tied up in sheaves; and as the rainy season is not then quite over, it is dried with some difficulty. When the *Ragy* is in flower, the crop is apt to be spoiled by heavy rain; which may be a reason why it does not thrive well to the westward. The produce of *Ragy* in a good crop is reckoned to be ten seeds, which, unless the seed is sown much thicker than usual, is very poor. This is probably in some measure the case, as at *Shiva-mogay* this crop is allowed little or no manure; but the people who gave me the account certainly concealed the quantity of produce, as the rent paid for the *Ragy-land* amounts to the value of almost ten seeds. All the dry-field being at a distance from the town, I had no opportunity of ascertaining the extent of a *Colaga* of *Ragy-land*.

Huruli.

For *Huruli*, the field, having been previously manured, is ploughed three times during the month which precedes the autumnal equinox, at the interval each time of three days. The seed is sown broadcast, and covered with the *Coradu*. It ripens in four months; four seeds are reckoned a good crop, and three a middling one.

CHAPTER XVIII.

April 2.

Wages and labour.

The greater part of the cultivation is carried on by the tenants, and their own families. In agriculture, some hired servants, but no slaves, are employed. The yearly wages for a labouring servant are from four to five *Ikeri Pagodas*, one blanket, one pair of shoes, and a handkerchief, amounting in all to about two guineas. He finds his house and victuals. In weeding time, women are hired, at four *Seers* of rough rice a day. A man, when hired by the day, gets five *Seers*. These wages are very high, when it is considered that no servant works here more than six hours. The labourers gave me the following account of the manner in which they pass their time. About eight o'clock of our day they rise from bed, and smoke tobacco; they perform their evacuations, and ablutions; and having been purified, they worship the gods. They then eat, an operation in which two hours are expended. They then rest themselves half an hour, when they proceed to the field, and work six hours. On their return, they again pray, and take a little of any cold victuals that they have ready. They then look after the cattle, and give them water and fodder. The labour of the day is now over; and the workman, having again washed and prayed, takes his supper, and about seven o'clock goes to bed, where he remains thirteen hours. This is their employment during the six months of toil. In the remaining half of the year, little cultivation being carried on, they repair their houses, lay in a stock of firewood, carry out dung, and do other little jobs about the farm. Masters, of course, work still less.

Tenures.

In this vicinity there are two kinds of tenure. The first comprehends gardens, and lands formerly granted in *Enam*. Both of these the occupants have a right to sell. *Hyder* laid half the usual rent upon the lands held by *Enam*, and this tax was increased by the *Sultán;* but *Purnea* has again reduced it to *Hyder's* assessment. The other tenure is that of what are called *Shist*, or valued lands; these are the absolute property of the government; and the occupants may be turned out at will. Each field is valued at a certain rent to be paid in money, which was first determined by *Sivuppa Náyaka.* The *Rany Viru Magi* added a half of the amount, and *Hyder* doubled her assessment; but no partial raisings upon any man's possessions have been permitted. Rice ground pays from four to eight *Sultany Pagodas* a *Candaca;* at this rate, the field which I measured, being of the worst soil, pays about 3*s.* 8*d.* an acre; its produce in a good crop being about ten bushels of clean rice, which is reduced to eight by deducting the expense of cleaning. Dry-field pays from sixteen to twelve *Pagodas* a *Candaca:* the produce, therefore, must be much greater than the ten seeds stated by the cultivators; for ten *Candacas* of *Ragy* are only worth about seventeen *Pagodas.* CHAPTER XVIII. April 2.

Four ploughs are here reckoned a large stock; and require four men, two boys, and eight or ten oxen. These four ploughs are said to be able to cultivate one *Candaca* and a half of rice land, with one *Colaga* of dry-field; but, even allowing for the extreme indolence of the labourers, this must be under-rated in the very worst soils. Stock.

The breed of cattle, when compared with that of the hilly country to the west, begins to improve at *Shiva-mogay.* None, however, that are bred in this district, are fit for the carriage of goods; but the oxen are of a short thick breed, well adapted for ploughing rice ground. Some are exported to the westward. The oxen are not wrought more than four or five hours in the day. From about the end of July till toward the end of January, they are fed on grass, some of which is cut, and at night is given to them in the house. During the remainder of the year they are fed on straw, and husks of *Huruli;* to which, when they are in danger of perishing, some of that grain is added. Very few buffaloes are employed in the plough; but many females are kept for giving milk, and the young males are exported. Immediately on leaving the forests of the western hills, asses become numerous. A few sheep and goats are Cattle.

CHAPTER XVIII.

April 2.

to be seen, but they are not bred in the country; very few indeed are reared on the west side of the *Tunga-bhadra.* For the use of traders, the public reserves some pasture land; and for each head of cattle they pay two *Dudus* a month. The farmers send their cattle to pasture in the hills and woods, where they pay nothing.

Manure.

The cattle are never littered; and the only manure used is their dung, collected in a pit, together with the grass and straw which they did not eat in the night. To these are added the ashes and sweepings of the farmer's house.

Strata.

At the entrance into the open country, the *Laterite* seems to stop. The last that I have seen was at *Baikshavâni Mata.* Between that place and *Shiva-mogay* the *strata* are not very observable. In some places they appear to run east and west, in others the rock seems not to be stratified. In one place only, since I came up to *Karnata,* have I observed the large veins of quartz so common to the eastward, and I saw none in any place below the western *Ghats.*

April 4. Appearance of the country.

4th *April.*—I went four cosses to *Kudali.* The country all the way is plain; but it contains many detached hills, some of which, toward the north, are pretty high. The whole country is bare, and almost entirely waste.

Inhospitable disposition of the natives.

Mid-way I came to a village, where the inhospitable disposition of the natives fully manifested itself. Near this village, I overtook a *Sepoy* lying in the utmost agony from a rupture. Having with some difficulty reduced it, the pain in his groin was succeeded by a violent colic, which contracted his limbs; and, had any exercise been at all proper for a man in his condition, rendered him totally unable to walk. I therefore went into the village, in order to procure a cot or bedstead, of which a litter could be readily made. As I had left all my attendants with the sick man, except an interpreter, the villagers held me in contempt. I found the *Gauda,* his brother, and some head men of the village, all *Sivabhactars,* standing in conversation, and wrapped up in their blankets. Having made known to them my case, the *Gauda* replied, that they had no cots, and his brother talked very loud, and in an insolent manner. This was checked by the coming up of a superior officer of revenue, who informed me that there were cots in every house; but neither offers of payment, nor threats of complaint, were of more avail than humanity. In excuse for these people it may however be said, that the *Sepoy* belonged to the *Bombay* army, a detachment of which had enabled *Purseram Bhow* to commit all his cruelties. Not that the *Bombay* army had any share in these excesses; but without its assistance he either would not have ventured into the country at all, or would have been assuredly defeated at *Shiva-mogay*. April 4.

About a coss from this inhospitable village, I crossed the *Tunga*, and from thence to *Kudali* some part of the country is cultivated. The principal crops are *Jola* and cotton.

Kudali.

Kudali, or the *Joining*, is an *Agraram*, or village given in *Enam* to the *Bráhmans*, and is situated between the *Tunga* and *Bhadra* rivers at their junction, whence the place derives its name. It was plundered and burned, as I have already mentioned, by a party of the *Marattah* army, who put all the *Súdra* inhabitants to the sword, although the place is quite defenceless, nor did the people attempt to make any resistance. After this, the *Bráhmans* went to complain to the *Bhow*, who gave each of them one *Rupee* as in duty *(Dharma)* bound.

Bráhmans.

I found, that the *Guru* or *Swami* was at *Hara-punya-hully*, employed in begging, as it is called. He had with him all his principal disciples; so that the *Bráhmans* who remained at *Kudali* were not men of great intelligence; but they gave me a copy in the *Marattah* character, of the *Sankara Acharya Cheritra*, or an account of the life and actions of that very celebrated personage. It is esteemed a book of great authority, and has been delivered to the Bengal government.

Sankara Acharlu, and his successors.

The *Bráhmans* whom I found at *Kudali* said, that *Sankara* appeared on earth in that character only once, and that he lived about two thousand years ago. At the time of his coming, the sect of *Buddha*

XVIII. April 4. and other heretics were very numerous; and most of the *Bráhmans* who were then living had fallen into the error of worshipping the sun, moon, and stars. The *Matam*, or college, of *Sánkara Acharya* was at *Sringa-giri*, and he appointed one *Sannyási* only to be his successor, and to occupy his *throne*. The *Matam* of *Sringa-giri* is still called the *throne* of *Sankara;* but each *Swami* that occupies it as his successor has a peculiar name, although they are all acknowledged to be gods, and incarnations of *Iswara*. The successors of *Sankara Acharya* have at different times found it necessary to appoint agents for the management of their remote followers; and, to render these agents sufficiently respectable, it has been found necessary to reveal to them the *Upadésa* peculiar to the rank of *Sannyási*. By this mean a portion of *Iswara* is incorporated with their bodies, in such a manner that the worship offered to them becomes of equal efficacy with the worship of that portion of the deity which remains in heaven. They are not supposed to be possessed of any extraordinary power, which indeed would be a pretension very difficult to support with credit for ages. Several of these agents, who managed their followers with skill, established *Matams* of their own, and appointed successors, who, according to their success, either acknowledged a dependance on the *Sringa-giri throne*, or have pretended to be equal to its *Swami*. Among these, the most conspicuous of whom I have heard is the *Swami* of *Kudali*. About 400 years ago, the first founder of this *Matam* was appointed a *Sannyási* by the *Sringa-giri Swami*, and was entrusted with the management of all the *Smartal* of the *Marattah* nation. These all continue to consider his successors as their *Gurus;* and the present opulence and power of the *Marattah Bráhmans* have raised the *Mata* of *Kudali* to a greater splendor than that of *Sringa-giri*.

Inscription. I procured from the *Bráhmans* of *Kudali* a copy of an inscription engraven on a copper-plate, and belonging to the *Swami*. It is dated *Sal.* 1043, in the reign of *Purandara Rájá*, of the *Cadumba* family at *Banawási;* and a copy has been given to the government in Bengal.

CHAPTER XVIII.

April 4. Three ancient temples.

At *Kudali* are three temples of the great gods, all reckoned celebrated by the *Bráhmans*, and all accompanied by miraculous traditions. The buildings are mean, and have the appearance of being ancient. The oldest, according to tradition, is that dedicated to *Brahméswara*, one of the names of *Siva*. Many *Yugams* ago, it rose spontaneously from the earth. In the same manner the second sprang up three *Yugams* ago, and is dedicated to *Narasingha*, one of the incarnations of *Vishnu*. At this there is an inscription on stone, but it is no longer legible. The third, compared with the others, is modern, and was built by *Ráma* only a few hundred thousand years ago, and dedicated to *Siva*, under the name of *Raméswara*, in order to wash away the sin which *Ráma* had incurred by killing *Walli* king of *Kiskinda*, a place that is near *Vijaya-nagara*, and is now called by the vulgar name of *Humpay*. This happened immediately after *Ráma's* return from *Lanca*, or *Ceylon*. When I tell the *Bráhmans* here, that the English have now conquered this celebrated island, they do not venture to call me a liar; but what they think is evident.

Inscriptions.

At the temple of *Raméswara* are four inscriptions on stone, of which one only is entirely legible. It is written in the *Nagara* character, but in the *Karnataca* language intermixed with *Sanskrit*. A copy of it in the character of *Karnata* has been delivered to the Bengal government. Another, that is partly legible, is also in the *Nagara* character. Two, that are in the character of *Karnata*, are only legible in part. The one is dated in *Cara Sal*. 1214, in the reign of *Vira Narasingha Ráya Maha Ráya*. Who this prince was I cannot say. The date is 44 years before the foundation of *Vijaya-nagara*, according to *Ramuppa's* chronology. The other is in the year of *Sal*. 1242; the *Rájá's* name, however, is not legible.

April 5. *Tungabhadra* river.

5th *April*.—I went four cosses to *Sahasiva-hully*. I recrossed the *Tunga* immediately above its junction with the *Bhadra*, where both rivers are nearly of an equal size, and even at this season contain considerable streams. The united rivers form the *Tungabhadra*,

CHAPTER XVIII.

April 4.

the channel of which is very little, if at all, wider than that of either of the parent streams: but its water is of course more copious. The water at this season is sunk very deep in the channel; so that the forming dams for irrigation would be very expensive.

Face of the country.

The country on the west side of the river is in general level, but is interspersed with hills. The whole is exceedingly bare. Near the river are many small villages, each provided with a round tower, near which the houses are crowded for protection. The cultivation near these villages is pretty considerable, and at present is confined almost wholly to the dry grains, about two thirds *Ragy* and *Tovary*, and one third *Jola* and *Harulu*. The other crops are of little importance. On the higher lands, near the hills, there is no cultivation. The soil in many places there is indeed very poor; but in others it is a fine red earth, reckoned particularly favourable for *Ragy;* and, if there were people, would be cultivated for that grain. The greater part of the tanks have gone to decay, so that there is very little wet land; and, even when the country was in its best state of cultivation, irrigation seems to have been much neglected. The *Kilidi* family, to whom this part of the country belonged, from having lived in a district where artificial watering was not requisite, seem not to have been sensible of its advantages. The *Amildar* says, that by constructing reservoirs much dry-field might be converted into rice ground. Below *Sahasiva-hully*, the river taking a bend to the south-west, I crossed it at the angle, and ascended the right bank to that village. Its name signifies *Along with Siva*, as it is supposed to be a place where that deity resided some time together with his wife. It has a small mud fort, and about a hundred houses. In this open part of the country there are very few fences, which in many points of view is a great loss. The crops here rarely fail from want of rain, and the epidemic disease among cattle is seldom so general as to the eastward. Tigers seem to be more destructive here than in the woods. The want of game makes them bold, and they frequently carry away the inhabitants from their beds.

This part of the *Nagara Ráyada* entirely resembles the *Mysore* country. The cultivators live in villages, their cattle are large and white, they rear sheep, the country is naked, and the people subsist chiefly on dry grains. Many of the inhabitants are *Cunsa Woculigas*, a laborious and intelligent class of farmers, strongly contrasted with the *Sivabhactars* of the west, who appeared to me to be as stupid and lazy a class of men as I have ever seen.

CHAPTER XVIII.

April 5.

Inhabitants.

The hills here, however, are not so rugged as toward *Mysore*; but the *strata* run north and south, and contain many lumps of quartz. In all the open country, where there is no *Laterite*, the limestone *nodules* abound. Although the natives in general think that calcareous stone in the ground diminishes its fertility, I have an idea that the want of this substance in the countries to the westward, more than any absolute sterility in their soil, may be the cause why the dry grains do not thrive.

Strata.

Before the invasion of *Purseram Bhow*, this country was in a very good state. After his destructive march, not above one fourth of the inhabitants remained alive, and these were left destitute of every thing which the *Marattahs* could either carry away or destroy. The wretched remnants of population had again begun to recover, when *Dundia* came among them. He did not put any one to death; but he plundered the houses, and even burned some of the villages, the inhabitants of which he suspected of concealing their property.

Desolation.

The dry-field of this village is very hard, and full of small stones, being what is called *Darray*; yet it seems to be productive, or at least the people seem willing to acknowledge the real returns which they obtain from its cultivation. Almost every kind of dry grain is raised on it, without attention to rotation, or any idea among the farmers that one grain is more exhausting than another. The soil is never rested, and contains limestone; but it is well dunged. The two great crops are *Ragy* and *Jola*. This has been a remarkably favourable year, and the *Ragy* produced forty seeds.

Dry-field.

CHAPTER XVIII.

April 5.

Allowance of grain for a labouring man.

A hard labouring man is supposed to eat daily the following quantities of the different kinds of grain; the *Mana* of this place containing $84\frac{375}{1000}$ cubical inches.

	Peck.
$1\frac{1}{2}$ *Mana* of *Ragy*, which is weekly -	$1,\frac{6419}{10000}$
1 *Mana* of *Jola* - -	$1,\frac{0989}{10000}$
1 *Mana* of cleaned *Shamay* -	$1,\frac{0989}{10000}$
$1\frac{3}{4}$ *Mana* of cleaned rice - -	$1,\frac{923}{1000}$

The allowance of *Jola* is reckoned the most nutritious.

		Pence.
1 *Ikeri Pagoda* purchases	192 *Manas Ragy*. 1 bushel costs	$12\frac{83}{100}$
	120 ditto *Harulu* - -	$20\frac{54}{100}$
	120 ditto *Tovary* - -	$20\frac{54}{100}$
	160 ditto *Jola* - -	$15\frac{4}{10}$

Rent and produce.

Having ascertained these preliminaries, I went to the fields with the cultivators, and officers of revenue; and found, that in the public accompts they were not valued by any measurement, nor by the quantity of seed which they were supposed to require; but that each field was rated at a certain rent. Having fixed on one that pays two *Rupees*, or half a *Pagoda* yearly, I found that it contained 55608 square feet. The soil is very stony, and apparently poor. The rent is at the rate of 3*s*. $1\frac{875}{1000}$*d*. an acre. The farmers gave me the following account of its average produce, and seed, in four different kinds of cultivation.

CHAPTER XVIII.

April 5.

Crop.	Seed.			Increase Folds.	Produce.				
	Of the Field.	Of one Acre.			Of the Field.		Of an Acre.		
					Quantity.	Value.	Quantity.	Value. Gross.	Value. Deducting seed and rent.
	Manas.	Bush. dec.	Pence dec.		*Manas.*	*Sul Pag. An*	Bush. dec.	Pence dec.	Pence dec.
1st *Ragy* -	12	0,3689	4,7347	20	240	1 4	7,378	94,694	
Avaray -	4	0,12296	not sold.	15	60	not sold.	1,8445	not sold.	not sold.
Total -	16	0,489186			300		9,2225		
2d *Ragy* -	12	0,3689	4,7347	20	240	1 4	7,378	94,694	
Harulu -	12	0,3689	7,5755	5	60	0 8	1,8445	37,8775	
Total -	24	0,7378	12,3292		300	1 12	9,2225	132,5715	82,3673
3d *Jola* - -	6	0,18445	2,8408	$20\frac{1}{3}$	122	0 $12\frac{1}{5}$	3,7505	75,763	
Tovary -	5	0,1537	2,3671	$12\frac{1}{5}$	64	0 $8\frac{8}{15}$	1,9675	30,3	
Total -	11	0,33815	5,2079		186	1 $4\frac{11}{15}$	5,718	88,063	44,9801
4th *Shamay* -	24	0,7378	not sold.	10	240	not sold.	7,378	not sold.	not sold.

Ráya Paditti, or chronological table.

I here received from *Subaia*, a *Bráhman* of *Holay Honuru*, a short *Ráya Paditti*, of which the chronology is very different from that of *Ramuppa*. *Subaia* says, that the original was copious, but was burnt by the *Marattahs*. The present short extract was made up from books and memory, and inaccuracies must therefore be expected. The general chronology is that of the eighteen *Puranas* The following is a translation:

" The *Kali-yugam* will contain 432,000 years. Particulars:

Yudishtera era - -	3,044 years
Vicrama - - -	135*
Salivahana - -	18,000
Naga Arjuna - -	400,000
Kali Bupati - - -	821
Total-	432,000

* Query—10,135?

CHAPTER XVIII. April 5.

Of this there have elapsed to the present time (being *Raudri* of *Salivahana* 1722), 4901 years. Particulars:

Yudishtara era - - - -	3044
Vicrama - - - - -	135
Salivahana - - -	1722
	4901 years.

Particulars of the *Rávaru* family.

Woragulla Pritapa Rájá
Son of *Campila Rájá*
Son of *Comara Rájá*

The end of his reign was in the year of *Sal.* 1150, *A. D.* 1227. In the year *Servadavi* of this *Rájá Woragulla Pritapa Ráya* the house guards of the treasury were *Hari-hara* and *Buca Ráya.* According to his order, these two men came to *Vijaya-nagara.* The year *Servadavi* is the commencement of the kingdom of the *Ráyaru.* This year, on Monday the 5th of *Chaitra,* they placed the pillar (a ceremony similar to ours of laying the foundation stone) for building *Vijaya-nagara.* The *Rájás* were placed on a throne of jewels.

Here follows a *Slókam,* signifying, "In this manner thirteen princes sat on the throne, governing every cast according to its own customs, and hearkening to the word of God with pleasure."

Particulars:

1 *Hari-hara Ráya*	8 *Virupacsha Ráya*
2 *Buca Ráya*	9 *Deva Ráya*
3 *Hari-hara Ráya*	10 *Rama Rájá Ráya*
4 *Virupacsha Ráya*	11 *Malicarjuna Ráya*
5 *Buca Ráya*	12 *Rama Ráya*
6 *Deva Ráya*	13 *Virupacsha Ráya*
7 *Rama Rájá Ráya*	

Total 13 princes reigned 232 years, till the year of *Sal.* 1382, *A. D.* 1459.

After that came the following kings.

Prowuda Ráya reigned 12 years. He was a son adopted from *Penu-conda*, and died in the year *Nundina* of *Sal.* 1394, *A. D.* 147$\frac{1}{2}$. April 5.

After that *Vira Narasingha Ráya* reigned 10 years. He died in the year *Chubucrutu* of *Sal.* 1404, *A. D.* 148$\frac{1}{2}$.

After that *Solva Narasingha Ráya* reigned 12 years. He died in the year *Anunda* of *Sal.* 1416, *A. D.* 149$\frac{3}{4}$.

After that *Achuta Ráya* reigned 3 years. He died in the year *Pingala* of *Sal.* 1419, *A. D.* 149$\frac{6}{7}$.

After that for 9 months there was a *Nava Náyakara.* This literally means nine *Náyakas* or petty princes; but implies an anarchy, where every chief is contending with his neighbour, and plundering the vicinity.

After that came the following kings.

Krishna Ráya reigned 40 years. He died in the day time on the 5th of the moon *Kartika*, being Monday, in the year *Hevalumbi* of *Sal.* 1460, *A. D.* 153$\frac{7}{8}$.

After that *Sedasiva Ráya* reigned 2 years. He died on the *Amávásya*, or last day of *Margasírsha* in the year *Shervari* of *Sal.* 1462, *A. D.* 15$\frac{39}{40}$.

After that, *Rama Rájá* reigned 24 years. He died on Wednesday the 14th of the dark moon in *Mágha*, in the year *Ructachi* of *Sal.* 1486 (*A. D.* 1563), and the city *Vijaya-nagara* was destroyed.

Total seven princes 103 years.

Grand total twenty princes 335 years.

The chronology will be found totally incompatible with the inscriptions. A copy of the original has been delivered to the Bengal government.

6th *April.*—I went three cosses to *Baswa-pattana*, in order to avoid a steep mountainous road, called a *Ghat*, that lies in the direct route between *Sahasiva-hully*, and *Hari-hara.* On the open country through which I passed, there are scattered several small hills. The soil in general seems to be capable of cultivation; but in other parts

April 6. Appearance of the country.

CHAPTER XVIII. April 6.

the rock comes to the surface, and much of it is waste. The farther I advanced into the open country, I observed that the villages are more strongly fortified. The country is very bare, and, like that to the eastward, is covered with bushes of the *Cassia auriculata*, and *Dodonæa viscosa*.

Baswa-pattana was formerly a part of the dominions of *Kingalu Náyaka*, the *Terricaray Polygar*. His successors were expelled by *Renadulla Khan*, who was succeeded by *Delawer Khan*, both *Mogul* officers. *Delawer Khan* resided here twenty years, and under his government the place seems to have been very flourishing. He was expelled by the *Marattahs*, who held it for seven years, when they were driven out by *Hyder*. This Mussulman destroyed the fort, in order to prevent it from being of use to the *Marattahs*, who in their next incursion destroyed the town; and till after the fall of *Seringapatam* it continued waste. The fort has now been repaired, and about two hundred houses have been erected in the town. It has two reservoirs, one of which is tolerably large. South east, about two cosses from *Baswa-pattana*, is one of the most celebrated works of this kind, which was erected by a dancing girl from the gains of her profession. It is called *Solicaray*, and the sheet of water is said to be three cosses in length, and to send forth a constant considerable stream for the irrigation of the fields. It is built on a similar plan with the reservoir at *Tonuru*, near *Seringapatam*. A bank has been erected between two hills, and thus confines the water of a rivulet which had originally found a way between them.

Baba Bodeen, and Vira Belalla Ráya.

Near the fort is a mosque, celebrated among the Mussulmans for being the first place where *Baba Bodeen* took up his abode. He afterwards went, and resided on a hill toward the south, which now is called after his name. The people of the mosque say, that he was a saint of the greatest reputation, who, although he performed a number of miraculous things, suffered many persecutions from *Vira Belalla*, the infidel king of this country. The saint at length invited *Jan Padisha*, a prince of the Faithful, from the north, and the infidel was taken prisoner. The saint then put the *Rájá* and all his family into a pit under his hill, and there they still continue to live, suffering the punishment due to their want of faith. April 6.

Near my tent a farmer was at work, expressing the juice from sugar-cane, and boiling it to form *Jagory*. He said that his field contained a *Wocula* land. The taxes amounted to 20 *Pagodas*, or 8*l.* 2*s.* 3*d.* The whole expense he calculates at 26 *Pagodas*, or 10*l.* 10*s.* 11*d.* The crop season will last 30 days; and on each he will boil three times, getting 2 *Maunds* of *Jagory* from every boiling. He therefore expects to get 180 *Maunds*, which sells at the rate of 3½ *Pagodas* for 10 *Maunds*. The whole produce therefore will be 63 *Pagodas*, or 25*l.* 11*s.* 1½*d.*, leaving a neat profit of 6*l.* 17*s.* 11½*d.*, or 17 *Pagodas*, or very nearly 27 *per cent.* on the gross produce. I did not measure the field. The cane was *Maracabo*. Sugar-cane.

7th *April*.—I went three cosses to *Malaya Banuru*. This last word is a common termination in the names of villages in this part of the country, and signifies a place behind any other; thus *Malaya Banuru* signifies the place behind the hill. On the left of the road, are the low bare hills which form the *Ghat* between *Sahasiva-hully* and *Hari-hara*, and which render that road very bad; but among the hills are many villages, and cultivated places, which from their situation are said to have escaped better than those in the plain. All to the right of this day's route is a fine level country, but it is exceedingly bare of trees and fences. Near the road at least nine tenths of the soil appear to be good; but a very large proportion of the country is waste, having been desolated by *Purseram Bhow*. The natives say, that two-thirds of the whole plain are of so poor a soil as to be unfit for cultivation. They are very unskilful in making reservoirs, and of course are negligent in the cultivation of rice, and never take a second crop. On being asked the reason of this, they say, that in the dry season the soil is too hot for cultivation. There is, however, no end to the foolish reasons which unskilful farmers assign for their conduct. Sugar-cane is a good April 7. Face of the country.

CHAPTER XVIII. April 7.

deal cultivated, but the kind is the *Maracabo*, which yields a very small quantity of juice, and that contains little saccharine matter. When the farmers are asked a reason, why they do not cultivate the *Putta-putty*, or *Restali*, they say, that these canes are so sweet, that it is impossible to keep the wild hogs from devouring them. Little or no credit can therefore be given to the reasons assigned by such farmers for their practices, or for the state of the country; especially, as is generally the case, when it is found, that no two people give the same reason; for the ignorant and lazy are in general abundantly unwilling to confess their weaknesses, and, rather than acknowledge them, assign some random excuse for their conduct.

Malaya Banuru.

Malaya Banuru has a small fort surrounded by a *Petta*, which contains about two hundred houses. It formerly belonged to the *Terricaray Polygars*, who were at one time very powerful; but their territory became a prey to various invaders. The Mussulmans of *Sira* took *Baswa-pattana*. The *Sivabhactars* of *Ikeri* took from *Mainhully* to *Lacky-hully*. The *Mysore Rájá* took *Banawara*. When *Hyder* seized the remainder, it consisted of *Terricaray*, with the adjacent country to the value of a hundred thousand *Pagodas* a year. *Hyder* permitted the family to remain at *Terricaray* with a yearly allowance of thirty thousand *Pagodas*. The whole of this was stopt by the *Sultán*. On his fall, one of the family returned, seized on the fort, and intended to set himself up as an independent prince. He was, however, betrayed by some of his ragamuffin followers, who, after wounding him, hanged him by the orders of the new government. Some of the family now remain, but they have no pension nor allowance.

Terricaray. Polygars.

Saline earth.

In some of the wells here the water is saline, and culinary salt has formerly been made at the place. The saline earth is found in low moist places. In this respect also the *strata* here agree with those to the eastward. No saline earth nor springs are to be found in the hilly western tract, nor in the country below the western *Ghats*.

CHAPTER XVIII.

April 8. Appearance of the country.

8th *April.*—I went a very long stage, called four cosses, to *Hari-hara*, and by the way crossed a large empty water-course, and afterwards a wide channel containing a considerable stream, which comes from the *Solicaray*, and is therefore called the *Solicaray holay*. It falls into the *Tungabhadra* immediately above *Hari-hara*, and never dries, except in very extraordinary seasons. The country in general near this day's route is plain, with a few hills scattered at great distances. Much of it is what the farmers of *Malaya Banuru* consider as totally useless; but the people of *Hari-hara* are of a different opinion, and think that two thirds of the whole level country is fit for cultivation, and would be employed in that way were there a sufficient number of inhabitants. A great proportion of it has, however, been long waste; for far beyond the reach of human memory the country has been a scene of warfare, and the wars of the natives are carried on in a most barbarous and destructive manner. The country is exceedingly bare, and at this season is very ill supplied with water.

Marattah territory.

The bank of the *Tungabhadra* opposite to *Hari-hara* forms a part of the *Marattah* dominion, and at present belongs to *Appa Saheb*, the son of *Purseram-Bow*: the natives here speak in raptures of the *Savanuru* district, including *Darwara, Hubuli*, and *Nilagunda*, and compare its air and fertility to those of *Cashemire*. The territory south of the *Varada*, although fertile, is greatly inferior to the other. Both are fast becoming desert.

Hari-hara.

I remained three days at *Hari-hara*, which was formerly an *Agraram* belonging to the *Bráhmans* of its celebrated temple of the same name. After the death of *Rám Rájá*, and the destruction of *Vijayanagara*, it became subject to the *Adil Shah* dynasty, and was given in *Jaghire* to a *Sheer Khan*, who built the fort. On the conquest of the *Decan*, it was taken by the *Savanuru Nabob, Delil Khan*, who was an officer of the court of *Delhi*. From the house of *Timour* it was taken by the *Ikeri Rájás*, who were expelled by the *Marattahs*; and these again, after fifteen years possession, were driven out by

CHAPTER XVIII. April 8.

Hyder. Since that time these free-booters have taken it thrice; the last time was by *Purseram Bow.* He did not kill any of the people, nor did he burn the town; but he swept away every necessary of life so completely, that many of the inhabitants perished from hunger. They have since enjoyed quiet. The fort contains the temple, and a hundred houses occupied by *Bráhmans;* the suburbs contain three hundred houses of the low casts. The temple, for a *Hindu* place of worship, is a tolerable building, but is kept in the usual slovenly manner. Many families live within its walls, and the area is defiled by cow-dung, mud, broken bricks, straw, dunghills, and other similar impurities. The idol resembles that of *Sankara Narayana* at *Gaukarna,* having part of the attributes or symbols of *Siva,* and part of those of *Vishnu.* Its name also implies its being a representative of both deities; for *Hari* is an appellation of *Vishnu,* and *Hara* one of the titles of *Siva.* Within the walls of the temples are twenty fine inscriptions on stone.

Manners of the people.

The most numerous class of cultivators near *Hari-hara,* and as far at least as *Savanuru,* are the *Sivabhactars.* There are scarcely any Marattahs among them, that is to say, *Sudras* of pure origin belonging to *Maháráshtra Désam.* Very few of the poorer inhabitants marry, the expense attending the ceremony being considered as too great. They content themselves with giving their mistress a piece of cloth; after which she lives with her lover as a wife, and both she and her children are as much respected, as if she had been married with the proper *Mantrams* and ceremonies: very few of the women live in a state of celibacy, to which indeed in most parts of India, I believe, they are seldom subjected. Few of the men go to foreign countries, and the rich have always more wives than one, which makes up for the men who live as bachelors.

The tenants, I am told, are remarkably fickle, being constantly changing from one side of the river to another, and of course at each time change their sovereign. They appear to me to be remarkably stupid, but they pique themselves on being superior to their northern neighbours, who, they say, are no better than beasts. Even the *Bráhmans* here are stupid, which is certainly a defect not common in that sacred order of men. April 8. Out of the hundred houses, I could not get one man who could copy the inscriptions at their temple with tolerable accuracy. During my stay I employed twelve *Bráhmans*, and two *Jangamas*, paying them whatever the *Amildar* judged proper; and he kept a man with them to rouse their industry; but I obtained copies of four inscriptions only; and it was necessary to have these corrected by my interpreter, although I could ill spare his services.

Of the inscriptions that I had copied here, the most ancient is dated in *Sal.* 1444, according to the *Slokam* in which the date is involved. Inscriptions.

The next is dated *Sal.* 1452, in the reign of *Vira Pritapa Achuta Ráyá.*

The next is dated *Sal.* 1453, in the reign of *Achuta Ráyá.*

The last is dated in *Sal.* 1477, in the reign of *Vira Pritapa Sedasiva Deva Maha Ráyá.*

All remarks that have been suggested by these inscriptions have already been anticipated in my commentary on the *Ráyá Paditti* of *Ramuppa.*

This year the crops have been remarkably bad, owing to too much rain; a circumstance of which I have not heard a complaint in any other part of *Karnata.* Season.

The common currency here being gold *Fanams*, and thirteen of these exchanging for an *Ikeri Pagoda*, this must be valued at the quantity of pure gold contained in the thirteen *Fanams*, which is somewhat more than it is actually worth. The *Rupee* is worth one fourth of a *Pagoda.* Money.

The *Cucha Seer* here weighs 24 *Rupees.* The *Maund* of cotton contains 48 *Seers*, or is $29\frac{12}{100}$ lb. nearly. The *Taccady* contains 36 *Seers*, or is $21\frac{84}{100}$ lb. This is the weight used by the farmers. The *Bazar*, or market *Maund*, contains 40 *Seers* of 24 *Rupees.* Weights.

CHAPTER XVIII.

April 8. Liquid Measure.

A *Cucha Seer* of oil, &c. measures $16\frac{1125}{10000}$ cubical inches.

Dry Measure.

The grain measure is founded on the *Chitty* of $159\frac{3}{4}$ cubical inches; 4 *Chitties* make 1 *Gydna*; 20 *Gydnas* make 1 *Colaga*; 20 *Colagas* 1 *Candaca*, which contains $118\frac{883}{1000}$ bushels.

Land Measure.

Land here is estimated by *Mars*, the extent of which the natives have two methods of ascertaining. The most common is, to call a *Mar* that extent of ground which requires $2\frac{1}{2}$ *Gydnas* of *Jola* for seed. I measured a field said to require twelve *Gydnas* of seed, and found it to contain 17,67,684 square feet. According to this, the *Mar* is $368267\frac{1}{2}$ square feet, or somewhat less than eight acres and a half. The other method of ascertaining the extent of a *Mar* is by counting the number of rows of pulse or *Acadies* contained in it, when it has been sown with *Jola*. A square field containing 120 of such rows is called a *Mar*. If the rows are from 3 to $3\frac{1}{2}$ cubits distant, this extent would coincide with that given by my measurement. I did not ascertain this to be the case at *Hari-hara*, but I found it to be the actual distance in other parts of the neighbourhood.

Harvest price of the produce.

The merchants here give the following as the average rate at which the produce of the country sells by wholesale immediately after harvest:

Cotton wool with the seed	per *Maund*,	$\frac{1}{6}$ *Pagoda*	Cwt.	$62,\frac{41}{100}$	Pence
Do. cleared from do.	do.	12 *Fanams*	do.	$345,\frac{6}{10}$	do.
Cotton seed	do.	$\frac{1}{20}$ *Pagoda*	do.	$18,\frac{72}{100}$	do.
Jagory	do.	4 *Fanams*	do.	$138,\frac{25}{100}$	do.

One *Ikeri Pagoda* purchases		Which therefore sells at
Gydnas	20 of *Jola*	pence 16,378 per bushel
do.	18 *Avaray*	18,298
do.	12 *Tovary*	27,307
do.	10 *Hessaru*	32,757
do.	20 *Madiky*	16,378
do.	20 *Huruli*	16,378
do.	16 *Alasunda*	20,473
do.	10 *Callay*	32,757
do.	20 *Navonay*	16,378
do.	18 *Sujjay*	18,298
do.	12 *Gur Ellu*	27,307
do.	12 *Harulu*	27,307
do.	20 *Ragy*	16,378
do.	10 *Rice*	32,757
do.	9 *Wheat*	36,396

April 8. Spinning of cotton wool.

In this neighbourhood much cotton thread is spun. The women of the cultivators spin part of the produce of their husbands farms; and others receive the cotton wool from the merchants, and spin it for hire; but the women of the *Bráhmans* are as averse from spinning, as their husbands are from holding the plough. The merchant always purchases the cotton with the seed, and employs people to clean it. From four *Maunds* of raw cotton he gets one of cotton wool, at the expense of four *Fanams*, which is one third of the value of the whole cotton thus cleaned. The instrument is a small mill, consisting of two horizontal cylinders moved by a perpetual screw, and turned by the hand; while a semi-cylindric cavity behind forces back the cotton to the person who feeds the mill. (See Plate XXVII. Fig. 74.) The rudeness of the machinery, as usual in India, renders the expense of the operation great, in comparison with the value of the raw material. The *Maund* of cotton wool, in beating with a bow, the manner universally used in India and China for preparing it for the wheel, loses an eighth part, expense included; that is to say, the merchant gives forty *Seers* of cotton wool to the cleaner, who returns thirty-five fit for spinning. When this is spun, the thread weighs only from thirty to thirty-two *Seers*, owing I suppose to its having been imperfectly cleaned. The coarsest thread made here costs $8\frac{1}{4}$ *Fanams* for the spinning of the 35 *Seers* of prepared wool, which has been procured from 40 *Seers* of raw cotton. At this rate, to make a pound of cotton wool into thread, costs a very little less than $2\frac{3}{4}$ pence, and it loses in the operation from one fourth to one fifth of its weight. The thread is remarkably coarse. The finest made here costs double the former price. When a woman does no other work, she can in one day spin three quarters of a *seer* of the coarsest kind; and therefore she makes about $1\frac{639}{1000}$ penny a day.

Commerce.

From this part of the country, cotton and thread are the principal exports, and there are few traders of any note. Two months before crop season, the merchants advance to the poor cultivators, and

CHAPTER XVIII.

April 8.

charge for interest half a *Fanam* on each *Pagoda*, or about 23⅐ *per cent. per annum.* They say, that they are contented with this profit, and when the crop is ripe take so much of the produce, at the market price, as pays the advance with interest. The farmers however allege, that when they receive advances, what the merchants call the market-price is lower than what a man, who is not necessitous, can get for his cotton. According to their account, the common price of cotton in the seed is 7 *Taccadies* for the *Pagoda*, or 71⅐ pence for the cwt., which is a little lower than the price stated by the merchants.

The great cultivation here is that of dry grains. The extent of land fit for the plough is very great; but a small proportion only is occupied, and in the best of times much has always been waste. If any farmer, or even an intelligent officer of revenue, be asked, why such or such a piece of ground is not cultivated, he will immediately say that it is impracticable, and assign some reason for this being the case. At first, I was inclined to pay much attention to these reasons; but finding that two people seldom gave the same reason, and that what two men, equally qualified by experience, alleged, was often totally contradictory, while no difference was observable between the soil and situation of the fields now cultivated, and those that are condemned as useless, I began to doubt; and after having questioned many natives, and having considered carefully what they said, I am persuaded, that the soil may be rendered productive, wherever it is not too hard or steep for the plough. The natives talk of one third of the land near the *Tunga-bhadra* being useless from these two causes; but I think that they over-rate its extent. In the land of many villages the soil is very full of small stones, especially of quartz; but the natives of these places are far from reckoning these useless; on the contrary, they allege that the stones are advantageous by keeping the soil cool, and retaining the moisture. In other places, these stones are reckoned a loss, as is the case at *Hari-hara.*

CHAPTER XVIII.

April 8. Different qualities of soil, and their rents.

The ground here is divided into three kinds. The first, called *Eray*, consists of a black mould containing much clay, and is valued in the rental at one *Pagoda* a *Mar*, or at 11½ pence an acre. The second kind of land, called *Kingalu*, or red soil, is valued at ¾ of a *Pagoda* a *Mar*, or at 8½ pence an acre. The third kind, called *Cul' Maradi*, or stony soil, is valued at ½ *Pagoda* a *Mar*, or at 5¾ pence an acre. This was the account given me at my tents; but when I went to a field to measure it, accompanied by the owner, the *Amildar*, and the *Shanaboga* with the public rental, I found that it paid 15 *Pagodas*, or at the rate of 3⅛ *Pagodas* a *Mar*, or nearly 3s. an acre. In general, it was of a fine black soil; only about one acre of it was rather stony, although the whole was reckoned of the first quality. The immense difference in the rent, as stated at my tents, and again in the field, did not strike me at the time, so that I got no positive explanation; but it, no doubt, arose from the following circumstance. This *Shist*, or valuation of the country, was first made by the *Ráyarus*. It was increased by the *Savanuru Nabobs* in the proportion of 8 to 3; and *Hyder* added to this an increase of ⅛ part. Both he and his son imposed some new assessments; but these were not included in the rental, and have been remitted by *Purnea*. The people at the tents mentioned the tax imposed by the *Ráyarus*, which by way of eminence is probably called the *Shist*; while at the field the whole land-tax that is now levied as brought into the accompt. The *Mar* of land of the best quality pays therefore 3⅛ *Pagodas*, or at the rate of 3s. an acre; the *Mar* of the 2d quality pays $2\frac{5\frac{1}{2}}{16}$ *Pagodas*, or at the rate of 2s. 3d. an acre; and the worst pays $1\frac{9}{10}$ *Pagoda* a *Mar*, or 1s. 6d. an acre. Rice-ground pays no higher than dry field; so that the only advantage government has by watered-land, is an excise of three *Pagodas* on every 1000 sugar-canes planted. Some soils here contain saline matter; and if the water be allowed to lodge on low spots, these become so impregnated with salt, as to be of little value for cultivation; but with proper pains this may be avoided. In some of the clay-land, there is a kind of soil,

CHAPTER XVIII. April 8.

which, though it is black, and to all appearance of the kind called *Eray*, yet it does not retain water, and very soon becomes dry; but, by a proper management of the manure, it may be rendered productive.

Division of village lands.

The three kinds of ground being of very different qualities, every man's share of each is scattered up and down in various places, in order to make the assessment fall equally; but hence arises an inexplicable obscurity in the accompts, and a great hindrance to improvement. All the cultivators live in fortified villages, and each man's share is scattered in small patches through the village lands.

The *Gaudas*, or chiefs of the villages, are hereditary; but in case of their incapacity, the villages may be let to *Gutigaras*, or renters. These renters and *Gaudas* force the cultivators to labour more than they are willing, which is a pernicious practice. The extreme indolence of the people in this neighbourhood is, however, an excuse that bears at least the appearance of reason. The *Amildar* says, that without compulsion they would not cultivate more than $\frac{2}{3}$ or $\frac{3}{4}$ of what they are able. A subsistence is all that they look for, and with little labour that can be procured. Superfluities, or riches, they have some reason to consider as mere temptations to the plunderer: so long as a man cultivates his fields, he cannot be deprived of them; but they cannot be mortgaged, or sold, to pay his debts. If he allow his lands to become waste, the government can give them to any person who will undertake their cultivation; but the original proprietor may at any time resume them, when he is able to find sufficient stock.

Size of farms.

The greater number of the farmers here have only one plough each; but all such as have not more than three ploughs are reckoned poor men, and are in general obliged to borrow money to pay the rent, and to carry on the expenses of cultivation. The crop is a security to the lender, who is repaid in produce at a low valuation. Farmers who have 4, 5, or 6 ploughs, are able to manage without borrowing, and live in ease. Those who have more stock are

April 8. Servants wages.

reckoned rich men. Each plough requires one man and two oxen, and can cultivate two *Mars* of land, or about 17 acres. In seed time and harvest, some additional labourers must be hired. All the farmers, and their children, even those who are richest, *Bráhmans* excepted, work with their own hands, and only hire so many additional people as are necessary to employ their stock of cattle. A servant's wages are from six to nine *Jimshiry Pagodas* a year, together with a blanket and pair of shoes. The *Jimshiry Pagoda* is four *Dudus* worse than that of *Ikeri*, which is rather less than $1\frac{1}{3}$ *per cent.* The wages are therefore from 2*l.* 7*s.* 10*d.* to 3*l.* 11*s.* 9*d.* Out of this they find every thing but the shoes and blanket. Men labourers get daily half a *fanam*, or $3\frac{1}{4}$*d.* and women receive one half of this hire, which is seldom paid in money, but is given in *Jola* at the market price. The man's wages will purchase daily about a quarter of a bushel. The people here work from eight in the morning until sun set, and in the middle of the day are allowed twenty-four minutes to rest and eat. The cattle work from eight in the morning until noon. They are then fed for an hour, and work from one until about five o'clock.

Cattle and manure.

Many of the farmers keep no cows, but purchase all their cattle. They, of course, can sell at least one half of their straw to the *Bráhmans* of the town, who in general keep many milch cows, and who in return sell the young oxen and the manure to the farmers. Although the cattle are always kept in the house, except during the two months immediately following the rains, no litter is used. Their dung is collected in pits, with the sweepings and ashes of the family, and sells for from six to twelve *Dudus* for the load of a cart which is drawn by eight oxen, but which does not appear to contain more than a single-horse cart. The price is from about 5*d.* to half that amount. The farmers also hire flocks of sheep to manure their fields, and say, that for folding his flocks on a *Mar* of land, they give the shepherd one *Colaga* of *Jola;* this, however, must be a gross exaggeration.

CHAPTER XVIII.

April 8.

Jola, with its accompanying grains.

The most considerable crop in this neighbourhood is *Jola (Holcus sorghum)*, which is always accompanied by one or more of the following articles, *Avaray (Dolichos Lablab)*, *Tovary (Cytisus Cajan)*, *Hesaru (Phaseolus Mungo)*, *Madiky*, a kind of pulse that seems to be peculiar to this part of the country, and of which I have seen only the seed; *Huruli (Dolichos biflorus)*, and *Alasunda (Dolichos Catsjang)*. These articles being intended chiefly for family use, a portion of each is wanted, and every man puts in his *Jola* field a drill or two of each kind.

Jola.

Jola thrives best on black clay, but is also sown on the red earth, and even sometimes on the stony soil. In *Chaitra*, the field is hoed with a *Heg Cuntay* (Plate XXVIII. Fig. 75,) which requires from six to eight oxen to draw it; for this is the month following the vernal equinox, when the soil is very dry and hard. In the following month the field is ploughed once, and then manured. In the month preceding the summer solstice, the seed is sown after a rain by means of the drill; while the rows of the accompanying grains are put in by means of the *Sudiky* or *Acadi*. The drill here differs from that of *Banawasi*, (Plate XXVI. Fig. 73,) in wanting the iron bolts that connect the bills with a wooden bar which crosses the beam. The *Sudiky* is a *bamboo* with a sharp point, which is tied to the drill, and through which the labourer drops the seed of the pulse, as he follows that implement. After having been sown, the field is smoothed with the *Bolu Cuntay*, a hoe drawn by oxen, and entirely resembling the *Heg Cuntay*, but of a lighter make. On the 20th day the field is weeded with the *Edday Cuntay*, (Plate XXVIII. Fig. 76), and on the 28th day this is repeated. In five months the *Jola* ripens, without farther trouble. The *Mar* of land usually produces 7 *Colagas* of *Jola*, or 56 fold, worth 7 *Pagodas*; deduct for rent 3 1/8 *Pagodas*, and for seed 1/8 *Pagoda*, and there remains to the cultivator for stock and labour 4 3/4 *Pagodas*, or about 68 *per cent.* of the gross produce, besides the pulse and straw; but this last must be allowed to go for manure. Besides, in favourable seasons, the farmer from the high-rented *Jola* land procures a second crop of *Callay, (Cicer arietinum)* as follows. CHAPTER XVIII.

If after harvest there be any rain, the field is ploughed in the month preceding the winter solstice. It is then ploughed across, and by means of the sharp pointed *bamboo* the seed is dropt into the furrows after the plough, and is covered with the *Heg Cuntay.* The *Mar* of land requires 8 *Gydnas* of seed, and produces 4 *Colagas,* or 10 seeds. This, deducting the seed, is a neat produce of 72 *Gydnas,* worth 7⅕ *Pagodas.* It is only from the very best ground that this can be taken, and each farmer's share of this kind is very small. April 8. *Callay.*

A few rich spots are reserved solely for the cultivation of *Callay,* and these are cultivated in the following manner. In the month following the vernal equinox the field is ploughed once, then manured, and in the following month is hoed with the *Heg Cuntay.* Between that period and the month preceding the shortest day, the grass is ploughed down twice, and the seed is sown with the sharp *bamboo* following the plough, and covered with the *Heg Cuntay,* as before described. It ripens in three months, and produces 8 *Colagas;* which, deducting seed, leaves 152 *Gydnas,* worth 15⅕ *Pagodas;* from which if 3⅛ be taken for rent, the cultivator has better than 12 *Pagodas* for his trouble and stock.

Cotton is raised entirely on black soil, and is either sown as a crop by itself, or drilled in the rows of a *Navonay* field. In the former case, two crops of cotton cannot follow each other, but one crop of *Jola* at least must intervene. In the 2d month after the vernal equinox, the field is ploughed once, then manured, then hoed with the *Heg Cuntay;* and the grass is kept down by occasional hoeings with the *Bolu Cuntay,* until the sowing season in the month preceding the autumnal equinox. The seed is sown by a drill having only two bills, behind each of which is fixed a sharp pointed *bamboo,* through which a man drops the seed; so that each drill requires the attendance of three men, and two oxen. The seed, in order to allow it to run through the *bamboo,* is first dipt in Cotton.

CHAPTER XVIII. April 8.

cow-dung and water, and then mixed with some earth. Twenty days after sowing, and also on the 35th and 50th days, the field is hoed with the *Edday cuntay.* The crop season is during the month before, and that after the vernal equinox. The *Mar* of land requires three *maunds* of seed, worth $\frac{1}{10}$ of a *Pagoda.* The produce is 50 *Tacadies,* at 7 for a *Pagoda,* and therefore amounts to $7\frac{1}{7}$ *Pagodas.* From this deduct $\frac{1}{10}$ of a *Pagoda* for seed, and $3\frac{1}{8}$ *Pagodas* for rent, and there remains to the cultivator for trouble and stock very little less than 4 *Pagodas.* When these weights, measures, and values, are reduced to the English standard, the produce of an acre appears very small. The seed is about $10\frac{1}{5}$ lb. worth two-pence. The produce is about $1\frac{181}{1000}$ cwt. worth, according to the cultivators, $82\frac{1}{4}$ pence: deducting 36 pence for rent, and two-pence for the seed, there will remain for the cultivator $44\frac{1}{4}$ pence, or about 53 *per cent.* of the gross produce.

Navonay, or *Panicum Italicum.*

Next to *Jola,* the most considerable crop in this neighbourhood is *Navonay,* which is cultivated on both the black and red soils, but by far most commonly on the latter. On the black soil it is usually accompanied by cotton in the rows between the drills; on red soil, it is accompanied by rows of *Jola, Sujjay, (Holcus spicatus)* and *Gur' Ellu,* which is the *Huts Ellu* of *Seringapatam (Verbesina sativa* Roxb. MSS.). In black soil, the ploughing commences in the month following the vernal equinox. After having been ploughed, the field is manured, and in the following month is hoed with the *Heg Cuntay,* and, after eight days rest, with the *Bolu Cuntay.* In the month following mid-summer, the seed is sown with the drill, and the accompanying grains by means of the sharp *bamboo.* The seed is covered by two hoeings with the *Bolu Cuntay,* one lengthwise and the other across. On the 20th and 28th days the weeds are removed by the *Edday Cuntay.* In three months the crop is ripe. In the red soil, the ploughing does not commence until the beginning of the rainy season; but the seed time, and all the process of agriculture, are the same as in the black soil. The *Mar* of land requires for

April 8.

seed 5 *Gydnas* of *Navonay*, worth $\frac{1}{4}$ *Pagoda;* together with one *Maund* of cotton seed, worth $\frac{1}{20}$ *Pagoda;* or $\frac{1}{4}$ *Gydna* of *Jola*, worth $\frac{10}{216}$ *Pagoda;* or 1 *Chitty* of *Sujjay*, worth $\frac{1}{72}$ part of a *Pagoda;* or 1 *Chitty* of *Gur' Ellu*, worth $\frac{1}{48}$ of a *Pagoda*. The produce in a middling crop is 12 *Colagas* of *Navonay*, worth 12 *Pagodas*, together with 15 *Tacadies* of cotton, worth $2\frac{1}{7}$ *Pagodas;* or $1\frac{1}{2}$ *Colaga* of *Jola*, worth $1\frac{1}{2}$ *Pagoda;* or 1 *Colaga* of *Sujjay*, worth $1\frac{1}{9}$ *Pagoda;* or 1 *Colaga* of *Gur' Ellu*, worth $1\frac{2}{3}$ *Pagoda*. It must be evident from this, that the people who gave me the account diminished the real produce of the *Jola*, which would never be the common object of cultivation, while *Navonay* was so much more profitable.

Sujjay, or Holcus spicatus.

Sujjay is here the next most common crop, and is always accompanied by *Huruli*, or *Alasunda*, or *Tovary*, or *Hessaru*. This is the crop commonly taken from the red soil, or that of the second quality. In the month preceding the summer solstice, the field is ploughed once, then manured, and then hoed with the *Heg Cuntay*. At the end of the month the seeds are sown with the drill, and covered with the *Bolu Cuntay*. On the 20th and 28th days, the field is weeded with the *Edday Cuntay*. In three months the crop is ripe. The *Mar* requires for seed $\frac{1}{2}$ *Gydna* of *Sujjay*, worth $\frac{1}{36}$ *Pagoda;* together with 2 *Gydnas* of *Huruli*, worth $\frac{1}{10}$ *Pagoda;* or 1 *Gydna* of *Alasunda*, worth $\frac{1}{16}$ *Pagoda;* or 3 *Gydnas* of *Tovary*, worth $\frac{1}{4}$ *Pagoda;* or $1\frac{1}{2}$ *Gydna* of *Hessaru*, worth $\frac{3}{20}$ of a *Pagoda*. The average produce is 12 *Colagas* of *Sujjay*, worth $13\frac{1}{6}$ *Pagodas;* together with $1\frac{1}{2}$ *Colaga* of *Huruli*, worth $1\frac{1}{2}$ *Pagoda;* or $1\frac{1}{2}$ *Colaga* of *Alasunda*, worth $1\frac{7}{8}$ of a *Pagoda;* or 2 *Colagas* of *Tovary*, worth $3\frac{1}{3}$ *Pagodas;* or 1 *Colaga* of *Hessaru*, worth 2 *Pagodas*. The rent is about $2\frac{11}{32}$ *Pagodas*. From these *data*, the share which the farmer gets for his stock and labour may readily be calculated. For instance, the gross produce of a *Mar* sown with *Sujjay* and *Huruli* is $14\frac{2}{3}$ *Pagodas;* while the rent and seed are rather more than $2\frac{1}{2}$ *Pagodas*, or $17\frac{1}{4}$ *per cent.* of the gross produce. This is another proof, that the cultivators concealed

CHAPTER XVIII.

the real produce of *Jola* and cotton, which are their most common crops.

April 8.

Huruli, or *Dolichos biflorus*.

Huruli, or what the English of *Madras* call *Horse-gram*, is at *Harihara* the next most usual crop, and is cultivated entirely on the poorest and worst soil, which pays as rent $1\frac{9}{16}$ *Pagoda* for the *Mar*. The field is ploughed once in the end of the 2d month after the summer solstice. In three or four days afterwards it is ploughed again; and with the sharp *bamboo* the seed is dropped into the furrow, after the plough, in rows about 9 inches distant from each other. It is then covered with the *Heg Cuntay*. On the 20th and 28th days, the hoe called *Edday Cuntay* is employed to remove weeds, and in five months it ripens without farther trouble. A *Mar* of land requires for seed five *Gydnas*, worth $\frac{1}{4}$ *Pagoda*; and the common produce is 3 *Colagas*, worth 3 *Pagodas*; so that the farmer has here only $1\frac{3}{16}$ *Pagoda* out of 3 of the gross produce; but he gives no manure, and the trouble is very small, and performed at a season when little else is doing.

Harulu.

On the 2d quality of soil some considerable quantity of *Harulu*, or *Ricinus*, is raised. In the month preceding the summer solstice, when the rainy season commences, the field is ploughed once. Fifteen days afterwards the seed is dropped into furrows made by the plough, in rows two cubits distant from each other, and is covered by another furrow. At the end of a month from sowing, the weeds are removed by the *Edday Cuntay*; and every 15 days afterwards, until the month preceding the autumnal equinox, the intervals between the rows must be ploughed. At this time the plants begin to flower; and the fruit ripens at various times between the month following the autumnal equinox, and that following the winter solstice. A *Mar* of land requires $2\frac{1}{2}$ *Gydnas* of seed, worth $\frac{5}{24}$ of a *Pagoda*. The produce is six *Colagas*, worth ten *Pagodas*. It is sold to the oil-makers, who extract the oil by boiling, as is the usual practice in India. The seed is first boiled for about an hour, when it bursts a little. It is then dried in the sun three days, and beaten into flour in a large mortar. The flour is then put into a pot with a little water, and boiled for about two hours. The oil floats above the flour, which forms a thick mass in the bottom of the pot. The oil is very bad, and thick. Two *Gydnas* of seed give sixteen *Seers*, *Cucha* measure, of oil; so that a bushel gives about 2 wine gallons.

Ragy (Cynosurus corocanus), *Shamay (Panicum miliare* E. M.*)*, *Harica (Paspalum frumentaceum* Roxb. MSS.*)*, *Baragu (Panicum miliaceum)*, *Wull' Ellu (Sesamum)*, and *Udu (Phaseolus. minimoo* Roxb. MSS.), are also cultivated at *Hari-hara;* but in such small quantities, that a particular account of each will not be required.

Allowance of grain for a man.

The usual daily allowance of grain for one person's eating, is ½ *Chitty*, or about 27 bushels, a year. The *Navonay* and *Sujjay* are chiefly consumed by the *Bráhmans*, and other people in easy circumstances, as being a more light and delicate food; while the labourers feed upon *Jola*, or *Ragy*, purchased from other districts. *Jola* straw, being the most common, is reckoned the most wholesome fodder for cattle.

Watered lands.

The watered lands are here of little importance; for in the whole district, which produces annually 15,000 *Canter' Raya Pagodas*, there are no dams, and only six reservoirs. The rains are quite inadequate to the cultivation of rice. Very little of this grain is therefore sown. Orders, however, have been issued by *Purnea* to erect dams on the *Solicaray Holay*. The *Amildar* says that there are three places in the district where reservoirs might be constructed with advantage. He thinks that forming dams on the *Tungabhadra* would be attended with great expense; nor could they be so constructed as to irrigate much ground. Below *Hari-hara* indeed, towards *Anagundi*, there are very fine ones, which supply with water rice-grounds worth 100,000 *Pagodas* a year. These are situated partly in the territories of the *Nizam*, and partly in those lately ceded to the Company.

Sugar-cane.

Sugar-cane is here the most considerable irrigated crop, as it

CHAPTER XVIII. April 8. requires but a small supply of water. In the intervals between the crops of cane, a crop of rice is taken, should there be a sufficient supply of water; but that is seldom the case, and the intermediate crop is commonly some of the dry grains. The land, when cultivated for grain, pays the usual rent; when cultivated with sugar-cane, it pays three *Pagodas* for every 1000 double cuttings planted. Land that pays 10 *Pagodas* of rent is called a *Wocula* land, which, as it plants 6000 double cuttings, pays, when under sugar-cane, 18 *Pagodas*, with two *Pagodas* for the use of the boiler, making in all a rent of 20 *Pagodas* for the *Wocula*, as stated by the man at *Baswapattana*.

The account that follows was taken from a principal accomptant (*Sheristadar*), who says that he is proprietor of a field, and is well acquainted with the process. The cane may be planted at any time; but there are only three seasons which are usually employed. One lasts during the month before and another after the summer solstice. This is the most productive and most usual season; but the cane requires at this time longer to grow, and more labour, than in the others; so that, although it pays the same tax only, it yields to the cultivator but little more profit. The other two seasons are the 2d month after the autumnal equinox, and the 2d month after the shortest day. Those crops arrive at maturity within the year. I shall confine myself to an account of the process in the first season. The kind of cane cultivated is the *Maracabo*, of which, according to the *Sheristadar*, 4800 canes are required to give one *Maund*, or about 24¼lb. of *Jagory*. When asked why he does not raise a better kind, the *Sheristadar* says, that the soil is too poor, and the climate too dry; both of which are, to all appearance, ill founded excuses for an obstinate adherence to old custom. In the second month after the vernal equinox, the field must be watered, and eight days afterwards it is ploughed once. After another rest of eight days, it must be ploughed again with a deeper furrow, four oxen having been put into the yoke. After another interval of eight days it is

CHAPTER XVIII. April 8.

ploughed, first lengthwise, and then across, with a team of six oxen. Then, at the distance of three, or three and a half cubits, are drawn over the whole field furrows, which cross each other at right angles. In order to make these furrows wider, a stick is put across the iron of the plough. In the planting season, two cuttings of the cane, each containing two eyes, are laid down in every intersection of the furrows, and are covered slightly with mud. The furrows are then filled with water, and this is repeated three times, with an interval of eight days between every two waterings. A little dung is then put into the furrows; and when there happens to be no rain, the waterings once in the eight days are continued for three months. When the canes have been planted forty days, the weeds must be removed with a knife, and the intervals are hoed with the hoe drawn by oxen. This operation is repeated on the 55th, 70th, and 85th days, and the earth is thrown up in ridges toward the canes. In the beginning of the fourth month, the field gets a full watering. Fifteen days afterwards, the intervals are ploughed lengthwise and across; and to each bunch of plants a basket or two of dung is given and ploughed in. The weeds are then destroyed by a hoe drawn by oxen; after which, channels must be formed between the rows; and until the cane ripens, which varies from fourteen to seventeen months, these channels are filled with water once in fifteen days. The crop season lasts from one month to six weeks. The mill is excessively rude, being two cylinders moved by a perpetual screw, and turned by a beam, to which four oxen are yoked. The *Wocula* land plants 6000 double cuttings, and the bunch springing from the two cuttings planted at each intersection contains from eight to twenty canes. The average may be fourteen, or altogether 84,000. These, at 4800 for the *Maund*, should produce not quite eighteen *Maunds*, which is only one tenth part of that which the man at *Baswa-pattana* mentioned, and he may be considered as having given a true account. The *Sheristadar* however, on being pressed, acknowleges 120 *Maunds;* but he is evidently a liar, and no dependence

CHAPTER XVIII. can be placed on what he says concerning the produce. I did no get any satisfactory account concerning the extent of ground called

April 8. a *Wocula;* but there is no reason to suppose any difference between the *Wocula* of *Baswa-pattana* and that of *Hari-hara.* If we take 6000 squares, of $3\frac{1}{2}$ cubits, as the extent of a *Wocula*, it will give $3\frac{3}{4}$ acres, which pay a tax of 20 *Pagodas*, or at the rate of 2*l.* 2*s.* 9*d.* an acre.

April 11. Appearance of the country. *April* 11th—I went three *cosses* to *Dávana-giri.* Near the road, three small hills excepted, the whole country is fit for the plough. Much of it however, even where the soil is of that fine black mould called *Eray*, would appear never to have been cultivated, and is overgrown with bushes. The soil of a very small proportion indeed, so far as I can judge, appears to be too barren for cultivation; much of it, however, is *Marulu*, or a poor stony land, and some of it is a red soil, fit for the cultivation of *Ragy.*

Dávana-giri. *Dávana-giri* contains above 500 houses, and a new *Bazar* (or street containing shops) is now building. In the centre of the town is a small mud fort. Some years ago, it was a poor village; and its rise is owing to the encouragement given to settlers by *Apojee Ráma*, a *Marattah* chief, who, having entered into the service of *Hyder*, obtained the place as a *Jaghire.* He died without heirs, but *Tippoo* continued to give encouragement to settlers, and ever since it has been gradually increasing. It is the first place in the *Chatrakal* principality *(Ráyada)* towards the west; and the *Amildar* of the district *(Taluc)* usually resides at it, although properly it is not the *Kasba*, or chief town.

Manufactures. At *Dávana-giri* some coarse cotton cloths are made; and at every village of the district three or four looms are employed in the manufacture. The staple commodity, however, of the *Chatrakal* prin-

Cumlies. cipality consists of *Cumlies*, or a kind of blankets which in their fabric greatly resemble English camblets. They are four cubits broad, by twelve long, and form a piece of dress, which the natives of *Karnata* almost universally wear. They are not dyed, but are of the natural colour of the wool, which in the finer ones is almost always a good black. The best are made at *Hara-punya-hully*, in the territory lately ceded to the company, and at *Dávana-giri*. Each of the blankets, made of the wool from the first shearing of the sheep, sells for from two to twelve *Pagodas*, or from 16*s*. 2¼*d*. to 4*l*. 17*s*. 4*d*. Those at four *Pagodas* are the finest made for common sale; and these, with all of an inferior value, are brought to weekly markets, and purchased by the merchant for ready money. If any of a higher value are wanted, advances must be made. The great excellence of these blankets is their power of turning rain; and, the finer they are, the better they do this. Some have been made, that were valued so high as from two to three hundred *Rupees*, and that were considered to be impenetrable by water.

Wool.

Before the sheep are shorn, they are well washed. The wool, when it has been shorn, is teased with the fingers, and then beaten with a bow, like cotton, and formed into bundles for spinning. This operation is performed both by men and women, partly on the small *Hindu* cotton wheel, and partly with the distaff. Some tamarind-seeds are bruised; and, after having been infused for a night in cold water, are boiled. The thread, when about to be put into the loom, is sprinkled with the cold decoction. The loom is of the same simple structure with that usual in *India*. The new made cloth is washed by beating it on a stone; and, when dried, is fit for sale. From this account of the process it will be evident, that the great price of the finer kinds is owing to the great trouble required in selecting wool sufficiently fine, the quantity of which in any one fleece is very small.

Commerce. Carriage.

Dávana-giri is a place of considerable trade, and is the residence of many merchants, who keep oxen, and send goods to distant places. Some of the merchants hire their cattle from *Sivabhactars*, *Mussulmans*, and *Marattahs*, who make the carriage of goods a profession, and are called *Badigaru*. The load is reckoned 8 *Maunds* of 48 *Cucha Seers*, or about 233lb., and the hire is estimated by this quantity, whatever load the owner may choose to put on his cattle.

CHAPTER XVIII.

April 11.

The hire for a load to any place near, is one *Fanam*, or almost $7\frac{1}{2}$ pence, for every *Gau* or *Gavada* of 4 cosses, which amount upon an average, I suppose, to between 12 and 14 miles; but to the great marts at a distance there is a fixed price; for instance, the load from *Sagar*, near *Ikeri*, to *Wallaja-petta*, near *Arcot*, costs 3 *Pagodas*, or 1*l.* 4*s.* $4\frac{1}{2}$*d.* The distance may be about 320 miles.

Customs.

Far from considering the customs exacted at different places on the road as a burthen, the traders here consider them as advantageous; for the custom house is bound to pay for all goods that may be stolen, or seized by robbers, within their respective districts. This seems to be an excellent regulation, which is in general use throughout the peninsula.

Trade with *Arcot*.

The most valuable trade here is that which is carried on with *Wallaja-petta*. The goods carried from hence are *Betel-nut* and pepper, and those brought back are *Madras* goods, imported from Europe, China, Bengal, and the Eastern Islands, together with salt, and some of the manufactures of the coast of Coromandel.

Trade with the *Nagara* principality.

There is also a great trade carried on between this and *Nagara*, and *Sagar*. From thence are brought *Betel-nut* and pepper, and from this are sent *Cumlies*, salt, and *Madras* goods.

Trade with the ceded district.

Next to these, the trade with *Rayá-durga*, and *Hara-punya-hully*, in the newly-ceded district, is the most considerable. The exports from *Dávana-giri* are coco-nuts, *Jagory*, tobacco, turmeric, *Betel-nut*, pepper, and *Capsicum*. The returns are, a little cotton wool, and cloth, *Cumlies*, and a large proportion of cash.

Trade with the *Mysore* principality.

To *Caduru*, and other places south from this, are sent cotton, cloth, and *Terra Japonica*; and from them are brought coco-nuts, tobacco, turmeric, fenugreek, garlic, and *Danya*, a carminative seed. The manufacturers of this neighbourhood frequently carry their blankets to *Seringapatam*.

Trade with the *Marattah* country.

Merchants from the *Marattah* territories beyond the *Tungabhadra* bring hither silk cloths, cotton, *Terra Japonica*, and wheat; and take away *Callay (Cicer arietinum)*, *Jagory*, and coco-nuts. At present this trade is at a very low ebb; parties of the *Marattah* troops seizing on whatever they meet. As these are not robbers, but persons regularly employed by government, the custom-house is not held answerable for their depredations. April 11.

From this it would appear, that the trade of *Dávana-giri* chiefly consists in exchanging the produce of one neighbouring country, for those of another. The only articles of export produced in the neighbourhood are *Cumlies, Jagory* (inspissated juice of sugar cane), and *Callay (Cicer arietinum)*.

April 12th.—To-day I was prevented from advancing by no less than seven of my people having been seized with the fever in the course of the night, and from its being impossible, without some delay, to provide means for their being carried. Fevers have of late been very prevalent among my servants, although the country is perfectly dry and clear. The weather is now very hot in the daytime, with strong irregular blasts of hot wind, which often comes in whirls. The nights are tolerably cool. Early this morning we had a very heavy rain, with much thunder, but little wind. April 12.

As I was detained here, in order to save time I sent for the principal sheep-breeders in the neighbourhood, and obtained from them the following account. Throughout the principality, and in the neighbouring country of *Hara-punya-hully*, which belongs to the Company, sheep are an object of great importance, and are of the kind called *Curi* in the language of *Karnata*. They are kept by two casts, the *Curubaru*, and *Goalaru*. A man of either cast, who possesses a flock of sheep, is by the Mussulmans called a *Donigar*. The *Curubaru* are of two kinds; those properly so called, and those named *Handy* or *Cumly Curubaru*. The *Curubaru* proper, and the *Goalaru*, are sometimes cultivators, and possess the largest flocks; but they never make blankets. The *Handy Curubas* abstain entirely from cultivation, and employ themselves in tending their flocks, and manufacturing the wool. The flocks kept by the two former casts contain from 30 to 300 breeding ewes; those of the *Handy Curubas* Sheep.

contain only from five to one hundred and fifty. All the shepherds have besides some cows, buffaloes, and *Maycays*, or long-legged goats; but the sheep form the chief part of their stock. They are pastured in waste places; for which a *Hulibundu*, or grass renter, is appointed by government; and to him each family pays a certain rent, fixed by an old valuation of their property. This rent varies from ½ a *Fanam* to 20 *Fanams* a year, or from $3\frac{1}{4}d.$ to $12s.\ 5\frac{3}{4}d.$ It is said, that changes in the quantity of a family's stock are not common, and that it is rare for a man to possess thirty more or less than his ancestor had at the time of the valuation. If any man's flock, however, should increase much above the number originally belonging to the family, the *Hulibundu* may increase the tax. The office of *Hulibundu* is not hereditary; but there are certain families of shepherds hereditarily annexed to the *Hulibundu* of each district; that is to say, they must pay their tax into his office. They are at liberty to pasture their flocks wherever they please, even into the territories of a different sovereign. Thus a shepherd of this place may feed his flocks in *Hara-punya-hully;* but he pays his rent to the *Hulibundu* of *Chatrakal.*

The sheep are allowed no food but what they can procure in the pastures, which are open uncultivated lands containing a few scattered bushes, but which are here called *Adavi*, or forests. In the rainy season, the sheep at night are driven into folds made of prickly bushes. In the dry season, they are at night confined on the arable lands, for the purpose of manuring them; and, as a reward, the cultivator gives victuals to the shepherds and their dogs. Four rams are reckoned sufficient for a hundred ewes. Owing to the temperate nature of the climate, the females breed at all seasons indifferently, and they bear six months in the womb. They have their first lamb at eighteen months old, and breed once a year, but never have twins. After bearing three lambs, the ewe is sold. If allowed to live, she would breed five times, but afterwards she would not be saleable. Sheep are never fattened for the market, farther than can be done by pasture, with which in India a sheep seldom becomes fat; but I think the meat of those here is better than I have seen any where else in India, where the animal has not been stall-fed. For stall-feeding, they are preferred by the gentlemen of Madras, who used formerly to be supplied from Bengal. CHAPTER XVIII. April 12.

The males, except those intended for breeding, are sold by the shepherds when under two years of age. At a year old, the best males are selected for breeding, the others are castrated. A female at one year old, sells for about a quarter of a *Pagoda*, or rather more than two shillings, and continues of the same value until after having had her third lamb. A male of a year old is worth the same money. A wether two years old is worth about a third of a *Pagoda*, or 2*s.* 8½*d.* A good ram for breeding sells for half a *Pagoda*, or rather more than four shillings.

Wool.

The fleece is shorn twice a year; in the second month after the shortest day, and in that which follows the summer solstice. The first fleece is taken when the sheep is about six months old, and is by far the finest in quality. From this alone can *Cumlies*, of any considerable fineness, be made. Every successive fleece becomes worse and worse, and does not increase in quantity. The sheep are never smeared. They are commonly black; and the deeper this colour is, the more valuable the wool is reckoned. The finer biankets are all of an excellent native black, without dye. Each fleece weighs from 1½ to 3 *Seers*, or from $\frac{91}{100}$ of a pound, to 1$\frac{82}{100}$ lb. The fleeces, as shorn, are divided into three qualities; which sell for 13, 8, and 7 *Fanams* the *Maund;* or for 1*l.* 11*s.* 2½*d.*, 19*s.* 2½*d.*, and 16*s.* 9½*d.* for the hundred weight.

Handy Curubaru.

The *Handy Curubaru*, or in the singular number *Curuba*, are a cast living in the *Hara-punya-hully* and *Chatrakal* districts, and are of *Karnata* descent; but many of them have now settled on the banks of the upper part of the *Krishna* river, in the *Marattah* dominions. All those who have settled in that country being horse-men, they are called *Handay Ravalar*, a name pronounced *Rawut* by the

CHAPTER XVIII. April 12.

Mussulmans, and by them frequently applied to every kind of *Curuba*. In this country they confine themselves entirely to the proper duties of their cast; which are, to rear sheep, and to work up wool into blankets. They can eat with the other tribes of *Curubaru*, but do not intermarry with them. They are allowed a plurality of wives, and their women continue to be marriageable after the age of puberty. Widows may live with a second husband as left-hand wives (*Cutigas*), and their children are not thereby disgraced; for in this tribe there is no inferior *Cutiga* cast. A woman who commits adultery is always excommunicated; nor can her paramour take her for his *Cutiga*. The *Handy Curubas* eat sheep, fish, venison, and fowls. They hold pork to be an abomination, and look upon the eating of the flesh of oxen, or of buffaloes, as a dreadful sin. They are allowed to drink spirituous liquors. When a *Curuba* dies, his property, as is usual with that of all *Hindus* in *Karnata*, is divided equally among his sons; and his wives and daughters are left entirely at the discretion of the males of his family.

The Deities, whom this cast consider as their peculiar objects of worship, are *Bira Deva*, and his sister *Máyava*. *Bira* is, they say, the same with *Iswara*, and resides in *Coilasa*, where he receives the departed spirits of good men. Bad men are punished in *Nuraca*, or by suffering various low transmigrations. There is only one temple of *Bira*, which is situated on *Curi-betta*, or the sheep hill, on the banks of the *Krishna*, near the *Poonah*. There is also only one temple dedicated to *Máyava*. It is near the *Krishna*, at a place named *Chinsulli*. Once in ten years, every man of the cast ought to go to these two temples; but a great many do not find leisure for the performance of this duty. These deities do not receive bloody sacrifices, but are worshipped by offerings of fruit and flowers. The priests (*Pújáris*) at both these temples are *Curubaru*; and, as the office is hereditary, they of course marry. Once in four or five years they go round, distributing consecrated powder of turmeric, and receiving charity. Besides the worship of the deities proper to the cast, the

Curubas offer sacrifices to some of the destructive spirits, such as *Durgawa*, *Jacani*, and *Barama Deva*. When sick, or in distress, they vow sacrifices to these spirits, provided they will no longer exert their baneful influence. The *Curabaru* have no trouble from *Pysachi;* and ordinary *Butas*, or devils, they believe, are expelled by prayer addressed to the deities of the cast. At *Hujiny*, in the *Hara-punya-hully* district, resides *Rávana Siddheswara*, the *Guru* of this cast. His office also is hereditary; and he is able to read, an extent of knowlege to which no other person of the tribe has pretensions. The *Guru* attends at feasts and sacrifices, to receive his share, and punishes transgressions against the rules of cast by fine and excommunication. At the principal ceremonies of the *Curabaru*, such as marriages, building a new house, or the like, the *(Panchanga)* astrologer of the village, who is a *Bráhman*, attends; and, having read the prayers *(Mantrams)* proper on the occasion, receives the accustomed due.

April 12.

April 13th.—I went what was called four cosses, but the stage was exceedingly long, and I halted at *Coduganar*. Except two small hills between which I passed, all the country near this day's route is sufficiently level for the plough, and very little of it appears to be too barren for cultivation. Some of the soil is black clay, some is red mould, but by far the greater part of it is poor stony land. I saw several villages, but a very small proportion of the country is cultivated, and from time immemorial much has been waste. A long continued scene of Indian warfare has prevented by far the greater part from having been cultivated. The most severe loss, however, that the natives remember, was what they suffered in *Purseram Bow's* invasion, when the whole *Chatrakal* principality was reduced to nearly a desert. The *Amildar* of *Mahiconda*, who met me at *Coduganar*, says, that almost the whole country is capable of cultivation, and with manure will produce either *Ragy* or *Jola*.

April 13. Appearance of the country.

In the forenoon a leopard was killed by the people of the village in a garden near the town, and brought to my tent in great triumph, with every thing resembling a flag, and every instrument capable

Leopard, or panther.

CHAPTER XVIII. April 13. of making a noise, that could be collected. First he had been shot in the belly, and then he was driven to the banks of a reservoir, where he stood at bay; and, before he was killed, wounded three of the men who attacked him with spears; one of whom was severely torn. He agreed very well with the description in Ker's translation of Linnæus, and was about four feet from the snout to the root of the tail. He had killed several oxen; and in this country, it is not unusual for leopards to attack even men. Although I have called this animal the leopard, there is reason to think that it does not differ from the panther of India; for I am persuaded that we have no larger spotted animal of the feline genus. The Indian panther and leopard I consider, therefore, as two names for the same animal. The African panther may, however, be different, as certainly is the hunting leopard of India.

April 14. Face of the country. 14th *April*.—I went a very long stage, called four cosses, to *Aligutta*. For some way, near the middle of this day's route, the road passed among low hills that are rather barren. On both sides of these there is a great deal of fine land; for much of the soil is of the fine black mould called *Eray*. Almost the whole is waste, owing chiefly to the invasion of *Purseram Bow*. Many of the fields, however, would appear to have remained longer uncultivated, which is attributed to invasions by the *Marattahs* that happened during the government of *Hyder*. I do not think that more than a tenth part of the arable fields is now occupied. *Ragy* and sugar-cane seem to be what the farmers attend to most; yet there is much land fit for *Jola* and cotton. Some sheep are reared; but all the wool is sent to other places, where it is manufactured. In the villages of this district are scattered a few weavers of coarse cotton cloths. In the *Chatrakal* principality there are no plantations of palm-trees; but there are many gardens in which kitchen stuffs *(Tarkari)* are raised. Among these, the carrot thrives remarkably well, and in flavour is superior to any that I have seen in India. *Aligutta* is a sorry place, situated among some rocky heights that are fortified. Contiguous to it is a very good reservoir. Distant from it about three cosses to the south, is a reservoir, which in size almost equals *Solicaray*, and is named *Bhima Samudra*, or the sea of *Bhima*, who was one of the five sons of *Pandu*, celebrated in *Hindu* fable. April 14.

April 15. 15th *April.*—I went a very long stage, called also four cosses, and encamped in the plain near *Chitteldroog*, as we call it. Most of the country through which I passed is tolerably good, but very thinly peopled, and poorly cultivated. After having passed over a low ridge of hills, I came to a small rivulet, named *Jenigay holay*, which has its source from *Bhima Samudra*, and from various mountain torrents. It runs towards *Gudi-cotay*, the chief town of a district in this principality, and contains water at all seasons. It forms some fine reservoirs, and in several places is also conveyed by canals to irrigate the fields for cultivation.

Chitteldroog. The plain of *Chitteldroog* is two cosses and a half from north to south, and one coss from east to west; the coss here being at least four miles. It is every where surrounded by low, rocky, bare hills, on one of which stands the *Durga*, or fort, formerly the residence of the *Polygars* of this country. By the natives it is called either *Sitala-durga*, that is to say, the spotted castle, or *Chatrakal*, which signifies the umbrella rock; for the *Umbrella* is one of the insignia of royalty. During the government of the *Ráyarus*, the tributary *Polygars* of *Chatrakal*, who by descent were hunters (*Baydaru*), governed a country valued at 10,000 *Pagodas* a year, or 3120*l.* 8*s.* 4*d.* On the decline of the royal family of *Vijaya-nagara*, these enterprising hunters, by gradually encroaching on their neighbours, increased their territories until they became worth annually 350,000 *Pagodas*, or 109,213*l.* 10*s.* 10*d.* The *Moguls* had no sooner settled at *Sira*, than they began to covet the *Chatrakal* principality, which being entirely an open country ought to have fallen an easy prey to their cavalry. *Sida Hilál*, *Nabob* of *Sira*, made the attempt, and besieged the town for two years, but without success. He then retired to *Sira*, having received a promise of an annual tribute, the

CHAPTER XVIII.

April 15.

payment of which he probably did not expect. *Hyder*, soon after taking *Bidderuru*, attacked *Chatrakal*. The first siege lasted five months, and was unsuccessful. After the second siege had continued six months, there was little prospect of success, and *Hyder* had recourse to corruption. Partly by money, and partly by the influence of a common faith, he obtained the treacherous assistance of a *Mussulman* officer, to whom the *Rájá* had given a high military command. At this time the town was very large, and filled a great portion of the plain; but owing to the removal of its court it has since gradually decayed. Still, however, it is a considerable place, and seems to receive particular encouragement from *Purnea*. It is now confined entirely within the walls, which are near the foot of the rock. They were strengthened by *Hyder;* and the town, after the peace granted by Lord Cornwallis, having become a place near the *Marattah* frontier, *Tippoo* had employed *Dhowlut Khan*, one of his slaves, to add much to its strength. The new works are now completing, and will render it totally impregnable against such invaders. Indeed, as it was before, *Purseram Bow* made no attempt to besiege it, that kind of warfare being little adapted for his troops, or indeed for those of any native prince; for the walls that resisted the two years siege of the troops of the haughty *Mogul*, were built entirely of mud. From the hereditary *Shanaboga* of this place, named *Shimuppa*, I received a history of the *Polygars* of *Chatrakal*, which I have delivered to the Bengal government.

April 16. Sickness prevalent in the hot weather.

16th *April*.—I unfortunately found, that the *Subadar*, or chief officer of the principality, was absent, and that his inferiors were little disposed to render me any assistance; of which I was much in want, owing to the number of my people who were sick, and who were daily attacked with fevers. The whole neighbouring country is reckoned exceedingly unhealthy, although it is perfectly dry and clear; and indeed, ever since I have come upon the open country near the *Tunga*, my people have been suffering very much. The natives say, that every country is unhealthy in which the black soil called *Eray* abounds. In the neighbourhood of *Chatrakal* there is also a deficiency of water. To reach it, the wells must not only be very deep, but all that is procurable is of a bad quality. This may be in part attributed to the common nastiness of the *Hindus*, who wash their clothes, bodies, and cattle in the very tanks or wells from which they take their own drink; and, wherever the water is scanty, it becomes from this cause extremely disgusting to a European. CHAPTER XVIII. April 16.

Finding that the agriculture of this country differed in nothing material from that at *Hari-hara*, and *Dávana-giri*, and wishing to remove my people to a more healthy situation, I determined to make no longer stay at the inhospitable *Chatrakal*, but to go to *Heriuru*, where the air and water are reckoned wholesome.

17th *April.*—I went two cosses to *Siddamána-hully*, a mud fort containing sixty houses. The first half of the way led through the plain of *Chatrakal*, which is mostly uncultivated, but consists of a fine black soil. Beyond the hills surrounding this plain, toward the east, is an extensive level bounded by *Nunnivala* hills and fort. The soil most common in this plain also is black. The number of inhabitants now in the country is not above a third part of what were in it before the *Marattah* invasion. The two great articles of cultivation here are *Jola (Holcus sorghum)* and *Navonay (Panicum italicum)*, of which about equal quantities are raised. The next most considerable crops are *Sujjay (Holcus spicatus)* and cotton. The quantity of wheat and *Callay (Cicer arietinum)* is small. There are no reservoirs, but some might be constructed. Near the village is said to be a place where one might be built that would water as much land as would sow 10,000 *Seers* of rice. The chief *(Gauda)* at *Siddamána-hully* is a *Sivabhactar*, as indeed is common in this principality; for since the overthrow of their chief by *Hyder*, the *Baydaru* have become almost extinct. April 17. Appearance of the country.

18th *April.*—I went three cosses to *Imangula*, and had on my right all the way a prolongation from the hills on which *Chatrakal* stands. April 18.

CHAPTER XVIII.

April 18.

The country near my route is chiefly level, and most of the soil is black; but it is almost entirely waste, and has very few tanks. Near *Imangula* is a small one that waters some rice ground.

Eggs of fishes very tenacious of life.

Although almost every year, before the commencement of the rainy season, this tank becomes dry, and has no communication with any rivulet, yet it contains many small fishes, all of which are caught whenever it dries. It would appear, that their eggs, although no doubt they become dry with the mud and stones, retain life, and are hatched so soon as they are moistened by the next rain. This shows the practicability of transporting the eggs of fishes from one country to another with very little trouble.

Imangula. Practice of swinging before idols.

Imangula is a large fort, but much space within is empty, and it contains only about 90 houses. The chief *(Gauda)* is hereditary, as is usual throughout the *Mysore Rájá's* dominions, and he acts as *Pújári* to the image of the village god. Almost every village has a peculiar deity of this kind, and most of them are believed to be of a destructive nature. That of *Imangula* is *Kalikantama*, a female deity. To her image an annual feast is given by the *Gauda*, who offers sacrifices, while her wrath is appeased by the people, who are swung round before the shrine, as they are suspended from the end of a lever by a hook of iron, that is passed through the skin of their backs. This cruel worship is never performed before the great gods; and the *Bráhmans* of the south consider it as an abomination, fit only for the groveling understandings of the vulgar.

Singular manner of cultivating the dry field.

In the black soil which forms a large portion of the fine plains east from *Chatrakal*, a singular manner of cultivation prevails. The plough used is drawn by from eight to sixteen oxen, and is heavy in proportion. In Plate XXIX. Fig. 80, is represented one that was drawn by eight oxen, the iron of which weighed 12 *Seers*, or about $7\frac{1}{4}$lb. The largest is exactly of the same shape, but much stronger, and its iron is double the weight. The reason of the number of cattle which the farmers here employ seems to be, the hardness acquired by the black soil in the dry and hot season during which the labour must be performed. After the commencement of the rains it becomes so sticky, that cattle cannot walk on it. In many parts of the *Marattah* country, I am told, the same mode of cultivation prevails, and that the plough is often drawn by 12 yoke of oxen, worth each from sixteen to twenty *Rupees*. With the strong team in use here, the field every third year receives two or three ploughings. In the two intermediate years it is only hoed with the *Cuntay*. It requires no manure, and is never rested, but constantly gives a crop of *Jola (Holcus sorghum)* or *Navonay (Panicum italicum)*, which are sown without any attention to rotation. On the year in which the field is ploughed, rows of *Callay (Cicer arietinum)* accompany the *Jola;* but in the two intermediate seasons nothing is sown with this grain. The *Navonay* is always accompanied by rows of cotton, at the distance of two cubits and a half. Both seeds are sown with the drill. The crop on the second year after ploughing is reckoned the best. When the country becomes inhabited and acquires a good system of agriculture, this part of the *Chatrakal* principality, which consists of *Eray*, or black soil, seems likely to be a source of great wealth; but its present desolation must for a considerable time keep it poor, and, adding to the natural unhealthiness of the climate, will make the increase of population slow.

CHAPTER XVIII. April 18.

April 19th.—I went three cosses to *Heriuru*, near which a great change takes place in the appearance of the country. The soil is mostly stony, and at this season exceedingly parched; so that there is scarcely any grass, and the only green things to be seen are a few scattered *Mimosas*.

April 19. Appearance of the country.

Owing to the sickness among my people, and an accident having befallen my horse, it became impossible for me to proceed farther; and as I had found it impracticable, when at *Sira*, to procure a palanquin bearer there, it became necessary to wait until some conveyance should be sent from *Seringapatam*. This delayed me fourteen days, nor could a set of bearers by any means be procured at

Delay owing to sickness.

CHAPTER XVIII. April 19. *Seringapatam*. I should have been reduced to the necessity of walking, had not the *Dewan* obligingly sent a positive order for the bearers of *Sira* to enter into my service. The common bearers of India are unwilling to enter into the service of a traveller, although the wages he gives are immense, when compared with what they get at home; for he takes them far from their families, to places which they consider as another world. All objects of enquiry having been soon exhausted, while the desert nature of the country precluded any resource from botany, my stay at *Heriuru* proved very tedious.

Climate. The winds in the day-time were hot, and came generally from the south. Slight whirlwinds from the same quarter were common. At night the winds were westerly, and tolerably cool. There were a few slight showers of rain, with some heavy squalls of wind, which changed all round the compass, and were accompanied by a terrible cloud of dust.

Fish. I procured much comfort from a small clear stream, called the *Vedawáti*, in which I cooled myself every evening, and whence I procured the three species of *Cyprinus* from which the accompanying figures (Plates XXX. XXXI. XXXII.) were taken, and of which the following are the scientific characters:

1. *Cyprinus Carmuca* B.

C. cirrhis duobus; corpore elongato; capite callis tuberculato; radiis pinnæ analis octo, dorsalis undecem.

Karmuka Telingorum.

Habitat in fluviis *Karnatæ*. Piscis aliquando tres pedes longus.

2. *Cyprinus Ariza* B.

C. imberbis cauda bifida; corpore elongato; maxilla inferiore carinata; radiis pinnæ analis septem, dorsalis duodecem.

Kincla Minu Tamulorum

Bangun Batta Bengalensium.

Arija Telingorum.

Habitat in fluviis Indiæ australis. Pisces hos numquam vidi trium palmorum longiores.

3. *Cyprinus Bendelisis* B.

C. cirrhis duobus; cauda biloba, corpore elongato, semi-fasciato; radiis pinnæ dorsalis novem, ani undecim.

Bendelisi Telingorum.

Habitat in fluviis *Karnatæ.* Pisciculus digiti longitudinem vix exsuperans.

This fine little river seldom or never dries up, and comes from *Sakra-pattana.* Its water is clear, and is reckoned wholesome. Four cosses below *Heriuru* it is joined by the *Cuttay-holay,* which comes from *Muga-Nayakana-Cotay* and *Hagalawadi,* and forms the boundary between the *Chatrakal* principality and *Sira.* Although this receives a small stream from *Sira,* yet in the hot season it commonly becomes dry. The natives here say, that the *Vedawáti* joins the *Utara Pinákani,* or northern *Pennar,* after having received the *Jaya-mangala* river, which comes from *Nandi-durga;* but this is a clear proof of their extreme ignorance in topography. The *Vedawáti* is the river which Major Rennell calls *Hogree,* and it joins the *Tungabhadra.*

Heriuru.

Heriuru signifies "a head place." It is situated on the east side of the *Vedawáti,* and during the government of the *Chatrakal Rájás* contained 2000 houses, with an outer and inner fort, and several temples of the great gods, one of which is of considerable size. This temple, called *Gunavunti,* possesses an inscription engraven on stone, dated *Sal.* 1332, in the reign of *Deva Ráya;* of which a copy has been delivered to the Bengal government. In the reign of *Hyder,* the town suffered considerably from the *Marattahs,* and was plundered by *Purseram Bow.* The ravages of this chief were followed by a dreadful famine, which swept away all the inhabitants. When the British army arrived last before *Seringapatam,* about 50 or 60 houses had again been occupied. Some of the dealers in grain that followed the camp found their way even to this distance, and plundered the wretched inhabitants. At the same time *Barama Nayaka,* a chief of the *Chatrakal* family, assembled some banditti,

CHAPTER XVIII. April 19. and entered the territories of his ancestors, to try what could be done. He had constant skirmishes with the *Sultan's* garrison in *Chatrakal*, and in each of these two or three villages were plundered by one or other of the parties. After the capture of *Seringapatam*, this chief wisely entered into the service of the *Mysore Rájá*, and is now employed in the command of 3000 men acting against a *Polygar*, who by us is called the *Bool Rájá*. When Colonel Dalrymple arrived with his detachment, giving protection to this part of the country, the number of inhabited houses in *Heriuru* was reduced to seven. About 300 have since been rebuilt, and the place is the chief town of a *(Taluc)* district.

Strata. The *strata* at *Heriuru* run nearly north and south, and are almost quite vertical. The basis of the country is somewhat between an *argillite* and *schistose hornblende*. It contains no veins that I observed; but in some places I saw large amorphous masses of reddish fat quartz imbedded in its substance. When exposed to the air, it readily decays, and is then covered with a cinereous crust. For building, it is a very poor stone; at least what is near the surface; but in a temple of *Iswara* without the walls I observed some pieces of it that have been squared, and resemble much the fine hornblende slate from *Batuculla*. It is probable, therefore, that by digging quarries excellent materials for building might be procured. Of these, however, there is no want any where in *Karnata*.

The only other common rock here is called the Black stone, and it may be considered as forming large beds between the strata of the argillaceous hornblende slate. This is an earthy quartz or hornstone, impregnated with hornblende. When exposed to the air, its masses do not readily acquire a crust, but separate into irregular quadrangular pieces, truncated at both ends. In the fissures may sometimes be observed yellow shining *nodules*, which I take to be the *mica aurata*. It contains no other venigenous matter, and does not cut with the tools of the natives; but from the angular shape of its fragments, the smooth surface with which they break, and its great durability, it is excellently fitted for rough walls.

April 19. Dry measures.

The *Seer* measure used in the market *(Bazar)* here for grain contains 76½ cubical inches; 72 *Seers* make one *Wocula* or *Colaga*. The farmers measure is founded on another plan: 2 *Seers* make 1 *Arecal* which contains 176⅘ cubical inches; 2 *Arecals* make one *Gydna*; 16 *Gydnas* make one *Wocula*; and 20 *Woculas*, or *Colagas*, make one *Candaca*, which therefore contains a little more than 52½ bushels, The *Wocula* of the *(Bazar)* market, and that of the farmers, are commonly considered as the same; but in fact the former contains 5508 cubical inches, and the latter 5652.

Price of grain.

The following is the average price of grain, calculated to the nearest farthing.

	Canter' Ráya Pagodas.		pence
1 *Candaca* of *Sujjay* worth	8	The bushel is worth	11½
Huruli	8		11½
Navonay	8		11½
Harica	5		7¼
Wheat	18		26
Ellu	15		21¾
Callay worth	12		17¼
Ragy	8		11½
Paddy, or rough rice	8		11½
Rice cleared from the husk	18		26

Cotton, cleared of the seed, is worth 12 *Fanams* for the *Maund* of 48 *Seers*, each weighing 22 *Dudus*, or 1*l.* 10*s.* 8½*d.* a hundred weight.

Dry field.

In this neighbourhood, the cultivation of dry field is the grand object, and differs very considerably from that in the western parts of the principality, where the black mould prevails. Here all the land is a poor stony soil. In some places it contains nodules of limestone; but these are considered as unfit for any kind of cultivation.

Tenures.

The whole lands are the property of the government. Some are still called *Enam*, but this is merely in remembrance of their former

CHAPTER XVIII. April 19.

tenure; for the holder of the *Enam* has no fuller right than any other tenant. No lands can be sold, mortgaged, or let to sub-tenants. They are let from year to year, and the possessions are changed from man to man at the pleasure of the officers of revenue; but the rent of each field is fixed by an old valuation. The cultivators never at any time gave more than this rent; and being at present few in number, considerably less is exacted, in order to encourage them to cultivate as much land as possible; for they are totally inadequate to the cultivation of the whole.

Plough of land.

The extent of dry-field is estimated by the plough, and all ploughs are said to be of nearly the same dimensions. I measured one, which I found contained 562,280 square feet, that is, very little less than 13 acres. One plough can not only cultivate this extent, but also a little of the watered land, the rent of which is paid by a division of crops. In doing this, the officers of revenue *(Amildars)* say, that it is impossible for the government to be defrauded, which appears to me incomprehensible. I have myself no doubt, partly from the division of crops, and partly from the power which they have of changing the cultivators possessions, that the officers of revenue have very lucrative appointments. The rent on dry-field at present amounts to from 10 to 60 *Fanams* a plough, or at from $5\frac{1}{4}$ to $34\frac{1}{4}$ pence an acre. That which I measured was an exceedingly poor stony field, and paid 34 *Fanams* a year, or $18\frac{1}{2}$ pence an acre.

The *Sultan's* management of the revenue.

The rent paid to *Tippoo* did not amount to one half of the valuation; for all parties united to defraud him, each getting a share. Although, during the *Sultan's* government, the rent fell thus light on the cultivators, they were, even by their own account, much worse off than they are at present; for there was no end to the arbitrary exactions which the lord lieutenants *(Asophs)* levied. The most intolerable of these, however, arose from the contribution which the *Sultan* demanded, to make good the sum that he was bound to pay to Lord Cornwallis by the treaty of *Seringapatam.* *Tippoo* ordered three millions *(crores)* to be collected; and the people here say, that by paying their share of this they would not have been distressed. In place of three *crores*, however, ten were collected, and of these seven were embezzled by the officers of revenue. These again were obliged to bribe their superiors; but *Tippoo* did not molest them, and many of the *Bráhmans* are said still to possess very considerable sums which were then accumulated. *Hyder* and his son acted on totally different plans. The father protected the cultivator, but was very apt to squeeze his officers in an arbitrary manner. The *Sultan* seldom molested his officers, but he cared not how much they fleeced the people. He, however, was probably ignorant of the lengths to which they went, especially after his unsuccessful war with Lord Cornwallis; from which period he was almost inaccessible to his subjects, and continued to brood over his misfortunes in sullen solitude. April 19.

Four ploughs are here reckoned a large stock. Two ploughs are common; but by far the greater part of the farmers have one only; and many, as is indeed usual in every part of the country, are necessitated to unite their stocks before they can furnish two oxen, and the miserable implements which are necessary to accompany one plough. The extent of land cultivated here by one plough is greater than usual in India; for it requires little labour. I am persuaded, however, that in every part of *Karnata* a plough, fully wrought, is capable of labouring at least thirteen acres of dry field; from six to seven acres may be taken as the average extent of a plough of watered-land. Each plough requires two oxen and one man, and additional women must be occasionally hired. Size of farms.

At *Heriuru* there are no slaves. Most of the labour is performed by the families of the tenants; but a few hire men servants by the year, and in seed time and harvest employ women by the week. A man gets from 50 to 70 *Fanams* a year, or from 1*l.* 11*s.* $2\frac{1}{2}$*d.* to 2*l.* 3*s.* $8\frac{1}{4}$*d.* This is paid entirely in money, without any addition, except that, for himself and family, he generally obtains room in Wages and servants.

CHAPTER XVIII.

April 19.

his master's house. Women get one *Fanam*, or $7\frac{1}{2}d.$ a week. Advances to servants are not common, and of course they are entirely free.

Hours of labour.

The hours of labour in this country are from eight in the morning until noon, and from two o'clock till sunset; in all, about eight hours. The labourers get up about sun rise; but an hour is spent in their evacuations, in which all *Hindus* are excessively tardy; and another hour is spent in ablutions, prayer, marking their faces with consecrated ashes or clay, and in eating their breakfast. They eat three times a day, their principal meal being at noon.

Sujjay.

The most common article of cultivation is the *Holcus spicatus* of Linnæus, called by the natives *Sujjay*, or *Cambu*. It is generally accompanied by *Huruli (Dolichos biflorus)*. The custom here is, to cultivate the *Cambu* fields three years, and then to give them a fallow of the same duration; and while thus allowed to rest, they pay no rent. Each man's farm is therefore divided into two portions; one of which is cultivated, and the other fallow. Other dry grains are also sown on the *Cambu* field, and that without any attention to rotation. The only manure that is given is, for some nights, to make a flock of sheep sleep on the field. They are not folded, but merely gathered together by the shepherds and their dogs. After the first heavy rain in the two months following the vernal equinox, the *Cambu* field is ploughed, lengthwise and across, with two oxen in the yoke. After the next rain this is repeated. It must be observed, that the rain must be of considerable duration; for in this arid soil and season the heaviest shower produces no sensible effect. After the second ploughing, the field is hoed with a *Heg Cuntay* drawn by four oxen. When the rainy season has fairly commenced, which happens about the summer solstice, the seed is sown with the drill, the *Cambu* being put in the *Curigy*, and the *Huruli* in the *Sudiky*. After having been sown one month, the field is weeded with the *Edday Cuntay*; and after an interval of eight days this is again repeated. The *Cambu* in five months ripens; the *Huruli* is a month later. Thirty-two *Seers* of *Cambu*, and six *Seers* of *Huruli*, are sown on one plough of land, and produce about 1280 *Seers* of the former, and 128 of the latter. The produce is therefore worth 80 *Fanams* for *Sujjay*, and 8 for *Huruli*; in all, 88. The seed and rent may on an average amount to about 36 *Fanams*, or about 40 *per cent.* of the gross produce. An acre of ground, at this rate, will produce nearly four bushels of *Cambu*, and $\frac{4}{10}$ of a bushel of *Huruli*; a strong proof of a miserable soil and wretched cultivation, yet the former is allowed to produce 40, and the latter above 21 fold; but I have already pointed out the fallacy of judging, concerning the productiveness of either soil or crop, by means of the increase on the seed that has been sown.

Cotton.

In a few places of this district (*Taluc*) cotton is put in the (*Acadies*) rows between the drills of *Cambu*; but it requires a much richer soil than is to be usually found, and is thought to exhaust the land. The quantity raised in the country is not equal to the consumption. In a few places *Harulu*, or *Ricinus*, is put in the drills with *Cambu*.

Navonay.

The next most considerable crop is *Navonay*, or the *Panicum italicum*. The field is ploughed twice in the month following the summer solstice, and at the end of the month it is hoed with the *Heg Cuntay*. In the following month, after a heavy rain, the seed is sown with the drill; and a month afterwards the weeds are removed by the *Edday Cuntay*. In three months it ripens, but is a very uncertain crop; for it is liable to be spoiled by either too much or too little rain. A farmer who has a plough, and sows 32 *Seers* of *Sujjay*, commonly sows 2 *Seers* of *Navonay*, and, when the season is favourable, will get 3 *Colagas*, or 96 seeds; which, after deducting the seed, is worth $11\frac{1}{4}$ *Fanams*. This, I suspect, ought to be considered as a part of what the plough of land produces, and will make its gross amount 100 *Fanams*; from which is to be deducted less than $36\frac{1}{2}$ *Fanams* for seed; and rent. The gross value of the

CHAPTER XVIII.

April 19.

produce of an acre of poor land, such as that I measured, by this estimate, will be about 4*s.* 10*d.* By the people here, the straw of *Navonay* is reckoned better fodder than that of *Cambu*, which is indeed exceedingly coarse. The grain of the *Cambu* is reckoned the most nourishing food for labouring men; while that of *Navonay* is preferred by the *Bráhmans*, and others, who are not under the necessity of performing hard work.

Horse-gram, or Dolichos biflorus.

With respect to quantity, the other crops are very trifling; but, as each man cultivates some of them, at seasons when his stock would be otherwise idle, they are of importance, as reducing the price of labour. The most considerable of them is that of *Huruli*, or *Horse-gram*, which *Purnea* has lately encouraged, in order to procure a plentiful supply for the cavalry that are stationed towards the *Marattah* frontier. The land employed for the purpose is the poorest in the country, and gets no manure. In the second month after the autumnal equinox, the field is once ploughed. About the beginning of the following month, it is ploughed again, and the seed is dropped into the furrows, after the plough, by a sharp pointed *bamboo (Sudiky)*. It is then covered by a hoeing with the *Heg Cuntay*. The seed is sown twice as thick as that of *Cambu*, ripens in three months, and produces five folds; one half of which goes to the public revenue. The produce of an extent of land equal to one plough is therefore worth twenty *Fanams*; of which ten go for rent, two for seed, and eight to the farmer. The produce of an acre is about one bushel, and is worth less than a shilling.

Harica.

On the same kind of soil, and in the year following the *Horse-gram*, is sown *Harica*, or the *Paspalum frumentaceum* Roxb. MSS. In the second month after the vernal equinox, the field is ploughed, and the seed is dropped into the furrow, after the plough, with the sharp bamboo, and covered with the *Bolu Cuntay*. Three months afterwards, the weeds are removed by the *Edday Cuntay*. It requires much rain, and eight months elapse before it ripens. Four *Seers* of seed produce two *Woculas;* but I do not know the extent of ground required. The rent is ten *Fanams* for the plough of land. CHAPTER XVIII.

In the bottoms of reservoirs, when they are dry, are sown wheat, *Ellu*, or *Sesamum*, and *Càllay*, or *Cicer arietinum.* For rent the government takes one third part of the produce. April 19.

Rice-land.

The quantity of rice-land in the *Chatrakal* principality is very small. In this district *(Taluc)*, eight or ten villages are partly employed in this kind of agriculture; and in favourable years they have two crops from the same field, which is not the case any where to the westward. There were formerly five reservoirs. Two of them have lately been put into repair; one is now undergoing that operation; and money has been allotted for the two others. There are many places in which new ones might be formed with great advantage, were there stock sufficient to cultivate the lands which they would irrigate; but, in the present desolate state of the country, all expense bestowed on erecting new reservoirs would be fruitless. In the principality there are a few *Betel-nut* gardens, which are cultivated in the same manner as those to the southward, which I have already described; but the soil here is little favourable for the *Areca.* Having formerly given a full account of the cultivation of rice in the neighbouring *Taluc* of *Sira*, it would in this place be superfluous to say any thing on the subject. The revenue is paid by a division of the crop.

Cattle and manure.

The village cattle during the whole year are kept in the house, but are not littered. Their dung is collected in pits, and mixed with the ashes and other soil of the family. This manure is reserved for the rice-land. The dry field gets nothing, except the dung of the sheep, which, at any season, are herded on it at night. A flock of 500 in two nights are supposed to manure fully a plough of land. The farmers say, that when they have not sheep of their own they hire in the flocks of the shepherds, and give them two or three *Fanams* for manuring the plough of land. But this is

CHAPTER XVIII. April 19. denied by the shepherds, who allege, that, except permission to feed their flocks on the fallow lands, they get nothing; and this, I believe, is true. The want of attention to increase the quantity of manure is a gross defect in the agriculture of *Heriuru*, and may account for the wretched produce of its field.

Sheep. The *Donigars* in this neighbourhood keep a good many sheep. Some very rich families possess 1000 ewes, and 200 *Maycays*. Those in middling circumstances have four or five hundred ewes. Those who have from fifty to a hundred only are reckoned poor. The wool is much coarser than at *Dávana-giri*, nor will even the first shearing make fine *Cumlies*. The sheep are also smaller, and by the natives are reckoned inferior meat; but, whether or not this would coincide with European taste, I cannot say. This inferiority of the sheep and wool is attributed to the difference of soil; for all over the good sheep country, especially in the *Harapunya-hully* district, the *Eray*, or black soil, is prevalent. The natives, when asked how much it is usual for the meat or fat of a good sheep to weigh, stare with as much astonishment, probably, as that with which an English feeder would behold a butcher who was ignorant of what he considered to be so obvious a matter of enquiry. The sheep here are never driven into a house. In the rainy season they are taken to the wastes, and at night are secured by a fence of dry thorns, to keep off the tigers, which are very numerous among the bushes; for in the neighbouring forests there are no trees. In the dry season, the flocks are at night brought near the villages, and kept on the arable lands. Even there, according to the account of the shepherds, it is necessary to surround them with a fence of thorns. At this season the sheep must have drink twice a day, at noon and in the evening. In the rainy season they are never brought from the wilds; but folds are raised in the driest spots that can be found, and within the enclosure of thorns the shepherds erect for themselves small huts. The rent is on the same footing as at *Dávana-*

giri, and varies from 1 to 40 *Fanams*, or from $7\frac{1}{2}$ pence to almost 25 shillings a year, according to the value of the flock. A flock containing, young and old, 500 sheep and 50 *Maycays*, requires four men and four dogs. These are able to drive away small animals of the feline kind, but have no arms that would enable them to attack the tiger or leopard. In the rainy season, the ewes are milked, and four of them give daily a *Seer*, which contains 72 cubical inches, or a little more than an ale quart. It sells for three *Dudus* a *Seer*, or $1\frac{1}{2}$*d.* a quart. It is of the same value with cow's milk, and is made in a similar manner into *Ghee*, of which 22 *Rupees* weight requires eight *Seers* of milk; that is to say, to make one pound of butter, boiled into *Ghee*, requires $14\frac{3}{4}$ quarts of milk, ale measure. Cheese, for which ewes milk is best fitted, is not known at *Heriuru;* nor any where, I believe, in India, except where it has been introduced by Europeans. The ewes breed once a year, but at all seasons indifferently. After having given five lambs, they are sold, and then bring from $2\frac{1}{2}$ to 3 *Fanams*, or from $18\frac{3}{4}$ to $22\frac{1}{2}$ pence. The males are emasculated at eighteen months old, and are sold from six to eighteen months afterwards. They are never fattened, except by the natural pasture; and it is only during the rainy season that they are in tolerable condition. In the dry season the fields produce scarcely a green herb. A wether at two years old brings five *Fanams*, and one three years old brings six *Fanams*, or double the price of a ewe. Lamb is never used. Seven *Fanams*, or 4*s.* $4\frac{1}{2}$*d.*, is reckoned a high price for a breeding ram; which ill-judged œconomy, probably, contributes to render the breed worse than that of *Chatrakal.*

Cows. In the wastes of this part of the country some *Goalas* keep herds of breeding cows. They are never brought near the villages, and are exceedingly fierce; so that no dog nor stranger can with safety approach them, and the males attack and kill the tiger. To the *Goalas*, however, they are very tractable, and follow, like dogs, the man who leads the herd to pasture; while the other *Goalas* follow.

CHAPTER XVIII. April 19. to bring up the young, and the stragglers. Some of the cows are however so vicious, that no milk can be taken from them. They are all white, but are not fit for carriage, being too small. They are very hardy in the plough, or machine for raising water called *Capily*; but are rather unruly, even after emasculation; so that an ox of this breed does not bring more than 40 *Fanams*, 1*l.* 4*s.* 11½*d.*; while the more tractable, but weaker cattle, bred in the villages, sell for from 60 to 70 *Fanams*, or from 1*l.* 17*s.* 5¼*d.* to 2*l.* 3*s.* 8*d.* Bulls for breeding sell for from 50 to 80 *Fanams*, or from 1*l.* 11*s.* 2½*d.* to 2*l.* 9*s.* 11*d.* The forest males are emasculated when between two and three years old; and are sold off at four, when they are fit for labour. The cows have a calf once in two years, and generally breed five times. In the rainy season, a cow gives daily 1¼ *Seer*, or 90 cubical inches, and in the hot season ½ *Seer*, or 36 cubical inches. The village cows being kept in the house at night, and being fed there, give about two *Seers* a day, or rather more than two ale quarts. These forest cattle are always kept in herds, which contain about 150 young and old, male and female. A herd of this kind requires the attendance of five men. One man carries the milk home to the village, and brings provisions; for the women dare not approach. The other four men lead the herd to pasture. The calves are secured in a fold strongly defended by thorns; and on the outside of this the *(Goalas)* cowherds build a small hut, in which they sleep surrounded by the cattle, and defended by them from the tigers. When water or grass fail in one part of the country, they remove to another, and are under the grass renter *(Hulubundi)* of *Chatrakal*, exactly on the same footing with the *(Donigars)* shepherds.

Buffaloes. In the wastes buffaloes are never kept; but in every house the women of the *(Goalas)* cowherds, and the people of the villages, keep at least one or two female buffaloes; for the greater part of the milk used in the country is procured from this kind of cattle.

Each female ought daily to give three *Seers*, or a little more than three ale quarts. In the rainy season, this sells at three half pence a quart, in the dry season at two-pence. The village cows and buffaloes are pregnant one year, and give milk the other. During the latter, the cow, besides supporting her calf, should give 30 *Seers* of butter, or $22\frac{1}{2}$ of *Ghee*, worth about $7\frac{1}{2}$ *Fanams;* that is, she gives $16\frac{64}{100}$lb. of butter, or $12\frac{1}{2}$lb. of *Ghee* worth, 4*s.* $4\frac{1}{2}$*d.* The female buffalo, besides rearing her calf, should give 35 *Seers* of butter, or $24\frac{1}{4}$ of *Ghee*, worth $8\frac{3}{4}$ *Fanams*, or $\frac{1}{6}$ more than the cow. If this be accurate, the buffalo milk must be poorer than the cow's, as she gives one half more. The contrary opinion is commonly entertained.

Sickness among my servants.

Although the air and water of *Heriuru* are reckoned salutary, and my people were well accommodated, they did not recover their health, and all my stock of medicines had been long expended. My cook died rather unexpectedly. His fever never had been severe; the paroxysms had come on as usual in the morning, and, after it was over, had left him tolerably well; but in the evening he suddenly became insensible, was convulsed, and died in about an hour. He was a very thoughtless man, and much addicted to intoxication; those, therefore, who fancy that all spirituous liquors are pernicious, especially in warm climates, will have no difficulty in accounting for his death:

Dicunt ah! nimio pocula dira mero.

But let me add,

Vobis si culpa est bilis, sua quemque sequuntur
Fata; quod immeriti crimen habent cyathi.

For my own part, I am persuaded, that intoxication is much seldomer a cause of disease, than is commonly alleged; and that it chiefly proves injurious to the health of our seamen and soldiers in warm climates by making them imprudently expose themselves to other causes of sickness. The two persons in my service that are most subject to fevers, are my interpreter and painter, although

CHAPTER XVIII. April 19.

from their situation in life they are exempted from all hardships; but from their cast they ought never to taste spirituous liquor, and are really sober men, avoiding not only liquor, but every intoxicating drug. At the same time, a man who takes care of my tents, although he is exposed to all weathers, and at times to much fatigue, enjoys perfect health, and probably keeps off the fever by copiously drinking spirituous liquors, to the use of which he is exceedingly addicted.

Superstitious fear of ghosts.

The arrival of a set of fresh men, and the consequent preparations for our departure, caused great joy among my people, notwithstanding their weak state. When the cook was taken ill, I had given orders to secure his effects for the benefit of his wife and children; but, on inspection after his death, no money could be found. Whether he had been plundered as soon as he became insensible, and that a guilty conscience occasioned fears among his companions, or whether the sudden manner of his death occasioned suspicions, I cannot say; but it was immediately believed that he would become a *Pysachi,* and all my people were filled with terror. The butler imagined, that the *Pysachi* appeared to him at night with a black silk handkerchief tied round its head, and gave him instructions to take all the effects of the deceased to his family; upon this, the butler, being a man of courage, put his shoes at the right side of the door, which he considered to be a sure preventive against such intruders. Next night a cattle-driver, lying in all the agonies of nocturnal terror, saw the appearance of a dog enter, and smell round the place where the man had died; when, to his utter dismay, the spectre gradually grew larger and larger, and at length, having assumed the form of the cook, vanished with a shriek. The poor man had not the courage to use the slippers, but lay till morning in a kind of stupor. After this, even the minds of the *Sepoys* were appalled; and when I happened to be awake, I heard the sentries, by way of keeping up their courage, singing with a tremulous voice.

CHAPTER XIX.

JOURNEY FROM HERIURU TO SERINGAPATAM, THROUGH THE WESTERN AND MIDDLE PARTS OF THE MYSORE DOMINIONS.

CHAPTER XIX.

May 2. Appearance of the country.

MAY 2d, 1801.—In the morning I went four cosses to *Ellady-caray*, which is situated among the low hills running S. E. from *Chatrakal*. I saw no houses by the way; but some must have been near my route, as in different places I observed a few fields that were cultivated. I passed through several ruined villages. The appearance of the country is desolate, and it is said never to have been much better, in the memory of man. The soil is entirely poor stony land; and the naked rocks, in a state of decay, come frequently to the surface. The grass in many places is long, but at this season it is quite withered; and the only things green, that are visible, are a few wild date palms *(Elate sylvestris)*, most of which are young. In moist places they grow spontaneously, and produce juice, which is often boiled into *Jagory*. The hills are of no considerable height, and among them there is much plain ground. By the natives this is considered as of very little use; but to me, much of it appears to be very capable of being rendered productive, whenever labourers and stock can be found.

Strata.

Between *Heriuru* and *Ellady-caray*, the *strata* are all nearly vertical, and of a slaty structure; but near the surface they are in such a state of decay, that it would be difficult to determine the species. Some appeared to be the same with the quartz impregnated with hornblende, that is found in the western *Ghats*. The layers or plates are in general very thin. There are no veins of quartz; but

CHAPTER XIX. May 2. many of the *strata*, or rather thin plates, of which united the *strata* are composed, are fat quartz. These strata or beds of quartz are from a quarter of an inch to two feet in thickness, and are often stained of a livid colour, which I have no where else observed.

Slate. The talcose argillite of *Heriuru* is here very common, and passes at times entirely into pure argillite, like the slate used for the roofs of houses. The transitions from the one stone to the other are so gradual, that it would be difficult to say where the one ends, and the other begins. The slate here is grey, blue, and purple. All that I saw, being near the surface, was in a state of decay, and therefore useless; but that is the case on the surface of the best slate quarries in Scotland.

Iron. Iron was formerly smelted at *Ellady-caray* from black sand, which was brought from a hill about two miles to the westward. Much of the *vitreous scoriæ* remains where the furnaces stood; but the work has been abandoned these sixty years: the want of fewel is indeed a sufficient reason.

Ellady-caray is a small fort with about thirty houses. It has a plantation, containing a few coco-nut palms; and a garden, containing *betel-leaf* and plantain trees, the verdure of which is very refreshing to the eye of a person coming from *Heriuru*. Near it there is a pond of dirty water full of reeds; but no tank, as its name would seem to imply. The cultivation consists of *Sujjay*, (*Holcus spicatus*), *Harica*, (*Paspalum frumentaceum Roxb:*) *Navonay*, (*Panicum italicum*), and *Huruli* (*Dolichos biflorus*).

Weather. This day has been cloudy and cool, with a threatening of rain. The natives are persuaded, that it is the commencement of the two months of showery weather which precede the rainy season.

May 3. *May* 3d.—I went three short cosses to *Chica-bayli-caray*; that is, the little hedge tank. The country is very hilly, as we crossed the highest part of the ridge coming from *Chatrakal*. The soil in general is very poor, and incapable of being rendered arable. I passed a ruined village surrounded by some good land, and a

CHAPTER XIX.

small fort with eight or ten houses. On the hills, there are a good many stunted trees.

May 3.

Chica-bayli-caray is a small fort containing about forty houses. The fields around, although very stony, are arable; and between the stones the soil is good. Near it is a torrent, which comes from the hills, and runs toward the *Vedawáti.* It is dry in the hot season, but during the rains fills a large reservoir. On its bank is a fine coco-nut garden, where the trees grow to a large size, are well loaded with fruit, and are allowed no water after having been transplanted, and having fairly taken root. The ground of the garden is ploughed every year, and produces *Horse-gram, Harica,* and other dry grains.

Iron smelted.

At *Chica-bayli-caray* is a furnace for smelting iron ore, brought from a mine called *Cudera Canavay,* and which is supplied with charcoal from the hills to the westward. The ore is brought upon buffaloes and asses. It is in small slaty fragments, that are broken to pieces with a stone, and thus separated from much sand and earth. These small pieces, when fit for the furnace, are about the size of a hazel-nut. The operation ought to be performed at the mine, to lessen the expense of carriage; but the danger from tigers prevents the people from staying there longer than is absolutely necessary. The number of these ferocious animals having increased of late, has forced the people to relinquish a mine named *Buca Sagurada Canavay,* which is distant from the other one coss toward the N.W. Even *Cudera Canavay* has now become very dangerous, and in the course of the last year three people have been destroyed.

The manner of smelting and forging the iron is exactly similar to that used at *Doray-guda,* which I have described in the seventh chapter of this Journal, Vol. II. p. 35, 38. At the two furnaces here are employed twenty-two men: nine to make charcoal, one to dig the ore, one to bring it from the hill (he is supplied by the proprietor with two buffaloes), one iron-smith at the forging

CHAPTER XIX. May 3. furnace, six bellows-men, and four hammer-men. They can smelt twice a day; but the sickness of any one of the party stops the whole operation, and they meet also with frequent interruptions from holidays, and from heavy rain. On such occasions, some of the workmen remain entirely idle, and others take day labour from the farmers. Each smelting requires five baskets of prepared ore, one basket weighing 1172 *Dudus*, or rather more than $29\frac{1}{2}$ lb. The smelting also requires ten baskets of charcoal; each weighing 514 *Dudus*, or $13\frac{81}{100}$ lb. The weight of the charcoal is therefore nearly equal to that of the ore; but the imperfection of the furnace renders the operation very incomplete. The metal is never liquefied by the greatest heat which the natives can excite; the particles are only so softened as to adhere together, while the earthy matters are half vitrified. When the smelting succeeds properly, the mass of iron is forged into twenty-one plough-shares; when it succeeds ill, it yields only fifteen. Those pieces of iron weigh on an average 75 *Dudus*; so that the greatest produce of the ore is less than 27 *per cent.* of malleable iron; while the workmen sometimes are able to extract little more than 19 *per cent.*; but this is probably more owing to their want of skill, than to the poverty of the ore. The plough-share is worth $\frac{1}{4}$ *Fanam;* so that the iron sells for rather more than 7*s.* $3\frac{3}{4}$*d.* a hundred weight. The workmen are paid by a division of the iron. Every 42 plough-shares are thus distributed;

To the proprietor - - - -	11
To the 9 charcoal makers - - -	9
To the iron-smith - - - -	$3\frac{1}{2}$
To the 4 hammer-men - - -	7
To the 6 bellows-men - - -	8
To the miner - - - - -	1
To the buffalo driver - - -	$2\frac{1}{2}$
	42

May 3.

By this it would appear, that the expense of the fire amounts to $\frac{9}{42}$ parts of the whole value of the iron. The utmost that a common labourer can make at this work is $1\frac{1}{2}$ penny a day; but should the operation succeed ill, he may get only $1\frac{35}{100}$ penny. This being very small wages, the workmen have probably concealed some part of their profit. The expenses of the proprietors are as follow;

For bellows - - -	*Fanams* 100
For sacrifices - - - - - -	30
For tax to government - - - -	375
	505

For this, when the operations succeed, he is repaid by 45 days working, and all the remainder of what he receives is clear profit; for the workmen build the huts and furnaces, which are exceedingly rude; and the iron-smith provides hammers, anvils, forceps, and every implement except the bellows.

Nail makers.

There is here a small manufacture of horse-shoes and hob-nails. It contains three anvils, at each of which are employed five men; one who manages the iron, and who furnishes all the tools; one who manages the fire; one to work the bellows; one to hammer the iron, as it is held by the foreman; and one who finishes the nail by giving it a head. The utmost that five men at one anvil can make in a day is 1200 nails. The four last mentioned workmen provide charcoal. Their wages are,

To the foreman 2 *Jumshiry Pagodas* for the month of 30 working days, or rather less than $6\frac{1}{4}$ pence a day.

To each of the other workmen 1 *Pagoda*, or $3\frac{1}{8}$ pence a day. One half of their time is probably employed in preparing charcoal. 36,000 hob-nails cost for manufacturing 6 *Pagodas*, or almost 2*l.* 6*s.* $9\frac{3}{4}$*d.*

May 4. Appearance of the country.

4th *May.*—I went one coss south, to see the mine at *Cudera Canavay*; and having examined it, I returned to *Chica-bayli-caray*. The road passes through a valley surrounded by low hills, and about half way there is a fortified village. At the bottom of the hill on which

CHAPTER XIX. the mine is, there is a plain of a very good soil, which would be the most proper place of residence for the smelters.

May 4. A *Jatram* of *Hanumanta.* On the road, I met with an image of *Hanumanta*, going on an annual visit that he makes to his master at a *temple* called *Raméswara*. From the neighbouring villages he was attended by all the better sort of inhabitants, male and female, young and old; the *Sivabhactars* excepted, who abominate both this idol and that of his master *Vishnu*. The people composing the train of the god were very irregular and disorderly; but they had collected together a number of flags, and insignia of honour, with every thing that could be found in the country capable of making a noise. The men who carried the idol said, that the god would rest himself at a *Mandapum* near *Raméswara*, and allow his followers to assemble, and form themselves into some order; after which he would visit the image of *Ráma;* and, having returned to the *Mandapam*, he would sit in state, while for his amusement the people played before this building. The *Bráhmans* would then sell them some victuals, which were consecrated by having been dressed in the temple, and offered to the god with the proper incantations (*Mantrams*). Having feasted on these, the image would return to his own temple, attended as on his outset. This is what is called a *Jatram;* and had the image been that of one of the great gods, it would have been carried in a *Rath*, or chariot; but for *Hanumanta* a litter is sufficient.

Mine at *Cudera Canavay.* *Cudera Canavay*, or the horse-hill, is a hummock about a hundred and fifty feet in perpendicular height. The north end is steepest, the slope toward the south being gentle. The east and west sides also are pretty steep. The natives say, that *Doray-guda* is about ten cosses to the S.E. and that there is a continued ridge of low hills extending the whole way between the two mines; but none of them contain ore.

The surface of *Cudera Canavay* is smooth, and is not interrupted by rocks. The soil is a poor red earth. I saw only one lump of *hæmatites;* and that, when compared with the fine masses lying on the surface of *Doray-guda*, is very poor, and ill-formed. The whole extent of the hill is not great, and the miners have contented themselves with digging the ore from the surface of the hill near its summit. No shaft nor pit having been made, I cannot form any estimate of the quantity of ore remaining. The mine appears to be much richer than that of *Doray*; for the quantity of barren stone intermixed with the ore is very small. This barren stone resembles the ore very much; and, no doubt, could the natives extract it, contains much iron. The specimen which I have brought away, has concentric layers somewhat like a log of wood. The superficial earth in most places is not above a foot thick. On digging into it, the miner comes to a mixture of ochres, earth, and ore, in a tabular form. This mixture sometimes extends in depth so far as has been wrought, which no where, that I saw, exceeded five or six feet. In other places the miner meets with large masses of ore, consisting of a number of plates united together like schistus. This by the miners is called black iron-stone. These masses have a tendency to divide into rhomboidal fragments. In other places, the ore is found in a number of flat pieces, divided by fissures into parallelograms, perhaps three inches long, two broad, and one thick. These fragments are placed in layers contiguous to one another; but they are separated by the slightest force, the fissures being filled up with reddish ochre. By the workmen this is called red-ore; and because it is taken out of the mine with the least trouble, it is most esteemed. All the kinds, when broken to small pieces, and rendered proper for the furnace, are quite the same. The manner of working is very simple. The miner forms a cut with a perpendicular surface, and throws all the rubbish down the declivity. He then continues cutting down from the hill, with his perpendicular surface, two or three feet in height. He works with a pick-ax, and cuts promiscuously through earth, stones, and ore. Having brought down a sufficient quantity, he rubs the fragments; and, having picked out the smaller pieces of ore,

CHAPTER XIX. May

he throws down the hill all the earth, ochres, barren stone, and larger masses of ore; for the trouble of breaking any of these into lumps the size of the fist, is greater than that of cutting down more from the hill. I observed nothing like strata in the mine, and look upon the present shape assumed by the ore, as of very recent date. From the rubbish thrown down by former miners, which consists in a great measure of ferrugineous particles, these have, I imagine, united into their present form; and the layers may be often observed intermixed with the roots of vegetables. Indeed, the process is probably now regularly going on; and until the hill be entirely consumed, the mine may be continued to be wrought in the same manner as it is at present.

Strata near the mine.

On the N.E. side of the hill, from which I ascended, the strata are in general vertical, and run from S. easterly to N. westerly. They are of quartz blended with hornblende, forming a hard, very tough, and sonorous stone, intersected with fissures, but free from venigenous matters, and having a slaty structure, with plates from an inch to a foot in thickness. In other places, this stone is not vertical, but has only a dip toward the east. In this I frequently observed the quartz and hornblende disposed in alternate layers; that is to say, certain alternate thin portions of the quartz were less impregnated with the hornblende than those that intervened. From the disposition of these, the stone looked as if at one time it had been fluid, and had then undergone an undulating motion; for the different coloured portions were disposed somewhat like the colours on marbled paper, or like the fibres in a knot of timber. To give a proper idea of this would require a specimen ten feet in diameter; but even in the specimen which I brought away, it is observable, although that has suffered a considerable decay. I had no means of breaking a specimen from the centre of the rock.

Here I also observed a rock of a similar nature, but divided into rhomboidal fragments by wide fissures, some of which were empty, and others filled with veins of fat quartz, which must therefore be of later origin. This resembled the rock described in the seventh chapter of my Journal, Vol. II. p. 43, at *Malaiswara Pagoda*, near *Madana Mada*, which is about eight cosses from hence toward the S.E. There, however, the veins of quartz formed a complete net-work, involving the fragments of the original stone, which contained little or no hornblende. CHAPTER XIX. May 4.

5th *May*.—I went to *Muteodu*, distant three cosses. On the way I passed through three little vallies, containing a good deal of rice-ground, with plantations of coco and *betel nut* palms. These seemed to be very ruinous. In the first valley I passed a large fortified village, named *Cagala Cutty*, which on each side had a fine tank. Where I crossed the second valley, there were also two fine tanks, that supplied the rice-grounds of thirty villages, among which the most distinguished was called *Lacky hully*. These villages having been laid waste, the valley has since become so infested by tigers, that the few remaining inhabitants are daily deserting it. The third valley is the smallest. May 5. Appearance of the country.

Muteodu is situated in a valley similar to the others, but much wider. Near it is a fine reservoir, which however at a moderate expense might be greatly improved. When the rainy season commences early, this tank supplies water for two crops of rice in the year, and never fails to afford a supply for one crop. The farmers do not commence cultivation until the *Tank* is full, as then they are secure from all accidents. The *Vedawáti* is distant one coss to the west. Its banks, according to the natives, afford many places where dams might be formed to great advantage. At a place called *Mari Canavay*, they say, that by building a mound between two hills 500 yards distant, an immense reservoir might be formed, which would convert a large proportion of the *Heriuru* district *(Taluc)* into rice-grounds. It would, however, inundate the present situation of many villages. At *Cangundy*, in the *Garuda giri* district, a dam might be constructed for 3000 *Pagodas*, that in three years would repay itself by the increase of revenue. Irrigation.

CHAPTER XIX.

May 5. History of the *Mutcodu Polygars.*

In the reign of *Krishna Ráya*, a native of *Lacky hully*, named *Ghiriuppa Nayaka*, was in the service of the king at *Anagundi*, and was a person of extraordinary strength and courage. An elephant, having broken loose, had got into the court-house, and could not be secured, until *Ghiriuppa* boldly seized on him by the tusks, and, having fastened a rope to his trunk, led him to the stables. As a reward for his intrepidity, the king created *Ghiriuppa Polygar* of his native town *Lacky hully*, with villages in the neighbourhood to the annual value of 9000 *Pagodas*, or 3120*l.* 8*s.* 4*d.* His tribute was 300 *Pagodas* a year, and he was bound to support 700 foot soldiers. In case of war, he left 300 of these in the country for its defence, and for the maintenance of order; and he was bound to join the king's standard with 400 men, whom he commanded in person. While on this service, he received five *Pagodas* a day, or about 31*s.* 3*d.* for his own subsistence; and the same sum for the subsistence of his whole corps. There have been twelve *Polygars* of this family; and *Haluppa Nayaka*, the present representative, from whom I have this account, is an elderly man. He says, that the nephew of *Ghiriuppa* removed the seat of government to *Muteodu*. When the *Chatrakal Polygars* became powerful, those of *Muteodu*, who, although they wear the *Linga*, are of the same family, submitted to the authority of their kinsmen. Their tribute was increased to 500 *Pagodas* a year, and they supported the former military establishment. *Haluppa* married a daughter of the last *Chatrakal Rájá;* but although she is still living, he has no children. When he observed the power of *Hyder* increasing, he was induced to assist that artful chief in the first siege of *Chatrakal*. After that was raised, his father-in-law, justly enraged at his conduct, attacked his country. In the month *Ashádha* of the year *Velumbi*, he laid siege to *Muteodu*, and three days afterwards took it by assault. Having plundered the town, he carried his rebellious son-in-law to *Chatrakal*, where he was kept in close confinement, but without ill usage, until he was released by

Hyder, who took that city in *Mágha* of the same year, or about the beginning of the year of our Lord 1778. *Haluppa*, although released from prison, was entirely neglected by *Hyder*, and never was restored to any part of his territory; a treatment that he richly merited. He retired at first to *Hagalawadi*; but twelve years ago he returned to *Muteodu*, where he occupies a hut, and lives in great poverty. His palace has in a great measure gone to ruin; but some portion of it has been lately repaired for a public office, and for the residence of the *Amildar*.

CHAPTER XIX. May 5.

Muteodu.

The fort of *Muteodu* never was strong: but in *Haluppa's* government it contained about 2000 houses, which are now reduced to 120.

Glass manufactory.

The most remarkable thing about the place is a manufacture of the glass that is used for making the rings which are worn round the wrists of the native women, and are called *Ballay* in the language of *Karnata*, and *Bangri*, or *Bangadi*, in that of the Mussulmans. The glass is very coarse and opaque, and much mor eof it is made than is here wrought up into ornaments. Great quantities of it are bought by the *Bangri-makers* from the westward. It is of five colours; black, green, red, blue, and yellow: the first is in most demand.

All the materials for making the glass are found in the neighbourhood; but their value cannot be ascertained, as the glass-makers pay a rent for them, and collect them by means of their own workmen; so that they are never sold.

Soulu Munnu, or soda.

In the hot season, the *Soulu Munnu*, or *soda* in the form of a white efflorescence, is found in several places near this, on the surface of sandy fields. Little of it now remains; for there have been several showers, which have washed away the greater part. For the exclusive privilege of collecting it, the glass-makers pay 48 *Ca. Pagodas* (14*l.* 19*s.* 8¼*d.*) They make it into cakes, in the same manner as the people of *Chena-pattana* do; a process that I have described in the third chapter of this Journal, Vol. I. p. 150, &c. The intention of making it into these cakes is probably to free it from earthy

CHAPTER XIX. May 5.

matter; but for making glass, this is perhaps no advantage, as the earth with which it is mixed is chiefly a quartzose sand. These cakes contain at least one half of their bulk of cow-dung, and from that cause are in fact inflammable. They are prepared for making glass by being burned, and of course afford an exceedingly impure alkali. It might be procured pure by lixiviation, and filtrating it through barrows of earth, as is usually done in India with culinary salt. The only objection to this is the scarcity of fewel, although much of the evaporation might be performed by the sun.

Glassmaker's furnace very bad.

The glass-maker's furnace here is rather better than that of *Chena-pattana*; but still it is extremely rude. The manufacturers say, that when the army of Lord Cornwallis left *Seringapatam*, they gathered with much pains a great number of broken bottles, which they found where he had encamped. These they thought a treasure; but, after having been at the expense of bringing the bottles to *Muteodu*, they found, that their furnace was not sufficiently strong to liquefy European glass. The bottles were then reduced to powder, and mixed with alkali; but these materials produced only an useless white mass. Our glass, therefore, is considered by them as useless as our cast iron; for neither of these substances are in a state upon which the fires of the natives have any effect.

Form of the furnace.

The furnaces are constructed in a high terrace, which is built against the inside of the town-wall, and are in form of a dome, or like an oven, eight feet in diameter, and about ten feet in height. The annexed section of one furnace (Plate XXXIII. Figure 81) will assist the reader to comprehend the description. The oven is not arched, but contracted above into a circular opening, about eighteen inches in diameter, by making the upper rows of stones project beyond those below them. At the bottom of the furnace, in the side opposite to the town-wall, is a small opening, through which the fewel is supplied. The crucibles are oblong, as in the figure, and would contain about 5½ Winchester gallons. Having been filled with the materials, they are lowered down into the furnace by the aperture in the top, by which also the workmen descend. They first place a row of the crucibles all round the furnace, with their bottoms to the wall, and their mouths sloping inwards. In this position they are secured by a bed of clay, which covers the crucibles entirely, leaving their open mouths only exposed. Above this row another is placed in a similar manner, and then a third and a fourth. The furnaces vary in size, from such as can contain fifty crucibles thus disposed, to such as can contain twice that number. The fewel consists of small sticks, which having been gathered a year are quite dry. A quantity having been put in the bottom of the furnace, the workmen ascend, and some burning coals are thrown upon the fewel. By the opening below, fresh fewel is added night and day, until the time allowed for vitrifying the materials has expired. The fire is then allowed to burn out, and the furnace to cool. Afterwards the workmen descend, and take out the crucibles, which must be broken to get at their contents.

Frit, or *Bilizu.*

The first operation is to make a frit, called *Bilizu*. The materials for this are, powdered white fat quartz 1 part; and prepared soda, or *Soulu*, 6 parts: the crucibles are filled with these mixed; and the fire is kept up five days. Every crucible gives a *Maund* of 40 *Cucha Seers*, or $24\frac{1}{4}$lb. of *Bilizu*.

Black glass.

To make the black glass: for every 40 crucibles, take prepared soda 1 *Candy*, or $18\frac{08}{100}$ bushels; and powdered frit $\frac{1}{4}$ *Candy*, or $4\frac{52}{100}$ bushels: mix them, and fill the crucibles. The crucibles having been put into the furnace, a fire is kept up for eight days and nights; so that the flame rises three cubits above the aperture at the top of the dome. Each crucible gives a *Maund*, or $24\frac{1}{4}$ pounds of glass, of a black, or rather of an intensely dark grass-green colour. It sells for 4 *Fanams* the *Maund*, or 11*s.* $6\frac{1}{4}$*d.* a cwt. It is evident from this, that only $\frac{1}{35}$ of the materials employed are silicious earth; the remainder is the impure salt called prepared *Soulu*. During the operation, part of this is dissipated; and part of it forms on the surface of the glass a pure white crust, an inch in thickness. This is

CHAPTER XIX.

used by the inhabitants for culinary salt, but in fact it is chiefly soda.

May 5. Green glass.

To make green glass: for 40 crucibles, take 1 *Candaca*, or $18\frac{98}{100}$ bushels of prepared *Soulu*; 5 *Colagas*, or $4\frac{51}{100}$ bushels of powdered frit; 1 *Maund*, or $24\frac{1}{4}$lb. of the powder of an ore called *Kemudu*; 4 *Seers*, or $2\frac{2}{10}$lb. of an ore called *Cari-cullu*; and 24 *Seers*, or $13\frac{2}{10}$lb. of calcined copper reduced to powder. These materials having been mixed and put into the crucibles, these are properly disposed in the furnace, and a fire is kept up for nine days and nine nights. For the first five days the fewel is added slowly, so that the flame just rises to the aperture; and afterwards it is not necessary to occasion quite so great a heat as for the frit, or black glass. The copper is calcined by burning it, on the fire-place in the bottom of the furnace, during the whole nine days that are required to make this glass. Each crucible produces 1 *Maund* and 12 *Seers* of green glass, which sells at 6 *Fanams* the *Maund*, or 17*s.* $3\frac{1}{4}$*d.* a cwt. The saline crust, formed on the surface of this glass, is considered by the natives as unfit for eating.

Red glass.

To make the red glass: for every 40 crucibles, take the same quantity of prepared *Soulu*, and frit, together with 5 *Maunds*, or $121\frac{1}{4}$lb. of powdered *Kemudu*. For fifteen days and nights these must be fused with a moderate fire. Each crucible gives $1\frac{1}{4}$ *Maund* of glass, which sells for 6 *Fanams* a *Maund*, or 17*s.* $3\frac{1}{4}$*d.* a hundred weight.

Blue glass.

To make the blue glass: for every 40 crucibles, take the same quantity of prepared soda, and powdered frit, as for the others. To these add 24 *Seers*, or $13\frac{2}{10}$lb. of calcined copper, and an equal quantity of powdered *Cari-cullu*. For fifteen days and nights these materials also must be burned, with a moderate fire. Formerly, the workmen used to put in only twelve *Seers* of calcined copper, with an equal quantity of a blue substance called *Runga*. The merchant, however, who supplied them with this article, having died, they have not for some time past procured any, and have been obliged to make up the deficiency by a double proportion of copper. What the *Runga* is, I cannot say. The natives know that it is not blue vitriol: it may perhaps be smalts.

CHAPTER XIX.

May 5.

Yellow glass.

To make *Hulledi*, or yellow glass: for every 40 crucibles, take the usual quantity of prepared soda; add to it 5 *Colagas*, or 4 $\frac{52}{100}$ bushels of native soda, from which all the small stones have been picked, but which of course contains a good deal of sand. For fifteen days these are burned with a slow fire. Each crucible gives a *Maund* of a wax-coloured glass, which sells for four *Fanams* a *Maund*, or 11*s.* 6$\frac{1}{4}$*d.* a cwt. When this glass is wrought up into rings (*Bangris*), it receives a bright yellow colour by enamelling it with the melted *calces* of the following metals: 5 parts of lead, and one of tin are calcined together. Then one part of *Sotu*, or zinc, is calcined in a separate crucible. The two *calces* are then mixed, and farther calcined, until they begin to adhere together. They are then powdered in a mortar. When the (*Bangri*) ring-maker is at work, he melts some of this powder; and, while the ring is hot, with an iron rod he applies a little of the powder to the surface of the glass.

May 6th. Weather.

6th *May*.—In the evening of the 5th there was much thunder, with heavy squalls of wind from every quarter of the compass, and some severe showers of rain. The thunder continued all night, and the morning looked so threatening that I did not set out till after breakfast. The weather, however, has now become so cool, that I did not feel the least inconvenience from being all day in the open air.

I had intended going to *Hosso-durga*, and had sent my spare tents to that place; but, finding it necessary to look after the mines, which produce the ores called *Kemodu* and *Cari-cullu*, I was obliged to alter my plan. Neither could I get any accurate information concerning the situation of these mines; some of those even, who were employed in bringing the ore, called them two

CHAPTER XIX.

cosses distant, while others stated their distance at three times as much.

May 6. Mine of *Cari-cullu.*

I went first in search of the *Cari-cullu*, and proceeded on the way by which I came yesterday, till I reached the small valley nearest *Muteodu*, distant from thence about ½ of a coss, or two miles. Here I passed a small village named *Sida Gondana hully*, and came to a low hill, which is called *Malaya Maluppa*, after a temple dedicated to *Siva*. This hill forms the eastern boundary of the valley, and is of no considerable height. The mine of *Cari-cullu* is on its ascent, and is readily discernible from a number of bluish-black stones, that lie on the surface of the ground. No excavation has been made. The *Cari-cullu* is found, in detached masses, on the surface, mixed with the stones. These stones are often so much tinged by the metal, as hardly to be distinguishable from it; but are known by being broken, when their stony nature appears evident. Some of them, when broken, appear internally to have undergone little change, and are evidently fat white quartz; the appearance of the internal parts of others has been so much altered, that had I not observed them in all intermediate gradations, I should never have supposed them to have been of a quartzy nature. The masses of stone are much more numerous than those of the *Cari-cullu*, owing probably to the quantity of the last that has been removed from the surface. Deeper in the earth it is probably found in a great proportion, but there has been no occasion to make any experiment by digging. The extent of ground which the mine occupies may be about 200 yards square. The *Cari-cullu* literally signifies the black stone. It is found in masses about the size of the fist, and has a very strong resemblance to the black ore of *Manganese*. By the usual process, however, for discovering the *calx* of that metal, I have not been able to obtain any; nor indeed any thing else, except a brown *calx* of iron. The ore however, when heated, readily gives out a considerable quantity of *oxygene*.

CHAPTER XIX.

May 6.

Strata near the mine.

Immediately N.W. from the mine, and on the declivity of the same hill, is a singular *stratum* of rock. It has every appearance of a rock that has formed the channel of a river, being water-worn, and excavated into round pits or pots, exactly like the rocks on which a rapid stream has long acted. This is an appearance, concerning which any one, who has been accustomed to a mountainous, well-watered country, can hardly be mistaken; yet, as the rock is situated on the declivity of a hill, and has a valley immediately below it, and parallel to its course, it is impossible, without a total change having taken place in the face of the country, that it could have formed the bottom of a river. At present there is no stream in the valley. This rock runs nearly north and south, and is quite vertical. It is a *Sienite;* sometimes of a homogeneous grey colour, and at other times composed of alternate grey and white layers, which last consist of the quartz and felspar entirely. These layers are of very various thicknesses, and are sometimes straight, and sometimes disposed in swirls, like a knot of timber. Although it has the appearance of having suffered much decay, this stone possesses a very high degree of toughness.

Appearance of the country.

Having examined this mine, I returned almost to *Muteodu*, and then proceeded south to a small village, named *Cadu-caray*, three cosses distant. The country is not hilly, and in most places is fit for the plough; but almost the whole is waste. I saw only one village, named *Chica Taycu-lawati;* but I passed several small collections of huts belonging to *Goalaru*, or keepers of cattle. Toward the east was a range of hills, running from *Chatrakal* to *Chica Nayakana hully*. Toward the west is a level country, interspersed with a few low detached hills. On the most remarkable of these is placed *Hosso-durga*, or the new castle.

Strata.

The soil is in general poor, and the rocky *strata* frequently come to view. Among these are very extensive *strata* of quartz, and of quartz intermixed with felspar of a white colour. Intermixed with

CHAPTER XIX.

these are *strata* of white quartz, and black mica, disposed in alternate layers, firmly united, and forming a very hard stone.

May 6. *Budihalu Taluc.*

Cadu-caray is in *Budihalu* district, and is under the management of the *Amildar* of *Muteodu*, although it does not form a part of the *Chatrakal* principality. The *Amildar*, therefore, accounts to the *Subadar* of *Chatrakal* for *Muteodu*, and to the *Dewan* of *Mysore* for *Budihalu*. In the time of the kings of *Anagundi* the districts of *Budihalu* formed the territory of a *Polygar*, named *Shirmia Nayaka*, who was of the *Goala* cast. It was then valued at 12,000 *C. Pagodas*, or 3744*l.* 9*s.* 7*d.* a year; but of this he paid one half as tribute. After the Mussulmans had taken *Sira* from the *Ratna-giri Polygars*, and had made it the residence of a *Nabob*, or *Subadar*, they seized on *Budihalu*, and soon afterwards it was given in *Jaghire* to *Ismael Mummud Khan;* he transmitted it to his son of the same name; from whom it was taken by *Hyder*, after he had conquered *Sira*. *Ismael Mummud Khan* raised the revenue to 20,000 *Pagodas* a year (6240*l.* 15*s.* 11$\frac{1}{4}$). Owing to a want of inhabitants, *Purnea* has reduced the revenue to 15,000 *Pagodas;* but were there plenty of cultivators, the former revenue, it is said, would not bear hard on them. North from *Cadu-caray* is a small river, that never entirely dries, and is named *Marana Canaray holay*. It comes from the hills to the westward; and after filling two *tanks*, runs into the *Vedávati* at *Niruvugullu*.

May 7. Mines on *Doda Rashy Guda.* Smelting of the ore.

7th *May*—I went in the morning to examine the mine of *Kemodu*, and another of iron, concerning which I had received intelligence on the preceding evening. The ore is smelted here in the same manner as at *Chica-bayli-caray*. When the process fails, a brittle porous mass is obtained, which has a greater resemblance to our cast iron than any thing that I have seen produced in India. This mass is fused in a furnace of lower power, and gives an iron softer than the common kind; and from this soft iron are usually formed the hoes, and other digging instruments of the natives.

CHAPTER XIX.

May 7. Appearance of the hill.

Doda Rashy Guda, or great heap hill, which contains the mines, is a peak about three hundred feet in height, and a mile in length, that forms part of a ridge running nearly north and south, and lying east from *Cadu-caray*. Between the mine and this village is another ridge, on the northern extremity of which is a temple dedicated to *Ranga*, and named *Mavana Canavay*, from which the rivulet so called has its source.

Strata.

As I ascended this nearest ridge, the first rock which I met was an earthy quartz, or hornstone, divided by fissures in all directions, and having some of these fissures filled with veins of white quartz. This rock is not vertical, but dips much toward the east. Further on, the common rock consists of alternate parallel layers, firmly united, of white arid quartz, and of brown iron shot quartz, or hornstone. These layers are sometimes plain, and at others disposed in swirls; and as the stone in decay, by the attrition of its longitudinal angles, has a great tendency to assume a cylindrical form, and always breaks in masses truncated at right angles to the layers, it is often found in pieces which have a strong resemblance to petrified wood. The stone does not break regularly in the direction of the layers, which are disposed in the same line with the strata. These are vertical, and run nearly north and south. I am by no means sure of the nature of the brown part of this stone. It may very possibly be hornblende overcharged with iron; and the *Sienite* found yesterday nearly in the direction of its strata, strongly confirms this opinion.

Kemodu.

Between the two ridges I came to the channel of a rivulet, named *Aladi-holay*, which at present is quite dry. Heré I found the place whence the glass-makers procure the ore called *Kemodu*. For about three quarters of a mile the bed of the rivulet is filled with stones of a steel-grey colour. Many of these are the iron ore called *Kemodu*. It is in water-worn masses, from the size of a man's head downwards, and possesses the external characters of the grey ore of *Manganese*. When powdered, it is attracted by the magnet.

CHAPTER XIX. May 7.

Intermixed with the *Kemodu* are other masses of a similar appearance, but which are useless. On breaking these, they are found to be in all intermediate stages of maturation, from the common rock before described, to almost perfect ore.

Source of the *Kemodu*.

On ascending the eastern bank of the rivulet, beyond the mine of *Kemodu*, I came to a conical peak on the eastern ridge; and observed, that all the stones on its side were stained with the steel grey of that ore. I saw none perfect on it; but on breaking the stones I found them in all stages, from the rude rock, to a state approaching to maturity. Indeed, many grains of pure *Kemodu* were very discernible, imbedded thickly in the substance of these stones.

Common iron ore.

Immediately south from this, is the peak called *Doda Rashy Guda*, whence the iron ore which supplies the forges is procured. This ore is quite the same with the black kind at *Cudera Canivay*, but it is disposed in a different manner. It is imbedded in large irregular cavities of the barren stone, or matrix. This consists of plates that are separable without much difficulty, and which, I have no doubt, are the brown layers of the common stone of the hill separated by the white ones having been corroded by iron. It is, no doubt, a primeval rock; and its strata may be traced running in the direction of the meridian, and in general vertically. The ore is similarly composed of plates; and fibres of the roots of plants are found to have penetrated into the interstices; but this, I am inclined to think, has happened after the surface has been exposed by the miners. I also suppose, that the ore has once been the common stone of the hill, and has afterwards been more and more impregnated with iron by some process unknown to us; in the same manner as, I suppose, has taken place in the ore called *Kemodu*. The various gradations from the perfect stone to the perfect ore is the circumstance that induces me to form this opinion. A portion of the rock, having been cut down with a vertical smooth face about three feet deep, presented an appearance similar to that in

Plate XXXIII. Fig. 82. The central parts are of the ore, and contain the roots of plants between their plates. The upper layers are of the barren matrix. I brought away, as a specimen, the upper extremity of the ore, with part of the matrix adhering. Owing to the nature of the mine, the manner of working it is somewhat different from that used at *Cudera Canivay*, and the workmen are forced to dig the ore from under the caverns of the matrix. I no where saw that they had ventured in farther than ten or twelve feet; so that I cannot say, whether or not the internal parts of the hill contain any veins, or rather beds, of ore. Openings have been made in various places for about a quarter of a mile in length, which seems to be the extent of the mine.

CHAPTER XIX. May 7.

Fine reservoir in ruins.

Having examined *Doda Rashy*, I descended by the banks of the *Aladi-holay*, till it came opposite to the temple of *Ranga*, where it joins the *Mavana Canavay*. Here both streams pass between the hill on which the temple stands, and one placed at no great distance to the north. The opening has been filled up by a mound, which, so long as it remained entire, formed a fine reservoir that watered a hundred *Candacas* of rice-land. The mound has long ago been broken; and it is said, that to repair it would cost three thousand *Pagodas*, or 936*l.* 2*s.* 4½*d.* As *Paddy*, when very cheap, sells at one *Pagoda* a *Candaca*, and as the government receives one half of the produce, which is here on an average forty seeds, even allowing that there should be only one crop in the year, the expense of rebuilding the tank would be repaid by less than two years rent.

Effects of low and high rent.

All over the *Chatrakal* principality, of which *Hosso-durga* forms a part, the rice crop is of little importance; the rent is no higher than that for dry grains, and little labour has been bestowed on irrigation. Here the rent is high, being one half, or even more, of the produce; the fields are very productive, and many excellent *Tanks* have been constructed. Most of these were made during the government of the *Shirmia* family.

CHAPTER XIX.

May 7. Unhealthiness of the climate.

From this ruinous *Tank* I went about two cosses to a fortified village, containing about forty houses, and called *Doda Tayculawati.* It is situated in the open country of the *Budihalu* district. The country is at present extremely unhealthy, even to those born in it. Almost every family has some person ill with the fever; and no less than eight persons in the house of the *Amildar* of *Budihalu* are now labouring under that disorder. The natives say, that the fever will stop immediately after the commencement of the rainy season. This year has been uncommonly unhealthy, owing to its having been unusually hot.

Wild date.

In every part of the *Budihalu* district the wild date *(Elate sylvestris)* is very common, but is of little use except for fuel. The present number of inhabitants cannot consume a hundredth part of the juice that could be extracted from it. This tree might be a source of considerable advantage, could a good spirit be extracted from its *Jagory*, of which I think there is little doubt; but from the wretched stills of the natives this can never be expected.

May 8. Appearance of the country.

8th *May.*—I went three cosses to *Belluguru*, and by the way passed two *Tanks* and villages. All the country near the road is level enough for the plough, and clear from trees; but, the army of *Purseram Bow* having passed this way, very little of it is cultivated. Some of the soil is rocky; a good deal is rich land; but by far the greater part is poor gravelly land; fit enough, however, for raising *Huruli (Dolichos biflorus)*, *Shamay (Panicum miliare* E. M.) and other such crops.

Belluguru.

Belluguru is a small fortified village with 150 houses. It suffered less than usual from the *Maruttahs*, as before the invasion of *Purseram* its houses amounted to only two hundred. It is a part of the *Garuda-giri* district, which has long formed a part of the dominions of the *Mysore* family. Near it is a very large reservoir.

Reservoir.

Owing to the mud deposited by the water, these *Tanks* fill gradually at the bottom; so that once in three or four years this mud must either be removed, or an addition must be made to the height of the bank; otherwise the reservoir becomes useless. The mud being an excellent manure for the neighbouring dry lands, as much of it as possible should be taken away, and spread on them. In other respects, the raising of the bank is the most advantageous manner of repairing a *Tank*, as it requires the least outlay of money. It offers also another advantage. If the sluice, through which the water is let out to irrigate the fields, were always raised to a level with the mud in the bottom of the *Tank*, as that was deposited, the extent of ground, which the *Tank* could irrigate, would always increase. This, it is true, would be attended with a considerable expense, and is never practised; so, in order that the plug which shuts the sluice may be kept clear, there is often a necessity of sinking a well ten or twelve feet in depth. The *Tank* here receives a stream forced by a dam from a rivulet, that comes from *Garuda-giri*, and which afterwards falls into a *Tank* called *Belallu Samudra*, which is one coss and a half N.W. from *Belluguru*.

CHAPTER XIX.

May 8.

Rice-ground.

In this district, and in the neighbouring one of *Budihalu*, all the rice-ground is cultivated as sprouted-seed. The seed, the natives here say, is sown equally thick in the two districts; yet in *Budihalu* the land often produces sixty fold, and the ordinary crop is forty seeds; while in this district of *Garuda-giri*, the usual produce is twenty seeds. I measured a field, said to sow three *Colagas* of seed, or 2673 cubical inches. It contained 46,636 square feet. The acre, therefore, requires 1 $\frac{161}{1000}$ bushel for seed, and produces here, in an ordinary crop, almost 23$\frac{1}{4}$ bushels of rough rice; while in *Budihalu* it produces twice, or even three times, as much. In the course of one year, there are frequently from the same field two crops of rice. The grain in the husk is worth one *Bahadery Pagoda* a *Candaca*, or 11 $\frac{66}{100}$ pence a bushel. The produce of one crop is, therefore, worth about a guinea an acre.

May 9.

9th *May*.—In the evening and night there was much loud

CHAPTER XIX.

May 9. Face of the country.

thunder, with heavy rain from the southward, but little wind. I went four cosses to *Garuda-giri*, or the hill of *Garuda*, the eagle on which *Vishnu* rides. It is often pronounced in the oblique case *Garudana-giri*, which, by the Mussulmans, is usually corrupted to *Gurruna-giri*; and in a map which I received, I find it called *Gurgan-droog*. The country through which I passed is flat, but the soil is rather poor. Almost the whole of it, however, is capable of being cultivated; but by the *Marattah* invasion it has been quite depopulated, and I passed only two small villages.

History of *Yagati*.

At one of these villages, named *Ana-giri*, in the *Yagati Taluc*, I met the *Amildar*. He says, that his district produces an annual revenue of 10,000 *Pagodas*, or 3120*l.* 8*s.* 4*d.* It formerly made a part of the *Garuda-giri* district, and belonged to the *Mysore Rájás*. On the occasion of an invasion by the *Nizam*, *Hunnama Nayaka*, *Polygar* of *Terri-caray*, rendered such assistance to the *(Curtur)* sovereign of *Mysore*, that he was rewarded by a cession of the *Yagati Taluc*. *Hyder* deprived the *Terri-caray* family of all their territories, ordered them to reside at *Manzúr-ábád*, and allowed them an annual pension of 2000 *Pagodas*, or 625*l.* 1*s.* 8*d.* They were by cast *Baydaru*, but of a different family from the *Rájás* of *Chatrakal*. During the reign of the *Sultan*, the present heir of the family enjoyed his pension. On the fall of *Seringapatam* he joined *Dundia*, and hanged three or four *Bráhmans*, who were his servants, and who refused to follow him in his mad enterprise. He afterwards repented, and, having submitted, was kept in irons for some time at *Seringapatam*. About two months ago, the *Amildar* says, this *Polygar* was liberated, and received the grant of a pension of thirty *Pagodas* a month.

Garuda-giri.

Garuda-giri at one time belonged to the *Ikeri Polygars*, from whom it was conquered by the family of *Mysore*. These built the *Durga*, or fort, which occupies the highest part of a short abrupt ridge, that by a strong imagination has been fancied to resemble one of the rude images of *Garuda*. The suburb *(Petta)* stands at the foot of the hill, and is fortified. During the government of *Tippoo*, it was the nominal capital *(Kasba)* of an *Asoph*; but that officer resided at *Chica-Nayakana-hully*, which is twelve cosses distant. *Garuda-giri* never was a large place, and at present contains only about forty houses. The *Amildar* is a *Sivabhactar*; as are also, according to him, by far the greater part of the neighbouring people; but in the public accompts, to be hereafter mentioned, very few of this sect are reported. CHAPTER XIX. May 9.

In all the country between this and *Seringapatam*, *Ragy* is the most common crop; and the cultivation of that grain prevails all the way towards *Baba Bodeens* hills, where the rice and *betel-nut* country begins. The rice-ground, according to the *Amildar*, produces on an average twenty fold.

In this part of the country there are many sheep, but few black cattle. The shepherds and their families live with their flocks. The men wrap themselves in a blanket, and sleep in the open air among the sheep. The women and children sleep under hemispherical baskets, about six feet in diameter, and wrought with leaves so as to turn the rain. At one side a small hole is left open, through which the poor creatures can creep, and this is always turned to leeward, there being nothing to cover it. I have not in any other country seen a habitation so very wretched. Shepherds.

Throughout the *Chatrakal* principality the roofs of the houses are terraced with mud, and this custom also commonly prevails over the eastern parts of *Mysore*, *Sira*, and *Colar*; but the fashion here is pent roofs. Although in every part of *Karnata* the materials for building huts are excellent, yet those with pent, and those with terraced roofs, look equally mean and rugged. Houses.

In a hill lying south from *Garuda-giri*, and called *Hiricul*, there are found both sandal-wood and lac. Owing to the increasing number of tigers, the collecting of this last has of late been given up. Lac and sandal.

10th *May*.—I went two long cosses to *Banawara*. The country May 10.

CHAPTER XIX. May 10. Appearance of the country.

through which I passed is scarcely any where too steep for the plough; but it is almost entirely waste, and much of it is overgrown with the wild date, which at present is only used for firewood. The chief cause of the desolation which is here visible is said to be the rapacity of the *Marattahs.* Within the memory of man this country has suffered two inroads, one about thirty years ago by *Trumbaca Mama,* and another by *Purseram Bow.*

Banawara.

Banawara is one of the best mud forts that I have seen; and, owing to its strength, it escaped from the fangs of the *Marattahs.* It is situated in a fine open country, on the side of a large *Tank* which is at present dry. The people are very subject to fevers, which cannot be attributed to the black clay; for the soil is dry and sandy. It formerly belonged to *Hari Hara Swaméswara Ráyá,* a *Polygar* descended from *Belalla Ráyá,* and of course of a most ancient family of the *Jain* religion. The ruins of their palace still occupy a considerable space, and are surrounded by a very high wall, which even now is in good repair. The buildings within have been mean, and are almost entirely ruinous. This family was destroyed by *Ballu Khan,* a *Mussulman* chief. He was expelled by a *Bayda* named *Timuppa Nayaka;* he again was driven out by the *Shivabhactars* of *Ikeri;* and from them the place was taken by *Chica Deva Ráya Wodear* of *Mysore,* the 7th in ascent from the *Curtur* whom *Hyder* confined. On that chief's getting possession of the government, *Banawara* contained about 2000 houses; but most of the inhabitants, with those of five other towns, were removed to occupy a new city, named *Naga-puri.*

Naga-puri.

In order, probably, to secure these people and their effects from the *Marattahs, Hyder* built the fort of *Naga puri* in a small valley, which is about half a coss in extent each way, and is surrounded on all sides by low hills, like those of *Chatrakal.* These hills appear to extend about two cosses from east to west, and three cosses from north to south. *Naga-puri,* which stood three cosses from *Banawara,* was found to be excessively unhealthy; and its situation did not prevent it from being plundered by the *Marattahs*. *Hyder*, therefore, eighteen months after having built it, allowed the people to return to their former abodes. CHAPTER XIX. May 10.

Tippoo bestowed some attention in encouraging the people of *Banawara*. On the fall of *Seringapatam*, *Hunnama Nayaka*, an uncle of the *Polygar* of *Terri-caray*, seized on the fort, and kept possession for two months and a half. On the approach of a detachment of British troops, his followers dispersed; and the newly appointed *Amildar*, who was in the neighbourhood with 300 *Candashara*, seized him, and hung him up directly. At present, *Banawara* contains 500 houses, many of which are inhabited by *Bráhmans*. *Banawara.*

The cultivators being scarce, the officers of revenue fall on a curious plan of increasing the appearance of cultivation, and of thus getting credit for having their districts in good condition. This is a very common practice, I am told, in every part of the south of India, and is as follows. In place of letting at the full rent, to the few inhabitants that remain, as much land as they can cultivate, the *Amildars* give no man more than what his family originally possessed; but, when he has finished the cultivation of his paternal farm, the tenant is forced to plough and sow as much of the waste fields as he can; and, in order to increase the quantity, no money rent is demanded; but the government is contented with a share of the produce, which is very small, the cultivation having been performed in a very imperfect manner. Lands forced on the cultivators.

Some of the rice-lands here are let for a money rent, and some by a division of crops, which the *Amildars* allege is much the best mode of assessment in a country where the quantity of rain is so uncertain. If the rains do not come, the tenant cannot pay his rent; and if they come in abundance, it is but fair, that the government should reap a part of the benefit. This reasoning is specious; but the division of crops, except under the immediate inspection of a small proprietor, gives such opening to fraud, that it ought to be utterly discarded. For the uncertainty of the seasons an easy Division of crops.

CHAPTER XIX. May 10.

remedy occurs. As, before the cultivation commences, it is exactly known, what extent of ground the water in the *Tank* will irrigate, those persons, in case of a scarcity of rain, may be exempted from rent, who cannot cultivate their fields; and there is no occasion for any favour being shown to those who can get a supply of water.

Rice-land. In this district *(Taluc)* good rice-land lets at twenty *Bahadury Pagodas* a *Candaca*, which the cultivators say is equal to the value of one half of the grain produced; for they acknowledge, that this ground produces forty fold, and value each *Candaca* at one *Pagoda*. This, however, is a low valuation; for the *Candaca* here contains 24,480 cubical inches; so that at this rate the bushel of rough rice would cost rather under $8\frac{1}{4}$*d.* The produce of the soil here, and in the *Budihalu* district, is acknowledged to be nearly the same; while in the intermediate district of *Garuda-giri*, the people acknowledge only half the quantity. The people of *Banawara* say, that their neighbours did not impose upon me; but that their soil is actually inferior. I measured a plot, which was said to require a *Colaga* of seed, and found that it contained 23,255 square feet. At this rate, the acre will require for seed $1\frac{967}{1000}$ bushel nearly, which agrees very well with the measurement at *Belluguru*. The acre here produces $42\frac{67}{100}$ bushels of rough rice, and pays 15*s.* 1*d.* of rent, which is reckoned the value of one half of the grain produced; but this is valued by at least one fourth too little.

Tobacco. In the neighbouring districts of *Garuda-giri*, *Banawara*, *Caduru*, *Hárana-hully*, *Honawully*, and *Chin'-ráya-pattana*, the cultivation of tobacco is very considerable. It is exported in large quantities to all the countries toward the north and west. It is sown in the dry field, cultivated for *Ragy* and other similar grains, of which a crop must intervene between every two crops of tobacco. When the season proves very wet, it cannot be cultivated, and it requires a good *Ragy* soil. A few small stones do no harm, but it will not grow on the hard soil called *Darray;* and, in fact, the soil of the first quality is that usually employed, though sometimes the tobacco is planted on the best fields of the second quality. In the three months following the vernal equinox, the field ought, if possible, to be ploughed ten times; but some of these ploughings are often neglected. After the 4th or 5th time, sheep and cattle must for some nights be kept on the field for manure. During the last fifteen days of the second month after midsummer, small holes are made throughout the field. They are formed with the hand, and disposed in rows distant from each other 1½ cubit; and in every hole a young tobacco plant is set. This being the rainy season, the tobacco requires no watering, unless during the first ten days from its having been transplanted there should happen to be two succesive fair days. In this case, on the second fair day, water must be given with a pot. On the 15th day a little dung is put into each hole, and the field is hoed with the *Cuntay.* Every fourth or fifth day, until the tobacco is cut, this is repeated, so as to keep the soil open and well pulverized. At the end of a month and a half, the top shoots of the plants are pinched off, and every eight or ten days this is repeated; so that six or seven leaves only are permitted to remain on each stem. In the month preceding the shortest day, it is fit for cutting. The stems are cut about four or five inches from the ground, and are then split lengthwise; so that each portion has three or four leaves. These half stems are strung upon a line, which is passed through their root ends; and then for twenty days they are spread out to the sun and air. Every third day they are turned, and they must be covered with mats should there happen to be rain; but at this season that seldom comes. The tobacco is then taken into the house, put into a heap, and turned four or five times, with an interval of three days between each time. It is then fit for sale, and by the merchants is made up into bundles, which include the stems. It is sold by weight; and on an average the farmer gets one *Sultany*

CHAPTER XIX. May 10. *Pagoda* for every four *Maunds*, each containing 40 *Seers* of 24 *Rupees* weight. This is at the rate of very nearly a penny a pound, being 9*s*. 3½*d*. a hundred weight. In order to prepare the seedlings, a plot of ground must be dug in the month which precedes the longest day. It must be then cleared from stones, and separated by little banks into squares for watering, in the same manner as in this country is done to kitchen gardens. The tobacco seed is then mixed with dung, and sown in the squares, which are smoothed with the hand, sprinkled with water, and then covered with branches of the wild date. Every third day it must be watered. On the 8th day the plants come up, and then the palm branches must be removed. If the plants be wanted soon, they ought to have more dung, and to be kept clear from weeds. With this management, they are fit for transplanting in from a month to six weeks. If they are not wanted for two months, or ten weeks, the second dunging is omitted, and the growth of the plants is checked by giving them no water for eight days after they come up.

Value of land cultivated for tobacco.

A *Wocula* of *Ragy* land plants 4000 tobacco stems, and in a good crop produces 16 *Maunds*, worth four *Sultany Pagodas*. This ground would sow one *Colaga* of *Ragy*, and produce two *Candacas*, or forty fold, worth 2 *Pagodas*. The *Colaga* or *Wocula-land*, of the first quality used for tobacco, pays a tax of one *Pagoda*; of the 2d quality it pays ¾ of a *Pagoda*; of the 3d, or worst quality, it pays half a *Pagoda*. I measured a field said to require 1½ *Colaga* of *Ragy* for seed, and found it to contain 15,000 square feet. The *Wocula* land, therefore, should contain 100,000 square feet; but, if a *Wocula* plants 4000 tobacco stems at 1¼ cubit distance, which I found to be the actual thickness, more than one fourth of this extent cannot be allowed for it. The number of 4000 plants, that can be put in a *Wocula* of land, was afterwards confirmed to me at *Jamagullu*. I am quite uncertain, however, whether the actual measurement, or a calculation founded on the number of plants, ought to be preferred. By the former, the acre of the first quality of land would pay a little more than 3*s.* 6*d.* as land tax, and would produce 169 lb. of dried tobacco, worth 14*s.* 0¼*d*; or it would sow almost two gallons of *Ragy* seed, and produce almost ten bushels, worth 7*s.* 0¼*d.* On the other supposition, the rent, seed, and produce, would be four times as great; but that would render this land almost as valuable as rice ground, which cannot be the case. CHAPTER XIX. May 10.

11th *May.*—I went three long cosses to *Jamagullu.* The country is rather more broken than that through which I have come for the last two days, and is equally deserted. The wild date has even overgrown much of the rice-land. *Jamagullu* at present contains about eighty houses, and has a fort. Before the invasion of *Triumbaca Mama,* it was a large place, but has never since recovered. May 11 Appearance of the country.

Here is a temple dedicated to *Narasingha,* and built entirely of *Balapum,* or potstone. It is highly ornamented after the *Hindu* fashion, and on the outside every part of its walls is covered with small images in full *relievo.* Both the general structure of the fabric, and the execution of the component figures, are utterly destitute of either grandeur or elegance; indeed, I have not yet had the good fortune to meet with a *Hindu* image that was tolerable. This temple is said to have been built by *Sholun Ráya,* and the architect that he employed was named *Jacanachery.* This prince lived about a thousand years ago; and having killed a *Bráhman,* in order to wash away his sin, he employed twenty years in travelling between *Kási* and *Raméswara,* and in rebuilding temples. The one here entirely resembles in its style the others that I have seen which are attributed to the repentance of this personage. It has an inscription on stone, but that has been defaced. The annual revenues formerly belonging to the temple amounted to 250 *Ikeri Pagodas* (100*l.* 6*s.* 4½*d.*). These were entirely removed by the *Sultan. Purnea* allows it 50 *Canter' Ráya Pagodas* a year in money, or 15*l.* 12*s.* 0½*d.* Temple built by *Sholun Ráya.*

Many of the *strata* around this are of potstone. They are quite vertical, and run north and south in the usual direction of the other *strata* of the country. In general, the potstone breaks into *Strata* of potstone.

CHAPTER XIX.

May 11.

small fragments, and is full of fissures; but in the neighbouring country there are many quarries, where masses of great size may be procured. It forms an excellent material for building, being very easily cut, and at the same time being excessively tough. The good kinds resemble entirely the stone at *Maru-Hully*, described in the eighth chapter of my Journal, Vol. II. p. 146; and, in fact, are somewhat between a hornblende and a potstone.

Climate and soil.

For the two last nights there has been much thunder, but no rain. To-night there was both thunder and very heavy rain. The soil here is very fertile; for the farmers acknowledge 50 fold to be the usual crop of both *Ragy* and rice, that have been sown on good ground properly cultivated. From what I have stated at *Banawara*, the produce by the acre, at this rate, may be easily estimated.

Bull Rájás.

The fort of *Jamagullu* was built by a *Baydaru Polygar*, named *Eijuru Vencatuppa Nayaka.* His family were related to the *Polygars* of *Raya-durga*, and south and west from hence possessed very considerable territories. *Jamagullu* was taken from them by the *Mysore* family, who annexed it to *Banawara*, under which it has ever since continued. In the reign of the *Sultan*, the descendants of *Eijuru Vencatuppa* had no lands, but still retained the title of *Bull Rájás*, and had an annual pension of 5000 *Pagodas* (1560*l.* 3*s.* 9½*d.*). On the fall of *Seringapatam*, *Kristuppa Nayaka*, the heir of the family, seized on *Manzúr-ábád*, *Bailuru*, and other parts of his ancestors dominions, and has made an obstinate struggle to retain them. In this he has had little success, and he has lately been forced to retire to the almost inaccessible forests near the *Ghats.*

May 12. Weather.

12th *May.*—I went to *Hullybedu*, a stage of about 10 miles, but it is called only two cosses. By the last night's rain the rivulets were swollen, and the natives consider the rainy season as commenced; but for the first two months, showers once only in four or five days are expected. On this day's route much of the soil is good, but the country is quite deserted. By the way I observed some small hills, consisting entirely of calcarious tufa, mixed with a little earth. *Hullybedu*, at present, is a small mud fort, with a suburb *(Petta)*

May 12.

containing about eighty houses, and abounding with beggars. It stands on the side of a large *Tank*, that waters a great deal of fine rice-ground, much of which is planted with sugar-cane, and some with palm gardens. This *Tank* was formerly in the centre of a great city, which was named *Dorasamudra*, and was the residence of several of the *Belalla Rayas*, who once reigned over a great part of the peninsula of India. According to the natives, the walls of this city may be traced, extending three cosses in circumference; and the site of the palace is shown, and is readily distinguishable by having been placed in an inner fort, or citadel.

Jain.

The *Belallu* family having been originally *Jain*, some traces of that religion still remain. There are here several people of that persuasion; and within a common inclosure there are three of the temples called *Busties*. Here are three inscriptions; one defaced, and two legible. I had the latter copied, and left the copies that they might be written in a fair hand; but they were not forwarded, according to promise.

Fine temple of *Siva*.

The most remarkable building at *Hullybedu* is a temple of *Siva* erected by *Vishnu Verdana Ráya*. From an inscription on the wall, this must have been before the year of *Sal.* 1203, or A. D. $128\frac{0}{1}$. A copy of this inscription has been delivered to the Bengal government. This temple is built of similar materials, and in a similar style of architecture, with that at *Jamagullu;* but is larger, and more crowded with ornaments. Its walls contain a very ample delineation of *Hindu* mythology; which, in the representation of human or animal forms, is as destitute of elegance as usual; but some of the foliages possess great neatness, as may be seen by a drawing made of part of one, and given in Plate XXVII. figure 83. The temple has long been without a *Pújári*, or public worship, and has gone so far to decay, that it would be repaired with great difficulty. This is a pity, as it much exceeds any *Hindu* building that I have elsewhere seen.

Fine stones.

Before the temple are placed two images of the *Baswa*, or bull of *Siva*. The one is of *Balapum*, or the potstone impregnated with

CHAPTER XIX. May 12. hornblende, of which the temple is built, and which does not admit of a marble polish. This stone, which as usual represents the bull in a lying posture, is sixteen feet long, ten feet high, and seven feet broad. The other image is not quite so large; but its materials are finer, and admit of a marble polish. It seems also to be a potstone, or perhaps a talc impregnated with hornblende, and contains small irregular veins of a green shining matter. Its general colour is black, with a tinge of green. Some of the pillars in the inner part of the temple are of the same fine black hornblende that is used in *Hyder's* monument, and are highly polished. Some of them reflect objects double, which by the natives is looked upon as miraculous. These temples having been built when this was the seat of empire, and the inhabitants for many centuries having had no occasion for such costly materials in their buildings, the knowlege of the quarries from which they were supplied has been lost; and the natives believe that the stones were brought from *Kási*, on the banks of the *Ganges*.

Rock called *Cariculu*. A very common rock here is called by the natives the black-stone (*Caricullu*). It seems to be a hornblende porphyry; but the basis, having a slight degree of transparency, probably consists of an intimate union of hornstone, or quartz, with hornblende. It is black, with a greenish tinge, and greasy appearance, and contains white felspar in pieces of various sizes. It sometimes also contains veins of quartz, and on that account might perhaps be called a *Sienite*. It does not cut well for fine buildings; but breaks into quadrangular masses, which, from their being excessively tough and durable, make excellent rough work. For the same reason it is frequently hollowed out into the mortars of oil mills.

May 13. Appearance of the country. 13th *May*.—I went three cosses to *Bailuru*. The country is very bare; some of it is hilly, and full of stones; much of it is a good *Ragy* soil; but very little is cultivated. I crossed a small river called the *Bhadri*, which comes from *Baba Bodeens* hills, and runs into the *Caveiy*. It never dries entirely, and receives the water from all the country south from *Banawara*. To the west of the *Bhadri* river the country is called *Malayar*, or the hills; while that on the eastern side is called *Meidán*, or the open country. I remained at *Bailuru*, taking an account of the cultivation there, as an example of that which prevails in the hilly region whence the *Cavery* has its sources.

CHAPTER XIX.

May 13.

Country called *Malayar*.

The nature of the *Malayar* country resembles that of the sea coast below the western *Ghats*, in so far as rice is the principal object of cultivation, and as little attention is paid to the rearing of dry grains upon which the people to the north and west of the *Bhadri* chiefly subsist. In the *Malayar* country, however, there are no pepper gardens, nor plantations of *betel-nut* palms, for which it seems as well fitted as the *Nagara* principality. It is said entirely to resemble the *Codagu Ráyáda*, or *Coorg* country. At *Bailuru* there is no brickstone, and the country abounds with the calcareous *tufa*. The hills are overgrown with wood, and are considered as quite useless. The vallies only are cultivated.

Rice-ground.

On the *Bhadri* there was formerly a dam, the water from which irrigated forty *Candacas* of rice-land; but this has gone to decay, and to repair it would require two or three thousand *Pagodas*, or about ten years rent. The rains in all the *Malayar* country are very heavy, and in general bring one crop of rice to maturity; but unless there be small *Tanks* to give a supply for any intervals of fair weather that may occasionally happen, the crops are rather uncertain. This circumstance occasions the rice-lands to be divided into two kinds; the one, called *Niravery*, is supplied from *Tanks;* and the other, called *Mackey*, depends entirely on the rains.

Rent and quantity of seed.

Each kind of rice-ground, according to its soil, is divided into three qualities. The extent is estimated by what are called *Candacas;* but these vary much in size, and in general require much more seed than one *Candaca*. A *Candaca* of *Muckey* is always larger than one of *Niravery;* and the rent not only depends on the nature of the soil, but on the extent of the *Candaca*. The *Candaca* of grain,

CHAPTER XIX.

May 13.

it must be observed, contains 4095 cubical inches, and consists of twenty *Colagas*, each divided into nine *Cucha Seers*. I measured a field of rich *Mackey* land, which was called a *Candaca*, and required thirty *Colagas* of rice-seed. It not only produced annually a crop of rice, but one also of *Callay (Cicer arietinum)*; on which account it paid a rent of three *Ikeri Pagodas* a year, which is the highest rate in this district *(Taluc)*. I found that it measured 64932 square feet. At this rate, an acre would sow $1\frac{9155}{10000}$ bushel, and pay 16*s.* 2½*d.* as rent. I then measured a field of *Niravery*, of a very poor soil, but well supplied with water. It is said to require thirty-three *Colagas* of seed, and its rent is also three *Pagodas*. In order to make up for the poverty of soil, a quantity of dry-field is thrown into the field, and pays no additional rent. This dry-field sows four *Seers* of *Ragy*, *(Cynosurus corocanus)*, and two of *Huts' Ellu (Verbesina sativa*, Roxb: MSS.). I found, that the *Niravery* contained 28566 square feet, and the *Ragy* ground 7100 square feet. The rent upon the acre, including both kinds of ground, is therefore 1*l.* 9*s.* 6½*d.* The seed of rice is at the rate of $4\frac{192}{1000}$ bushels an acre; that of *Ragy* at the rate of rather more than one peck $1\frac{17}{100}$; and that of *Huts' Ellu* at the rate of about half a peck an acre. In the following table will be seen the kinds of rice cultivated here.

Kind.	Land.	Cultivation.	Quality.	Months required to ripen.
Hassoday	*Niravery*	Dry-seed	Large	8
Chipiga	do.	do.	do.	7
Kiaseri	do.	do.	do.	7
Cumbara Kiaseri	Both	do.	do.	7
Balla Mulligay	*Niravery*	do.	Middle sized	8
Sana Butta Bily	do.	do.	Small	8
Do. *Kempu*	do.	do.	do.	7
Modara	Both	All 3 methods	Coarse	7
Kirwinnna	*Niravery*	Dry-seed transplanted	do.	8
Putta Butta	do.	Dry and sprouted-seed	Small	8

May 13. *Niravery* land.

On *Niravery* land, or that which has a supply of water from *Tanks*, the rices most commonly cultivated are *Kiriwunna* and *Hassoday*. All the three kinds of cultivation are in use; but in ordinary seasons the dry-seed is by far the most prevalent. In extraordinary wet seasons a good deal is transplanted, and some is sown sprouted.

Dry-seed.

The cultivation of the dry-seed is conducted as follows. In the month following the winter solstice, the ploughing commences, and in the course of two months the operation is eight times repeated. The little banks, inclosing the plots for confining the water, are then repaired, and the field is manured. In the month preceding the vernal equinox, after a shower of rain, the clods are smoothed with the *Ada*, or *Gydday Maram*, which is the same implement with that which at *Nagara* is called *Noli*, Plate XXIX. Figure 79. Eight days afterwards the field is again ploughed, and again smoothed with the *Ada*. The seed is sown by the drill, according as the rainy season commences, during the two months and a half which follow the vernal equinox. It is then covered by the *Ada*. On the 23d day after having been sown, the field is hoed with the *Edday Cuntay*, Plate XXVIII. Figure 76, and this is repeated twice, with an interval of four days between each time. The field is then inundated by confining the water, and the *Cuntay* is drawn a 4th time in the mud. On the day following, the soil is smoothed with the *Ada*. Eight days afterwards, the field is drained until the weeds can be removed by the hand. After a month or six weeks, this must be repeated. The rice is cut with the straw, and trodden out by oxen. It is sometimes sold by the cultivators in the husk, and sometimes after having been cleaned, eight parts of which are equal in value to twenty parts in the husk. The farmers estimate their rough rice at six *Candacas* for a *Bahadury Pagoda*, or their rice at 30 *Seers* for the *Rupee*; but in the market (*Bazar*) none is sold lower than 23 *Seers* for a *Rupee*. The wholesale price for rough-rice, therefore, is a small fraction less than $8\frac{1}{2}$*d.* and

CHAPTER XXI. May 13.

for rice a small fraction more than 1*s.* 9*d.* a bushel. This, however, is only the price for which necessitous persons sell it at harvest-time; the average value is probably a fifth part more. The farmers say, that on a good soil the crop is about 25 *Candacas* on a *Candaca* land, which, according to my measurement, is about 72½ bushels an acre, worth 2*l.* 11*s.* 2½*d.* deduct for seed 3*s.* 4½*d.* and for rent 1*l.* 9*s.* 6½*d.* and there remain to the tenants, for stock and labour, 18*s.* 2½*d.*

Advantage of sowing thick.

Nothing can better show the great error into which the *Hindu* farmers fall, in sowing too little seed; a practice which seems to have arisen from their usual poverty, and from the constant cropping of their land, which, without plentiful irrigation, or rich manuring, is thereby too much exhausted to produce a full crop. The farmers here, probably, under-rate their produce as much as their neighbours; but as they sow their seed almost four times as thick, they have from the same extent of land at least three times as much produce. It is true, that here they speak of a small increase of seventeen or eighteen fold, while in other places they talk largely of an increase of forty, and even sixty seeds; but here an acre produces for the support of man from sixty-five to seventy bushels of rough rice; while in the others from twenty to twenty-four may be considered as a usual crop.

Transplanted crop.

When the rains are heavy, a good deal of rice is raised by transplantation. For every *Candaca* land, two *Candacas* of seed must be sown; and the produce of this, on the best land, is only twenty-one or twenty-two *Candacas.*

Sprouted seed.

Very little sprouted-seed is sown; but it seems to be the cultivation that would answer best. For a *Candaca* land fifteen *Colagas* of seed are sufficient, and the produce is little less than in the dry-seed. The reason that the natives assign for neglecting the sprouted-seed cultivation is, that it requires the ploughing to be performed while the field has by irrigation been reduced to mud, and that their cattle are not adequate to this labour. The cattle however, are not worse than those of the sea-coast, where the dry seed is seldom sown.

May 13. *Mackey* land.

On the *Mackey* land, or that which depends entirely on rain for a supply of water, the seed is always sown without preparation, and managed exactly in the same manner as on the *Niravery*. The produce, on the best land, is 22 *Candacas* from thirty *Colagas* sown on a *Candaca* field. According to my measurement, this makes the produce of the acre rather more than 28 bushels, worth 19*s.* 10*d.* deduct 1*s.* $4\frac{1}{2}$*d.* for seed, and 6*s.* $2\frac{1}{2}$*d.* for rent, and there would only remain 2*s.* 3*d.* for stock and labour; but it must be observed, that my estimate of the rent is formed from a very rich field, that produces a second crop of *Callay*, and that the rent of fields giving only a crop of rice is not more than half as much as what I have here stated.

The *Callay*, or *Cicer arietinum*, is sold as it ripens; so that the farmers cannot, or at least will not, say what the produce is.

Dry-field.

The only dry crop cultivated here is *Ragy* mixed with *Huts'Ellu.* When the rains are scanty, these thrive very well; but the seasons are often so wet, as to destroy them all together. The whole quantity sown is very small. The ground is ploughed four times, and then manured during the month following the vernal equinox, or in the beginning of the next month. The field is then ploughed twice more. The *Ragy* seed is sown with the *Curigy*, or drill; while the *Huts' Ellu* is disposed in rows, by means of the *Sudiky*, or sharp pointed *Bamboo* tied to the drill. After this, the field is smoothed with a plank, and harrowed with a bunch of thorns. On the 12th day it is hoed with the *Cuntay*, and this is repeated four times, with intervals between every two, of from five to eight days. The produce in a good crop is said to be forty seeds of *Ragy*, and nine of *Huts' Ellu.* According to my measurement, this will make the produce of an acre $16\frac{7}{10}$ bushels of *Ragy*, and $1\frac{1}{8}$ bushel of *Huts' Ellu.*

The lands here, both dry and watered, are let by a fixed rent in

CHAPTER XIX. May 13. Tenures.

money, according to an old valuation. They are seldom kept separate; but a little of the dry field is thrown into the contiguous plots of rice land. In this district, the *Bráhmans* have lands in free gift *(Enam)* to the annual value of 500 *Pagodas;* and a *Mussulman* has an estate of the same nature worth 24 *Pagodas.* These lands may be transferred by sale. All the remainder is the property of the Government; but, if a farmer pay the full valuation, he cannot legally be turned out of his possession. Many of them, however, will not consent to give the full rent, and these may be dispossessed whenever a better tenant offers. The *Niravery* is valued at from two to three *Bahadury Pagodas* a *Candaca.* The *Mackey,* except where it is extraordinarily rich, is only valued at from 1 to 1½ *Pagoda.*

Price of labour.

In the *Malayar* there are no slaves. Most of the labour is carried on by the farmers, and their own families. Servants are hired by the year, month, or day. A man's wages when hired by the year are annually three *Pagodas,* a pair of sandals, a blanket, and daily a meal of ready-dressed rice; worth all together about five *Pagodas,* or about 2*l.* He eats another time daily, but this is at his own expense. A servant hired by the month gets half a *Pagoda,* or about four shillings, without any addition. The daily hire is ⅓ of a *Canter'-ráya Fanam,* or 2¼*d.* Hired servants work from eight in the morning until six in the afternoon; but half an hour's intermission is granted, to give them time to eat some ready-prepared victuals.

Stock.

Each plough requires two oxen, and one man, and can cultivate two *Candacas* of land. Suppose these to be of the best quality, then the rent will be six *Pagodas,* the man's hire five *Pagodas,* extra labour at seed-time and harvest three *Pagodas,* seed half a *Pagoda:* total expense, besides interest for the stock, fourteen *Pagodas* and a half. The produce, according to the farmers, is fifty *Candacas,* worth 8⅓ *Pagodas.* From this it is evident, either that the farmers greatly over-rate their expenses, or under-rate the produce and extent of the land cultivated by one plough; and probably they do both; but what the real state is, I could not ascertain.

Cattle and manure.

The only manure used here is from the dunghill, in which, with all the cow-dung, the ashes and sweepings of the house are collected. The cattle sleep the whole year in the house, but are never littered, which is a very great defect in the agriculture of a country. On the *Malayar* side of the *Bhadri* rivulet, the size of the cattle diminishes, and sheep will not thrive; and in that country neither asses nor swine are bred.

Commerce.

A considerable trade is carried on between *Bailuru* and *Jamál-ábád.* The goods imported from the country below the *Ghats* are *betel-nut*, ginger, pepper, *Cassia (Laurus)*, *Cachora (Acorus)*, *Casturi* (a kind of turmeric), turmeric, and salt. The goods sent from *Bailuru* are tobacco, *Jagory*, capsicum, cummin-seed, *Danya*, (a seed like anise), tamarinds, iron, grain, buffaloes, onions, mustard, cotton cloth and thread, and blankets *(Cumlies)*.

Cochineal.

I found here two men whom an officer now stationed at *Arcot* employed in rearing cochineal. They have been in this country one year, have sent to their employer fifteen *Maunds*, have fifteen *Maunds* ready for sale, and, before the insects have consumed all the *Nopals* *(Cactus)* that are near the town, they expect to have ten *Maunds* more. When this happens, they will carry two men's load of branches filled with the insect, and apply these to the *Nopals* of some other place; where they will remain until the insects breed, and consume all the plants. The *Nopals* have been raised by the farmers as fences round their gardens, but were sold by the officers of revenue for four *Bahadury Pagodas*, or about a guinea and a half. So soon as all the plants have been consumed, such of the insects as have not been collected will perish; and the *Amildar* says, that he will then compel the farmers to plant new hedges of the *Nopal;* but I suspect that few plants will be reared, unless the farmers get a large share of the profits, as indeed they ought in reason to do. The hedges

CHAPTER XIX.

will grow up in three years, when it is expected that some other person rearing the insect will come and buy the plants.

May 13.

This seems to me to be the most rational plan of any that has been hitherto proposed for rearing the cochineal in India; and to be deserving of the attention and encouragement of government. The men employed here say, that the young insects ought to be put upon the new hedges immediately after the rainy season is past. In six months they will have increased so, that they may begin to be collected; and a year more will elapse before the whole plants are consumed. During the course of this year, whenever a leaf is fully loaded, it ought to be cut, and the insects scraped from it with a small stick, and collected in a basket. While they are in this, a little boiling water is poured on them, by which they are killed. They are then well agitated in the basket, to remove the hair with which they are covered, and dried for two days in the sun, when they are fit for sale. These men say, that, all expenses included, the cochineal, thus prepared, will cost here three *Madras Pagodas* a *Maund* of forty *Seers*, each weighing twenty-four *Rupees;* which is rather less than 11*d.* a pound. The cochineal is of the bad kind that has lately been introduced into India, and the plant is the *Cactus* that is the aboriginal of the country.

History of *Bailuru.*

Bailuru, or *Bailapuri*, as it is called in the *Sanskrit*, is situated at a little distance from the *Bhadri* river, and has a good fort built of stone, and a suburb *(Petta)* which contains about six hundred houses.

In order to get some historical information, I assembled the *Bráhmans* who are proprietors of free estates *(Enams);* but I found them, as usual, grossly ignorant. They either could not or would not read any of the inscriptions that are at their temple; and I was obliged to employ my interpreter to get one of them copied. It contains a grant of lands from *Narasingha Ráya*, son of *Vishnu Verdana*, to *Narasingha Swami*, one of the incarnations of *Vishnu)*, and is dated in the year of *Sal.* 1095. A copy has been given to the

CHAPTER XIX.

May 14.

Bengal government. I found among the *Bráhmans* a poor man who had no *Enam*, and whose poverty had sharpened his understanding: he read the inscriptions with the utmost facility, and I set him to work at them on the second morning of my stay; but I found his industry not equal to his intelligence; and in the evening, when I went to see what progress he had made, I found that he had scarcely commenced; and all the idle *Bráhmans* of the place having asembled on the occasion, the day had been passed in conversation. I found, however, that he possessed a manuscript that had been written by his ancestors, and which, he says, contains an account, collected from the inscriptions here, of the repairing the temple of *Cayshava Permal* by *Vishnu Verdana Ráya* in the year of *Salivahanam* 1039; and of all the gifts made to that celebrated place of worship by the three sons of this prince. This manuscript was in a very old character; but the *Bráhman's* necessities induced him to follow me to the next stage, and to give me a copy, which has been presented to the government of Bengal.

The temple in its present form was built by *Vishnu Verdana*, after his conversion by *Ráma Anuja Achäryá*, of which I have given an account in the seventh chapter of this Journal, Vol. II. p. 81. It is in good repair, and is a large building, which, although inferior to those of *Hully-bedu* and *Jamagullu*, is much ornamented after the *Hindu* fashion.

The *Bráhmans* whom I had assembled say from tradition, that this country, meaning *Karnata*, was divided among nine brothers of the *Belalla* family, who were all destroyed by the *Turcs*, except one young man. The *Mussulmans* found it afterwards necessary to restore this prince to the dominions of his ancestors; and on his first accession he was called *Bita Deva Ráya;* but afterwards, having rebuilt the temple here, and that of *Siva* at *Hully-bedu*, he took the name of *Vishnu Verdana.* He sometimes resided at the one place, and sometimes at the other; but *Hully-bedu* seems to have been by far the largest town. He had great success against the

CHAPTER XIX. May 14.

Mussulmans, and expelled them entirely from all the country south from the *Krishna*. His son *Narasingha* governed quietly, and was succeeded by his son *Vira Belalla*, who was destroyed by a *Mussulman* prince that *Baba Bodeen* invited. His residence had been chiefly at *Bellagami*. The *Mussulman* prince is by the *Bráhmans* called *Hussein Khan*. He took up his abode in the great temple here, and was succeeded by his son *Runnadulla Khan*. This *Mussulman* was expelled by two of his *Hindu* officers, named *Rama Ráya* and *Achuta Ráya*, who established themselves at *Anagundi*. They were succeeded by their two brothers *Krishna* and *Narasingha Ráyáru*. Here these *Bráhmans* are jumbling together all the traditions of the country. What follows has more resemblance to probability.

The *Ráyaru* distributed all their dominions among their servants. The ancestor of the *Mysore Rájás*, for instance, was the person who made the king's bed. The person who carried the *Betel* box was *Vencatadri Nayaka*, ancestor of *Krishtuppa*, the present *Bull Rájá*. The chiefs descended from *Vencatadri* were originally of considerable note in the country, and had three places of residence, *Bailuru*, *Sakra-pattana*, and *Narasingha-pura*. When driven from these by the *Mysore* family, they retired to the hills of *Manzúr-ábád*, around which they possessed a territory worth annually 18,000 *Pagodas*, or 5616*l.* 13*s.* 4*d.* *Hyder* rendered them tributary, and the present heir was driven by *Tippoo* into the *Marattah* dominions. Five years afterwards he solicited a pardon, which was granted, and he was taken into the service on an allowance of 2000 *Pagodas* a year. This was afterwards increased to 5000. On the fall of *Seringapatam*, he demanded the restoration of his ancient family domains; which was refused, and he was offered the same allowance that he received from the *Sultan*. The people here think that he would be satisfied with being put on the same footing that he was in the reign of *Hyder*; but, as a war has commenced, he is not likely to get any thing. At first he had some success, and seized on *Bailuru*, but he is now cooped up in the woods of the western *Ghats*.

May 15. Appearance of the country.

15th *May*.—I went three cosses to *Haltoray*. I first recrossed the *Bhadri*, and then proceeded through a country fine by nature, but very bare. It does not seem so destitute of cultivators as most parts through which I have lately come; but at least one half of the arable lands are waste. There is much rice-land. Some of the *Tanks* are large; and the crop which they irrigate is raised chiefly in the dry season, after the quantity of water which they are to collect for the season has been ascertained. A great part of the rice-land is *Mackey*, which is cultivated in the rainy season, without a supply from *Tanks*. The farmers here acknowledge forty seeds as the usual produce of good rice-lands. The dry ground is very fit for *Ragy*; and on the east of the *Bhadri* much of that grain is raised.

Sankety Bráhmans.

Near *Haltoray* are some fine *Betel-nut* gardens, the property of a kind of *Sri Vaishnavam Bráhmans*, called *Sankety*. They are all *Vaidika*; but are not on that account exempted from gross ignorance, and they never read any thing, except accompts, or letters on business. They are originally from *Dravada* proper, and now speak a strange mixture of the *Tamul* and *Karnata* languages.

Having assembled these *Bráhmans*, they gave me the following account of their gardens.

Plantations.

Betel-nut plantations are found no farther west than *Haltoray*, and from thence they extend all the way to *Sira*. As soon as the garden begins to produce, the proprietors pay one half of the nut, as rent to government, and are at the whole expense, not only of rearing the plantations, but of forming the wells and *Tanks* by which these are watered. The government gets no share of any other part of the produce, which consists of plantains and *Betel leaf*. A man may sell his garden; but if he allows it to become waste, the soil is public property. The plantation is not allowed to die out; but, when one tree decays, a new one is planted in its stead. After the trees have grown up, they are allowed neither dung nor water; but the garden is hoed three times in the year; and once in five years the channels for carrying off superfluous water are cleared, and

CHAPTER XIX. May 15.

some fresh earth is put on the beds. When *Betel leaf* is reared upon the palms, the garden must be regularly watered and manured, and on that account becomes more productive. Pepper vines, it is said, have been tried here, but without success. The *Bráhmans* say, that in the *Malayar* district they have in vain tried to rear the *Betel-nut* palm. How this should have happened I cannot understand, as the climate there very exactly resembles that of *Nagara.* Perhaps the *Bráhmans* have neglected to shelter the young plantations from the setting sun, which in the open country, owing to its greater coolness, is not requisite. A garden of 300 bearing *Arecas* produces ten *Maunds* of boiled *Betel-nut*, worth one *Bahadury Pagoda* a *Maund*, or 1*l.* 17*s.* 2½*d.* a cwt. To give one *Maund* of prepared *Betel* requires 4000 nuts; so that the average produce, acknowledged by the proprietors, for each tree of a bearing age, is 133⅓ nuts, that are worth, when boiled, 3¼ pence, of which one half is paid for rent. That this may be the amount received by government is very probable; but few will be inclined to credit that it really exacts the fair half of the produce.

Sandal. Sandal-wood trees are planted in the hedges that surround these gardens. The government has the sole right of cutting and disposing of this article of commerce; but the proprietor of the garden expects for his trouble in rearing it, and with justice receives, a gratuity. The planted *Sandal* is here reckoned of as good a quality as that which has grown spontaneously.

Haltoray. *Haltoray* is a ruinous mud fort, but it contains some good houses, which belong to the *Sankety Bráhmans.* Most of the other houses are in ruins, and were reduced to that state by the troops of the *Sultan;* who, in their marches to and from *Mangalore* and *Nagara,* frequently passed this way. The discipline of this prince did not extend to prevent his troops from being rapacious, even in his own territory. In *Hyder's* government the people had no reason to complain of the army. *Haltoray* was never a large place. Its name is thus explained: *Hal* signifies milk, and *Toray* a stair leading down to a *Tank* or river. It formerly belonged to the *Hásina* district; but when the conquests of the *Mysore* family extended that length, it was annexed to *Bailuru*. Before this family rose to power, *Hásina*, *Gráma*, *Chin'-raya-pattana*, and *Narasingha-pura*, belonged to the ancestors of *Krishtuppa Nayaka*, the *Bull Rájá*. At *Haltoray* are the ruins of a temple dedicated to *Bira Linga*, a deity of the *Curubaru*. There are at it two inscriptions on stone. One of them is partly legible; and of all that could be made out in a connected form I procured a copy, which has been delivered to the government of Bengal. It is dated in the year of *Sal.* 1116, and in the reign of *Boca Rájá*, of whom I have no where else heard.

CHAPTER XIX. May 15.

Aray, or *Marattah* robbers.

In this vicinity robbers have for many years been very numerous. They are the farmers in the *Malayar*, or hilly country to the westward, and are all of *Marattah* extraction, on which account they are by the *Bráhmans* called *Aray;* for, in the *Arabi* or *Tamul* language, that is the name of a *Marattah*. These ruffians come in bands of from twelve to twenty men, and steal, or rob, whatever comes in their way. Murder and torture are frequently added to their other outrages. At present, this class of men have entirely given up agriculture, and have entered into the service of *Krishtuppa*, the *Bull Rájá;* nor are the troops of the *Mysore Rájá* able to prevent small parties of them from issuing out of the woods, and committing occasional depredations.

May 16. Appearance of the country.

16th *May*.—I went three *Sultany* cosses to *Hásina*, which derives its name from one of the *Saktis* that is the village deity (*Gráma Devata*). The country through which I passed is fine *Ragy* land, but very little of it is cultivated.

In good rice-land at *Hásina*, twenty seeds are reckoned the usual produce. In this district, since the *Marattah* invasion, not above a fourth part of the former cultivators remain.

Change of climate.

The natives say, that formerly the rains were so copious, that by means of small *Tanks* a great part of the country could be cultivated

CHAPTER XIX. May 16.

for rice. These *Tanks* were only sufficient to contain eight or ten days water, and to supply the fields when such short intervals of fair weather occurred. For forty years past, however, a change having taken place in the climate, no rice has been cultivated, except by means of large reservoirs. The truth of this allegation is confirmed by the number of small *Tanks*, the ruins of which are now visible; and by the plots of ground levelled for rice that are near these *Tanks*, and which are now quite waste.

Hásina.

Hásina formerly stood at some distance from its present situation, toward the south; but one of the *Anagundi Ráyarus*, being here on a hunting party, discovered, by the usual means of the hare turning on his dogs, that the place where it now stands was *male ground.* He therefore built a fort on the auspicious ground; and, while he was thus employed, an image of *Siva* rose out of the ground, and was called *Virupacshéswara*, after the celebrated idol at *Anagundi*. A temple was of course built over the image, and it is called *Siddhéswara.* At this temple two inscriptions on stone remain. The one, in the reign of *Achuta* and *Krishna Ráyaru*, is dated in the year of *Sal.* 1454. The other is in the reign of *Sedasiva Ráya*, son of *Achuta Ráya*, and is dated in the year of *Sal.* 1412, but that is evidently a mistake of the copyist for 1512, the *Karnata* cyphers for four and five having a strong resemblance. Copies of these inscriptions also have been delivered to the government of Bengal. The place was originally in the *Polyum*, or feudatory estate of the ancestors of the *Bull Rájá.* It was taken from them by *Renadulla Khan*, a *Pattan*, whose family held it sixty years. This family of Mussulmans seems to be the same with that which the *Bráhmans* of *Bailuru* confounded with the prince who destroyed *Vira Belalla Ráya.* The Mussulmans were expelled by the *Sivabhactars* of *Ikeri*, who held *Hásina* a hundred years. The *Mysore* family then kept it ten years; but were obliged to restore it again to the descendants of *Sedasiva*, the chief of *Ikeri*. Thirty years afterwards, hovever, they finally annexed it to their territories, and this happened 180 years ago. The whole

CHAPTER XIX.

of the periods in this tradition seem to be lengthened out greatly beyond the truth.

May 16.

The fort at *Hásina* is by far the best that I have ever seen constructed of mud and rough stones, and is in excellent repair. *Hyder* made the covered way, and a central battery, or cavalier, which serves as a citadel. In his reign the fort contained about fifteen hundred houses, and in the suburbs *(Petta)* there were five hundred. At present, in both places there are only five hundred houses, of which one hundred are occupied by *Bráhmans*, and twenty by *Jain*. These have a temple of the kind called *Busty*, which is by far the neatest place of worship in the town. At *Hásina* there are scarcely either trade or manufactures.

May 17. *Gráma.*

17th *May.*—I went two *Sultany* cosses to *Gráma*, which signifies merely a village. It is, however, the *Kasba*, or capital of a *Taluc* (district), and is a considerable mud fort, containing about two hundred houses. It would not appear to have ever been more populous. It was not taken by *Purseram Bhow*, but suffered exceedingly in *Triumbaca Mama's* invasion. The officers of revenue say, that only one fourth part of the arable lands are waste. The rains never were so copious here as to admit of the cultivation of rice without large reservoirs; but the soil is abundantly good, and, according to its quality, produces from 15 to 40 seeds, both of rice and *Ragy*. The best *Ragy* land lets for eight *Sultany Fanams* a *Colaga;* which of course, at forty seeds, produces two *Candacas*.

May 18. Appearance of the country.

18th *May.*—I went, what appeared a long stage, to *Chin'-raya-pattana*. It was called four *Sultany* cosses. The country is naturally pretty; but, like all that between *Bailuru* and *Seringapatam*, it is exceedingly bare, and has hardly either trees or fences. Some of it is hilly, and much of it poor land; but, to me, by far the greater part of it appears to be arable. Not above one fourth part is now cultivated. On the way, there is one considerable village. Near the road are several fine *Tanks;* and the quantity of rice which this district produces almost equals that of *Ragy*. These *Tanks* also

CHAPTER XIX.

supply water to several palm gardens; and a considerable quantity of sugar-cane is raised on the land that they water.

May 18. *Chin'-raya-pattana.*

Chin'-raya-pattana signifies the city of the *little* prince, one of the names of *Vishnu*, who has a temple there. At this is an inscription on stone, of which a copy has been given to the Bengal government. It is dated in the year of *Sal.* 1400, in the reign of *Virapacsha Maha Râyaru.*

Mysore family.

The fort is well built of stone and lime, and was made by a man named *Baswa-rajya*, in the service of *Canterua Nursa Râjâ Wodear.* This was the first prince of the *Mysore* family who acquired great power. From the inscription, of which a copy has been given to the Bengal government, and which is engraved on a stone at *Chin'-raya-pattana*, it would appear, that this *Râjâ* had acquired this town on or before the year of *Sal.* 1561, or of Christ 163⁸⁄₉, and that then he acknowleged no superior. Here is also another inscription by the *Mysore* family, a copy of which has been delivered with the former. It is dated in the year of *Sal.* 1585, and in the reign of *Deva Râjâ Wodear*, who, I believe, was the prince that extended the conquests of this family to *Banawara*, *Garuda-giri*, *Budihalu*, and other districts toward the north-west. Previous to the conquest by the *Mysore* family, *Chin'-râya-pattana* was a *Grâmam* belonging to the *Brâhmans* of *Vishnu's* temple; and it was subject to a *Polygar*, whose name the present inhabitants do not remember, but who must have been the ancestor of the *Bull Râjâ*. *Purseram Bhow* did not attempt to take it, although the garrison consisted only of 500 *Candashara*; but the taking of towns was not his object. With a small suburb *(Petta)* it contains between eight and nine hundred houses, of which sixty are inhabited by *Brâhmans*, and 200 by the *Candashara* that form the garrison. It has a weekly fair, but no considerable trade.

Cycle of sixty years.

I procured from the *Brâhmans* here a table of the years that compose their cycle, to which I have often referred. I annex the years of *Salivahanam*, and of the Christian era, in which, according to the

May 18.

Brâhmans of this town, each year of the present cycle commences. It must, however, be observed, that very great variations take place concerning this in different parts, and also apparently in the same part at different times; which renders this chronology of cycles of very little use to the historical antiquary.

Year of Christ.	Year of Cycle.	Year of *Salivahanam.*	Year of Christ.	Year of Cycle.	Year of *Salivahanam.*
1747	*Prabava*	1669	1777	*Hevalumbi*	1699
1748	*Vibava*	1670	1778	*Velumbi*	1700
1749	*Sucla*	1671	1779	*Vicari*	1701
1750	*Promoduta*	1672	1780	*Shervari*	1702
1751	*Prejotapati*	1673	1781	*Pluvva*	1703
1752	*Anghirsa*	1674	1782	*Chubucrutu*	1704
1753	*Srimoca*	1675	1783	*Shobacrutu*	1705
1754	*Bava*	1676	1784	*Crodi*	1706
1755	*Iva*	1677	1785	*Visuavasu*	1707
1756	*Dat'hu*	1678	1786	*Parabava*	1708
1757	*Ishura*	1679	1787	*Plavunga*	1709
1758	*Bohudania*	1680	1788	*Kilaca*	1710
1759	*Primadi*	1681	1789	*Sovumia*	1711
1760	*Vicrama*	1682	1790	*Satarana*	1712
1761	*Vishu*	1683	1791	*Virodicrutu*	1713
1762	*Chitrabanu*	1684	1792	*Paridavi*	1714
1763	*Suabanu*	1685	1793	*Premmdicha*	1715
1764	*Tarana*	1686	1794	*Anunda*	1716
1765	*Partiva*	1687	1795	*Racshasa*	1717
1766	*Veya*	1688	1796	*Nalla*	1718
1767	*Servajittu*	1689	1797	*Peingala*	1719
1768	*Servadavi*	1690	1798	*Calayucti*	1720
1769	*Virodi*	1691	1799	*Sidarti*	1721
1770	*Vicrotu*	1692	1800	*Raudri*	1722
1771	*Cara*	1693	1801	*Durmati*	1723
1772	*Nundina*	1694	1802	*Dundubi*	1724
1773	*Juja*	1695	1803	*Rudrodagari*	1725
1774	*Visia*	1696	1804	*Ructachi*	1726
1775	*Munmuttu*	1697	1805	*Crodona*	1727
1776	*Durmutti*	1698	1806	*Acchaya*	1728

In *Nepal*, the year 1802 was *Srimoca;* whereas at *Chinroyp'pattana* it was *Dundubi*; a difference of 11 years.

May 19. Appearance of the country.

19th *May.*—I went two *Sultany* cosses to *Sravana Belgula.* To me the country appears to be almost entirely waste, although the

CHAPTER XIX. May 19. *Amildar* will only allow that one fourth part of all the arable land in his district is unoccupied; but it must be always remembered, that very few of the native officers have an idea of any lands being arable, except such as are rated in public accompts. By the way I passed several fine *Tanks*; and the rains have already been so considerable, that one of the *Tanks* has been filled, so as unexpectedly to overflow, and break down its bank, which has deluged all the subjacent fields.

Sravana Belgula. *Sravana Belgula* is a village containing 120 houses, and its name is said to signify *here is the white Solanum;* for in its neighbourhood a species of that plant grows very copiously.

Jain. This place is celebrated, as being now the principal seat of the *Jain* worship, which once was so prevalent over the greater part of *India*. In the village is a *Matam* belonging to a *Sannyási*, who claims a precedency over the person with whom I conversed at *Carculla*. This *Sannyási* and his chief disciples were absent when I was at *Sravana Belgula*. Near the village is a *Tank*, a very handsome work. It was built by a *Jain* merchant of *Seringapatam*. Near the village also are two rocky hills. On the one, named *Indra Betta*, is a temple of the kind called *Busty*, named *Bundara;* and a high place (*Betta*), with a colossal image of *Gomuta Ráya*. This I was not able to visit, owing to an inflammation that attacked my eyes the day before, and rendered the light almost intolerable. I sent my painter and interpreter to inspect the hill. The painter gave me the accompanying sketch of the image, Plate XXXIV. Figure 84, for the accuracy of which I cannot answer. Its height is seventy feet 3 inches. Sir Arthur Wellesley, who has visited the place lately, thinks the drawing rather more clumsy than the image. He is of opinion, that the rock has been cut until nothing but the image remained. The interpreter brought copies of six inscriptions on stone, which have been given to the Bengal government. I then sent him to the other hill, named *Chandra-giri*, on which there are said to be fifteen *Busties*, or temples belonging to the *Jain*. There he found many inscriptions on stone; but having no time to copy them, he contented himself by noting down the dates and princes reigns of those which were in best condition. A copy of these notes also has been given to the Bengal government. From two of these dates it would appear, that *Vishnu Verdana Ráya* continued to reign in the years of *Sal.* 1045 and 1050. May 19.

Having assembled the most learned *Jain* here, they gave me a copy of a writing on *Palmira* leaves, which they said was a copy of an inscription on copper belonging to the *Sannyási*, their *Guru.* It is dated in the year of the *Kaliyugam* 600, and in the reign of *Rájá Mulla*, king of the south. A copy has been delivered to the Bengal government. They say, that the *Betta*, or high place, with its colossal image, were made by a certain *Chamunda Ráya*, descended from whom were the nine *Belalla Rájás.* The first eight of these princes resided chiefly at *Hully-bedu.* The 9th lived at *Tonuru*, and changed his religion to become a worshipper of *Vishnu.* I have already given the history of his conversion, according to the *Bráhmans* of *Tonuru.* I shall now relate what the *Jain* say on the subject. This prince had become enamoured of a dancing girl, who, having been educated in the temples of *Vishnu*, had a great respect for the *Bráhmans* that follow the doctrines of *Vyasa.* This prostitute one day artfully upbraided the king, by saying that his *Guru* would not receive any thing out of his hands. The king insisted that the *Guru* respected him more; and at length it was determined, that if the *Guru* accepted the present of the king, then the favourite should change her religion; but if the present was rejected, that the king should receive the *Sri Vaishnavam Bráhmans* as his spiritual guides. On the first visit that the *Guru* made to court, the matter was decided. The king had lost a finger; and it being an abomination with the *Jain Bráhmans* to take any thing from the hands of a mutilated person, the offerings of the prince were rejected with obstinacy. The king then, according to his promise, destroyed all the *Jain* and their temples, and, having taken the name of *Vishnu*

CHAPTER XIX. May 19. *Verdana*, built many temples in honour of his new god. Among these is that at *Bailuru*, which, according to an inscription already mentioned, was built, or repaired, in the year of *Sal.* 1039, which must have been after the conversion of this prince.

The *Jain* of this place differ considerably from those of *Tulava*. They deny that the *Bunts* of *Tulava* are *Sudras*, and say that they are *Vaisyas*. They will not indeed acknowledge that any *Sudras* belong to their sect. A person of any of the three casts into which they are divided may become a *Sunnyási*, or act as a *Pújári*. The office of *Purôhita* only is exclusively in possession of the *Bráhmans*. The *Jain* originally inhabited all the six *Khandas* of the world. This, in which we live, is *Aria*, or *Bharata-khanda;* and at present few *Jain* remain in it; but there are still many in two *Khandas*, named *Puruovideha*, and *Aprovideha;* which, they say, mean the east and west. They judge of these places from their books; for they have had no communication with the *Jain* there, nor can they give any geographical account of their situation. The books in highest authority among the *Jain* are called *Sara*, and they are three in number; the *Gomuta*, the *Triloca*, and the *Lubda Saras*. These they consider as holy, as the other *Bráhmans* do the *Vedas*. They were composed by *Ady Brahma*, or *Adyswara*, one of the perfect beings who has become a *Sidaru*, and who must not be confounded with the *Brahma* of the followers of *Vyasa*, who is looked upon by the *Jain* as a *Devata* only, and is the chief servant of *Gomuta Ráya*. Next in authority to the *Saras*, is a commentary on them in 24 *Puranas*, or books, composed about 1700 years ago by *Jenaseanu Acharieru*, a *Sannyási*.

My eyes now became so very painful, that I could bear the light no longer. I was obliged to leave this place, therefore, with a much less perfect knowledge of its antiquities than I could have wished; and I proceeded to *Seringapatam*, where I continued some days in great pain, and unable to read or write. By the way I passed one night at *Sindy-gutta*, and another at *Tonuru*. At this last place I obtained from the *Bráhmans* an extract from a book called *Guru Para*, written by *Rám'Anuja Achárya*, partly in *Sanskrit*, and partly in the *Tamul*. The words of the former in the *Grantha* character, those of the latter in the *Arabi*, or vulgar letters. This extract, of which a copy has been delivered to government, contains a life of this extraordinary personage; who, according to his own account, was born in the year of *Sal.* 939. It is therefore certain, that both he and his convert, *Vishnu Verdana*, must have lived to great ages; as the king would appear, from the inscriptions above mentioned, to have been living in the year of *Sal.* 1050.

June 2. *Rám Anuja Achárya*

3d *June*.—My eyes having now so far recovered as to allow me to write, I resolved to set out on my return; and accordingly sent my tents a little way, intending to sleep at them, and in the morning to proceed; but in the afternoon there came a severe storm of thunder, wind, and rain, which kept me another night with my kind and hospitable friends in *Seringapatam*.

June 3.

During my stay there, I procured the *Caneh Sumareh* of the *Mysore Rájá's* dominions. It contains a list of villages, public edifices, houses, families, ploughs, and a few other particulars, with a classification of the inhabitants in each *Taluc*, or district. In this, due attention is neither paid to cast nor possession; nor can great reliance be placed on the accuracy of its statements. I have, however, thrown as much as relates to the population and stock into the form of a table; as a nearer approximation to the truth than any that has been yet given.

Caneh Sumareh of Mysore.

CHAPTER XIX.

June 3.

Abstract of the Caneh Sumareh of the Territories belonging to the Rájá of Mysore.

Talucs in the *Chatrakal Ráyada.*	Families.	Houses.	Ploughs.
Kasba Chatrakal - - -	3824	3859	1330
Onaji - - -	2014	2043	1338
Mola-calu-muri - - -	1510	1533	669
Mahi-conda - - -	2995	3080	2417
Heriuru - - -	2305	2403	2224
Gudi-cotay - - -	2967	3019	1620
Canacupay - - -	2918	3072	1915
Bhima-samudra - -	1186	1382	602
Tulloc - - -	1656	1645	903½
Holalu-caray - - -	2143	2414	1528
Doddery - - -	2297	2297	1144
Muteodu - - - -	1355	1409	994
Hosso-durga - - -	2109	3164	3021
	29289	31320	19705½

Talucs in the *Nagara Ráyada.*			
Hyder Nagara Kasba - - -	4870	4960	2696
Shiva-mogay, or Shimogay, - -	5368	5368	3209
Surabha - - - -	1584	1584	1055
Chandra-gupti - - -	3119	3150	1302
Tavanundy - - -	1354	1455	904
Ananta-para - - -	1896	1899	1303
Honali - - - -	2963	2973	2305
Holay-honuru - - -	3219	3219	2413
Udaguni - - - -	4452	4452	3098
Shikári-pura - - -	3760	3768	1931
Ikeri and *Sagar* - - -	4691	4691	3365
Cumashi - - - -	3091	3585	1649
China-giri and *Basava-pattana* - -	9071	9071	6224
Danivasa and *Lacky-hully* - -	4138	4138	2582
Hari-hara - - -	1931	2164	1011
Holalu - - - -	595	700	321
Copa - - -	6612	6612	3944
Anawati - - -	3544	3544	2138
Cowl-durga - - - - -	6615	6615	5017
	72873	73948	46467

CHAPTER XIX.

June 3.

Talucs in the *Pattana Ráyada.*	Families.	Houses.	Ploughs.
Mahásura Nagara - - -	5653	5748	3352
Mahásura Ashta-grám - -	4527	4527	2280
Pattana Ashta-grám - - -	5075	5075	3078
Hardena-hully - - - -	3701	3701	1592
Bucana-caray - - - -	1512	1394	1098
Bettada-pura - - - -	3252	3105	2500
Taiuru and *Moguru* - -	5054	5056	2770½
Arculagodu Conanuru - -	4416	4337	3707
Nunjinagodu - - -	963	960	445
Edatory - - -	2188	2188	1678
Priya-pattana - - - -	2507	2431	1569
Goruru - - -	2627	2612	2473
Kanyakarna-hully vulgo *Cancan-hully*	3728	3633	2996
Honganuru - - - -	1186	1186	513½
Ellanduru - - - -	2652	4464	829
Callalay - - - -	3893	6265	1999
Ki-caray - - - -	2079	2114	1664
Cayragodu - - - -	4731	4932	2708
Sosila and *Talacadu* - - -	4204	4324	2338
Gundal and *Tirucanambi* - - -	7025	7235	3914
Capala-durga - - -	583	604	453
Tonuru and *Mail-cotay* - -	3153	3196	2385
Mahá-ráyana-durga - - -	2071	2071	1136
Malawully - - -	4033	4075	2743
Cuttay Malalawady - -	2142	2162	1481
Cotagala - - - -	1589	1590	1050
Hegodu-devana-cotay - -	6251	6251	4123
Sali-gráma - - - -	1177	1261	1015
Narasingha-pura - -	5664	5893	3448
Maduru - - - -	4415	4415	2621
Deva-Ráya-Durga - -	5359	5364	4052
Budhi-cotay - - -	2971	4347	2297
Ercalavy - - -	2873	4432	2089
Magadi - - -	4426	4326	3522
Sunacul - - -	1092	1557	687
Silagutta - - -	5566	7848	3729
Devund-hully - -	4449	4976	3857
Bhairawana-durga - -	934	934	931
Coruta-giri - -	2092	2182	1152
Total carried over	131813	142771	86275

CHAPTER XIX.

June 3.

Pattana Ráyada continued.	Families.	Houses.	Ploughs.
Brought over	131813	142771	86275
Chin'-ráyan'-durga	2399	2849	1838
Chica Bala-pura	5503	8184	3652
China-pattana, vulgo *Chenapatam*	5069	4950	3514
Colar	7059	10209	4922
Hosso-cotay	8408	14681	5666
Madhu-giri	4803	4950	2540
Pauguda	4452	4981	1596
Ambaji-durga	5188	8472	3574
Huliculla	923	1251	796
Nidjagul	3146	5165	2807
Nellavungul	2766	4498	2416
Gudibunda	4160	4879	2346
Anicul	2484	4147	1599
Doda Bala-pura	7166	10187	5201
Hangaluru	11532	17506	8245
Mahá-káli-durga	1766	2320	1497
Jangama-Cotay	2684	3909	1596
Guma-Naiada-Pallia	3187	4147	2005
Malavagul	7623	10012	5990
Rama-giri	1757	1798	1905
Huliuru-durga	4803	4803	3394
Tayculum or *Maluro*	5988	8783	4081
Tamcuru	3855	3840	2854
Honawully	3492	2664	4545
Budihalu	1598	2181	1130
Niddygul	2598	2601	1207
Sira	6673	6593	2756
Nughi-hully	1786	1786	1416
Caduba	3992	3998	3336
Bailuru	7447	7447	5741
Gubi	1237	1319	781
Gráma	1817	1881	1609
Hebburu	2754	4131	2122
Garudana-giri	1449	1673	1103
Banawara	2483	2611	1875
Sakra-pattana	2270	2265	1526
Turiva-caray	3738	4782	2658
Hárana-hully	2598	3071	2280
Chin'-raya-pattana	3684	3994	3731
Cunda-Caray	1481	1483	1216
Carried over	289551	343772	198341

CHAPTER XIX.

June 3.

Pattana Ráyada continued.	Families.	Houses.	Ploughs.
Brought forward	289551	343772	198341
Belluru	2329	3315	1919
Cunigul	3604	3716	2357
Chica-Náyakana-hully	2266	2461	1697
Naga-mangala	4268	4992	2963
Hasina	4505	4459	3484
Hagalawadi	5832	7317	3878
Wostara	3013	3013	2317
Ajim-pura	3536	3855	3011
Terri-caray	3422	3606	2333
Chica Moguluru	4893	5175	3528
Caduru	1782	1833	1106
Yagati	2128	2638	1708
Total	331129	390152	228642

Recapitulation.			
13 *Talucs* in *Chatrakal Ráyada*	29289	31320	19705½
19 Ditto in *Nagara Ráyada*	72873	73948	46467
91 Ditto in *Pattana Ráyada*	331129	390152	228642
Total	433291	495420	294814½

History of the *Mysore Rájás*.

I also procured from my friend Captain Marriote a history of the *Mysore Rájás*, which the present *Dalawai* composed in the *Marattah* language. A copy has been presented to the government of Bengal.

Seringapatam I found recovering apace. Some more openings for parades, and other public uses, have been made in the town; but it still continues to be a sink of nastiness. The suburb called *Shahar Ganjam* is increasing rapidly, and care has been taken to form the streets wide and straight. A new magistracy has just now been established, under the superintendance of Captain Symmonds, an establishment that was much wanted; for the officers of the garrison have neither time nor inclination to investigate civil affairs. Provisions are good, and, bread excepted, are cheap. Artificers have

CHAPTER XIX. June 3. been assembled, and are now busy in preparing military stores; such as gun-carriages, leather accoutrements, tents, and cordage of the aloe leaves (*Agave vivipara*). This employs many people, and will turn out a great saving to the Company. Trade is beginning to be restored, and considerable quantities of the produce of *Malabar* again pass this way. The lands are increasing in value; and people, who had formerly deserted to adjacent districts, are now returning, and with the utmost eagerness are reclaiming their former possessions. This climate, however, continues to be very unhealthy; and a damp is thrown on every thing by the sickness of the Resident, Colonel Close. Owing to this, I have been much disappointed by not receiving any answers to the queries which I proposed.

CHAPTER XX.

JOURNEY FROM SERINGAPATAM TO MADRAS.

JUNE 4th.—Early in the morning I left *Seringapatam;* on coming to where my tents had been pitched, I found, that in the storm of the preceding night they had been blown down, and that my people were dispersed into the neighbouring villages. I was, therefore, necessitated to halt a day, in order to put my tents into some kind of repair, and to reassemble my people. In this I had great difficulty, most of them being intoxicated.

CHAPTER XX. June 4th. Storm.

Kari-ghat, near which I halted, is a high peaked hill, which consists chiefly of schistose mica, that is composed of white quartz, and silvery mica, disposed in an undulating manner. When the stone is split in the direction of the *strata,* the mica is most conspicuous, and makes a very beautiful appearance.

Strata of *Kari-ghat.*

5th June.—I went three cosses to *Banuru.* The country through which I passed belongs to the *Pattana Ashta-grám* district. Near *Kari-ghat,* I passed chiefly through rice grounds watered by the great canal, and bounded toward the north by low hills at no great distance from the *Cavery.* Two cosses from *Kari-ghat,* I passed the *Array caray,* the great reservoir in which the canal terminates, and which, collecting the superfluous water of that noble work, irrigates much land. From thence to *Banuru* the level country widens, and is mostly arable; but little of it is watered. It looks very well, many of the fields being enclosed, and interspersed with *Babul* trees (*Mimosa indica* Lamarck). These do, not injure the corn

June 5. Appearance of the country.

Babul tree.

CHAPTER XX. June 5. growing under them, and hinder so much ground only from being productive as is occupied by the diameter of their stems. Although it does not grow to a large size, the *Babul* is very useful in making the implements of agriculture. Its bark is valuable to the tanner. At reasonable distances, therefore, throughout the *Ragy* fields, young plants of it are allowed to grow.

Banuru. *Banuru*, under the government of *Hyder*, contained five hundred houses, which are now reduced to one hundred and fifty. In order to prevent it from being of use to Lord Cornwallis, it was plundered by *Tippoo's* troops; and in the late war it was again plundered by the dealers in grain (*Lumbadies*) who followed Colonel Read's detachment. It has a very fine *Tank*, that receives a branch from the great canal.

Rent of dry-field. Not having been satisfied with the former accounts which I received of the rent of dry-field in this part of the country, I took the officers of revenue and the farmers to the field. They say, that the rent varies from two to ten *Sultany Fanams* for what is called a *Wocula* or *Colaga* land, according to the quality of the soil, of which there are four distinctions. They confess that in general the *Wocula* land sows more than a *Colaga* of seed, which contains thirty-two *Sultany Seers*. The poorer soils not only pay less rent, but in them the extent of a *Wocula* land is greater than in a rich mould. I found great difficulty in getting them to say any thing upon which I could depend; but at length I got a measurement, which I believe, so far as it goes, may be considered as accurate. I measured a field, said to sow forty-eight *Seers* of *Ragy*, besides *Avaray*, *Tovary*, and the like, and which in the books of revenue is rated at one *Colaga* and a half. The rent was twelve *Fanams* for grain, 25 *per cent.* on the above for straw, and a certain quantity of grain, which was originally paid in kind; but in place of it four *Fanams* are now added to the rent. The whole field measured 109,848 square feet, and paid nineteen *Fanams*, or at the rate of 4*s.* 8½*d.* an acre. It was divided into two portions of 60,480 and 49368 square feet; which, although thus unequal in size, and apparently of the same soil, were estimated at the same value, and were allowed the same quantity of seed. The soil was of the best quality, and was a fine red earth, which in favourable seasons is very productive of *Ragy*. The seed is at the rate of 2 $\frac{54}{100}$ pecks an acre. This is about 11$\frac{1}{2}$ *per cent.* thicker than what was given by my former measurement at *Seringapatam;* but in such accounts as a traveller in *India* can procure, that is no material difference. To this we must add one fourth part of the above quantity of the seed of the accompanying pulses. June 5.

6th *June*.—I went two *Sultany* cosses to *Sosila*. The country is plain, with a few small hills interspersed. Some of the soil is very sandy; but there is much rice-land, supplied chiefly by canals from the river. That of *Sosila*, according to an old valuation made by *Deva Ráya*, amounts to what was estimated to sow five hundred *Candacas* of seed, at 225 *Seers* each. This land is watered by a canal coming from *Rám Swami Anacut*, which dam is two cosses below the island of *Seringapatam*. The farmers commonly employ the dry-seed cultivation, which requires only $\frac{4}{5}$ of the *Candaca* of seed for the extent of land called a *Candaca*. They find, however, by experience, after three or four crops cultivated in this manner, that the soil is improved by taking a transplanted crop. They have only one crop of rice in the year, and that grows in the rainy season, as is usual with land watered by canals from the *Cavery*. Good land produces 25 *Candacas* of rough rice from the *Candaca* land. The rent of the whole, good and bad, is on each *Candaca* land 5$\frac{1}{2}$ *Candacas* of rice in the husk for the grain, and 7$\frac{1}{2}$ *Fanams* for the straw. The *Candaca* of rice in the husk is worth fifteen *Fanams*. The rent, therefore, is eighty *Fanams* for the *Candaca;* and the average rent and seed makes only 28 *per cent.* of the produce of the best land, besides the straw, which from the vicinity of *Seringapatam* sells very high, and therefore pays part of the rent. The lowness of this tax, compared with that at *Seringapatam*, where the rice- June 6. Watered lands.

CHAPTER XX. June 6. grounds pay ten seeds, is owing to the want of a sufficient supply of water; so that one quarter of the fields cannot produce rice, and are cultivated for *Ragy*.

Appearance of the country. A little *Jola* and cotton are raised here, in the same manner as on the opposite side of the river, which I have described in the eighth chapter of this Journal. The dry lands seem mostly waste; and the country which I saw to-day is neither so well wooded nor so well enclosed as that through which I passed yesterday. *Sosila* is a town that contains about 250 houses, and has a large fort constructed of mud and rough stones. It is situated on the banks of the *Cavery*, opposite to the junction of the *Kapini*, and has long been subject to the *Mysore* family.

June 7. 7th *June*.—I went three cosses and a half to *Kirigavil*. The country through which I passed is mostly dry arable land; but much of it is waste. I crossed one small ridge of hills, consisting of naked rocks of white granite. *Kirigavil* has once been a large village; but after the affair at *Malawully* the *Sultan*, in order to prevent it from being of use to the army under General Harris, destroyed it, and few of the houses have been rebuilt. The greater part of its inhabitants are *Mussulmans*; for, during the former government of the *Mysore Rájás*, it was given in *Jaghire* to a *Mahomedan* family in their service. The heir of this family now lives at the place, and has a considerable pension from the Company, for which he appears to be grateful.

June 8. 8th *June*.—I went three cosses to *Malawully*. All the country through which I passed seems capable of cultivation; and there are vestiges remaining to show that the whole has once been ploughed, and enclosed with quickset hedges. Much of it is now waste, and the fences are very ruinous. There is little irrigation.

Malawully. *Malawully* is a large mud fort, separated into two portions by a transverse wall. The upper portion, reserved for the *Bráhmans*, is in good repair; but the works made to defend the low casts have become ruinous. This place formerly belonged to the *Rájás* of

Talacadu, which is said to be only four cosses distant; a circumstance which from the maps I cannot explain. The *Talacadu Rájás* were conquered by those of *Mysore*, and this must have happened previous to the year of *Sal.* 1595; as there is here an inscription of that date, in which *Deva Rájá Bupala*, commonly called *Deva Ráya* the great, is styled sovereign of the country. A copy of this has been given to the Bengal government. After the conquest, a village, half a coss east from *Malawully*, and named *Ancanahully*, was given to the *Talacadu Rájá* in *Jaghire*. This the family retained till the government of *Hyder*, when they were obliged to fly; and the people here are ignorant of the place to which they have retired. CHAPTER XX. June 8.

Orchards of the late *Sultans*.

Hyder gave *Malawully* in *Jaghire* to his son *Tippoo*, and of course it enjoyed considerable favour, and contained a thousand houses. Adjoining to the town is a very fine reservoir, that gives a constant supply of water to a fruit-garden which the *Sultan* planted. This is of great extent; but the soil is poor; and some of it is indeed so bad, that the trees have died, and the ground has been again converted into rice-fields. The establishment kept in this garden consists of one *Daroga*, or superintendant; one writer; and ten labourers, who, as they cultivate the rice-fields, are not able to keep the fruit trees in decent order, much less to prevent the walks from being in a most slovenly condition. The trees are 2400 in number; and of these one half are *Mangoes*. They are loaded with fruit, and some of the oranges are very fine. The *Mangoes* that I saw were but ordinary. One kind, if the account of the superintendant is to be credited, is very curious. It annually produces two crops, one in the hot season, and the other during the rains. In the centre of the garden is a small, but neat cottage *(Bungalo)*, from which grass walks diverge in all directions.

Engagement at *Malawully*.

About two miles south-west from *Malawully* is a large reservoir, near which the *Sultan* made a trial of his army with that of General Harris. After having by this found that his troops were totally inadequate to face the English, he shut himself up in *Seringapatam*.

CHAPTER XX. June 8.

The trial was absurd; but it is said, that *Tippoo* was not to blame. The officers whom he sent to reconnoitre, with the flattery usual among the natives, gave him false information, and induced him to bring his forces down into the open country, on the supposition of the English army being a small advanced party which he could intercept. Before he was undeceived, he had advanced so far, that he must have either engaged, or lost all his guns. Being afraid of dispiriting his people by the sacrifice of his artillery, he preferred the former. While, therefore, he began to withdraw his guns, he formed his army and made an attack with a part of it, which was entirely lost; but with this sacrifice he was able to carry off all his guns, and to bring away the remainder of his troops without much disorder. After the action, *Tippoo* sent and destroyed *Malawully*; and only about five hundred of its houses have as yet been rebuilt.

June 9. Appearance of the country.

9th *June.*—I went four long cosses to *Hulluguru.* For the first half of the way the country resembled that through which I came yesterday. Afterwards it became poorer and poorer, and was covered with low *Mimosas.* At one coss distant from *Huluguru,* is the *Madura* river, which was so much swollen by the rains, that the loaded cattle had some difficulty in fording. It never dries entirely, and has its source from a large *Tank* at *Caduba,* near *Gubi.* Its proper name is the *Caduba.*

Iron mines.

Between *Malawully* and this river are two villages, *Bana-samudra* and *Halasu-hully,* at which iron ore is smelted; and from thence *Seringapatam* receives its chief supply. I was in search of the forges; but was informed that they were at *Hulluguru;* nor was I undeceived until I had gone too far to return. On my arrival at *Hulluguru* I found no smelting forges; but a manufacture of iron boilers for sugar works, and of the common implements of agriculture. The iron comes from mines near *Chenapatam* and *Rama-giri.*

Hulluguru.

Hulluguru is an open village, containing about 120 houses. Both in the invasion under Lord Cornwallis, and in that under General

Harris, it was burned. It is situated three cosses south from *Capala-durga*, and four north from *Baswana kéda*, a ford in the *Cavery* one coss below the junction of the *Caduba* with that river. The road certainly leads nearer the *Cavery* than, from the situation of the principal stages in the best maps, I have, for want of better authority, placed it. CHAPTER XX. June 9.

There are in this neighbourhood two hills producing sandal wood: *Baswana-Betta*, in the *Malawully* district, from which this year were procured 250 trees; and *Capala-durga*, which produced somewhat less. No more will be obtainable for eight years. On these hills there are no valuable timber trees, but abundance of *bamboos*.

10th *June.*—I went two *Sultany* cosses to *Satnuru*, through a pretty wide valley, with hills on both sides of the road. The soil is in general poor, and much of it is over-run with low *Mimosas*, and other bushes. From *Capala-durga*, *Satnuru* is distant one coss; and is a poor open village, containing about thirty houses, of which ten are occupied by *Mussulmans*. These are now betaking themselves to agriculture. In the public accompts, *Satnuru* is called an *Usul Grám*, or principal village; but in India we must guard against high-sounding names. The chief *(Gauda)* is the poorest creature that I ever saw. Half a coss from *Satnuru* is a forge for smelting the black sand ore of iron. June 10. Appearance of the country.

11th *June.*—I went three cosses to *Canicarna-hully*, commonly called *Cancan-hully*. The former name is universally said by the natives to be the proper one; but the derivation which they give of it seems very forced. *Canicarna*, they say, is the genitive case of *Canicar*, which in the *Tamul* language signifies a proprietor of land: and *Hully*, in the language of *Carnata*, is a village. * The road by which I came passes through a valley, in some places narrow and rocky, and in others wide, partly cultivated, and partly overgrown with low trees. The hills surrounding it are very rocky, and are said to be much infested by tigers. June 11.

* The name of this village is properly *Kanya-karna*, composed of two *Sanskrit* words, *Kanyá* virgin, or the goddess *Bhawáni*, and *Karna* ear.

CHAPTER XX.

June 11. *Cancan-hully, and Jagá-deva Ráya of Chena-pattana.*

Cancan-hully is the residence of an *Amildar*, and is a pretty fotr built by *Jagá-deva Ráya* of *Chena-pattana*, whom, in the tragical story of *Sivana Samudra*, I have already mentioned, as having been in his time one of the most powerful princes of this neighbourhood. A *Bráhman* here possesses a grant of land from *Imudy Ancusha Ráya* of *Chena-pattana*, son of *Pedda Ancusha Ráya*, son of *Jagá-Deva Ráya*. He acknowledges the superiority of *Sri Ráma Deva* of *Penu-conda*, son of *Sri Ranga Ráya*, who must have been one of the royal family of *Vijya-nagara*, that on the destruction of the empire retired to *Penu-conda*, and by the *Polygars* of this vicinity was nominally acknowledged as a master. This grant is dated in *Sal.* 1546, which, according to *Ramuppa*, is 35 years after the destruction of *Vijya-nagara*.

Rájás of Mysore, or Mahásura.

The descendants of *Jagá-deva* were subdued by the *Mysore* family. At a temple here are two inscriptions on stone. The one is in the reign of *Chica Deva Ráya Wodear* of *Mahásura*, for so in all inscriptions is *Mysore* written. The word is said to signify the great warrior. The other inscription is in the reign of *Deva Ráya Wodear*, who in the year of *Sal.* 1589 grants certain lands to a *Jangama's Matam*; for the *Mysore* family are much under the influence of that priesthood, as all the females wear the *Linga*; although the reigning prince declares himself a follower of the *Sri Vaishnavam Bráhmans*.

Krishna Ráya of *Mysore* rebuilt the great temple of this place; which, as usual, is supposed to have been of great antiquity. According to fable, it was founded by *Valmica*, a celebrated *Bráhman*, the author of the *Ramayena*, who lived in the *Tritaia Yugam*, many hundred thousand years ago. Previous to the invasion by Lord Cornwallis, the country was fully cultivated. The devastation was commenced by *Tippoo*, who blew up the works in order to prevent them from being useful to the British army. After this the *Anicul Polygar* ravaged the country, Colonel Read having invited him back to his dominions. According to the accounts of the *Amildar*, this *gentle Hindu* has rendered two fifths of the whole arable lands a waste; and, from the small number of inhabitants, the beasts of prey have increased so much, that, during the two last years of the *Sultan's* government, eighty of the inhabitants of *Cancan-hully* were carried away by tigers from within the walls of the fort. These have been since repaired, and the people can now sleep with safety. To keep off these destructive animals, every village in the neighbourhood is strongly fenced with a hedge of thorns. On the approach of the army under General Harris, *Tippoo* burned the town, and he did not allow to escape this favourable opportunity of destroying an idolatrous place of worship. He broke down the *Mandapam*, or portico of the temple, and nothing remains but the gateway, and the shrine; to destroy which, probably his workmen, durst not venture. *Cancan-hully* at present contains about two hundred houses. Before the invasion of Lord Cornwallis there were at least five hundred. It stands on the west side of the *Arkawati* river.

CHAPTER XX.

June 11.

Arkawati.

The river *Arkawati* comes from *Nandi*, and passes through the great *Tank* named *Nagaray caray* at *Doda Bala-pura*. It then passes *Magadi* and *Rama-giri*, and falls into the *Cavery* six cosses from *Cancan-hully*, and one coss below the ford, or passage of *Baswana Kéda*. For three months in the hot season, it contains no stream; but, by digging a little way into the channel, good water may always be procured.

June 12.

12th *June*.—Having been troubled with an irregular tertian fever ever since I left *Seringapatam*, I halted to-day at *Cancan-hully*, in order to take medicine. I employed my time in taking some account of the state of agriculture, in which I was assisted by the *Amildar*.

Villages.

A great impediment to good cultivation arises from a practice, very common in India, of all the farmers living in towns and villages. The fields that are distant from the houses cannot receive manure, and of course produce little, and pay a small rent. It is true, that in the revenue accompts all the lands, according to the

CHAPTER XX. June 12. quality of the soil, are valued at the same rate; but no one will give more than a fourth of the valuation for lands that are distant from his village. Indeed, the present number of inhabitants is not adequate to cultivate more than the fields that are near the towns.

Wages. Most of the cultivation is performed by the hands of the farmers, and of their own families. A few hired servants, but no slaves, are employed. A man servant gets annually of *Ragy* four *Candacas* of 200 *Seers* of 72 inches, or nearly 26½ bushels, worth at an average 28 *Fanams*, with 12 *Fanams* in money. In all, he receives 40 *Fanams*, or 1*l.* 4*s.* 11¼*d.* The hours of work are from 6¼ in the morning until noon; and from two in the afternoon until sun-set. The number of holidays allowed is very small; but the servant occasionally gets four or five days to repair his house. At seed time and harvest, a day-labourer gets from ⅓ to ¼ of a *Fanam*, or from 2½*d.* to rather more than 1¼*d.* a day. Women get daily from ¼ to ⅕ of a *Fanam*, or about 1¼*d.*

Stock, and size of farms. No farmer here has more than six ploughs. Those who have four, or more, are reckoned very rich. For each plough, one man and two oxen are kept. The *Amildar* says, that each plough can cultivate ten *Woculas* of dry-field, of which one half will be *Ragy* land; or that it will cultivate five *Colagas* of dry-field, and five of watered land. The chiefs of villages *(Gaudas)* say, that, if a man cultivates five or six *Colagas* of rice land with one plough, he can sow no dry grains. The account of the *Amildar* (chief of a district) is evidently that upon which most dependance ought to be placed.

I measured a field said to require seven bullas, or 1¾ *Woculas* of *Ragy* for seed, and found it to contain 73884 square feet. The *Wocula* or *Colaga* land contains at this rate 42218 square feet; and the plough, if confined to dry-field, should cultivate only 9$\frac{7}{10}$ acre. The rate of seed on rice ground has been ascertained at *Ráya-cotay* by Colonel Read from actual experiment; and, according to my information, the five *Colagas* here, at this rate, would sow almost an acre and a quarter. So that a plough can also cultivate 1¼ acre of rice land, and 4 $\frac{52}{100}$ acres of dry field. This small quantity, it must be observed, is the estimate of the *Amildar*: that of the *Gaudas* deserves no attention.

Sugar-cane

The quantity of watered land here is not considerable; but a large proportion of it is employed to raise sugar-cane. This is all of the *Restali* kind; the *Puttaputti* not having as yet found its way into this district. The rent is paid by a division of the crop. The government should have one half, and usually receives 500 *Seers* from the *Wocula* land, or about 11 cwt. an acre. This is so great a return, that I suspect some mistake. After sugar-cane, the ground must be cultivated with rice one year, before sugar-cane be again taken.

Rice lands.

When, in a favourable season, the *Tanks* are filled, two crops of rice might be procured from the same ground in the course of one year; but the farmers, being few in number, can cultivate one half of the rice grounds only at one season, and the remainder afterwards; nor can the inhabitants of the villages, where dry grains only are cultivated, be induced to settle near the watered lands, although the profits on these are much greater to the farmer than those on *Ragy* land. The natives of *Karnata* seem indeed to be immoderately attached to their birth-place; and so many of them having deserted their native huts during the reign of *Tippoo* is a strong proof of his tyranny.

Ragy and Shamay.

Ragy (Cynosurus corocanus) pays a fixed rent, which in the lands near the villages varies from five to two *Fanams* a *Wocula* land, which, at the rate of my measurement, would be from 3*s.* 2½*d.* to 1*s.* 3½*d.* an acre. *Shamay (Panicum miliare. E.M.)*, the next most common crop here, pays one half of the produce as rent. According to the *Amildar's* account, a *Wocula* land of the best quality produces as follows:

Seed					
Ragy	*Wocula*	1	produce 2 *Candacas*	worth	14 *Fanams*.
Avaray, or *Tovary*.		¼	6 *Colagas*	-	$\frac{4}{11}$

The rent is 5 *Fanams*, or not quite 28 *per cent.* of the produce.

CHAPTER XX.

June 12.

The same land cultivated with *Shamay*, which is done in places that are too distant to manure, requires $1\frac{1}{4}$ *Colaga* of seed, and produces 15 *Colagas*, worth 6 *Fanams*, of which the government gets one half. Although this requires less trouble than the *Ragy*, the farmer has most profit by the latter grain.

Coco-nut plantations.

On the banks of the river above *Cancan-hully*, there are many coco-nut plantations. A few *Arecas* are intermixed; but in a general point of view, these are of no importance. The coco-nuts are sold in the shell to the people of the *Bára-Mahál.* The ground is the property of government; but the trees belong to the farmer; and so long as these grow, the public has no right to the soil. When an old tree dies, another is planted in its stead, and must be watered for six or seven years; after which it begins to bear, and requires no more irrigation. They live for about a century, and are in full vigour for one half of that time. They are never cut until they are dead. These palms, in this country, are never manured with salt, and eight months in the year produce ripe fruit. In the month following the summer solstice, owing to the cold and rain, all the fruit which is then on the trees falls off; and during the three following months none arrives at maturity; but there are plenty of green nuts, which contain a juice fit for drinking. Each of the trees annually produces from 10 to 200 nuts, which are worth five *Fanams* a hundred. Of the produce the government takes one half. Some of them are planted on dry-field, and others on watered land, and the soil under the trees is cultivated with the appropriate grains. If the trees be sufficiently thick, the crop of grain is poor, and the farmer is allowed to keep the whole; but, if he neglect his gardens, and have only a few trees scattered through a large space of ground, the government takes one half of the grain also; which is but reasonable. There is, however, no space defined for each tree; their being too distant, so as to allow a demand of rent for the grain, is left to be determined at the discretion of the *Amildar*, which is an error. The *Amildar* says, that they may be planted at five or six fathoms distance from each other. At 36 feet, an acre will plant about 33 trees; the produce of each of which may be estimated at five *Fanams*, or a little more than three shillings. It is very seldom, however, that a piece of ground is fully planted.

June 13. State of the country.

June 13th.—I went three cosses to *Malalawady*, a village of the *Chena-pattana* district. The greater part of the country through which I passed is overgrown with low trees and bushes, and very little of what is arable is actually cultivated. By the way I crossed three times the channel of a small river named the *Swarna-réká*. It comes from *Anicul*, and joins the *Arkawati* a little above *Kanyakarna-hully*. *Malalawady* is a small town, with a ruinous fort. Before the invasion of Lord Cornwallis, it contained three hundred houses. *Tippoo*, in order to prevent its being of use to his enemies, burned it. Most of the wretched inhabitants perished from hunger and disease; and although it met with no disturbance in the last war, it now contains only sixty-eight houses. It stands eight cosses from the *Cavery*, and is surrounded by some good dry fields. *Ragy* and *Horse-gram* form the chief part of the crops, sell at about the same price, and are equally used in the common diet of the inhabitants.

June 14. Company's territory.

June 14th.—I went four cosses to *Tully*. Soon after leaving *Malalawady*, I entered a hilly country, which continued until I reached *Tully*, the first place in the districts belonging to *Karnata* that have been added to the Company's province of the *Bára-mahál*. To-day I crossed the *Swarna-réká* again three times.

Tully.

Tully is an open village near a small fort, and contains about sixty houses. Before the invasion of Lord Cornwallis it contained about five hundred. After the capture of *Bangalore*, many of the inhabitants retired to *Tully*, and obtained from the *Sultan* a guard of five hundred horse, and two thousand foot. The detachment from the British army at *Hoss'uru*, having heard of this, marched all night, and at day-break surprised *Tully*. The garrison were roused

CHAPTER XX.

June 13.

in time to be able to run away without loss, for they did not attempt to resist. The assailants obtained a great deal of plunder, and destroyed the town. An officer *(Phousdar)* of *Tippoo's* came some days afterwards, and dug up a large quantity of grain that had been concealed under ground. A party of dealers in grain *(Lumbadies)* came after this, and swept every thing clean; so that a large proportion of the inhabitants perished of hunger. During the government of *Tippoo*, few of the remainder came back; but most of them retired to the *Bára-mahál*, in order to obtain Colonel Read's protection. They are now daily returning.

Denkina-cotay family.

Tully formerly belonged to the *Denkina-cotay Polygar*, who, from being possessed of a town named *Bala-hully*, took the title of *Belalla Ráya*; but he was no relation of the *Belalla* monarchs of *Karnata*. He was deprived of his dominions by *Jaga Deva Ráya* of *Chenapattana*, whose successors were in their turn expelled by the *Mysore* family.

Districts annexed to the *Bára-mahál*.

Tully forms a part of the *Denkina-cotay Taluc*, which with several other districts of *Karnata* were annexed to the *Bára-mahál* after the fall of *Seringapatam*. These districts are the *Talucs* of *Hosso-uru*, *Denkina-cotay*, *Kella-mangalam*, *Ratna-giri*, *Vencata-giri-cotay*, and that portion of the *Alumbady Taluc* which lies on the left of the *Cavery*, together with the *Polyams*, or feudatory lordships, of *Punganuru*, *Pedda-Nayakana-Durga*, *Bagaluru*, *Suli-giri*, and *Ankusa-giri*.

Polygars.

All the *Polygars* have been restored to their estates, and put on a footing very similar to that of the *Zemindars* of Bengal. They pay a fixed rent, or tribute, for their lordships; but have no jurisdiction over the inhabitants, for whose protection an officer *(Sheristadar)*, appointed and paid by the government, resides at each lordship. The establishment of officers of revenue and police are paid by the *Polygars*, whose profits may now be about a fourth of the revenue; but, as the country recovers, these will greatly increase.

June 13.

In this district the natives of the *Bára-mahál* will not settle, on account of the coldness of the climate during the rainy season, which they find not only very disagreeable but also unhealthy.

State of cultivation.

The chief officer, *Tahsildar*, of *Denkina-cotay*, a very sensible man, says, that at present he has 2700 ploughs, and that it would require 6000 more to cultivate the whole arable land in his district. The proportion of waste land in the other districts of *Karnata*, which have been added to the *Bára-mahál*, is nearly similar; and, so far as I can judge, I think they are in as good a state as the best districts now belonging to the *Mysore Rájá*, and infinitely better than any of those through which the *Marattah* army passed.

Barren lands.

The *Tahsildar* estimates the land in his district that is too steep or rocky for the plough to be about a fourth of the whole.

Iron.

In the neighbouring woods some black sand ore is smelted into iron.

Sandal.

South from hence, in the *Alumbady* district, is a hill producing sandal wood. Captain Graham, the collector, sold to a renter all the trees that were fit for cutting, and received for them 300 *Pagodas*. The condition of the sale was, that only the old full-grown trees should be cut; but the fellow has taken every stick of any size, and there will be no more fit for cutting in less than ten years.

Lumbadies.

In the woods west from *Tully*, the *Lumbadies*, after a trading expedition, refresh their cattle for eight or ten days. They then carry to *Dravada*, or the low country, a cargo of *Ragy*, *Avaray*, *Tovary*, *Ellu*, and *Hessaru*, and return from thence with a cargo of salt and a little rice.

Watered lands.

In this district all the reservoirs for irrigation are in repair, but seven or eight of them only are of any consequence. Indeed, the cultivation of rice, in these districts annexed to the *Bára-mahál*, is by no means important. There are, however, many *Cuttays*, or small *Tanks*, from which the water is raised by machinery to irrigate

CHAPTER XX.

Turkari, or kitchen gardens, a most valuable kind of cultivation. There are also many plantations of coco-nut and *Areca* palms.

June 13. Manufactures.

All the manufactures of the annexed districts, except at *Bagaluru*, are coarse, and fit only for the use of the lower classes. A great supply for the rich comes from *Saliem*, and from *Bangaluru*.

Bráhmans.

The temple of *Gópála* at *Tully*, as appears by a (*Sunnud*) deed now extant, was built, or rebuilt rather, by *Vira Rájaia* son of *Dalawai Dodaia*, in the reign of *Krishna Ráya Wodear*, the *Curtur* of *Mysore*, and in the year of *Sal.* 1640. Although little more than 80 years old, it has fallen into great decay. Its *Rath*, or chariot, is remarkably indecent, and has now become useless, the whole property of the temple having been reassumed by *Hyder* and *Tippoo.* The *Bráhmans* on this account are not a little clamorous; but the want of endowment seems to have sharpened their wits, and I found among them some very intelligent men.

Mysore family, its divisions, and customs.

These *Bráhmans* informed me, that the males of the *Mysore* family are divided into two great branches, the *Rájá-bundas*, and the *Callalays.* A *Rájá-bunda* man can marry only a *Callalay* girl, and the men of the *Callalay* family are only allowed to marry the daughters of a *Rájá-bunda.* The head of the *Rájá-bundas* is the *Curtur*, or sovereign. The head of the *Callalays* is the *Dalawai*, whose predecessors, although they always acknowledged the superiority of the *Curtur*, yet frequently possessed all the authority of the state. When any action is said to have been performed by such or such a *Mysore Rájá*, it is by no means necessarily implied, that the actor was one of the *Curturs;* for the *Dalawais* also enjoyed the titles of *Mysore Rájá*, and *Wodear*. Some of the males of each family are of *Vishnu's* side, and some of them of *Siva's*; but none wear the *Linga*, and all acknowledge the *Bráhmans* as their *Gurus*; and the *Curtur*, immediately on ascending the throne, in whatever religion he may have been educated, always adopts the ceremonies at least of the *Sri Vaishnavam.* The ladies of both families wear the

Linga, refuse the authority of the *Bráhmans*, and are under the spiritual guidance of the *Jangamas*. This is one of those circumstances which among any other people would be considered as extraordinary, but which in the religion of the *Hindus* are common. The *Mysore* family are of *Karnata* extraction, and were not introduced by the *Telingana* princes who so long governed this country.

CHAPTER XX.

June 13.

Rachewar.

The *Rájáwar*, or *Rachewar*, must not be confounded with the *Rájá-bundas*, although they pretend to be *Kshatriyas*. They are originally from the north of India, and probably from the country which in our maps is called *Rachoor*.

Property of the *Bráhmans* seized on by government.

The *Bráhmans* conducted me to a fine *Tank*, and showed me an inscription, from which it appeared, that this reservoir had been constructed by a *Banijiga* merchant of *Naga-mangala*, a town in this vicinity. The work was done in the reign of *Achuta Ráya*, and in the year of *Salivahanam* 1452, which agrees very well with the chronology of *Ramuppa*. The whole ground irrigated from the *Tank* was originally intended for the use of religious men, *Jangamas*. *Bráhmans*, &c; but it has now fallen into the powerful hands of the state, which afflicts its former proprietors by applying its revenue to the administration of justice, the defence of the country, and other such worldly purposes.

Irrigation.

The reservoir is filled by a small torrent named the *Sanat-kumára*, which comes from a hill at a little distance toward the N.W. and, after going through many *Tanks*, and watering much rice land, falls into the *Cavery* near *Alumbady*.

June 15. Appearance of the country.

15th *June*.—I went three cosses to *Panch-akshara-pura*. This name is derived from some foolish charm, and signifies *the five-letter-city*. The place is a small village without a shop. The country is quite open, and consists mostly of lands fit for cultivation, with many small *Tanks*, and spots of irrigated land, and palm gardens; but, on the whole, it is very bare. One half at least of the arable land is said to be waste; but it seems to be in a better condition

CHAPTER XX.

June 15.

than most of the dominions of *Mysore*. *Panch-akshara-pura* was plundered and burned by some part of the British army under Lord Cornwallis; and on the approach of General Harris it suffered the same fate from *Tippoo*. This year an epidemic fever has been very destructive; it raged with the utmost violence for the five months preceding the vernal equinox, but is now on the decline.

June 16.

16th *June*.—I went three cosses to *Kellamangalam*, and by the way crossed two barren ridges covered with wood. Much of the intermediate arable land is waste.

Lumbadies, or Banjaries.

These woods and wastes are much frequented by the traders in grain called *Lumbadies*, or *Banjaries*, who even in the time of peace cannot entirely abstain from plunder. In the small villages near the forest, they occasionally rob, and commit murder; nor is it safe for one or two persons to pass unarmed through places in which they are. On account of their services during the two last wars, they have hitherto been treated with great indulgence. This has added audaciousness to the natural barbarity of their disposition; and, in order to repress their insolence, it was lately necessary to have recourse to a regular military force.

Districts added to the *Bára-mahál*.

I remained two days at *Kellamangalam*, taking an account of the state of its neighbourhood, as an example of that which prevails in the territories annexed to the *Bára-máhal*.

Kellamangalam.

Kellamangalam is a small fort with two reservoirs, and two suburbs (*Pettas*), and is the residence of a *Tahsildar;* for the country here is exactly under the same excellent administration that prevails in *Coimbetore*. Before the invasion of Lord Cornwallis, it contained five hundred houses; but, having been burned, both then, and in the late war, most of the inhabitants had dispersed, when Captain Graham, the collector of the *Bára-mahál*, took possession. Since that time three hundred houses have been rebuilt. *Kellamangalam* and *Hosso-uru*, which now form two districts, originally belonged to the *Polygar* of *Bagaluru*. Both these places, being rather weak, were long ago seized upon by the *Mysore Polygars;* but *Bagaluru* resisted all their attempts, and until the government of *Hyder* was not subjected to the authority of *Seringapatam.* In the war of Lord Cornwallis, the heir of *Bagaluru* joined Captain Read, and was very serviceable to him in procuring provisions for the army; and on the peace he followed that gentleman into the *Bára-mahál.* When, by the fall of *Seringapatam*, *Bagaluru* was annexed to this province, he was restored as *Polygar* (feudatory lord) to such part of the family domains as *Hyder* had seized; but the two districts of *Kellamangalam* and *Hosso-uru* are considered as the property of the state.

Weights and measures.

The *Candaca* here is equal to - $5\frac{693}{1000}$ bushels
The *Maund* of *betel-nut* to - $30\frac{315}{1000}$ lb.
The *Maund* of tobacco and *Jagory* to $24\frac{261}{1000}$ lb.

Average price of the produce of the country.

The following is given by the traders, as the average price of the most common articles of commerce, which are chiefly the produce of the country.

	Sultany Fanams.		Shillings.	Pence and decimal parts.
Rice in the husk, *per Candaca*	8	per bushel	0	10,523
Ragy, Cynosurus corocanus, do. -	8	do. -	0	10,523
Avaray, Dolichos Lablab, do. -	11	do. -	1	2,46933
Tovary, Cytisus Cajan, do. - -	12	do. -	1	3,785
Hessaru, Phaseolus Mungo, do. -	20	do. -	2	2,30825
Udu, Phaseolus Minimoo Roxb. do.	16	do. -	1	9,0465
Callay, Cicer arietinum, do. -	35	do. -	3	10,039
Shamay, Panicum miliare, E. M. do.	4	do. -	0	5,261425
Ellu, Sesamum, do. - -	30	do. -	3	2,56363
Huts' Ellu, Verbesina sativa Roxb. do.	14	do. -	1	6,46933
Huruli, Dolichos biflorus, do. -	5	do. -	0	6,577
Harulu, Ricinus, do. - -	18	do. -	1	11,67722
Wheat, do. - - -	40	do. -	4	4,61425
Danya, a seed like anise -	16	do. -	1	9,0465
Womum, a seed like cummin, do.	32	do. -	3	6,093
Salt, do. - - - - - -	28	do. -	3	0,93866
Tobacco, *per Maund* - -	7	*per Cwt.*	20	1,944
Jagory of sugar-cane, do. - -	4	do. -	11	4,7
Boiled *Betel-nut,* or *Areca,* do. -	25	do. -	57	2,05

CHAPTER XX.

June 16.

Oxen fit for the plough sell for from 30 to 40 *Fanams*, or from 19*s*. $8\frac{1}{2}$*d*. to 1*l*. 4*s*. $11\frac{1}{2}$*d*.

A sheep or goat fit for killing costs three *Fanams*, or 1*s*. $10\frac{1}{2}$*d*.

Dry-field measure.

Here the dry-field forms by far the greatest part of the arable land. Its extent is estimated by the quantity of *Ragy* seed that it requires. On measuring a field, said to require six *Colagas* of seed, I found it to contain 168,249 square feet; the *Colaga*, therefore, is nearly equal to $\frac{81}{100}$ parts of an acre.

Rent.

In every district, the dry-field of each village, according to its soil, is divided into three qualities. In some villages, of course, the best lands are of no more value than the worst in others; which occasions a great difference in the assessment, or rent. The valuation of the best lands in some villages is ten *Fanams* a *Colaga*, while in others it is only three. The rent at this place, for the best dry-field, is six *Fanams* the *Colaga;* for the second $4\frac{1}{2}$ *Fanams;* and for the third 3 *Fanams;* or 5*s*. $9\frac{3}{4}$*d*., 4*s*. $4\frac{1}{2}$*d*. and 2*s*. 11*d*. an acre.

Farmers forced to cultivate by the *Wudary*.

It is the land near the villages only that can be let at this rate. The farmers are not at all willing to cultivate any of the distant fields; and after they have cultivated as much of the fields near the villages as they are able to do at a proper season, and in a proper manner, it is the peculiar duty of a low village officer, named here the *Wudary*, assisted by the watchman *(Toty)*, to compel them to cultivate a certain portion of these remote fields; which receive no manure and little labour, and pay only a trifling rent, or a share of the produce in kind.

Crops taken from land of the best quality.

When the rainy season commences early enough, the first quality of dry-field is reserved for *Ragy*, and its accompaniments. If the rains are too late, this land is sown with *Shamay;* and should the season for that grain pass, it may be sown with *Huruli*. The seeds that are sown along with *Ragy* are *Avaray*, *Tovary*, *Pundrica (Hibiscus cannabinus)*, and *Harulu*. This last is seldom used; but in every field a portion of each of the others is commonly sown.

Ragy, &c.

After the first rain in spring, the field gets a double ploughing;

that is, once lengthwise, and once across. Eight days afterwards, this is repeated, and then the manure is given. In eight days more it gets two other double ploughings. After a rain in the month following the summer solstice, the seed is sown with the drill, or *Curigay*, and rows of the accompanying grains are put in by means of the pointed *bamboo (Sudiky)*. The field is then harrowed with a bunch of thorns. On the 15th day afterwards, it is broken with the hoe drawn by oxen, and called here *Guntivay;* and six days after that, the hoe is used in a direction crossing the former at right angles. On the 35th and 40th days, the same is repeated, and the weeds are then removed with a spade. The *Ragy*, four months after sowing, is ripe. It is cut with the straw, and trodden out by oxen. Its straw is reckoned better fodder than that of rice, and the grain in a storehouse will keep ten years; whereas after a third part of that time rice in the husk is quite spoiled. Along with a *Coluga* of *Ragy*, may be sown $1\frac{3}{16}$ *Colaga* of *Avaray*, or $\frac{1}{8}$ *Colaga* of *Tovary*. The *Pundrica* is sown in very small quantities. Its bark makes a bad rope for the use of the farm, and its acid leaves are used in the family as a green; but in the account of the produce it may be altogether overlooked. The seed for an acre is $\frac{442}{1000}$ bushels of *Ragy*, with $\frac{525}{1000}$ parts of a bushel of *Avaray*, or $\frac{055}{1000}$ parts of a bushel of *Tovary*. The produce of a *Colaga* land is 20 *Colagas*, of *Ragy*, worth 8 *Fanams*, and 5 *Colagas* of *Avaray* worth $2\frac{3}{4}$ *Fanams;* in all, $10\frac{3}{4}$ *Fanams;* which is probably greatly under-rated by the farmers who gave me the account, as it is not double the amount of the rent.

June 16.

Shamay.

When the rains begin later than usual, this first quality of land, called *Awal Bumi*, is sown with *Shamay*, and produces about the same quantity of that grain as it does of *Ragy;* but this produce is only worth four *Fanams*, which is only two thirds of the rent, and the field next year requires an extraordinary quantity of manure.

Huruli.

When the rains fail altogether, or nearly so, *Huruli* or *Horse-gram* is sown, to prevent or mitigate the horrors of famine.

CHAPTER XX.

June 16. Second quality of soil. *Ragy, &c.*

On the second quality of dry-field, or *Duim Bumi, Ragy* and its accompaniments are frequently sown. The produce is only one half of what it is on the first quality of soil, which would amount to no more than the seed and rent. The farmers here evidently conceal at least one half of the produce; forty seeds of *Ragy* being allowed, in the neighbouring districts, as the common produce of a good soil. In place of *Avaray* or *Tovary*, on this kind of land, *Navonay*, or common millet *(Panicum italicum)*, is sometimes sown in the drills of *Ragy* fields.

Shamay.

On the second quality of soil, however, the most common crop is *Shamay*. After the first rain of spring, the field gets five double ploughings, with an interval of six days between each. *Shamay* is not allowed manure, is sown broad-cast during the two months which follow the summer solstice, is then ploughed in, and the field is harrowed with the rake drawn by oxen. The seed required for a *Wocula* land is half a *Colaga*, or $\frac{321}{1000}$ parts of a bushel for an acre. On this soil it produces only 20 seeds, or two *Fanams* worth of grain. The rent is four *Fanams* and a half; from which an estimate may be formed of the veracity of my informers.

On this soil *Hessaru, Udu, Ellu,* and *Harulu*, are also sown, but in no considerable quantities.

Horse-gram, third quality of land.

In bad seasons *Huruli* is sown on this second quality of land; but in neither the first nor second qualities of soil does it thrive so well as on the poorest fields, where in common seasons it forms the usual crop. In the two months preceding the autumnal equinox, the field gets two double ploughings. The seed is then sown broad-cast, and is covered by the plough. The seed required for a *Colaga* land is half a *Colaga*, or $\frac{321}{1000}$ bushel an acre. The produce is ten seeds, or five *Colagas*, worth $1\frac{1}{4}$ *Fanam*. This is evidently as much under-rated as the others, the rent being three *Fanams*.

On this kind of ground, small quantities of *Huts' Ellu* and *Harica* are also sown.

The dry-field is frequently let to those who cultivate gardens

June 16. *Tarkari Tota*, or kitchen-gardens.

watered by the *Yatam*. A garden consisting of five *Woculas*, or a little more than three acres, can be watered by one *Yatam*, on the balance of which one man walks. This man and two others are adequate to cultivate the whole. It lets for only one or two *Fanams* a *Wocula* more, than if it were cultivated for *Ragy*. These gardens are partly cultivated by *Tigular*, that is, persons whose ancestors were originally of *Dravada Désam*, and who live entirely by the profession of gardening; and partly by the farmers who cultivate the fields. The articles raised in these gardens for sale are, wheat, *Maize*, *Ragy*, *Tovary*, *Mentea*, or fenugreek, *Nayla*, *Sunicai*, or *Arachis hypogea*, onions, garlic, turmeric, tobacco, poppies, *Cossumba* or *Carthamus tinctorius*, capsicum, and the carminative seeds *Danya* and *Womum*, together with greens, cucurbitaceous fruits, and other kitchen stuffs for the use of the cultivators' families. The articles produced in these gardens, that are exported, are wheat, *Danya*, *Womum*, poppies, *Cossumba*, tobacco, garlic, and turmeric.

Although most of these gardens are dry-field, and are watered by the *Yatam* from wells, yet some are on rice-land, and receive their supply of water from a reservoir. The ground is in constant crop, and often produces at the same time four or five articles.

Tobacco.

Tobacco is cultivated not only in gardens, but also in rice-land and dry-field. In the first and last cases, the cultivator pays the usual rent. When it is cultivated on rice-land, the state gets one half of the produce. When raised on dry-field, the water must be brought in pots from the nearest well. In the month preceding the summer solstice, the field is ploughed fourteen or fifteen times. In the month following, furrows at the distance of two cubits are drawn throughout the field, and are filled with water. In these, young tobacco-plants from the seed-bed are placed, at nine inches distance, and a little dung is put at their roots. The young plants are then covered with broad leaves, and for four times are watered once a day. The leaves having been removed, the plants for three

CHAPTER XX. June 16.

times get water once in four days; and even again on the 20th day, should the rainy season not have then commenced. At the end of the month the whole field is hoed, and the earth is thrown toward the plants in ridges. At the end of the second month this is repeated, and at the same time all the leaves, except from six to nine, are pinched from every plant; and all new leaves, that afterwards shoot from the centre, are once in eight or ten days removed. When it begins to whiten, the tobacco is fit for cutting. After having been cut by the ground, the stems are allowed to lie on the field until next day, when they are spread on a dry place, and exposed to the sun. Here the tobacco remains nine days and nine nights. On the 10th morning some grass is spread on the ground; on this heaps of the tobacco are placed, and the roots are turned toward the circumference. The heap is covered with straw, and pressed down with a large stone. In these heaps the tobacco remains for nine days. The stems are then removed from the leaves, of which from six to ten, according to their size, are made up into a small bundle. These bundles are again placed in a heap, covered with straw, and pressed with a large stone. Every evening the heap is taken down; and, each bundle having been squeezed with the hand, to make it soft, the whole is again replaced as before. On the fifth evening the tobacco is spread out all night to receive the dew. Next day the heap is rebuilt, and this process of heaping, squeezing, and spreading out to the dew, must be in all performed three times; the tobacco is then fit for sale. The larger leaves of this tobacco seem to me to be well cured for the European market, being not so dry as usual with that cured in India, but moist and flexible: of the flavour I am no judge. A *Wocula* land in a *Tarkari* garden produces twenty *Maunds* of cured tobacco, worth, according to the merchants, 140 *Fanams*. According to this, an acre produces about 6 cwt. 2 qrs. 25 lb. worth 6*l.* 15*s.* 8½*d.* The cultivators, however, only value their tobacco at five *Fanams* a *Maund*. The tobacco is cut in the 1st and 2d months after the autumnal equinox. For three successive years, three crops of tobacco may be taken from the same field: but before a fourth crop, some other article must intervene for at least one year; and after this plant, even in gardens, no second crop is admitted.

Common manner of cultivating gardens. Garlic.

The most common crop in these gardens is garlic, followed by poppies, *Cossumba*, and radishes. The manner of conducting this will suffice to give an idea of the progress made in gardening, which much exceeds that in managing arable lands. In the month preceding midsummer, the plot intended for garlic is dug with a hoe. It is then dunged, and ten days afterwards is again hoed. It is then divided into small squares, which, in order to confine the water, are separated by low banks; and between every two rows of squares, channels for conveying the water from the *Tank*, or well, are constructed. In each of these squares, lines are then drawn at four inches distance from each other; and in these, at similar distances, are placed single cloves of garlic, which are covered by smoothing the area of the square with the hand. The squares are then filled with water; and once a day, for eight times, this is repeated. On the tenth day a little dung is given; and, when it does not rain, some soils require water every third day, while others only require it once every fourth day. Care must be taken to remove the weeds, as they spring. In the month following the autumnal equinox, the roots are full grown, and are then dug up.

After a month's rest the plot is again hoed and manured. On the tenth day the hoeing is repeated, and then the little squares and channels for watering the plot are formed. The poppy seed, having been mixed with an equal quantity of dust, is then sown in the squares, and covered by drawing the hand over the mould, which gets a little manure and water. At every two cubits distance, all over the small banks that separate the squares, a seed of the *Cossumba* is then placed, and the interstices are sown with radishes. For the first eight days, the squares are allowed, morning and evening, a little water. Afterwards, for twenty days, they are

CHAPTER XX. June 16. irrigated once in twenty-four hours, and then every fourth day. At the end of the first month, the weeds are removed with the end of a sharp stick, and a little manure is given. Any weeds that afterwards appear must be plucked as they spring.

Radishes. At the end of the second month the radishes are pulled.

Poppy-seed. Some few poor *Tigular* make opium; but in general the poppy is allowed to ripen its seed, without receiving injury in its fruit; for the operation of extracting opium diminishes the quantity of seed; and here this is much esteemed, and enters largely into the sweet-meats and cakes which the wealthy eat.

Opium. In the beginning of the third month the poppies are fit for producing opium. The fruit is scratched with a thorn; and the juice that exsudes, after it has thickened by exposure to the air, is scraped off with a shell, and seems to be very good opium. According to the cultivators, this sells at fifteen *Fanams* a *Seer*, which is about fifteen shillings a pound. How such an enormous price can be required for it, I cannot conceive, except on the supposition of the late government having prohibited, by severe penalties, the use of this intoxicating substance.

Post. Where the seed has been allowed to ripen, the husks, or *capsulæ*, are beaten with *Jagory* and water, so as to form an intoxicating liquor, which in the *Marattah* and *Karnata* languages is called *Post*, and which is much used for inebriation both by *Mussulmans* and *Hindus*.

Cossumba. In five months the *Cossumba* pushes out its flowers, which are collected at three different times, between each of which is an interval of eight days. The petals, *flosculi*, are not pulled until they are in a state of decay; so that their removal does not prevent the seed from coming to maturity. It is either eaten parched; or beaten with a little water into an emulsion, which is mixed with boiled rice and *Jagory*, and forms a dish called *Paramana*, that is a favourite delicacy with the natives. The *flosculi*, after having been pulled, are dried in the sun two or three days, and are then old to the dyers at half a *Fanam* for the *Seer*, or at about sixpence a pound.

June 16. Watered lands.

The extent of the watered lands is estimated by the quantity of rice which they require for seed. I measured a field, said to require three *Colagas*, and found it to contain 33146 square feet. At this rate, therefore, the *Candaca* of land is $5\frac{914}{1000}$ acres, and the acre requires nearly $1\frac{1}{8}$ bushel of seed.

On this ground, rice forms by far the most common crop, and in favourable seasons two crops of this grain are procured from the same field. That which grows in the rainy season is called *Hainu;* that which grows in the hot weather is called *Caru.* When the quantity of water for either crop is not sufficient to irrigate rice, a crop of some other grain is sown in its stead.

The kinds of rice cultivated here are as follow:

Kinds.	Quality.	Months required for this crop.	Crop in which it is cultivated.
Gydda Byra - -	Thick grain -	6	*Hainu* and *Caru.*
Doda Byra - -	Large grain -	7	*Hainu*
Doda Caimbutty - -	ditto.	6	ditto
Sana ditto - -	Small grain -	6	ditto
Indigay - - -	Large grain -	5	*Hainu* and *Caru*
Potapalu - -	ditto.	4	ditto ditto
Cari Nellu - -	ditto.	4	ditto ditto

The length of time required for each kind of rice includes the time that is occupied in the whole process of cultivation.

The *Hainu* crop, which grows in the rainy season, is commonly *Gydda*, or *Doda Byra*; and the former also most usually composes the crop of the dry season, except where the *Doda Byra* has preceded it; in which case, some of the kinds that are more quick of growth must be used. The grains that require six or seven months take

CHAPTER XX. June 16.

two more ploughings than those that come to maturity in less time, which is the only difference in the process of cultivation. The only cultivation in use here is the *Mola*, or sprouted seed.

Hainu crop.

In order to cultivate *Gydda Byra* in the rainy season, the field is watered in the month preceding midsummer; and then, having been drained, it is ploughed first lengthwise, and then across. Next day the double ploughing is repeated, and the field is inundated. On the fifth day the field is again drained, the double ploughing is repeated, and then the water is again admitted. These steps are repeated on the 8th, 11th, and 14th days. At the 3d or 4th double ploughing the field is manured with dung; and immediately after the last it is smoothed with a plank drawn by oxen *(Maram)*, sown broad-cast with the prepared seed, and then covered two inches deep with water. On the third day after sowing, the field is drained, and sprinkled with dry dung, which has been rubbed to dust. On the fifth day an inch of water is admitted, and ever afterwards the field is inundated; the depth of water being increased as the rice grows, and care being taken that the young plants should be never entirely covered. On the 20th day the field is harrowed with the rake drawn by oxen; and on the 30th, 40th, and 90th days, the weeds are removed by the hand. At this last weeding, all superfluous stalks are destroyed by pinching them between the toes. When ripe, this crop is cut with the straw, and put up in heaps. Next day it is trodden out by oxen. The straw is sometimes spoiled by the rain, and thrown into the dung-hill; but at other times it is preserved for fodder.

Caru crop.

The cultivation for the crop raised in the dry season is quite similar to that before described; but the ploughing season is different. The straw of this crop is always well preserved, which renders it valuable; but the quantity of grain is smaller.

Produce.

On good soils, the crop raised in the wet season produces forty fold of *Gydda Byra*, or almost forty-five bushels an acre, worth 1*l.* 19*s.* 4¼*d.* In the crop coltivated in dry weather, on good soils the produce is thirty seeds, or rather more than $33\frac{1}{2}$ bushels an acre. The rice of both crops keeps equally well, and is of equal value.

CHAPTER XX.

June 16. Expense of removing the husks.

If a man beat out his own grain, a *Candaca* of rough rice gives half a *Candaca* of clean grain; but if he hire labourers, they return him only four tenths of a *Candaca* of clean rice; so that a fifth of the grain is the expense of removing the husks; and this may be considered as the expense of this operation that is usual in every part of India. The operation is commonly assisted by boiling, and is performed by beating the grain in a mortar with a stick five or six feet long, three inches in diameter, and shod with iron.

Seed.

The quantity of seed required for bad land is the same with that given to good; and in neither does the quantity actually sown measure a *Seer* more or less than that contained in the estimate of the public accompts. When the rains commence rather late, the crop cultivated immediately afterwards is taken of some of the kinds that grow quickly; otherwise, those which are slow of growth are always preferred.

Grains substituted in place of the *Hainu* crop.

When soon after the commencement of the rainy season there is not in the *Tank* a quantity of water sufficient for a crop of rice, in its stead the following grains are cultivated: *Ellu, Hessaru, Udu*, and *Jola.*

Sesamum.

Of these, *Ellu* is most used. In the second month after the vernal equinox, the field is ploughed twice. On the sixth day it is again ploughed twice; then with the first rain in this, or the following month, the seed is sown broad-cast, and covered with the plough. In three months the crop ripens without farther trouble. It is supposed to injure the following crop of rice. A *Wocula* of land requires $\frac{1}{8}$ *Colaga* of seed, and produces two *Colagas*, or 16 seeds. For an acre, therefore, the seed will be $\frac{14}{100}$ parts of a bushel, and the produce about $2\frac{1}{4}$ bushels, worth 7*s.* $2\frac{1}{2}$*d.*

The other grains are cultivated exactly in the same manner.

Phaseolus Mungo.

The seed required for a *Wocula* land is $\frac{1}{4}$ *Colaga* of *Hessaru*, which produces three *Colagas*, or twelve seeds. The acre, therefore,

CHAPTER XX. requires $\frac{28}{100}$ parts of a bushel for seed, and produces $3\frac{364}{1000}$ bushels worth 7*s.* $4\frac{1}{2}$*d.* This, next to *Ellu*, is the most usual crop.

June 16. *Phaseolus minimoo* Roxb. *Udu* is the next most common crop, and its seed is sown of the same thickness; its produce is one third less. An acre, therefore, produces $2\frac{345}{1000}$ bushels, worth 3*s.* $11\frac{1}{4}$*d.*

Holcus sorghum. The quantity of *Jola* raised is very small. The seed and produce, owing to the imperfect manner of cultivation, are not greater than those of *Udu.*

Grains substituted in place of the *Caru* crop. When the water in the *Tank* is not sufficient to raise a crop of rice in the dry season, the following grains are raised in its stead, *Hessaru*, *Callay*, and *Jola.*

Phaseolus Mungo. *Hessaru* is the most common. In the month preceding the autumnal equinox, the field is ploughed twice in one day; which on the third day is repeated. On the 6th or 7th day it is ploughed once, the seed is sown broad-cast, and covered by the plough. In three months it ripens. The seed for a *Wocula* land is the same as in the rainy season; but it produces twelve fold, or $3\frac{366}{1000}$ bushels an acre, worth about six shillings.

Cicer arietinum. Much less *Callay* is sown, as it requires the very richest soils. The field, in the month preceding the shortest day, gets four double ploughings, with an interval between each of two days. A few days afterwards the seed is dropped into the furrows, after a plough, at nine inches distance, and is covered by another set of furrows drawn by a second plough. In three months it ripens. A *Wocula* land requires $\frac{1}{4}$ *Colaga* of seed, and produces one *Colaga.* The seed for an acre is therefore $\frac{14}{100}$ parts of a bushel, and the produce $1\frac{12}{100}$ bushel, worth 4*s.* $3\frac{1}{4}$*d.*

Holcus sorghum. The quantity of *Jola* sown is very small, and not more productive than in the rainy season.

Division of crop. The rent on watered land is paid by a division of the crop, and the following is the manner in which that is conducted with a *Rashy*, or heap of rice, which usually contains the produce of five *Colaga* lands, and may amount to about $7\frac{1}{2}$ *Candacas*, or more than 400 bushels.

CHAPTER XX.

June 16.

	Colagas.
The *Shanaboga*, or village accomptant, gets with a bundle of unthrashed corn.	1
Toty, a watchman, all that adheres to the *Chaps* or marks, and with some straw.	$1\frac{1}{2}$
Nirgunty, or conductor of water	$2\frac{1}{4}$
Wudary, a kind of beadle	$1\frac{1}{2}$
Gauda, or chief of the village	2
Ditto for the annual sacrifice which he makes to the village god	1
Ditto for marking the heaps	1
Washerman, barber, and blacksmith	$2\frac{1}{2}$
The temples in the village	1
To poor *Bráhmans*, and other religious mendicants	1
	$14\frac{1}{4}$;

or, on account of the first share, say 15 *Colagas*, or ten *per cent.* The remainder is divided equally between the public and the cultivator; but while this is doing, the latter makes a spring at the heap, and usually carries off about four or five *Colagas*. The government pays for the *Tanks*, or canals, by which the ground is watered, as will be hereafter explained.

Sugar-cane.

In this country a considerable quantity of sugar-cane is raised. There are four kinds; *Restali, Puttaputti, Mara-cabo*, and *Chittuwasun*. The soil required for each kind is different; so that they continue to be all cultivated, although the quantity of *Jagory* given by the two last is a fourth less than that which the two first kinds afford. The *Jagory* of the *Restali* sells higher than that of the others, and the *Puttaputti* cane is preferred for eating without preparation. The *Restali* and *Puttaputti*, with a fifth kind, called *Cari-cabo*, and nearly related to the *Puttaputti*, require a rich soil. The *Mara-cabo* and *Chittuwasun* will grow any where, and will thrive even on a middling soil.

The *Restali* and *Puttaputti* are cultivated as follows: in the

CHAPTER XX. June 16. month after the shortest day, the field is twice ploughed. On the 4th, 8th, 12th, and 16th days, it gets two double ploughings. With a billet of wood the mould is then broken small, and is manured with dung. After this the field is ploughed twice, and, in order to distribute the water, it is formed into ridges with channels between them. These channels are nine inches wide and deep, and nine inches apart. The cane intended for seed is cut into pieces, each containing three joints. The channels having been previously filled with water, a row of cuttings is laid in each, and sunk into the mud of its bottom, so as just to be covered. The cuttings are placed horizontally, in a line parallel to the channels, and their ends are nine inches from the ends of those which are nearest. Every fifth day the channels are filled with water. On the 10th day the weeds are removed with a spade. On the 20th day the field is hoed, and the earth from the ridges is thrown down upon the plants between the rows, so that channels are formed where at first the ridges were. The leaves of the young canes are at this time about nine inches high, and they require no water until the 30th day; when channels are formed so as to wind in a serpentine manner, with two rows of canes between each bend, as is explained by the sketch in Plate XXXIII. Figure 85. When there is no rain, these channels must be filled with water, once in eight days, until the cane be ripe. When the stems begin to appear, they are brought together in clusters of from three to five, and bound round with leaves, so as entirely to exclude the light; and this must be carefully done, as the stems rise from the ground; otherwise the rind will be thick, and the quantity of juice very small. The crop season begins in the second month after the shortest day of the second year, and in the course of thirty days all the canes must be cut. The space occupied by this crop, therefore, is fourteen months. A *Wocula* land produces eight *Maunds* of *Jagory*, and plants a thousand cuttings. The acre will therefore plant 3942 cuttings, and produce about 6 cwt. 3qrs. 7lb. worth 3*l.* 17*s.* 4*d.*

The *Mara-cabo* and *Chittuwasun*, which is also called *Hullu-cabo*, are cultivated exactly in the same manner; only they do not require to be tied in clusters, and they ripen a month earlier. A *Wocula* of land produces only five *Maunds* of *Jagory*; so the acre produces 4 cwt. 1qr. 4lb. worth 2*l.* 8*s.* $7\frac{1}{4}$*d.*

CHAPTER XX. June 16.

Between every two crops of sugar a crop of rice must intervene; but this is reckoned better than usual where no cane is cultivated.

The rent of sugar-cane is also paid by a division of the crop, which is conducted as follows with a field that may produce about 360 *Maunds*, and about which eight or ten farmers will be concerned.

Daily expense.	*Seers.*	*Fanams.*
Rent of the iron boiler belonging to the government -	$1\frac{1}{2}$	1
Mill rent - - - - - - -	$1\frac{1}{2}$	1
Nirgunty, or conductor of water - - -	$1\frac{1}{2}$	0
Shanaboga, or village accomptant - -	$1\frac{1}{2}$	0
Iron-smith, as a workman - - -	$1\frac{1}{2}$	0
Ditto as priest, or *Pújári* of *Ganésa* - -	$0\frac{3}{4}$	0
Oil, butter, and quick-lime - - - - -	0	0
	$8\frac{1}{4}$	$2\frac{1}{2}$

The mill commonly goes 60 days, and produces daily 6 *Maunds*.

	Fanams.
Daily expense at 60 days, *cash* at $2\frac{1}{2}$. -	150
Jagory at $8\frac{1}{4}$ *Seers*=*Maunds* $12\frac{3}{4}$ at 4 *Fanams* -	51
	201
Total produce, 360 *Maunds* at 4 *Fanams* -	1440
Balance	1239
Annual expense for each mill,	
Custom-house - - - - - - -	5
Carpenter and iron-smith, - - - - -	5
Sacrifice of two lambs, - - - -	4
	14
This deducted from the former balance, -	1239
leaves a balance of - *Fanams*,	1225

CHAPTER XX.

which is divided equally between the farmer and the state, as proprietor of the soil.

June 16. Plantations of *Areca* palms.

In this part of *Karnata* there are a good many *Betel-nut*, or *Areca* plantations. To carry off the water, the ground is divided by channels into beds. In the centre of each bed is set a row of plantain trees (*Musa*), and at each side a row of young *Arecas*. When these grow up, the plantains are sometimes allowed to remain; and sometimes they are removed, and then the beds are cultivated with the plants called *Tarkari*, especially with turmeric. The man who makes the garden is at the sole expense of inclosing, digging, and planting. Sometimes he also makes the *Tank* or reservoir; but in this case, should the rent be paid by a division of the crop, he gets a fourth part of the government's share; or should the rent be paid in kind, he gets a proportional deduction.

Produce, according to the officers of government.

The chief officer of the district (*Tahsildar*), and the farmers, differ exceedingly in their account of the produce. The former says, that a *Candaca* land should plant 2000 *Arecas*, which should produce 50 *Maunds* of boiled nut. One *Bulla* contains 120 nuts in the husk. The *Candaca*, therefore, contains 9600 nuts; which, when peeled, measure 8 *Colagas* of raw nut; and these, when boiled, weigh $2\frac{1}{2}$ *Maunds*. The 50 *Maunds* will therefore require 192,000 nuts; so that every tree will give 96 nuts. At this rate, an acre will plant $394\frac{1}{5}$ trees, and produce $37843\frac{2}{10}$ nuts. These, as they come from the tree, will measure $22\frac{443}{1000}$ bushels; when peeled, will measure $8\frac{977}{1000}$ bushels; and when boiled, will weigh 299lb., worth 7*l.* 12*s.* $9\frac{1}{4}$*d.* I have entered into this detail, that the reader may be able to compare all the foregoing accounts concerning the produce of the *Areca*.

Produce, according to the cultivators.

The proprietors of the garden allege, that a *Candaca* land will plant only 1000 *Arecas*, and 500 plantain trees. The produce they state at $12\frac{1}{2}$ *Candacas*, or 120,000 nuts; which, for each tree, is at the rate of 120; but they probably reckon only a certain proportion of the whole trees, excluding the others, as not productive, while the *Tahsildar* includes every one.

All these plantations formerly paid one half of the produce as rent; but *Tippoo* agreed with some of the proprietors for a rent in money, which was to be fixed by a kind of jury, as before described. A *Candaca* of land, in this manner, pays from 100 to 120 *Fanams*, or at the rate of from 15*s.* 6*d.* to 18*s.* 7*d.* an acre. By this, according to the *Tahsildar's* statement, the government is a great loser; as it got at least one half of the produce, or 25 *Maunds* a *Candaca* land, worth 575 *Fanams.* The cultivators acknowlege themselves well pleased with the change. They say, that when they have a fixed rent they are industrious, knowing that the rent must be paid, and that whatever more they can get will be their own; but with the division of crops, however slothful they may be, they are sure of something.

June 16. Rent.

The ground cultivated for *Betel-leaf* is rice-land, and pays four *Fanams* a *Colaga*, or 9*s.* 10*d.* an acre; which is much about the actual receipt of the government when the land is cultivated with rice.

Betel-leaf, Piper Betle

In these districts, the property of all the soil is vested in the state, except in the *Polyams*, and a few small free estates (*Enams*), which have been granted to *Vaidika Bráhmans*, to the temples, to pious Mussulmans, to the petty officers of police and revenue, and to a set of men called *Caray-cuttu Codigy*, who have acquired this property by constructing reservoirs, and keeping them in repair. The *Enams* of the petty officers, such as *Gaudas, Shanabogas, Nirgunties*, and the like, are saleable; but the office, which is hereditary, is always transferred with the land.

Tenures. *Enam*, or free estates.

When a rich man undertakes at his own expense to construct a reservoir for the irrigation of land, he is allowed to hold in free estate (*Enam*), and by hereditary right, one fourth part of the lands so watered; but he is bound o keep the reservoir in repair. Such a proprietor is called *Caray-cuttu Codigy.* The *Tanks* to which there is a person of this kind are notoriously kept in better repair,

Lands granted to those who erect *Tanks*, or other public works.

CHAPTER XX. June 16. than those which the government supports, either when they have been constructed originally at the public expense, or when the *Enam* of the founder, from a failure of heirs, has reverted to the sovereign. The reason assigned for this by the natives is perfectly satisfactory. They say, that they can compel the holder of the free estate to perform his duty; but the state has no master. It would seem adviseable, therefore, to encourage the rich natives to undertake this business; and, where the *Enam* has reverted to the government, it would be better to sell the estate to some other family, than to retain it and repair the *Tank;* and, if the practice of raising the rent by a division of crops be still continued, it would be yet more advantageous for the public to grant the *Caray-cuttu Codigy* one fourth of the government's share of the crop, which ought to be the same as his half of the produce of a fourth part of the land. This would not only prevent the free estates from growing in size, a thing that very usually happens, but it would be a check upon the revenue officers who superintend the division. A few free estates *(Enams)* have been granted to those who have built forts, and undertaken to keep them in repair.

Stock, and size of farms. Five ploughs are here reckoned a great stock. Each plough can cultivate five *Colagas* ($1\frac{1}{4}$ acre) of rice land, and five *Colagas* ($3\frac{1}{4}$ acres) of dry-field. This is all that the farmers will voluntarily undertake to do; but, when they have completely laboured this extent, the beadle *(Wudary)* is sent, and compels the lazy fellows to cultivate five *Colagas* more of dry-field. This is done in a very slovenly manner, as might be expected; and the custom, although established by long practice, seems to me very prejudicial.

Wages. Most of the labour is performed by the farmers and their own families. A few rich men hire yearly servants; and at seed-time and harvest additional daily labourers must be procured. There are no slaves. A ploughman gets annually $3\frac{1}{2}$ *Candacas* of *Ragy* (20 bushels), worth 28 *Fanams*, with a hut; and 16 *Fanams* in money.

His wages, besides a hut, are therefore 1*l.* 7*s.* 5½. The additional expense attending a plough is 3¼ *Fanams* for implements, and 2 seeds for the hire of day-labourers, or one *Candaca* of grain, worth eight *Fanams*, for what the plough will cultivate; in all 55¼ *Fanams*. Add 30 *Fanams* for the rent of the dry field, and we have 85¼ *Fanams* of expense, besides the interest of the value of the two oxen, which, however, is a mere trifle. In an ordinary year, the produce, after deducting the seed and the government's share of rice, with the stoppages for village officers, according to the farmers will be:

June 16.

	Fanams.
Ragy 55 *Colagas*, worth - - -	22
Avaray 19 *Colagas* - - - -	10¼
Rice, Hainu crop, 85 *Colagas* - - -	35
Caru crop, 57½ *Colagas* - - -	23
Fanams	90¼

This amounts to just about the expense; but I have mentioned that the produce of the dry grains is in this account under-rated by at least one half; and I have not brought into the account the half produce of the five *Colagas* which the farmers are compelled to cultivate, and which costs little or no additional expense.

Condition of servants.

The farmers in general consent to advance money to their servants for marriages, and other ceremonies. This money is repaid by instalments out of the wages that are given in cash; for the people here are not anxious to keep their servants in bondage, by a debt hanging over them. A day-labourer, whether man or woman, gets daily $\frac{1}{8}$ *Colaga* of rough rice, or $\frac{316}{1000}$ parts of a bushel. Of this, it must be observed, one half is composed of husk.

Manure.

Leaves are not in use here as a manure. The cattle are never littered; but the straw which they do not eat, the rice straw that rots, with that of *Hessaru*, *Ellu*, and the like, are all collected together in one pit with the dung, ashes, and other soil of the house. A great defect in this manner of procuring manure is, the not

CHAPTER XX. June 16. using the *Hessaru* straw and leaves for litter. Sheep and goats are at night gathered on the arable lands, but are not confined by folds, which seems also an error.

Cattle. In this neighbourhood there are no herds of breeding cattle, but every farmer keeps some cows and female buffaloes, the profit of which is clear gain. Many *Bráhmans*, and other rich people, keep, for the milk, a considerable number of both cows and female buffaloes. The males, when fit for labour, are sold; so that a considerable number are exported from hence. The breed is bad, and fit only for the plough. The dealers in grain (*Lumbadies*) have a great many cattle, male and female; but they are no better than the common breed of the villages, and would not be used for carriage by the merchant, still less would they be fit for the camp. The farmers keep a good many sheep and goats, which during the day are fed in the woods, and at night sleep on the arable lands near the villages. Asses are numerous, and lean swine are common. The lower casts in every part of *Karnata* eat pork; the swine, therefore, are not here employed as scavengers, which in some parts of India is the case. The number of cattle in these districts was formerly very great, especially in the villages of *Alumbady* that are surrounded by woods; but the stock has been exceedingly reduced by an epidemic distemper, that raged after Lord Cornwallis invaded the country, and by the depredations which in the last war the troops of the *Nizam*, and the *Lumbadies*, committed.

Seasons. The only account of the seasons that I could procure here was as follows. For one month before, and two after, the vernal equinox, the weather is clear and hot. In the two months of midsummer, the weather is cloudy, and cold, with thunder, lightning, rain, and strong winds from the west. This is the season that now prevails, and to the feelings of a European it is exceedingly agreeable. The air resembles that of a cloudy day in an English summer. In the two months before the autumnal equinox, the rains are very heavy, and come from the west, and the air is not so cold as in the two precedin months. In the two months after the autumnal equinox, there are moderate rains, which probably come from various directions, as on this point the natives have made no observation. These rains are, however, part of the monsoon which comes from *Madras*. In the three remaining months, the weather is cool, with fogs and dews in the mornings, but clear days, which no doubt appear hot to a European.

CHAPTER XX. June 16.

Strata.

The *strata*, the whole way between *Seringapatam* and *Kéllamangala*, lie north and south, and are all vertical. Many of them are grey granite. In the eastern part of *Karnata* I have observed no pot-stone. The nodules of lime-stone are very common, as is also iron-ore in the form of black sand.

June 18. Appearance of the country.

18th *June*.—I went two cosses to *Waragan-hully*. The country consists of low rocky hills overgrown with brushwood. Interspersed are considerable portions of arable land. Of this, according to the *Tahsildar*, the soil of the first or best quality forms a fifth part; of the second quality, two fifths; of the third and fourth qualities, each one fifth.

Produce of the dry field of the first quality.

The soil of the best quality is sown entirely with *Ragy*, and its accompaniments; and should produce forty seeds, which is double the quantity admitted by the cultivators of *Kellamangalam;* but there is no observable difference in the soil, climate, or cultivation; and there can be no doubt, that the crops in the two places are nearly equally productive.

Produce of the second quality.

On the second quality of land are sown *Ragy (Cynosurus corocanus)*, *Shamay (Panicum miliare E. M.)*, *Harica (Paspalum frumentaceum* Roxb.*)*, *Navonay (Panicum italicum)*, *Ellu (Sesamum)*, *Udu (Phaseolus minimoo* Roxb.*)*, and *Hessaru (Phaseolus Mungo)*. *Ragy* on this land produces twenty seeds. When the rains fail, it is sown with *Huruli*, and *Huts' Ellu*. *Navonay* produces ten seeds, and the seed is sown as thick as that of *Ragy*. *Shamay* produces the same quantity as *Ragy*, that is, one *Candaca* from a *Colaga* land, and requires only three quarters of a *Colaga* for seed.

CHAPTER XX.

June 18. Produce of the 3d quality.

On the third quality of dry-field are sown *Huts' Ellu (Verbesina sativa* Roxb.), *Huruli (Dolichos biflorus), Udu (Phaseolus minimoo* Roxb.), and *Hessaru (Phaseolus mungo)*. A *Colaga* land sows a quarter *Colaga*, and produces twenty seeds. *Huruli* gives the same increase, and is sown four times as thick.

Produce of the 4th quality.

On the fourth quality of land nothing is sown except *Huts' Ellu*, and it produces only five seeds.

This account, I believe, may be relied on, and applied to correct the information given at *Kellamangala* relative to dry grains, the produce of which the farmers at that place were most interested to conceal.

Colonel Read

Waragan-hully is a small village in the *Ratna-giri* district, which has been placed under the management of the *Tahsildar* of *Ráya-cotay*, one of those native officers who have been brought up under Colonel Read, and who are much superior to those with whom one usually meets in India.

ascertains the quantity of seed.

He says, that at *Ráya-cotay*, where all the lands have been actually measured, the quantity of seed required for the different grounds was ascertained by Colonel Read, assisted by the most intelligent natives.

Ragy.

One *Colaga* of *Ragy* was found to sow forty *Guntas*, each of which was 35 feet 2 inches square. Although this is a trifle more than an acre, the chain with which I measured may have stretched a little, so as to make the difference; and I think it probable, that the *Colaga* is exactly an acre. The *Puddy* of *Ráya-cotay* contains $52\frac{87}{100}$ cubical inches. The acre therefore sows rather less than $\frac{1}{10}$ of a bushel.

Rice.

Ten square *Guntas*, or one rood, sow a *Colaga* of rice; so that an acre sows $\frac{4}{10}$ of a bushel. This differs greatly from my measurement; yet there is no apparent reason, why the seed should be sown of a different thickness at *Ráya-cotay*, and *Kellamangala*. Unless the *Tahsildar* has mistaken, it is evident that Colonel Read's measurement is the one on which by far the greatest reliance ought to be placed.

June 18. Uniformity of measures introduced by Col. Read.

In every part of the country under his management Colonel Read succeeded, without much trouble, in introducing a uniform standard for weights and measures.

Telinga language introduced.

Ratna-giri and *Ráya-cotay* formerly belonged to *Jaga-deva Ráya* of *Chena-pattana*. From him they were taken by a *Marattah;* and from him again by the *Mysore Rájás*. The people in this neighbourhood speak about an equal proportion of the dialects of *Telingana* and *Karnata*, although it is situated in the latter country; but the *Polygars* and all their followers were of *Telinga* descent, which has occasioned the mixture.

June 19. *Bára-mahál* and *Dravada Désam*.

19th *June*.—I went three cosses to *Ráya-cotay*, where my survey ended; but I shall continue to note down what I observed on my return to Madras. *Ráya-cotay* is the last place in *Karnata Désam*, and is commonly reckoned in the *Bára-mahál*, because it was added to that province by the peace which Lord Cornwallis granted to *Tippoo*. The twelve places properly constituting the *Bára-mahál* are all in *Dravada Désam*, which is bounded on the west by the *Ghats*, and on the east by the sea. These 12 places are, *Krishna-giri, Jacadeo, Varina-ghadá, Cavila-ghada, Máhá-raj'-ghada, Bujunga-ghada, Catora-ghada, Tripaturu, Vanambady, Gagana-ghada, Sudarashana-ghada*, and *Tatucallu*. *Ghada*, it must be observed, signifies a fort, and *Giri* a hill. On the fall of the *Ráyaru* of *Anagundi*, the *Bára-mahál*, with *Ráya-cotay* and many other districts, became subject to *Jaga-deva*, the *Polygar* of *Chena-pattana*. On the overthrow of this powerful family, its territories were divided between the *Nabob* of *Cudapa*, or *Curpa*, and the *Rájás* of *Mysore*. The former took the *Bára-mahál*, and the latter the dominions of the *Chena-pattana* family that were situated in *Karnata*. *Hyder* annexed the *Bára-mahál* to the dominions of *Mysore*.

Ráya-cotay.

In the war of Lord Cornwallis, *Ráya-cotay* was taken by Major Gowdie, and has ever since continued in the possession of the British. Being the chief key to *Karnata*, pains have been taken

CHAPTER XX.

June 19.

to strengthen the works, which consist of a high fortified rock, and a fort at its bottom. Comfortable houses have been built by the officers, who enjoy very good health, although surrounded by rocks, hills, and woods.

Mildness of the air in *Karnata.*

The air of *Ráya-cotay* is very temperate. The commanding officer, Colonel Leighton, informed me, that in April last, which was a hot season, and which is the warmest month in the year, Fahrenheit's thermometer in the shade never rose higher than 82°. At the present season, it is usually about 72° at noon, and 64° at day-break.

Language.

The people of *Ráya-cotay*, being on the frontier, speak a strange mixture of the languages of *Karnata*, of the *Tamuls*, and of the *Telingas.*

June 20. Appearance of the country.

20th *June.*—I went 17 miles to *Krishna-giri.* The road is good, and most of the way leads through narrow defiles among hills covered with brushwood. The descent is very gentle. Towards *Krishna-giri* I crossed the *Dakshana Pinakani*, or *Pennar.* The former is the *Sanskrit*, the latter the vulgar name of this river. Near *Krishna-giri* the country consists of a plain, in which are scattered high rocky hills.

Krishna-giri.

That on which the fort of *Krishna-giri* is situated is about 700 feet in perpendicular height, and remarkably bare and steep. Much of the plain is rice-ground; but the soil, although well watered, is in general poor. A new village has been founded, excellent roads have been made, and convenient houses for the European gentlemen have been built. The weather at this season is cool, with strong westerly winds, which bring many clouds to mitigate the power of the sun.

June 21.

21st *June.*—I remained at *Krishna-giri* with Captain Graham, the collector, a gentleman educated in the school of Colonel Read. My intention was, to have returned from *Krishna-giri* to *Madras* by the way of *Gingee*; but Captain Graham prevented me from adopting this plan, by informing me, that the country through which I must have passed had become so desolate, that I should find great difficulty in procuring a subsistence. June 21.

22d *June.*—I went twelve miles, by an excellent road, to *Malapaddy*. The country, like that near *Krishna-giri*, consists of a plain, in which are scattered high detached rocky hills. The soil of the plain is poor, and much of it is waste, and overgrown with brushwood. *Malapaddy*, although placed in the heart of the *Bára-mahál*, never belonged to that province, and has long been annexed to *Arcot*. The *Nabob* has given it in *Jaghire* to the husband of one of his sisters. It is a very sorry place. Here the language of the *Tamuls* is almost the only one that is spoken. June 22. Appearance of the country. *Malapaddy.*

23d *June.*—I went about fifteen miles to *Tripaturu.* The plains on this day's route are wider than those I saw yesterday, and are also better cultivated. The hills are lengthened out into ridges. *Tripaturu* is a large open village, containing some good houses neatly roofed with tiles. This is to be seen no where in *Karnata*, and these roofs have been probably constructed by workmen from *Madras*, where a long intercourse with Europeans has greatly improved the natives in all the arts. At this place an attempt was made by Colonel Read to introduce the manufacture of sugar, and the rearing of silk-worms. A Mr. Light, from the *West Indies*, and a native of *Bengal*, were procured to superintend; but both have failed. June 23. *Tripaturu.*

24th *June.*—I went fourteen miles to *Vanambady*, a village fortified with a mud wall. It looks well, as it is surrounded by trees, of which the *Bára-mahál* has in general very few, and as it is situated on a fine plain surrounded by hills. It is placed on the banks of the *Palar*, or milk river, which in the *Sanskrit* is called *Cshira Nuddi*. It has its rise near *Nandy Durga*, or the *Bull-castle*, and in the rainy season frequently commits great devastation. It rises highest when the rains prevail on the coasts of *Coromandel*. At present its channel is apparently quite dry; but, by digging a June 24. *Vanambady.*

CHAPTER XX.

June 24. Many inscriptions on stone.

small canal in the sand of its bed, a stream of water is procured. In *Vanambady* are two temples of some note. At that of *Iswara* are above twenty inscriptions on stone, some of which are said to be of great antiquity, being of the age of *Vicrama Ditya*. At the temple of *Vishnu*, under the name of *Allaha Perumal*, are six inscriptions carved on the wall. I had only time to procure copies of three, and unfortunately commenced with such as are of little importance. One, of which a copy has been given to the Bengal government, contains the grant of a village to *Allaha Perumal*, from *Narasingha Deva Maha Ráya*, dated the 2d of *Magha* of the year *Servajittu*, but no era is annexed. The second, of which also a copy has been given to government, is dated *Parabova* of *Sal.* 1460, *Chaitra* 12th. By this, *Naia Deva*, son of *Vira Pritapa Sedásiva Ráyaru*, gives a village to *Allaha Perumal* on account of the decease of his father. The third, also delivered to government, is dated 15th *Kartika* of the year *Visuavasu*, being of the era of *Sal.* 1464. By this, *Vencatadri Rájá*, and *Rama Rájá*, grant each a village to the god, on account of the decease of their departed parent, *Sedásiva Ráya*. These persons granting the villages, probably, were of the house of *Anagundi*, although this is not ascertained by any thing in the inscriptions; but the date cannot be reconciled with the chronology of *Ramuppa*.

Appearance of the country.

The country through which I came to-day is tolerably well cultivated, and resembles what I saw yesterday. The air, although warmer than at *Ráya-cotay*, is still temperate; for clouds and strong westerly winds moderate the violence of the sun.

June 25. *Amboor.*

25th *June.*—I went thirteen miles to *Amboor*. The road leads through a fine valley watered by the *Palar*. Near *Vanambady*, this valley seems to be tolerably well cultivated and inhabited. Near *Amboor*, it is overgrown with *Palmira* trees (*Borassus*), and seems to be mostly waste. This is, no doubt, owing to the devastation which *Hyder* committed in his two inroads into what we call the *Carnatic*; for near *Amboor* the *Bára-mahál* ends, and the territories of *Arcot* commence. The road all the way from *Krishna-giri* is excellent, and very level. *Amboor*, having been long a frontier place, is a town built under the protection of a hill fort that still retains a British garrison.

CHAPTER XX.

June 25.

Jesuit Missionary.

I here found a Jesuit Missionary, a native of France. He has a small flock, who seem to be in great poverty; but, by their contributions, I imagine they are able to support him. He is educating one of them to be his successor, as *Guru;* for so he is called by his converts. He favoured me with his company at dinner, and was a very lively, pleasant man. To avoid offending the prejudices of the natives, he abstains from the use of beef.

June 26. *Anavun Nelluru.*

26th *June.*—I went thirteen miles to a small village named *Anavun Nelluru.* The road is good, and leads through a very pretty valley, watered by the *Palar.* There is a good deal of rice-land, most of which seems to be occupied; but the dry-field forms a large part of the arable land, and is much neglected.

Indigo.

A good deal of indigo has been lately introduced. It grows on the higher parts of the rice-land, from which, in the rainy season, a crop of grain will be procured.

Irrigation.

The whole of the rice land is irrigated by means of canals, which are either dug across the dry channels of rivers, below the surface of which a small stream is always found; or conducted from places in which subterraneous springs have been discovered. These canals are here called *Cashay.* A canal supplied from a river, in which there is a perennial stream above ground, is in the *Tamul* language called *Vakial.*

June 27. *Viranchi-pura.*

27th *June.*—I went eleven miles down the *Palar* to *Viranchi-pura,* an open town situated on the south side of the river. It formerly was a large place, and possessed many public buildings, both *Hindu* and *Mussulman;* but all these have suffered much, from the towns having been repeatedly destroyed in *Hyder's* wars. A large temple of *Iswara* has escaped, having been surrounded by a very large and strong wall of cut granite, that excluded irregulars; and

CHAPTER XX.

June 27. *Hyder* took no delight in the destruction of temples. On the walls of this temple, there are many inscriptions, which are written in the *Grantham* character, and some of them are said to be of great antiquity. The *Bráhmans* promised to send me copies, but this they neglected to do. They were very clamorous in complaining against the *Nabob*, although he annually allows the temple 2000 *Pagodas*, or 800*l.* The town seems to be recovering fast.

June 28. *Vellore.* 28th *June.*—I went eight miles, and halted at a little distance east from *Vellore.* There I visited the buildings preparing for the families of *Hyder* and *Tippoo.* They are built with accommodations similar to those used by *Mussulmans;* and the architecture is more elegant, and the apartments are more commodious, than those in the palace of *Seringapatam.* The building would have been still more elegant, had not the custom of those who were to occupy it required long dead walls, and narrow staircases, with other things that by us are considered as deformities.

In order to give the reader a correct idea of the countenance of the Indian *Mussulmans,* I have procured the accompanying ENGRAVINGS (PLATES XXXV. XXXVI. XXXVII.) of *Fatah Hyder,* the eldest but illegitimate son of *Tippoo,* said to be remarkably like his father and of *Sultan Mohay ud Deen,* and *Moiz ud Deen,* the two eldest legitimate sons of that prince.

June 29. *Wallaja-petta.* 29th *June.*—I went about fourteen miles to *Wallaja-petta,* or *Wallaj'-abad,* on the north side of the river, about two miles from *Arcot.* The valley leading from *Vanambady* to *Vellore,* or *Velluru,* opens here into a level country containing both dry-field and rice-ground. The weather in the day, although there are strong winds from the west, is very hot. There are occasional showers of rain, that have brought forward the crop of *Bajeru* (*Holcus spicatus*), which is that commonly raised on the dry-field.

June 30. 30th *June.*—I remained at *Wallaja-petta,* in order to give my people rest. This town was built by the orders of the late *Nabob, Mahummed Aly Wallaja,* and called after his own name. The people were removed from *Laal-petta* and other places, which with the *Mussulman*-princes of India is a common practice. Soon after it had the misfortune to fall into the hands of *Hyder;* but on the restoration of peace, the *Nabob* heaped benefits on his favourite, and it has risen to a great size, and is regularly built, rich, and populous. Its fortifications are mouldering to decay; but, as the place is now far from an enemy, it is not soon likely to regret the loss. Almost the whole of the trade, between the country above the *Ghats* and the sea-coast, centres here; and a larger assortment of goods can, it is said, be procured at *Wallaja-petta* than in any town of the peninsula, *Madras* itself not excepted. Provisions are plenty and cheap.

CHAPTER XX.

June 30.

1st *July.*—I went a short stage to *Wochuru Choultry,* having passed through a fine country very well irrigated from numerous reservoirs. Owing to the excellent supply of water, some of the rice-ground is even now in crop.

July 1. Appearance of the country.

Wochuru is an inn *(Choultry)* with a pent roof of tiles, and was built for the accommodation of travellers. This kind of building, in the native language, is called *Chauvadi,* from which perhaps the English term *Choultry* is derived. The same kind of building, which consists of one long hall open in front, is also used by the native officers, for the place in which they transact business. When behind the hall there is a square court, surrounded by buildings for the farther accommodation of travellers, the inn is by the natives called *Chitteram;* by the English this also is called *Choultry.* Every where within 40 or 50 miles of *Madras* such useful buildings are very common, and have been erected and endowed by the rich native merchants of that flourishing city.

Choultry.

At *Wochuru* there is also a very handsome *Tank,* formed by digging a square cavity into the soil. Its sides are lined entirely with cut granite in the form of stairs. Such a *Tank,* when intended for the accommodation of travellers, or of the people of the neighbourhood, in the *Tamul* language is called *Colam;* in the *Karnataca*

CHAPTER XX. July 1. dialect it is called *Cúntay;* and by the *Telingas*, and southern Mussulmans, it would be called *Gunta*. Similar *Tanks*, that are within the walls of a *Covil*, or temple, are called by the *Sanskrit* names *Calliany*, *Sarovara*, *Tirta*, or *Puscarany*.

July 2. 2d *July*.—I entered the Company's *Jaghire*, and went to *Conjeveram*, which by the natives is universally called *Kunji*. The country has more verdure than it had last year when I visited it. The rains usual about this season had not then commenced; but they have this year been unusually favourable.

Weather. All over the coast of *Coromandel*, it is common in May, June, and July, to have occasional showers, and at some period of that time to have even three or four days heavy rain, which somewhat cools the air, and enables the cultivation for dry grains to take place. The weather now, although hot, is cloudy, with strong winds from the west. Such weather usually prevails about this time for eight or ten days; and at *Tanjore* is well known to precede the rising of the *Cavery*, which is at the highest when the periodical rains prevail in *Mysore*. These clouds seem to be an extension of those which before and during the violence of the monsoon collect over the western *Ghats*. When these have poured down, and have occasioned the swelling of the river, the rains even in *Karnata* abate, and the weather clears in the countries below the eastern *Ghats*, until October, when the easterly monsoon brings on the proper rainy season of the sea-coast. In the interval, the weather at Madras is often excessively hot, and the sea breeze frequently fails; or, what occasions more uneasiness, blows from the south, and is then called the long-shore wind.

July 3. Dubashies of Mădras. 3d *July*.—I went to *Vira Permal Pillay's Chitteram*, or inn built by *Vira Permal*, a *Madras Dubashy*. At *Madras* there are three casts of *Sudras*, who act as *Dubashies*, that is, interpreters. The persons of the first cast seem to be somewhat analogous to the *Káyâstas* of Bengal, and are called *Canaca-pillays*, which by us is commonly written *Canacopily* or *Canacoply;* and this name by

CHAPTER XX. July 3.

Europeans is also frequently extended to all persons, whether *Bráhmans* or *Sudras*, who follow the same profession. The *Canaca-pillays* are a cast of the *Tamuls* of *Dravada*, and throughout that *Désam* were originally in possession of the hereditary office of village accomptant, in the same manner as the *Bráhmans* possess the similar office of *Shanaboga* above the *Ghats*, or as the *Kayastas* of Bengal possessed the analogous office of *Canongó*. The next cast, who follow the business of *Dubashies*, are the more learned *Goalas*, or *Yadavas*. Some of these are of *Telinga*, and others of *Dravada* extraction, and the proper business of the cast is to tend herds of black cattle. The *Dubashies* of this cast, however, have given up all communion with those who follow the original profession of their tribe; and value themselves very highly, as being related to the god *Krishna*, who was born of a *Goala* woman. On this account they all assume some of the names of *Vishnu*, such as *Ráma Pillay*, *Narayana Pillay*, &c. The third cast, who perform the business of *Dubashies*, are the *Vaylalars*, of the labouring class among whom I have in the tenth chapter of this Journal, Vol. II. p. 329, given an account. Those who are men of learning have separated from the cultivators, and call themselves *Modalies*. They are a *Tamul* tribe, and more numerous in *Chéra Chóla*, and *Pandava*, and I believe in the adjacent island of *Ceylon*, than in *Dravada*. Each of these casts pretends to a superiority of rank over the others; and as, at Madras, they are all possessed of great wealth, many ingenious arguments from the books which they esteem sacred have been advanced, to support their various pretensions, which frequently occasion bickerings, and always great heart-burnings and bad neighbourhood. The pride of cast is indeed that which is most prevalent with the *Hindus*; and there is scarcely a creature so wretched or ignorant, but who on this account holds in the utmost contempt many persons in easy circumstances, and respectable situations; for the rank of the different casts is by no means well ascertained; the only one

CHAPTER XX.

point that is clear is, the immensurable superiority of the *Bráhmans* above the rest of mankind.

July 4. *Sri Permaturu.*

4th *July.*—I went to *Sri Permaturu*, or *Varam-phuthur*, a celebrated temple and *Agrarum*, or abode of *Bráhmans*, which is situated about a mile out of the road; but I was desirous of visiting a place rendered remarkable by its having given birth to *Ráma-Anuja Achárya.* The temple has from government an annual allowance of 250 *Pagodas*, or 100*l*; but this would be totally inadequate to the maintenance of the fifty-three families of *Vaidika Sri Vaishnavam Bráhmans* who live in the place. By the contributions of the sect, however, they are supported in considerable affluence. The *Amin*, or civil officer, having assembled the *Bráhmans* whom he considered as most learned, they said, that originally there was at the place a small temple of *Vishnu;* but that, after the celebrity of *Ráma Anuja* had thrown lustre on the place of his nativity, the temple was enlarged, and received an image of this great teacher. In the reign of *Krishna Ráyaru* it was enlarged to the present size, which is very considerable. This was done by *Paran Cusha*, a *Yecang*, that is to say, a *Satany* who has assumed *Sanyási*, and dedicated his life to religious austerity. It was afterwards repaired by a *Dubashy* of Madras; and at present is putting in complete order, at the joint expense of a *Dubashy* and a *Satany.* There are at this place no inscriptions of any antiquity; but it is reported, that when *Paran Cusha* enlarged the temple some were buried in the earth. Near this is the spot where the great man was born. A stone chamber has been erected over it; and between this and the temple is one of the finest *Mandapas*, or porticos, that I have seen erected by *Hindus.* It is of great size, and supported by many columns; but, as usual, it is neglected, and has become ruinous and dirty. Adjoining to the place where *Ráma Anuja* was born, is a temple dedicated to a prophet named *Curat' Alwar.*

The *Sri Vaishnavam* believe in eighteen great prophets, ten of

CHAPTER XX.

July 4.

Eighteen prophets worshipped by the *Sri Vaishnavam*.

whom are called *Alvars*, and eight *Achâryas*. Some of the *Alvars* were *Sudras;* nay even *Parriar* have arrived at this dignity; but all the *Achâryas* were *Brâhmans*, and among others was *Râma Anuja*. In order to prove himself an *Alvar*, a man must abstain from women, and all carnal delights; and give a proof of his being divinely inspired, by foretelling some very great and extraordinary event that is about to take place. When this has happened, and his inspiration has been thus fully established, he delivers in poetry some histories concerning the gods; and by the *Sri Vaishnavam* these are received as canonical. This sect erect images of the eighteen prophets; nor can a *Brâhman* of this kind perform worship, eat, or sleep, in any temple, where such an image is not to be found. From the *Sri Vaishnavam* these images receive divine honours, but not from either *Smartal* or *Madual;* nor do these two sects acknowledge the prophecies to be of divine authority. It is, however, admitted by all parties, that these personages are mentioned in the eighteen *Puranas* as very holy and extraordinary men.

Eighteen *Puranas*.

Although the *Brâhmans* of the south frequently asserted to me, that different events of the *Kali-yugam* are mentioned in the eighteen *Puranas*, yet I was inclined to doubt this; as they thought, perhaps, to confirm the truth of what they were relating, by referring to so high an authority. Having consulted a learned *Pandit* in *Bengal*, he says that my doubts are well founded, and that in the writings published by *Vyása* no particulars of the history of this degenerate age are to be found. The books quoted by the *Brâhmans* of the south as the eighteen *Puranas*, were probably the *Ityhass*, or the *Upu-purana*, which give an account of the transactions of the *Kali-yugam*. Other learned persons allege, that the *Upu-purana* is also the work of *Vyása*; for all such matters are subject to innumerable doubts.

Guru Para, written by *Râma Anuja*.

I have already mentioned, that the book called *Guru Para*, or *Guru Parum Paray*, of which, while at *Tonuru*, I obtained an extract

CHAPTER XX.

July 4.

that contained the life of *Ráma Anuja*, is said to have been written by that personage. In it, according to the *Bráhmans* of his native place, he modestly writes, that he is an incarnation of four deities. The book contains also a similar account of the lives of the other seventeen prophets; and the *Bráhmans* here look upon it as of excellent authority, although several of these prophets lived after *Ráma Anuja* was dead. The *Bráhmans* here, on consulting their copy of the *Guru Para*, agree with those of *Tonuru* concerning the year in which their chief was born, namely, in the year of *Sal.* 939 *A. D.* 1016.

Sri Vaishnavam.

The *Sri Vaishnavam* look upon their *Gurus*, both *Sannyásis* and hereditary, as men highly favoured by God; but not as actual divinities. They have the power of exempting from future transmigrations all persons on whom they bestow *Upadésa* and *Chakrantikam*. The souls of the happy people who are thus exempted from change live in a heaven called *Veicunta*, and there serve *Vishnu*. This sect do not admit of the absorption of the spirits of good men into the essence of the deity, a doctrine that seems to prevail chiefly among the worshippers of *Siva*. The *Sri Vaishnavam* say, that *Brahma* is the son of *Vishnu*, and the father of *Siva*; but they pray to *Vishnu* alone, as the preserver of all living beings, and as the supreme deity.

Heretical sects.

Before the appearance of *Ráma Anuja*, the most prevailing sects in this neighbourhood were the followers of *Buddha*, and the *Charvaca*. Both now seem to have become quite extinct.

Rent and tenures of rice-ground.

The officer of revenue *(Amin)* says, that the *Tank* here waters 1000 acres of land, each containing 100 *Guntas* of 24 feet square. The extent of irrigated ground is therefore rather more than 1322 English acres. This land pays 1700 *Pagodas* a year to the government, and 600 *Pagodas* to temples, revenue officers, &c. &c; in all, 2300 *Pagodas*, worth at the Tower mint 845*l.* 12*s.* 10½*d.* which is at the rate of 12*s.* 9¼*d.* an acre. This land is private property, and may be either sold or mortgaged, in a manner exactly similar to that used in *Malabar*. An acre, according the nature of the soil, will mortgage for from 5 to 100 *Pagodas;* which shows, that the rent is very moderate, considered as such; but considered as a land tax it must be allowed to be very high. Each village now pays a fixed rent, for which all the proprietors are jointly answerable. Among themselves, they determine each man's share by some old valuations.

July 4.

Rájá Paditti.

The hereditary *Canaca-pillay* here gave me a copy of an old *Rájá Paditti* belonging to his family. A copy has been delivered to government, and I here give a translation.

"The form of the *Kali-yugam* will be as follows. The *Kali-yugam* will contain 432,000 years. The men of this age will be four cubits high, and live 100 years.

Particulars of the names of the *Rájás* in the *Kali-yugam.*

Dynasty of the Deva Rāyas.

Parachittu Maha Rájá, grandson of *Dharma Rájá*, and son of *Abimunna*, reigned	64 years.
Jennamya Jya	143
Rájá Narendra	140
Saringa Panry	214
Susta Studica Maha Rájá	154
Vicrama Ditya	1746
Salivahanam	80
Boja Ráya	144
Danta Chicraverti	62
Tribuvana Chicraverti	57
Shanda Deva Maha Rájá	60

Total of the government of 11 *Deva Rájás*, 2864."

The whole account of this dynasty is evidently full of error and confusion. Some person of no discernment has probably extracted it from the books esteemed sacred. The eras of *Vicrama* and

CHAPTER XX.

July 4.

Salivahanam, two of the best established points in *Hindu* chronology, are by this account most horribly distorted. The author has followed an opinion, commonly prevailing among the *Hindus*, of a great monarchy, that extended all over *India* under princes descended from *Yudishtara* the son of *Pandua*, and which commenced with the beginning of the *Kali-yugam*; that is, according to the chronology usually adopted here, 3100 years before the birth of Christ; but with regard to the era of the *Kali-yugam* the *Bráhmans* differ considerably. This dynasty the author supposes to have reigned 2864 years, or until the year 236 before the birth of Christ. However, to return to our author.

Dynasty of *Sholun Ráyaru*, kings of *Naraputti*.

"After this *Naraputti*, *Gaja-putti*, and *Ashaputti*, three thrones were established.

Naraputti throne was possessed by

Utinga Sholun - -	32 years.
Culatunga Sholun - -	18
Rajaendra Sholun - -	11
Tiramudi Canda Sholun - -	13
Carical Sholun - - -	21
Arundavan Sholun - -	13
Womyuru Sholun - -	17
Shayngun Sholun - - -	15
Munalinda Sholun - -	12
Mavanedi Canda Sholun -	15
Vacula Sholun - -	14
Alaperinda Sholun - -	8
Tiraveratu Sholun - -	15
Arleunu Cadamay Canda Sholun -	62
Jeyum Canda Sholun -	12
Kirimi Canda Sholun - -	20
Tondaman Sholun - -	12
Buddum Cuttum Sholun - -	45

CHAPTER XX. July 4.

Shomuman Sholun	reigned 11 years.
Ghingui Conda Sholun - -	11
Sundra Pandia Sholun - -	40
Pottapu Sholun - - -	24
Shingu Wullanda Sholun - -	14
Deva Sholun - - -	10
Shaynahutti Sholun - -	15
Vira Sholun - - - -	30
Shayngara Sholun - -	24

Total of the *Sholun Rájás* 27, who reigned 534 years."

Here we have a dynasty that no doubt existed, and of which many traces remain in *Karnata*, *Dravada*, and the countries toward the south. It is probably not mentioned by *Ramuppa*, because *Tulava* did not belong to the throne of *Naraputti*. Our author makes its end to have been in the year of our Lord 298. The tradition at *Jamagullu*, where one of the temples built by a prince of this family remains, makes them to have been about five centuries later. There is also some reason to think, that the *Sholun Permal*, from whom *Cheruman Permal*, the viceroy of *Malayala*, rebelled, was one of this family. If so, the tradition of *Malayala* agrees with that of *Jamagullu*, and fixes the last princes of this family to have lived about a thousand years ago. After the overthrow of this *Sholun* dynasty, *Karnata* and *Dravada* seem to have been separated from the southern portions of the *Naraputti* sovereignty; for our author goes on thus:

"*Chéra*, *Chola*, and *Pandava Désas* were possessed by

Dynasty of the *Maha Rájás* who governed *Madura*, *Tanjore*, and *Coimbetore*.

Udiamara Maha Rájá - -	18 years.
Jeyadeva M. R. - -	19
Lohita M. R. - -	10
Gungadira M. R. - -	11
Vama Deva M. R. - -	13
Terupulinda M. R. - -	34
Puttaviran M. R - -	43

CHAPTER XX. July 4.

Sri Devanata M. R.	- -	38 years.
Malica Arjina Maha Rájá	reigned	7
Adi Raer	- - -	13
Maha Sustra M. R.	- -	16
Visuveshura M. R.	- -	8
Chindrabuti M. R.	- -	9

Total, 13 princes of *Chéra, Chola,* and *Pandava,* who reigned 239 years."

This brings the chronology down to the year 537 of the Christian era, to which we must add 500, the probable error. It was, perhaps, this dynasty that erected the palace of *Madura,* which in greatness and elegance is said to exceed all other remaining *Hindu* buildings, and would indeed seem to be an admirable work. The last dynasty of *Madura Rájás,* named *Trimula Nayakas,* were *Polygars,* who on the fall of *Vijaya-nagara* assumed independence.

Belalla Rájarus who governed *Karnata.*

" *Belalla Rájar* dynasty.

Rájá Belalla Rájen	- reigned	18 years.
Vira Belalla Rájen	- -	11
Chenna B. R.	- - -	22
Deva B. R.	- - -	14
Vishnu Verti B. R.	- -	28
Hurry B. R.	- - -	19
Imudi B. R.	- - -	17
Visia B. R.	- - -	16
Buca B. R.	- - -	22
China Buca B. R.	- - -	8

Total, 10 *Canudia Belalla Rájar* governed 175 years."

The residence of this, and most of the following dynasties, being far removed from *Madras,* little accuracy relative to them is to be expected in this *Rájá Paditti.* Our author's chronology brings the end of the *Belalla Rájar* government to the year of the Christian era 712. But *Vishnu Verti* is no doubt the same with *Vishnu Verdana,* who, although younger, was contemporary with *Ráma Anuja*, born in the year of *Sal.* 939, or 1016 of the Christian era. This confirms the tradition at *Jamagullu*, and *Malayala*, concerning the time of the *Sholun Rájás*, and brings all the other dynasties much lower down than the *Rájá Paditti* places them.

CHAPTER XX.

July 4.

Adeva Rájás.

" *Adeva Rájás* government.

Sri Ranga Ádeva Ráyaru	reigned	25 years.
Vira Narayana A. R.	- -	23
Wobala A. R.	- - - -	21
Siruvaynguda A. R.	- -	22
Pirungei Endia A. R.	- -	15
Canda Gopala A. R.	- -	32
Narasingha A. R.	- - -	13
Cambuli A. R.	- - -	15
Bucun A. R.	- - -	22
Vira Narasingha A. R.	-	12
Narasingha A. R.	- - -	8
Duia A. R.	- - -	12
Sri Pandia A. R.	- -	9
Vasu Deva A. R.	- - -	12
Siric Virindi A. R.	- -	15
Cutia Deva A. R.	- -	14
Rájá Visia Bujinga A. R.	-	12
Shalica Narayana A. R.	- -	10
Pritiwadi Bacukera Shadicun A. R.		87

Total, 19 *Adeva Ráyás*, governing 370 years."

There can be little doubt, but that this dynasty is the same with the 18 ancestors of *Pritapa Rúdra*, mentioned in the *Ráya Paditti* of *Ramuppa;* in such loose hints as can be procured of *Hindu* history, the difference of one person being of little importance. The immoderate length of the last reign is probably owing to some

CHAPTER XX. July 4.

mistake; and then the coincidence between the two *Ráya Padittis* will be greater; for *Ramuppa* allows only 211 years for these princes. The *Sri Permaturu Ráya Paditti* brings this dynasty down to the year of the Christian era 1082; but that must be corrected as above. It then goes on to state, that

Pritapa Rudrun.

"*Uricundy Pritapa Rudrun* governed 58 years, and *Anna Pemma Ruddi* 77 years."

It is probable, that *Anna Pemma* may have been a prince descended from *Pritapa Rudra*, who established himself here after the overthrow of that king by the *Mussulmans*, and was not brought under subjection to the first prince of *Vijaya-nagara*; for *Hari-hara* the first is not mentioned in this succession of princes.

Tuluva Ráyar dynasty.

"*Tuluva Ráyár* government.

Buca Ráyar -	reigned	14 years.
Vijia Buca Ráya - -		13
Hari-hara R. - -		14
Casi Deva R. - - -		8
Rama Deva R. - - -		7
Virupacshi R. - - -		5
Malica Argina R. - - -		7
Rama Chandra Ráyar - -		9
Shalava Conda Deva Maha Rájá -		14
Deva Ráya Maha Rájá - -		15
Cambudia Deva M. R. - -		5
Comara Cambudia M. R. - -		4
Sholava Canterua Deva M. R - -		6
Sholava Narasingha Deva M. R. -		40
Imudia Dharma Ráyar - -		11
Piravida Deva Maha Ráya -		30
Rama Chindra M. R. - - -		18
Vicunta M. R. - - -		19

CHAPTER XX.

July 4.

Padma Nava Maha Ráya reigned 6 years.
Damudera M. R. - - 16
Narasingha M. R. - - - 11
Vira Narasingha M. R. - - 21

Total, 22 *Tulava Ráyas*, governing 293 years."

This brings the chronology down to the year of Christ 1510. The account here given of this dynasty is remarkably different from that of *Ramuppa*, and is totally unsupported by such inscriptions as I have collected. The author then proceeds to the celebrated *Krishna Ráyaru*, as of a distinct family.

" *Ráyar* government.

Krishna Rayar.

Krishna Ráyar - governed 20 years.
Achuta Ráyar - - - 13
Total 33.

Ráma Rájá.

Ráma Rájá - - - - - 22
Tirumala Deva Maha Ráyar - 8
Sri Ranga Deva M. R. - - 14
Peria Vencata Pati Maha Ráyar - 29
Ráma Deva M. R. - - - 15
Anagundi Vencata M. R. - - 12
Sri Ranga M. R. - - - 5

Total 7 *Rájás* from *Ráma Rájá* to *Sri Ranga*, who governed 105 years."

Total from the beginning of the *Kali-yugam* till the year *Veya*, 4748.

Ráma Rájá is, no doubt, the prince who was killed on the banks of the *Krishna*, and whose death was immediately followed by the destruction of *Vijaya-nagara*; which, according to this chronology, would have happened in the year of the Christian era, 1565. According to *Ramuppa*, however, that event happened about the year 1588; and in this point, I imagine, his chronology is not

CHAPTER XX. July 4. materially erroneous. The princes that follow *Ráma Ráyaru* are probably those of a branch of the *Anagundi* family; which, after the fall of *Vijaya-nagara*, settled at *Chandra-giri*, north from *Tripathi*, and which for some time possessed a considerable territory in that vicinity.

Mussulmans. " Afterwards, beginning with the year *Servajittu* (that is, the year following *Veya*, or 1648), were the *Turcanum* (that is to say, the *Mussulmans.*)

The *Golconda Rájá*, called *Toluta Abdulla*, reigned 26 years.

Hussun Cudumusta reigned 14 years. Total of the *Golconda* government, 2 reigns and 40 years. Total from the commencement of the *Kali-yugam* 4788 years (*A. D.* 1688).

Afterwards, from the year *Parabava* in the month *Kartika*, were the *Delhi Sultans*, *Ashaburi Padishas*.

Aburung Shai governed 19 years. His sons were *Asumudar*, *Salem*, and *Cam Bucshi*.

Asumudar governed 3 months.
Salem governed 3 years.
Cambucshi did not govern.
Baba Shean governed 6 years.

The government of 4 kings of *Delhi* continued in all 28 years and 3 months, ending in the year of the *Kali-yugam* 4816 (*A. D.* 1716.)

After this, in the month *Ani* of the year *Munmutta*, came other *Rájás*."

The author's knowledge of the *Mussulman* kings, living at a great distance, has been very imperfect.

July 5. 5th *July*.—I returned to *Condatura*, and on the day following arrived at *Madras*; having observed, ever since passing the *Ghats*, more and more signs of improvement, the nearer I approached this European city.

I was here greatly disappointed at not finding any answers returned to the queries which I had proposed to the gentlemen who managed *Bára-mahál* and *Coimbetore;* as I had depended on this assistance, and as their great knowledge and abilities would have enabled me to correct many errors into which I must have fallen, and to obtain much information which a traveller cannot procure.

July 6.

APPENDIX.

REPORT of the PRODUCTIONS, COMMERCE, and MANUFACTURES, of the SOUTHERN DISTRICTS in *MALLEAM* (*Malayalam*) framed by the Resident at *Calicut*, agreeably to the Instructions of the Commissioners appointed to inspect the Countries ceded by *Tippoo Sultan* on the *Malabar* Coast; and comprized under the following Heads, *viz.*

1st, ACCOUNT of the several ARTICLES of COMMERCE produced or manufactured, and which are also consumed in the Country.

In calculating the probable profit on the following List of Articles, a deduction must be made for Inland Duties, Customs, and other Charges, which are very considerable, but which cannot be accurately ascertained; for this reason, the difference between their respective local value, and when ready to be sold at, or exported from, the sea-coast, has been put down as the profit arising on the trade. Many of the Articles inserted in this List, are of too trifling a nature to yield any advantages worth mentioning in a commercial point of view.

Natural Productions of the Soil.	Local Value.	Probable Profit arising on the Trade.	Explanatory Remarks.
Betle-Nuts -	230 *reas per* 1000	When dried and prepared, 50 per cent.	100 *reas* = 1 *rupee*
Black Wood -	$3\frac{1}{2}$ *rupees per candy*	200 per cent.	
Bamboos	2 *rupees per* 100	50 ditto	
Buzarbut-Nuts, a country-medicine	18 *rupees per candy*	25 ditto	
Betle-Nut Leaves	1 *rupee per* 4000	25 ditto	
Butter	6 *rupees per maund*	25 ditto	
Coco-Nuts	14 *rupees per candy*	3 *rupees per mill* (1000)	Extremely variable in their Prices
Cardamums, 1st sort	800 *rupees per candy*	80 *per cent*	Little used in the Country. — *Vide* List of Goods exported.
Ditto, 2d ditto	600 ditto ditto	50 ditto	
Ditto, 3d ditto	450 ditto ditto	40 ditto	
Ditto, 4th ditto	300 ditto ditto	20 ditto	
Cassia (*Laurus*)	30 to 40 *rupees per candy*	50 ditto	Occasionally bought up by the Europe Ships; and which, in London, they mix with the real Cinnamon.
Coir, Rope of Coco-Nut Husks, 2 sorts	18 *rupees per* ditto	50 ditto	
Capoor Catchree	3 *rupees per maund*	10 ditto	A Country Medicine
Colenzun	12 *rupees per candy*	5 ditto	Used in Medicine
Cassia Leaves (*Laurus*)	10 *rupees per* ditto	25 ditto	
Cultee - -	$1\frac{3}{4}$ *rupees per robin*	40 ditto	Horse Gram. *Dolichos biflorus*
Chowla - -	$2\frac{1}{4}$ *rupees per* ditto	50 ditto	A Country Grain, *Holcus Sorghum*
Castor Seed -	$1\frac{3}{4}$ ditto *per maund*	25 ditto	*Ricinus*
Dry Ginger - -	35 *rupees per candy*	50 to 100 ditto	
Eggs - -	$1\frac{1}{2}$ *rupees per* 100	25 ditto	
Honey - -	5 *rupees per maund*	50 ditto	
Heavy Pepper -	100 *rupees per candy*	80 *per cent.* last year: now 100 *per cent.*	It is said, that the French at *Mahé* now give 210 *rupees per candy*
Jack Wood -	$1\frac{1}{2}$ *rupee per candy*	100 ditto	*rtocarpus*
Jeer Kulchla -	5 ditto ditto	Not to be ascertained	A Medicine
Jeer Mui - -	12 *rupees per candy*	Not to be ascertained	Kind of Nuts used in Medicine
Jinjely Seed -	$2\frac{1}{2}$ *rupees per robin*	50 *per cent.*	*esamum*
Jacks Fruit -	8 *per a rupee*	Ditto	*Artocarpus*
Kud Ebrumee -	10 *rupees per candy*	Not to be ascertained	

Natural Productions of the Soil.	Local Value.	Probable Profit arising on the Trade.	Explanatory Remarks.
Light Pepper -	100 *rupees per candy*	100 *per cent.*	The Reason of Light Pepper bearing apparently so high a Price, is from the vast Quantity of it which goes to one *candy* in weighing it.
Lowlungar Wood -	1½ *rupees per candy*	Not to be ascertained	A heavy hard Wood, which sinks in the Water; occasionally used by *Tippoo* in launching his Ships, to put beneath them when hauled into the Water. *Hopee Buch.* MSS.
Mug (Mung) -	2 *rupees per robin*	50 *per cent.*	*Phaseolus Mungo L.*
Mangoes, Fruit -	2 *rupees per* 100	Not to be ascertained	*Mangifera*
Nag Kasur, Flower of *Cassia*	35 *rupees per candy*	25 *per cent.*	
Poon Wood for Masts -	5 to 100 *rupees per* piece	Variable, and not to be ascertained	In great demand for large Ships, *Callophyllum*
Paddy, or Rough Rice -	1 *rupee per robin*	50 *per cent.*	
Plantains, or *Bananas*	5 *rupees per* 100	Ditto	*Musa*
Plantain Leaves -	1 ditto *per* ditto	25 ditto	*Musa*
Sapan Wood -	10 ditto *per candy*	60 ditto	Used in Dying, *Guilandina Sapan*
Teak Wood (*Theca*) -	3 *rupees per* ditto	200 ditto	*Vide* Remark at the End of this Report
Turmerick -	25 *rupees per candy*	50 to 100 *per cent.*	
Tamarinds -	10 to 15 *rupees per* ditto	50 *per cent.*	
Toor, a Grain -	1½ *rupee per robin*	Ditto	Produced in small Quantities. *Cytisus Cajan*
White Pepper -	220 *rupees per candy*	175 ditto	Picked from the heavy Pepper; and produced in small Quantities.
Jams, a Fruit -	10 ditto ditto	25 ditto	*Calyptranthes Jambulana*
MANUFACTURES.			
Bees Wax -	8 *rupees per maund*	25 *per cent.*	Produced in small Quantities
Baskets - -	30 to 60 *per a rupee*	5 ditto	
Coco-Nut Oil -	3 *rupees per maund*	50 ditto	
Castor Oil - -	Variable	— —	Ditto ditto
Coir Ropes -	25 *rupees per candy*	25 *rupees per cent.*	Made of Coco-Nut Husks
Ditto Cables -	27 ditto	40 ditto	
Copra - -	30 ditto	25 ditto	Dried Kernels of the Coco-Nut
Chunam (Lime) -	2 *rupees per* 1000 *noye*	10 ditto	
Cadzans - -	5 *rupees per* 1000	25 ditto	Mats, made of the Coco Leaf
Dammer (Resin) -	1½ *rupee per maund*	10 ditto	
Dry Coco-Nuts	47 *rupees per* 1000	25 ditto	
Gold -	Variable	Not to be ascertained	Produced in small Quantities
Iron - -	Ditto	Ditto	Ditto ditto ditto
Jenjily Oil (*Sesamum*)	5 *rupees per maund*	15 *per cent.*	Ditto ditto ditto
Jagary of *Toddy*	17 *rupees per candy*	25 ditto	Inspissated Juice of Palm Trees
Mats of *Bamboos* -	1½ *rupee per corge* of 20	25 ditto	
Red *Betle-Nuts* -	30 *rupees per* cwt.	25 ditto	
Ditto *Chuqueenee* ditto	45 ditto	20 to 50 ditto	
Rice, boiled -	1½ *rupee per robin*	25 ditto	
Small *Cumberbands* -	½ *rupee per piece*	Not to be ascertained	The only Cloth manufactured in the Country.
Summer Heads, or *Chitries*	Variable	Ditto	Parasols
Toddy - -	¾ *rupee per maund*	20 *per cent.*	Juice of Palm Trees
Twine - -	2½ *rupees per maund*	25 ditto	Produced in small Quantities
Toor Dholl, a Grain	2 *rupees per robin*	25 ditto	Ditto ditto ditto, *Cytisus Cajan*
Towker - -	16 *rupees per candy*	25 ditto	
Wax Candles -	22 *rupees per maund*	20 ditto	Ditto ditto ditto
White *Betle-Nuts* -	34 *rupees per candy*	25 ditto	

2dly, ACCOUNT of GOODS EXPORTED, and to what Places.

Natural Productions of the Soil.	Local Value.	Whither exported.	Probable Profit.	Explanatory Remarks.
Betle-Nuts	230 *reas per* 1000	To all Places in *India*	Not to be ascertained	
Black Wood	3½ *rupees per candy*	Ditto	50 *per cent.*	*Pterocarpus*
Bamboos	2 *rupees per* 100	Different Places along the Coast	Ditto	
Black *Gram*, a Pulse	2½ *rupees per robin*	Ditto ditto	15 ditto	Very little produced in the Country
Buzarbut Nuts	18 ditto per *candy*	To all Places in *India*	20 ditto	A Country Medicine
Betle-nut Leaves	1 *rupee per* 4000	To all Places along the Coast	2 ditto	
Butter	6 *rupees per maund*	Bought up in small Quantities by Vessels	10 ditto	
Cardamums, 1st sort	800 *rupees per* cwt.	Ditto and Europe	Not to be ascertained	
2d ditto	600 Ditto			
3d ditto	450 Ditto			
4th ditto	300 Ditto			
Cassia (Laurus)	30 to 40 *rupees per* cwt	Ditto and ditto	Ditto	Very little produced in the Country
Coco-Nuts	14 *rupees per* 1000	To all Places in *India*	5 *per cent.*	
Coir Coco-Nut rope, 2d sort	18 *rupees per* cwt	To all Places in *India*	Not to be ascertained	
Capoor Cutchree	3 *rupees per maund*	Ditto and *China*	Ditto	Used in Medicine
Colenzun	12 *rupees per candy*	Ditto	Ditto	Ditto ditto
Cassia Leaves (Laurus)	10 *rupees per candy*	Ditto	5 *per cent.*	
Cultee, a Pulse	1½ *rupee per robin*	Different Places along the Coast	Ditto	Horse Gram. *Dolichos biflorus*
Chowla (*Holcus Sorghum*)	2¼ ditto	Ditto	Ditto	A Country Grain; very little produced in the Country
Castor Seed	1½ *rupee per maund*	Ditto	Ditto	
Dry Ginger	35 *rupees per* cwt	To all Places in *India*	Not to be ascertained	
Eggs	1½ *rupee per* 100	Bought up in small Quantities by Vessels	Ditto	
Honey	5 *rupees per maund*	Ditto ditto ditto	Ditto	Very little produced in the Country
Heavy Pepper	100 *rupees per candy*	Europe, and all Places in *India*	Ditto	
Jack-wood	1½ *rupee per* ditto	To all Places in *India*	10 *per cent.*	*Artocarpus*
Jeer Kutchla	5 ditto	Ditto	Not to be ascertained	Used in Medicine
Jeer Moi	12 ditto	Ditto	Ditto	
Jenjily Seed (Sesamum)	2½ *rupees per robin*	Ditto	Ditto	Very little produced in the Country
Jacks, Fruit	8 *per a rupee*	Ditto	Ditto	*Artocarpus*
Kud Ebramee	10 *rupees per candy*	Ditto	Ditto	
Light Pepper	100 *rupees per* cwt	Ditto	50 *per cent.*	
Limes	2½ *rupees per* 1000	Ditto and Coast	5 ditto	
Lowlungar Wood	1½ *rupee per candy*	Ditto	10 ditto	
Mug, *Phaseolus Mungo*	2 *rupees per robin*	Ditto ditto	5 ditto	Ditto ditto
Mangoes Fruit	2 *rupees per* 1000	To all Places in *India* and Coast	Not to be ascertained	
Nagkesur, or Flower of *Cassia*	35 *rupees per candy*	To all Places in *India*	Ditto	Very little produced in this Country
Poon Wood for Masts	5 to 100 *rupees per piece*	*Bombay*, and bought up by the *Lingys*.	Ditto	*Calophyllum Inophyllum*
Paddy, or Rough Rice	1 *rupee per robin*	To all Places in *India* and Coast	Ditto	
Plantains, or *Bananas*	5 *rupees per* 1000	Ditto	2 *per cent.*	*Musa*
Plantain Leaves	1 *rupee per* ditto	Ditto	Ditto	
Sapan Wood	10 *rupees per candy*	To all Places in *India*	5 ditto	Used in Dying. *Guilandina Sapan*
Teak Wood	3 ditto	Ditto ditto	25 ditto	*Theka Jussieu*
Turmerick	25 ditto	Ditto ditto	Not to be ascertained	
Toor, Pulse	1½ *rupee per robin*	Ditto ditto	5 *per cent.*	Very little produced in the Country. *Cytisus Cajan*
White Pepper	120 *rupees per candy*	Europe, and to all Places in *India*	Not to be ascertained	Ditto ditto
Jams, Fruit	10 *rupees* ditto	To all Places in *India* and Coast	Ditto	*Calyptranthes Jambulana*

Natural Productions of the Soil.	Local Value.	Whither exported.	Probable Profit.	Explanatory Remarks.
Sandal Wood, 1st, 2d, 3d and 4th sorts	60 *rupees per candy*	*China*, *Europe*, and Places in *India*	Not to be ascertained	Where the *Sandal* Wood is produced, it is bought up without being picked, or divided into the 1st, 2d, 3d, and 4th sorts; which is always done afterwards
MANUFACTURES.				
Bees Wax	8 *rupees per maund*	To all Places in *India*	10 *per cent.*	
Baskets - -	30 to 60 *per a rupee*	To all Places in the Coast	4 ditto	
Coco-Nut Oil -	3 *rupees per maund*	To all Places in *India*	Not to be ascertained	
Castor Oil - -	Variable	— —	Ditto	Very little produced in the Country
Coir Ropes of Cocoa-Nut	25 *rupees per candy*	To all Places in *India*	10 *per cent.*	
Ditto Cables -	27 ditto	Ditto	Ditto	
Copra, dried Coco-Nut Kernel	30 ditto	Ditto	Not to be ascertained	
Chunam (Lime)	2 ditto *per* 1000 *noye*	Different Places along the Coast	Ditto	
Cadjans, Mats of Coco-Nut Leaves	5 ditto *per* 1000	Ditto ditto	5 *per cent.*	
Dammer, Resin	1¼ *rupee per maund*	To all Places in *India* and ditto	Not to be ascertained	Ditto ditto
Dry Coco-Nuts	17 *rupees per* 1000	To all Places in *India*	Ditto	
Gold - -	Variable	— —	Ditto	Ditto ditto
Iron - -	Ditto	— —	Ditto	Ditto ditto
Jenjily Oil, *Sesamum*	5 *rupees per maund*	Different Places along the Coast	5 *per cent.*	Ditto ditto
Jagree of *Toddy* -	17 *rupees per candy*	Ditto ditto	Ditto	Inspissated Juice of Palm Trees
Mats of *Bamboos*	1½ *rupee per corge*	Ditto ditto	Not to be ascertained	Corge means 20, or score
Red *Betle-Nut*	30 *rupees per candy*	To all Places in *India*	Ditto	
Ditto *Chuqueenee* ditto	45 ditto ditto	Ditto	Ditto	
Rice, Boiled	1¼ *rupee per robin*	Ditto and the Coast	Ditto	
Small *Cumberbands*	¼ *rupee per piece*	To all Places in Coast	5 *per cent.*	
Summerheads, or *Chitries*	Variable	Ditto	Not to be ascertained	Parasols
Toddy -	3 qr. *rupee per maund*	Ditto	Ditto	Palm Wine
Twine - -	2½ *rupees per maund*	Ditto	Ditto	Ditto
Toor Dholl -	2 *rupees per robin*	Ditto	Ditto	Grain of the *Cytisus Cajan*
Towker - -	16 *rupees per candy*	To all Places in *India*	6 *per cent.*	*Malabar* Grain
Wax Candles -	22 *rupees per maund*	Ditto	5 ditto	
White *Betle-Nut*	34 *rupees per candy*	Ditto	Not to be ascertained	

3dly, ACCOUNT of GOODS IMPORTED.

List of Articles.	From whence imported.	Quality.	Average Price.	Remarks.
Alum	*China*	*Dapotas*	35 *rupees per candy*	
Almonds	*Muscat*, *Mocha*, and *Judah*	Bags	4 to 6 *rupees per maund*	
Amber	*Diree Mahall* ditto (*Arabia*)	Wooden Boxes	3 to 400 *rupees per pound*	
Aloes	*Muscat*	Bags	6 *rupees per maund*	
Benjamin	*Bengal* and *Achin*	Chests	12 to 20 *rupees per maund*	
Black Grapes	*Muscat* and *Mocha*	Bags	4½ *rupees per maund*	
Brimstone	Ditto	Ditto	60 to 90 *rupees per candy*	
Black Cummin Seed	Ditto, *Surat*, and *Guzerat*	Ditto	80 to 100 ditto ditto	
Black *Gram*, a Pulse	*Bombay* ditto and ditto	Ditto	18 to 35 ditto ditto	
Bole, Medicine	*Muscat*	Ditto	8 *rupees per maund*	
Batty, Rice in the Husk	*Bombay*	—	35 to 45 *rupees per morah*	
Black *Dooties*, a Cloth	*Surat*, *Guzerat*, and *Madras*	Bale	110 to 130 *rupees per corge*, or 20 pieces	
Broad Cloth	*Bombay*	Ditto	45 to 80 *rupees per piece*	
Camphire	*China* and *Achin*	Chest	80 to 100 *rupees per pecul*	
Cotton	*Bombay*, *Surat*, *Guzerat*, *Rajapore*	Bale	80 to 130 *rupees per candy*	
Cutch Cotton	*Cutch*	Ditto and *Dokras*	60 to 90 ditto ditto	
Chilly, *Capsicum*	*Bombay* and *Goa*	Bags	40 to 70 ditto ditto	
Castor Oil	*Surat* and *Guzerat*	*Dupper*	60 to 80 ditto ditto	
Chintz	*Bengal*, *Madras*, *Bombay*, and *Guzerat*	Bales	30 to 80 *rupees per corge*	
Cinnamon	*Ceylon* and *China*	Chests	40 to 50 *rupees per* cwt.	
Coffee	*Muscat* and *Mocha*	Bags	8 to 10 *rupees per maund*	
China Root	*China*	*Dapotas*	45 *rupees per candy*	
Copper in Sheet, Plate, and Bar	*Bombay*, *Bengal*, *Muscat*, and *Batavia*	Chests	16 to 18 *rupees per maund*	
Creat	*Bengal*	Ditto	8 *rupees per maund*	
Cloves	*Batavia* and *Malacca*	Ditto	3 to 4 *rupees per* pound	
China Cabob	*China*	Ditto	15 *rupees per maund*	
Cummin Seed	*Bombay*, *Surat*, *Guzerat* and *Muscat*	Bags	100 to 150 *rupees per candy*	
Dholl, a Pulse	*Bengal*, *Bombay*, *Surat*, and *Guzerat*	Ditto	25 to 30 *rupees per* cwt.	
Dry Dates	*Bussorah*, *Muscat*, and *Mocha*	Ditto	25 to 30 ditto	
Dry Ginger	*Bengal*	Ditto	65 to 75 ditto	
Dammer, Resin	*China*, *Achin*, and *Malacca*	Chests	50 *rupees per* cwt.	
Eyes Medicine	*Muscat* and *Juddah*	Bags	10 *rupees per maund*	Refined Antimony
Essoop Gool Seed	Ditto ditto	Ditto	50 *rupees per* cwt.	
Figs, Dry	Ditto ditto	Ditto	10 *rupees per maund*	
Gram, a Pulse	*Bengal*, *Bombay*, *Surat*, and *Guzerat*	Ditto	22 to 35 *rupees per candy*	
Green Paint	*Surat* and *Guzerat*	Ditto	20 to 35 *per maund*	
Ghee, Boiled Butter	*Bengal*, *Sind*, *Surat*, and *Guzerat*	*Dupper*	6 to 8 *rupees per maund*	
Gunny Bags	*Bengal* and *Bombay*	Bale	3 to 4 *rupees per corge*	Made from the *Crotolaria juncea*
Gunny in Pots	Ditto	Ditto	2½ *to* 3 *rupees per* ditto	
Gum *Arabic*	*Muscat*, *Surat*, and *Guzerat*	Bags	5 to 8 *rupees per maund*	
Hartall, Cinnabar	*China* and *Muscat*	Ditto	110 *rupees per* cwt.	
Hing, Asafœtida	*Muscat* and *Sindia*	Jar	30 to 50 *rupees per maund*	
Hengraw	*Muscat*	Ditto	5 *rupees per maund*	
Iron	*Bombay*	—	65 to 80 *rupees per* cwt.	
Jenjily Oil	Ditto *Surat* and *Guzerat*	*Dubler*	70 to 100 *rupees per candy*	*Sesamum*
Jagree	*Bombay and Rajapore*	Earthen Pots and Baskets	55 *rupees per candy*	Inspissated Juice of Sugar Cane
Jestomud, Medicine	*Bussorah*, *Muscat*, and *Mocha*	Bags	30 *rupees per* ditto	Liquorice
Kincob, Cloth	*Bombay*, *Surat*, and *Guzerat*	Bales	20 to 100 *rupees per* piece	
Kismiss, Raisins	*Mocha* and *Muscat*	Bags	4 to 5 *rupees per maund*	
Long Pepper	*Bengal*	Ditto	30 to 40 ditto ditto	
Lime Pickles	*Mocha* and *Muscat*	Jar	12 to 15 ditto *per* 100	
Lead	*Bombay*, *Malacca*, and *Batavia*	Cask	4 to 5 *rupees per maund*	
Mug, Pulse	Ditto, *Bengal*, *Surat*, and *Guzerat*	Bag	18 to 35 *rupees per candy*	
Mustard	Ditto *Guzerat* and *Sindia*	Ditto	30 to 40 *rupees per* ditto	
Mace	*Batavia*, *China*, and *Sindia*	Wooden Box	3 to 500 *rupees per* pound	

List of Articles.	From whence imported.	Quality.	Average Price.	Remarks.
Mugadooties, Silks	*Bengal*	Bales	30 to 40 *rupees per corge*	
Musroo	*Bombay*, *Surat*, and *Guzerat*	Bales	90 to 200 *rupees per ditto*	
Munzett, Madder	*Mocha*, *Bussorah*, and *Sindia*	Bags	160 *rupees per candy*	
Mortooth, or Blue Vitriol	*Surat*, and *Guzerat*	Ditto	15 to 25 *rupees per maund*	
Moytee, Fenugreek	Ditto	Ditto	35 to 45 *rupees per* cwt.	
Medicine	*Bengal*, *China*, *Bombay*, *Surat*, *Guzerat*, and *Mocha*	Ditto and Chests	Not to be ascertained	
Nutmegs	*Batavia* and *China*	Wooden Box	10 to 12 *rupees per* pound	
Nuckla	*Muscat*	Ditto	15 *rupees per maund*	
Opium	*Bengal*, *Bombay*, and *Mocha*	Chests	70 to 180 *rupees per maund*	
Oil of Mustard Seed	*Surat*, *Guzerat*, and *Sind*.	Jars	70 to 90 *rupees per candy*	
Onions	*Bombay*	Baskets	20 to 50 *rupees per* ditto	
Purpets, Cloth	*Bombay*	Bales	16 to 27 *rupees per* piece	
Piece Goods, Silk and Thread	*Bengal*, *Madras*, *Bombay*, *Surat*, and *Guzerat*	Ditto		
Pistachio Nuts	*Muscat*	Bags	6 *rupees per maund*	
Pepul Mull	*Bengal*	Ditto	22 *rupees per maund*	Root of the Long Pepper
Pearls	*Muscat*, *Bombay*, and *Surat*	Buts		
Pomegranate	Ditto	Baskets	16 to 20 *per a rupee*	
Persia Gul	Ditto	Jars	22 *rupees per candy*	
Persia Salt	Ditto	Bags	10 *rupees per* cwt.	
Quick Silver	*Bombay*, *China*, and *Batavia*	Jars	45 to 50 *rupees per maund*	
Rice	*Bengal*, *Mangalore*, and *Sindia*	Bags and *robin*	7½ to 12 *rupees per* bag	
Rattans	*Batavia*	Bundles	2½ *rupees per* 100	
Red Earth	*Muscat*	Bags	15 *rupees per candy*	
Rose Flowers	Ditto	Ditto	4 *rupees per maund*	
Rose Water	Ditto	Bottles	1 *rupee* per bottle	
Rose *Mallos*	Ditto	Jars	121 *rupees per candy*	Mallows?
Red Lead	*Bombay*	Casks	4½ *rupees per maund*	
Salt	*Bombay*; *Muscat*, and *Mocha*	Bags	¾ *per* bag	
Shark Fins	*Muscat*	Ditto	30 *rupees per pecul*	
Sweet Limes	Ditto	Baskets	15 to 20 *per rupee*	
Sheep	Ditto and *Mocha*	—	8 to 12 *rupees* each	
Salem	Ditto ditto	Bags	2 to 4 *rupees per* pound	
Sunsull Karr	Ditto	Ditto	2 *rupees per maund*	
Sona Makee	Ditto	Ditto	3 ditto ditto	
Saw Cummin Seed	Ditto *Surat*, *Guzerat*, and *Sind*	Ditto	160 *rupees per candy*	
Saffron	*China*, *Bombay*, and *Goa*	*Dupper* and Tin Box	20 to 25 *rupees per* pound	
Shawls	*Bombay*, *Surat*, and *Guzerat*	Bale	20 to 100 *rupees per* piece	
Steel	*Bombay*	—	90 *rupees per candy*	
Sugar in *Dapotas*	*China*	*Dapotas*	18 *rupees per pecul*	
Ditto in Bags	*Bengal*	Bags	16 ditto	
Ditto in Cannister	*Batavia*	Cannister	80 *rupees per candy*	
Sugar Candy	*China* and ditto	Tub and Cannister	120 to 160 *rupees per candy*	
Salt Petre	*Bengal*	Bag	60 to 70 *rupees per candy*	
Silk	Ditto and *China*	Bale and Chest	4 to 600 *rupees per pecul*	
Tobacco	*Surat*, *Rajapore*, and *Coimbetore*	Bale	60 to 100 *rupees per candy*	
Sandal Wood	*Rajapore* and *Mangalore*	—	10 to 15 ditto	
Tuthnagne	*China* and *Batavia*	—	8 *rupees per maund*	
Tortoise Shells	*Batavia*	Bale	5 *rupees per* pound	
Tin	Ditto	—	10 *rupees per maund*	
Vermillion	*China* and *Surat*	Wooden Box and Bundle	1¼ *rupee per* bundle	
Wheat	*Bombay*, *Surat*, *Guzerat*, and *Muscat*	Bag	20 to 35 *rupees per candy*	
Wallnuts	*Muscat*	Bag	2 to 3 *rupees per* 1000	
Wet Dates	*Muscat* and *Mocha*	Ditto	20 *rupees per candy*	

Teak wood is at present very scarce at *Calicut* and the sea-ports, owing to the elephants which were employed in this trade being taken away by the *Nabob* (*Tippoo*) for the use of his army. Before the *Teak* Timber can be brought from the forests, the process is very tedious. It is, in the first instance, necessary to cut off all the branches from the trees intended to be cut down; to cut the tree nearly two-thirds through, and to make long incisions in the bark; in which state it must remain one year to dry, during which time the bark falls off of itself; after which it is cut down, pushed into the rivers contiguous, during the rains, by elephants, and floated down them to different places. The *Teak* wood, when green, is very heavy; and sinks in water.

The *Poon* spars are got in nearly the same manner, but the *Jack* tree can be cut down at any time.

An ABSTRACT of the GOODS IMPORTED and EXPORTED by SEA, for the different Years, taken from the Custom-House Account of *Tellichery* Circle.

Malabar Year 973.		974.	975.
IMPORTS.			
A			
Arrack, *Columbo*	16 *leaguers* 75 *gallons*	210 *leaguers* 10 *gallons*	73½ *leaguers*
Ditto *Batavia*	73 ditto	32 ditto 11 ditto	
Ditto, *Cochin* - -	42 ditto 100 ditto	97 ditto 12 ditto	25 *leaguers* 43½ *gallons*
Ditto, *Anjengo* - -	25 ditto 118 ditto	11 ditto	23 ditto 128 ditto
Ditto, *Canara* - -	2 ditto 48 ditto	3 ditto	
Almonds - -	8 *candies* 0 *maunds* 16 *lb.*	15 *candies* 18 *maunds* 20 *lb.*	2 *candies* 7 *maunds*
Aloes - -	3 ditto 1 ditto 13 do.	2 ditto 14 ditto	
Aguam Seed - -	100 ditto 17 ditto 16 do.	21 ditto 16 ditto	11 ditto 15 ditto 16 *lb.*
Asafœtida - -	19 ditto	2 ditto 13 ditto	2 ditto 10 ditto
Alum —	— —	5 ditto 6 ditto 16 *lb.*	6 ditto
B			
Betle-Nuts - -	3 *candies* 12 *maunds* 16 *lb.*	16 *candies* 1 *maund*	41 *candies* 2 *maunds*
Ditto, *Cut* - -	13 ditto 16 ditto 16 do.	16 ditto 4 ditto 8 *lb.*	7 ditto 6 ditto 8 *lb.*
Ditto, Green	27,900	7000	343,000
Beads - -	20,000	3000	1 *candy* 18 *maunds*
Benjoin - - -	36¾ *peculs* = 133 *lb.*	12 chests	5 ditto 10 ditto
Barley - -	5 kegs and 3 chests	11 kegs	6 kegs
Boots - - -	1 trunk	4 trunks	35 pairs
C			
Confectionary - -	1 box	2 boxes	5 boxes
Cutlery - -	2 ditto	11 ditto	6 chests
Coffee - - -	2 *candies* 16 *maunds* 12 *lbs.*	1 *candy*	
Chelly Pepper (*Capsicum*) -	16 ditto 13 ditto 16 do.	16 *candies* 7 *maunds* 10 *lb.*	10 *candies*
Coir, or Coco-Nut Cordage	271 ditto 18 ditto 8 do.	151 ditto 15 ditto	347 ditto
Cointer Seed - -	11800 *edangallies*, 108 cub. in.	8415 *edangallies*	590 *edangallies*
Cotton - -	247 *candies* 11 *maunds*	374 *candies*	250 *candies* 18 *maunds* 16 *lb.*
Ditto, Yarn - -	3 ditto 13 ditto	1 ditto 2 *maunds*	15 ditto
Corks - -	5 boxes and 108 gross	1 dozen	50 gross
Cheese - -	8 boxes and 318 *lb.*	11 boxes	12 boxes
Cummin Seed - -	24 *candies* 13 *maunds* 8 *lbs.*	9 *candies* 10 *maunds*	21 *candies* 4 *maunds* 16 *lb.*
Coco-Nuts - -	191,085	60730	88553
Copra, or Coco-Nut Kernel	20¼ *candies*	13 *candies*	12 *candies*
Cowry Shells -	17 ditto 14 *maunds* 16 *lb.*	15 *maunds*	4 ditto
Cassia -	1 ditto 7 ditto 24 do.	1⅓ *candies*	3 ditto
Copper Pots - -	49 ditto 14 ditto	18 *candies* 11 *maunds*	4 ditto 6 *maunds*
Castor-Nuts, *Ricinus* -	3 *duppers*, or leather bags	12 *Duppers*	2 ditto 10 ditto
Carpet - -	6 *corges*, or scores	3 *Corges*	17 *corges*, or scores
China Ware -	16 chests	18 chests	16 chests and 23 boxes
Cloves - -	1 *candy* 1 *maund* 28 *lb.*	29 chests	5 *candies*
D			
Dammer, or Resin -	12 *candies*		
Dates - -	771 bundles	243 bundles	1440 bundles
Doll, or Pulse -	58 *candies* 2 *maunds*	128 *candies* 11 *mounds*	53 *candies*

Malabar Year 973.		974.	975.
IMPORTS.			
E			
Europe Liquors	91 dozen	83 dozens	
Ditto ditto	42 chests	41 chests	24 chests
Ditto ditto	9 boxes	3 boxes	
Ditto ditto	12 pipes	14 pipes	20 pipes
Ditto ditto	7 casks	9 casks	8 casks
Ditto ditto	13 hogsheads	14 hogsheads	
Ditto ditto	1 trunk	5 trunks	
Ditto ditto	5 cases	18 cases	
F			
Frying Pans	150 sets	312 Sets	
G			
Ganjaw, or Hemp Leaves	6 *candies* 17 *maunds* 16 *lb.*	8 *candies* 16 *maunds*	7 *candies* 10 *maunds*
Gram (Pulses) *Mung*	199 ditto 8 ditto 1 do.	748 ditto 17 ditto 24 *lb.*	219 ditto 10 ditto 15 *lb.*
Ditto ditto	59 *robins*	231 *robins*	206 *robins*
Ditto, *Cully*	717 ditto	154 ditto	321 ditto
Ditto, *Guzerat*	334 *candies* 18 *maunds* 3 *lb.*	618 *candies* 11 *maunds* 30 *lb.*	187 *candies* 15 *maunds*
Ditto, *Towra*	— —	6 *robins*	8 *robins*
Ditto, Matt	— —	11¾ *candies*	
Ghee, or Boiled Butter	89 *candies* 1 ditto	41 *candies* 8 *maunds*	34 *candies* 13 *maunds*
Garlick	12 ditto	11 ditto 16 ditto	15 ditto 17 ditto
Ginger	158 ditto 1 ditto	87 ditto	25 ditto
Gunny Bags, *Crotolaria juncea*		12500 bags	2000 bags
Goat Skins	102 gallons 10 pints	43 gallons 3 pints	59 gallons 15 pints
Glass Ware	35 chests	41 chests	8 chests
Ditto ditto	12 trunks	14 trunks	
Ditto ditto	2 casks	16 casks	
Ditto ditto	1 case		
H			
Hartal Cinnabar	— —	12 *maunds*	2 *candies* 10 *maunds*
Hemp	12 *candies* 18 *maunds*	— —	6 ditto
Hams	1 box	10 boxes	6 boxes
Ditto	22 in number	15 in number	
Ditto	24 pounds	140 *lb.*	
Hats	1810	700	18 dozen
I			
Jagree Cane, or Inspissated Juice of Sugar Cane	35 *candies* 8 *maunds*	93 *candies* 18 *maunds*	95 *candies* 4 *maunds*
Iron Nails	1 *candy*	2 ditto	
Ditto	128 ditto 11 ditto	— —	4 ditto
K			
Kismish Raisins	9 *candies* 13 *maunds*	18 *candies* 13 *maunds* 24 *lb.*	10 ditto
L			
Liquorice Root	20 *candies*	45 *candies* 12 *maunds* 8 *lb.*	3 ditto 7 ditto
Looking Glasses	60 *corges*, or scores	14 *corges*	80 dozen
Leather	8 ditto	19 ditto	15 *corges*

Malabar Year 973.		974.	975.
IMPORTS.			
M			
Mace	7*lb.*	8 *maunds*	15 *maunds*
Mustard Seed	10 *candies* 16 *lbs.*	24 *candies* 12 *maunds* 8 *lb.*	15 *candies*
Mats	10 *corges*, or scores	133 *corges*	152 *corges*
Ditto, *Bamboo*	20 ditto	112 ditto	130 ditto
Malabar Medicines	17 *candies* 2 *maunds*	13 *candies*	2 *candies* 10 *maunds*
N			
Nelly, rough rice	594,642 *edangallies*, 108 cub. in.	865,000 *edangallies*	26,050 *edangallies*
Nutmeg	2 *candies* 3 *maunds*	4 *candies* 15 *maunds*	3 *candies* 5 *maunds*
O			
Oil, Coco-Nuts	923½ *paddahs*	9,049 *paddahs*	115 *paddahs*
Opium	1 box	13 baskets	9¼ *maunds*
Ditto	1 chest	3 chests	
Oil, Castor	15 *maunds*	19 *maunds*	
Ditto *Gingely, Sesamum*	20½ *candies*	28½ *candies*	5 *candies*
Ditto. ditto	1½ *dupers*, leather bag		
Onions	184 *candies*	215 *candies*	160 *candies*
Ollibanum	—	24 ditto	26 *maunds*
P			
Paper	96 reams	129 reams	678 reams
Pickle, Europe	5 boxes	14 boxes	20 boxes
Ditto ditto	3 cases	13 cases	
Ditto, Country	11 *candies* 10 *maunds* 16 *lbs.*	20 cases	30 barrels
Pork, Salt	—	15 casks	12 ditto
Perfumery	2 chests	13 chests	15 chests
Ditto	1 box	12 boxes	
Ditto	1 trunk	3 trunks	
Pepper	520 *candies* 16 *maunds*	711 *candies* 6 *maunds*	849 *candies*
Planks	1934 *guz.* or cubits	1,450 *guz.* or cubits	2,000 pieces
Padlocks	—	3 dozen	25 dozen
Piece Goods, *Guzerat*	16,781 *corges* 3 pieces	85,800 *corges* 14 pieces	75,400 *corges*
Ditto ditto *Bengal*	127 ditto 10 ditto	342 *corges* 10 pieces	425 *corges* 3 pieces
Ditto ditto *Palgawt*	383 ditto 11 ditto	843 ditto 15 ditto	725 ditto 12 ditto
Ditto ditto *Madras*	211 ditto 13 ditto	486 ditto 2 ditto	480 ditto 12 ditto
Ditto ditto *Manapar*	1680 ditto 14 ditto	870 ditto 13 ditto	550 ditto 16 ditto
Ditto ditto *Colletchy*	231 ditto 4 ditto	420 ditto	325 ditto 13 ditto
Ditto ditto *Palamcotah*	798 ditto 15 ditto	384 ditto 15 ditto	733 ditto 10 ditto
Ditto ditto *Canara*	27,184 ditto	87,385 ditto 4 ditto	75,430 ditto 10 ditto
Ditto ditto *China*	408 ditto 3 ditto	601 ditto 4 ditto	640 ditto 3 ditto
R			
Rafties, Cotton Cloth	69 pieces	25 pieces	230 pieces
Red Dye	10 *candies* 16 *maunds* 16 *lbs.*	43 *candies* 18 *maunds* 16 *lb.*	
Red Earth	18 Kegs	10 kegs	
Rice, *Bengal*	—	42,000 bags	2000 bags
Ditto, *Canara*	100,323 *robins*	360,440 *robins*	72,500 *robins* [illegible]/41 cub. in.
Rose Water	70 bottles	141 bottles	196 bottles
Rice, *Malabar*	9315 *robins*	85,000 *robins*	7,300 *robins*

Malabar Year 973.		974.	975.
IMPORTS.			
S			
Sugar -	- 22 chests	121 chests	275 bags -
Ditto -	- 200 bags	456 bags	70 chests
Ditto -	- 126 *candies* 16 *maunds*	421 *candies* 15 *maunds*	326 *candies*
Ditto -	- 138 *piculs* 133 *lb.*	146 *piculs*	
Ditto, *Candy*	- 82½ ditto	935 ditto	825 *piculs*
Ditto ditto -	- 180 tubs	342 tubs	416 tubs
Summerheads (parasols)	- 16 *corges* 16 pieces	14½ *corges*	16 *corges*
Ditto, Silk -	- 1 ditto 4 ditto	3¼ ditto	4 ditto 3 pieces
Sweetmeats -	- 1695 bundles	486 bundles	1,650 bundles
Sago -	- — —	14 small bags	18 bags, small
Salt - -	- 282,000 *edangallies*, 108 cub. in.	469,046 *edangallies*	362,500 *edangallies*
Ditto - -	- 3152 bundles	14,000 bundles	
Ditto - -	- 56¼ *candies*	83½ *candies*	107 *candies* 17 *maunds*
Shoes -	- 8 trunks	10 trunks	5 trunks
Ditto - -	- 33 *corges*, or scores	80 *corges*	90 *corges*
Stationery -	- 3 chests	10 chests	11 chests
Ditto -	- 4 boxes	1 box	
Spars -	- 20 pieces	61 pieces	82 pieces
Small Shot -	- — —	30 bags, small	29 bags, small
Soap - -	- 82,400 pieces	18,456 pieces	216,700 pieces
Stockings -	- 8 dozen	14 dozen	20 dozen
Ditto -	- 1 trunk	3 trunks	2 trunks
Ditto -	- 3 *corges*, or scores	1 *corge*	
Snuff - -	- 51 *lb.*	31 *lbs.*	
Sapan Wood -	- 19¾ *candies*	15 *candies*	3 *candies*
Sandal Wood -	- 61 ditto 16 *maunds*	93 ditto	105 ditto
T			
Tobacco, *Palighat*	- 2,210 ditto 8 ditto	1,531 *candies* 16 *maunds*	2,342 ditto
Ditto, *Guzerat*	- 36 ditto 15 ditto	86 *candies*	43 ditto
Ditto, *Canara*	- 43 ditto 10 ditto	40 ditto 5 ditto	82 ditto
Tamarinds -	- 96 ditto 17 ditto	16 ditto	19 ditto 15 *maunds*
Turmerick -	- 12 ditto 18 ditto	17 ditto	18 ditto 16 ditto
Tea -	- 43 boxes	81 boxes	73 boxes
Teeth, Elephant	- 4 *maunds*	2 *maunds*	
Twine -	- 20 *lb.*	40 *lb.*	60 *lb.*
Timber -	- 17 pieces	401 pieces	76 pieces
Tin -	- 2 *candies*	12 *candies*	8½ *candies*
V			
Ulva Seed -	- 20 ditto 5 ditto	63 *candies* 10 *maunds*	54 *candies* 15 *maunds* 24 *lb.*
Vermillion	14 ditto	3 ditto	— 18 ditto 18 do.
W			
Wheat -	- 850 ditto 1 ditto 5 *lb.*	904 ditto 12 ditto 3 *lb.*	475 ditto 15 ditto 18 do.
Wax Candles	- 2 ditto 17 ditto 22 ditto	4 ditto 18 ditto 14 do.	6 ditto 17 ditto

Malabar Year 973.		974.	975.
EXPORTS.			
	A		
Arrack -	- 20 leaguers 75 gallons	18 *leaguers* 25 *gallons* -	28 *leaguers* 12 *gallons*
Assafœtida -	- 7 *maunds*	14 *maunds*	10 *maunds*
	B		
Betle-Nuts -	- 327 *candies* 12 *maunds* 16 *lb.*	385 *candies* 14 *maunds* 24 *lb.*	518 *candies* 13 *maunds* 18 *lb.*
Ditto, Cut -	- 39 ditto 9 ditto 8 do.	20 ditto 13 ditto 8 do.	42 ditto 10 ditto 24 do.
Barley -	- 2 kegs	3 kegs	5 kegs
	C		
China Ware -	- 10 *corges*	15 *candies*	12 boxes
Cotton -	- 125 *candies*	130½ ditto	73 *candies* 16 *maunds* 8 *lb.*
Chilly Pepper (*Capsicum*)	- 6 *maunds*	8 *maunds*	— 15 ditto 18 do.
Cloves -	- 14 ditto	12 chests	2 ditto — 16 do.
Cardamums -	- 6 *candies* 9 *maunds* 26 do.	19 *candies* 2 *lb.*	25 ditto — 18 do.
Coco-Nuts, Dry -	- 721,120 in number	1,786,900	551,000
Ditto, containing Water	- 637,300 in ditto	897,900	305,400
Coprah, Coco-Nut Kernel	- 575 *candies* 4 *maunds* 8 *lb.*	1,450 *candies* 6 *maunds*	292 *candies* 2 *maunds*
Coir, Coco-Nut Cordage	- 25 ditto 15 ditto	67 ditto 9 ditto	15 ditto 18 ditto 17 *lb.*
Copper -	- 17 ditto 18 do.	2 ditto 13 ditto 16 *lb.*	1 ditto 6 ditto 15 do.
	D		
Dates -	- 107 bundles	88 bundles	108 bundles
	E		
Europe, Liquors	- 85 chests	44 chests	36 chests
Ditto, ditto -	- 14 hogsheads	11 hogsheads	18 hogsheads
	F		
Fish Sounds -	- 8 *maunds*	13 *maunds*	2 *maunds*
	G		
Gram Moong, Pulse	- 16½ *candies*	18 *candies*	12 *candies* 11 *maunds* 12 *lb.*
Ditto, *Guzerat*, Pulse	- 18¾ ditto	46 ditto	12 ditto 18 ditto —
Ganjaw, Hemp Leaves	- 13 *maunds*	17 *maunds*	— 13 ditto 18 do.
Garlick -	- 5 *candies*	7 *candies*	7 ditto 12 ditto 11 do.
Ghee, Boiled Butter	- 36 ditto	24½ ditto	2 ditto 18 ditto 19 do.
	H		
Hams -	- 80 *lb.*	101 *lb.*	28 *lb.*
Hats -	- 4 dozen	8 dozen	13 dozen
	I		
Iron - -	- 12 *candies*	16 *candies*	10 *candies* 14 *maunds* 14 *lb.*
Jagree, Inspissated Juice of Palm Trees -	26½ ditto	18¾ ditto	8 ditto 12 ditto
	K		
Kismish Raisins -	- 13 *maunds*	18 *maunds*	19 *maunds* 21 *lb*

Malabar Year 973.		974.	975.
EXPORTS.			
	L		
Liquorice Root	3 *candies*	11 *maunds*	12 *maunds* 28 *lb.*
	M		
Mace	21 *lb.*	8 *lb.*	1 *maund* 18 *lb.*
	N		
Nutmegs	6 *lb.*	18 *lb.*	8 *lb.*
Nelly, or Rough Rice	26,010 *edangallies*	46,300 *edangallies*	56,500 *edangallies*
	O		
Oil, Coco-Nut	18 *paddahs*	3 *paddahs*	12 *paddahs*
	P		
Pepper	5221 *candies* 17 *maunds* 16 *lb.*	2,306 *candies* 7 *maunds* 8 *lb.*	1,850 *candies* 10 *maunds* 23 *lb.*
Ditto, Light	— —	85 ditto 15 ditto	57 ditto 9 ditto 8 do.
Perfumery	4 chests	2 chests	3 boxes
Piece Goods	270 *corges*	107 *corges*	267¾ *corges*
	R		
Rice	18,670 *robins*	3,786 *robins*	8,007 *robins*
	S		
Sugar	25¾ *candies*	63 *candies* 14 *maunds* 18 *lb.*	24 *candies* 10 *maunds* 10 *lb.*
Ditto, Candy	24 tubs	18 tubs	17 tubs
Sandal Wood	567 *candies* 5 *maunds*	548 *corges* 2 *maunds* 27 *lb.*	1,056 *candies* 11 *maunds* 27 *lb.*
Ditto, Sawings	52 ditto 14 ditto	143 ditto — 15 do.	4 ditto — —
Sharkfins	9 ditto 1 ditto 16 *lb.*	7 ditto 14 ditto 16 do.	11 ditto 2 ditto 16 do.
Spars	11 score 12 pieces	1 score 9 pieces	16 pieces
Sapan Wood	4 *maunds*	16 *maunds*	18 *maunds*
	T		
Tobacco	76 *candies* 18 *maunds*	86 *candies* 11 *maunds* 13 *lb.*	93 *candies* 13 *maunds* 10 *lb.*
Tea	8 chests	13 boxes	10 chests
Timber	632 *candies* 5 *maunds* 3 *lb.*	200 *candies* 18 *maunds* 16 *lb.*	103 *candies* 16 *maunds* 13 *lb.*
	V		
Ulva Seed	3 *candies*	9 *candies*	11 ditto 16 ditto 8 do.
	W		
Wheat	73 *candies* 16 *maunds* 16 *lb.*	28 *candies* 18 *maunds* 18 *lb.*	16 ditto 13 ditto 18 do.

TOTAL QUANTITY of different ARTICLES EXPORTED by SEA from *BETTUTANADA*, in the Years 974 and 975.

Articles.	Quantity in 974.	Quantity in 975.
Betle-Nut	170 *candies* 4 *tulam*	157 *candies* and ¾ *tulam*
Brass	14 ditto	— 4 ditto
Cassia	16½ ditto	1 *candy* 4 ditto
Chappungum Wood (*Sapan*)	130 Ditto 16 ditto	147 ditto
Chinakai, a Fruit	21 Ditto 4½ ditto	17 ditto 17 ditto
Chilly	1 Ditto 13 ditto	— 16½ ditto
Clay, White	None	1½ *tulam*
Coolty, a Grain	370 *morahs*, or *robins*	527 *morahs*, or *robins*
Coco-Nuts, Dry	32,34265	2731520
Ditto, Green	10,06590	2,20070
Coir, or Coco-Nut Cordage	25 *candies* 8 *tulam*	14 *tulam*
Coriander Seed	None	50 *edungarry* (*edungallies*)
Cotton	7½ *tulam*	13¼ Ditto
Ditto, Yarn	None	6 Ditto
Dates, Dry	1 *candy* 2½ *tulam*	2 *candies* 9½ *tulam*
Ditto, Wet	None	16 *tulam*
Fish, Salt	182½ ox loads and 292 bales	366 bales
Gingly, *Sesamum*	819 *morahs*, or *robins*	1155 Ditto
Ginger, Wet	2 *tulam*	9 *tulam*
Ditto, Dry	63 *candies* 19½ *tulam*	86 *candies* 16 *tulam*
Garlic	2 Ditto 7¾ ditto	16½ *tulam*
Ghee	None	1 Ditto
Gunja. Dried Leaves of *Cannabis sativa*	50 bales	None
Kemp, *Crotolaria juncea*	11 *candies* 14 *tulam*	6 *candies* 2 *tulam*
Iron	90 Ditto 10 ditto	90 *candies*
Ditto Ware	None	654 pieces
Jagory, or Inspissated Juice of *Brab* Tree	3 *tulam*	None
Kastury	50 *candies* 18 *tulam*	63 *candies* 12 *tulam*
Kopra, dried Coco-Nut Kernels	19 Ditto 5 ditto	29 Ditto 11 ditto
Kolakai	12 Ditto 16 ditto	26 Ditto 6 ditto
Kuwa Flower	4 Ditto 8 ditto	7 Ditto 1 ditto
Ditto Root	None	78 Ditto 6 ditto
Medicine, *Weppumtoly*	10 *tulam*	None
Ditto, *Ramacham*	None	½ *tulam*
Ditto, *Weralary*	16½ *tulam*	150 *edungarry* (*edungallies*)
Ditto, *Kuwahottamura*	None	3 *tulam*
Ditto, *Kutumarana*	16½ *tulam*	None
Ditto, *Karingaly*	None	1 *candy* 6 *tulam*
Ditto, *Konepuwa*	25 *edungarry* (*edangallies*)	None
Ditto, *Nerengilla*	None	1 *tulam*
Ditto, *Wengakathil*	2 *tulam*	None
Ditto, *Karkolari*	None	62½ *edungarry* (*edangallies*)
Ditto, *Takaram*	10 *tulam*	None
Ditto, *Waimba*	None	2 *candies* 1½ *tulam*
Ditto, Stink Wood	1 *tulam*	None
Ditto, *Pachotytoly*	2 Ditto	None
Moong, Pulse, *Phaseolus Mungo*	29 *morah*, or *robin*	224 *morahs*, or *robins*
Mats, Grass	None	50
Nellikai, *Phyllanthus Emblica*	3625 *edungarry* (*edangallies*)	270 *edungarry* (*edangallies*)
Oil, Coco-Nut	None	30 pots
Oil *Gingly*, *Sesamum*	54¾ *Chothana*, or Pots	None
Ola, Writing Palm Leaves	None	1000
Onions	8 *tulam*	4 *tulam*
Paddy, or Rough Rice	43,840 *parahs*	4600 *parah*
Pepper, Black	120 *candies* 19 *tulam*	214 *candies* 19½ *tulam*
Ditto, Long	None	15 *tulam*
Rice	665 *morah* (*robins*)	57 *morah* (*robins*)

Articles.	Quantity in 974.	Quantity in 975.
Resin - -	None	1½ *tulam*
Salt, Coarse - -	45,80½ *parah*	4681½ *parah*
Ditto, White - -	2 *tulam*	None
Ditto, *Peppara* -	3 *candies* 3 *tulam*	1 *candy* 8 *tulam*
Sandal Wood - -	10 Ditto 2 ditto	3 Ditto 16¾ ditto
Sugar, Moist - -	1 *tulam*	2 *tulam*
Sheep Skins - -	None	4½
Tamarinds - -	4 *candies* 10 *tulam*	10 *tulam*
Tobacco - -	100 bundles, small	190 bundles, small
Tonies, Canoes -	None	9 new ones
Turmerick - -	28 *candies* 10¾ *tulam*	10 *candies* 4 *tulam*
Wax - - -	23¼ *tulam*	½ *tulam*

TOTAL QUANTITY of different ARTICLES IMPORTED by SEA, in *BETTUTANADA*, in the Years 974 and 975.

Articles.	Quantity in 974.	Quantity in 975.
Betle-Nut - -	37 *candies* 15½ *tulam*	None
Cloth, *Mannapar* -	117½ *corge*, or score pieces	100 *corge*
Cedar - -	None -	1¼ *tulam*
Ditto, *Kolichy* - -	24½ Ditto	25 *corge*
Ditto, *Kotarum* -	None	12½ Ditto
Ditto, *Kangy* - -	2 pieces	None
Fish, Salt - -	138 bales	None
Salt - -	590 *parah*	2000 *parah*
Sublimate (of Mercury) -	6 *tulam*	None

(Signed) J. W. Wye, Collector.

TOTAL QUANTITY of ARTICLES EXPORTED by SEA from *PARUPA-NADA*, in the Years 974 and 975.

Articles.	Quantity in 974.	Quantity in 975.
Betle-Nut - -	9 *candies* 9 *tulam*	9 *candies* 3 *tulam*
Cassia Laurus - -	3 *tulam*	None
Chuppungom Wood (*Sapan*)	15 *candies* 2½ *tulam*	16 *candies* 10 *tulam*
Chinakai - -	15 *tulam*	15 *tulam*
Coco-Nuts, Dry -	1,081,540 in number	832800
Ditto, Green - -	None	134650
Coir -	62 *candies* 12 *tulam*	52 *candies* 5 *tulam*
Coriander Seed - -	200 *edungarry* (*edangallies*)	None
Coolty, Pulse, *Dolichos biflorus*	45 *morah* (*robins*)	25 *morah* (*robins*)
Fish, Salt - -	2 bales	None
Garlick - -	1 *tulam*	None
Ginger, Wet - -	17 Ditto	13 *tulam*
Ditto, Dry - -	43 *candies* 13 *tulam*	38 *candies* 4½ *tulam*
Gingly Seed (*Sesamum*) -	326 bales	423 bales
Hemp, *Crotolaria juncea* -	18 *candies* 18 *tulam*	None
Iron - -	10 Ditto 13 ditto	27 *candies* 19 *tulam*

Articles.	Quantity in 974.	Quantity in 975.
Kastury, a kind of Turmerick	10 *candies* 16 *tulam*	17 *candies* 14 *tulam*
Kolakal -	1 Ditto 16 ditto	7 Ditto 6 ditto
Kopra, Dried Coco Nut Kernel	4 Ditto 5 ditto	21 Ditto 9 ditto
Kuwa Root - -	16 *tulam*	None
Ditto, Flower - -	7 *candies*	7 *candies* 12 *tulam*
Moong, a Pulse, *Phaseolus Mungo*	None	2 *morah* (*robins*)
Medicine, *Weralary* -	2 *tulam*	1 *tulam*
Ditto, *Neringila* -	None	½ Ditto
Ditto, *Waimbu*, *Acorus aromaticus*	2 *tulam*	
Ditto, *Karinguly* -	None	½ *tulam*
Nellikai, *Philanthus Emblica*	3050 *edungarry* (*edangallies*)	900 *edungarry* (*edangallies*)
Oil, *Gingly* (*Sesamum*) -	8 pots	None
Paddy, Rough Rice -	1400 *parah*	Ditto
Pepper, Black - -	41 *candies* 18 *tulam*	21 *candies* 4 *tulam*
Rice - -	None	25 *morahs* (*robins*)
Sandal Wood - -	2 *candies*	14 *candies* 5 *tulam*
Salt - - -	34,300 *parahs*	7350 *parahs*
Shells for *Chunam* (Lime) -	None	600 *narui*
Tobacco - -	10 *tulam*	None
Turmerick - -	1 *candies* 11 *tulam*	11 *candies* 15½ *tulam*
Tonies (Canoes) New -	None	14
Twine, Hempen, *i. e.* of the *Crotolaria juncea* -	Ditto	2 *candies* 10 *tulam*

TOTAL QUANTITY of ARTICLES IMPORTED by SEA in *PARUPA-NADA*, for the Years 974 and 975.

Articles.	Quantity in 974.	Quantity in 975.
Betle-Nut - -	27 *candies* 6 *tulam*	None
Cloth, *Mannapar* -	15¾ *corges*, or scores of pieces	127½ *corges*
Ditto, *Kolichy* -	3 Ditto	None
Cotton - -	5 *candies*	Ditto
Dates, Dry -	5 Ditto 4 *tulam*	Ditto
Resin - -	8 *tulam*	Ditto
Rice - -	None	150 *morahs* (*robins*)
Sugar, Moist -	10 *tulam*	None

(Signed). J. W. Wye, Collector.

TOTAL QUANTITY of ARTICLES EXPORTED by LAND from *MANAR-GHAT*, in the Years 974 and 975, commencing 14th September, 1798 and 1799.

Articles.	Quantity in 974.	Quantity in 975.
Betle-Nut, *Areca* -	729⅛ *tulam* 2½ *palom*	1042½ *tulam* 5 *polam*
Ditto, Leaf, Piper Betle -	None	6760 small bales
Cassia Laurus -	10½ *tulam*	26½ *tulam*
Cardamoms -	¾ Ditto	4 Ditto
Cedar - -	None	½ Ditto
Chappungum Wood (*Sapan*)	19 *tulam*	20½ Ditto

Articles.	Quantity in 974.	Quantity in 975.
Chinakai	4 *tulam*	None
Coco-Nuts	70	7663
Coir, Coco-Nut Cordage	None	1¼ *tulam*
Fish, Salt	None	98 bales
Dubbers, New, Leather Bags	None	30
Dates, Wet	None	15 *tulam*
Ginger, Dry	347 *tulam*	255½ Ditto
Hing, Asafœtida	½ *tulam*	None
Hides	2	
Honey	None	13 pots
Jagory, of the Brab Tree	1¼ *tulam*	19½ *tulam*
Jagory, of Sugar Cane	None	2 Ditto
Kastury, a Turmerick	None	28 Ditto
Medicine, *Weralury*	2 *tulam*	
Ditto, *Nagapuwa*	½ Ditto	
Oil Wood	None	25⅓ pots
Oil, Coco-Nut	20¾ pots	30½ Ditto
Oil, *Gingly* (*Sesamum*)	None	26 Ditto
Pepper, Black	281¼ *tulam* 11 *polam*	279 *tulam* 8½ *polam*
Pepper, Long, Root of	9½ *tulam*	5 *tulam*
Puwatta, a Red Dye	5¼ Ditto	None
Ragy, a Grain	28 *parahs*	None
Resin	3 *tulam*	None
Rice	51½ *parahs*	405½ *parah*
Sandal Wood	93¾ *tulam*	2½ *tulam*
Salt	None	1 Ditto
Ditto	870½ *parahs*	1222 *parah*
Shells for *Chunam* (Lime)	None	21½ *parah*
Sugar, Moist	None	1½ *tulam*
Turmerick	418⅓ *tulam* 7½ *palam*	540⅜ Ditto
Wax	75⅞ Ditto 7½ ditto	2⅝ Ditto

TOTAL QUANTITY of ARTICLES IMPORTED by LAND to *MANAR-GHAT*, in the Years 974 and 975.

Articles.	Quantity in 974.	Quantity in 975.
Buffalo, Female	27	10
Ditto, Male	1	106
Cardamoms	11½ *tulam*	5½ *tulam*
Chappungom Wood (*Sapan*)	3½ Ditto	None
Cloth, *Coimbetore*	5269¼ pieces	3514½ pieces
Chilly, or *Capsicum*	227 *parah*	118½ *parah*
Castor Oil Seed	41¼ Ditto	44 Ditto
Chinakai	3 *tulam*	None
Cotton Yarn	205½ Ditto	364½ *tulam*
Cummin Seed	4¼ Ditto	10¼ Ditto
Cooliy, a Pulse	29 *parah*	33 *parahs*
Coriander Seed	33½ Ditto	36 Ditto
Dill Seed	446 Ditto	157½ Ditto
Dholl, Split Pease, of the *Cytisus Cajan*	536½ Ditto	17¾ Ditto
Ditto, Whole	None	421¾ Ditto
Garlick	2745¾ *tulam*	2107¼ *tulam*
Gunja, or Hemp Leaves	8394 bales, small	3536 bales, small
Gram, Pulse	119 *parahs*	331 *parahs*
Ginger, Wet	6 *tulam*	None
Ghee, or Boiled Butter	674¼ pots	1762⅜ pots

Articles.		Quantity in 974.	Quantity in 975.
Hemp, *Cratolaria*	-	3 *palam*	None
Honey -	-	None	25½ pots
Jagory -	-	21 *tulam*	105¾ *tulam*
Kadukai -	-	23 Ditto	12 Ditto
Lac -	-	½ Ditto	None
Medicine, *Waimber*	-	5 Ditto	501 *tulam*
Ditto, *Neringilla*	-	None	1 Ditto
Ditto, *Weralary*	-	4 *tulam*	4½ *parah*
Moong, Pulse -	-	5¼ *parahs*	30 Ditto
Mustard Seed -	-	1873 Ditto	1401½ Ditto
Onions -	-	130 *tulam*	45½ *tulam*
Oil of *Weppu* -	-	None	1 pot
Ditto, Coco-Nut	-	None	4 pots
Pepper -	-	70½ *tulam* 10 *polam*	
Poppy Seed -	-	15½ *parah*	None
Resin -	-	15 *tulam*	None
Sheep -	-	111	182
Sandal Wood	-	18¼ *tulam*	36½ *tulam*
Tamarinds -	-	128¼ Ditto	32¼ Ditto
Tobacco -	-	176966 bales, small	189742 bales, small
Urced, Pulse	-	80½ *parahs*	279 *parahs*
Wax - -	-	None	73 *tulam*

(Signed) J. W. Wye, Collector.

An ACCOUNT of the GOODS EXPORTED and IMPORTED by the *TAMARACHERY GHAT*, for the *Malabar* Year 975.

EXPORTS.	Quantity.	IMPORTS.	Quantity.
Water Coco-Nuts -	19000	Bags of Rice - -	115 value, from 3 to 4 *rupees* each
Dry *Sooparcys*, or *Betel-Nuts*	47 *tulam*		
Coco-Nut Oil -	57 ditto	Ditto *Nelly*, or Rough Rice	268 value from 2 to 3 *rupees* each
Silk - -	12 pieces		
Dungaree Cloth, coarse Cotton Cloth -	8 *corges*, or scores of pieces	Country *Lac* -	9½ *tulam*
		Bees Wax - -	10½ ditto
Maonds, or Waist Cloths	13 ditto	*Ghee*, or boiled Butter -	13½ ditto
Soap - -	600 pieces	Tobacco - -	3½ ditto
Sugar - -	3 *maunds*	*Gunjar* (Hemp Leaves) -	22¼ ditto
Chapungam Wood, *Sapan*	30 ditto	Bullocks, Oxen -	94
Blankets, Country -	10	Country Blankets -	4 *corges*
Salt - -	343 bags	*Jagory* - -	3 *tulam*
Jagary - -	1230 bundles, 10 pieces in each	*Dholl*, Pulse - -	3 bags
Salt Fish - -	7400	Red *Chilley*, *Capsicum*	56 *tulam*
Ditto, small -	59 bags	Red Onions - -	40 ditto
Cochin Arrack -	10 gallons	White ditto -	12 ditto
Country ditto -	167 pots	*Bapennah* (Castor Oil) -	18
Dates - -	10 *tulam*	*Euenah* (a small grain) -	140 *dungallys* (*edangallies*)

(Signed) R. Coward, Collector.

An ACCOUNT of the EXPORTS and IMPORTS of the various ARTICLES into the *PYE-NADA* DISTRICT, for the *Malabar* Year 975.

EXPORTS.	Quantity.	IMPORTS.	Quantity.
Water Coco-Nuts -	315700	Rice, *Moodahs* (*robins*) = 108000 cubical inches	3292 *moodahs* (*robins*)
Dry ditto - -	163000	*Pyroo*, a Pulse -	39 ditto
Soopareys (dry) *Betel-Nut*	443¼ *candies*	Red *Sooparys*, or *Betel-Nut*	136700
Coco-Nut Oil -	48¾ ditto	Dates - -	5½ *candies*
Pepper - -	56 ditto	Red Onions - -	1½ *tulam*
Coprah, White, Coco-Nut Kernels - -	66 ditto	*Manapar* Cloth -	10 *corges*, or scores of pieces
Ditto, Black - -	10½ ditto	Salt - -	13000 *dungallys* (*edangallies*)
Manucil - -	2 ditto	*Oringna* - -	140 *moodahs* (*robins*)
Ditto *Chuckoor* -	4 *maunds*		
Karookar - -	1¼ *candy*		
Ghee, or boiled Butter -	2 *maunds*		
Ginjaly, Oil of *Sesamum*	2¼ ditto		
Coir, Coco-Nut Cordage	59 *candies*		
Mats, *Bamboo* -	31600		
Iron - -	1½ *candy*		
Chapingar, *Sapan* Wood	1 ditto		

(Signed) R. COWARD, Collector.

ABSTRACT of GOODS IMPORTED by SEA, from 1st January to 31st December, 1799.

Quality.	Quantity.	Quality.	Quantity.
		Bamboos - -	13,800
A		Boots - -	4 trunks
		Beef - -	4 casks
Almonds - -	12 bundles	Ditto - -	4 kegs
Arrack - -	485 *canadas*	Bellows, Smiths -	2
Ditto - -	96½ leaguers	*Bagery*, Grain of the *Holcus Spicatus*	7 *candies*
Ditto - -	31 casks	Ditto - -	5 *cappats*
Ditto - -	15 kegs	Ditto - -	2 *maunds*
Ditto - -	11½ cases	Ditto - -	8 bags
Ditto - -	5 jars	Blue Cloth -	49 *corges*, or scores of pieces
Ditto - -	21 pipes	Ditto - -	5 pieces
Ajuan Seed, an umbelliferous Plant	10½ *candies*	Ditto - -	2 bales
Ditto -	20 *maunds*	Ditto - -	1 bundle
Ditto -	52 bags	*Bamboo* Mats -	208 *corges*
Ditto -	12 *capats*	Books - -	46
		Ditto - -	1 chest
B		Beer - -	2 chests
		Ditto - -	12 dozen
Bengal Rice -	59 bags	Blankets - -	10 pieces
Betel-Nut - -	2 *maunds*	Ditto - -	3 *corges*, or scores
Ditto - -	74,000	Brandy - -	4 chests
Ditto - -	2 bags	Ditto - -	kegs
Ditto - -	300 bundles		

Quality.	Quantity.
Brandy	14 dozen
Ditto	2 casks
Ditto	29 cases
Bottles of Ale	1 ditto
Ditto ditto	1 hogshead
Barley	2 casks
Ditto	1 keg
Ditto	2 chests
Brooms	100
C	
Columba Arrack	16⅛ leaguers
Ditto	5 casks
Ditto	4 kegs
Ditto	7 pipes
Ditto	15000 bottles
Cochin Arrack	4 leaguers
Ditto	4 pipes
Ditto	2 casks
Ditto	92 bottles
Country Arrack	4 leaguers
Ditto	110 pipes
Ditto	392 *canadas*
China Ware	2 baskets
Ditto	8 chests
Ditto	707
Country Boots	5 pair
Coco-Nuts	104660
Copper Pots	37 bags
Ditto	90 *maunds*
Cointer Seed	6615 *edangallies*
Ditto	15 *candies*
Ditto	9 *maunds*
Ditto	5 *cappats*
Ditto	4 bags
Corks	6 ditto
Ditto	76 gross
Ditto	1000
Ditto	1 chest
Coffee	20 bags
Ditto	1 bundle
Ditto	26 *maunds*
Cummin Seed	23 bags
Ditto	40 *maunds*
Claret	3 chests
Ditto	45 dozens
Cotton Lace	24 bundles
Ditto	40 pieces
Cruet Stands	2
Cloves	2 *maunds*
Ditto	1
Cully Gram, a kind of Pulse	15 *maunds*
Ditto	18 *robins*
Chilly Pepper, *Capsicum*	23¾ *candies*
Ditto	62½ *maunds*
Ditto	4 bags
Candles	2 bales
Ditto	35 *maunds*
Ditto	850 *lbs.*
Canvas	26 bolts
Coir, Coco-Nut Cordage	19¼ *candies*
Ditto	10¾ *maunds*
Ditto	
Cotton	6 *candies*
Ditto	12 *maunds*
Ditto	22 bales
Cherry Brandy	1 box
Ditto	2 dozen
Cheese	5 boxes
Ditto	2 chests
Cards and Pomatum	1 box
Coco-Nut Oil	48 *chodanas*
Ditto ditto	8 jars
Ditto ditto	660 *paddoms*
Ditto ditto	1155 pots
Ditto ditto	172 candies
Ditto ditto	81 *dubers*, or leathern bags
Ditto ditto	11 *cutys*
Country Mats	186 *corge*, or score
China Mats	122 pieces
Common Cups	4 chests
Combs	10 *corges*, or score
Cutlery	4 chests
Ditto	1 bundle
Chintz	5 *corges*, or score
Country Beans	15 *robins*
Chandrose	5 bundles
Combla Mas	12¾ ditto
D	
Dholl, a kind of Pulse	19 *candies*
Ditto	10 *maunds*
Ditto	5 *edangallies*
Ditto	64 bags
Dates	73 *cappats*
Ditto	2½ *maunds*
Ditto	8 bags
Dorca, a kind of Muslin	14 pieces
Dungary, Cotton Cloth	67½ *corge*, or score
Ditto	4 bundles
E	
Europe Cloth	1 trunk
Ditto	1 chest
Empty Bags	3200
F	
Flannel	1 bag
Ditto	4 pieces
Frying Pans	23 sets
G	
Gram, a kind of Pulse	82 *candies*
Ditto	132 *cappats*
Ditto	96 bags
Ditto	20 bales
Ghee, or Boiled Butter	109 *duppers*, leather bags
Ditto	31½ *maunds*
Gingelly, Oil of *Sesamum*	11 *duppers*
Gun Powder	1 bag

Quality.	Quantity.
Gun Powder	1 barrel
Glass Ware	12 dozen
Ditto ditto	10 chests
Ditto ditto	2 boxes
Gin	244 cases
Ditto	5 chests
Ditto	1 leaguer
Garlick	18 bags
Ditto	4 baskets
Ditto	7½ *candies*
Ditto	4 *cappats*
Ginger	1 *candy*
Ditto	25¼ *maunds*
Ditto	2 bundles
Ganjah, or dry flowers and Leaves of Hemp	75 ditto
Ditto	10 *maunds*
H	
Handkerchiefs	5 *corges*, or score
Hams	2 boxes
Ditto	27 chests
Ditto	2 cases
Hira Cassy, a Dye	5 *maunds*
Hemp, that is of *Crotolaria juncea*	60 ditto
Ditto	37 *lbs.*
Hats	6 chests
Ditto	1 box
Ditto	1 trunk
Ditto	183
Hooka Snakes	1 chest
Hock	3½ dozen
I	
Iron	30 bars
Ditto	289 pieces
Ditto	4 *maunds*
Ink Powder	10 bundles
Ditto ditto	3 dozen
Jagory	38½ *candies*
Ditto	118½ *maunds*
Ditto	87 pots
Ditto	4 *duppers*, or leather bags
Ditto	6 bags
Ditto	10 bales
K	
Kismiss, or small Raisins	62 *maunds*
Ditto	1 bag
Kascas, Poppy Seed	3 ditto
L	
Looking Glasses	1 dozen
Ditto	14½ *corge*, or score
Ditto	2 bundles
Linseed Oil	4 *lbs.*
Lamps	3 chests
Lemon Juice	24 bottles
Lutestring	1 piece
Ditto	3 chests
Long Drawers	11½ *corges*, or score
Leather	16¾ ditto
Lisbon Wine	2 quarter casks
M	
Madeira Wine	12 casks
Ditto	4 boxes
Ditto	39 chests
Ditto	4½ pipes
Ditto	160 dozen
Malmsey Wine	8 chests
Ditto	3 boxes
Medicine, Europe	1 dozen
Ditto, ditto	2½ boxes
Ditto, *Malabar*	5½ *maunds*
Manapar Onions	4 bundles
Mowrah	1½ pipe
Ditto	2 leaguers
Mustard	2 dozen
Ditto	8 bags
Ditto	40 *robins*
Mung, a kind of Pulse	25 ditto
Ditto	2 bags
Ditto	2 *cappats*
Ditto	4 *candies*
Methy Seed, *Fenugreek*	1 *candy*
Ditto ditto	7 bags
N	
Nelly, or Rice in the Husk	254,000 *edangallies*
Ditto	9330 *parahs*
Ditto	22 *robins*
Ditto	331 bags
Nellika Phyllanthus Emblica	1185 *edangallies*
Nutmegs	1 bundle
Ditto	67 *lb.*
Nackeny, the grain of the *Cynosurus Corocanus*	165 *robins*
Needles and Pins	24 papers
Nankins	5 chests
Ditto	111½ *corges*, or score
Nails	1 cask
Ditto	1 *maund*
O	
Opium	3 bundles
Ditto	11½ *maunds*
Ditto	55 *Seers*
Ditto	
Onions	4 bags
Ditto	204 *candies*
Ditto	5 *maunds*
Ditto	20 *cappats*

Quality.	Quantity.
P	
Port Wine -	6 quarter casks
Paper - -	198¾ ream
Ditto - -	9 chests
Ditto - -	200 sheets
Pomatum -	2 cases
Peppermint -	3½ dozen
Pickles - -	38 boxes
Ditto - -	1 chest
Ditto - -	4 cases
Ditto - -	6 *maunds*
Piece Goods -	3 chests
Ditto - -	4 boxes
Ditto - -	2390 *corges*, or score
Ditto - -	44 bundles
Ditto - -	283 ditto
Ditto - -	11,823 pieces
Ditto - -	8 bags
Powder Horns -	1½ dozen
Purpet Cloth -	20 pieces
Pepper - -	4½ *candies*
Pen Knives -	1½ dozen
Paint of Sorts -	7 kegs
Ditto ditto -	½ *maund*
Perfumery -	36 chests
Ditto - -	5 boxes
Pale Ale - -	2 casks
Ditto - -	2 kegs
Ditto - -	2 chests
Paint Brushes -	2 dozen
R	
Rum - -	2 chests
Ditto - -	20 cases
Rice - -	6934 *robins*
Ditto - -	422 bags
Ditto - -	20000 *edangallies*
Ditto - -	350 bundles
Ditto - -	375 *padys*
Rose Water -	37 bottles
Razors - -	2 dozen
Rosin - -	1½ *candy*
Ditto - -	8 *cappats*
S	
Soap - -	6 bolts
Ditto - -	3442 pieces
Ditto - -	143½ *maunds*
Ditto - -	100 bags
Ditto - -	2½ *corges*, or score
Sundry Articles -	3 chests
Sago - -	1
Shoes - -	89 *corges*, or score
Ditto - -	14 pieces
Ditto - -	2 chests
Ditto - -	1 dozen
Ditto - -	1 box
Salt - -	4 *candies*
Ditto - -	16 *maunds*
Ditto - -	34 *cappats*
Ditto - -	3000 *edangallies*
Sugar - -	9 *candies*
Ditto - -	35 *maunds*
Ditto - -	37 baskets
Ditto - -	210 bags
Ditto - -	177 tubs
Small Cups -	4 baskets
Ditto Jars -	25
Sindy Salt -	22 *cappats*
Saucers - -	2 dozen
Shot - -	20 bags
Ditto - -	2 kegs
Sadlery -	1 trunk
Ditto - -	3 chests
Saddle - -	1
Sersekar - -	1 piece
Shawls - -	55 pieces
Shirts - -	19¾ *corges*, or score
Ditto - -	211 pieces
Sinamon (Cinnamon) -	5½ *maunds*
Spying Glasses -	4
Scissars -	2 dozen
Sweet Oil -	1 ditto
T	
Tooth Powder -	1 dozen
Tea - -	1 ditto
Ditto - -	4 chests
Table Cloths -	21
Tobacco -	11½ *candies*
Ditto - -	1 box
Ditto -	85½ *maunds*
Ditto - -	8049 bundles
Ditto - -	239 bales
Ditto - -	8 bags
Ditto - -	129 *chipms.*
Tent Lace -	7½ *maunds*
Thread - -	1000 *skeins*
Ditto - -	10 bags
Ditto - -	5½ *lbs.*
Turmerick -	3½ *candies*
Ditto - -	53½ *maunds*
Table Sheds -	9 pairs
Tamarinds -	65 *maunds*
Ditto - -	73¾ *candies*
Ditto - -	11 *cappats*
Ditto - -	33 bundles
Ditto - -	30 bales
Ditto - -	55 bags
Tape - -	14 bundles
Twine - -	39 *maunds*
Ditto - -	2 bags
Ditto - -	1 bundle
Tooth Pick Cases -	3 dozen
Trowsers - -	5 ditto
Tin Ware -	1 chest
Tongues -	1 cask

Quality.	Quantity.	Quality.	Quantity.
Tutanague -	2 *maunds*		
Ditto - -	20 pieces	W	
Tea Cups and Saucers	9 sets		
		Wheat - -	332 bags
V		Ditto - -	73⅓ *candies*
		Ditto - -	22¼ *maunds*
Vinegar - -	1 dozen	Wax Candles -	500 *lbs.*
Ditto - -	1 case	Ditto - -	1 box
		Wooden Dishes -	23¾ *corge*, or score
U		Ditto - -	41 pair
		Wafer Stamps -	1 dozen
Ured, a kind of Pulse	250 *edangallies*		

Cannanore,
31st December, 1799.

(Signed) Bri. Hodgson,
C. Mr.

ABSTRACT of GOODS IMPORTED by SEA, from 1st January to 31st December, 1800.

Quality.	Quantity.	Quality.	Quantity.
		Bamboos - -	3900
A		Barley - -	2 kegs
Almonds -	7 bags	*Bengal* Soft Sugar -	98 bags
Ditto - -	2 *cappats*	Broad Cloth -	1 piece
Ditto - -	6 *maunds*	Ditto - -	71 yards
Amanick Oil -	4 jars	Brass Lamp -	1
Anee Bans -	4 pieces	Ditto - -	1 bag
Ajvan, Seed of an umbelliferous Plant	39 bags	*Botty* Wood, perhaps *Fili* or Black Wood	32 *candies*
Ditto - -	1 *robin*	Brass Pots -	11 bags
Artal Cinnabar -	¾ *maund*	Ditto - -	11 *lbs.*
Anjengo Arrack -	3 leaguers	Beer - -	12 hogsheads
Ditto - -	19 casks	Ditto - -	20 dozen
Arrack - -	1 leaguer	Blue - -	5 *maunds*
Ditto - -	14 casks	Boat Cloak -	6 pieces
B		*Bepo* Oil -	2 jars
Bamboo Mats -	100¾ *corge*, or score	*Bamboya* - -	2 *maunds*
Boots - -	1 box	Brandy - -	2 chests
Ditto - -	1 trunk	Ditto - -	2 quarter casks
Bengal Piece Goods	2 bundles	C	
Ditto - -	1148 pieces	Country Mats -	34 *corge*, or score
Bealen Rice -	29 *robins*	*Catcha* Cloth -	37 pieces
Ditto - -	450 *edangallies*	Ditto - -	14 bundles
Blankets -	76 pieces	Ditto - -	10 bales
Betel-Nuts -	1 bale	*China* Hams -	1 chest
Ditto - -	9 *pullon*	Ditto - -	1 box
Ditto - -	21 *maunds* 18 *lbs.*	Copper Pots -	1 chest
Ditto - -	13,200	Ditto - -	8 bags
Ditto - -	21 *robins*	Ditto - -	4 *maunds*
Blue *Doties*, a Cotton Cloth	59 pieces	Cummin Seed -	36 bags
Blue Cloth -	9 *corge*, or score	Ditto - -	1 *maund*
Benjamin - -	10 chests	Country Shoes -	10 *corge*, or score

Quality.	Quantity.
Cait Lace, a kind of Tape	3 bundles
Coir, or Coco-Nut cordage	200 ditto
Ditto - -	6 *candies*
Chintz - -	9 *corge*, or score
Ditto - -	5 pieces
Cutlery - -	1 chest
Chandroose -	16 bales
Ditto - -	5 bags
Ditto - -	30 *cappats*
Ditto - -	5 chests
Ditto - -	20 *maunds*
Cotton - -	21 bales
Ditto - -	19 bundles
Camphire -	1 box
Ditto - -	1 chest
Carla - -	34 *corge*, or score
Catcheria -	7 *candies*
Cointer Seed -	3 bags
Ditto - -	162 *edangallies*
China Summerheads, Umbrellas -	12
Chapa Ramal, Handkerchiefs	120 pieces
Cassia Laurus -	17 ditto
Chana Gram, a kind of Pulse	20 *candies*
Ditto - -	50 bags
China Handkerchiefs	16 pieces
Chellas -	3 ditto
Comillis -	2 bales
Cochin Arrack -	10 leaguers
Ditto - -	8 casks
Chickney Betel-Nut	2 *candies*
Ditto - -	5 *maunds*
Ditto - -	9 *robins*
Ditto - -	6 bales
Country Twine -	5 *maunds*
Cotton -	18 bundles
Country Combs -	26 *corge*, or score
Ditto *Challums* -	900
Copra, or Dried Coco-Nut Kernels -	10 *maunds*
China Wax -	5 chests
Coriander Seed -	230 *edangallies*
China Flowered Sattin	1 bundle
Canvas -	3 ditto
Cloth - -	1 piece
Candles - -	3 boxes
Ditto - -	1 chest
Coco-Nuts -	154,100
Country Thread -	1 bag
Chilly Pepper, *Capsicum*	2 ditto
Ditto - -	140 *pharas*
Ditto - -	3 *maunds*
Coco-Nut Oil -	4 skins
Ditto -	6 jars
Ditto - -	409 *paddas*
Ditto - -	65 *maunds*
Ditto - -	
Castor Oil -	2½ *maunds*
Culty Gram, a kind of Pulse	42 bags
Ditto - -	42 *robins*
Cherry Brandy -	2 chests
Claret - -	1½ ditto
Confectionary -	2 boxes
Cheese -	8 ditto

Quality.	Quantity.
Corks - -	1 bag
Copper Sheets -	5 *maunds*
Cootnys, a kind of Cloth, Silk and Cotton	52 pieces
D	
Dry Dates -	38 *cappats*
Ditto - -	15 bags
Ditto - -	15 *maunds*
Dungary, Cloth -	67 pieces
Ditto - -	10 *corge*, or score
Dooties, Cloth -	82 pieces
Dry Ginger -	11¼ *maunds*
Ditto - -	10 bundles
Doll, Split Pease of the *Cytisus Cajan*	32 *pharas*
Ditto - -	20 *maunds*
Ditto - -	100 measures
G	
Glass Ware -	1 box
Ditto - -	6 chests
Ditto - -	1 case
Gram Moong, a kind of Pulse -	22 *cappats*
Ditto - -	18 *robins*
Ditto - -	11 bundles
Ganjah, Dry Flowers and Leaves of Hemp	44 ditto
Ditto - -	1½ *maund*
Googal, a kind of Incense	9 *maunds*
Ginger - -	2 *candies*
Ditto - -	3½ *maunds*
Ditto - -	15 bundles
hee, Boiled Butter	17 *duppers, or skins*
Ditto - -	8 pots
ram, a kind of Pulse	5 *candies*
Ditto - -	5 *maunds*
Garlick - -	17½ ditto
Ditto - -	5 bags
ingham, a Cotton Cloth	280 pieces
Ditto - -	2 bundles
Gin - -	37 cases
Ditto - -	2 chests
H	
Hooka Snakes -	1 bundle
Hemp, *Crotolaria Juncea*	2 *candies*
Hats - -	1 chest
Ditto - -	3 boxes
Handkerchiefs -	18 pieces
Hair Powder -	3 dozen
I	
agory -	43 bundles
Ditto - -	[illegible] *lbs.*
Ditto - -	5 pots
Ditto - -	1½ *candy*

Quality.	Quantity.
Jagory	19 *maunds*
Ditto	4 bags
Iron Gridles	10
Iron Gridle Spoons	1 bundle
Ditto	17½ *corge*, or score
K	
Kincob, Silk Cloth	1 piece
L	
Lanthorns	2 sets
Lutestrings	4 pieces
M	
Manapar Cloth	119 bundles
——— Onions	2 *maunds*
Medicine	1¼ *candy*
Ditto	1 bundle
Madeira Wine	½ chest
Ditto	3½ pipes
Ditto	7 dozen
Mung, a Pulse, *Phaseolus Mungo*	16 *cappats*
Ditto	5 bags
Mustard Oil	1 jar
Methy Seed, *Fenugreek*	20 bags
Ditto	1 *maund*
N	
Nelly, Rice in the Husk	385 *robins*
Ditto	370,536 *edangallies*
Nachany, a Grain	60 *robins*
Nankins	1 chest
Ditto	5 *carge*, or score
Ditto	3 bundles
Nilacka, Fruit of the *Emblica*	2 ditto
O	
Opium	1 bundle
Oil	771¾ *chodana*
Ditto	59 pots
Ditto	350 *coolies*
Ditto	18 *duppers*, or skins
Ditto	10 *maunds*
Onions	1½ ditto
Ditto	3 bags
P	
Perfumery	4 boxes
Pomatum	1 ditto
Pedrum	3½ *maunds*
Paulghaut, Piece Goods	4673 pieces
Ditto	1 chest
Ditto	3 bales
Ditto	42 bundles
Plates, *China*	150 pieces
Ditto	35¾ *corge*, or score
Pine Apple Cheeses	10
Pantaloons	6 pieces
Pickles	3 cases
Ditto	1 box
Pale Beer	1½ chest
Ditto	5 casks
Painted Red Pearls	20 *corge*, or score
Pots of *Spear*	6
Paddy, Rice in the Husk	1675 *edangallies*
Ditto	2 bundles
R	
Rum	1 pipe
Ditto	2 leaguers
Rice	4909 *robins*
Ditto	250 dozen
Ramnath Cloth	2 boxes
Raisins	1 chest
Ditto	3 *cappats*
S	
Stockings	1 chest
Shirts	6 *corge*, or score
Sugar	14 bags
Ditto	3 tubs
Ditto	50 *maunds*
Ditto	14 chests
Sugar Candy	9 boxes
Ditto	15 tubs
Ditto	2 chests
Saddy	17½ *corge*, or score
Soap	2 bags
Ditto	380 pieces
Ditto	60 *maunds*
Shoes	3 chests
Siniman (Cinnamon)	5 *maunds*
Shellas Cloths	17 pieces
Silk Piece Goods	30 ditto
Sadlery	1 box
Ditto	1 chest
Salt	2100 *edangallies*
Shark Fins	11¾ *maunds*
Ditto	1700 pieces
Sindy Salt	6¼ *candies*
Ditto	6000 dozen
Stationery	2 boxes
Surat Tobacco	1 bundle
Surat Gram, a kind of Pulse	88 *candies*
Saffron	2 *maunds*
Shaving Boxes	3
Sauce, Fish	2 kegs
Sundries	1 bag
Ditto	2 boxes
Sneakers	550
T	
Tea	3 chests
Tea Pots	3 pots
Tutanague	5 *maunds*
Thread	8 *lbs.*

Quality.	Quantity.	Quality.	Quantity.
Towra, a Pulse -	1 *robin*		
Tongues -	2 kegs	U	
Turmerick -	2½ *candies*		
Ditto - -	51 *robins*	*Ured Gram*, a kind of Pulse	14 *robins*
Ditto - -	81½ *maunds*		
Ditto - -	4 bundles	W	
Tobacco - -	1 chest	Wafers -	1 box
Ditto - -	260 *chippons*	Wooden Dishes -	40 pieces
Ditto - -	13,669 bundles	Wheat - -	65 *cappats*
Ditto - -	69 bales	Ditto - -	161 bags
Ditto - -	4½ *candies*	Ditto - -	9½ bundles
Ditto - -	52 *maunds*	Wine - -	1 chest
Tape - -	23 rolls	Whips, of sorts -	5
Twine - -	8 *maunds*	Vermillion -	1 bundle

Errors excepted,

Cannanore,
31*st December*, 1800.

(Signed) Bri. Hodgson,
C. Mr.

ABSTRACT of GOODS EXPORTED by SEA,
from 1st January to 31st December, 1799.

Quality.	Quantity.	Quality.	Quantity.
		Coco-Nuts -	1 *candy*
A		Ditto -	23900
Arrack -	36½ leaguers	*Cointer* Seed -	145 *edangallies*
Ditto -	16 kegs	Country Mats -	400
Ditto -	150 bottles	*Comblams*, Country Blankets	1050 pieces
Aniseed - -	1 chest	*Chelly* Pepper, *Capsicum*	7 bags
		Cardamums -	6 *maunds*
Ajuan, Seed of an umbelliferous Plaut	5 bags	*Chilly* Pepper, *Capsicum*	22½ ditto
		China Bowls -	2400
Ditto - -	2 *maunds*	Coco-Nut Oil -	7 pots
Almonds -	1 bale	Cummin Seed -	4 bags
B		Ditto -	3 *maunds*
Betel-Nut -	12 *candies*	*Coir* Rope of Coco-Nut Husks	½ *maund*
Ditto -	17 *maunds*	Cheese -	84 *lbs.*
Ditto -	2000	Cotton Rope -	7½ *maunds*
Brandy -	7 chests	Coffee -	1 box
Beer - -	9 dozen	Ditto - -	2 *maunds*
Barley -	1 box	Canvas -	15 pieces
Bottles, Empty -	650	*China* Ware -	2 chests
Budgery, a Grain -	2 bundles	Ditto - -	4 dozen
Bomblos (Dried Fish) -	60 ditto	*China* Sweetmeats -	2 jars
Blue *Duty*, Cotton Cloth	11 *corge*, or score	Copper Pots -	5 bags
Blue Scarlet Cloth -	6 pieces	Ditto - -	22½ *maunds*
C		D	
Churats, Tobacco rolled, for Smoking	4000	*Dholl*, a kind of Pulse	2 *candies*
Cotton -	12 bags	Ditto - -	20 bags
Ditto -	27 bales	Dates - -	7½ *candies*
Ditto -	24 *maunds*	Ditto - -	15 *maunds*

Quality.	Quantity.
Dates - -	4 bundles
Ditto - -	2 *cappats*
G	
Gin - -	53 cases
Gram, a kind of Pulse	18 bags
Ditto - -	34 *candies*
Ditto - -	5 *maunds*
Garlick	2 *candies*
Ditto - -	6 *maunds*
Ganja, Dried Flowers and Leaves of Hemp	7 bundles
Ghee, or boiled Butter	34 *duppers*
Ditto - -	1 *candy*
Ditto - -	7½ *maunds*
Glass Ware -	1 chest
Gloucester Cheese -	2 ditto
H	
Hing, or Asafœtida	4 bottles
Hams - -	1 *candy*
Ditto - -	1 chest
Hooka-Snakes -	2
Hats and Hosiery -	2 chests
I	
Iron - -	3 *candies*
Ditto - -	11½ *maunds*
Jagory - -	10 pots
Ditto - -	14 bundles
Ditto - -	1 *candy*
Ditto - -	9½ *maunds*
Ironmongery -	10 chests
Ditto - -	1 box
Jackets -	2 *corge*, or score
K	
Knives - -	1½ *corge*, or score
L	
Leather - -	14¾ *corge*, or score
Limes - -	1 bundle
M	
Mung, a kind of Pulse	28 bags
Ditto - -	5 *candies*
Ditto - -	5 *maunds*
Madeira - -	3½ pipes
Ditto -	8 chests
Ditto -	32¾ dozen
Moodra - -	10 *robins*
Mustard Seed -	1 bag
Ditto - -	9 *maunds*
Metty Seed, *Fenugreek*	2 ditto

Quality.	Quantity.
N	
Nankins -	58 *corge*, or score
Ditto - -	15 pieces
Nelly, Rice in the Husk	4 *robins*
Ditto - -	12800 *edangallies*
O	
Onions - -	6 *cappats*
Ditto - -	27 bags
Ditto - -	27 *candies*
Ditto - -	13 *maunds*
Opium - -	1 bag
Ditto - -	1 bundle
P	
Pepper - -	32 *candies*
Ditto - -	13 *maunds*
Paper - -	66½ reams
Port Wine -	9 dozen
Pantaloons -	12 *corge*, or score
Piece Goods -	4050 pieces
Ditto - -	69½ bundles
Ditto - -	92 *corge*, or score
R	
Rose Water -	1 bottle
Rice - -	2057 *robins*
Rum - -	4 pipes
Rum Shrub -	2 boxes
Red *Camblys* -	2 *corge*, or score
Raisins - -	4 *cappats*
Ditto - -	3 *candies*
Ditto - -	15 *maunds*
S	
Sandal Wood -	7 pieces
Salt - -	7 bales
Ditto - -	22500 *edangallies*
Sindy Salt -	2 bundles
Ditto - -	6 *cappats*
Ditto - -	3 *maunds*
Shoes - -	1 chest
Ditto - -	41½ *corge*, or score
Sugar - -	7 bundles
Ditto - -	43 bags
Ditto - -	4¾ *candies*
Ditto - -	1 *maund*
Shirts - -	17 *corge*, or score
Summerheads, Umbrellas	2 ditto
Sundry - -	1 trunk
Ditto - -	17 bundles
Ditto - -	1 case
Soap - -	450 loaves
Ditto - -	22 bags
Stationery -	1 chest
Surat Tobacco -	7½ *candies*

Quality.	Quantity.	Quality.	Quantity.
T		V	
Tea - -	1 box	Vinegar - -	7 bottles
Ditto - -	22 chests	*Ured*, a kind of Pulse	96 bags
Ditto - -	15 *lbs.*		
Tortoise Shells -	1 *maund*		
Ditto ditto -	4 *lbs.*		
Twine - -	3 bundles	W	
Ditto - -	7½ *maunds*		
Tutanague -	4 pieces	Wheat - -	115 bags
Tamarinds - -	2 *candies*	Ditto - -	45¾ *candies*
Ditto - -	17 *maunds*	Ditto - -	5 *maunds*
Ditto - -	7 bundles	Wax Candles -	2 chests
Tobacco -	62 ditto	Ditto - -	2 *maunds*
Ditto - -	12 *candies*	Ditto - -	34 *lbs.*
Ditto - -	23 *maunds*		

Errors excepted,

(Signed) Bri. Hodgson, C. Mr.

Cannanore,
31*st December*, 1799.

ABSTRACT of GOODS EXPORTED by SEA, from 1st January to 31st December, 1800.

Quality.	Quantity.	Quality.	Quantity.
A		C	
Ajuan, Seed of an umbelliferous Plant	1 *candy*	Confectionary -	2 pots
Ditto - -	4 *maunds*	Coco-Nut Oil -	12 *puddas*
Ditto - -	14 bags	Ditto - -	50 *cooties*
Arrack -	4 casks	*Cointer* Seed -	31 bags
Almonds -	25 *maunds*	Camphire -	½ *maund*
Ditto - -	1 jar	Cotton - -	6 *candies* 9¾ *maunds*
Ditto - -	1 bag	Ditto - -	40 bundles
Ditto - -	1 *cappat*	*Chandroise* -	2 bales
		Curtain Cloth -	2 pieces
B		*Chilly* Pepper, *Capsicum*	8½ *maunds*
Bengal Piece Goods -	155 pieces	*Calumbo* Arrack -	15 leaguers
Betel-Nut -	2½ *maunds*	Ditto ditto -	30 gallons
Boots - -	24 pair	*Cadys* - -	20 pieces
Barley - -	1 bundle	*Cochin* Shoes -	7 *corge*, or score
Beer - -	7 casks	*Chella* Cloth -	67 pieces
Ditto - -	28 dozen	*China* Shoes -	1 chest
Ditto - -	½ leaguer	Chints - -	238 pieces
Blue *Doty*, Cotton Cloth	59 pieces	Copper Pots -	40 *maunds*
Ditto - -	23 *corge*, or score	*China* Summerheads, Umbrellas)	1 bundle
Blue - -	5 *maunds*	*Camblies*, Country Blankets	1½ *corge*, or score
Brass Pots -	6	Ditto - -	1 bundle
Benjamin -	1 chest	Cot Lace, a kind of Tape	4 ditto
Ditto - -	1½ *maund*	*China* Ware -	20 chests
Bruces (Brushes?) -	1 chest	Ditto - -	1 basket
Brandy - -	2 ditto	Ditto - -	5 dozen
		China Paper -	1½ quires

Quality.	Quantity.
Country Medicine -	2 bags
Country Thread -	19 *lbs.*
Country Twine -	1 bundle
Ditto - -	1½ *maund*
Ditto - -	4 *lbs.*
Coco-Nuts -	19700
Combla Mass (Fish) -	60500 pieces
Ditto ditto	26 bundles
Coffee - -	6 chests
Ditto - -	6 *maunds*
D	
Dry Coco-Nuts -	5 bags
Dupatts, a Cotton Cloth	6 *corge*, or score
Dates - -	37 *cappats*
Ditto - -	3 *candies*
Ditto - -	71 bales
Ditto - -	20 bundles
Dimity -	18 pieces
Dholl, a kind of Pulse	141 *maunds*
Ditto - -	1 bag
Dungary, a Cotton Cloth	15 *corge*, or score
E	
Europe Cloth -	6 pieces
Ditto, Chints -	9 ditto
Empty Bottles -	109 dozen
Europe Twine -	2 bundles
Ditto Thread -	6 *lbs.*
G	
Ginghams, a Cotton Cloth	2 *corge*, or score
Ditto - -	8 pieces
Gram, a kind of Pulse	500 *edangallies*
Ditto - -	1½ *candy*
Ditto - -	28 bags
Gin - -	10 chests
Ditto - -	2 cases
Glass Ware -	13 chests
Ghee, Boiled Butter -	43 *duppers*, or skins
Ditto - -	2 pots
H	
Hooka-Snakes -	1 chest
Horse-Shoes -	10 pair
Hams - -	15 chests
Hats - -	3
Handles - -	10 bundles
Handkerchiefs -	2 pieces
I	
Izary, Cotton Cloth -	3 pieces
Iron, Brass (Bars?) -	2 *candies*
Jack Wood, *Artocarpus*	25 pieces
Issence (Incense?) -	1½ *maund*
K	
Knives and Forks -	6 dozen
L	
Leather Gloves -	1 dozen
Large Nails -	225
Lime Pickles -	6 jars
Ditto - -	200
M	
Methy Seed, *Fenugreek*	1 *maund*
Maneary -	2 chests
Mowdah -	9 ditto
Manapar Cloth -	57½ bundles
Ditto - -	34 pieces
Madeira Wine -	3 chests
Ditto - -	½ pipe
N	
Nankins -	54 pieces
Nutmegs -	12 *lbs.*
Nelly, Rice in the Husk	2500 *edangallies*
O	
Opium - -	12 *lbs.*
Orny, Gold Thread -	5 pieces
Onions - -	7 *candies*
Ditto - -	3 bags
Oil - -	13 *duppers*, or skins
P	
Piece Goods -	8 *corge*, or score
Ditto -	37½ ditto
Ditto -	671 pieces
Portuguese Paper -	2 chests
Ditto ditto -	128 reams
Ditto ditto -	5 quires
Padlocks - -	15 dozen
Palighat Tobacco -	2 bales
Ditto Piece Goods -	200 pieces
Perfumery -	2 boxes
Pins - -	1 bundle
Port Wine -	2 chests
Pickles - -	2 cases
R	
Rice - -	500 *edangallies*
Ditto - -	1542 *robins*
Razors - -	30 dozen
Rum - -	1 chest
S	
Super San -	3 pieces
Surat Tobacco -	3 *candies* ½ *maund*

Quality.	Quantity.	Quality.	Quantity.
Surat Tobacco -	9 bundles	Tobacco -	32 *cappats*
Soap - -	274 bags	Turbands -	20 pieces
Silver Epaulettes -	1 pair	Taffetas - -	4 *corge*, or score
South Cloth -	5 pieces	Ditto - -	15 pieces
Sandal Wood -	14325 ditto	Turmerick -	2 *maunds*
Saddy - -	388 ditto		
Sugar - -	16 chests		
Ditto - -	5 *candies* 3 *maunds*		
Ditto - -	18 bags		
Spanes Glass (Spying Glasses)	7	V	
Sugar Candy -	10 chests		
Ditto -	15 tubs	*Ulva* Seed -	4 bags
Stationery -	3 chests	Vinegar -	2 chests
Sundry Europe Articles	6 ditto	Ditto - -	3 casks
Scissars - -	3 dozen		
Salt - -	1 bale		
Ditto - -	7 *cappats*		
Stockings -	1 trunk	W	
Salmon - -	1 cag		
Shot - -	2 bags		
Silk Handkerchiefs. -	1 piece	Wax Candles -	1 chest
		Ditto - -	3½ *maunds*
T		Wine Glasses -	1 chest
		Wetery - -	1 ditto
Tobacco -	1 *candy* 5 *maunds*	Wheat - -	6½ *candies*
Ditto - -	93 bundles	Wine and Claret -	2 chests

Errors excepted,

Cannanore,
31*st December*, 1800.

(Signed) Bri. Hodgson,
C. Mr.

ABSTRACT of GOODS EXPORTED by LAND, from 1st January to 31st December, 1799.

Quality.	Quantity.	Quality.	Quantity.
		Chilly Pepper, *Capsicum*	30 *maunds*
A		*Canga* - -	3½ *corges*, or score
		Cloves - -	4 *lbs.*
Almonds -	28 *maunds*		
		D	
B			
		Dates - -	8½ *candies*
Betel-Nut -	1000	Ditto - -	79 *maunds*
		Ditto - -	24 bales
C		*Dholl*, a kind of Pulse	10 *maunds*
		Doria, a Cotton Cloth	2 pieces
Caddy - -	14 pieces		
Coco-Nut -	1200	G	
Cotton - -	30 *maunds*		
Ditto - -	14 bags	Garlic - -	5½ *maunds*
Coco-Nut Oil -	22 *paddams*	*Gram*, a kind of Pulse	5 ditto
Catcha Cloth -	10½ pieces	*Ganjah*, Dried Flowers and Leaves of Hemp	14 bundles
Comblies, Indian Blankets	5 *corge*, or score		

Quality.	Quantity.
Ganjah, Dried Flowers and Leaves of Hemp	96 *lbs.*
Glass Ware -	1 box
Ditto - -	1 chest
H	
Hats - -	1 chest
Handkerchiefs -	17 pieces
Hing, or Asafœtida -	2 *maunds*
I	
Jagory - -	1 bag
K	
Kissemis, Raisins -	1¼ *candy*
Ditto - -	10 *maunds*
M	
Mung, a kind of Pulse	16 *maunds*
Mustard Seed -	½ ditto
Maniary, Beads -	3 boxes
Ditto - -	2 chests
Ditto - -	1 bag
N	
Nankins -	10 pieces
Nails - -	1½ *maunds*
O	
Opium - -	4 *lbs.*

Quality.	Quantity.
P	
Post Paper -	19½ ream
Ditto - -	1 bundle
Piece Goods -	2104 pieces
Ditto -	29 bundles
R	
Raisins -	4 bundles
Ditto - -	14½ *maunds*
S	
Sugar - -	3½ *candies*
Ditto - -	4 *maunds*
Salt - -	12 bags
Ditto - -	18700 *edangallies*
Shirts - -	½ *corge*, or score
Soap - -	195 pieces
Ditto - -	3 bags
Shoes - -	2 *corge*, or score
Scissars - -	3 dozen
Surat Gram, a kind of Pulse	3 bags
Saddy - -	1 piece
Sindy Salt -	5 *maunds*
T	
Tobacco - -	25½ *maunds*
Tamarinds -	1 *candy*
Ditto - -	6 *maunds*
Tatton - -	3 pieces
W	
Wax Candles -	1 box

Errors excepted,

Cannanore,
31st *December*, 1799.

(Signed) BRI. HODGSON,
C. Mr.

ABSTRACT of GOODS EXPORTED by LAND, from 1st January to 31st December, 1800.

Quality.	Quantity.	Quality.	Quantity.
A		*Doty*, a Cloth -	2 pair
		Dongary, a Cotton Cloth	22 ditto
Almonds - -	40 *maunds*		
C		M	
		Manapar Cloth -	57 pieces
Country Medicines -	2 bags	Ditto ditto -	8 bundles
Comblies, or *Indian* Blankets	1 *corge*, or score	Ditto ditto -	6 *corge*, or score
Coco-Nut Oil -	50 *cootys*		
Chella - -	3 pieces	S	
Cotton - -	39½ *maunds*		
Comblies, or *Indian* Blankets	10 pieces	Summerheads (Umbrellas)	1½ *corge*, or score
Camphire -	½ *maund*	Salt - -	1,03,0080 *edangallies*
Catcha Cloth -	4 bales	Sugar - -	6 *cappats*
		Ditto - -	7½ *maunds*
D		Ditto - -	9 tubs
		Scissars -	3 dozen
Dholl, a kind of Pulse	1 *maund*	Soap - -	1 *maund*
Dates - -	34 *cappats*		
Ditto - -	1 *maund*	T	
Ditto - -	3 *candies*		
Ditto - -	33 bales	Turpentine Oil	1½ dozen

Errors excepted,

Cannanore,
31*st December,* 1800.

(Signed) BRI. HODGSON,
C. Mr.

GENERAL INDEX.

GENERAL INDEX.

Anamulu, a kind of pulse. See *Dolichos Lablab*.
Ananda and his kinsmen kings in India, iii. 96.
Anavun Nelluru, iii. 463.
Ancola, iii. 176.
Andhra or *Andray*, the poetical dialect of the *Telinga* nation; also the Sanscrit name for the nation itself. See *Telinga*, and i. 253. iii. 90.
Andulay conday, a place in *Malabar*, i. 499.
Anethum Sowa Roxb. MS. a carminative seed cultivated, ii. 164.
Angada-puram, a town of *Malabar*, ii. 434.
Angaraca, a kingdom, ii. 200.
Angaru, a river of *Canara*, iii. 108.
Angedira, iii. 78.
Ani Duclu, a copper coin with the impression of an elephant. See *Dub*.
Ani-malaya, town of *Coimbetore*, ii 331.
———--, a passage in the mountains between *Coimbetore* and *Malabar*, ii. 332.
Apogodal, a town, ii. 226.
Appearance of the country, and general state of cultivation and population between *Madras*, and the *Ghats*, or passages up the mountains, i. 1, 5, 8, 10, 15, 16, 18, 19, 23.
Idem in the *Mysore* or *Patana Ráyada*, i. 37, 41, 44, 48, 49, 50, 53, 54, 56, 58, 82, 137, 170, 190, 191, 265, 271, 272, 276, 310, 316, 342, 344, 357, 360, 398. ii. 2, 4, 15, 16, 23, 24, 33, 34, 44, 58, 60, 63, 65, 68, 69, 80, 85, 87, 88, 89, 91, 92, 97, 118, 129, 137, 142, 146, 149, 150, 155, 156. iii. 359, 363, 367, 375, 380, 382, 384, 389, 392, 403, 405, 407, 409, 419, 422, 424, 425, 431, 435, 457, 460, 461, 462, 465.
Idem, in the *Nagara Ráyada*, iii. 253, 259, 283, 284, 286, 287, 288, 289, 292, 309, 311, 313.
Idem, in the *Chatrakal Ráyada*, iii. 330, 337, 338, 343.
Idem, in the districts belonging to the Company above the Eastern *Ghats*, i. 28, 29, 33. ii. 164, 173, 175, 179, 181, 186, 285.
Idem, in the province of *Coimbetore*, ii. 186, 189, 192, 199, 226, 228, 235, 238, 244, 245, 248, 249, 275, 278, 282, 286, 287, 291, 293, 299, 301, 307, 318, 331,
Idem, in the province of *Malabar*, ii. 346, 347, 364, 387, 389, 390, 413, 419, 422, 432, 434. 460, 462, 470, 494, 496, 500, 501, 510, 514, 516, 517, 540, 544, 553, 555, 558, 559, 563, 565.
Idem, in the province of *Canara* below the *Ghats*, iii. 1, 8, 9, 12, 14, 15, 19, 61, 62, 64, 67, 73, 74, 80, 87, 88, 89, 101, 104, 108, 134, 135, 136, 138, 152, 158, 162, 166, 175, 178, 186, 189, 190, 201.
Idem, above the *Ghats*, iii. 203, 206, 207, 210.
Idem, in *Soonda* or *Sudha*, above the *Ghats*, iii. 211, 217, 229.
Arabian colony in India. See *Moplays*.
Arachis hypogæa L. a kind of pulse, i. 329.
Aravay-courchy, a town of *Coimbetore*, ii. 302.
Aray, the *Canarese*, or *Karnata* name for a *Maruttah*, i. 237.
Architecture. See Bridge, House, Inn, Palace, Temple.
Arcola, a village of *Canara*, iii. 61.
Arcot, or *Arrucate*, a town, capital of a country, i. 17.
—— *Rupee*, a silver coin, ii. 210.
Areca Catechu Lin. or *Betel-nut* palm. See Gardens, Plantations, i. 153, 384. ii. 52, 110, 259, 365, 454, 458, 487, 504, 524, 552, 561. iii. 2, 45, 54, 59, 84, 86, 151, 154, 220, 270, 277, 403, 452.
Arhitta, a sect considered now as heretical. See *Jainas*, also their Gods, iii. 77.
Aritta parumba, a place in *Malabar*, ii. 559.
Arkawatí river, iii. 427.
Artocarpus integrifolia, or *Jack*, a fruit tree, ii. 365, 402, 454, 458, 463, 487, 524, 552, 561. iii. 47, 86.
Arts, state of. See Agriculture, Architecture, Calendar, Canal, Gilding, Iron, Manufactures, Measures, Quarries, Reservoirs, Survey, Weights, Wells, Varnish.
Arulu-gupay, a town, ii. 57.
Arya, a region of the world. See *Bhárata*.
Asagaru, a cast which contains washermen, i. 337.
Asoph, chief governor of a large district under *Tippoo*, ii. 2.
Ass, an animal, i. 7, 206, 356. ii. 180, 383.
Assur-khana, a kind of Mussulman temple, i. 347.
Astrology. See *Cunian*, *Panchanga*, i. 235. ii. 425, 528.
Asura, a devil, iii. 78.
Attavany, a messenger, ii. 215.
Avanasi, a town of *Coimbetore*, ii. 276.
Avaray, a kind of pulse. See *Dolichos Lablab*.
Avatar. See Incarnation.
Avila-gotna, iii. 189.
Baba Bodeen, a Mussulman saint, iii. 310.
Bacadaru, a cast of slaves in *Canara*, iii. 106.

GENERAL INDEX.

GENERAL INDEX.

Funerals. See each cast for its customs.
Gajina guta, a hill in *Mysore* producing minerals, ii. 46.
Game, i. 169. ii. 127, 414.
Ganagaru, a cast containing oil-makers, i. 228. See also *Jotyphanada*.
Ganapatyam, a religious sect of *Hindus*, i. 143. ii. 74.
Ganesa, or *Ganeswara*, a deity of the *Hindus*, i. 36, 52, 245, 335. iii. 83.
Ganga-rájá, his city and history, ii. 170.
Gangawali river, iii. 174, 218.
Ganges river, ii. 306.
Gardens in general, in opposition to fields, and termed in native accompts, *Bagait*, *Tota*, and *Parum*, i. 83, 111, 401. ii. 255, 365. iii. 218.
——, *Betel leaf*. See *Piper Betel*.
——, Flower, i. 56, 115.
——, Kitchen, or *Tarkari*, i. 41. iii. 293, 327, 339, 355, 383. ii. 56, 110, 255, 281, 299, 314, 402, 450, 524. iii. 44, 85, 441.
——, palm, or orchards and plantations. See *Areca*, *Cocos*, *Borassus*, Plantations, *Musa*, *Artocarpus*, *Piper nigrum*. i. 113, 153, 384. ii. 64, 67, 90, 109, 151, 165. iii. 153.
——, public, i. 24, 46, 73.
Garlic, iii. 443.
Garse, a weight. See Weights, i. 6.
Garsopa, iii. 137.
Garuda, a mythological eagle of the *Hindus*, ii. 78.
Garuda-giri, iii. 382.
Gauda, or *Gaur*, chief officer of a village or manor in *Mysore*, or *Karnata*, i. 82, 124, 268, 298, 388. ii. 64, 67, 90, 109, 151, 165. iii. 342.
Gaukarna, iii. 166.
Gauly, a person who sells milk, i. 116.
Gaunda, called also *Munigar*, chief officer of a manor in the countries where the *Tamul* language prevails, ii. 213, 216.
Gavada, a day's journey. See Measures of Length.
Gaynicara, a tenant in *Tulava*, iii. 32, 38.
Ghats, or passes, applied peculiarly in southern India, to those which lead up from the low-country, towards the sea, and *N. Pennar* river to the table-land, in the centre of the Peninsula, i. 25. ii. 181, 183, 186, 435, 490. iii. 203.
Ghee, butter preserved by boiling. See Butter.
Ghenugu-guti, iii. 259.
Ghentala, a kind of corn. See *Halcus spicatus*.
Ghosts, superstitious fear of, iii. 358.
Gilding, false, i. 74.
Gingeli oil. See *Sesamum*.
Ginger, ii. 273, 335, 450, 469, 502. iii. 85.
Glass, and glass-ware, i. 147. iii. 369, 370.
Goalaru, a cast who rear black-cattle, ii. 5, 13.
Goat, i. 120, 164. ii. 12, 13, 276, 383. iii. 57.
Godi Juri, a kind of wheat. See Wheat.
Gola, a treasurer, ii. 215.
Gold dust, ii. 441.
Gollaru, or *Gollawanlu*, a cast who transport money, i. 347.
Gomasta, an agent, ii. 215.
Gomuta Ráya, one of the Jain deities, iii. 73, 82, 84. Image of, 410.
Goni, or Indian hemp, and sack-cloth. See *Crotolaria*.
Gopaly, *Hana*, *Palam*, or *Fanam*, a gold coin, ii. 210.
Gopi-chitty, iii. 185.
Gorippa, a male deity of the *Hindus*, i. 337.
Goray. See *Cassutium*.
Graham, Capt. the collector at *Krishna-giri*, iii. 460.
Grain, manner of preserving it. See each kind of corn and pulse, also i. 90. ii. 374. iii. 145, 276, 316.
———, price of, iii. 347.
Grama, a village or manor, the lowest territorial division in *Mysore*, i. 299. iii. 407.
———, or *Gramam*, is also peculiarly applied to manors, bestowed in charity on *Bráhmans*, i. 82. ii. 352. iii. 99.
Granite, a kind of rock, i. 17, 27, 53, 132, 164, 182. ii. 60, 85, 386, 440, 460, iii. 66, 87, 89.
Gubi, a town of *Mysore*, ii. 29.
Gudada, a female deity of the *Hindus*, ii. 37, 42.
Gudy, a temple of the *Bráhmans*, iii. 75, 82, 131.
Guddy, *Shanaboga*, or *Sheristadar*, register of a district, called *Hobly*, in *Mysore*, i. 270.
Guides, ii. 242. iii. 62.
Gujah, a measure of length, i. 131.
Gum, produced by various trees, i. 168, 204.
Gungoma, one of the deities called *Saktis*, i. 242.
Gungricara, a cast occupied in agriculture, ii. 119.
Gunta, a land measure of *Canara*, iii. 2, 102.

GENERAL INDEX.

GENERAL INDEX.

GENERAL INDEX.

GENERAL INDEX.

GENERAL INDEX.

GENERAL INDEX.

GENERAL INDEX.

GENERAL INDEX.

THE END.

Printed by W. Bulmer & Co.
Cleveland-Row, St. James's.